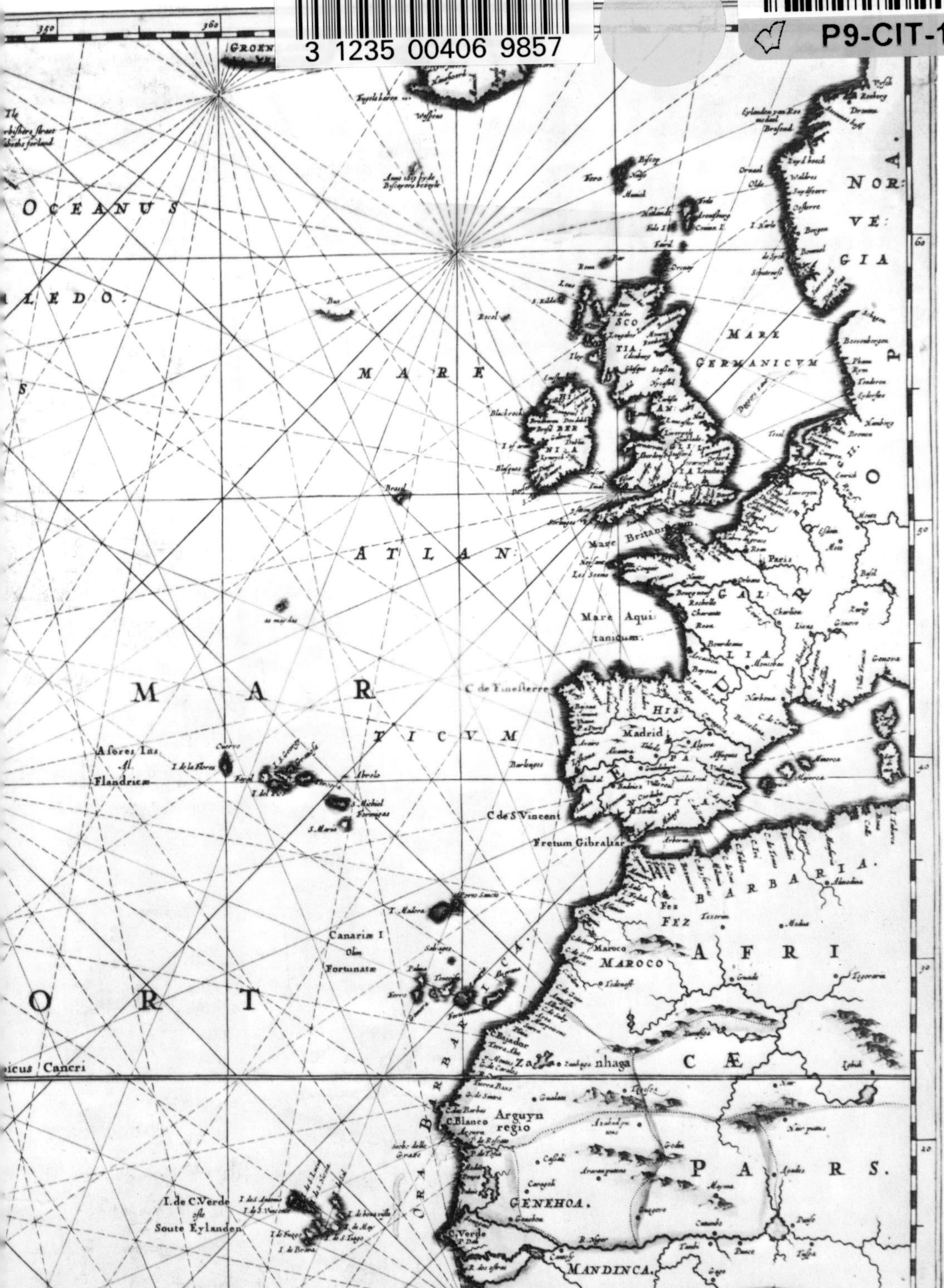
OCEANUS
MARE
ATLAN
M A R
TICVM
O R T
picus Cancri
Circulus Æquinochalis
OCEANI ÆTHIOPICI
Asores Ins
Al. Flandricæ
Canariæ I
Olim Fortunatæ
I. de C.Verde
ofte
Soute Eylanden
C de Finesterre
C de S.Vincent
Fretum Gibraltar
Mare Britannicum
Mare Aquitanicum
MARE GERMANICVM
NOR VE GIA
SCO TIA
BER NIA
GAL LIA
HIS
Madrid
Paris
BARBARIA.
FEZ
MAROCO
AFRI
CÆ
PARS.
C.Blanco
Arguyn regio
GENEHOA.
C.Verde
MANDINCA.
GUINEA
ORA GVINEÆ.
350
360
10
20
30
40

THE SHAPING OF AMERICA

THE
SHAPING
OF
AMERICA

A GEOGRAPHICAL
PERSPECTIVE
ON 500 YEARS
OF HISTORY

Volume 1
Atlantic America,
1492–1800

D. W. MEINIG

Yale University Press
New Haven and London

Designed by Nancy Ovedovitz and set in Goudy Old Style type by The Composing Room of Michigan, Inc. Printed in the United States of America by Vail-Ballou Press, Binghamton, N.Y.

Library of Congress Cataloging-in-Publication Data
Meinig, D. W. (Donald William), 1924–
    The shaping of America.
    Bibliography: pp. 461–79.
    Includes index.
    Contents: v. 1. Atlantic America, 1492–1800.
    1. United States—History 2. United States—Historical geography I. Title.
E178.M57 1986   973   85–17962
ISBN-0–300–03548–9 (v. 1)

10 9 8 7 6 5 4 3 2 1

*for
Lee*

Think of the past as space expanding infinitely beyond our vision. . . . Then we choose a prospect. The higher it is, the wider and hazier our view. Now we map what we see, marking some features, ignoring others, altering an unknown territory . . . into a finite collection of landmarks made meaningful through their connections. History is not the past, but a map of the past drawn from a particular point of view to be useful to the modern traveler.

Henry Glassie

CONTENTS

PART THREE
REORGANIZATIONS:
THE CREATION OF
AN AMERICAN MATRIX

PART FOUR
CONTEXT:
THE UNITED STATES
circa 1800

ILLUSTRATIONS

TABLES

PREFACE

Atlantic America is the first in a projected set of three volumes that will view the United States as a gigantic geographic growth with a continually changing geographic character, structure, and system. It is a historical view but from a different perspective than that commonly taken by historians. The result is a new map of some important features of the American past.

I hasten to emphasize that by geographic *growth* I do not imply some kind of quasi-natural process, but refer to the historical development from a group of precarious European footholds to a transcontinental nation and, in our own time, a macroculture of world impact. And by *geographic* character, structure, and system I do not imply the determination of history by the fundament of nature, but refer to the human creation of places and of networks of relationships among them. Geography is not just a physical stage for the historical drama, nor just a set of facts about areas of the earth; it is a special way of looking at the world. Geography, like history, is an age-old and essential strategy for thinking about large and complex matters.

Geography and history are not only analogous, but complementary and interdependent, bound together by the very nature of things. This relationship is implied by such common terms as space and time, area and era, places and events—pairs that are fundamentally inseparable. In practice the two fields are differentiated by the proportionate emphasis each gives to these terms. *Atlantic America,* with its special attention to localities and regions, networks and circulations, national and intercontinental systems, is in this sense a geographic complement to the work of historians. It is a different reading of the past but it cannot be a substitute for more orthodox studies because it makes no attempt to deal with many of the persons, issues, and events that are generally accepted as basic to history. Yet it is more than simply an addition to the expanding array of topics treated by historians. It is a synthesis of important themes and a critique of standard histories as being seriously deficient in certain respects. It asserts the need for important alterations in scope and emphasis in common understandings of our past, and such changes will require a rethinking and recasting of history.

The need for such an undertaking testifies that in practice, and especially in America, geography and history have not been complementary and interdependent fields at all. Why that should be so cannot be analyzed here. The pertinent fact is that despite some encouraging recent developments in both disciplines there has not been sufficient interaction and convergence in major topics to have had significant effect on interpretations of American history. *Atlantic America* can be no more than an example of some possibilities relating to the larger task of bringing the two fields more fruitfully together. It must not be taken as representative of the methods or purpose of historical geography in any full sense. It is idiosyncratic; I have focused on a few themes of strong personal interest and virtually ignored others of intrinsic importance. For example, I have not paid close attention to changes in the land with reference to environmental and ecological matters, and my intermittent mention of crops and commerce and of center-periphery relations barely hints at the kinds of geographic analyses of economic activities and systems relevant to historical interpretation. My emphasis upon social and cultural patterns reflects not only what I enjoy learning about areas but, more important, my conviction that the geography of such things has been seriously undervalued in descriptions and assessments of the United States. This conviction arose from my own experience of living for several years in the regional capital of a subtle but powerful subculture in the western United States.

The special themes and concepts of this particular view of the shaping of America will become clear enough in the text and need no adumbration here. Nevertheless, because geographic interpretations of history are as yet uncommon it may be useful to mention at the outset a few basic principles that have informed this work.

1. *Geographic context.* Every area is part of a larger mosaic, and its own character cannot be adequately assessed without reference to some encompassing pattern. Thus, although the United States is our central topic it is held in broader focus. The United States emerges within an Atlantic World and it everafter must share the continent and adjacent seas with other peoples and powers; relationships with these bordering areas have therefore a claim on our attention at all periods of development.

2. *Geographic coverage.* Although areas will vary greatly in their significance for particular topics, the geographer works with the full map at hand and must not completely ignore some areas and give attention only to parts of a whole. One simple but important corollary is that all resident populations are thereby

encompassed and recognized. Although the various "peoples" (however defined) of the United States are diverse and uneven in their effect upon major patterns of development, together they constitute "the American people" and each group must be recognized as continuing participants in American history and essential pieces of the American mosaic.

3. *Geographic scale.* Even after the nation becomes a powerful force people continue to live in a locality, a state, and a region, and it is important not to impose a dominating national perspective on all topics. Indeed, patterns and problems arising from the coexistence of these several scales of group life are topics of continual significance in this complicated nation.

4. *Geographic structure.* One of the elementary ways to make sense out of a complex whole is to study it as a set and a system of parts. Although routine in the consideration of the geopolitical structure of a federation, such an approach is not so obvious with respect to less formal areas. Most geographic regions are abstractions and approximations rather than discrete parts, yet it is necessary to give attention to the diverse character and relationships of regions and to the interests and networks that bind them into larger associations.

5. *Geographic tensions.* Large territorial structures are necessarily internally diverse and uneven in the patterns of power and influence. Center-periphery relationships are inherent in many modes of administration and service, several centers may compete in any particular activity, and regions may develop very divergent interests. Such conditions tend to generate pressures and resistances among various points and areas, which if not ameliorated may create stress and even threaten the integrity of the whole.

6. *Geographic change.* All human geography is subject to change, and the emergence of the United States and its ongoing development constitute one of the greatest exhibits of the continuous reshaping of the geographic character of areas. Such alteration is the generalized result of changes in the many elements of an area; it is always uneven in incidence, may be gradual and unappreciated at the time, and can never be fully controlled or predicted. Continual assessment of such internal geographic dynamics is an essential dimension of historical analysis.

Like most principles, these seem virtual truisms when stated. They deserve rehearsing only because they have been so often neglected or ignored.

There is one other matter that requires prefatory comment. It relates to the concept of *geographic growth,* but it carries us quickly beyond matter-of-fact principles into areas of fervent controversy. The reader will find that *imperialism* is an important theme in this study. That word is so loaded with ideological, historiographic, and emotional connotations that one might be tempted to avoid it altogether. Instead, I have tried to use it carefully in a restricted historical geo-graphic sense. I have done so because, given the facts of the case, I see no reasonable alternative. I wish to make clear that I use *imperialism* as a generic term, to refer to a type of geopolitical relationship: the aggressive encroachment of one people upon the territory of another, resulting in the subjugation of the latter people to alien rule. Such events are apparently as old as human history; they have happened in all times and in all places. To say that is not to suggest that all, or any particular, imperialism was inevitable, only that it is impossible to imagine the development of the world we live in without such actions. The European conquest of the Americas may be seen as one vast episode in the age-old and continuing workings of imperialism in history.

But we cannot leave it at that. Such historical processes are more than bloodless abstractions—they are violent collisions, with victors and victims. Those who triumph usually go on to create larger and stronger societies, and they also create their own versions of history. As A. P. Thornton has observed, they are wont to "expatiate on 'a great heritage,' but . . . not stop to consider those who were not mentioned in the will." I think that it is important for Americans to understand more clearly than they do that their nation has been created by massive aggression against a long succession of peoples. That is an ineluctable part of the "frontier," the "westward movement," the "growth" of the republic and similar themes so long celebrated in American history. Just as in the case of China, Rome, Russia, and other macrosocieties and empires, such expansion resulted in the destruction or displacement, capture, and deep deformation of all societies in its path. That such drastic changes were wrought in region after region is a fact that must receive attention in this kind of geographic interpretation. That there has always been an ugly, destructive side to American expansionism seems to me a truth worth stat-ing. That truth of course is no discovery of mine. It has always been known by those most heavily affected by it, and it has upwelled into prominence in recent years as part of a broad and diverse critique of American policies. Many historians are working on ways of incorporating something of this very different view of American development into their interpretations. I believe that the perspectives of *Atlantic America* and subsequent volumes will offer some help in that task. The purpose is not to allocate blame but to enlarge understanding. This attempt at a consistent view of America as a geographic growth developing into a world mac-roculture and of imperialism as an age-old kind of geographic process, structure, and system provides a framework for reassessment.

Imperialism is only one of many important topics being reassessed these days. For some years now there has been under way an examination so far-ranging and radical, a going to the roots of all major themes of American history, that the eventual result will be nothing less than a new "invention" of America: a new coherent and widely disseminated and received description and interpretation of what America is like and how it got that way. I hope that *Atlantic America* and subsequent volumes on the shaping of America will be welcomed as a small part of that exciting endeavor. While geography alone cannot provide that new version of America, I am convinced that we will never come near to a satisfactory view of this nation and its past until Americans draw far more than they have as yet done upon this venerable but neglected field.

D. W. Meinig
Syracuse, New York

ACKNOWLEDGMENTS

My most obvious debt is displayed in the bibliography: to the many scholars, mostly historians, who have specialized in the eras and areas, specific topics and general themes pertinent to this work. Anyone from another field who steps into the realm of early American history is in immediate danger of smothering in the mass of literature—perhaps an appropriate fate for academic interlopers. A newcomer with only a few years to linger cannot hope to master any considerable part of it, nor even absorb all the technical studies bearing directly upon any major theme. One tries to get acquainted with a few classics and major recent works, skims the journals for specific topics and review essays; one becomes especially grateful for collections of papers that have been given some real focus, and for the succinct summations of recognized authorities. At its best it is a splendid literature and I came to admire many of its authors and envy their command of both subject and language. I must resist a desire to name a few of the best, knowing that I could never decide just where to stop. Some of them are mentioned in the text and I hope that they will not find that I have misused their work. Their service is not specified on every page because footnotes would be a cumbersome clutter in a book designed to be more a panorama and synthesis than a research reference. However, sources of all specific quotations are listed at the back.

Some of my colleagues at Syracuse have generously taken time to review portions of the manuscript, and I thank John Western, Ralph Ketcham, Stephen Webb, and John Agnew for their valuable critiques as well as their encouragement. The meticulous work of my copyeditor, Elizabeth Casey, saved me from some of my worst tendencies with the language—but I was headstrong about a few matters and she must not be held accountable for what remains.

The general standards and the support I have received from Yale University Press are the best I have known in a fair range of experience with publishing. The director, John Ryden, not only strongly endorsed the work but allocated additional resources to enhance it with more maps and illustrations. I am especially grateful to my editor, Judy Metro, who expressed confidence in the project from an early prospectus and whose encouragement has been particularly important to me over the past two years as I labored to complete this first volume. I thank Nancy Ovedovitz for her fine work on design and Lorie Freed for very efficient assistance in the search for illustrations.

The forty-three original maps and diagrams were prepared from my sketches by Marsha Harrington and Nienke Prins under the supervision of Michael Kirchoff in the Cartographic Laboratory at Syracuse University. I thank them for their careful work and patience. I have made eager use of the great generosity of John Reps in supplying me with historic maps, plans, and views—many more than the ones actually reprinted here. I thank David Tatham for help with pertinent New England illustrations, and Mrs. Erwin Raisz for permission to use the great "Landforms of the United States" map created by her husband.

I have occasionally asked graduate assistants to compile information for me and I thank Jay Bruff, Patricia Lambert, Patricia Rossi, Michael Roark, David Barnet, and Richard Schein for their conscientious responses. I am especially indebted to my typists, Dolores Green, Gitta Trippany, and Pamela Walker, whose good cheer never faltered in the face of great stacks of yellow sheets disfigured by my scrawl. I thank John Crist and Kay Steinmetz for help in preparing the index.

Through all the years of preparation of this book I have enjoyed the full support of and many practical aids from my departmental chairman, Robert G. Jensen, and the Dean of the Maxwell School, Guthrie S. Birkhead. Much of the cost of preparing the manuscript and illustrations has been covered by the Cressey-James Fund of the Department of Geography, Syracuse University.

Many years ago at the School of Foreign Service, Georgetown University, Carroll Quigley and Jules Davids showed me what an exciting field history could be. I later took a different route into some of the same topics and I have always been grateful for their superb, unorthodox introductions to Western civilization and American history. In a more recent stage of my life I have had the great good fortune of sharing closely an interest in the cultural geography of America with Peirce F. Lewis and Wilbur Zelinsky, both of Pennsylvania State University. We have explored countrysides and walked cities together, talked and corresponded about an endless stream of topics, and they have opened my eyes to so many things and taught me so much that their mark is on this book to a degree they cannot realize and in more ways than I could readily specify. By so saying I of course do not wish to burden them with any direct responsibility for a work whose shape and content they have never seen. I only hope they will find some satisfaction in a book they have so generously encouraged.

The book is dedicated with deepest thanks to the one who has lived it with me day by day.

PART ONE
OUTREACH:
THE CREATION OF
AN ATLANTIC WORLD

The world was "discovered" a long time ago, well before the Great Discoveries. . . . Europe's own achievement was to discover the Atlantic and to master its difficult stretches, currents and winds. This late success gained it the doors and routes of the seven seas.

Fernand Braudel

Prologue

We begin in Europe because it was the Europeans who reached across the Atlantic and initiated the radical reshaping of America. That outreach to and encounter with the American World was at once a sequence of events and a set of processes. We shall be concerned with both, but in a special and limited way. There is no need to rehearse all the rich history of the voyages of discovery and the trials of early colonization, for these have been recounted in a huge and splendid and continually expanding literature. Nor shall we attempt to assess and apply in any formal way the more specialized monographic treatments of the ways in which political, economic, and social institutions operated to initiate, sustain, and become themselves transformed by such transoceanic enterprise. We seek only for some landmarks that can guide a wide-ranging reconnaissance from which we can make a useful base map for this particular interpretation of the shaping of America.

Our theme is the creation of a vast Atlantic circuit, a new human network of points and passages binding together four continents, three races, and a great diversity of regional parts. We need to get a clear picture of just where those European thrusts came from, where they made connections with coastlands overseas, and what kinds of transformations they initiated. We shall hold to this oceanic focus until all of the major Atlantic societies of Europe have gotten something substantial under way across the seas. That will force us to find our way through at least a century and a half of increasingly complex activity and to try to discern some general patterns amidst the dense details of time and space.

1. America as a Continuation

In A.D. 1492 the last Muslim hold upon Iberia was broken and Columbus sailed forth and discovered America. After seven centuries of grinding effort the Spanish had burst through the final barrier and in an explosion of energy spanned an ocean to begin the conquest of a new world.

Such a statement is at once misleading and usefully symbolic. The fall of Granada and the voyage of Columbus were not deeply interdependent events. Granada was a mountainous remnant that had no essential bearing upon Christian ventures out into larger realms. If there was indeed a "burst through the barrier" it had come centuries earlier with the Castilian conquest of Andalusia when warriors from the lean highlands seized control of the richest lowlands, the very seat of Islamic civilization in the west. So too was the Columbus voyage the culmination of a long prelude of Iberian Atlantic reconnaissance and island conquests. Yet this superficial coincidence can be given significant meaning, for it was in thanksgiving for the fall of Granada that Isabella equipped Columbus's expedition, and it is quite appropriate to see the *reconquista* in Europe and the range of the *conquistadores* over the Americas as successive phases in the same broad movement: the powerful outward expansion of Western Christian society. Viewed at such a scale these events of 1492 do mark an ending in the Old World, a beginning in the New, and a convenient symbolic concatenation in the larger structure of history.

American beginnings of course involved more than Iberia, and to the north we can see a vaguely similar pattern wherein Cabot's voyage from Bristol in 1497 and the English and French enterprise that followed can be regarded as an overseas thrust by these peoples beyond their centuries-old Celtic frontiers. Viewed more closely, here too the actual patterns fail to sustain so simple a relationship, or indeed, any close similarities to Iberia. The British Celts had become Christians before their adversaries, and although their own rather different version of the faith had long ago been brought into basic conformity with the dominant Western pattern, in 1497 they were still a group of distinctive peoples holding out on the rainy rugged edge of Europe against the chronic pressures of the Normans and Anglo-Saxons; their conquest was not a prelude but a later integral part of this larger Atlantic history. Furthermore, the long delays and difficulties in getting anything firmly under way in the New World from this part of the Old hardly represent an explosive expansion but rather contrast starkly with the Iberian conquest of half the Americas in half a century.

Nevertheless, it is best to begin with the broader view: to see those first Spanish and Portuguese, French and English explorers, conquerors, and settlers as the vanguard of a common movement, the cutting edge of a powerful Romano-Germanic Christian culture that had burst out upon the World Ocean and would eventually bring the coastlands of every continent under siege.

It is also pertinent to see these two great Italian seafarers as emblematic of another important dimension within this broader context. For several centuries this Western Christian culture had also been thrusting eastward into Byzantine, Arabic, and Turkish waters. Now this variable Mediterranean combination of crusade and commerce was being redirected westward to lands beyond the Ocean Sea. Columbus, a Genoese financed in large part by fellow Genoese residing in Seville, and Cabot, a Genoese native and Venetian citizen long experienced in the eastern trade, were only the most famous figures among the thousands of seafarers and entrepreneurs who turned from the Mediterranean to the Atlantic and thereby forged a deep and complete continuity between the earlier and later phases of this great European outreach.

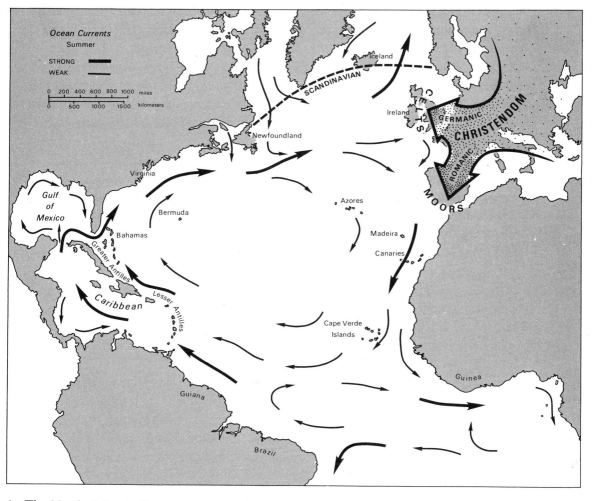

1. The North Atlantic Basin.

A GENERAL FORMULATION

All Atlantic-bordering European societies were advantageously located for the outreach to America. The general conformation of the North Atlantic and its circulations of water and winds lay open a very extensive and complicated coastline—reaching from the corner of Brazil to Labrador—to relatively ready access from any of the Atlantic ports of Europe. Within that broadly elliptical basin the ocean currents move clockwise, accompanied by relatively steady northeasterly trade winds on the south and the much more variable but prevailing westerly winds in the north. Mariners quickly learned to make use of this natural circulation: southwesterly outbound directly into the American Indies, returning northeasterly, arching parallel with the trend of the North American coast. Therefore this entire continental seaboard and the attenuated archipelago shielding its tropical seas became a single arena of action for the competition of Atlantic Europe. For more than two centuries events in one sector might ramify into others with important impact thousands of miles away on this western rim. Thus, even though we are concerned ultimately with the United States, this entire North Atlantic littoral is the necessary beginning framework.

But position is only a potential. Transatlantic operations called for unprecedented vision and vigor, initially from a few score persons, eventually from a much larger body if anything significant was to be sustained. Although news of the discoveries quickly reverberated through the maritime systems of western Europe, not all societies were equally well prepared for American adventures.

Clearly the first requisite for transatlantic operations was *seafaring*. All Atlantic European societies made use of the sea, but not all were equipped to extend the range of their operations so drastically. Still there were at least half a dozen local maritime districts, from Andalusia to the Bristol Channel, which had the seaworthy vessels, the skilled mariners and craftsmen, the facilities and hinterland resources, and the commercial connections to undertake ventures across the ocean. Those long engaged in the North Atlantic fishery as far north as Iceland could readily extend their reach to the Grand Banks, for this required no major alteration of routine practices. Transatlantic exploration, seasonal bartering, and coastal plundering could be carried out by individual entrepreneurs and small corporate associations backed by no more than local home resources. Such parties may have sought state approval, carried the flag, and laid claims in the name of the Crown, yet they were not essentially dependent upon state support.

But although the American seaboard was visibly empty along many stretches, it was not uninhabited. A European foothold, a trading post or exploration base, might be negotiated or even forced upon local Indians without great effort but anything larger would eventually meet strong resistance. Most of these European Atlantic societies were deeply predatory, quite ready to push in upon and plunder anything to their advantage. But again, not all had so institutionalized predation as to apply it toward effective control. Buccaneers might win a battle but the security of a large area required garrisons of soldiers under orderly administration, which in turn required (even if indirectly) the participation of the state much more critically. *Conquest*, the forced imposition of European rule upon American peoples, marked the initiation of true imperialism and represented a marshaling of far greater resources and more elaborate institutions than did sporadic bartering and plundering. The possibilities for such a successful extension of the state itself were obviously dependent upon a far greater complex of factors. We might well assume that those societies most freshly and extensively experienced in the conquest of territory and the governing of captive peoples would be the most likely to have eager visions of new conquests and proven institutions ready at hand, and thus be the most likely to seize upon and make the most of American opportunities.

Conquest may yield plunder and some exaction of tribute but it does not insure long-range returns. And of course the common American experience was that a coastal territory might be conquered only to have the native people withdraw into the interior, or die from new diseases introduced unwittingly by their conquerors, or disintegrate as a society and quickly diminish as a population from forced labor and brutal treatment. When such was the case, the only hope of realizing a benefit from conquest was to bring in a new labor force to work the land. Whether making use of African slaves, European bondsmen, or wage laborers, such an economy required local subsistence and support that could only come from the *planting* of settlers to cultivate the land, establish industries, and provide essential services. This true colonization demanded an even greater range of resources, institutions, and appropriate states of mind than mere conquest. Initial success in such transplantations had little to do with size or any assumed "surplus" of populations in the home country. All these European societies had potential colonists, but the recruitment of settlers and the support of an expanding European society overseas were fraught with enormous difficulties, and here again we may assume that experience counts, that those societies which had recently been involved in the colonization of new ground would be in the best position to make the first effective implantation of European civilization on American shores.

Seafaring, conquering, and *planting* may be taken as convenient labels for three kinds of activities undertaken by various European societies overseas. They can also be taken as three phases in the European encroachment upon the American seaboard, for seafaring is the obvious first essential and conquest a necessary prelude to any extensive planting. And since the planting of European settlers is clearly the most direct and effective means of rooting European culture onto the American seaboard, we may take seafaring, conquering, and planting as three essential components in the accomplishment of that end. We can expect that those European societies best equipped with the facilities, institutions, and attitudes of mind appropriate to these three components would be the earliest successful agents of that transfer, whereas a deficiency in any one would cause serious delays and difficulties.

This simple formulation is offered as a useful guide through a complex history, helping us to account for the great variations in responses and results in the decades following the discoveries. The variation that most attracts our interest at this point can be illustrated very simply: whereas only five years separate the voyage of Columbus out of Palos from that of Cabot out of Bristol, more than one hundred years separate the founding of Santo Domingo by the Spanish from that of James-town by the English. A quick review of these and some intervening ventures will not only illustrate the utility of our formulation but demonstrate some patterned interrelationships and provide the basis for a set of geographical generalizations about the whole process of transoceanic transfer and the interactions involved.

2. Iberian Initiatives

Columbus's sensational triumph of discovery and his dismal failure to accomplish anything substantial with what he discovered offers a telling application of our formulation, for the Columban voyages were an extension of seafaring and nothing more. That prior to his voyage Columbus was given such an extraordinary panoply of titles, authority, and rights to revenue over all that he discovered suggests that he was not expected to discover anything really extraordinary—a few more islands in the Ocean Sea perhaps, well beyond the Canaries and Azores. His expedition was capable of no more than limited barter or local plunder on encountering inhabited lands.

But of course discovery led to visions of conquest and exploitation. On his second voyage Columbus founded Isabella, an elaborate design for the first Euro-pean town in the New World. It was not a success. As Carl Sauer noted, "He wished a capital befitting his new station and ordered the building of an unneeded town in a wrong location." His attempts to exploit resources and establish a sound polity and society were little more successful, and Columbus died without having laid the foundations for the empire he so strongly desired. Much of this failure may be laid to the man's own vanities and personal limitations, but it also illustrates the more general proposition that successful imperialism is not simply a ready exten-sion from discovery. Columbus was an experienced seafarer but a novice at con-quest and colonization.

Once the Spanish Crown came to realize that there really was a New World to the west instead of a few new islands, and as the failures of Columbus as an individual entrepreneur became manifest, all the experience and institutions of a heritage of conquest, resettlement, and orderly administration were brought to bear upon these fresh opportunities. Which is to say that after the Columban ten-year prelude the reconquista, which after the fall of Granada had been carried by its centuries-old momentum on southward across the straits to Melilla and the Barbary Coast, was now redirected and projected westward across the Atlantic. It should be noted that Iberians had been gaining experience in combining seafaring, conquering, and planting for some years before Columbus in their subjugation of the Canary Islands. In this "trial laboratory of colonial matters," the indigenous people, the Guanches, resisted conquest, and Castille, which eventually obtained exclusive rights, had to replace various entrepreneurial efforts with more formal procedures. Parry notes that "in the Canaries, Spaniards served their first apprenticeship in the arts of colonial empire and had their first experience of converting and exploiting a primitive subject people." The apprenticeship was not in conquering and converting per se, but in doing so a thousand miles overseas against a people far different from the highly civilized Muslims. And the results were ominous. The liberty of baptized Canarians was recognized in law, but not always in fact. Those who resisted were fair game; thousands were sold into slavery and their lands taken by mainland opportunists (some of whom were themselves *conversos* who sought to escape the enmities and suspicions of home localities).

Thus the really firm beginnings in America date from Ovando's arrival in Santo Domingo in 1502 with a fleet of thirty vessels and twenty-five hundred men. Nicolas de Ovando, the experienced commander of a religious-military order in Spain, was sent as deputy of the Crown to be the governor general, the *adelantado* of the new *frontera.* He relocated and rebuilt his capital city (it had been destroyed by a hurricane shortly after his arrival) and founded a network of towns, all "a transplantation in general of the old Castilian municipality of the Middle Ages." Having administered large grants of conquered land and people in Spain, "he became the principal architect of the *encomiendo* system in the New World." The Church was an integral partner in the process, founding missions, building churches, and, in 1512, forming the first American bishopric. Within a few years there were perhaps ten thousand Spaniards living in Hispaniola, a colony supported by local produce and wealth extracted through the forced labor of the conquered population, administered through the Audiencia (established 1511), and connected routinely by commerce with the Casa de la Contratación (formed in Seville in 1503 to control this new Atlantic traffic). The vigor of this Hispaniola establishment soon faded as a result of the destruction of its Indian base and powerfully centrifugal attractions toward the mainland. But it does illustrate how the limitations of the individual entrepreneur were quickly overcome by experienced leaders working with tested tools and acting with the strong support of an old imperial society long involved in conquest, resettlement, and the administration of newly acquired ground.

The Portuguese sequence was not in general dissimilar. Oceanic seafaring developed only after the capture in 1415 of Ceuta, a Muslim stronghold on the African shore of the Strait of Gibraltar. Here, too, there was a strong historical logic in support of expanding such a foothold upon the Moroccan coast, but Prince Henry, who "made discovery an art and science; and . . . voyaging a national interest," directed explorations far to the south to tap the trans-Saharan gold trade nearer its source. These led to the discovery of Madeira and the Cape Verde Islands, as well as the Azores lying directly west, all of which were colonized.

About 1470 the Portuguese discovered Fernando Po, Príncipé, and São Tomé, uninhabited islands near the equator in the Bight of Biafra, which were quickly developed for sugar production by Portuguese entrepreneurs. Meanwhile they established trading stations and a few strong forts at key points along the African coast. Some attempts were made to evangelize the natives and to open diplomatic relations with African princes. But any hope of colonization was thwarted by the high mortality of Europeans due to African tropical diseases. Thus the Portuguese mainland venture remained primarily a coastal trading operation dealing in gold, slaves, and ivory. In this Atlantic and African prelude to their American enterprise the Portuguese displayed their superior skills in seafaring and an efficiency in planting without having to undertake much conquering.

Brazil had been discovered about 1500, but with more attractive commercial opportunities in Africa and India the Portuguese engaged in no more than occasional coastal bartering. When colonization was initiated in 1532, out of fear of French encroachment, it was done under the auspices of the Crown according to a comprehensive plan modeled on the "captaincy system already successfully tried in the Atlantic Islands." But the American mainland proved a rather more formidable environment than those benign Atlantic islands. The Indians often vigorously resisted their invaders and refused to provide a reliable labor force. Most of the *donatarios*, the proprietary landlords who were granted extensive hereditary powers in return for carrying out conquest and colonization, found the demands far beyond their skills or means. Some were repelled by the Indians; others failed for lack of colonists and profitable exports. The major early successful venture, in Pernambuco, drew upon fresh Portuguese tropical experience by the direct transfer of the sugar plantation and slave system from the Cape Verde and the Biafran islands. But in Brazil as in Hispaniola, more general success came only after the replacement of individual overlordship with a much larger measure of state control. The arrival in 1549 of Martin Afonso de Sousa, appointed to the new post of governor general and accompanied by several members of the new Jesuit order as well as a thousand colonists (many of them exiles), marks the beginning of much more direct initiative by the Crown and the Church, a shift analogous to that carried out by Ovando in Hispaniola nearly half a century earlier.

We can see this emergence of Brazil, therefore, as the culmination of more than a century of Portuguese seafaring, conquering, and planting, and a direct geographical extension of operations on the Atlantic islands and the African coast to this easternmost promontory of America. We can also see that the firm founding of Portuguese America lagged several decades behind that of Spanish America. This was certainly in part due to the greater commercial attractions of Africa and Asia. But their early Brazilian efforts also suggest that perhaps the Portuguese were less well prepared than the Spanish for conquest and planting on a continental scale. Their reconquista was further back in history, their recent colonization had been mainly on empty islands, and their national policies were more geared to overseas commercial adventuring than to systematic conquest and incorporation of land and people by state and church.

Nevertheless, both powers displayed an ability to carry forward a prodigious imperial enterprise, and that surely was related to their common Iberian and Atlantic experiences, which had given them a cast of mind and a set of institutions, military, civil, and ecclesiastical, by which they could implant their versions of civilization firmly on American shores long before their northerly neighbors in Atlantic Europe.

3. The Creation of New Spain

The American empire of Spain was indeed a prodigious creation—by 1600 it was a geopolitical structure extending from the Rio Grande del Norte to the Río de la Plata at the southern portal to Peru—but it was not simply an extension of European civilization across the high seas. If it was clearly Spanish (or, more specifically, Castilian) in concept and control, it had become distinctly Spanish-American in content and direction: a vigorous new hybrid from the intense encounter between old and unlike peoples.

The conquest itself was clearly a direct continuation of traditional processes, displaying both the freedoms and formalities of the reconquista. Thus the rapid, wide-ranging forays through the West Indies and mainland margins in search of riches to plunder and natives to exploit were a repetition on a larger stage of Iberian border warfare and the Canaries conquests, carried out in large part by adventurers on their own initiative and resources, outrunning any close supervision of the state. Yet leaders of major expeditions sought crown approval of their projects and confirmation of their gains; consequently, the imposition of a formal imperial system routinely followed in the wake of their conquests.

The initial thrusts into the American tropical seas were simple extensions. The lands and the inhabitants were neither a formidable challenge nor a powerful lure. Hispaniola, Puerto Rico, Cuba, and all the lesser islands were essentially a greater Canaries, a larger archipelago across a broader sea, the Arawaks and Caribs, like the Guanches, a primitive race to exploit or expel. Thus, in a macrocultural sense the real discovery of America was made in 1519 when Hernando Cortes broke in upon the core of the Aztec empire in the high-lying Valley of Mexico. Here amidst the mountains of Mesoamerica was a truly new world of peoples and cultures, an old civilization of great cities and rich countryside, many languages, and millions of citizens organized within a complicated set of theocratic and military states that shared a long, tumultuous history. Here was something more like the complex world of the Mediterranean than the simple insular scatterings of the Atlantic and the American tropical threshold.

And indeed, the early pattern of this imperial creation bears some likeness to that of the Roman conquest of the Greek world, wherein a simplified universal order was imposed upon a rich sociopolitical diversity. Thus the standardized Castilian conquest system, drawn out of its last great proving grounds in Andalusia and Granada and brought to bear upon the dense complexities of this American civilization, resulted in a New Spain which "at no point in its history" could be accurately characterized as simply "a Spanish society transplanted in the New World"; within a single generation it had all the marks of what all the world would come to recognize as distinctly "Mexican." The historical parallel must not be pushed too far. The Spanish impress upon America was greater than that of the Romans upon the Greeks, not because of an intrinsically more powerful imperial system but because a series of devastating epidemics reduced the Meosamerican indigenous population from more than twenty million to perhaps two million or less after the first century of contact.

Such drastic spasmodic depletions accompanied by the small but continual influx of Europeans radically altered the balance between the two peoples and forced them ever more closely together. The Crown originally defined a dual society, making the Indians wards of the state as a means to protect what rights they were to have and to provide an orderly basis for changes to be imposed, especially their conversion to Christianity. But the human substance of this legally defined *republica de los indios* dwindled so rapidly and the opportunity and need for drastic reorganization of the economy and society were so great that Indian and Spaniard were soon so intermingled and interdependent that miscegenation and acculturation resulted in a single complex hybrid creation in which Spanish formal institutions and systems were dominant but coexisted with and were increasingly articulated to an underlying folk culture, now much depleted and altered but everywhere vital and locally influential.

The richly developed Indian agriculture remained the principal basis of subsistence for much of the population, but the Spanish brought in wheat and barley, together with Andalusian plows and oxen, and established sugar plantations, vineyards, and other horticultural activities. The most profound change was the introduction of European cattle, sheep, swine, horses, burros, and mules. Thus a distinctive new Euro-American agricultural complex was rapidly formed, provid-

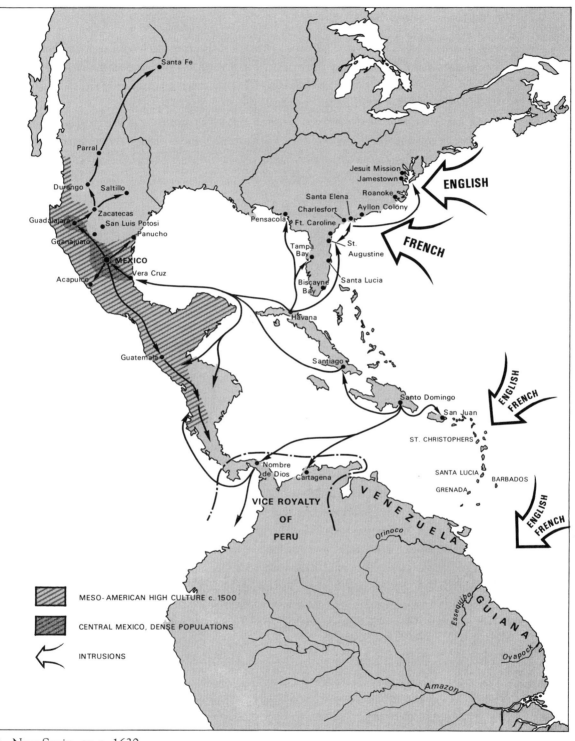

Santa Fe

Parral

Durango • Saltillo

Zacatecas
Guadalajara
San Luis Potosi
Guanajuato
Panucho

MEXICO
Vera Cruz

Acapulco

Jesuit Mission
Jamestown
Santa Elena   Roanoke
ENGLISH
Charlesfort   Ayllon Colony
Pensacola   Ft. Caroline
FRENCH
Tampa   St.
Bay   Augustine

Biscayne   Santa Lucia
Bay

Havana

Guatemala

Santiago

Santo Domingo
San Juan
ENGLISH
FRENCH

ST. CHRISTOPHERS

SANTA LUCIA   BARBADOS
GRENADA

Nombre
de Dios
Cartagena

VICE ROYALTY

OF

PERU

V E N E Z U E L A

Orinoco

ENGLISH
FRENCH

G U I A N A

Essequibo

Oyapock

Amazon

MESO-AMERICAN HIGH CULTURE c. 1500

CENTRAL MEXICO, DENSE POPULATIONS

INTRUSIONS

2. New Spain, to c. 1630.

ing an enriched subsistence, new industries, and even more surpluses for export to labor-poor colonies such as Cuba and Hispaniola. To the north, beyond the margins of Mesoamerican civilization, in the drier open lands of the Gran Chichimeca of the "barbarian" hunters and gatherers, the balance was far more European than native American. Here a ranching industry geared especially to supplying the mining districts with cattle and mules was established, drawing directly upon the resources and systems of the Iberian Meseta, the only area of western Europe where the management of large herds of cattle on horseback had been developed.

The Spanish intensively probed that north in search of precious minerals, making a series of discoveries of rich silver deposits, and establishing a number of great mining camps, as at Guanajuato, San Luis Potosí, Zacatecas, and far to the northwest at Parral, nine hundred miles from Mexico. Exploitation of these coveted resources required vast programs of regional development, involving the conquest of the local Indians in a series of destructive wars, the importation of laborers as well as whole colonies of Indians from the south to establish farms and provide stability, the organization of extensive systems of transport and supply, and the founding of many towns.

"The Spanish empire was an empire of towns." The municipality was the basic unit in the territorial hierarchy and the physical town was the anchor and focus of social and political life. "If the great symbol of the English colonist is the frontiersman clearing the land, the symbol of the Spanish colonization should be the *adelantado* pacing out the grids of a Spanish town." This rectangular plan with central plaza, varied in scale and detail but standard in general form, became one of the great instruments of conquest and colonization, defined in the basic codes. It had not been routinely applied in the *reconquista* and was not derived from any common form of Spanish town. But the idea was as old as the Romans; there were a number of examples of such plans in Iberia (whose lineage is probably traceable to the French *bastides* in the twelfth-century recolonizations just across the Pyrenees); and the design had been used by Castille for at least two new towns just prior to Columbus's voyage. Thus Ovando laid out Santo Domingo according to this general plan, Cortes superimposed it upon the ruins of the Aztec capital at Tenochtitlán, and within a few years it was being so routinely used for so many new settlements that a century later the grid-pattern town—full of houses roofed in red tiles, focused on a central plaza, the whole overshadowed by church or cathedral— had become the great symbolic landscape of Spanish America.

Such towns were full of varieties of people representative of this great encounter and sustained contact. In all of the larger centers there would be several different Indian groups, some representing displacements, migrations, or new associations

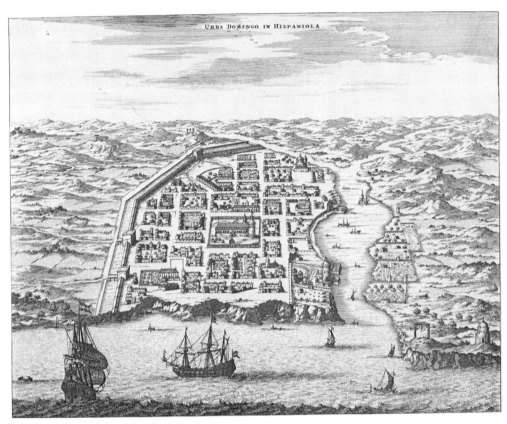

3. Santo Domingo, 1671.
Although Santo Domingo's prosperous days were long past, this depiction of the oldest European city in the Americas, published 169 years after its founding, displays a fine example of the common Spanish plan and the wealth and status of an early colonial capital. The cathedral, in which Christopher Columbus's bones were eventually interred, was begun in 1514, completed in 1540. The impressive stone castle at the river's edge was built by the discoverer's son Diego, who was appointed governor in 1509. The first settlement was on the opposite bank of the Rio Ozama, where fields are shown. The plate is from *De Nieuwe en Onbekende Weerld* by Arnoldus Montanus, and the appearance therein of views of this and other cities of the American tropics reflects the Dutch dominance in the seventeenth century. (Courtesy of John W. Reps)

from a wide area, and these were further varied by differing degrees of acculturation to Spanish forms as displayed in clothing, coiffure, language, and participation in civic life. By 1600 a large proportion of the urban population was of mestizo or *mulatto* origin, and such mixtures were so common and so complex as to defy any simple gradation of social status. Those of apparently pure European ancestry asserted and largely maintained social dominance, but these, too, became divided between those born in Spain (*peninsulares*) and those born in America (*criollos*), the latter soon outnumbering the former despite continual immigration. Regional identities, still strong in Spain, faded quite rapidly in the New World except for the Basques, few in number but influential in commerce, mining, and the royal bureaucracy. By 1600 Castilian had become the dominant language in the homeland and the official language of the empire.

Thus New Spain, that great Mexican portion of Spanish America, was much more than a superimposition of Spaniards upon a decapitated Aztec empire. It was a new creation resulting from the forceful application of a sharply honed and simplified imperial system to the programmatic reshaping of a highly developed civilization. As Octavio Paz has put it, the conquest of Mexico was "a historical act intended to create unity out of the cultural and political plurality of the pre-Cortesian world." The Spanish "postulated a single language, a single faith and a single lord" against that variety, and in less than a century had created a Spanish-speaking, Roman Catholic, civic-centered, land-based, multiracial, stratified society, organized within a rational hierarchy of territorial authority.

This territorial structure was a vast geopolitical system that recurrently showed great expansive power. Thus in 1600 a *New* Mexico was being created fifteen hundred miles north of the core of the first Mexico by a process still reflective of the reconquista. Juan de Oñate, from a family enriched by the mines of Zacatecas and Parral, had gained royal permission to subdue, at his own expense, the region of the agricultural Pueblo Indians whom Coronado had encountered sixty years before clustered along the upper Rio Grande and on several isolated mesas to the west, a population of perhaps well over 100,000 living in more than sixty towns. Oñate proceeded like many another predatory adventurer beyond the reach of official supervision, conquering, punishing, plundering whatever lay at hand, searching for mines and riches never to be found, settling in to exact tribute from a badly disrupted and sullen society. But as was also common to the process, such initial agents of conquest were soon overtaken by the formal institutions of the system and punished for their transgressions against the higher objectives of empire. Thus in 1606 Oñate was recalled, fined, and exiled from his new province; a new governor was soon sent to lay out a new capital town more closely following imperial instructions, missionaries moved in upon the largest of the nearby Indian pueblos, and the more orderly processes of incorporation of new lands and peoples into the larger imperial society was under way.

Jamestown, Quebec, and Santa Fe were founded within a year or two of one another, and are sometimes considered focal points for the earliest significant developments of regional societies in the United States and Canada. But these contemporaries were expressions of utterly different histories and phases of European expansion. For while the first two represent the precarious experimental struggle of the English and the French to get any substantial enterprise firmly attached to American shores, the new capital town near the southern end of the

Sangre de Cristo mountains was merely one more town added to the hundreds of such places already established by the Spanish in their century-old routine of conquering and planting in the Americas.

4. The Luso-African Contribution

Portugal's role in the history of America stems from an unintended imperial allocation and some early unexceptional commercial transactions, but it has been of enormous consequence. That their exploration of coastal Africa positioned the Portuguese to become the first Europeans in the trans-Atlantic slave trade is of course well known. What needs to be emphasized and clarified is that the Portuguese provided more than a mere seafaring link between Africa and America: they created the systems and societies that made possible and set the pattern for the creation of an Afro-American world. Before Columbus happened upon the American Indies a model for their colonization and exploitation was taking shape in the Luso-African tropics.

Shortly after Columbus's return from his first discoveries a formal division of imperial hemispheres was made by drawing a line through the vast emptiness of the mid-Atlantic, allocating to the Spanish whatever lands lay to the west, and reserving to the southward-probing Portuguese Africa and lands to the east. In 1494 this line was shifted somewhat farther to the west in recognition of Spanish retention of the Canaries, and only some years later did it become known that this diplomatic demarcation cut through a great eastward bulge of South America, giving the Portuguese claim to Brazil (a sequence which has made some historians wonder if the Portuguese knew more than they had revealed about the conformation of the South Atlantic). However, the foundations for a Portuguese America and for a wider impact upon the Americas had been laid in lesser lands some decades before.

Madeira, the Azores, and the Cape Verde Islands were all colonized in the fifteenth century. In the history of European discovery and exploration it is common to recognize these little Atlantic islands as stepping-stones across the ocean. But they were much more than stations on the route to the New World; they were themselves a New World and important proving grounds for new seafaring and planting systems, as Boxer notes:

> The settlement of these uninhabited islands initiated the Portuguese into the practice of overseas colonization, and the settlers were literally pioneers in a New World. This was something of which they were naturally conscious, as shown by the fact that the first boy and girl born on Madeira were aptly christened Adam and Eve.

It was an opportunistic movement, initiated by individual seafarers, entrepreneurs, small companies, and groups of nobles, with varying royal support or eventual endorsement, and it drew upon many strands of that Iberian convergence—Portuguese, Castilian, Italian, Norman, Flemish. Sauer emphasizes the routine procedure of colonization in the Azores: "In the span of twenty years the archipelago in mid-ocean had become part of rural Portugal, a land of country gentry, farmers, and fishermen with a sizeable Flemish enclave." Domestication of this little scattering of islands took several decades, but it was initiated under the general overlordship of Prince Henry. Sauer's description seems an echo of Stanislawski's stress upon the importance that Portuguese kings had placed upon the orderly resettlement of lands recovered from the Muslims in previous centuries. On the other hand, Verlinden emphasizes Italian precedents, noting the prominence of Genoese merchants and the close resemblance of forms and procedures to those they had long applied in the Aegean and the Levant. Thus a new combination of these planting and seafaring traditions was brought to bear upon this new Atlantic World.

The Azores were halfway to the Grand Banks and the Portuguese were among the earliest to probe and limn the North American coast. In 1521, Fagundes, a mariner from Viana do Castello in northernmost Portugal, got royal permission to establish a colony there as a more substantial base for fishermen, trade, and the manufacture of soap. Some evidence suggests that such a station was built on Cape Breton Island, but if so it did not last long and thereafter the Portuguese continued to be no more than a seasonal presence along with many others in the Great Fishery. It was in their southward rather than their westward voyaging that they would lay the basis for their crucial link with America.

The Cape Verde Islands, discovered in the 1450s, were also uninhabited but were considerably less attractive than Madeira and the Azores. Lying in the latitude of the southern Sahara two thousand miles from home this archipelago of semi-arid volcanic peaks provided a convenient base for explorers but rather meager possibilities for colonization. Pushing on to the south and east along the trend of the African coast the Portuguese seemed to have reached their original main objective of all this voyaging in 1471 when they came upon peoples amply supplied with gold ornaments, which they readily exchanged for iron, brass, and cloth. A decade of annual trading voyages (challenged on occasion by Castilian forays) proved profitable and the Portuguese decided to establish a permanent foothold on El Mina ("the mine," their term for this area, which soon became known as the Gold Coast). Thus in 1482 an expedition brought stonemasons and carpenters to build the fortress of São Jorge da Mina, as well as officials, priests, clerks, doctors, workers, and soldiers to staff and garrison it. Working through established networks of African traders they succeeded in diverting a profitable

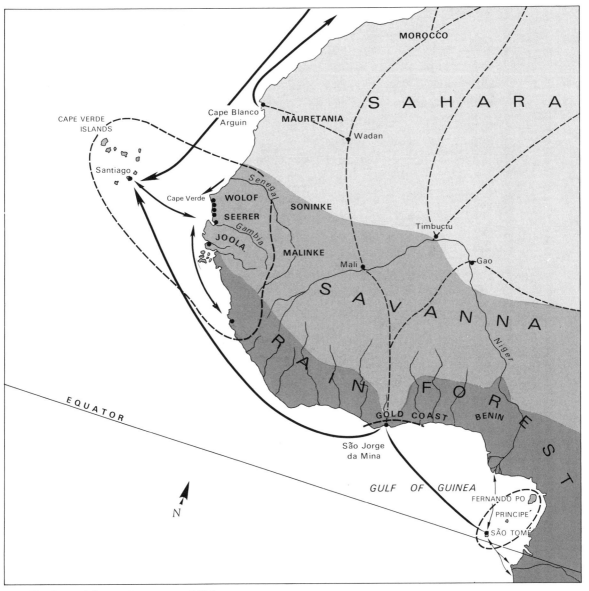

4. The Luso-African System, c. 1500.

portion of the gold mined in the interior highlands from long-established trans-Saharan traffic ways.

Gold was the great focus of Portuguese interest in Africa. It became basic to the homeland economy and central to royal support of overseas operations, as it was the incentive and means for continuing exploration and speculations. But all the while another African resource was emerging as profitable and apparently capable of extension to serve new and expanding markets. Portuguese seafarers first made connection with the African slave trade in the 1440s after reaching Cape Blanco. From a small station on Arguin Island in the lee of that bold promontory they opened trade with Mauretanian merchants and soon attracted Muslim caravans. For a time they even had an inland post at Wadan on one of the main trans-Saharan routes. The several hundred slaves obtained annually by such means were readily disposed of in Lisbon, the Algarve, and Madeira. Slaves had long been a common part of the Mediterranean and Iberian scene. Some were worked in small gangs on galleys or on large estates, but mostly they were artisans or domestics of one sort or another, part of the service and adornment of a rich household, and integral if restricted members of the family and local community. In general, the system worked toward increasing acculturation and incorporation of such people through the generations, while being sustained by fresh additions from the sporadic trade in new captives taken from some distant military frontier, such as the Balkans (the word itself perhaps derived from "Slav," from peoples seized in the bitter fourteenth-century Turkish conquests of southeastern Europe). Similarly, slavery was an old institution in Africa. Throughout West Africa slaves were a part of most societies. They were "outsiders," people who had been captured in war or purchased or born in captivity lacking proper affiliations with clan or caste to give them a legal claim on ordinary freedoms. Most were employed in family households, and all had a recognized status as part of the community. In some of the larger African states royal slaves, like those in the Turkish empire, were persons of special talents and privileges; used in administration and as specialized military units, such groups were often quite powerful and not always under close control.

These ancient systems became transmuted by stages in the early decades of this new Atlantic World into what would become the distinctive American type of slavery. The general marks of that type were as follows:

1. the extensive use of mass labor in specialized agricultural or mineral production for export;
2. the exploitation of such laborers as a commodity to be used up and replaced by purchase;
3. an extensive system to supply large numbers for sale annually at a reasonable price;
4. the heavy male bias in such use and trade, inhibiting the comprehensive formation of families;
5. the formalized debasement in custom, and in part in law, of such people as unworthy of acculturation and incorporation into the general community; and
6. the linkage of status with color, by which Blacks but not Whites were subject to slavery.

The sugar boom in late fifteenth-century Madeira offers an early hint of this new type. The first mill was erected in 1452; within a few years shipments were being made to England and Flanders, improvements in refining soon made Madeira sugar a superior product, and for a brief while these intensively terraced little islands became Europe's greatest source of an increasingly valued commodity. Sugar cane is a South Asian plant that the Arabs had brought to Egypt and Palestine, from where it was carried to various Mediterranean districts and to the Algarve and southern Morocco. The heavy hot labor of cultivation and harvesting had long been done in large degree by some sort of coerced labor; Galloway states that the sugar-slave link "became firmly forged in Crete, Cyprus, and Morocco" using war captives marketed by the Turks. The Madeira beginning coincided with the firm Portuguese connection with Muslim traders at Arguin, providing an ample supply of Black slaves from tropical Africa.

The Madeira industry soon reached its limits, and the Cape Verde Islands were too dry to provide more than a minor extension. The next major development was the discovery of another set of uninhabited islands lying off the great bend of the African coast in the Gulf of Guinea: São Tomé, tiny Príncipe, and mountainous Fernando Po (Bioko). Colonization of São Tomé began about 1485. The rich volcanic soils of its rainy lower terraces proved superb for sugar cane, and the "strange company of young Jews, exiles, officials, traders, and slaves" who pioneered here soon made it a major source of European supply. And here slavery began to take on a new scale and character. The Portuguese at São Jorge da Mina had been dealing in slaves, primarily buying from coastal traders to sell to other African merchants for use as porters in the expanding traffic to the interior mining region. Trade was now quickly broadened to include the Congo and later Angola, to supply the demand for thousands of laborers. The estimate of 50,000 slaves imported into São Tomé by 1550 indicates the intensity of the sugar boom, the high mortality of slavery's victims, and the rapid emergence of a mass procurement and marketing system.

São Tomé would remain the largest slave importer for several decades and would thereafter long serve as a major entrepôt for the assemblying and seasoning of slaves for marketing to Brazil, but the transatlantic traffic in slaves was begun from other sources and the early destination was Spanish, not Portuguese, America. In Hispaniola as in the Canaries the Spanish first tried to make use of natives, but the devastations of disease and enslavement so quickly depleted this labor supply that other sources were sought. Ovando arrived with authorization to bring in *ladinos* (Iberian Christianized Negroes) to work in the mines and in 1510 shipments of *bozales* (Negroes not yet Christianized but untainted by Islam or Judaism) were allowed. By 1517 Genoese entrepreneurs and Canarian technicians had gotten sugar production underway and the first licenses were issued for direct importations from Africa. Thus, when Cortes left Cuba for Mexico in 1519 "the basic machinery for importing slaves to the Indies had been established." That "machinery" was entirely in Portuguese control, and the principal center for the development of the trade was in the Cape Verde Islands.

These islands, lying three hundred miles out from the westernmost headland of

Africa, had served well as a revictualing station, providing dried goat meat, grain, yams, fruit, and salt for Portuguese fleets working the Gulf of Guinea and, after da Gama's voyage, the Indian Ocean trade. Now they became pivotal in a new Portugal–Africa–West Indies traffic, and slave procurement was intensified on the adjacent mainland. Hence "Guine de Cabo Verde," the Portuguese term for the hinterland of the Senegal, Gambia, and Casamance rivers and the many estuaries on south to Sierra Leone, became the first major source of the African contribution to the repopulation of the American tropics and "the key region for cultural interchange between Africa and the West through a series of Afro-European communities in the coastal towns."

It proved impossible to establish any substantial European enclave on the coast of West Africa because endemic diseases, especially yellow fever and malaria, proved as deadly to Europeans as European measles, smallpox, and pneumonia were to American Indians. The mortality of European residents and visitors was often eighty percent or higher. Hence they tended to stay on ships, work through African traders, and tarry as briefly as possible. The semi-arid Cape Verde Islands were somewhat less dangerous, but, more important, because few Portuguese families could be lured to such distant and niggardly lands, there rapidly developed a mulatto population, an amalgam from the various Portuguese, Genoese, Castilian, and other European settlers and sojourners and from the Wolof, Sereer, Malinke, Joola, and other African captives and associates. Such offspring were generally immune to African diseases and could make familial or ethnic connection with mainland societies. Therefore, here on the Cape Verde Islands and adjacent Africa a racial and cultural fusion took place, resulting in the first Africanization of a European society. To European eyes the great majority of the Cape Verdeans were a "colored" people, mostly mulatto, with Black Africans, slave and free, a routine part of every community; yet the ruling polity, language, religion, dress, and social norms were dominantly Portuguese. Black clergy served as priests in the cathedral on Santiago and as missionaries on the African coast; Black merchants, industrialists, and craftsmen provided the goods for trade; Black deckhands and canoemen manned the distinctive vessels (a Portuguese and African blend) of local commerce; and, critical to the entire system, the lançados, a mulatto trading class—"speaking both creole and African tongues, professing Christianity and practicing paganism, tolerated by African societies but not part of them, imbued with certain European racial concepts, and wedded to the notion that they were 'Christian', 'Portuguese', and 'white'"—became the resident brokers in the coastal and river towns of Senegambia who worked with the indigenous Muslim juula trading caste to procure slaves from old and far-reaching networks. The trade itself came to depend a good deal upon a Cape Verde Island textile industry, which, through extensive use of both slave and free artisans, developed a highly valued cloth from African cottons featuring blends of African, Moorish, and Portuguese designs. So, too, this region, islands and mainland together, became the first major area for the exchange of African, European, and American crops and the creation of new agricultural systems therefrom. African rice, yams, and millet were taken to America, and American maize and manioc entered into Senegambian agriculture. The provisioning of slave ships became an important part of the regional economy.

Here, therefore, in the Cape Verde Islands–Senegambia in the late fifteenth and early sixteenth century a region was formed that became literally fundamental to the creation of America and to its enormous and variegated Afro-American component.

In the 1530s that regional role began to be modified and shared as the trans-atlantic slave traffic began to swell and diversify into new markets. In 1531 the first direct shipment from São Tomé to Santo Domingo and San Juan was made. In this decade sugar production got underway in several other parts of Spanish America, including several mainland districts. But the conquest of Mexico lured the Spanish far more heavily into mining and ranching and governing than into plantation agriculture. Slaves continued to be imported annually through the Portuguese system but this interimperial traffic became far overshadowed by the belated rise of Portugal's own American colony to preeminence in world sugar production. Drawing upon Madeira and Cape Verdean sources, Genoese entrepreneurs implanted a sugar industry in Brazil and began to ship to European markets in the late 1530s. But there were many difficulties and success came only after the shift in policy from the early *donatario* system to more direct governmental initiative in the planting of a major Portuguese emigrant colony with authority to import African slaves. From the miscellaneous band of adventurers and exiles, a wealthy European and mulatto planter class rapidly emerged, to preside over households of Black and mulatto servants and large gangs of enslaved African fieldhands on rude estates hacked out of the forests of Bahia and Pernambuco. This process was in all essentials a demonstration of how during the half century preceding the small African equatorial island of São Tomé had been "a portent of the future, the pilot project for new world sugar plantations." In the last quarter of the sixteenth century Brazil suddenly became the largest slave-importing region in the world; it was the onset of an insatiable appetite: "For three centuries Brazil would consume more African slaves than would any other portion of the Atlantic world." The enduring legacy of this horrendous appetite was the creation of the largest and most densely Africanized region in mainland America and, more broadly, of one of the greatest, most complex, and vital mulatto societies of the world.

Thus Portugal developed the system that bound Europe, Africa, and America together. For well over a century the Atlantic slave trade was essentially a Por-

tuguese monopoly (recurrently challenged but never seriously depleted by interlopers and smugglers), a system continually adjusting to new supplies and demands, extending its impact ever more powerfully upon the human geography of
the Atlantic World. The Atlantic islands and the Lisbon market had provided an
impetus and the Cape Verde Islands–Senegambia procurement and marketing
system was effectively in place by the time Columbus opened the way to the New
World. The Spanish were able to connect readily with that system and extend it
across the Atlantic to help lay the foundation of the first Euro-American empire
and they continued to draw upon it year after year so that an African ingredient,
while varying in strength and never dominant, became laced through the whole
body of Spanish America. Meanwhile on little São Tomé the new Euro-African
sugar production system was rapidly perfected to a form that would readily transfer
to the grand stage of Brazil and thereby establish across the equatorial Atlantic the
most powerful bonds between Africa and America.

By 1600, it is estimated, about 275,000 Africans had been sold into slavery
within the European-dominated Atlantic world. Nearly 50,000 of these had gone
to Europe itself, but that sizeable total becomes a trickle when spread over the
century and a half of shipment, and some portion of these slaves were reexported.
The Atlantic islands accounted for another 25,000, São Tomé over 75,000,
reflecting the emergence of the firm sugar–Black slave link. Thus the American
imports account for less than half of the total to that date, but America was clearly
the great market of the future. In the last quarter of the sixteenth century more
than eighty percent of this mounting outflow was directed to Spanish and Portuguese America.

Thus the system and pattern of the tragic African diaspora were also in place
long before the northern Europeans got a firm hold upon any part of America, and
African slaves and Brazilian sugar had joined Mexican and Peruvian gold and silver
as powerful lures to avaricious and nationalistic seafaring predators. It was through
their opportunistic forays into this tropical realm that small strands of this African-
American connection would become attached to North American shores and
introduce one of the most fateful additions to American diversity.

5. Initiatives in the North and Huguenot Enterprise

John Cabot's voyage from Bristol in 1497 and his discovery of a mainland directly
across the western sea is a famous but increasingly controversial event. Dispute
arises over the geographical question of exactly which coastland he sighted, and
over the historical question of whether he was the first to have sailed that far and
sighted that land. Inferential evidence suggests that Bristol mariners may already

have known of that North American shore and been harvesting its rich seas for a decade or more, a reading which led Sauer to assert that "the English were first to cross the western sea . . . by private initiative of seamen and merchants of Bristol, experienced in trade with Iceland, Madeira, and the Azores." But even if true this minority view does not seem to alter the common version of subsequent events. As Quinn states,

> It did not greatly matter whether men from Bristol or men from Terceira [Azores] first saw land in the west, so long as they did not align their sovereigns behind them to obtain exclusive rights and thus manipulate discovery and control exploitation in these areas.

There were several attempts to follow up the first Cabot voyage with larger exploring and trading expeditions, but with little result, and thereafter there is little evidence of substantial English activity toward American shores for many years; at most some continued participation in the Great Fishery may be inferred. This brief flurry of initiative seems critically dependent upon the Bristol link with Azorean seafaring and Italian mariners, while the long lapse may suggest that in general the English were not yet ready in mind and institutions for a sudden extension into transoceanic enterprise. They were seeking a passage to Cathay, and the newfound land was itself an insufficient lure.

The French rather than the English were the most immediate and prominent successors of Cabot. Norman, Breton, Basque, and Rochellais mariners working the fisheries of the Grand Banks and Newfoundland and Labrador shores were the vanguard of wide-ranging French transatlantic initiatives. Verrazzano, Italian-born but long resident in France, sailed from Dieppe to conduct an extensive exploration of the North American coast in 1524 and then helped open trading with Brazil, where French vessels were soon more frequent than those of the Portuguese and where a number of ephemeral outposts were set up. In the 1530s Cartier, a St. Malo mariner who was probably well acquainted with the Brazilian as well as the Newfoundland coasts, made two voyages, investigated the St. Lawrence River as far as the Indian settlement of Hochelaga (Montreal), and spent a winter near Stadacona (Quebec). Both men became interested in the colonization of this part of America. Verrazzano (who was killed by Carib Indians in 1528) was reported to have returned from his first great voyage with strong ambitions "to people the regions he discovered with French colonists, to introduce European plants and domestic animals, and to bring the 'poor, rough and ignorant people' of North America to Christianity"—in short, to transplant European civilization onto American shores. Cartier's program on his return in 1541 was narrower in concept, for the main purpose of his colony on the St. Lawrence at Charlesbourg-Royal (near Quebec) was a base for further exploration for a Northwest Passage and

conquest of a rumored rich kingdom of Saguenay. He was able to obtain only a few
colonists, mostly convicts, and after one season of Indian harassment, scurvy, and
winter hardship he abandoned the place. A reinforcement party, led by Roberval,
of two hundred settlers, including some women, arrived soon after and built a more
substantial settlement, but after another winter of sickness and cold they too gave
up and went home.

These were important experiences. France certainly had the requisite seafaring
skills and was applying them to the search for wealth in an expanding oceanic
world. The lure of plunder, whether of treasure-laden Spanish ships or mythical
American kingdoms, was primary, but trade with the Indians for furs had been
initiated even though it was not as yet of compelling interest, and the idea of
colonization was becoming an integral part of French plans. These voyages,
backed by the king, were well equipped; had the barrels of iron pyrites and quartz
crystals that Cartier brought back from Canada turned out to be the gold and
diamonds he thought they were, we may assume that the New France he proclaimed on these deep probes into northern America would have become substan-
tiated by a major colony long before the days of Champlain.

By mid-century Protestantism was rapidly gaining strength in many parts of
France, particularly among some sections of the nobility and the bourgeoisie. The
severe religious and political tensions arising therefrom provided a new impetus
and a new kind of colonist for American ventures. Gaspard de Coligny, Admiral of
France, became strongly sympathetic to the Protestant cause and when the soldier
of fortune Villegaignon proposed the idea of a Huguenot colony on the coast of
Brazil, Coligny saw an opportunity to unite humanitarian and strategic objectives.
Thus in 1555 an expedition sailing from the naval base at Le Havre established a
settlement on an island in Rio de Janeiro harbor. In the following year nearly three
hundred reinforcements were sent to this "Antarctique Gaul," including fourteen
Genevans selected by John Calvin himself (Villegaignon and Calvin had been
contemporaries at the University of Paris). More were preparing to go but the
colony was soon in severe trouble. Villegaignon, sensing the tide of affairs in
France, declared his Catholicism and came into bitter conflict with the Protestants. This dissension together with great practical difficulties in getting the settlement established led to a disintegration, the return of most, and the slaughter of
the remnant by the Portuguese in 1560.

The Huguenots were strong, however, in the western and northern coastal
regions, and the idea of Huguenot colonies in America was now very much alive.
Attention was now turned to the northern margins of Iberian America, lured
especially by the possibilities of preying upon the Spanish treasure fleet in its
annual voyage through the Florida Strait. The Spanish had made several attempts
to establish a permanent presence on the mainland coast of Atlantic Florida but

without success. In 1523 Ayllon, a wealthy entrepreneur from Hispaniola, brought a party of several hundred colonists, slaves, and missionaries to a site on the "Rio Gualdape" (presumably the Savannah River or vicinity). But Ayllon suddenly died and dissension and Indian pressures soon caused a withdrawal. In 1559 a new governor of "Florida and Santa Elena" undertook a major strategic program to establish a colony on the Gulf Coast of northern Florida as the base of an overland route across the peninsula to an outpost at Santa Elena, but this, too, was a failure. By the time the French arrived in force the Spanish had just made a careful coastal reconnaissance as far north as Chesapeake Bay but had failed to establish a permanent foothold.

In 1562 another group of largely Huguenot colonists—sponsored by Coligny and led by Jean Ribault, an experienced French buccaneer—sailed from Le Havre and set up a small base, Charlesfort, on Port Royal Sound. Ribault returned for reinforcements but found that religious warfare had broken out and Le Havre was under siege, so he fled to England. The small colony soon broke up from internal conflict. As soon as peace was restored in France another party under Laudonniere, who had been second in command under Ribault, was sent out in 1564 and established Fort Caroline on the St. John's River in Florida. But weak leadership, a neglect of subsistence in favor of a frantic search for gold, and troubles with the Indians put the colony in severe difficulty. A fleet carrying reinforcements led by Ribault arrived the next year but was almost immediately dispersed and damaged by a severe storm. The colony was then attacked and taken by the Spanish, and in a savage retribution for this intrusion all but a few of the captured French were executed. The French retaliated with various forays but the outbreak of much more extensive religious warfare within France, culminating in the Massacre of St. Bartholomew's Day in 1572 (in which Coligny was murdered), and the suppression of Protestantism brought a cessation of sponsored colonization projects.

These French thrusts prompted the Spanish to strengthen their hold upon the tropical borderlands. The destruction of Fort Caroline was part of a comprehensive geopolitical program entrusted to an Asturian naval commander, Pedro Menéndez de Avilés. Menéndez envisioned a strategy of development anchored on Havana, pivoted on Florida, and reaching from the Pánuco River on the northwest shore of the Gulf of Mexico far up the Atlantic coast to Chesapeake Bay. With a large force brought over directly from Spain he established St. Augustine as a major mainland base, and a number of smaller garrisons and missions, including forts on the sites of the two abortive French colonies. In 1570 a Jesuit mission was begun somewhere in the vicinity of the Powhatan Indians in the lower James River area, and in the next few years a considerable number of Asturian farmer-colonists were sent to Santa Elena. But by now a long history of brutality and treachery had made nearly all the Indian tribes of southeastern North America enemies of the Spanish. The

Chesapeake missionaries were soon murdered, the colonies were harassed and dwindled in strength and resolve, French privateers reappeared, and in 1586 St. Augustine itself was devastated in a raid by Sir Francis Drake. That was a powerful signal of the entry of a new contestant for American empire, and indeed, an English colony had already been initiated in the northern reaches of what the Spanish regarded as their Florida.

6. The Emergence of the English

The abrupt collapse of Huguenot initiatives toward America was followed by the emergence of the English as a major transatlantic force. Although the cessation of the one was not simply the cause of the other the sequence was significant, for the English learned directly, variously, and extensively from the French. Rowse noted: "It seems that the idea of American colonization came to us out of that Huguenot circle."

English seafaring only gradually realized the full oceanic possibilities of the new age, first in voyages of trade and privateering to Brazil and the West Indies, then by corporate mercantile ventures to Morocco, Guinea, and, by way of a new north-east sea route, Muscovy. Meanwhile Bristol and West Country fishermen rose to prominence in the Grand Bank and Labrador fisheries. As Morison notes, it was not until the 1550s and 1560s that "Englishmen were acquiring experience of deep water and long voyages which qualified them to contest empire with mighty Spain"; and in the 1580s in his argument for extensive American undertakings Hakluyt laid great stress on the much-needed benefits to English seafaring: "For it is the long voyages . . . that harden seamen and open unto them the secrets of navigation." In most of these activities French influence was apparent, arising in part from long-standing maritime connections across the Channel, in part from close links in political and intellectual circles, and perhaps most forcefully from direct involvement with the Huguenot cause. In 1546 sixty French mariners, pilots, and hydrographers, all Huguenot sympathizers, were in temporary service with the now Protestant English king. Ribault, the naval leader of French Florida, was one of them and when he again came to England in 1562 he soon organized a joint Anglo-French colonization scheme for that same coast. Queen Elizabeth gave Stukeley, the English coleader, a license to plant a colony there but no expedition was sent. John Hawkins had similar ideas and on his second slave-trading circuit to the West Indies visited Fort Caroline in 1565 just before its destruction by the Spanish; as mayor of Plymouth and a leading seafarer, Hawkins became heavily involved in assisting the Rochellais against the siege by French Catholic forces. Hawkins, Drake, Gilbert, and Raleigh are only the most famous among the leaders in Elizabethan oceanic and American ventures who were directly involved with the Huguenots. Richard Eden, the Cambridge geographer whose translations from Spanish accounts presented "for the first time in English or in England a substantial body of information on the new age," entered Huguenot service in 1562 and may be presumed to have paved the way in England for the enormously influential work of the two Richard Hakluyts, and in France for the comprehensive foraging by the younger Hakluyt (during his five years as chaplain to the English ambassador in Paris) for all matters relating to voyages and colonizations. Among the most famous of this Hakluyt's finds and early publications were the official reports of French Florida, which presumably were of considerable practical value in giving good firsthand information about America and the opportunities and difficulties of planting there.

Howard Mumford Jones has called attention to the fact that the very words *colony* and *plantation* seem to appear in English only in the 1550s, suggesting that despite decades of activity by the Spanish, Portuguese, and French, "English thinking about the nature of a colony had to begin virtually *de novo*." It is also of interest to note that the first appearance of the former word is in one of Eden's translations of Spanish-American experience, and the first appearance of *plantation* is in a 1558 history of Ireland. And reference to Ireland in such a matter at just this time points to the interacting significance of Ireland and America in the Elizabethan and Stuart experience of conquering and planting.

"Ireland was on the way to America," averred A. L. Rowse, and he went on to emphasize that it was a West Country group with hard-won experience in Ireland that carried forth the first English colonizing efforts in America. The stress should be put on the connection, not the sequence, for to a large degree English efforts in Ireland and America were contemporary, and even where Ireland served as experience it offered no model of how to conquer and plant effectively.

At mid-century "the English Pale" seemed an accurate label to the English for their position in Ireland. Military conquest, treaties, garrisons, punishments had repeatedly failed to produce a secure English hold, and it remained a pale, "a country embanked against marauders." That was of course an imperial view: the "marauders" were the native Irish desperately trying to regain their own land. In 1556 after yet another Irish rebellion had been crushed, the idea of systematic plantation was put forth as a fresh and permanent solution. Irish land would be confiscated from hereditary local chieftans, vested in the Crown, shired (that is, divided into formal counties as juridical and administrative territories), and allocated to English proprietors who would survey and further partition their lands into leaseholds for new loyal British settlers. Applied to an area just west of the Pale, the program had no immediate success for few capable proprietors or settlers could be lured to such desolated and dangerous lands in the woods and bogs of Ireland. But it did serve to launch the idea of colonization. Subsequent Irish "plantations" were elaborations upon the same program and we may well assume that those in America were in some degree also.

The famous half brothers from Devon, Humphrey Gilbert and Walter Raleigh, together with their cousin Richard Grenville, provide the best illustration of the links between Ireland and America, and with France as well. Gilbert was captain of an English force sent to help the Huguenots in 1562. Returning, he was soon sent to fight in Ireland, and while there he wrote his *Discourse* on the need for a vigorous English outreach to the New World and through the Northwest Passage to the riches of Asia. In this treatise he argued the advantages of colonies as supports to trade and as an outlet for the unemployed. Meanwhile, Grenville was leading a group of Devonshire men in an attempt to set up estates in Munster, the southern quarter of Ireland. When the Munster Irish revolted, Gilbert led the force that defeated them and became a leader in formulating new English schemes for the permanent pacification of Munster and also Ulster, the rebellious northern region. Next he was sent by the queen to lead an English army assisting the Dutch in their revolt against Spain. Returning from there Gilbert considered a variety of ventures and then in 1578 obtained from Queen Elizabeth a charter to take possession of lands and found a colony anywhere on the coast of America between Labrador and Florida. His first fleet, hastily assembled that year, never got out of British waters, but in 1580 a reconnaissance was made and in 1583 Gilbert led an expedition from Plymouth. Landing in Newfoundland he asserted formal English possession of that long-used island fishing base and then sailed southward to seek a favorable site for a colony. But the season was late and a variety of troubles made him decide to return to England and come back the next year better prepared. Gilbert never got home, for he went down with one of his small ships in the stormy Atlantic, and Raleigh, who had also soldiered in France and Ireland, now took hold of the enterprise. He obtained a similar patent from the queen and sent out a reconnaissance party in 1584, which returned with glowing reports of the Carolina Banks area. In the next year Grenville led a party of over one hundred men to Roanoke Island and oversaw the founding of a settlement. This group gave up and came home the next year just before Grenville came again with more supplies. In 1587 Raleigh sent another, directing them to Chesapeake Bay as a more favorable region. However, the naval commander of the expedition (a Portuguese who had piloted Gilbert) was so eager to go on the hunt for Spanish treasure ships that he hastily dumped the settlers on the old site on Roanoke Island. This predilection for plunder dogged the enterprise. The ships sent out with supplies and reinforcements in 1588 were diverted by their captain to the taking of prizes and were thereby crippled and never crossed the ocean. Later that year the Armada appeared and the war with Spain delayed the sending of a supply vessel until 1590, when no trace of the inhabitants could be found: a mystery implanted in the American epic as "the Lost Colony." Having invested so much effort and money to so little avail in Virginia Raleigh and Grenville now turned again to Ireland where both had obtained large estates in another and much larger plantation scheme initiated after the Munster Rebellion of 1585.

Thus the English were rapidly gathering experience, but they had much to learn. They became superb seafarers, but had so honed their skills in preying upon the Spanish that they found it difficult to apply them consistently to less daring and less profitable purposes. They enlarged their sphere of conquest in Ireland, but it was the continuation of an experience so harsh and frustrating that it engendered attitudes about "natives" that in turn gave rise to policies of ruthless expulsion or near extermination as the only hope for sustained control. They were developing ideas about the objectives and means of planting but their test in practice had as yet produced no satisfactory result. They dreamed of and inferred great wealth awaiting in America but had yet to produce any compelling evidence.

Gilbert's *Discourse* and the elder Hakluyt's careful instructions to Frobisher some years later on how to organize a colony show that they were thinking more of a trading post or an overseas base ancillary to trading or mining operations than of a permanent plantation. As one historian comments, Hakluyt had not yet grasped the first principle of colonization, "that colonies must first be able to feed themselves." In 1584 the younger Richard Hakluyt drew up a "Particular Discourse on the Western Planting" that was much the most comprehensive statement of the time and the best reflection of English perspectives over the next thirty years. Prepared at the behest of Raleigh for presentation directly to Queen Elizabeth, it was a rigorous argument in support of extensive American undertakings by a man whom we now regard as "one of the directing minds of the new age," who spoke "with the voice of the new nationalism." Hakluyt's views are important not only because of his influence but because of his unprecedented study of the whole question. He had schooled himself in everything available regarding the colonial experiences of the Portuguese, Spanish, and French. Resident in Paris part of each year, he drew extensively and explicitly upon the "late plaine examples of the Frenche" and served as a major link in the diffusion of ideas about colonization across the Channel. Hakluyt argued that English settlements in America would serve to "inlarge the glory of the gospell and . . . plante sincere religion" and also "staye the spanische kinge from flowing over all the face . . . of America," a land which England had every right to claim as her own. But the main purpose, it seems clear, was to tap and to create wealth by harvesting the natural products that abounded in America and by introducing into cultivation and preparation all those commodities now obtained in "our olde decayed and dangerous trades in all Europe, Africa, and Asia." A further natural result of this expanding enterprise would be the invigoration of English seafaring and of a host of related trades, as well as the export of English goods as the Indians were brought to a state of civility. If such arguments were not really new, the scale of the undertaking envisioned and the concern for how it should be accomplished were. Although not specified in geographical detail, Hakluyt certainly hoped that England would quickly "plante upon the mouths of the greate navigable Rivers" all along the coast from Florida to Cape Breton Island.

Those plantations were to be from the outset naval bases strongly fortified against challenge from the sea, missionary and trading bases for the Indian nations upriver, and firmly rooted settlements drawing their basic sustenance from the land itself. It was this last feature, which we now accept as the obvious "first principle" of colonization, that represented the greatest advance. Hakluyt not only listed all the provisions needed for the proper support of a major expedition, but also the domestic animals and plants (wheat, rye, barley, oats, beans, peas, buckwheat) to sustain a permanent colony.

But who would be the colonists? Here again Hakluyt explored the question more thoroughly than had others. It is clear that mainly he regarded the poor and unemployed of England as the great potential source. It is in fact one of his strongest arguments in favor of colonization that it would provide a productive outlet for "multitudes of loyterers and idle vagabonds," for petty criminals "that for trifles may otherwise be devoured by the gallows," for the children of "wandering beggars," for great numbers who "dare not or cannot for their debtes shewe their faces," for "soldiers and servitors" idled by the cessation of war who might be sent to America "to the common profit and quiet of this Realme." The argument was certainly not new; Gilbert had used it in his *Discourse* eighteen years before, and concern for the individual miseries and the social dangers of high unemployment was chronic in Elizabethan England. But if there seemed therein an obvious human resource for American undertakings Hakluyt's extensive discourse on the topic falls short of declaring the absolute necessity for *family* colonization. That there were women as well as men who were vagabonds, beggars, criminals, and debtors may have been so apparent as to need no reference, but the need for stable families, and especially experienced rural families, to create a firm local foundation for any plantation appears not to have been so obvious. Most of the categories of colonists mentioned were in some way wards or potential wards of the state and thus, as Hakluyt suggested, "might be condempned for certen yeres in the western partes." Such people would be more appropriately thought of as sojourners than settlers, exiles hopefully earning their way back to civilized life in their homeland.

But if the idea of permanent emigration overseas was not yet central to concepts of English planting, it was nevertheless emergent. Gilbert regarded his whole enterprise as a social experiment and planned to offer free land to poor emigrant families. The first Raleigh expedition of 108 colonists contained no women, but the second included a number of extended families totaling eighty-nine men, seventeen women, and eleven children. Armed with elaborate plans for the "City of Raleigh" they clearly intended to found "a genuine self-perpetuating colony, not a mere trading post or garrison."

The "late plaine examples of the Frenche" had suggested another category of colonists to Hakluyt and he did add to his argument that the English plantations would "provide a safe and sure place to receave people from all parts of the worlde that are forced to flee for the truthe of gods worde." But he seems to have regarded this as simply doing a good deed to help French and Flemish Protestants rather than seeing such religious refugees as an unusual and peculiarly valuable type of colonist. Gilbert had proposed to make use of English Roman Catholics as a nucleus for his colony, for such persons were now under severe public restriction in England. Whether many would have actually emigrated at this time (as they later did to Maryland) remains uncertain because the queen for various political reasons did not approve. But in 1593 England created a new set of religious refugees when Parliament decreed that English nonconforming Separatists must either stand trial for their lives or leave the country. Holland was the most obvious refuge, but one group petitioned the queen to be allowed to go to a "foreign and far country which lieth in the West from hence in the Province of Canada." Specifically, this group had made connection with English mariners who wanted to wrest control from Bretons and Basques of the rich walrus fishery around the Magdalen Islands in the Gulf of St. Lawrence. The English entrepreneurs, with the essential help of a Basque (and probably Huguenot) navigator, had already reconnoitered the area and in 1597 they sent a party including a clergyman and a farmer to inspect the feasibility of the island for a permanent Separatist colony. However, the resistance of the rival fishing fleets thwarted the enterprise, and these Separatists eventually joined the larger group of their exiled brethren in Holland.

In 1598 Parliament recognized banishment to lands beyond the seas as an acceptable punishment for rogues and beggars. In that same year a Breton arranged with the French government to ship some convicts to Sable Island, a low bleak sandy strip of land near the continental shelf a hundred miles off the coast of Cape Breton Island, to exploit the walrus and seals there and provide a base for wide-ranging operations in Acadia. Two years later a Norman rival set up a trading post at Tadoussac, the first wintering place on the St. Lawrence since that of Roberval in 1542. Such initiatives might well spur the English into further action for they were more than a fresh set of "plaine examples"—they were a French challenge to English claims over the fishery and northern coastlands. How to implant a permanent colony to substantiate such claims remained a problem for both the French and the English. As Morison has forcefully reminded us, "It is difficult for Americans, north or south, to accept the fact that for a century after Columbus's discovery, the ordinary sort of European had to be bribed, drugged, or beaten to go out to this 'land of promise,' unless to fish." But the idea of America as a religious refuge

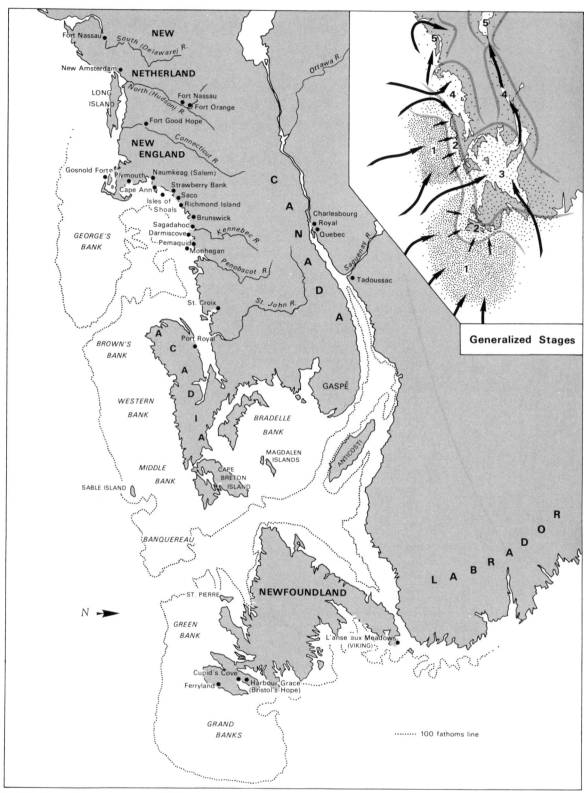

NEW NETHERLAND
Fort Nassau
South (Delaware) R.
New Amsterdam
LONG ISLAND
North (Hudson) R.
Fort Nassau
Fort Orange
Fort Good Hope
Connecticut R.

NEW ENGLAND
Gosnold Forte
Plymouth
Cape Ann
Naumkeag (Salem)
Strawberry Bank
Saco
Isles of Shoals
Richmond Island
Brunswick
Sagadahoc
Darmiscove
Pemaquid
Monhegan

GEORGE'S BANK

Kennebec R.

CANADA
Ottawa R.

Charlesbourg Royal
Quebec

Saguenay R.

Penobscot R.

St. Croix

St. John R.

Tadoussac

BROWN'S BANK

A C A D I A
Port Royal

WESTERN BANK

GASPÉ

BRADELLE BANK

MAGDALEN ISLANDS

ANTICOSTI

MIDDLE BANK

CAPE BRETON ISLAND

SABLE ISLAND

BANQUEREAU

L A B R A D O R

ST. PIERRE

NEWFOUNDLAND

N →

GREEN BANK

L'anse aux Meadows (VIKING)

Cupid's Cove
Ferryland
Harbour Grace (Bristol's Hope)

GRAND BANKS

·········· 100 fathoms line

Generalized Stages

5. Northern America, to c. 1630.

was now alive in England. Such an emigration would also be impelled by threats and persecutions, but it offered a new conception of the "promise" latent in a new land.

Meanwhile, other English seafarers and entrepreneurs were probing for a Northwest Passage to Asia, an old geographic concept revived in part by the success of the English in opening a Northeastern trade route beyond Norway to Archangel. Martin Frobisher, backed chiefly from London, explored the Arctic seas along western Greenland and Baffin Island on three annual voyages in 1576–78. The last of these was a major expedition of fifteen vessels and more than a hundred workers to establish a mining camp on a small island at the entrance to Frobisher Bay to exploit the riches inferred from an ore sample brought back on the first voyage. But the loss of supplies en route defeated the plan for the colony, and the failure of persistent efforts to smelt any riches from the cargoes of rock bankrupted the enterprise. A decade later John Davis, with the support of various West Country investors (including Humphrey Gilbert's brother Adrian), made three voyages, probing much further north along the west of Greenland, but the war with Spain caused a long interruption before any more westward channels of the polar sea could be determined.

7. Implantations from Northwest Europe

Those tiny tentative French footholds of 1600 on the great fragmented rockbound promontory of nearest America were evidence of a growing realization of the possibilities for profits from the land as well as the sea, possibilities that owed as much to the spread of a fashionable craze for beaver hats in Europe as to the animal riches of northern America.

The Breton entrepreneur, La Roche, who came to Sable Island with the king's franchise for control of the whole region, had obtained a patent for some such colony as early as 1577 and in association with some French Basques had projected an outpost on the Gulf of St. Lawrence in 1583 (the same year a Rouen merchant was prospecting the Bay of Fundy with similar intent). The Sable Island colony of convicts ended in mutinous chaos in 1603; meanwhile rival promoters had connived to intrude upon La Roche's monopoly. The post at Tadoussac, set up by Chauvan, a Dieppe Huguenot who had obtained rights to the lower St. Lawrence, was a logical step following upon twenty years' growth in the seasonal trading for furs, chiefly by crews from St. Malo. This fine anchorage at the mouth of the Saguenay had become a great summer rendezvous for Montagnais and Algonkian Indians from a wide area.

There is direct continuity between these little enterprises initiated in the sixteenth century by local Breton and Norman syndicates and the emergence of Acadia and Canada as substantial regional societies. And that continuity is primarily represented in the remarkable career of Samuel de Champlain, a Saintongese native who became associated with and was sent out to the Tadoussac venture in 1603. After returning to France he came back the next year with de Monts, the new head of the company who had been granted enlarged privileges by the king but also assigned the responsibility of planting sixty colonists a year to create a substantial New France. De Monts decided to go back to the system of summer trading from shipboard on the St. Lawrence, and shift to the ice-free Bay of Fundy as a more suitable area for a colony as well as a forward position against English encroachment northward upon his territories. A post was built at the mouth of the St. Croix, but after one harsh winter it was shifted across the Bay of Fundy to the sheltered basin behind Digby Gut. Here at Port Royal a substantial beginning was made, but in 1607 the company's commercial monopoly was revoked and it was decided that the prospects did not warrant continuance. However, after a two-year interval, Poutrincourt, who had been a resident lieutenant of de Monts, obtained a bit of financing to reopen a small operation at Port Royal. Meanwhile, de Monts obtained a brief reprieve and in 1608 sent Champlain back to the St. Lawrence to gain a larger measure of the profitable fur trade. Champlain now established a post at Quebec, a bold defensible site at the narrowing of the great river.

For more than twenty years the Port Royal and Quebec establishments were no more than little seafaring outposts by which a French presence was asserted over two closely related sectors of North America. In the 1620s the Crown and the Church drew up new programs for development (with Huguenots now officially excluded), but only in the next decade did colonization actually get underway. Despite that long interval, it was Champlain, now as royal governor, who oversaw the emergence of a substantial New France from these precarious nuclei.

The French concern over English intrusion was justified: "While the crews were loading the ships for departure [from Port Royal] in August, 1607, far to the south 105 Englishmen were establishing a base at Jamestown. Another group was making a similar attempt to the north on the Kennebec River, well within the confines of the territory ceded to de Monts." These landings at two widely separated locations were the result of an English colonization program of impressive sponsorship and substance, a quick culmination of a marked reassertion of transatlantic activities that included increasing aggressiveness in the fishery, several testings of resources along the many estuaries and islands of the northern coast, and renewed concern for the Chesapeake and the fate of Raleigh's Roanoke. In 1606 many of the varied interests behind these ventures were brought together in the charter for the Virginia Company, in which that name was now broadened to embrace a continental segment stretching from the St. Croix to Cape Fear, divided into a northern sector allocated to a Plymouth-based association of West Country interests and a southern sector dominated by Londoners.

The Plymouth Company was quick off the mark, sending out two vessels later that year, but only one actually got to the designated locale, and not until 1607 was the colony initiated at Sagadahoc on the Kennebec River. However, despite a good beginning the death of two major backers and a hard winter caused a withdrawal of the settlement the next year and a shift to summer trading by ships. English activity continued over a broad reach of northeastern coastlines. What would prove to be a more enduring hold was implanted two years later on the Avalon Peninsula by a quite separate Bristol company, to be followed in a few years by two more nearby colonies, backed by other companies, on this southwestern corner of Newfoundland. Although small and unstable affairs, these were genuine colonies of men and women, aimed at providing year-round bases to enhance competitive positions in the fishery as well as to develop fur, timber, and mineral resources, and, so it was stated in the proposal of 1610, to serve as a halfway station between England and Virginia. And in these same years English interests became focused more fully on the lands lying toward the tropics from this promontory as they largely gave up hope of a Northwest Passage after the voyages of Hudson (1610) and Button (1612) had limned the general shape of Hudson Bay.

In 1614 John Smith turned from the controversies of management at Jamestown to survey a portion of the northern coast for another entrepreneur, and after a brief look he named and extolled it in book and map as "New England," a term which the Plymouth Company soon incorporated into its renewed charter. There was sustained interest in the area by various investors and mariners but the fateful beginning was an accidental intrusion. Many of the English Separatists exiled in Holland became increasingly dissatisfied with their lot and prospects. The general attention being given to America in both Holland and England brought a reassertion, twenty years after the meager and aborted Magdalen Island scheme, of their consideration of America as a better prospect for social survival. Contact with a member of the London Company led to an invitation to emigrate to some district in its sector of Virginia. Apparently such was the intent, but blown off course by winter storms they made their landfall at Cape Cod in December of 1620 and decided to search for a suitable location in that vicinity. Subsequent negotiations with the Plymouth Company confirmed their rights to a large district opposite the Cape Cod Peninsula. As the Indians of that area had been nearly exterminated by diseases a few years before, no conquering was needed, and as these "Pilgrims" came as an autonomous settler group, rather than as wealth-seeking agents of a company, planting was the primary task. The creation of Plymouth colony proceeded without grave institutional impediments.

While this nucleus of Separatists slowly took root on Plymouth Bay a number of commercial posts were founded by various entrepreneurs at other harbors nearby. It was through connection with one of these, the outpost of the small Dorchester Company, originally located at Cape Ann (1623) but later shifted to Naumkeag, that a group of prominent Puritan leaders turned to Massachusetts Bay as the site for an American colony. The arrival of the first party of this far larger and more powerful body of religious dissidents at Naumkeag (Salem) in 1628 would soon become the boldest mark of a new phase in the outreach of European civilization to North American shores.

Meanwhile, a far more substantial English foothold had been implanted at great expense of men and resources in the southern sector of Virginia. This enterprise was a knowing successor to the Roanoke failure and aimed for the capacious embayment to which Raleigh's second expedition had been sent but never reached. The initial party of 1607 entered Chesapeake Bay, sailed up the south-ernmost of its many large estuaries, and after extensive reconnaissance, having in mind the elaborate instructions that the council had provided for the selection of "the strongest, most wholesome and fertile place," chose a swampy but defensible and deep-water site forty miles up the "Powhaton" (James) River along the north shore some distance from any Indian village. Here they constructed their fort, laid out their settlement, and began their increasingly chaotic and frantic search for riches. Jamestown was intended to be a permanent base but not necessarily the nucleus of a large colony of English settlers. The whole venture was a speculative commercial undertaking: there were no women in these first vessels and the men were all company employees, whose main task was to develop a profitable enter-prise, not to initiate a new society overseas. The hardships, near failures, but ultimate success of this Virginia colony are so well known as to need no descrip-tion. One clear implication of those early years of desperate struggle is that the English were still inexperienced at planting. The fundamental necessity of recruit-ing a solid nucleus of farmers and artisans and establishing first of all a local base for subsistence was understood by some individuals but ignored by the company, which insisted upon the earliest possible return on the investment.

The shift from company control to royal province in 1624 brought traditional institutions to bear upon problems of polity and society but there was little to bring from that tradition to aid in effective colonization, despite the long English experi-ence in Ireland and some close relationships between Irish and American opera-tions. The last years of Elizabeth's reign had seen the greatest of the Irish uprisings, harsh reconquests, and new programs for colonization. Much the largest and most drastic of these imperial schemes was applied to Ulster in 1606, in the same year and drawing upon some of the same investors and talent as were involved in the Virginia Company. A comprehensive plan for the redevelopment of six counties in the north was defined and within a few years a dozen companies and many individual proprietors were at work luring English and Scottish Protestants to form a new geography of towns and estates.

The simultaneity of the Ulster experiment precluded it from serving as a model for Virginia, and although the dozen years (1585–98) of the second (and again, abortive) Munster Plantation were surely an important experience for both, the Irish and American contexts were significantly different. Thus while Quinn emphasized the "web of interconnection between Munster and America," he also carefully noted that in the former the English worked through long-established Irish ports and commercial networks, under an existing Dublin-based administrative framework, amidst a labyrinth of Munster land claims, and in considerable degree directly with local Irish and Old English tenants as well as with newly transported colonists. Such features limited the pertinence of Irish precedents. If Ireland was "the blueprint for America," as Rowse broadly put it, it was a dim print difficult to read and one that would need so much altering as building proceeded that the resulting structures would bear little resemblance. Thus whereas the Ulster project has been cited as "the first reasonably successful attempt at regional planning in Ireland," by which this northern area was "changed from being the last stronghold of pastoral, non-urban Gaelic traditions to become the powerful bastion of peoples whose speech, habits, traditions, unwavering loyalties and resolute Protestantism differed totally from native ways, and whose new towns and villages, commercial and industrial enterprise, and land-use methods were to transform the landscape," the Virginia plantation was at the outset almost formless and opportunistic, although it had an impact as dramatic and far-reaching.

But if successful planting was too new an experience in Ireland to shape American ventures, the long history of successive conquerings could hardly fail to have some influence. Although the Jamestown settlers were under instructions to avoid overt intrusion upon Indian grounds, they were quickly embroiled in a maze of disputes and ill feelings and in general they treated the Indians as Englishmen had come in general to treat the Irish: as a wild, savage, barbarian, unprincipled race that would have to be subdued by force, broken as a society, and, if still rebellious, cleared from the land. The concerted Indian attack upon the Virginia settlement in 1622 in which about 350 colonists were killed was a response to such treatment, and the ruthless retaliation that followed was but an American version of an old English practice in Ireland, the essential imperial prelude to whatever "regional planning" might then be applied.

Despite heavy losses of life, year after year the Virginia Company continued to send over people by the hundreds; women and children first arrived with the reinforcements of 1609. The company also began to modify its land policies so as to allocate free land to every head of household, and as tobacco began to emerge as a profitable staple Virginia was soon transformed from a speculative mercantile project into a permanent implantation of Englishmen, attractive alike to capitalists and colonists. In 1612 Bermuda was settled by a subsidiary company as a useful outlier in the western Atlantic, following lengthy experience with this uninhabited island by the survivors of a Jamestown-bound vessel wrecked upon its shores in 1609.

In England at this time Guiana and southern Virginia were considered to be comparable realms, each a place of probable wealth in tropical products and gold and each prudently marginal to the main Spanish holdings. Thus they became competitive for the energies and resources of speculators and adventurers. Raleigh was the obvious embodiment of this connection, turning after his early Virginia disappointments to become obsessed with "the large, rich, and beautiful Empire of Guiana," whose coast he explored on several voyages. He was grossly deluded about its ready wealth, but several entrepreneurs attempted to establish colonies, one in 1604 along the "Wiapoco" (Oyapok) River, whose failure was followed by a larger French attempt in 1607, and that by another English venture in 1609, which lasted about four years. Soon after, the English set up posts at several points along the Amazon only to be expelled by the Portuguese. All of these were intended to be trading posts, plantations for the raising of tobacco and other crops, and bases for the search for gold and silver. By the 1620s these failures and the growing success of Virginia made it difficult to raise funds for further ventures in Guiana and the English turned away from the South American mainland to the nearby islands.

The wars with Spain had brought a much more aggressive and extensive assault upon Spanish shipping and installations in the West Indies, and the evident weakening of Spanish defenses led to ideas about the seizure of more permanent operational bases. In 1598 the English took San Juan, Puerto Rico, and were thwarted in their plans to make it such a base more by yellow fever than by the Spanish. In that same year Hakluyt had called attention to the fact, well known to those experienced in the area, that the "great multitude of . . . small isles called Las Antillas . . . are either utterly desolate, or inhabited by a few Salvages." Such was the condition of many of these islands after a century of ruthless raiding by the Spanish to provide labor for their plantations on the larger islands. Buccaneers of various nationalities had long used many of their anchorages. Abortive colonizations had been undertaken by the English in 1604 (St. Lucia) and 1609 (Grenada); the first sustained venture was headed by an English entrepreneur who had been at one of the Amazon posts and who then spent some months on St. Christopher (St. Kitts) making friends with the Indians and testing the ground for tobacco. He returned with a small group of colonists in 1624 and soon thereafter came to terms with a French party to share the island and thereby strengthen defense against any Spanish retaliation. These small beginnings were quickly followed by larger ventures from each country. Barbados, uninhabited and somewhat detached from the main string, was colonized in 1627 and became the main English holding, under patent to the "Lord Proprietor of the Caribbees"; the Companie des Iles d'Amerique undertook French development of Guadeloupe and Martinique. Tobacco and tropical woods were the first main exports.

By this time the English and French had been joined by a new and ominously vigorous rival on the high seas. The Dutch, long established in the North Sea and Baltic trade, suddenly reached out across the oceans following their successful revolt from Spanish Hapsburg rule in the 1580s. The Spanish had reconquered Flanders and Brabant but were halted at the great waterways where, with English help, the Netherlanders held on to Zeeland, the islands commanding the greatest river entrance into the body of Europe. Antwerp, long the great fulcrum of northwest European finance and commerce, was recaptured by the Spanish, and as a result thousands of Flemish and Walloons, and especially those of Protestant sympathies, including a large proportion of the mercantile and artisan communities, fled into northern Netherlands. Thus Amsterdam soon doubled in population and became the center for a surge of fresh undertakings. Antwerp had long had close commercial and financial connections with both Portuguese and Spanish imperial operations. As the Portuguese were now chafing under Spanish royal dominance, mariners and merchants from Dutch ports were often welcomed at Portuguese overseas ports. Thus in the 1590s Dutch vessels began trading to Africa, Brazil, and the Orient; in 1602 the Dutch East India Company was formed with state assistance and by 1609 not only was it competing actively along the main eastern routes but it had engaged the experienced English seafarer, Henry Hudson, to search for a westward passage through America. He found instead two great rivers whose estuaries had lain obscured and unexplored behind the broad sandy shields of coastal New Jersey and Long Island. The northern one reached 150 miles into the continent; though not the Northwest Passage it was clearly a strategic portal and, by his account, led through very attractive country. Thus began Dutch interest in, and soon assertion of claim to, all the land between New England and Virginia, tributary to the Hudson and the Delaware (the North River and the South River, in Dutch usage). Fur trading posts were set up near the head of navigation on each of these rivers and later on the Connecticut.

In 1621 the Dutch West India Company was formed as a new instrument specifically to gain dominance over the Atlantic trade. Such an objective meant a primary focus on capture of the Spanish treasure fleets and domination of the sugar and slave trade, but the company's directors were familiar with the fervor in England for planting and gave attention to colonization projects as well. The Hudson Valley and Guiana were the chief areas of interest. An earlier scheme to make use of English Separatists (the Pilgrims) as the nucleus for a colony on the

Hudson had been refused by the Dutch government, so the new company turned to Flemish and Walloon Protestants who had already indicated their willingness to go to America by their petition to the London Company of Virginia a few years before. That petition had not been refused but neither had it been supported by the special aid that had been sought and thus no emigration had taken place. Thus these religious refugees now formed the main body of the first Dutch colonies in North America.

In what would become a famous exchange, the Dutch purchased Manhattan Island from local Indians and soon laid out New Amsterdam on its southern tip. The Dutch planting in the Hudson was immediately successful, in part surely because the company leaders were alert to learn from the experiences of their neighbors. The detailed instructions on "conditions for colonies" drawn up to guide proprietors emphasized all the essentials for firm beginnings, detailing the appropriate equipment and supplies and the necessity of giving priority to subsistence production. It was a planting which grew slowly, however, because the company was far more interested in more profitable ventures.

Dutch plantations were begun on the "Wild Coast" (Guiana) at this same time and grand designs upon the Spanish and Portuguese imperial systems were drawn up, but the chief focus was upon Spanish and Portuguese commerce. As early as 1598 Dutch seafarers had intruded upon the Guinea Coast and in the next year they sacked São Tomé. In 1617 they seized the little island of Goree lying in the shelter of Cape Verde and began to move boldly in upon the Senegambian slave trade and upon its main markets. In 1630 the Dutch seized Pernambuco and rapidly expanded their hold upon this northeastern coast. In the creation of this "Netherlands Brazil" the Dutch did not oust the Portuguese planters nor implant many new colonists but concentrated on controlling the profitable sugar trade. Meanwhile bold plunderings of the Spanish culminated in the Dutch capture of the main treasure flotilla off Cuba in 1628.

By 1630 seafaring, conquering, and planting, even though highly varied in application and uneven in results, had become recognizable components of American enterprise for all major Atlantic societies of Europe. The entire Atlantic front and marginal embayments of North America had been mapped and to some degree evaluated.

That continental coastline presented two markedly different faces to those approaching across the Atlantic, with some contrasting attractions for seafarers and planters. North from Cape Cod to Hudson Strait the uplands and ancient shield so recently scoured by continental ice were studded with harbors but nearly devoid of arable lands behind. The dense forests and summer meadows deluded many a viewer as to the prospects for settlements, even though most of the early entrepreneurs were envisioning no more than modest coastal footholds. Only the glacial outwash lowlands of Massachusetts Bay and the narrow limestone margins of the St. Lawrence trench offered possibilities for extensive and continuous settlement. Furthermore, the winters were shockingly harsh to sojourners and settlers from similar latitudes in Atlantic Europe.

South from Cape Cod the most common features of the American shore were the long smooth margins of the coastal plain guarded by dangerous surfs, offshore bars, and shallow lagoons backed by monotonous stretches of pine barrens or swampland, inhospitable to seafarers and planters alike. The early challenge to seafarers was to find the great natural punctuations through this sandy barrier. By 1630 they had sounded all the main bays and estuaries and sailed up the tide-mingled flood of the great American rivers as far as their ocean vessels could carry them. These rivers varied greatly as entryways. The Hudson and St. Lawrence provided deep corridors into the continent, but the Connecticut, Delaware, Susquehanna, Potomac, and James offered much shorter penetrations, while the rivers of Carolina and Florida provided little more than estuaries for anchorage. Conquest and planting would be shaped by what lay beyond these many portals, by what kinds of men and institutions an outreaching society could bring to bear upon the peoples and the resources latent in the great variety of hinterlands.

The concept of planting overseas had developed slowly in northwest Europe. Plundering and trading were compelling attractions to these seafaring nations but the idea of transferring Europeans permanently onto American shores was far from obvious as to purpose or possibility. The Huguenots were in the vanguard and though their colonies were pitiful failures their composition and intent were strong hints of a new pattern. Sixty years later when Richard Eburne wrote in A *Plain Pathway to Plantations* that "it be the people that makes the land English, not the land the people," there was a New England to exhibit the argument, and a New Netherland and a New France already on the maps and soon to give similar substance to the proposition that societies of Europeans could indeed be established in lands an ocean away from home. That was of course a proposition which Ovando had begun to demonstrate well over a century before in a New Hispania, and by 1630 Ovando's implantation in those islands was a mere threshold of a Spanish empire that reached deep into the continent to a New Mexico thirteen hundred miles north of its old Mexican core.

8. Generalizations: European Source Regions

Geographically the topic of American beginnings leads to a focus upon southwestern Iberia. Seville and Lisbon were the first great seats of American enterprise, the pivotal points linking American operations to all the wider European world. Although both centers prospered as a result of America, both were as much involved in the cause as in the effect. Each had grown from rich surroundings, the plains of Andalusia and Estremadura, which had been brought to a state of intensive cultivation and high productivity under the Muslims, before being conquered by Christian kingdoms from the north.

Of greatest significance for the outreach to America was the encounter, interaction, and intricate convergence in these two areas—and only in these areas in anything like this magnitude—of two great cultural traditions: imperial conquest and commercial seafaring. The former was brought to these lowlands by the Castilians and the Portuguese from their long continuous history of recovery of lands from the Muslims; the latter was brought by the Genoese, Venetians, Catalans, Jews, and others from the ancient cosmopolitan centers of the Mediterranean. It is not that seafaring and conquering had never been combined before; the Crusades are but one example among many from the history of the Mediterranean littoral to suggest otherwise. But never had such a highly developed set of institutions for the seizure, administration, and resettlement of new territories and their populace, an entire system of conquest, become so fully articulated with such a highly developed set of institutions for the financing, production, shipment, and marketing of goods. Furthermore, these traditions were compatible in numerous ways, reinforcing one another with different techniques and experience applicable to the same purpose. Both were fundamentally aggressive and predatory. Plunder and conquest were as much a part of the intensely competitive commercial world of

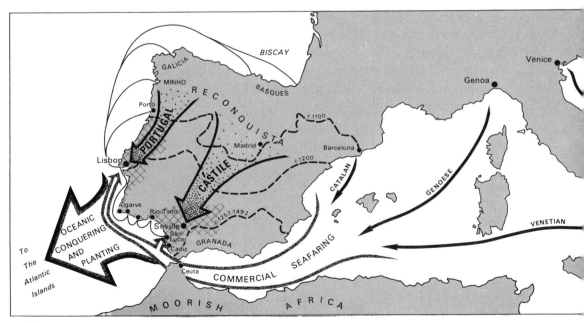

6. The Iberian Culture Hearth.

the Mediterranean as of the landed world of Iberia, as demonstrated by the Cata-lans in the Balearics, the Genoese in Corsica, and the Venetians in Crete. And both traditions included experience with planting as well as conquest. Mediterra-nean companies had often undertaken the development of new resources, recla-mation of wastelands, and repopulation of devastated districts.

The long process of the *reconquista* was at once spasmodic and continuous, reflecting a remarkable combination of formality and freedom, of state planning and local opportunism. In the larger view it was a sequence of major campaigns and formal treaties, followed by periods of consolidation of newly acquired territories; but in the marchlands there was almost continuous guerrilla activity, fostered by a class of rough settler-soldiers, or, more accurately, rancher-raiders, who in return for braving the dangers of such border zones were left "to do very much as they liked, and what they liked was plundering Muslim villages." Thus the cutting edge of empire was kept finely honed for the next major advance.

Out of long experience Castille, especially, had developed an elaborate and efficient system for dealing with conquered territories and captive peoples. Booty was distributed and lands reallocated by royal commissions in amounts graded by rank, service, and official favor. Mosques were transformed into churches and militant religious orders empowered to supervise baptisms and conformity of the Moriscos. Civic institutions were implanted, new towns founded and often granted greater freedoms than those in older regions, and a new set of names imposed upon major features of town and countryside. When Seville was taken after a two-year siege the Castilian leader insisted on the expulsion of all its Muslims, an unusually severe tactic designed to secure so great a city. As thousands fled to Granada and Africa, thousands of Castilians and others poured in from the Christian highlands, and hundreds of merchants and shippers came in from the Mediterranean to join the small colonies of such people already there. Such periods of massive change, involving the relocation of populations, restructuring of society, redistribution of wealth, and widespread acculturation, are times of stress and opportunity, calling forth new leadership and stimulating new ventures.

The process of convergence of this imperial system with a seafaring tradition and its orientation to an enlarging Atlantic World takes many forms and passes through distinct phases. An obvious example would be the movement of a number of Genoese merchants and financiers to Lisbon and Seville, their rapid rise to wealth and prestige from new enterprises, their gradual intermarriage with leading Portuguese and Castilian families, and their ultimate transition into the local aristocracies. Geographically, we can follow the shift of Mediterranean seafarers to Atlantic bases, first to the main ports of San Lucar, Seville, and Lisbon, gradually spreading to the many lesser harbors as Atlantic commerce expands until, in the close concatenation of local maritime districts from Cádiz to San Lucar, the Rio Tinto, the Algarve, and north to Lisbon, mariners of many different Mediterranean backgrounds are so intermingled with those native to these coasts—and also with those Minhotos, Galicians, and Basques who were also attracted to these fresh possibilities—as to enlarge and invigorate Iberian maritime culture. And it may properly be called Iberian, for, typical of maritime societies (and as this very process of migration suggests), such persons tended to be highly opportunistic, available for hire, ready to serve without rigid regard for national or dynastic political differentiations. Only after 1493 does the separation between Spanish and Portuguese seafaring enterprise become quite distinct.

And we can trace the development of new tools, especially of a new kind of ship with a stability, range, and capacity for truly oceanic service. Regular seasonal shipping from major Italian ports to Flanders did not begin until well into the fourteenth century. Such voyages revealed the need for new types of vessels and it was in pivotal Iberia that designers first "married Atlantic and Mediterranean technology" and began to evolve hulls intermediate "between the long and unstable Mediterranean war galley . . . and the ponderous merchant ships of northern Europe." Outfitted with larger sails, lateen rigs, and a strong sternpost rudder, these new caravels "became available to the Portuguese shortly after the conquest of Ceuta," and they are only the most obvious among the many inventions and adaptations that provided the basis for an oceanic imperialism.

While Columbus, a Genoese mariner sailing under a Castilian banner, was an appropriate symbolic vanguard of this new synthesis of Mediterranean and Iberian systems, John Cabot, the Venetian citizen sailing under an English banner five years later, did not prove to be the immediate forerunner of a comparable thrust across the Atlantic. When it did come, a century later, it too was a distinctive type that drew upon intensive experience and emanated from a highly creative sector of Europe.

We can see that region take shape in the turbulence of the sixteenth century as the pressures of the Reformation progressively narrowed and compressed the area of free-ranging Atlantic outreach. Seafarers from half a dozen maritime districts, from the Biscayan ports to the Bristol Channel, probed and gleaned the North American coast during the early years of the century. The Basques were leaders in fishing and whaling operations and Basque seamen were important in the service of many French expeditions. The prominence of La Rochelle in early colonizations may suggest an analogy with Iberia. In the wake of devastation and depopulation brought about by punitive crusades and plagues, large areas of southwestern France were recolonized in the thirteenth century through a network of *bastides*, new towns formed as centers for the development of the countryside into a great wine-exporting region. Such towns were new in kind as well, offering greater economic freedom and social equality as inducements to colonists. The resulting land promotion and resettlement, social experimentation and change, commercial speculation and vigorous marketing outreach led Vance to speak of Aquitaine as the

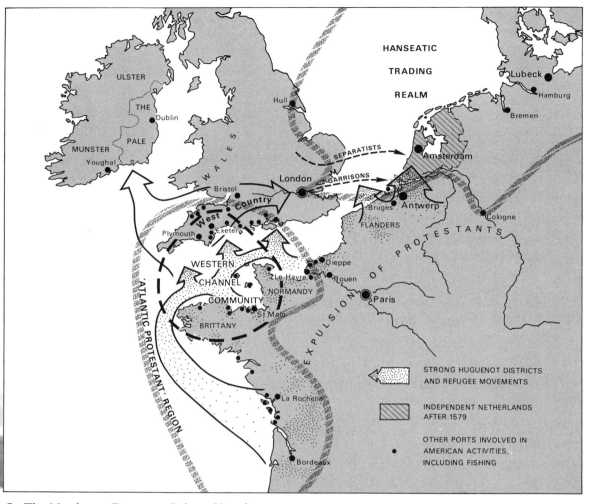

7. The Northwest European Culture Hearth.

laboratory for the later American operation. However, such a connection was made rather tenuous by the centuries intervening, although the Rochellais Huguenot mercantile culture was rooted in it. Huguenot colonization in the sixteenth century suffered from having no ready staple at hand and thus attempted to combine planting with privateering. The Huguenots were also soon crippled by religious persecution, so that the tragedy of the Albigenses themselves rather than the colonization of Albigensian lands came to be the more telling historical precedent. The Huguenots would eventually become an important ingredient in North American settlement, but chiefly as foreign refugees moving through English and Dutch channels.

The English were long deeply involved in southwestern France. Bristol had close ties with Bordeaux in the wine trade and Plymouth had particularly strong links with La Rochelle. Further north the bonds were more intimate. Amongst the many ports of Brittany and Normandy on the south, Cornwall and Devon on the north, and the Channel Islands in between there had developed out of a long complicated heritage of local commerce and smuggling, dynastic ties, political intrigue, military forays, and refugee movements "something like an Anglo-French Channel community." A series of transatlantic ventures was launched by local syndicates of merchants from such places as St. Malo and Rouen and from various West Country English ports. Yet none of these secured a firm foothold and in both nations there came a shift eastward to more substantial resources and power. The suppression of the Huguenots brought closer involvement of the state and subsequent schemes would more commonly emanate from Paris by way of its outport at Le Havre, although a good share of the commercial aspects of New France would remain in the hands of Rouen, La Rochelle, and Bordeaux merchants. On the English side, after Raleigh's failures it became increasingly evident that if they were to pursue anything like Hakluyt's program for development in "those large and spatious countries on ye easte part of America" there was a need for larger resources in the form of capital and skills and more direct support from within and around the royal court. Hence the inexorable shift toward London (a shift nicely symbolized by the benefices bestowed by the queen upon the Reverend Richard Hakluyt, who was made a canon of Bristol Cathedral in the 1580s and a canon of Westminster Abbey in 1600). In this way West Country enterprise was brought into closer connection with another rich mercantile tradition. London had long been a major foreign port of the great Hanseatic network of the North Sea–Baltic basins and had more recently been reaching out on its own to new lands: while Bristol and Plymouth were sending expeditions in search of a Northwest Passage to Asia, London had found a Northeast Passage to Muscovy. And just as it was becoming clear that American and Irish enterprise required a larger scale of operations, London commercial and financial resources and skills were being enriched by the influx from Antwerp and Huguenot France.

The Reformation reordered the human geography of northwest Europe. The English break with the papacy, the Calvinist revolt of the Netherlands, the suppression of French Protestantism, the return of Flanders to the Catholic fold, and the recapture of Antwerp by Spanish forces not only profoundly affected societies and politics but shifted the fulcrum of the European economic system, redefined the realms of relatively unrestricted commerce, and focused and fueled national rivalries. The estuaries and narrow seas connecting the Thames and the Zuider Zee emerged as the axis of a region of powerful forces, and London and Amsterdam came to dominate the next century of oceanic enterprise as Lisbon and Seville had the previous one.

On the eve of these disruptions Antwerp was the greatest commercial and financial center of the continent. Situated just off the great Rhenish waterway adjacent to the flourishing Flemish industrial district and at the convergence of traffic from north, east, south, and west, its large cosmopolitan merchant establishment, subdivided by family, national, and commodity networks, handled the myriad products of all the lands and seas of Europe as well as those of the new oceanic commerce: Asian spices, African gold, Atlantic sugar, and American silver. But twenty years of war, siege, and deprivation following upon the initial revolt of 1566 destroyed this preeminence, halved the population, depleted its resources, and reduced Antwerp to a regional trade center with special linkages across the new international Protestant-Catholic border. As Antwerp had succeeded Bruges, now it yielded to Amsterdam. That capital of Holland, central within the free provinces of the Netherlands and secure behind a labyrinth of waterways and polders, was suddenly swollen with talented, wealthy, and well-connected refugees, as well as thousands of common laborers. Opportunities for investment abounded: in the needs of the city itself, in the expansion of the polders and intensification of local agriculture, fishing, and industries; in the realignment of European trade and the capture and extension of overseas networks; in the invention of new commercial facilities, such as the formation of a central bank with unprecedented resources and powers. By 1625 Amsterdam had doubled in population (to 100,000) and become "a capitalist centre on a new scale."

All the while, England, too, was undergoing fundamental changes. The break with the papacy was followed by increasing social upheaval and the subsequent warring with Catholic Spain called forth an unprecedented national fervor. It was a period of shifts in power and wealth, a time of population movement, of rural migration to urban centers, of foreign immigration to London and cities of the south and east. England drove out some of her own dissidents but received a far larger number of Huguenot, Flemish, Walloon, and other Protestants. Such persons constituted an uncommonly valuable addition to English life, bringing in new skills, experience, and wealth in many forms and providing new links across local and distant seas. Thus southern England in general and London especially emerged as the vortex of the wider turbulence affecting all northwest Europe, and the coalescence of these several streams of foreigners with the great numbers of English alert to new possibilities resulted in "the most dynamic society in the Western World—perhaps on the entire globe," with direct implications for America:

> The extraordinary mobility of the people of the United States in the present century is customarily interpreted as a uniquely American phenomenon, but that this is far from so is made overwhelmingly clear to anyone who studies the local histories of seventeenth century England. The beginnings of American mobility are in Stuart England.

And, we should add, in the Netherlands of the House of Orange.

Thus, the America created out of this sector of Europe was one of the many manifestations of an explosive new movement rather than the continuation of an old one analogous to the reconquista. The tumultuous religious, political, social, and economic developments that characterized the Reformation were at their greatest intensity in Northwest Europe at just this time. Their suppression in France and Flanders helped to make London and Amsterdam centers of super-charged vitality while turning France toward the Iberian model of a centralized imperial system of state and church and ending Antwerp's primacy in European commerce. Among the countless evidences of social disruption emanating from the Reformation none was more portentous for America than the thousands of refugees: individuals, families, whole groups gravitating from a thousand localities into this intensifying urban commercial nuclear region. Dislodged from old patterns, such persons were forced to create new ones and they were made increasingly aware, by governments who wanted to get rid of them, entrepreneurs who wanted to make use of them, or their own kind who wanted to assist them, of America as a possibility for resettlement. Although the great impulse toward America from this corner of Europe does not begin as part of a religious movement and is only sporadically and intermittently dominated by cohesive religious groups, the prominence of persons carrying these new religious identities—those first Huguenots in Brazil and Florida, Separatists and Puritans, Flemish and Walloons (and Scottish Presbyterians in Ulster)—becomes a major feature. They are the most readily visible groups among the larger body of "vexed and troubled Englishmen" and others who would in time create something very new in a New World.

Whereas the great characterizing feature of Iberia was a formalized system of conquest, that of northwest Europe was a flexible system of commerce. Nurtured along the Baltic and North Sea coasts and various inland districts of specialized production, intensified seasonally in the trade fairs at regional crossroads, this system—through continual expansion and elaboration—had by the sixteenth century brought the whole of Europe into a primary commercial focus on the narrow seas of the northwest. It was a system of many parts, created and manipulated by individuals, families, syndicates, and guilds, rather than by kings and princes. That was the critical difference in this emergent capitalism: it operated internationally beyond the control of any one political ruler and without centralized authority of any kind. While it normally served to provide reasonably regular flow of an increasing range of goods to a growing population, it was inherently speculative and opportunistic, adaptable and expandable, for it operated, fundamentally, on the basis of private self-interest and thus it had participants ready to venture on any possibility of a new means to profit.

When Flanders and the Netherlands became part of the vast imperial federation under Charles V there was momentarily a direct political linkage between this Northwest capitalist system and the intercontinental geopolitical structures of

Iberia. As the financial burden of empire increased, the wealth of America, Africa, and Asia flowed in ever-larger proportions from Seville and Lisbon on to Antwerp and other northern financial centers, while at the same time the Flemish (a cosmopolitan term including those from merchant colonies, such as Italians and Sephardic Jews, as well as local Germanic peoples) infiltrated key commercial centers throughout the Spanish and Portuguese imperial networks. In the revolt against the constrictions of Charles's cumbersome structure the direct political link was broken but many informal (and often illegal) connections remained. The rapid shift from Antwerp to Amsterdam demonstrated the great adaptability of this capitalist system, and compressed by the new geopolitical boundaries but empowered by the newly intensified nationalism, northwest Europeans moved out upon the oceanic stage to challenge the Iberians anywhere on the globe.

Harnessing the deep philosophical and emotional drives of nationalism and religion to the old European zest for predation and profits created a powerful thrust but did not in itself provide an efficient instrument for implanting European civilization on American shores. The Dutch and the English were splendid at seafaring but had no well-tested formula for conquering and planting. And here we should note that Ireland was not quite analogous to those lesser Atlantic islands so pertinent to the Iberian advance. While it is commonly assumed that "Ireland and privateering were the battlefields on which Englishmen won their spurs as colonizers and seamen," they proved themselves much more readily on the sea than on the land. For the English never really completed their struggle to conquer and assimilate this great Celtic isle, and thus Ireland was no simple stepping-stone nor proving ground and it was surely in some degree an obstacle, an intervening opportunity that absorbed energies, manpower, and capital that might have been applied more directly and sooner to America had the English had an unobstructed view to the west. Similarly, Quinn suggests that the effort and resources expended upon the seafaring obsession with the search for an unobstructed northwest passage around America "postponed the application of capital and personnel to the solution of the problems of North American settlement."

Thus the America created out of this northwest sector of Europe was necessarily more invention than extension. There was important continuity in the commercial emphasis, and many of the financial systems were adaptations of Italian precedents, but there was no indigenous system for the colonization and administration of conquered lands and there was no possibility of simply borrowing such a thing from Iberian predecessors and rivals, despite multifarious connections, because it would require not simply a set of tools but patterns of attitude and behavior deeply rooted in cultural character and experience. French and especially English and Dutch colonization were therefore far more experimental, diverse in type, and uncertain in result.

Thus there were two great source regions for two great impulses toward America. Distinct in specific character and timing, they are nevertheless broadly analogous in important ways, and to identify them as source regions is not only to bring into geographic focus some well-known historical patterns, but to suggest a type and point to the pertinence of cultural theory relating to a fundamental geographic question. That general question is: why do creative cultural movements begin *where* they do? The theory relates to the concept of a "culture hearth," defined as an area wherein new basic cultural systems and configurations are developed and nurtured before spreading vigorously outward to alter the character of much larger areas. In their fullest sense, these matters represent the geographer's part of the general problem of the origins of civilization, and of "civilizations" or macrosocieties, those vast geographical entities within which a distinctive form of culture shapes the lives of millions of people over centuries, such as Ancient Egypt, China, the Roman Empire, Western Civilization, and others on the controversial lists of such historical creations.

While there is as yet no commonly accepted general theory on the processes critical to the emergence of such phenomena, there is a diverse literature that tends to converge on certain basic conditions that seem to have provided extraordinary stimulus to cultural change. The clearest formulation is that of Carroll Quigley in *The Evolution of Civilizations* (1961), which focuses on the invention of a new "instrument of expansion" as the result of the "mixture" of two ore more cultures. If our two European source regions of American enterprise are not necessarily culture hearths of great configurations on the world scale of "civilizations," they are nevertheless seats of creativity and vitality from which powerful forces initiated immense cultural change over large areas. It is therefore appropriate to assess, if only briefly, the applicability of this geographic theory to the origins of the European transformation of America.

Basic to the concept of "mixture" in the theory of culture origins is the adage that "isolation breeds stagnation, whereas contact fosters change." However, the kind of change required is not a mere borrowing by one culture from another, not a diffusion of elements but a compounding of new forms, a fusion which in its fullest expression may be called a cultural synthesis. Since every society has routine contacts with other societies along its borders, we may expect such radical change to come from some disruption of those routines, from some gross alteration that discredits old patterns and demands and opens up possibilities for new ones. The most obvious examples are cases of conquest followed by migrations, resettlements, and reorganizations, cases involving the penetration of peripheries and the imposition of contact at the edge or within the very core of the conquered state. An important corollary to this concept of cultural synthesis is that the greatest stimulus to change will come from contacts between societies of unlike but not grossly unequal levels of culture. We would expect, for example, that the Castilians would be far more stimulated by an encounter with the Muslims of Andalusia than with the Guanches of the Canaries.

In such adversarial encounter there is not only the stimulus of contact arising from the challenging display of a different way of life; there is also, to borrow a Toynbeean term, the "stimulus of pressures," arising from the challenge to survive the chronic threat to such marchland societies of subordination or extinction by a powerful neighbor. Such survival requires a high degree of social efficiency, putting a premium on skilled and courageous leadership, on social cohesion and esprit, on the employment of well-honed tools of political and military contest.

Such contacts and pressures may stimulate the creation of new systems and configurations, but the concept of a culture hearth implies the spread of these outward from the region of origin so as to transform a much larger area. In Quigley's formulation the creation of an "instrument of expansion" involves invention, saving, and investment; that is, it requires an incentive to find new and better ways of doing things, an accumulation of surplus wealth by some group that controls more than they wish to consume immediately themselves, and their application of that surplus to further creation and extension. In the longer view, such an instrument of expansion results in greater production of goods, a rise in the general standard of living, growth of population, an increase in knowledge and in artistic and philosophic activities, and an increase in territorial extent along with alterations in geographic structure to form distinct core and peripheral regions. We may characterize this process as the "stimulus of resource rewards," to denote a social system that generates an ongoing expansion of wealth rather than merely the episodic plunder of conquest. Such increases may come from the discovery and development of new resources, the application of new technology, or the organization of new systems of production and distribution.

Applying these concepts to the two source regions, one notes that the most obvious feature they shared was an unusual level of turbulence and disruption—warfare and conquests, persecutions and migrations—brought about by the confrontation of powerful and deeply antagonistic societies. Certainly the stimulus of pressures was apparent in the chronic encounter of Christians and Muslims and in the explosive hatreds of Protestants and Catholics, which upwelled with special intensity along the old Romano-Germanic borderlands. The stimulus of contact is equally clear in the Iberian case and recalls Dawson's emphasis upon the creative possibilities arising from "the coming of a new people into an old culture-field." Despite widespread expulsions, enough of the conquered population remained in Andalusia to introduce their conquerors to forms and levels of production and civilization beyond what they had known in Castile. In northwest Europe the relationship was more the reverse for the influx was of refugees rather than conquerors and it was they who stimulated new developments in what had been lesser centers. Amsterdam, in particular, though a prosperous regional entrepôt, had been markedly conservative in commercial technique. However, it is less easy to specify such stimulus of contact here amidst the swirl of the Reformation than in the simpler confrontations of the reconquista.

Castile's "instrument of expansion" was its highly honed conquest system, a tested integration of military, administrative, economic, social, and religious parts. Each major conquest brought the stimulus of further contacts and fresh resources as well as the challenge of integrating additional regions and administering an enlarged whole. The convergence in Andalusia with Mediterranean seafaring resulted in fresh invigoration and possibilities. The outreach to America brought contact with an array of new peoples, including the greatest of its civilizations. In the high Valley of Mexico the Spaniards were once again a "new people coming into an old culture-field," and the stimuli of pressure and resource rewards were enormous. The Spanish adapted their Iberian system to the tasks of overseas continental imperialism with remarkable energy and success, aided greatly by the heavy mortality of their opponents. But the very nature of their instrument of expansion required a recurrent infusion of new wealth to propel it onto new ground. A centralized bureaucracy has an insidious tendency toward rigidity and stagnation, a tendency, in Quigley's terms, to convert instruments into *institutions;* that is, for agencies to work with decreasing efficiency toward their original purpose and with increasing emphasis upon maintaining themselves. Hence the need for periodic reform. The Spanish empire surged forward on the basis of initial plunder and the discovery of rich extractive resources, but the costs of sustaining such an extensive imperial system were enormous and any surplus was increasingly squandered on fruitless European warfare. Having seized the wealth of half the Americas in half a century the Spanish monarchy underwent a series of declared "bankruptcies" immediately thereafter; it couldn't meet its payments on borrowed money. On the American side, of course, the more fundamental creative work proceeded generation by generation in the long process of cultural synthesis within the culture hearths from which a distinct Mexican and a more general Spanish-American culture would emerge.

The Portuguese case had its own peculiarities and importance. The initial instrument of expansion was state-supported seafaring, starting notably with Prince Henry, with investments producing improvements in nautical technology and increases in geographical knowledge that eventually tapped sufficient wealth in tropical Africa and Asia to sustain an incentive to further investment and expansion. Portugal opened the way toward a truly global commerce, but its more infamous contribution was the creation of another instrument of expansion: the tropical slave plantation system. Drawing first upon Mediterranean and Mauretanian antecedents, tested on Madeira, then on a larger scale on São Tomé, and finally, backed by the Cape Verde Islands–Senegambia procurement system and implanted on the massive stage of Brazil, it was a distinctive cultural synthesis developed within the new Atlantic World. It was a crude and costly instrument, requiring virgin ground and large annual replacements for its brutalized labor force, but it produced sufficient wealth to implant an expanding Portuguese America, and the capture of that colony by the Dutch provided the means to extend that system in new directions.

We may take that intrusion of the Dutch into Brazil as symptomatic of the character, the power, and the problems of northwest Europe's instrument of expansion. Drawing upon a long history of seafaring and commerce, including a critical infusion of Italian techniques, supported but not controlled by flourishing national states, at times focused and intensified by religious rivalries, commercial capitalism would prove to be an unusually creative and flexible instrument. Yet for decades its outreach to America was fruitless and fumbling. The basic fact was that private investment required relatively quick returns. Hence the frantic search for ready resources and the strong temptation to plunder. Colonization, even the establishment of a modest outpost overseas, proved to be extremely costly and therefore unattractive. Impelled by profits rather than empire, it was far easier to raise money to sail and seize the wealth already produced by the Spanish and Portuguese than to send shiploads of workers to try to extract something valuable from American ground. Whereas Spanish America was an imposed "normative order," for the Dutch and English "America was a business," and by 1630 the recent capture of the entire Spanish treasure flotilla and the extension of control over the Portuguese sugar-slave system were as yet more characteristic of northwest Europe's instrument of expansion than were Virginia, New Netherlands, New England, or New France. In the longer and broader view, of course, we may now see that northwest area and its nations as not only the source region for North American development but the culture hearth of the New Europe and the core-states of the modern world capitalist system.

9. Generalizations: Sectors and Circuits of the Atlantic World

The first European discoveries of wealth on the western rim of the Atlantic called into being two quite distinct maritime connections across the ocean to two utterly different Americas. The one trafficway led to Northern America, indeed a formidably northerly America of foggy seas, ice-scoured lands, and punishing winters, whereas the other led to Tropical America, a deceptive paradisaical America of green-mantled islands and perpetual warmth, but fragile in substance and lurking with the dangers of disease and storm. From these two thresholds Europeans

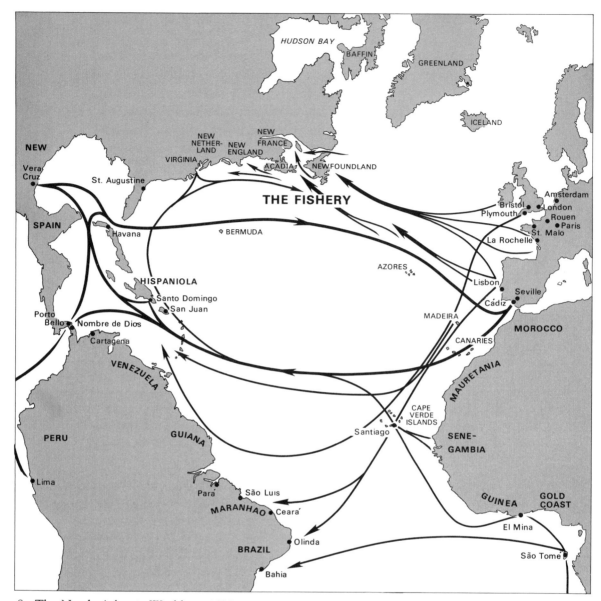

8. The North Atlantic World, c. 1630.

probed and pushed westward and inward upon the great landmass itself, and also laterally, northward and southward along the continental margins. In the broader view the creation of European North America was a geographical emanation from these two earliest oceanic axes.

The wealth of northern America lay ready to harvest in the teeming waters of the great banks, where according to a widely publicized remark attributed to Sebastian Cabot, there were "so great multitudes of certeyne bigge fysshes . . . that they sumtymes stayed [his] shippes." By simple extension from Atlantic Europe or a westward swing from Icelandic waters the gathering of such riches could be immediately undertaken by fishing fleets from Portugal and the Azores, Cantabrican and Basque ports, La Rochelle, Brittany, and Normandy, the Channel Islands, and the West Country. That the exact sequence, numbers, and changes in scale and proportion of these many groups remain so uncertain over so long a time is an indication of how diffuse and peripheral this activity was. It was an open commerce of hundreds of entrepreneurs projected from scores of local ports; it was by its very nature marginal to both continents; and it was a commerce in which traditional customs relating to fishing rights on the open sea quelled national assertions of dominance or claims to adjacent shores.

And so, too, its significance to a long sequence of American developments remains unappreciated. For in a very practical sense, one may say that every ship that sailed across the northern Atlantic in the 1600s was sustained by the experience and skills, the manpower and infrastructure, the assessments and visions developed from the routines of the Great Fishery. That is not surprising, considering that exploitation of this rich resource was one of the great economic activities of Europe during the latter sixteenth and the seventeenth centuries, an economic venture which every year lured hundreds of vessels across the ocean, drew upon and fostered seafaring support systems along much of the Atlantic fringe, and marketed its catch through a network that reached far into the European realm; thus it trained generations of mariners, employed thousands of craftsmen and suppliers, and involved families and friends, syndicates and whole communities in North American activities long before any Pilgrim or Puritan, Norman or Dutch colonist took root in American soil.

We can generalize a sequential geography of European exploitation of this northern sector, starting with the "wet fishery" on the unseen edge of the continent, followed by the shift to the summer shelter of a hundred rockbound anchorages and the assault upon the forest edge to build the flakes and fires for the "dry fishery"; thence through the straits on either side of this first-found land (if via Belle Isle, sailing unwittingly by the meager rubble where intrepid seafarers had implanted a Norse America five hundred years before) into the capacious compartment of the Gulf of St. Lawrence, especially attractive for its whales and the walrus on the sandy Magdalenes; next on past the cliffs of Anticosti, lying like a huge hull guarding the entryway, and riding the wind and tide up the Great River of Canada (whose broad flow must be powered by some immense continental reach or reservoir) still in pursuit of whales and cod, but pausing occasionally to trade for furs; then the transition in emphasis from fish to furs and the establishment of a trading post where the Saguenay offers the first break through the walls of this narrowing funnel; and soon on further skirting the Ile d'Orleans lodged in the very throat of this passageway, to set up a frontier entrepôt and bind two peoples into a single intercontinental system by which the furs from interior America would be sent to the fashionable marts of Europe (see figure 5 inset, above).

This entire thrust, reaching from the full breadth of the great banks through successive narrowings to the channel of the upper St. Lawrence, remained a singularly maritime operation, by which ocean vessels penetrated the continent a thousand miles from the open sea. It remained so because there was no wealth apparent in the ground itself. From the first contact after an oceanic crossing on up the great river as far as Quebec it all seemed well summed in Cartier's famous phrase: "the land God gave as his portion to Cain." Still farther upstream Indian fields came into view, but this scattering of riparian patches, apparently the northernmost edge of agriculture over against the endless boreal forest, offered little to lure European investors.

Lateral extensions from the fishery led, naturally, into markedly contrasting environments: northward along even more barren ice-scoured coasts and arctic seas; but southward into softer country, the cul-de-sac of Fundy and the muddy flats exposed by its enormous tides, a length of isle-studded granitic coast, and then a series of morainic estuaries, the broader lowlands of Massachusetts, and the great sandy hook of Cape Cod. The transitions to better ground and easier climate are neither sharp nor simple and geographically it is not inappropriate to see this complicated coastline as a southerly sector of Northern America, with many continuities in lands and seas and early activities. The European implantations here, so famous in the annals of America, in fact came out of a long succession of fishing stations, trading posts, mission sites, and colonization schemes. The Separatist flirtation with the Magdalenes and the deep West Country involvement underlying Sagadahoc and Salem are only the more obvious links. Even the Dutch, arriving late on the scene, sailed up the great trench of the Hudson to establish their first post as deep into Northern America as their oceanic system could carry them.

Thus, when we begin to assess the creation of America in its proper Atlantic context we see not only Newfoundland and New France but New England and New Netherland, all the many beginnings from Hudson Bay to the Delaware, as integral parts of a Northern America, each in some degree an emanation from this old annual harvest of the northern seas.

The other transatlantic connection was an exact opposite in several respects: a single route from a single port connecting to two portals on the American mainland, one the focus for the traffic of Mexico and the other for that of Peru; a rigidly controlled maritime axis of an enormous imperial system that asserted exclusive territorial rights to most of the American world (and in fact a system which had extended its reach on westward to the Philippines and its claim over the entire Pacific Ocean).

Nature's circulation of winds and waters carried the Spanish directly to the American tropics. They began in the islands, first on Hispaniola, central in the

Antillean chain; next to the adjacent large islands of Puerto Rico, Cuba, and Jamaica; then to the lesser isles, chiefly on the hunt for Indian slaves. But the European impact upon this American threshold was appallingly, almost incredibly, destructive, reducing the population from perhaps several million to a few hundred thousand in a single generation, and after 1521 this varied archipelago became a partially abandoned backwater as the lure of plunder and of labor and land and mines led to the creation of a far greater New Spain on the mainland, and Santo Domingo became a way station rather than the primary focus of empire. During the sixteenth century modest amounts of sugar, tobacco, hides, pearls, and salt were shipped from some of these tropical coastlands, but the primary value of this entire insular realm and its continental flanks of Florida and Venezuela–Guiana was to guard the annual fleets to and from Mexico and Peru.

That circulation of traffic of the famous Carrera de Indies reflected the broad simplicities of winds and currents and of the imperial system of official ports and passageways: sailing outward from Seville and Cádiz (the deep-water outport) to Las Palmas on Grand Canary, driven by the trade winds and north equatorial current across the Atlantic, threading the Lesser Antilles screen (most commonly by Mona or by Dominica Passage) to Santo Domingo, or sometimes without pausing there on to Vera Cruz or to Nombre de Dios, the Panamanian collection point for Peru (replaced in the 1590s by nearby Porto Bello). These were separate fleets, the one bound for Vera Cruz departing several months ahead of the Isthmian one. For the return, the Peruvian and Mexican fleets, having wintered in America, assembled at Havana, and, picking up the mighty flow of the Gulf Stream through Florida Strait, arched eastward, avoiding Bermuda and calling in at the Azores if desired or necessary, en route back to Cádiz and Seville. As French and later English and pirate attacks increased, this annual passage began to be made under armed convoy, and San Juan, Cartagena, and Havana were fortified as major naval bases.

Thus a Spanish Atlantic became firmly defined, not as a broad diffusion of ships across the ocean as in the north, nor a simple axis, but as a circuit along a relatively narrow routeway. Traveled by often a hundred or more vessels (with declines in numbers offset by increases in the size of ships), the annual volume and value of goods, though varying a good deal, tended toward a peak in the early seventeenth century. Until the 1580s outbound cargoes were chiefly grain, biscuits, olive oil, and wine, "which enabled these Mediterraneans exiled in the land of maize to keep up long-established eating habits." But increasing production of wheat and wine in America, decreasing creole prejudice against American cuisine, and the growing impossibility of sustaining such "economic lunacy" worked to replace such shipments with cloth and other manufactured goods from Italy and northern Europe. The return voyages of the famous treasure fleet laden with silver and gold, but also carrying a considerable variety of produce from these tropical lands and seas, was vital to the ongoing life of the entire imperial structure, and became the most obvious exhibit of wealth in America to envious rivals.

There was another sector of the American tropics in Brazil that was part of still another transatlantic circulation. This Portuguese network began as a Euro-African connection and took on a special American dimension only as the Brazilian sugar-slave production system developed. Santiago in the Cape Verde Islands was the principal pivot within this traffic pattern, although as the demands in Brazil increased direct shipments from African supply stations became more common. Portuguese America was a large claim upon the map but in effect more a set of discrete local districts confined to the narrow coastal lowlands. In function it was more a maritime commercial enterprise than a close kin to the continental empire of Spain. When these two were forcibly married under a common emperor in 1580 the Portuguese were allowed to take shipments of slaves directly to Cartagena, and later to Vera Cruz and Havana. There had of course been widespread smuggling of Africans into Spanish America for many years, but heretofore legal imports had been under monopoly license to traders who normally purchased slaves from the Portuguese in Lisbon or the Cape Verdes and shipped them via the main flotillas from Seville or the Canaries.

Thus there were three oceanic systems extending Europe's reach across the Atlantic, one to Northern America and two to distinct national and geographical sectors of Tropical America. Although each was anchored upon separate bases, they were in fact drawn into the general European commercial system focused, primarily, during most of the sixteenth century, at Antwerp. Within the Atlantic the earliest two, the Northern and the Spanish systems, were essentially separate, touching only incidentally at the Azores, overlapping in a minor way in the participation of Portuguese and Basque mariners and shipbuilders in both. The two Iberian systems were more significantly interlocked, in old and close connections between Lisbon and Seville and of both of these ports with Madeira and the Canaries, and more fatefully in the supply of slaves to Spanish America, at first indirectly, later with the Cape Verdes as the principal link, by which almost from the very first Africa became bound ever more deeply and extensively into the Euro-American relationships.

But the seas were open to any who dared enter. The shipments moving along these oceanic routeways, and especially the trunk lines of the tropical empires, were the most obvious displays of ready wealth and a lure toward America, which proved irresistible to the deeply predatory and increasingly nationalist societies of northwest Europe. Lacking adequate organized naval forces, governments made willing use of privateers and gave tacit encouragement to pirates in the pursuit of national objectives. Given the powerful animosities unleashed by the Reformation "the result was the creation of great areas of savage, unorganized conflict," with "an immense increase in the incidence of robbery and violence, spreading . . . southwards in the east Atlantic from the English Channel to the Guinea Coast and westwards to all the shores of America from the River Plate to Newfoundland." This preying of European upon European was an integral and important part of the transfer of European culture overseas and it increasingly entangled, altered, and complicated this basic sixteenth-century pattern of sectors and circuits in the Atlantic World.

The prospects for plunder produced some audacious forays celebrated in national and naval histories; lesser known but of greater significance were the more permanent intrusions of northwest Europeans into Iberian America and Africa. Such attempts to colonize and to develop or take control of commerce were mostly

> an affair of innumerable small ships, obscure promoters and many anonymous seamen, so many particles in the unorganized drift across the Atlantic that slowly gathered momentum. . . . Few of the great merchants of France, England and the Netherlands took any serious interest in this sort of business, which was essentially a shipowner's trade—among the Dutch, for example, the Zeelanders were the main promoters, and among the French, the men of Dieppe.

The savage destruction of the Huguenot colonies in Brazil and Florida showed how dangerous it could be to encroach upon these Iberian empires, but it proved impossible to defend them entirely against the rising maritime powers of northwest Europe. There was an increasing leakage of commerce through the connivance of local officials in outlying areas, such as Venezuela and Maranhão, and although no actually colonized part of either empire was lost more than momentarily until the Dutch seizure of Olinda in 1629, there was no hope of preventing footholds in the Lesser Antilles, Guiana, and the northern flank beyond Florida. The English colonies at Roanoke and Jamestown were encroachments upon lands claimed by Spain, as the unrealized strategic program of Menéndez and the Jesuit mission on the James declared, and each site was selected and fortified by the English with that fact uppermost in mind. These implantations were an attempt to gain a portion of the American tropics. The Raleigh expedition of 1585 came by way of the Canaries and Hispaniola and picked up sugar cane and other crops for trial; the later Virginia promoters extolled a long list of anticipated tropical productions, and the type of tobacco that finally opened the way to wealth was a transplant from the West Indies. Only as experience lengthened was it realized how marginally subtropical the Chesapeake region actually was.

Permanent footholds gave rise to more regularized Atlantic traffic, and the English began to develop a North Atlantic circuit that in some degree bound together the West Indies, Virginia, New England, and Newfoundland, with Bermuda as a new alternative way station. But it was the larger Dutch syndicates that created the most impressive and profitable system, and did so by moving in more directly upon the Portuguese and the Spanish, first by punishing raids, then by actual seizure and rule of productive districts and strategic stations. By the mid-1630s they had conquered much of Brazil, held a number of outposts in Senegambia, and had rapidly taken control of much of the slave trade (they ousted the Portuguese from El Mina in 1637); they dominated the Guiana and Venezuelan coasts, and had set up Curaçao and St. Eustatius as major entrepôts of Caribbean commerce; and they had created a New Netherland along the Hudson, with minor outliers on the Delaware and Connecticut, tapping into the fur trade of Northern America. Furthermore, Dutch "sack" ships began to alter the routines of the Great Fishery, with their seasonal voyages to Newfoundland to buy rather than catch fish themselves.

Thus the Dutch became the primary maritime power of the Atlantic and superimposed their own patterns upon earlier ones. Emphasizing commerce much more than colonization, they became the principal agents of contact and diffusions around this Atlantic circuit, the most important of which would be the spread of Africans and of more efficient plantation and marketing systems. It was a Dutch privateer that brought the first Blacks to Virginia, and a Dutch company that first shipped African slaves into Northern America, for the purpose of helping erect the first public buildings of New Amsterdam. Influences from Dutch Brazil would be critical to the emergence of English Barbados and French Martinique as wealthy sugar colonies, and these islands would become important in the transfer of English and French planter societies onto the North American mainland.

As an imperial type this Dutch creation was a maritime commercial system more like its older Mediterranean predecessors of Venice and Genoa than its Iberian rivals in the Atlantic, a network of collection centers and strategic points along critical trafficways. Small islands lying off a productive mainland were the ideal geographic base for such a system: secured by a natural moat, easily defended by a small garrison yet readily accessible alike to river, coastal, and ocean vessels; a natural compound for slave or indentured labor; and an obvious unit for separate political administration. It was a geographic type of empire that was therefore fragmentary, shallow in continental impact, irregular in territorial hierarchy. Because a large share of the Europeans came as sojourners rather than settlers, assigned for a tour of duty or attracted by the hope of profit, it was a system that tended to foster spatial and class segregation rather than the integration of European and local peoples. Such geopolitical systems were also unusually flexible and unstable. One outpost might be substituted for another, and there was little hope of or desire to invest in the comprehensive control of all islands or coasts as the Spanish had attempted. Thus the English, French, and Dutch were piecing together such networks simultaneously in the same regions; they picked up neighboring islands and coastal segments, and together with the remnants of the Portuguese system and the bastions of the Spanish began to create a highly fragmented geopolitical pattern of indelible consequence to important sectors of this Atlantic rim.

To the modern eye perhaps the most striking feature of that Atlantic World up to 1630 was the lack of any real competitive focus or vigorous development in middle-latitude North America, the very lands most amenable to the direct transfer of European crops and systems of living. This sector, extending from the Delaware to southern New England, was apparently of little interest (so little, in fact, that in the latter 1630s the Swedish flag would be raised over a newly implanted colony on the Delaware portion of New Netherland with no significant reaction from the Dutch for years). Yet these were lands that could be described in familiar terms and praised as equal to the best at home. But that was precisely why they had so little attraction to the commercial capitalists of northwest Europe, for the trade such people thrived on was based on the complementarity of *unlike* regions. The greatest profits came from exotics, from commodities given value by special demands, relative scarcity, and lack of substitutes.

Since the production of the familiar staples of home gave no promise of great wealth, the promise of social rather than economic gain seemed the obvious alternative to those who wished to promote the development of this sector: the lure of land in large blocks, land for manors, patroons, or seigneuries, land to be held more as a measure of prestige than as a means to quick profits. The patroons of New Netherland were an early example of such an attempt to extend an age-old European social pattern across the seas. But these proved a weak instrument for it was easier to attract initial investment than actual patroons and tenants and the costs of development surpassed the means of most aspiring squires. However, there was yet another possible social connotation, latent particularly in these middle-latitude lands and given its first full expression in "New England": not the replication of England across the seas, but an England new in social possibilities for a whole body of people, a new kind of England, a departure from rather than a transfer of traditional patterns. It was the outreach of Calvinist Protestantism, foreshadowed in those abortive Huguenot colonies, initiated by the Separatists at Plymouth, and vigorously undertaken by the English Puritans that would provide a new and powerful impetus toward America, directed toward these very lands that had proved so marginal to more fully commercial interests.

By the 1630s the Atlantic World had begun to display a good deal more differentiation and complexity than it had only a few decades before. The annual harvest of the sea remained the paramount activity in northern America, but after a long informal testing period the fur trade was emerging as an attractive prospect of wealth from the land. The key indication was the willingness of substantial entrepreneurs to invest in settlements in America, in small colonies supported in part by local produce rather than ephemeral outposts. It was a commerce dependent on the Indians and it was a geographically expansive system, which thereby spurred territorial rivalries among European nations and among their Indian allies. The English had formalized competitive imperialism in this sector by laying claim to Newfoundland in 1583, but only began to endanger the informal routines of the fishery by actual colonization thirty years later. The fur trade was basic to the initiation of Acadia, Canada, New England, and New Netherland. Emerging out of a swirl of commercial rivalries these imperial territories were not as yet very clearly delimited on the map, but English attacks upon Port Royal and Quebec and their proclamation of a New Scotland in place of Acadia were indications of a sharp intensification of European national interests in this nearest America. Furthermore, the presence of colonies of religious refugees in Massachusetts Bay, Plymouth, and New Netherland began to give a new regional diversity and a further divergence from the original and still basic commercial character of this broad thrust across the northern Atlantic.

In Tropical America imperial competition and new colonization had brought even more extensive change. The Spanish held firmly to their enormous continental empire, but had lost control over its outer Atlantic approaches and thereby over the security of its own imperial trunk line. Less notable at the time but more basic was the founding of English, French, and Dutch colonies and the beginnings of their own versions of tropical planter societies. In the subtropics a distinctly English empirical creation was taking shape out of the desperately difficult attempt at commercial colonization by the Virginia Company. The Portuguese had developed their part of Tropical America into the most productive commercial sector of the American seaboard, sustained by an expansive slave-procurement network along the West African coast. This African littoral was an important commercial area even apart from its primary human product, supplying gold, ivory, spices, medicinals, and dyewoods, as well as a still-valued amount of São Tomé sugar. In the 1630s the Dutch moved in upon both ends of this Portuguese equatorial axis, and other northern Europeans soon followed to introduce a new set of unstable and complicated patterns of maritime imperialism.

Generalizing more broadly once again, we can see that the two great thrusts out of the two creative source regions carried two distinct versions of European civilization across the ocean, initiating a Catholic imperial America in the south and a Protestant commercial America in the north. But these direct extensions were increasingly caught up into larger Atlantic circuits binding together four continents, three races, and several cultural systems, complicating and blurring the processes of extension and transfer. Distance and time, encounter and environment, events and experience would surely imperil any comprehensive replication of European society. Already two great mutations had appeared, the mestizo-creole society of Hispanic America and the mulatto-creole society of Luso-Afro-America, and there were hints of others in the tropical colonies of northwest Europe and in the refugee colonies in northern America. By 1630 Europe held dominion over every seaboard sector and huge portions of the interior. America had become incorporated into the routine concerns of European nations, but this was not simply an enlargement into a Greater Europe. It is better seen as a new Atlantic world. The ocean had become the "inland sea of Western Civilization," a "new Mediterranean" on a global scale, with old seats of culture on the east, a great frontier for expansion to the west, and a long and integral African shore.

10. Generalizations: Geographic Models of Interaction

The Atlantic World was the scene of a vast interaction rather than merely the transfer of Europeans onto American shores. Instead of a European discovery of a new world, we might better consider it as a sudden and harsh encounter between two old worlds that transformed both and integrated them into a single New World. Our focus is upon the creation of new human geographies resulting from this interaction, and that means those developing not only westward upon the body of America but eastward upon the body of Europe, and inward upon and laterally along the body of Africa. For it is certain that the geography of each was changed: radically on the American side, with widespread disruption of old patterns and imposition of new ones; more subtly on the European side, with new movements of people, goods, capital, and information flowing through an established spatial system and slowly altering its proportions and directions; slowly and unevenly on the African side, making connections with existing commercial systems but eventually grotesquely altering the scale and meaning of old institutions.

In search of guidance in thinking about so complex a matter, we may begin by recalling our simple formulation of *seafaring, conquering,* and *planting* as a common sequence in the European outreach to and encroachment upon America. These can be further subdivided to recognize some recurrent general patterns:

1. *Exploration:* reconnaissance, the search for basic information, the discovery of possibilities.
2. *Gathering:* exploitation of obvious coastal resources, such as fish, ship timbers, and salt, by extension of routine activities.
3. *Barter:* commercial opportunism, trade with local populations for exotic goods, testing for further development.
4. *Plunder:* brigandage, military opportunism, sometimes involving forays into the interior, seizing whatever might have value in European markets.

5. *Outpost:* fixing a point of commercial exchange; a commitment to overseas investment and assignment of personnel to overseas residence.
6. *Imperial Imposition:* assertion of formal claim and power over American territory; assignment of governor, soldiers, missionaries, and other agents of European state and society.
7. *Implantation:* transfer of Europeans as permanent settlers and initiation of self-sustaining colony.
8. *Imperial Colony:* logical development from imperial imposition and implantation—transfer of full complex of institutions, a selected transplant of European culture tending toward expansion and divergence from the home country.

It must be emphasized that this is not a rigid sequence. In some localities there were no immediate resources awaiting harvest; barter and plunder might be, often were, intermixed, alternating as phases of the same enterprise; formal imperial assertion might be simultaneous with the establishment of a commercial post and extensive colonization. But the list does offer a useful perspective on a general process in which we can view the first five categories as a *prelude,* a set of activities that required nothing more than seafaring backed by modest commercial interests and that could be readily discontinued without major loss or disruption. (See figure 9.) In contrast, subsequent categories clearly imply more substantial encroachment, made possible by conquering and planting to form a firm European nucleus upon lands overseas. (See figure 10.)

As soon as we begin to relate these phases to specific cases variations among the many transatlantic enterprises will be discernible, most notably in the differences among those of the several European states. But some of those differences are so commonplace that it is useful to stress for a moment the opposite. Columbus and the earliest Portuguese in Brazil were as involved in exploration, gathering, barter, plunder, and the establishment of speculative outposts as were the northern Europeans in northern America. Only in the later phases do these thrusts create rather different kinds of American colonies, reflective of their markedly different cultural origins.

Moreover, if we are to stress interaction we must broaden our perspective to bring both sides of the Atlantic into view and try to envision the simultaneous changes in Europe and America through this sequence, as diagramed in figures 9 and 10. The first four phases share fundamental similarities on both sides of the Atlantic: requiring only modest resources, they can be projected from small European ports; and being inherently sporadic and intermittent because of the lack of an obvious commercial infrastructure to connect with on the American side, they result in no fixed point of sustained contact. The commercial outpost marks an important step. In Vance's terms, the "impulse to trade" had now spun a thin

PRELUDE

AMERICA   ATLANTIC   EUROPE

accidental
momentary
contact with
small coastal
bands; new
perceptions.

speculators
from small ports
in search of
information;
new perceptions.

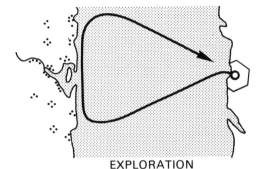

EXPLORATION

casual
seasonal
contact along
seaboard;
little
impact.

mariners and
fisherman from
provincial ports;
extension of
routine activities.

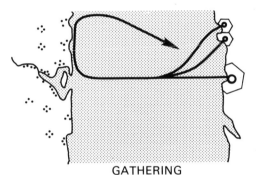

GATHERING

sporadic
intermittent
contact;
occasional
conflict;
new
diseases;
shallow
impact.

speculative merchants
and brigands; testing
of goods, costs, markets,
little impact.

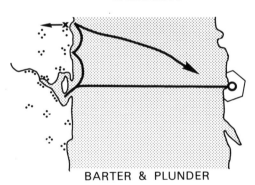

BARTER & PLUNDER

9. Transatlantic Interaction: Prelude Phases.

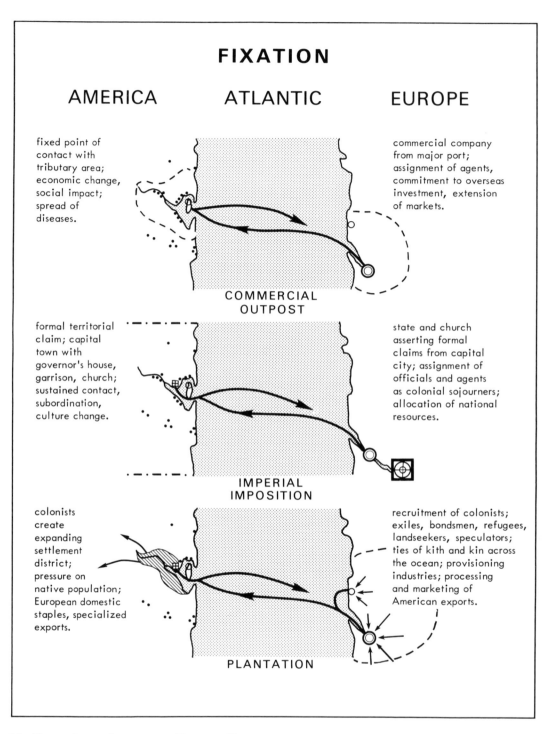

FIXATION

AMERICA   ATLANTIC   EUROPE

fixed point of
contact with
tributary area;
economic change,
social impact;
spread of
diseases.

commercial company
from major port;
assignment of agents,
commitment to overseas
investment, extension
of markets.

**COMMERCIAL
OUTPOST**

formal territorial
claim; capital
town with
governor's house,
garrison, church;
sustained contact,
subordination,
culture change.

state and church
asserting formal
claims from capital
city; assignment of
officials and agents
as colonial sojourners;
allocation of national
resources.

**IMPERIAL
IMPOSITION**

colonists
create
expanding
settlement
district;
pressure on
native population;
European domestic
staples, specialized
exports.

recruitment of colonists;
exiles, bondsmen, refugees,
landseekers, speculators;
ties of kith and kin across
the ocean; provisioning
industries; processing
and marketing of
American exports.

PLANTATION

10. Transatlantic Interaction: Fixation Phases.

strand between "points of attachment" on either side of the ocean, which would likely channel subsequent developments very markedly. Because such a distant outpost required a considerable investment it was likely to be a projection from a major port wherein entrepreneurs had ready access to capital and mercantile connections, although it might well draw upon the energies and earlier experiences of smaller ports as well; and because such an outpost became the focus of a newly constituted economic area it might have widely ramifying social and cultural impact. Imperial imposition expresses a formal link between commercial enterprise and political power, the axis between port and court (which were not always in the same city). On the American side it created a cluster of facilities representing government and church as well as commerce. Implantation begins to draw more fundamentally upon European hinterlands, which become catchment basins for the recruitment of colonists and thereby become bound by ties of kith and kin with these new overseas creations. On the American side such migration will lead inevitably to some degree of disruption of the indigenous population.

We can envision, therefore, general patterns of change spreading inwardly upon each continent as the strands linking them across the Atlantic thicken and multiply. It is a sequence broadly of increasing magnitude of change: in the number of people directly engaged and indirectly affected, in the number and scale of institutions extended across the sea, in the volume of capital invested and goods transported. Geographically it is a sequence involving shifts in location and scale that can be generalized within hierarchical territorial systems: from Atlantic-facing provincial ports or even lesser fishing harbors to larger commercial and political centers, with a concordant shift in the size of hinterlands affected. The obvious anomalous case was the state-enforced monopoly system of Spain, which after 1503 kept all American traffic rigidly focused on Seville. The internal commercial networks of all these European states in some degree reflected the agrarian medieval central place system, modified by the presence and function of a few major international entrepôts. The outreach to America augmented this latter mercantile dimension, in the need to expand the provisioning of ships and settlements overseas, to produce goods for trade, and to process new imports. Beyond these major ports, we might logically expect that the impact in Europe of American operations, including the spread of information, recruitment of personnel, attraction of capital, and marketing of produce, would move through these national systems in hierarchical patterns. We can be sure that there would be anomalies, and no doubt any attempt to identify and measure the amount of such geographical change in European cities, settlements, and systems would be as elusive and controversial as the long-pursued attempt to measure the relative impact of American bullion upon the European economy, but it does seem a worthy corollary task.

On the American side, except in those few regions where Europeans superim-

posed themselves upon dense and deeply rooted Indian societies, as in central
Mexico, there was no similar structured network of localities for European-induced
change to move through. Such change began of course from the moment Europeans and Americans caught sight of one another: their mutual discovery creating
new perceptions of the world of men, exciting new hopes and fears. Long before
Europeans took firm root in North American soil contact had effected important
changes. Disease was the most devastating, resulting at times in sudden and drastic
demographic deformations of Indian societies.

> When the isolation of the New World was broken, when Columbus brought the two
> halves of this planet together, the American Indian met for the first time his most
> hideous enemy: not the white man nor his black servant, but the invisible killers
> which those men brought in their blood and breath.

Barter could initiate economic change as Indians responded to supply new markets
and to do so with the help of new tools obtained from Europeans. It is important to
emphasize that there was no obvious imbalance in these early commercial relationships. Contact opened new opportunities that persons on each side warily but
avidly explored, seeking whatever advantage might be gained for themselves.
Completely separate cultural development had created an inherent basis for commerce: each side had utterly ordinary goods that proved amazingly attractive to the
other, allowing both to regard the exchange as highly profitable. Because the basis
of such commerce was new and because there was no network of market towns,
specialized system of carriage, or separate class or clans of traders already in place
along the American seaboard, the establishment of a European outpost was by its
very nature a transforming intrusion, which could not but have major social as well
as economic effects. But the more fragmented and less stable political and economic geography of Indian groups would lead to a less systematic and symmetrical
diffusion of such impacts over any considerable territory than in Europe.

A powerful European sense of superiority was latent in all such encounters.
Europeans initiated these contacts and any resisters to their intrusions were regarded as enemies. An imperial relationship was therefore assumed and its overt
assertion marked a critical stage and level of impact, for, however effective in fact
at any particular place and time, imperialism implies political subordination,
military coercion, economic exploitation, social stratification, and often some
attempt at religious alteration and other programs to enforce cultural change. The
influx of Europeans as permanent settlers would reinforce and insure the perpetua-
tion of such pressures. Resistance, conflict, and dislocations were sure to follow,
but there were marked differences in geographic results. In general, three basic
geographic types (see figure 11) were common:

1. expulsion of the native population from the colonized area and the creation of a
   firm frontier of separation between the two peoples, as in Virginia;

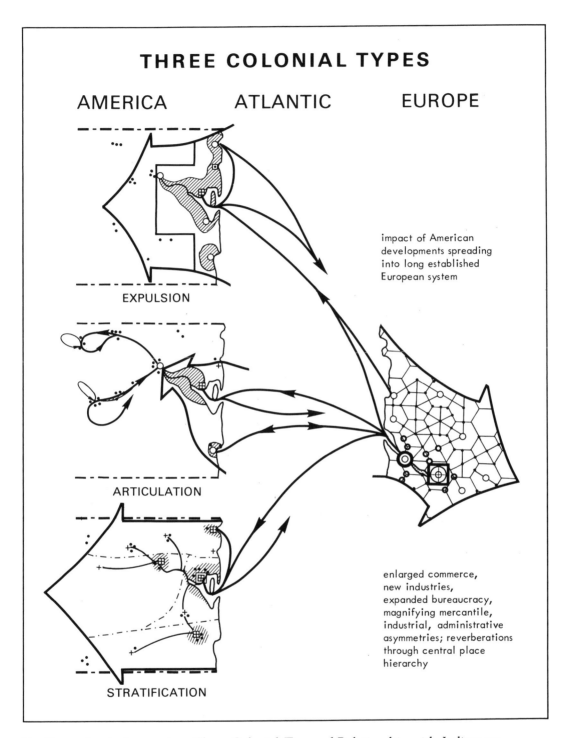

THREE COLONIAL TYPES

AMERICA   ATLANTIC   EUROPE

EXPULSION

impact of American
developments spreading
into long established
European system

ARTICULATION

STRATIFICATION

enlarged commerce,
new industries,
expanded bureaucracy,
magnifying mercantile,
industrial, administrative
asymmetries; reverberations
through central place
hierarchy

11. Transatlantic Interaction: Three Colonial Types of Relationship with Indigenous
Peoples.

2. benign articulation of the two peoples at a point of exchange, each group operating largely within a separate territory but bound together in an encompassing economic system, as in Canada; and
3. stratification within a single complex society, exhibiting varying degrees of racial and cultural mixture and fusion, as in Mexico.

Much has been written about the differing racial attitudes of the English, French, and Spanish as important causes of such patterns, but it would appear that different local circumstances, and especially basic differences in imperial objectives, were more critical. Miscegenation was apparent in all areas of encounter, but a fusion of peoples and cultures arose from the assumption of a comprehensive imperial purpose in the European outreach. An incomplete account of Spanish landholders in Hispaniola recorded 146 of 392 living there with their wives, of whom ninety-two were Spanish and fifty-four Indian; dated 1514, this report suggests how early such blending got under way where colonization was an integral part of a system of conquest. Racial attitudes are conditioned by cultural experience; they were more a product of the formative phases of this new encounter in America than rigid assumptions transferred from Europe.

One further variation must be added to these generalized patterns of geographic change wrought around the Atlantic rim. West Africa was bound into this European outreach from the very first and Africans became the principal population in some American sectors. The circuits of the slave trade were more triangular than directly reciprocal across the Atlantic, so that the main cultural impacts were those of Europe upon Africa and Africa upon America, with very little American influence directly eastward upon Africa (the introduction and spread of selected tropical crops being the most obvious). Because a traffic in slaves had long existed within Africa and because Iberians were well acquainted with the use of coerced labor, the critical prelude took place quite rapidly on the Atlantic islands, in Senegambia, and on São Tomé, and the sugar-slave plantation system could be implanted in Tropical America without long experimentation.

On the African side the common pattern was that of a European station on an island or peninsula, supervised by a few officials and agents, adjacent to or near an entrepôt manned largely by Europeanized mulattos and Blacks, which was in turn the base of an African-controlled slave procurement system reaching into the territories of vulnerable tribes in the interior. Here disease defeated ambitious imperial designs and the European presence was minimal, marginal, and unstable, so that cultural imports were primarily those selected by, rather than imposed upon, the Africans. Many detailed features remain obscure, but the cultural and economic incentives introduced and magnified by the European-controlled Atlantic system may be presumed, from the sheer scale of the trade, to have altered the human geography of West Africa in major ways, although with marked regional

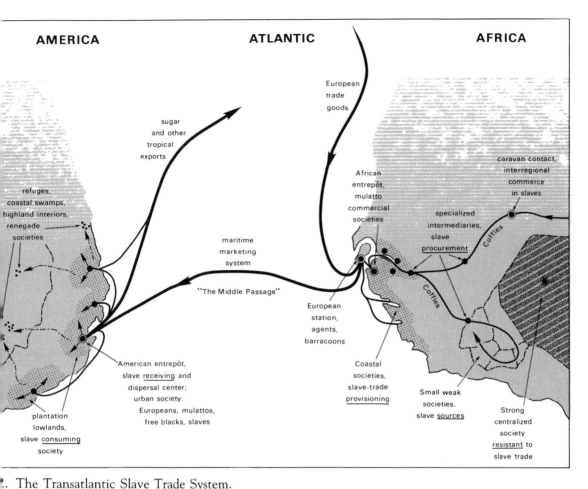

AMERICA   ATLANTIC   AFRICA

European trade goods

sugar and other tropical exports

caravan contact, interregional commerce in slaves

African entrepôt, mulatto commercial societies

refuges, coastal swamps, highland interiors, renegade societies

specialized intermediaries, slave procurement

Coffles

maritime marketing system

"The Middle Passage"

Coffles

European station, agents, barracoons

American entrepôt, slave receiving and dispersal center; urban society: Europeans, mulattos, free blacks, slaves

Coastal societies, slave-trade provisioning

Small weak societies, slave sources

plantation lowlands, slave consuming society

Strong centralized society resistant to slave trade

. The Transatlantic Slave Trade System.

variation, since some of the more powerful centralized societies, such as Benin and Dahomey, resisted participation.

On the American side slaves were marketed through established networks linking major ports, regional centers, and rural districts. Wherever they were used in any number they of course created a highly visible African presence on American soil, a presence recurrently reinforced by fresh importations. More subtle were their influences upon their European masters and upon any residual local Indians. Miscegenation was inevitably a widespread, ongoing feature among such closely associated and interdependent peoples. The human geography of these societies tended toward increasing complexities of stratification and segregation arising from racial and cultural mixtures, from the emancipation of individuals, from the emergence of unsupervised clusters of Africans in cities and marginal districts, and eventually from outlaw societies of renegades who fled to freedom in remote hinterlands. On a broader scale, of course, the Europeans controlled the spread of this African impact, but as servants, artisans, and laborers Blacks were taken in

13. Slave Trade on the Guinea Coast.
This remarkable seventeenth-century panorama displays one of the most intensely developed sectors of the Euro-African trading system. Within a stretch of about twelve miles five European forts cling to the mountainous margins of the Gold Coast: Mina (Elmina), the first great Portuguese bastion, seized by the Dutch in 1637 and so elaborated that John Barbot noted "it looks as if it had been made for the dwelling of a king, [rather] than for a place of trade in Guinea"; St. Iago, a Danish fort (c. 1670) on an adjacent height; Cabo Corso (Cape Coast), which the English had taken from the Dutch in 1664 and made into the chief base of the Royal African Company; half a mile on, Manfrou (Amanfro), established in 1600 as a base for the Danish African Company; and Mouree (Mouri) where the Dutch began trading in 1598 and built Fort Nassau in 1624. These substantial fortifica-

small numbers to many ports and districts and thereby exerted in some way the influence of Africa along almost the full length of the American seaboard.

Thus we can attempt to envision these changes as the effects of a single vast spatial system, a transoceanic network ever enlarging its extent and capacity, lacing itself ever more deeply and complexly into the body of Europe, encroaching ever more powerfully and drastically upon the lands and peoples of America, and

tions reflect not only these European rivalries but the insecurity of all Europeans, who operated on this coast only on the sufferance of local rulers. The canoes featured in the foreground emphasize another essential African role in the system. There are no good harbors along this coast; ships must stand well offshore and be served by African boatmen skilled in coping with the heavy surf. The original of this sketch dates from about 1680 when John Barbot was trading along here with the French Royal African Company (which had no forts in this area). His manuscript "A Description of the Coasts of North and South Guinea" evidently first appeared in print in 1732 in an English translation published in London as part of Churchill's *Collection of Voyages and Travels*. This print is a photograph of Johannes Kip's engraving in Volume V of that work.

drawing ever more extensively and destructively upon the societies of Africa. The great primordial circulation of the Atlantic had become the medium for an immensely complex and widely ramifying exchange of plants and animals, goods and money, men and women, tools, ideas, and entire systems of activity. By 1630 the impact was already enormous and the balance heavily weighted in favor of Europe. To use Wallerstein's formulation, the American and African sectors were parts of a new *periphery* of an emergent *core* now "firmly located in northwest Europe, that is, in Holland and Zeeland; in London, the Home Counties, and East Anglia; and in northern and western France," a relationship that heralded the birth of "the modern world-system" of capitalist economy. A key to that structure was the creation of a "geographical division of labor" in which some form of coercion was used in outlying areas for the production of valued goods, which products and the profits therefrom flowed to the capitalist groups who controlled the vigorously diversifying developments in the states of the core region. Such a pattern on a world scale can be traced to the Portuguese use of African slaves for sugar production on the Atlantic islands, not because that system was wholly new in form but because it was the first step in a vast geographical extension of such an economy.

Our principal focus is upon societies rather than economies, and here, too, the Europeans were the shaping agents. The social life and demographic patterns of a large portion of American and parts of Africa had been deeply disrupted and deformed. Disease, warfare, slave hunting, and cruel exploitation had nearly depopulated most of the West Indies, extensive stretches of the mainland coast, and some inland regions. Africans now formed the main population of several colonies and were present in nearly every European-developed locality in the American tropics and subtropics. Europeans, already many different kinds of Europeans, dominated by power if not everywhere by numbers from Labrador to the Río de la Plata.

Such an attempt to envision an Atlantic World ensnares us in an even larger web and leads logically to the necessity of seeing it as only part of a global system. We must hold that awareness of scale ever in our minds, but our major concern is with America and it is now time to shift our focus from this general system in this oceanic arena and look more closely at the regional variety of peoples and places created from these European footholds in North America and on islands closely related to North American developments.

PART TWO
IMPLANTATIONS: THE CREATION OF AMERICAN DIVERSITY

As a single story the recruitment, settlement patterns, and developing character of the American population in the preindustrial era . . . covers a long period of time. . . . Further, it involves population movements over a vast geographical area—an area stretching from the bleak island of Foula off the west coast of the Shetlands at the latitude of Greenland to the Lunda Kingdom deep in equatorial Africa, from the Baltic port of Flensburg and from Görlitz on the German-Polish border to Natchez and Pensacola. And, finally, the problems it involves lead naturally beyond history itself to other disciplines as they relate to history: anthropology, demography, and particularly, cultural geography.

Bernard Bailyn

Prologue

The Atlantic World bound together a vast diversity of peoples and places. At the broadest scale these would become defined by the aggressive European creators of this system in crude racial and continental terms: White, Red, Black; Europe, America, Africa. And by their conquests, migrations, and conversions Europeans would impose further broad religious and political differentiations: Catholic, Protestant, "heathen"; Spanish, Portuguese, French, Dutch, English.

We are concerned with diversities related to race, religion, and nation but we must come into focus on a much finer scale than any of the above. We cannot, of course, deal with persons and families, but we can try to recognize peoples in terms of some basic social identities that they carried by birth, choice, or assignment in the routines of the life they shared with other groups, identities relating to the color of their skin, the language they spoke, the church to which they belonged, the region they claimed as their ancestral home.

We seek to define diversity in these terms because Americans in general have always thought and acted as if such things mattered in personal and community life. They have made such features criteria for defining social status, bases for ascription and discrimination, badges of pride and prejudice. Although specific terms and attitudes have varied greatly with times, places, and peoples these basic features themselves have had profound connotations through the course of American history.

Similarly, in our concern for the diversity of places we cannot give attention to every town and countryside but we can focus on initial centers and expansions therefrom, and try to define areas in terms of place identities created by the presence, impress, and activities of these social groups.

Because our primary perspective is geographic our review is ordered in terms of areas and seeks to trace a diverse set of regional formations from the beginning of European colonization to about 1750. That will allow us to make an inventory of these diversities on the eve of a major change, the English takeover of French North America, soon to be followed by further far-reaching geopolitical reorganization.

1. Peoples and Places

EUROPEAN DIVERSITY

It is trite to observe that the American people emerged out of a great diversity of peoples, but it is not at all easy to define just what that diversity consisted of. That England, France, Spain, the Netherlands, and Sweden were directly involved in establishing colonies on the North American seaboard in the seventeenth century provides a geographical reference appropriate to diplomatic and military history but quite inadequate for any kind of cultural history. Those names refer to political states but they cannot yet refer to national cultures in any full sense of that concept, for none of them was yet a strongly developed, cohesive, self-conscious national unit.

Countering the all-too-common contrast of "European" with "American" in interpretations of the emerging character of colonial society, Michael Kammen has emphasized that the "colonials didn't come from Europe. They came from East Anglia, Bristol, London, Ulster, Leyden, and Nantes." That is a salutary reminder but his illustrative list, a mixture of regions and cities, is not a clear guide to the most relevant concept or scale of territory. Davies's similar emphasis, that "colonies were not founded by the French, Dutch, and English *nations* but by sections, usually geographical, sometimes religious, of those countries," gives a further clue to the kinds of groups we must recognize in our search for the constituent peoples of this transatlantic implantation. The cultural diversity we seek to identify, therefore, exists *within* the states of Europe, for the most part, and is fundamentally either regional or religious in character.

Regional culture refers to that which is characteristic of a group of people who are deep-rooted and dominant in a particular territory, who are conscious of their identity as deriving from a common heritage, and who share a common language and basic patterns of life. The Welsh, an old Celtic population long resident in a highland region of Great Britain, may serve as a good example. The Welsh are a vivid exhibit of an ethnic group, as well as of the complexities of that concept. At first encounter the Welsh and the English were sharply distinct peoples, but centuries of contact and subordination of the Welsh within the English polity altered and blurred the evidence of Welsh ethnicity. In the seventeenth century there was still a strongly "Welsh Wales" and "English England" but also a borderland and enclaves of English-speaking Welsh. One might thereby recognize gradations of "Welshness," but ethnicity is not simply a matter of regional differences in particular features, even in so basic a one as language; it is more a matter of feelings, of self-identity. Thus even in the late twentieth century when the entire region is articulated closely to English society and most Welsh speak only English, Wales is the seat of "a vigorous Anglo-Welsh society . . . which shows little sign of being simply a transition stage to Englishness."

If we move only a few miles to the south of that borderland, across the Bristol Channel, we encounter a more uncertain example of regional culture. Within England the West Country was long generally regarded as a distinct region. But, aside from its old Celtic-Cornish extremity, as a society it was clearly no more than a subdivision, somewhat vague in extent, anchored on Devon, with Exeter as the historic center of an area with its own traditions, dialect, and ancestral families, but with no really unmistakable "ethnic" distinctions. Here we deal with a relatively subdued form of regional culture, one which its members are conscious of but not normally militant about, though strong feelings of identity may be aroused under special circumstances (as in the case of certain rivalries with London in early American enterprise).

These two forms of regional culture, the one clearly ethnic in character, the other a much less obvious territorial variation, existed in many areas of western Europe, giving a culturo-geographic diversity to every major political state.

Whereas such regional cultures are typically the product of many centuries of group development in place, the religious diversity of seventeenth-century Europe was an unstable pattern reflecting the complexities of new movements. The Reformation broke the bonds of centuries-old Western Christian culture and produced an almost kaleidoscopic resorting of peoples.

Most rulers regarded religion as a central institution of the state and sought uniformity in religious allegiance within their own territories. Thus many populations were, in a broad sense, simply reclassified by political decision, a collective shift in allegiance from Rome to the state church. In such changes religion would become more directly ethnic in local character, as in the case of Lutheranism in the various Germanic lands. Major religious movements such as Calvinism often involved a more personal choice and led to new groupings in which people through conscious selection quite explicitly shared in certain basic beliefs and values. In some degree the groups formed by such individual choice represented new religious cultures, but these too could be only partial modifications of older ethnic identities. Thus Calvinism could not produce simply Calvinists, but Swiss, French, German, Dutch, English, and Scottish Calvinists. Those religious movements that gave greatest stress to individual conscience and regarded the church as a voluntary association represented the most marked departure from older territorial-based cultures. Quakers and various Anabaptist sects were rarely dominant even locally and thus emerged as religious subcultures within some encompassing society.

Our concern is not with all such regions and movements in Europe, but only with those that had significant impact upon American colonial areas. Even so, and whatever the uncertainties about what constitutes a "significant" impact, we are certainly dealing with diversities arising from nearly three dozen regional and religious cultures rather than a mere handful of political states.

NATIVE AMERICANS

Although we are not well accustomed to thinking so, the great diversity of the American people stems from more than European immigration—it includes those native to the lands they came to. Here, too, there are problems of identification, but of a special character. Columbus drew upon the geographical presumptions of his obsessive quest and categorized all the people he encountered with a single name that was soon diffused into the languages of subsequent explorers: *los Indios, Indianer, Indian* (the French never used the term, preferring *Sauvages*). Thus an identity that could initially have no meaning to these people themselves was eventually fixed upon the whole population of the New World. Columbus's voyages, encounters, and act of naming were of course powerful events in the emergence of a world defined at the broadest scale in crude continental and racial terms.

Yet Columbus himself reported on differences among the peoples native to various parts of these Indies, and every subsequent attempt to foster trade, impose rule, or implant a colony meant an encounter with the specific people of a particular locality. Each of these peoples had its own identity and a clear sense of its relationships with other peoples within the compass of its knowledge, just as each European group did of itself, but the culture worlds of the two were so different with respect to such concepts as authority, membership, and territory of a "people" that any quick and clear translation between them was impossible. Thus by the very nature of the encounter the identities of native American peoples became those fixed upon them by their invaders, whether or not such terms were at all concordant in name, concept, or extent with pre-European patterns. What Europeans labeled as an Indian "nation" might vary from an independent band of a hundred people to a loose confederation of many thousands, and the record of two centuries of encounters along the North American seaboard produced such a bewildering variety of names that there remain many uncertainties about the actual participants and patterns of particular localities. One general fact is clear, and further complicates the matter: the impact of European contact was so disruptive as to cause major change in the location, affiliation, and identity of many indigenous groups, and these changes, too, have been reported entirely through European interpreters.

To recognize that both the collective and specific identities of Native Americans have been fixed upon them by Europeans is to recognize a basic fact that still needs emphasis: conquering must precede planting, that is, American beginnings were everywhere shaped by imperial processes. It is naturally difficult for conquerors to have anything like a balanced and comprehensive view of all the peoples involved in such historical processes. It is insidiously easy to think of Indians in collective terms and to see them as victims of an unfortunate but necessary opening phase in the modern history of each region, to think of them very largely as an obstacle to "progress" or to the "march of civilization." But if we are serious about identifying the great diversity of peoples involved in the creation of the American people we must acknowledge that Indians were and remain active participants in that great ongoing process of creation and therefore deserve recognition at the same basic scale as that given to Europeans. Applying that view to the zone of early encounter extending from Hudson Bay and Newfoundland to the lower Rio Grande and San Antonio reveals at least forty distinct Indian groups who helped shape in some significant way the developing pattern of their region.

AFRICANS

Africans brought forcibly to America are a still different case and problem for interpretation. Slaves were procured from a very extensive area of the African coast and deep hinterlands, drawing upon scores of tribal groups and many regional cultures. But the slave marketing system worked directly against the transfer and maintenance of tribal or ethnic groupings in America. From the time of first assemblages on the beaches of Africa for shipment, masters in charge of any considerable number followed a practice of deliberate separation of such groups and a mixing of unlike peoples in order to forestall any kind of concerted resistance; further fragmentation was incidental to the dispersion of any one shipment to many buyers, and to further resale. The degree to which such unwilling immigrants passed on important elements of their native culture to subsequent generations and the ways in which these contributed to the formation and development of American regional and national cultures remain important and controversial topics, but there seems to be little evidence of the transplantation and continuation of any recognizable discrete African ethnic groups in local North American areas. As Huggins has noted: "The progeny of these Africans were to lose all vestiges of tribal difference, making one people and giving ironic validity to a coming nation's slogan: *e pluribus unum.*"

Thus these people too had a new identity fixed upon them by European aggressors, one even more drastic and rigid than that given to Native Americans.

Europeans made *African* and *Negro* synonyms of powerful social and legal meaning, a collective categorization of people firmly locked into American society at its lowest level and severed from viable connection with their specific ancestral cultures. Yet this common status and experience did not give rise to a single Afro-American people. For captives wrenched from their own society and immersed in a foreign one are perforce under powerful pressures of acculturation. Physical survival and service as a slave require at least some basic adaptations to the culture of the slave-owners. We can be certain that Afro-Americans reared in English Virginia, Spanish Florida, and French Louisiana could hardly develop a single Afro-American culture, and we might well assume that other regional differences would also become apparent. Since Blacks were an important feature of most of the societies from Rhode Island to Louisiana as well as those of the West Indies we could expect that the colonial Afro-American population displayed some of the variations to be found in that range of coastal and island cultures. However, we should not assume that such variations would simply reflect those of the host societies, for these involuntary immigrants were not simply imitative—they adapted their own African cultures in response to particular American circumstances, the most important of which were the proportions and proximities of Black and White in daily life. In all of this we are so dependent upon evidence gathered and interpreted by Whites rather than by the Blacks themselves that we cannot be confident of our understanding of the nature and significance of such variations, but we can at least insist that in place of the long-standing tendency to regard "the Afro-American community created by the [slave] trade as an alien body on the periphery of national life" we must see it, quite the contrary, as an ancient, integral, and central component of American development.

One last troublesome feature in this matter of identities of peoples should be noted. People who give routine recognition to "race," defined on the basis of skin color, hair, and physiognomy, will very likely recognize the products of racial mixture as distinct categories as well. Over the centuries out of many languages a number of terms have been used by Europeans to designate such people, from the general, such as "mixed-bloods," to more specific blends, such as "mestizo" or "metis," "mulatto," and "zambo," to attempts at designated proportions, such as "quadroon." Such terms have little objective content, other than to indicate recognition of mixture. We must always keep in mind that a good many persons labeled White, Red, or Black, European, Indian, or African were "mixed" in the same sense. Yet we must make use of such terms because they were given social significance, because they were made relevant to status, privilege, and group identity. They take on meaning only within specific societies, but in some of these they become very important indeed. That in so doing they become terms of value and may be regarded as offensive by the persons so categorized should be recognized but we may not forgo their use solely on that account. We must try to be sensitive to such concerns but we cannot avoid the fact of such categorization.

In this overview we cannot of course trace each of these European, Native American, and African peoples through their entire history as Americans. What we can and should do is to acknowledge their presence as participants in our national history and to insist that here in the early phases of our history the diversity we should seek to understand consists of seventy to eighty different peoples rather than the seven or eight who have long been most prominent in our literature.

AREAS

When we turn our attention from peoples to places we are faced with a somewhat similar problem. Because our primary perspective is geographic we must find the areal framework that will best suit our consideration of developments emanating from the various implantations on American shores.

It will be obvious that the most gross political areas will not serve. The broad sectors of the competing European powers, such as French America, British America, and Spanish America, were colorations on the world map of empires, realms of a sovereign, zones of diplomatic and military significance, but not actual units of administration or of anything else. Lesser regional groupings of common historical reference, such as New England, the Middle Colonies, the Southern Colonies, and the West Indies, are also inappropriate for a beginning framework. It will be important to discover the degree to which and the ways in which such labels become useful generalizations about functional coherence, cultural similarity, and regional consciousness, yet it is clear that any such regional integrity or identity could not be implanted, but could only emerge from effort and experience over many years.

It might seem obvious that not these groupings but the formal political units of which they are composed, the "colonies" in the most common use of the term, provide the logical framework. It is certainly true that these separate jurisdictions are relevant to a great many topics and thus have conveniently served as an effective matrix for a diverse range of historical analysis. Yet on close examination these political territories are not firm sociocultural compartments. Some contain more than one distinct social area and some cultural groups spread across political boundaries; if our concern is more with peoples than with politics such units are not necessarily the best framework.

Our search is for those *discrete colonization areas* that were created directly or very nearly directly from the migration of distinct groups of Europeans (and, in some cases, their African slaves). We seek to identify every nucleus that endured sufficiently to contribute in some significant way to the subsequent American scene. As Andrew Clark put it, in defense of his meticulous study of an Acadia that was eventually uprooted and nearly effaced, we must be concerned with all those early nuclei that "had a long enough life to leave the indelible stamp of their personalities on the regions in which they appeared, even if that personality was only the first trace on a palimpsest of superimposed regional character that succeeded in place with the passage of the centuries." It is through these areas that the diversity of immigrant peoples was first introduced to America.

There are, of course, problems in the definition of such areas, just as in the identification of peoples. Some degree of arbitrariness cannot be avoided. Selection is not simply a matter of scale. Every colony began in a locality, but there is no possibility or need to pay attention to every single landing place, every trading post, fishing village, or farmer's wharf along the American strand. We must focus attention upon those implantations that gained command of a considerable district, impressed a particular order upon the land, developed local resources, expanded a system of trafficways, and emerged as a substantial society amidst its own particular landscape, an area recognizably distinct from its neighbors. Here again, definition of distinctiveness may not be easy in every case. It may be clearly ethnic, rooted in obvious linguistic and religious identities and displayed in distinctive architecture and settlement forms, but it may be more subtle, a matter of a degree of social homogeneity and self-identity; or it may be more complex, a particular structural diversity of peoples and landscapes within some commonly recognized social framework. Colonization took place within legally defined territories (although often enmeshed in disputes over the legality of those definitions), and such areas might be altered in extent and would usually be subdivided into local administrative areas as the population and area of settlement expanded. Where expansion went beyond the bounds of chartered limits important discordances between cultural and political geography were created, and the inadequacy of purely geopolitical designations made manifest.

The result of this approach is the identification of more than two dozen areas as the basic sociogeographic entities in this Atlantic world that would have significant bearing upon the eventual creation of the United States of America. In a larger sense all of Spanish America is part of that context, but here only Florida and Texas are included as separate pieces, as each was established in response to border challenges along the Atlantic rim. Other early northern mainland colonizations in New Mexico, Sonora, and California may more appropriately be described in the context of an expanding Anglo-American nation.

These new geographic entities form the first layer of building blocks for the larger edifice. Ideally, we should wish to describe the cultural geographic development of each area in detail. Practically, we shall have to proceed with no more than summary characterizations and a quick outline of the changing contexts and results of a century and a half of colonial history. That in itself will be complicated enough, a marked contrast with the geographical simplifications characteristic of standard histories, and should thereby provide a fresh look at a number of basic features.

2. Northern Coasts: Beginnings

The nearest American land to Europe was long known but of little intrinsic interest. The seas were rich, the land poor. The main incentive to gain hold of land was to gain advantage in harvesting the sea. Gradually other resources, chiefly furs and ship timbers, and broader strategic concerns enlarged interest in the long, complicated coastlines between the Avalon Peninsula and Long Island. In the early seventeenth century several nuclei of settlement began to take shape.

By that time the West Country English had come to dominate the richest fishing grounds off Newfoundland. The common practice was for small firms in the ports of Devon, Dorset, and Bristol to send over ships and crews for summer fishing, making use of temporary flakes on shore to cut, salt, and dry the cod. Very gradually "overwintering" became more common, some of the crew staying on for a year or two to harvest resources such as salmon and seals, prevalent in fall and winter. Occasionally such men brought their wives along, and in time a few stayed on, children were born, and a permanently resident population accrued. Between 1610 and 1640 several organized colonizations were undertaken. These were, in general, attempts by London interests to break in upon this West Country domain. None were really successful as economic operations, but some of the colonists, drawn primarily from those same West Country ports, stayed on. The New-foundland fishery was considered an important national activity (for the produc-tion of seamen as well as a staple) and the English government tended to support the established West Country mercantile interests. As late as 1677 the govern-ment was pressuring for the removal of all permanent residents from the island.

Newfoundland's population was therefore an accumulation rather than an im-plantation. It began as a kind of flotsam washed up on the beaches from the intensive seasonal harvest of the sea and only gradually took on greater substance and a vaguely visible shape as a settlement region. This was a strand culture, facing the sea, each tiny village a jumble of simple houses and garden patches amongst the rocks at the head of an anchorage along the eastern shores of the Avalon Penin-sula. Behind lay a wilderness of little interest into which the Beothuk Indians had retreated after a century of sporadic harsh encounters along the coast. Unplanned

14. Fishing Station, Newfoundland, c. 1690.

This prosaic scene is a very rare thing indeed: a painting of activities in the Great Fishery by a seventeenth-century artist, based on his own on-the-spot sketches. Gerard Edema, born and trained in Holland, emigrated to England as a young man and quickly developed a clientele for his landscapes among prosperous merchants. One of his patrons, Sir Richard Edgcumbe of Devon, suggested that Edema accompany the local fishing fleet on its annual voyage to America. He spent a summer sketching the wild scenery; this large canvas featuring ramshackle storage sheds and drying racks in a typical Newfoundland cove on Placentia Bay needs only a drizzle of rain and the stench of rotting fish guts to seem fully authentic. (Courtesy of the Royal Ontario Museum, Toronto, Canada)

and unauthorized, it was an incoherent colonization, a scattering of pieces not held together by any visible framework. For many years there were no formal institutions. As each cove tended to be served by a particular merchant who had recruited crews and laborers from a particular port and hinterland, this large American island became bound to Europe by an array of kith and kin connections between very specific sets of places. This pattern and process would shape the peopling of Newfoundland well into the nineteenth century: "It is unlikely that any other province or state in contemporary North America drew such an overwhelming proportion of its immigrants from such localized source areas in the European homeland over so substantial a period of time."

To the southwest, across Cabot Strait, informal fishing settlements of varying duration also appeared along the coast but here traders were attracted to the fur resources as well. A number of posts were founded and larger schemes of colonization were envisioned. One of these, by a Scottish entrepreneur, affixed the name "Nova Scotia" on British maps, but the area took on substance as "Acadia" with the initiation of French colonization in the 1630s. The main focus was the long Port Royal Basin tucked in the eastern shore of the Bay of Fundy.

Begun by a French company in support of its fur trade operations, this colonization soon developed an independent and distinctive character. It was an unusual coastal environment, and these French colonists "chose to win farms with spades, rather than with axes, by dyking and ditching the vast salt meadows that Fundy's great tidal range had distributed so generously about its shores." The settlers were chiefly from Poitou and Aunis and it is assumed that they learned of the possibilities and techniques of such reclamation from the work of Dutch engineers who had been imported to dyke the tidal flats on the nearby Biscayan coast of France. The choice of this mode of agricultural colonization resulted in a noncontiguous settlement region as the pioneers expanded from one tidal basin to another, with the largest concentrations at Minas, Cobequid, and Beaubassin toward the head of this great maritime cul-de-sac with its tidal surges of twenty to forty or more feet. There were also outlying trading posts and farming footholds along the northerly coast, as at Miramichi and Chaleur Bay.

Thus Acadia developed into a distinctive cultural landscape: a French peasant population living a relatively comfortable colonial life in their heavy wooden houses (made of squared horizontal logs or boarded palisades) overlooking their dyked fields, gardens, orchards, and pastures on the rich tidal silts, which yielded an ample diet of grain, peas, cabbage, turnips, fruit, and meat, supplemented by local fish and game. It was a sequestered society of closely intermarried families, clustered in villages, making much use of communal labor, growing by natural increase, expanding by its highly specialized form of reclamation. Although the settlers held land nominally under seigneurial tenure, there was in fact little formal control of any kind. Port Royal was usually the local seat of French authority, but the Acadians did their best to stay away from any surveillance. Their principal contact with the outer world was through the New England trading ships that called at every little hamlet.

The Acadians also had an unusually harmonious relationship with the Micmac Indians, the chief basis of which was the clear separation of territories. The Micmac were nonagricultural and were therefore not bound to rich land likely to be coveted by Europeans, and the latter, by reclaiming their fields from the sea, could expand without serious encroachment on Indian sites. Thus the two peoples enjoyed the mutual benefits of trade, although this contact increasingly distorted the Indian ecology and society; and through the persistent efforts of French missionaries, the Micmac came eventually to share, at least nominally, the Acadians' Catholicism.

The island-studded coast trending southwest from Acadia became a battleground between the French and English and their respective Indian allies. In 1635 the French drove traders of the Plymouth Company away from their new outpost at Castine and they came to regard the Penobscot River as the western boundary of Acadia. But twenty years later the English occupied several of the French positions as far east as Canso, and there were further such advances and retreats through the rest of the century. Through it all the Acadian peasant communities were relatively undisturbed.

West of the Penobscot there were a good many fishing camps and trading posts, mostly of West Country origin, varying in permanency. Following the failure of Sagadahoc on the Kennebec, Ferdinando Gorges continued to dream of an elaborate formal Anglican colony of landed estates, and he obtained a new patent, jointly with John Mason, to "the Province of Maine," a coastal tract reaching from the Merrimack to the Kennebec. Gorges's plans again came to little, but several settlements were initiated along the lower Piscataqua and in 1629 the tract was divided, with Mason receiving the land lying west of that river as "New Hampshire." A thriving nucleus, eventually incorporated as Portsmouth, developed on the south bank of the Piscataqua estuary. It was entirely a secular mercantile foundation, nominally Anglican, largely West Country in origins and population, deriving its wealth from ship timbers, shipbuilding, fish, and furs, with wide trading connections.

Just to the south, at Cape Ann, a similar undertaking by a group of Dorset Puritans in 1623 was less successful. In 1626 a remnant shifted a few miles west to Naumkeag as a better agricultural site, and two years later this Dorchester Company was sold to a London-based group of Puritan merchants who incorporated the New England Company and sent a small group to Naumkeag to form the colony of Salem. In the following year, new elements in this Puritan enterprise succeeded in transforming this land patent into a royal charter to the Massachusetts Bay Company and began to foster the emigration of whole congregations of Puritans to America. What had started as a mercantile venture by a few Puritan entrepreneurs was transformed into a major religious emigration under powerful church leaders to found a new Jerusalem.

The sheer scale of this emigration (about two thousand in the first two years, nine thousand by 1640), the character and motivations of the people involved, and the wealth and organization that sustained it were unprecedented. The first party landed at Salem but the main focus was soon established in a small hilly peninsula in the larger complex bay to the south. From this center at Boston the inflow of colonists quickly spread out to the north and south to form an expanding Puritan nuclear area.

Just to the south of Massachusetts Bay lay Plymouth, settled ten years earlier by a small band of English Separatists who had emigrated to America after some years of exile in Holland. Separatists and Puritans represented manifestations of the same general movement of religious protest in England, but if broadly similar in doctrine they were distinct as social groups and colonizers. When the Puritans began to pour into Massachusetts, Plymouth was still a rather precarious colony of a few hundred people. They held a patent to a considerable wedge of land but there had been only a trickle of new immigrants each year. Their original plan to support the colonizing company by fishing and fur trading had failed, their mercantile connections with England were relatively limited, and they had to struggle to sustain themselves with a meager farming economy. Their attempts to live as a close-knit communal society had soon given way to private ownership and a dispersal of farmers onto their lands. Plymouth was a tiny formal village, centered on the governor's house, overlooked by the church-fort on the hill. It was the focus of a self-consciously religious people, the self-styled "Pilgrims," who saw their plantation as a distinct nucleus on this northern coast.

These several nuclei, diverse in character and unequal in demographic and social vitality, clinging narrowly to coastal footholds, would be brought into closer relationship and become parts of a major regional system in Colonial America. The principal creators of that system were the Puritans and their descendants. The implantation on Massachusetts Bay would lead to the creation of a major culture area and a powerful influence along a thousand miles of the North American coast.

3. New England

EMERGENCE OF NEW ENGLAND

In the early 1600s the Puritans in England were neither a cohesive sect nor a regional group. They were simply a broad and varied array of people who shared certain general opinions as to desirable directions in church reforms. They were to be found in every county but their numbers were greatest in the east and south, especially in the many commercial and industrial centers. Many of these places had long had close ties with the continent and their indigenous Protestantism had been augmented and stimulated by the influx of thousands of French, Walloon, and Flemish Calvinists. As many of these refugees were skilled artisans, they had been sought by towns and companies to help foster industrial development. Such persons were thus rather quickly integrated into English life, and at the same time their presence accentuated the emergence of numerous localities that were industrial and prosperous, dissenting in religion and in royal politics, ethnically mixed and socially fluid, with wide mercantile connections. When, coincident with a period of economic depression, severe political and religious pressures were suddenly brought to bear upon the Puritans, those who considered emigration saw a choice of Holland or America. In some years more crossed the narrow seas than the wide ocean, but over the years 1630–60 about 20,000 came to America, where they constituted an unusual and markedly aggressive colonizing population.

The first influx of Puritans resulted in the creation of half a dozen towns in the immediate vicinity of Boston. Continued immigration and a vigorous internal growth resulted in settlements all along the coast and in the attractive valleys and morainic lowlands. The power and pattern of this expansion was influenced by four important features of Puritan colonization: the fact that epidemics of European diseases had greatly reduced the Indian populations of this region; the sheer need for land to accommodate the sudden inflow of several thousand agricultural settlers and the rapid natural increase that soon followed; the fact that many emigrated as congregations seeking sites with ample room for expansion, well removed from existing settlements; the fact that the very nature of Puritanism, which aspired to combine strict doctrinal order, congregational rule, and individual access to the Scriptures, generated dissensions that often led to the splitting of a congregation and the exodus of one group to a new area to establish its own settlement. Within a very few years, these factors had led to the creation of several important nuclei that formed the matrix of a multicentered New England region.

The first major exodus from Massachusetts Bay pushed overland in 1635 to implant several towns in the midst of the very attractive Connecticut Valley. Whether impelled more by religious issues or by the desire for autonomy and economic opportunity (historians differ in their interpretations), this Connecticut nucleus was soon thriving and beginning to extend its reach. Springfield, established by an entrepreneur interested in the fur trade, was soon enveloped by Puritan settlers moving upriver. Expansion to the south was complicated by the presence of another vigorous colonizing effort. Here New Haven was founded in 1638 by a large group of Puritans from England who stopped in Boston only briefly while searching for an advantageous location. They were soon followed by several closely associated groups, each an English congregation with its minister, which formed settlements along the coast and across the Sound on Long Island. Further east, Saybrook, at the mouth of the Connecticut River, and New London, on the Thames, were initiated by Puritan investors who soon attracted settlers from Massachusetts.

The most important settlements that originated primarily from religious dissension within the Massachusetts Bay Colony grew up in and around Narragansett Bay. Roger Williams, banished from Massachusetts, soon attracted other refugees and wanderers to form the community of Providence. As one historian has put it:

> Emphatically this was not a colony founded by a colony, but a settlement of exiles and drop-outs who entered a plantation covenant to walk in the same way. They had no royal charter, no authorizing act from a parent colony, no proprietorial sponsor, and no mercantile backing. They were squatters.

Warwick was also founded by dissidents from Massachusetts, as was Portsmouth, from which a splinter group soon shifted to the other end of Rhode Island to establish Newport. Despised and feared by Puritan leaders, these independent parties were augmented by an influx of English Quakers in 1657. A few years later George Fox himself, the founder of the Society of Friends, visited; soon many prominent Rhode Island families joined the radical Friends and the religious exceptionalism of the colony was deeply reinforced.

Other exiles from Massachusetts moved north beyond the Merrimack to implant the Puritan towns of Exeter, Hampton, and Dover in New Hampshire; and some years later dissidents from the lower Merrimack Valley took refuge on Nantucket Island. Meanwhile the pressing growth of numbers and economic incentive led to expansion ever further inland from Boston and into vacant districts of the much less vigorous Plymouth Colony.

Within the swirl of this great swarming of Puritans we can therefore discern several major clusters: Massachusetts Bay, the Connecticut Valley, the New Haven shores, Narragansett Bay, and also encroachments upon the two adjacent earlier colonies of Plymouth and the Piscataqua. These clusters would take on clearer identity as they competed for firm control of areas. The Puritan migration took place during a period of political turmoil in England, which caused a neglect of close supervision of overseas ventures. That gave an unusual freedom for the founding of colonies, but left the legitimacy and extent of claims uncertain. Thus there followed intensive complicated efforts on the part of the leaders of these colonizations to gain official recognition as separate colonies with jurisdiction over as much territory as possible.

Such intense geopolitical rivalries had disastrous consequences for the Indians. Initial colonizations had not been seriously disruptive. The English usually negotiated with local tribes for rights to lands, and the Massachusetts Indians were so few and scattered that there was little direct encroachment upon their villages and fields. But the pressures for land were relentless, and colonial rivalries soon converged on the southeast sector where Connecticut, Massachusetts, and Plymouth coveted the rich lands and harbors of Narragansett Bay, an area claimed by the notorious dissenters of Providence and Rhode Island. It was also the territory of the

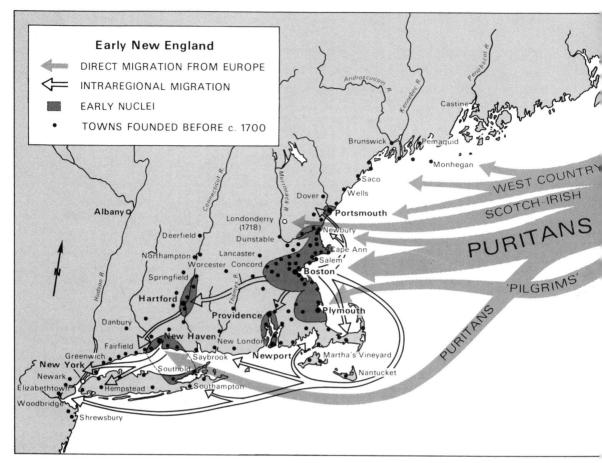

15. Early New England.

largest remaining Indian tribes, most notably the Pequots, Narragansetts, and Wampanoags, who were riven with rivalries themselves and thus open to the blandishments of European allies. In 1637 the Pequots were very nearly exterminated by a vicious English attack from Massachusetts. Shortly thereafter the first Puritan missionary program was undertaken. By the 1670s there were fourteen missions in eastern Massachusetts, each a village of "Praying Indians" settled on a small tract of land and taught the arts and mores of "civilization" under a Puritan minister. A somewhat similar but separate and more successful acculturation was taking place on Martha's Vineyard, where the proprietor had established good relations with the local Wampanoags. However, in the 1670s a renewal of complicated competition for territory in the southeast and northeast exploded into what is usually called King Philip's War, which killed between six and eight hundred English and perhaps three thousand Indians, shattering all the remaining tribes, reducing the fourteen missions to four, and causing most of the surviving Indians to find refuge in Canada or New York. It would take decades for the New England colonial frontier to restore its losses.

As for the direct competition among these several English colonies, Roger Williams soon obtained a parliamentary charter for a loose confederation of Narragansett settlements; after the Restoration this was affirmed by royal charter as the Colony of Rhode Island and Providence Plantations, but its eastern boundary was not finally fixed until 1741. Connecticut had early incorporated itself as a separate commonwealth and then worked to gain legal recognition to a large block of territory. It purchased title to the patent of Saybrook and in 1660 obtained a royal charter that recognized its claim to all the land south of Massachusetts Bay Colony and west of Narrangansett Bay, a vague definition that would bring it into recurrent legal conflict with neighboring colonies. Most important was the fact that the charter gave Connecticut claim to the whole of the New Haven colonies. New Haven leaders tried desperately to exert a concerted resistance to this absorption, but they failed to obtain royal recognition and when the English annexed New Netherland in 1664 they reluctantly agreed to accept Connecticut rule out of greater fear that they might be allocated to New York. Culturally the peoples of Connecticut and New Haven were identical, but they had developed certain detailed differences in politico-ecclesiastical concepts and, true to Puritan precedents, one group of New Haven resisters fled Connecticut rule by emigrating to New Jersey, where they founded Newark. Long Island, which had been in effect partitioned by treaty between Connecticut and New Netherland, was allocated to New York in 1664. Its several Puritan settlements were thereby legally severed from their mainland kin but they long ignored or resisted efforts of New York to impose effective administration.

The Massachusetts Bay Company began with a royal charter to a strip of land lying between the Merrimack and Plymouth Colony. This gave it jurisdiction over all the settlements that had been established from Connecticut upriver from Springfield. But Massachusetts was soon looking beyond its initial limits. An absence of firm local authority and uncertainty over land titles during this period of political turbulence in England induced the settlers of New Hampshire (in 1641) and Maine (1652) to accept the protection of administrative jurisdiction offered by Massachusetts. In 1680 New Hampshire was by London action again separated, but from 1689 until 1741 it shared the same governor with Massachusetts. During this time Puritan settlers colonized many tracts and set up business in many of the ports along this coast. In Maine, during a redevelopment period following extensive depopulation from the wars with the Abenaki and their allies, the Massachusetts systems of land allocation and town government were widely applied.

Massachusetts also exerted pressure southward upon Plymouth. This Separatist colony was thinly populated and development was sustained in part by sales of land to Puritans. Most of the towns on Cape Cod were established by Massachusetts settlers. The Plymouth Colony was a very loose association of settlements, with no cohesive authority, no strong leadership, and no influential political connections in England. Although its entrepreneurs had made various attempts to tap fur, forest, and fish resources over a broad region, the colony remained very largely agricultural, with limited mercantile connections. Thus it became increasingly dependent upon Boston for commercial services. Furthermore, as the Puritan movement also became increasingly a formal separation from the Church of England, ecclesiastical differences between the older and newer colony faded. The invitation to John Cotton, member of a prominent Puritan family and Harvard graduate, to become minister of the Plymouth Church in 1667 reflected this convergence in doctrines and the dependence of Plymouth upon the larger colony for leadership. Thus, when the Plymouth Colony was merged into Massachusetts in a major reorganization of English colonial charters and policies following the Revolution of 1688, there ensued a relatively easy commercial and cultural absorption. Although the Plymouth towns did not welcome such an end to their autonomy they were unable to mount effective opposition. The islands of Martha's Vineyard and Nantucket, settled from Massachusetts but included in the grant of New York in 1664, were also added to Massachusetts at this time. By these acquisitions the original Puritan colony doubled its area under effective settlement and gained 10,000 people and a dozen fine harbors. With Maine under its administration, Massachusetts had formal control of the entire coast between Narragansett Bay and the Bay of Fundy, excepting only the narrow segment of New Hampshire.

New Hampshire was, in fact, an increasingly important exception within this pattern of Massachusetts expansion. In the Massachusetts assumption of administration over New Hampshire the civil rights of non-Puritans were explicitly recognized, but the thriving merchant oligarchy at Portsmouth became increasingly restive under Boston domination and Puritan pressures. Reasserting their Anglicanism and making use of social and political ties in England, this group engineered a complete secession from Massachusetts, reestablishing New Hampshire as a separate colony in 1741. Such a move was opposed by a majority of the people, who were farmers and tradesmen in the interior, mostly of Massachusetts antecedents and suspicious of the social pretensions, royal political connections, and economic power of the Portsmouth group.

After the conquest and expulsion of the Abenaki the settlement of the rural areas of both New Hampshire and Maine had been accomplished under Massachusetts designs and largely by Puritan settlers, but the presence of other colonists also helped to distinguish this northeastern frontier from its Massachusetts center. The most important group was the Scotch-Irish. Several hundred of these Ulster Presbyterians were encouraged to come to Massachusetts by its governor in 1718 but found they were unwanted in any of the settled areas unless they became Congregationalists (Puritans). They were therefore directed to various frontier

tracts in Massachusetts, New Hampshire, and Maine. Reinforced by further immigration they came to dominate a number of local districts, especially in southwestern New Hampshire around Londonderry.

By the eighteenth century New Englanders were also reaching much farther east
into the maritime realm of the Great Fishery. With the growing availability of
American products New Englanders captured much of the provisioning trade for
Newfoundland. Boston offered more services over a longer season than Devon;
New England merchants worked through the residents, whose presence had been
so long opposed by West Country interests; and the numbers and character of that
resident population had changed in the eighteenth century with a change in
English practice. The old pattern of fishing on shares had given way to the use of
wage laborer and bonded servants, who were obtained from Waterford and other
seaports of southern Ireland, directly en route to the fishery. Every year some of
these workers stayed on and by mid-century two-thirds of the 10,000 people in
Newfoundland were Irish Catholics.

New England traders also captured much of the trade of the Bay of Fundy
settlements after the English seized that area from France in 1710. With the treaty
in 1713 peninsular Acadia and the western Fundy shore became officially Nova
Scotia, and Port Royal was renamed Annapolis Royal. The French settlers were
given a choice of pledging allegiance to their new overlords or leaving Nova
Scotia, but the new English governor and garrison at Annapolis had little contact
with the Acadians, tucked away on their scattered tidal marshlands, and no real
pressure was applied. A change in imperial overlordship was nothing new to the
region. To the extent that its well-rooted inhabitants had any connection with a
wider world it was through Boston and not Annapolis or directly to London.

By that same treaty the French retained control of Ile St. Jean, Cape Breton
Island, and the western coastlands of the Gulf of St. Lawrence. On Ile St. Jean a
French proprietor brought in a few colonists, primarily to the harbors and inlets of
Port la Joie (Charlottetown), Tracadie, and St. Pierre that nearly bisect this
narrow island. That particular company soon failed and later immigrants were
largely Acadians from the mainland. Much more dramatic and focused was the
construction, begun in 1720, of a major fortress at Louisbourg on Cape Breton
Island. Lying directly between Newfoundland and Nova Scotia, overlooking the
fishery and guarding the French entryway to Canada, Louisbourg quickly became
an entrepôt as well as a military center. The Acadians were soon trading, illegally,
with this new focus and its very presence helped to sustain a passive French
allegiance. Louisbourg was also a new point of opportunity for Yankee sea peddlers,
who were already provisioning and trading with the fleets off Canso and the Nova
Scotia Banks. New England was a better source of supplies than either France or
Canada and local officials connived to encourage what was technically an illegal

trade. Chronic concern over the vulnerability of New England made Nova Scotia of intense strategic concern to some New England leaders and brought about a strong intervention in the area during the renewal of general hostilities in the 1740s, culminating in an audacious Yankee foray that actually forced the surrender of Louisbourg, and calling forth proposals to expel all of the French, settlers as well as soldiers and officials, from the entire region. The treaty settlement restoring the prewar status quo, giving the famed and feared fortress back to the French, was naturally greeted with great disgust and concern as another indication of how little London understood or cared about her own people in North America.

However, the English did decide to build a counterweight to Louisbourg, thereby incidentally creating a shield for New England, and in 1749 they selected a splendid harbor midway along the Atlantic shore, laid out the city of Halifax as an administrative, military, and commercial headquarters, and brought in several thousand settlers to secure their hold upon the land as well as the town. The major group of agricultural colonists was composed of "Foreign Protestants" from the Rhineland, mostly German, with some Swiss and French. The recruitment of such people for Nova Scotia had been urged for some years by a philanthropist who had been associated with the new colony of Georgia. They were selected to be a reliable, industrious, antipapist population that could be settled alongside the Catholic Acadian villages. However, such allocation proved impractical at the outset and most were placed on a drumlinoid tract south of Halifax at Lunenburg, one of the few areas suitable for agriculture along the Atlantic coast of the peninsula. Nevertheless, this sudden English program heightened the fears of the Acadians, and within two years more than a thousand had left the mainland for Ile St. Jean, more than doubling the population of that remnant of New France.

Thus Halifax was the result of a chronic Atlantic imperial rivalry, a display of seafaring and conquering applied to an old planting of French colonists, and it made Nova Scotia a peculiar geographical structure with its new British capital town and Germanic outlier separated by fifty miles of wilderness road or two hundred miles by sea from the nearest Acadian settlers clustered here and there

---

16. Halifax, 1750.   ◆

This fine set of maps and views of the regional context, site, plan, and opening phase of settlement was hurried into print in 1750. The plan (inset) was reprinted from an engraving by Moses Harris, a naturalist who had visited Nova Scotia in 1749; the rest of the plate was prepared by Thomas Jefferys, "Geographer to his Royal Highness The Prince of Wales," and presented to the Board of Trade and Plantations. Who actually did the sketch "from ye Topmasthead" showing the temporary encampment within the fortified stockade as construction got under way is not known. (Courtesy of Public Archives of Canada, National Map Collection)

along the Fundy shore and with no direct contact whatever with the Micmacs who coursed the inland trails. It was a geopolitical pattern sharply discordant with the past, a shift in focus away from Port Royal–Annapolis Royal, creating a deeply segmented "colony" connected to a "mother country" that was at best a stepmother to most of the inhabitants.

GREATER NEW ENGLAND

By 1750 northeastern North America was to an important degree a Greater New England. Such a term does not refer to a homogeneous region nor a cohesive structure; it included six political units, several economic areas, and some cultural variation; but it was a functional realm dominated by a powerful people and focused on a major center. It had not been created by any conscious English design, but by American initiative, by the colonization, mercantile expansion, and political opportunism of a vigorous new American people.

Boston was the principal focus of this entire realm, the commercial and cultural capital, as well as the political capital of the most populous and influential colony.

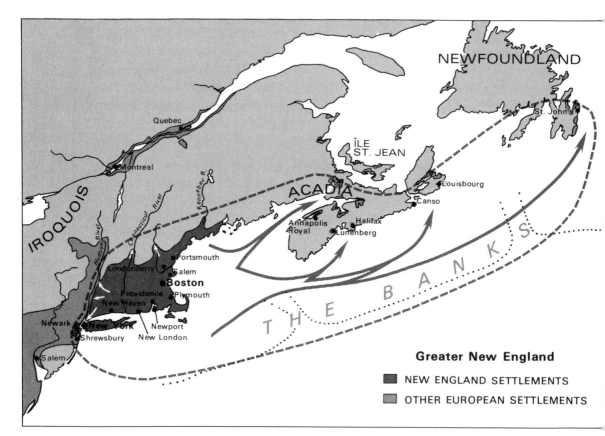

17. Greater New England.

It was the chief intelligence center, the point of gathering and dissemination of information between the region and the world. However, Greater New England was not a simple structure. Boston had its rivals, most especially in Newport, which served Rhode Island much as Boston served Massachusetts, and in such ports as Salem, Portsmouth, Providence, New London, and New Haven, which also had extensive direct connections overseas. Halifax, designed to be a major imperial seat, was also much less under Boston influence than most of the lesser ports.

The main body of this Greater New England was the contiguous settlement region dominated by descendants of English Dissenter colonists of the early seventeenth century. It extended from western Long Island and the Berkshires eastward over all the lowlands and adjacent island, with salients up the Connecticut and Merrimack valleys, and a fringe tapering along the Maine coast. This region was the result of expansions from six major nuclei, implanted directly from Europe or created by fission in the first years of colonization. Two of these, Plymouth and New Haven, had been absorbed by aggressive neighbors, leaving only a faint imprint of whatever distinctions they once had. Two others, Rhode Island and the Piscataqua, were confined to small coastal areas by the more aggressive expansion of others, but they had retained enough individuality to stand out as significant subregions. The Piscataqua was an expression of an old and basic difference in English origins; Rhode Island was an American creation, a culturo-geographic manifestation of the social logic of certain Reformation ideas. Although an emanation from Puritanism and thus of the same British culture as its neighbors, Rhode Island, by establishing a different polity and a haven for religious dissenters of many kinds, attracted the sort of people who sustained a social divergence from the main New England pattern.

That main pattern had been established by the remaining two nuclei, Massachusetts and Connecticut. Fully Puritan in heritage, these two colonies constituted the core area of New England. Their continuance as separate political units would remain an important geopolitical feature, but they differed only in minor detail as to social and political character and thus constituted a solid culture area dominating the lowlands of New England.

The basic character of New England was formed by the Puritans. The most distinguishing feature of Puritan colonization was its powerful emphasis upon the formation of "Christian, utopian, closed, corporate" communities. The Bible provided the precepts; the New England wilderness, isolated from the corruptions and complexities of the Old World, provided the space for the practical adaptation of the model community, which would be accomplished by a people who explicitly agreed upon fundamental issues and covenanted to work together to build a new society. Those who dissented on basic matters could not be allowed to remain and jeopardize the common task.

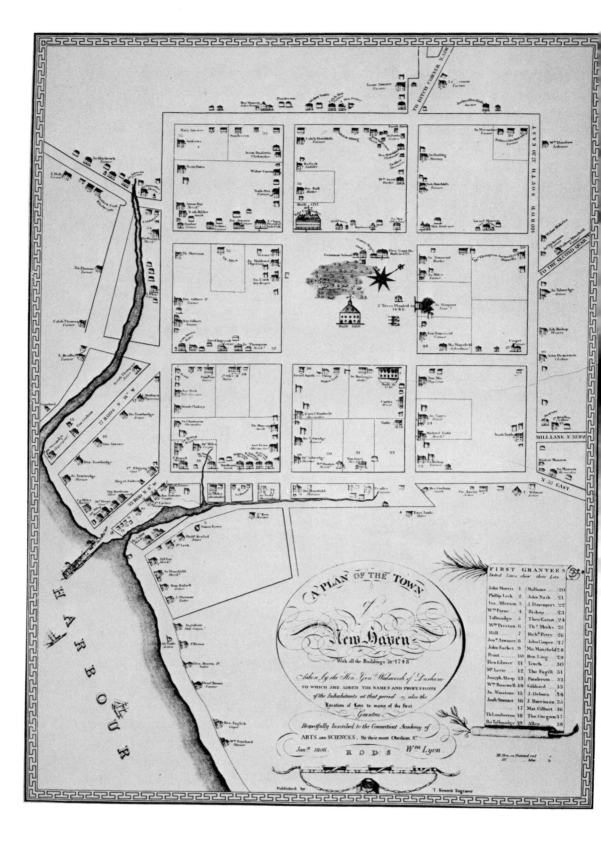

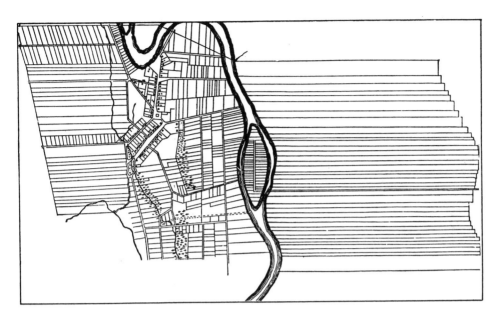

18. Two New England Settlements.

New Haven and Wethersfield are two of the best known—and least typical—of New England settlement patterns. The famous "nine squares" of New Haven were surveyed in 1638 by the founding proprietors of the new colony on the Quinnipiac. The central square was reserved for a marketplace and, as shown on William Lyon's 1806 redrawing of the Wadsworth Map of 1748 (*opposite*), eventually contained the meetinghouse, schoolhouse, courthouse, and jail. Few New England villages were as formal and focused in their ground plan. Wethersfield (*above*) was the first of the Connecticut Colony towns, laid out on the low terraces and meadowlands along the Connecticut River in 1634. Since this map first appeared as the frontispiece of Charles M. Andrews's authoritative monograph on "The River Towns of Connecticut" nearly a century ago, it has been reprinted time and again as an example of the special character of New England settlement. However, this striking threefold pattern of house lots, adjacent field lots, and outlying long lot strips has a greater symmetry and Old World look about it than most, in part because of the stronger congregational nature of these earliest Connecticut towns and in part because of the unusual physical possibilities in this broad valley floor. The house lots are in two distinct alignments joined at the meetinghouse on the green, reflecting the formation of the town by two groups of colonists, arriving in quick succession but uniting in the allocation of lands. (Lyon's version of the Wadsworth Map courtesy of Map Collection, Yale University Library)

Community formation was aided by the fact that the Puritans were self-selected by beliefs and an unusually homogeneous body of colonizers. They were comparatively well educated (virtually all were literate), skilled, and prosperous. In England most had been artisans and tradesmen, but some had been farmers and a number were mercantile entrepreneurs of considerable means and influential connections. They emigrated as nuclear families, some bringing along a few servants, and many families came as members of a congregation under the leadership of a minister.

The Puritan concept of community presupposed a clustering of people, a physical grouping that would enhance interaction and social cohesion. The basic areal unit for colonization was the town, a tract of a few square miles granted to a particular group. Near the center of the town a site was chosen for a village. Each family was given a house lot in the village and one or more parcels of farmland in the adjacent arable fields, and each was granted rights to share in the use of pastures, haylands, and woodlots. A building serving as church and assembly hall on the village commons was the symbolic center and periodic focus of community life. Land and rights were not allocated equally: community leaders and families of greater means could obtain larger portions. Nor was there a standard geometry to the settlement pattern. Some towns were rectangular tracts and a few villages, such as New Haven, were laid out in formal squares, but the great majority were nonsymmetrical adaptations to local conditions. Expansion took place by a similar process. When farming extended into lands beyond easy reach of the village or when the population outgrew local resources, the authorities of the town might sponsor the formation of a selected cadre to establish a new village in a far corner of the town or in some new town in another district. Because the community was a covenanted group and shared in rights and responsibilities, casual migrations were discouraged.

Such, briefly, was the ideal pattern of Puritan colonization and it was widely enough applied in some degree in the first years to create a very distinctive community form and landscape. Obviously English in many elements, it was nevertheless an indigenous creation, a new kind of community formed out of what had been no more than loosely associated fragments within the larger society of England. The New England town was an American version of the English parish, and the farm-village with its arable strips and common lands recalled the late medieval patterns of East Anglia, but there were significant differences in form, content, and function. There were neither manor houses nor tenant cottages in New England. It was a much less stratified, less complex society, one of property owners without sharp class or wealth distinctions, led by a local elite operating under congregational sanction, the whole body explicitly bound together to create a way of life whose nature was continuously under examination. That it was a distinctive Puritan creation was demonstrable from the evidence of adjacent Rhode Island, created simultaneously out of a rejection of the Puritan concept of authority, where the first town differed as much "from the layout of a Massachusetts town as the shapelessness of the Rhode Island religious organization differed from the orderliness of the Massachusetts system."

Actual practice, of course, varied considerably from this stereotype. From the outset Puritan emigrants differed in zeal and aspirations. Many towns were founded by loose aggregations rather than cohesive congregations and made little attempt to form rigidly theocratic communities. The availability of new land was a powerful lure to dispersal and to speculation. Increasingly, blocks of land were granted to companies that were interested in subdivision and resale rather than to congregations of would-be settlers. Economic development was accompanied by greater disparities of wealth and influence and by a stronger secular outlook, while chronic dissension weakened church authority. Thus, Puritan theocracy was transformed into a merchant-dominated civic polity. As the society expanded and loosened it came to accommodate, often grudgingly, other Christians: Anglicans, Baptists, and even Quakers, although most of the smaller settlements remained single-congregation communities. The core area was everywhere dominated by Congregationalism, heavily in Massachusetts, somewhat less so in western Connecticut where a return to Anglicanism had upwelled, initially out of contacts along the border of New York.

These changes marked the transformation of the Puritan into the Yankee, a second phase in the cultural development of this American people (the first being the formation of purely Puritan communities on American soil by English emigrants), but it was a change in emphasis, degree, and detail rather than in fundamentals. Throughout, the concept of a community as a body of morally conscious, industrious people working together to create a better society remained a powerful ideal. The great majority of the people were descendants of the Puritan colonizers, and their numbers and their homogeneity were an exhibit of the demographic power of that family emigration that took root so rapidly and successfully. With his characteristic flair (in the language of 1920) Samuel Eliot Morison presented the stereotype:

> The seventeenth-century stock completely absorbed its eighteenth-century accretions, both English and non-English. To outsiders, as late as 1824, the population of Massachusetts seemed, and was, racially homogeneous as that of Brittany. But the race was not Anglo-Saxon, or Irish. It was Yankee, a new Nordic amalgam on an English Puritan base; already in 1750 as different in its character and its dialect from the English as the Australians are today. A tough but nervous, tenacious but restless race; materially ambitious, yet prone to introspection, and subject to waves of religious emotion. Conservative in its ideas of property and religion yet (in the eighteenth century) radical in business and government. A people with few social graces, yet capable of deep friendships and abiding loyalties; law-abiding yet individualistic, and impatient of restraint by government or regulation in business; ever attempting to repress certain traits of human nature, but finding an outlet in broad, crude humor and deep-sea voyages. A race whose typical member is eternally torn between a passion for righteousness and a desire to get on in the world. Religion and climate, soil and sea, here brewed of mixed stock a new people.

Such a homogeneous culture left a distinct imprint upon the landscape of these glaciated lowlands. Although there was much unused land, settlement was essentially contiguous; the whole area was organized into towns, with the villages spaced not evenly but with a general regularity every few miles, wherever terrain and soil allowed. In the older, richer areas the architecture revealed a century of creative translation of the solid and often elaborate brick and stone town and country buildings of southeastern England into simpler, modest, often graceful wooden counterparts in New England houses, outbuildings, shops, and churches. In the more prosperous localities the restrained elegance of Georgian forms and ornamentation was becoming visible, reflecting the close social communications between this dissenting colonial area and the mother culture. The whole area was knit together by a fairly intricate network of roads, droving trails, rivers, and local ports. Agriculture was the main basis of livelihood but an uneven and changing one. Except in the larger river valleys, good soil was very erratically distributed and many fields soon declined in fertility. Wheat, the preferred staple, was widely afflicted with a blight, and was grown chiefly in newer lands. This led to a shift to maize and rye and to a greater emphasis upon livestock. A few districts tended to specialize in crops such as flax or in garden or orchard produce. Mills and forges were fairly widespread, and in the main ports an array of workshops, sugar refineries, and rum distilleries processed imported products for regional sale or reexport.

The two significant subregions were marked by their variation from the Puritan legacy. Rhode Island was the seat of Baptists and Quakers, who had spread their influence into bordering districts of Massachusetts and Connecticut as well. There was also a congregation of Sephardic Jews in Newport. Rhode Island was not only a separate colony and an enclave of religious toleration, it was a general community that lived quite autonomously within New England. The physical conditions were unusual: a more complex array of islands and coasts, harbors and estuaries, salt marshes, meadows, and fine silty soils, and a somewhat milder climate. Early proprietors had taken advantage of such conditions to develop a thriving livestock economy. They sowed English grasses, bred sheep, cattle, horses, and hogs (all easier to control and protect on islands), and traded far and wide. Bridenbaugh stresses the importance of the Quaker network:

> Through the meetings of Friends, the grandees of Rhode Island succeeded in marketing their agricultural surpluses profitably to other Friends located along the Atlantic Coast, in the West Indies, and in the British Isles, thereby rescuing the farmers and graziers of the Narragansett region from absolute dependence upon the Puritan caprice of Boston traders.

But there were other commercial families as well and none was in Boston's thrall. Newport was a major port and social center, a summer resort with strong connections with the West Indies and South Carolina. By 1750 Providence was also thriving, and both ports were developing direct connections with Europe. Thus Narragansett merchants and planters had developed their own little "commercial republic"; their handsome estates and fine livestock, tended by Black slaves and servants, represented a way of life quite divergent from the New England norm. Actually, Black servants were not uncommon in wealthy and even middling households in New England seaports. Of the estimated 13,000 Blacks in the region, about 5,000 lived in Rhode Island. Yankee merchants were of course much involved in the slave trade, which included Indians as well, mostly from South Carolina, and these too were most prominent in Rhode Island.

Narragansett Bay, Cape Cod, and the islands held at least two-thirds of the four to five thousand local Indians remaining in all New England. These Narragansetts and Wampanoags lived as small bands of families on small tracts of land allocated by colonial authorities; there were, for example, at least six separate congregations on Martha's Vineyard. To the west there were the remnants of the Pequots (about one hundred) in Groton, of the Niantics at Lyme, and of the Montauks on the eastern end of Long Island. Natick was the only remaining village of "Praying Indians" in the Massachuetts Bay area. In the west along the Housatonic there were also a few villages of Indians who had been pushed out of the Hudson Valley by the Dutch or the Mohawk. The most prominent was that of the Mahicans at Stockbridge, to whom an Anglican mission had been sent from Scotland in 1734. Fifteen years later it was reported that 125 of the 218 Indians there had been baptized, 55 children were in school, and 20 of the families lived in "English houses" and 33 in "Indian houses." Each family had been given an allotment within the township plot, but such land was held in common by the group as a whole. Some were using plows and all were dependent in some degree on trade with and assistance from the Whites. Stockbridge was an especially vigorous and formal effort, but every Indian group in New England had been under heavy pressure and exhibited much acculturation.

The lower Piscataqua district, focused on Portsmouth, was another small but distinct nucleus. Overshadowed by and long subordinate to Boston, it was never a Puritan colony. It had its own West Country antecedents and English connec-tions; it had prospered on the wealth of the pine forests of its own hinterland; it was the seat of a revived Anglicanism that stood apart from the evangelical Great Awakening, which swept so powerfully over New England in the 1740s; and it was the capital of a separate political entity that it had recovered from Massachusetts domination. It had in fact created a political hinterland it could not easily domi-nate or lead. This Piscataqua nucleus contained no more than a quarter of the 40,000 people of New Hampshire, most of whom did not share its social and cultural patterns. Portsmouth was also the focus of parts of southern Maine, but that was a minor augmentation.

Even outside the Piscataqua enclave, the Puritan-Yankee imprint was weaker in this northeast fringe. Along the coast it had been preceded at many points by West Country foundations; inland it was diluted by Scotch-Irish settlements, and even though Massachusetts had administrative control over Maine, the Yankee-sponsored settlements there were mostly speculative land promotions rather than the close congregational colonizations of an early Puritanism. The general difference in origins and character was well expressed in Cotton Mather's pained report of the visiting Massachusetts minister who urged a congregation on this rocky coast to "walk in the paths of righteousness and piety so that they would not 'contradict the main end of Planting this Wilderness,'" whereupon a prominent resident blurted out "Sir, you are mistaken, you think you are Preaching to the People at the Bay; our main End was to catch Fish."

The lands farther east lay beyond the domain of New England settlement, but were a sphere of strong Yankee influence, bound in many ways to Boston and its

19. St. John's, Newfoundland.
By the time H. P. Brenton made this drawing in 1798 the flags flying from the governor's house and fortifications atop the hill bespoke the significance accorded this strategic site after a long succession of imperial wars, but the hodgepodge of wooden buildings straggling up the steep slope from Water Street—"the oldest [European] street in North America"— still displayed the unplanned jumble so characteristic of Newfoundland's long development. (By permission of the British Library)

commercial system despite the strong British official presence at Halifax. At the farthest remove lay Newfoundland, separate in origins and people but ever more closely linked to the New England network in a relationship that was more than just commercial, for Newfoundland became an important source of seamen for Yankee fleets. The chronic rivalry with the French had finally brought an official English presence onto the island, and St. John's, with a governor, garrison, courthouse, and Anglican church, had emerged as a weak focus of the Avalon settlements. The eight Dissenter families listed as resident in St. John's in 1752 may have been New England agents, but there was little to attract Yankee settlers. The West Country Anglicans and Irish Catholics tended to cluster in separate villages but they shared a common pattern of life, bound entirely to the fishing industry with its summers of intense work and winters of idleness. It was a boisterous, disorderly society, with a heavy preponderance of males, an imbalance exaggerated every summer with the seasonal influx; a "household" in Newfoundland often referred to one free male (English) and several bonded male servants (Irish). The trend was gradually toward a more normal population structure but it was erratic, reflecting the general instability. There were few churches and no schools. Few residents were deeply rooted; many had good reason for squatting on this far wilderness edge beyond the easy reach of civil authority.

Halifax, Canso, and Newfoundland constituted a maritime border zone wherein New England seafaring competed with that reaching directly across the Atlantic from England. Here as elsewhere, westward into the Hudson Valley, southward upon Long Island and New Jersey, and northward toward Canada, New Englanders were exerting strong outward pressures, a power of expansion that was both demographic and cultural in origin, the thrust from a distinctive American region of a thriving, aggressive people.

4. Northern Entryways: The St. Lawrence

While this Greater New England was emerging along the northern coasts, other major seats of colonization were developing to the north and west, each anchored on a large river. Two of these rivers, the St. Lawrence and the Hudson, provided long penetrations for ocean vessels, contact with major Indian groups, and thus the potential for fur trading that reached deep into the continent. A third large river, the Delaware, proved disappointing as a continental entryway but led directly to an area rich in agricultural possibilities for northwest European colonists.

Canada, the lands bordering the St. Lawrence, was begun as a fur trading venture; it soon became an intensive Jesuit mission as well, but commercially it remained solely a fur trade operation for fifty years, and was largely sustained by the wealth and requirements of that trade throughout the French regime. However, when the great transatlantic imperial system that had developed the fur trade was broken and removed, a more basic creation was more clearly revealed: a deep-rooted New France, the solid core of one of the major culture areas of the Americas.

The Company of New France was required by its charter to foster colonization. It failed to satisfy the French government and in 1663 the latter assumed direct control. At that time there were about twenty-five hundred European residents in Canada, most of them in or near the three main posts of Quebec, Trois-Rivières, and Montreal (this last founded as a special militant missionary colony), and few rooted in the land. During the next thirty years the government sent over about five thousand colonists, and a lessening trickle thereafter, in an attempt to create a solid French Catholic base for a commercial and imperial enterprise of continental proportions.

As usual in colonial undertakings, the results were often discordant with designs. Both the company and the government attempted to colonize through a seigneurial system, by which land was allocated in large blocks to seigneurs who were in turn to pay for the importation of settlers to whom they would grant land on receiving an oath of fealty. As Harris has demonstrated, this "vestigial feudalism" created a nominal social structure but had little detailed effect upon the way the colony was actually settled and functioned. Settlers were not plentiful and they avoided firm enfeoffment; revenues were meager and seigneuries costly to manage. Thus, most seigneurs collected small annual dues and provided little in the way of services. They built few great manor houses (most chose to live in Quebec or Montreal) and their titles were symbols of social status more than of actual wealth and power. Both the company and the government attempted to create villages but the settlers preferred to live on their long lots, the narrow strips of land reaching from the river up across the arable terraces into the forest. There was so much frontage available along the St. Lawrence that in 1750 settlement area could, with little exaggeration, be described as two riverine strips over two hundred miles long and a mile deep on either side of the river; expansion had as yet proceeded up only a few tributary streams and hardly at all into lands behind the first tier of allotments.

So completely was the colony bound to its great artery that a visitor sailing up the river could watch virtually the entire domesticated colonial landscape pass before his eyes: the rural landscape of the côte parallel to the route with its sturdy steep-roofed Norman farmhouses of field stone and wooden barns spaced along the terrace, lot after narrow lot, each overlooking its river landing and backed by the endless forest; a scene punctuated from time to time by a church steeple, but rarely altered by a noticeable village cluster; the farmland occasionally interrupted by

20. The Côte of Canada, 1787.
This detailed depiction of a Laurentian landscape was one of many watercolor paintings by Thomas Davies during the last of his four postings to British North America. He had first come to Halifax in 1757 and was by now thoroughly familiar with Canada and practiced in the art of a military topographer. The view is downriver from Chateau-Richer, fifteen miles below Quebec, with the edge of Ile d'Orleans in the right background. This is one of the oldest districts of European colonization in North America. The great river highway and the narrow continuous riverine settlement pattern are apparent, as is the succession of long lot holdings, each reaching from the river through seine nets, water meadows, fields, road, farmsteads, orchards, and upslope into the forest. A twin-towered parish church, featured in another Davies painting, lay just upriver from this spot. (Courtesy of the National Gallery of Canada, Ottawa)

steep expanses of rock and forest. But the most striking scene came early in the voyage when after passing the intensely cultivated Ile d'Orleans the capital of New France loomed into view. The very look of the place symbolized the dominance of imperial over mercantile interests. In Lower Town on the narrow terrace between the cliff and the river were the docks, warehouses, customshouse, and taverns; above on the heights of the great rocky promontory were the baroque buildings of the Crown and the Church and the residences of the wealthier citizens:

> Dominating all was the Chateau St. Louis, residence of the governor general, with a row of cannon on its terrace overlooking the mile-wide river. Nearby were the cathedral, the seminary, the Jesuit college with a clock in its chapel steeple, the

convent of the Ursulines, the Hotel Dieu, the bishop's palace, and the unpretentious church of the Recollets. These steep-roofed buildings were of stone, walls several feet thick, with the clean, simple, but graceful proportions of northern France.

Near the upper end of the côte at the base of another bold height was the principal mercantile center and frontier garrison town, surrounded by a stone wall and containing its own set of important institutions. Montreal was the main base for an enormous wilderness region, which reached westward up the Ottawa River and up the St. Lawrence and through the Great Lakes into the heart of the continent, the largest area tributary to any North American colony.

Exploitation of that realm was critically dependent upon close and amicable relations with the Indians. The French entry up the St. Lawrence in 1600 brought them into direct contact with various Algonkian peoples whose friendship and assistance the French cultivated assiduously from the time of Champlain. The Algonkians were ideal allies, migratory hunting and fishing peoples whose birch-

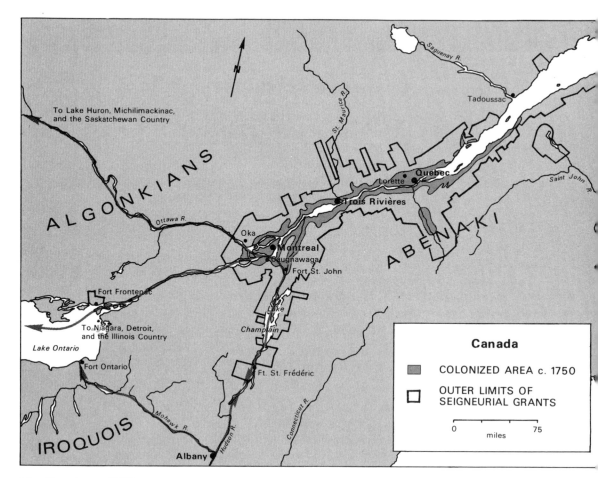

21. Canada, c. 1750.

bark canoes and snowshoes gave them far-ranging mobility through the water-laced northern woods, a culture readily adaptable to the gathering of furs, and a population not seriously dislodged by the French settlements along the river below Montreal. The success of the fur trade grew out of mutual acculturation and interdependence between the Algonkians and the French; by 1750 it was the most extensive and enduring alliance between Europeans and Indians in North America. The great convoys of furs and of trading goods moving down and up the Ottawa and the easy comings and goings of hundreds of Indians and voyageurs to Montreal were seasonal exhibits of this relationship. This alliance and dominance over so large an area had not been achieved without cost. Early and recurrent warfare between at first Dutch- and later English-supported Iroquois and French-supported tribes had brought destruction and dislocation over a broad swath of country as far west as Lake Huron. At Caugnawaga and Oka near Montreal, at Lorette near Quebec, and in other less cohesive camps in the protective shadow of the French militia lived tiny remnants or splinters of once-strong interior tribes: poignant evidence of the heavy human cost of the intensified and deadly rivalries among Indians backed by European allies.

This interior country was tapped by way of two main lines of outposts. The southerly one of Fort Frontenac (at the outlet of Lake Ontario), Fort Niagara, and Detroit was more a military than a mercantile line, guarding against British encroachment into the Lower Lakes and Ohio Country. The principal trade route was by way of the Ottawa and Lake Huron to Michilimackinac, a post which was pivotal to routes running west and north to Lake Winnipeg and the Saskatchewan Country and those turning southerly from Lake Michigan across the low portages to the upper Mississippi and the Illinois Country. Each of these main posts was a small colony, with farmers and missionaries as well as soldiers and traders, each a complex cluster of French, métis, and a variety of Indians.

French Canada was therefore a vast realm of two parts articulated at Montreal. Its Laurentian sector, the product of organized implantation and closely supervised development, was a coherent structured society dominated by a strong aristocratic, ecclesiastic, and military ethos. Its two prominent centers, containing over twenty percent of the population, the highest level of urbanization in any North American colony, sought with some success to display an urbanity "reflecting the polish and social graces of the French *noblesse.*" The European population was broadly homogeneous: virtually all of the stock had come from the west and north of France, with La Rochelle and Paris the principal urban points of origin, and Aunis, Saintonge, Poitou, and Normandy the principal rural sources. Yet this population was not internally cohesive. Most of these people did not emigrate as family and neighborhood groups, congregations, or refugee bands; most came as individuals but few came on their own. Of the approximately 10,000 immigrants during the French regime, about 4,000 came as *engagés* (indentured servants), 3,500 were

A View of the City of QUEBEC, the Capital of Canada
Taken partly from Pointe des Peres, and partly on Board the Vanguard Man of War, by Captain Hervey Smyth.

Gen.l Wolfe landing

To the Right Honourable William

These SIX VIEWS of the most remarkable Places in the Gulf and River of St. Laurence

London Printed for John Bowles at N.º 13 in Cornhill, Robert Sayer at N.º 53 in Fleet Street, Tho.ª Jefferys the corner of S.t Martins Lane in the Strand, Carington Bowles at N.º 69 in S.t Pauls Church Yard, and

Vue de la Ville de QUEBEC, Capitale du Canada

P. Benazech Sculp.

Prise en partie de la Pointe des Peres, et en partie abord de l'Avantgarde Vaisseau de Guerre, par le Cap.ᵗ Hervey Smyth

ne of his Majesties most Honourable Privy Council & Principal Secretary of State.

scribed, by his most Obedient humble Servant   Hervey Smyth.   Aid du Camp to the late GEN.ˡ WOLFE.

z S.ᵗ Charles River.

22. Two Views of Quebec.
This boldest townscape of North America was a favorite subject for visiting artists, especially after its dramatic capture by the British. This rendition of the citadel of New
France at the narrowing of the Great River, with its impressive skyline of church and state
and merchant's town below, was one of "Six Views of the most remarkable Places in the
Gulf and River of St. Laurence" by Captain Hervey Smith, printed in London in 1768
(*overleaf*). Note the double inscription, in English and French. It is interesting to compare
this comprehensive rendering by an army topographic artist with the rough sketch of the
military essentials of the place in a "Bird's-eye View of the Town of Quebeck besiegd by the
British Army, Sept. 1759" by Guy Carleton, who would soon be installed as its governor.
(Smith drawing courtesy of the Library of Congress; Carleton drawing courtesy of the
Rosenbach Museum & Library)

released soldiers, 1,000 were prisoners exiled (chiefly smugglers, an old and widespread coastal activity), and 1,000 were women shipped over to become wives.
They were mostly poor or dispossessed persons who had no secure niche in the
home country. Canada was a much harsher country than home but a century of
effort by expanding families on virgin soil under light taxation had provided a
subsistence base superior to that of most rural folk in France. Thus Canadian
habitants struck visitors from Europe as a remarkably vigorous and spirited people
who lived in a loosely structured society, with a good deal of social mobility and
independence. The fur trade provided many outlets for individual energies and a
break with the common patterns of settled life. Many people, rural and urban,
participated in some form of wilderness living and Indian contact during some part

of their lives. Yet this was balanced by a strong gregariousness and conviviality, with no great emphasis upon individual entrepreneurship and material achievement. As Harris has noted, "Even today, lines of closely spaced farmhouses have a gregarious feel—as if, in rejecting village for côte, the habitants had struck a balance between their wishes to be associated with their fellows and to be isolated from authority."

Forged over the span of a century of American experience, this rather loose Canadian society, clearly reflective of French, frontier, and Indian influences, would grow much more self-conscious and cohesive when it found itself cut off from its homeland and captive within an English-speaking empire.

5. Northern Entryways: Hudson Bay

Although the greatest of the northern embayments of America lay only a few degrees above the home latitudes of English seafarers, its approaches and the vast sweep of its shoreline lay ice-bound much of the year and were the most compelling exhibit of what could only seem a climatic anomaly to such explorers, a marked continentality of seasonal temperatures so different from the maritime climates of Atlantic Europe. Its general shape and limits were soon determined by various voyages in the wake of Hudson's initial probe and demise, but these very discoveries were read as a prolongation of the failure to find a Northwest Passage. There seemed nothing in the land of these bleak latitudes to attract further interest and it was only decades later, after episodic involvements with Acadia and Canada and the annexation of New Netherland, that the English began to sense the full scale and possibilities of the North American fur trade and thus to consider that Hudson Bay might serve as a threshold to a vast productive region.

A trading voyage in 1668 brought a handsome return and two years later the newly formed Hudson's Bay Company was granted exclusive rights to the entire drainage basin of the bay, an area now denominated Rupert's Land. Within a few years several posts were established in estuaries along the southerly margins (the "bottom of the Bay") and to the west, each carrying on a very profitable trade with the Cree bands in its hinterland.

The French did not at first acknowledge any English rights to this "Baye du Nord" and attempted various retaliations, some by sea, most across the watershed from the Montreal–Ottawa River route, but they failed to dislodge their rivals and they put their main efforts in shoving their highly successful St. Lawrence–Great Lakes trading system vigorously westward. Meanwhile the Hudson's Bay Company remained content to exploit its vast realm solely from posts along the shore, trying out various locations and systems of collection, but always dependent upon the

Indians to bring down their canoeloads of furs with the annual spring thaw for the brief exchange of English goods.

In 1750 the company had just been reconfirmed in its monopoly, having weathered a parliamentary enquiry initiated by rival British interests critical of what they characterized as its "sleep by the Frozen Sea." While it had certainly not been aggressive in territorial reach, the company had not been indifferent to development. It had begun to experiment with whaling, and had just established a post on the eastern shore to test some promising mineral deposits. Its local headquarters at York Factory and several of the older posts were substantial establishments with comfortable buildings, gardens, and a few livestock; the great stone fort at Churchill was an expensive testimony to the chronic French threat from the sea. Yet after eighty years of operations the European hold on this vast realm remained marginal and shallow. No attempt had been made to settle anyone permanently on or adjacent to these subarctic shores. The company's personnel were there on assignment for a tour of duty. Company regulations were designed to keep contacts with the Indians to the bare minimum needed to facilitate profitable commerce, a relationship often described, and by critics derided, as a "hole in the wall" form of exchange. But while this English system was a stark contrast with that of its French rivals to the south, it was not quite as simple in character or impact as either its policies or caricatures implied. There was a distinct cultural complexity to these Hudson Bay posts. Nearly all the masters and clerks were English, whereas the craftsmen, servants, and laborers were almost all Orkneymen, the product of systematic recruitment on outward voyages begun in the 1720s after it had become apparent that these hardy fishermen and crofters inured to cold and privation were far more dependable workers than the usual miscellany available around the docks of London. Despite official discouragement there were also scores and often hundreds of Indians at these posts now living interdependently with the Europeans, serving as fishermen, hunters, and fowlers (geese and partridge were a critical meat supply) in return for food (often oatmeal), alcohol, and tools. Despite strong company policies against cohabitation many of the Europeans had Indian mates, and a considerable mixed-blood population had grown up, some of whom took employment with the company. Aside from these "home Indians," the Cree bands in the hinterlands made seasonal visits and within these a distinct class of middleman had developed to serve as the critical agents in the procurement of furs from and the distribution of English goods to other Indian bands deep in the interior ("uplanders" was the bay term for these latter). Thus, in defiance of company policies, their posts had become settlement nuclei, and despite the lack of any direct thrust inland, the influence of these Europeans on the bay had radiated over a vast area.

At mid-century this English enterprise seemed threatened once again by the

French, this time not by direct assault but by severance of the richest part and potential of the North American interior. In the 1740s the French had rapidly extended their system from Lake Superior to Lake Winnipeg and on to the Saskatchewan. This was an intrusion into Rupert's Land and a direct encroachment upon the hinterlands of York and Churchill. As the Indians, trappers as well as traders, were astute participants in these commercial systems and welcomed such rivalry, such a challenge was beginning to cause the Hudson's Bay Company to reassess some long-standing policies.

6. Northern Entryways: The Hudson River

It was often remarked at the time that Dutch North America was a New Netherland in more than an obvious political sense. It took little imagination to see the majestic Hudson as an American Rhine, a broad avenue through the highlands to a rich interior, and to see its complex estuary of islands, bays, alcoves, narrow passageways, and radial rivers as a counterpart to the canal- and river-laced lands about the Scheldt and the Zuider Zee. New Amsterdam was established to command this portal to the continent, and it quickly became a miniature of its namesake in form and function. It never became more than a small commercial center during the Dutch regime because its hinterland was only thinly colonized and because the whole province was but a minor holding in the worldwide operations of Dutch mercantile enterprise.

Early trials tended to confirm explorers' assessment of the excellence of the Hudson Valley for European-style agriculture, but the Dutch West India Company was not much interested in such lands. Furs were the great source of wealth and at first they were obtained locally from the "River Indians," the many Algonkian bands of the Hudson Valley. But these sources were soon depleted, and a far greater wealth was tapped after the Mohawks, the easternmost of the Iroquois Confederacy, expelled the Mohicans from the upper Hudson and made direct contact with the Dutch traders at Fort Orange, situated at the strategic junction of the Hudson waterway with the Mohawk Valley route to the west. The Iroquois soon became extremely aggressive allies, competing for the trade of the entire Great Lakes region. After a few years the company did attempt to foster colonization by means of patroonships, large riverine grants to proprietors who were supposed to undertake the importation of settlers and the development of manors. But little was accomplished according to plan. Money and settlers were lacking, conflicts with the Indians thwarted various promising starts, and when, after forty years of Dutch activity, the English seized control in 1664 the colony had a total European population of only about 10,000. The great majority of these were on Manhattan

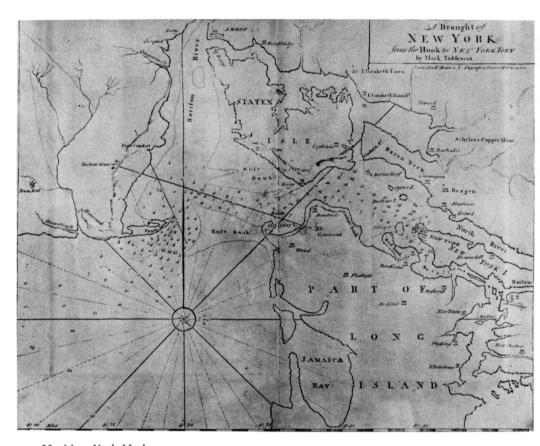

23. New York Harbor.

Mark Tiddeman's chart in the 1732 edition of the *English Pilot*, one of several available at the time, was used with only minor alterations for the next fifty years. It brings into appropriate nautical focus the narrow entryway between Sandy Hook and the East Bank, broadening out from "Cunny" Island, and the sharp turn to starboard necessary to follow the channel curving upriver to New York Town. The chart suggests something of the advantageous maritime complexities of this great estuary, and the twenty-seven villages named on the map attest to the attractiveness of the immediate hinterland of New Amsterdam–New York. (Courtesy of Map Collection, Yale University Library)

and adjacent shores; Esopus and Beverwyck (Fort Orange) were the only substantial colonies upriver. The Indians of the lower river and bay had been much disrupted and reduced. Conflict had begun with Hudson's voyage and remained endemic. The Dutch usually tried to negotiate for lands, but there were at least fifteen different bands to deal with and endless confusions over transactions and rights. The Indians were strongly attracted to the European settlements by the possibilities for trade, gifts, and theft; the colonists spread further outward. In the 1640s the accumulation of grievances on both sides exploded into bloody, intermittent, rather chaotic conflict, which, together with the toll of disease, left these Algonkian bands so depleted as to be unable to stem further European expansion.

The colony of New York was developed directly upon the foundations of New

Netherland. Names were changed and new peoples arrived but there was much continuity in basic character. Throughout the colony Dutch proprietors and tenants were generally confirmed in their lands. The change in name to Albany brought in a few English officials and soldiers but for many years thereafter the Dutch merchants of the Upper Hudson and Mohawk were little disturbed in their actual domination of the area and its commerce, despite lingering resentment over English regulations and courts. The English also enlarged upon the cosmopolitan and commercial patterns of New Amsterdam, but they eventually did more than that: they made it the principal strategic focus of their North American empire.

The English made some important geopolitical alterations almost immediately. They restored political unity to Long Island, which had been divided by treaty in 1650 between the Dutch on the west and the English in the center and east, and thereby severed several Puritan towns from their cultural kin across the Sound in New Haven and Connecticut and placed them under the jurisdiction of Anglican and Royalist New York governors. More important was the detachment of the large block of land between the lower Hudson and the Delaware to form New Jersey. This broke the political unity of the Hudson estuary, creating commercial and political complications and thereby some degree of tension between the two jurisdictions ever after. New Jersey was soon subdivided by its proprietors into East Jersey and West Jersey. The land of East Jersey was periodically further subdivided among many proprietors who eagerly peddled parcels to a variety of peoples. To a considerable degree the province was early settled by expansions westward from Manhattan and Long Island, and it long remained a rural area largely dependent upon New York City for mercantile services. The two Jerseys were reunited into a single royal colony in 1702, but each half continued to reflect in its social character and commercial orientations the broader Hudson or Delaware region with which it had been so closely associated.

The situation and significance of New York changed rather markedly in the 1670s as a result of a number of external factors. Imperial rivalries had intensified (indeed the Dutch reoccupied an undefended New York City for more than a year); there were serious disturbances in other major colonial areas, New England being ravaged by Puritan-Indian wars and Virginia by frontier rebellion; and the authoritarian Duke of York, heir to the throne, was determined to establish firm control over his extensive North American dominions. He sent over a governor-general who undertook a vigorous program. As Stephen Webb put it, "Edmund Andros found New York a village. He left it a city." Andros built a much enlarged and improved anchorage and public warehouses, established a mercantile exchange, rationalized regulations, and fostered commerce and milling in many ways. It was he also who forged a firm English alliance with the Iroquois, sought to curb New England expansion, and made New York the premier seat of British imperial authority. Thus the annexation of New Netherland together with these

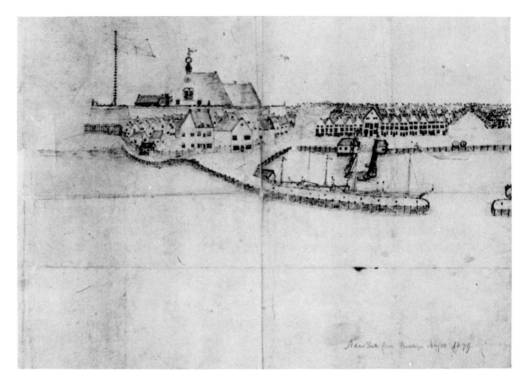

24. A View of New York, 1679–80.
This naive sketch from Brooklyn Heights by Jaspar Danckaert, who came to America to seek a suitable location for a colony of his fellow Freisian Labadists (they would eventually settle in Maryland), shows a town wholly Dutch in appearance. But Edmund Andros was now resident in the Governor's House adjacent to the great church, the two buildings looming within the walls of Fort James, and the picture really features the mark he had

new patterns and policies "shifted the gravity of American development from the older English colonies," transforming the geopolitical view of empire: "Now Eastern America was seen as a whole, with its political, diplomatic, strategic center not, as formerly, at Boston or at Jamestown, the capitals of the old colonial cultures, but, rather, at the headquarters of England's continental empire in America, Fort James, New York."

By the early 1700s English and Huguenot families were dominant and the Dutch a decreasing minority in the city, but the Dutch rural population continued to increase and expand into new ground. English governors continued and enlarged the previous official emphasis upon large land grants, and the connivance of officials and speculators resulted in great complexities over titles, rights, and availability to actual settlers. Many parcels remained speculative wilderness tracts, none of the estates represented the kind of feudal-manorial control that some proprietors had envisioned, and there were little clusters and scatterings of essen-

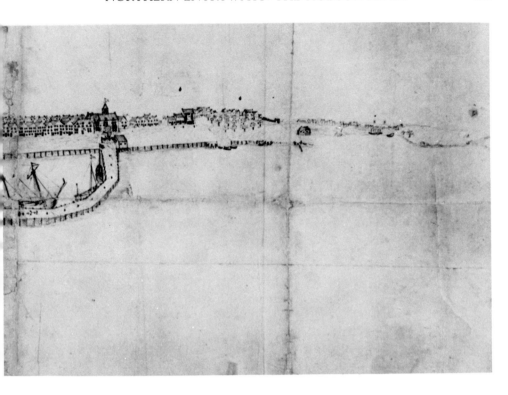

already made on the place: the arms of the Great Dock, providing the first sheltered anchorages, and the Market House, on piles across from the weighhouse at the base of the short pier. The old West India Company warehouse at the head of that pier was now the King's Warehouse and Customs House. The building with steeple and flag at the head of the right-hand dock was City Hall. (Courtesy of the Long Island Historical Society)

tially freehold farmers in every district, but there was enough evidence of a class-structured rural society to make the Hudson Valley estates—with their tenant farmers under the overlordship of a closely interlocked set of patrician families—widely understood to be a characterizing feature of the Colony of New York.

The first shipload of farmer colonists sent to New Netherland were Walloon refugees, and subsequent immigrations continued to reflect the many streams of movement into Holland and various other overseas adventures of Dutch enterprise. These latter resulted in the importation of African slaves from Dutch raids in the Caribbean, and in the influx of refugees, including a congregation of Sephardic Jews, after the Dutch lost control of northeastern Brazil. This heterogenity was continued and augmented under English rule. British and Dutch mercantile, religious, and kinship networks continued to provide contact with a wide area of western Europe, bringing in a trickle of Swedes, Norwegians, Germans, and Portuguese, as well as larger numbers of Dutch, Flemish, Walloon, Huguenot, and

Rhenish Protestants, with spasmodic additions of English Puritans and Quakers, Scottish Quakers and Presbyterians, and a continual small inflow of Anglicans. The importation of Africans increased until by the mid eighteenth century they made up about fifteen percent of the population, widely distributed through New York and East Jersey, especially in the Dutch-dominated areas. Not all were slaves, and a good many were artisans rather than laborers or servants. This diversity was further extended by migrations from New England, especially into East Jersey whose proprietors were sympathetic to Nonconformists. Thus six of the seven earliest towns in that province were organized by Puritan migrants from Long Island or New England, and although this preponderance was modified by the influx of various other peoples, a Puritan influence long remained a strong component in the life of the province.

A great characterizing feature of the lower Hudson region, therefore, was a population diverse in origin and not dominated by any one religious or ethnic group. To some extent it was a geographical mosaic of localities, each stamped with the strong imprint of a particular people, such as New Harlem and Flatbush (Dutch), Bergen (Flemish), New Rochelle (Huguenot), Perth Amboy (Lowland Scots), Newark and Elizabeth (New Haven Puritans), Piscataway (New Hampshire Baptist), and Shrewsbury (New England Quaker and Baptist). But while a stolid conservatism would long maintain such distinctions in many rural districts, there was also steadily increasing contact, intermingling, and some direct blending of peoples. New York City was of course the greatest seat of diversity and focus of contact, but there was also a broader interaction, for the lower Hudson was a lively commercial region. About fifteen percent of the total New York–East Jersey population lived in the city and another fifty percent lived within a day's journey by sloop or wagon of that center.

The processes of convergence and of the emergence of an encompassing coherent regional society were varied and sometimes subtle. Among some of the Dutch and Flemish and among various German groups distinctions based upon European roots faded as their sharing of an American locality lengthened. More powerful was the practical lure of the English language and institutions. Many Huguenots, who were chiefly a middle-class merchant and artisan group, rather quickly assimilated to English society. By the middle of the eighteenth century many of the Dutch in the lower Hudson area were bilingual and some had shifted to the Anglican Church in protest against the strong resistance to the use of English by conservative Dutch Reformed leaders. Such shifts were often associated with intermarriage. The leading families of New York City merchants and Hudson Valley landlords were often a blend of ethnic backgrounds. Thus a distinctly new American people was being formed in this colonial "melting pot," chiefly from English and Dutch ingredients, but laced with Huguenot, Scottish, Germanic, and other elements. This emerging "Yorker" population became the central com-

25. Hudson Valley Farmstead.
Sometime in the mid-1700s an itinerant artist painted this lively rural scene on a panel
(cropped here at right and left) that the Garrett van Bergen family could proudly fix over
its mantle. The van Bergen farmstead, initiated by Garrett's father in 1680 on a high
terrace three miles west from the landing on the Hudson and thirty miles south of
Albany, with its fine Catskill background, was thoroughly Dutch American: the brick
house built in 1729 (replacing an earlier small stone one), with its *stoep* and double doors
and red tile roof punctuated by small dormers; the distinctive Dutch hay barracks—a set
of poles supporting an adjustable pyramidal roof—and presumably corn or grain storage
barracks (with raised floor); the broad seventeenth-century barn; the heavy-wheeled
sloped-box wagon; the board fence and variety of livestock; and, as characteristic as the
architecture, the Black slaves, serving as milkmaid and servant. (Courtesy of the New
York State Historical Association, Cooperstown)

ponent of the larger regional society, which also included Puritans, Quakers,
Africans, and those who still clung strongly to European ethnic identities. Struc-
turally complex and riven by factions of differing interests, it was nevertheless a
coherent functioning regional society, which was sharply and self-consciously
different in its general character from that of adjacent New England.

Upriver, especially from Kingston (Esopus) on north, however, the pattern
became much simpler. There were clusters of Palatine Germans in the Schoharie
Valley and along the upper Mohawk; Scots and Scotch-Irish whom William
Johnson, a major landowner, speculator, and Indian agent, had recruited to settle
along the edge of the wilderness north of the Mohawk; and a few Scotch-Irish
migrants from New Hampshire in the upper Susquehanna country. But apart from
these frontier districts the population over much of the valley was almost solidly
Dutch. Albany was the bastion of merchants who had long prospered from the fur
trade; it was the seat of a society still so strongly rooted in its Dutch heritage, so
strongly protective of its commercial and social interests, and so indifferent or
antithetical to the concerns of New York City and its realm that it was widely
regarded as a distinct subregion: "Albany can best be described as a city-state. Its
frontier location, its almost totally Dutch character, and its fur-centered economy
all conspired to emphasize a separate, special, and unique position."

Something of the common geographic structure of New Netherland and New
France was still apparent in the New York and Canada of circa 1750 and a voyage

up the Hudson might readily remind a traveler of a natural similarity to a journey up the St. Lawrence. But there had been important divergences in developments and the details of settlement were quite different. The Hudson Valley was a considerably more complex and populous region (c. 100,000 compared to c. 60,000 in the St. Lawrence), and that population was more heavily concentrated in the lower reaches of the river axis. New York City, compactly sited on the southern tip of Manhattan, was four times the size of Quebec. It was the focus of a much richer and more diversified local hinterland, with expanding productions from farms, forests, and iron mines, and it was far better located for North Atlantic trade. Its safe, capacious, ice-free harbor gave ready access to the main seaboard trafficways. Furthermore, it lay between two vigorously developing neighboring regions; the Hudson passageway led directly to two major powers on the northern frontier, the Iroquois and the French in Canada; and its strategic role made it the major center for military contracts and procurement.

The rural hinterland along the river to the north was not at all a near-continuous côte of farmsteads on their long lots, but a highly uneven distribution: a small cluster, a scattering of individual farms, occasionally a somewhat larger country seat, with fields and orchards suggesting a pleasant prosperity but interrupted by long stretches of vacant land. There were river landings and a few small hamlets but no real towns. The stone houses and broad wooden barns were different from those in Canada and quite unlike anything in adjacent New England; and at the northern end on a steep slope on the west bank remained the most vivid representation of Dutch America: the step-gabled brick houses, shops, stores, and churches of Albany.

Albany was in general the counterpart and competitor of Montreal. It still handled a third to a half of English imports, but most of the actual trade now took place well to the west in the midst of Iroquois country. Over many decades the geography of contact between Europeans and Indians had shifted from the open frontier mart within early Albany itself to camps outside the walls and to the increasing intervention of such upriver outposts as Schenectady, Fort Hunter, and, after 1727, Fort Oswego on the shores of Lake Ontario. This last was mainly there to assert English claims against the encroachments of imperial France. By 1750 settlers lined the Mohawk Valley for eighty miles and the Mohawk Indians, famous for a century as "Keepers of the Eastern Door," were present in only two villages (Fort Hunter and Canajoharie); having suffered heavily in warfare over this strategic position and resenting such encroachments, the majority of that tribe had shifted to the St. Lawrence Valley and closer association with the French. The remaining members of the original Iroquois League, the Oneidas, Onondagas, Cayugas, and Senecas, were still aligned in their sequence of territories across the northern margins of the Appalachian plateau, their villages spaced out in the

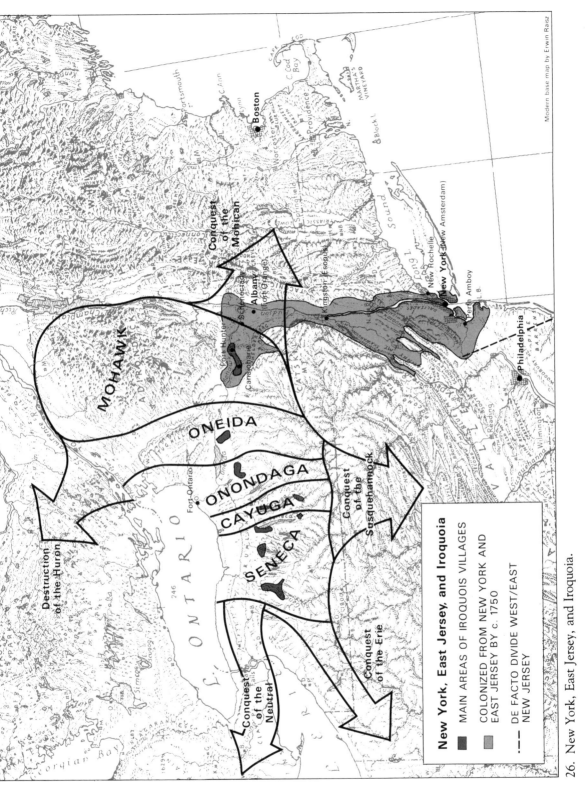

26. New York, East Jersey, and Iroquoia.

New York, East Jersey, and Iroquoia

MAIN AREAS OF IROQUOIS VILLAGES

COLONIZED FROM NEW YORK AND
EAST JERSEY BY c. 1750

DE FACTO DIVIDE WEST/EAST
NEW JERSEY

Modern base map by Erwin Raisz

glacial valleys and better drained uplands amidst the lake country between Oris-
kany and the Genesee Valley. To the west were their Tuscarora kin, who had
retreated from the North Carolina coast; to the south along the Susquehanna were
various client tribes, refugees from warfare and harassment in the Delaware and
Chesapeake regions.

There was a delicate complexity in political relationships in these matters. The
Iroquois League had at its core the five distinct but long closely associated nations
of this region, with an array of other tribes and peoples, some of whom had been
conquered by the Iroquois, in more or less subordinate affiliations. This whole
Indian complex was bound up with European partners in the Covenant Chain, a
set of oral treaties, contracts, and understandings recurrently renegotiated and
adjusted to achieve the mutual objectives of commerce, peaceful relations, and
defense against rivals. Thus New York, like Canada, was part of a much larger
bicultural geopolitical complex binding together in this case an Indian empire, a
European colony, and the king across the great sea. Albany rather than New York
City served as the de facto capital and although its English-Iroquois hinterland was
not as large nor by 1750 nearly as rich in production as that of Montreal, it was on
the basis of such formal long-standing relationships with this powerful Indian
leadership that the English laid claim to a huge western territory.

There were other claims to that territory, and not only from the imperial
French. The attenuated region of European colonization along the Hudson came
under pressure from another direction, which if less physically dangerous was
nevertheless keenly felt by some of its people. This north-south axis of New York
lay directly athwart the westward expansionism of New England. By 1750 Yankee
settlers were encroaching strongly upon vacant lands east of the river that Hudson
Valley proprietors claimed lay within their estates and New York governors insisted lay within their colonial jurisdiction. Uncertainties over exact boundaries
exacerbated such disputes for years, but this Yankee pressure was also exerted well
beyond lands claimed by Connecticut and Massachusetts. In the lower Hudson, on
Long Island, and in the Raritan Valley, they competed with Dutch farmers for new
ground, and Yankee peddlers and merchants joined in the thriving commercial life
of the region.

Such movements were regarded by many New Yorkers as an intrusion by a
grasping, conniving, self-righteous people, and the presence and perceived threat
of these Yankees gave Yorkers a heightened sense of their own identity. These two
regional cultures had little in common. The Hudson society was a moderately
prosperous, secularized, commercial society, rather strongly class-structured, dominated by patrician families who though extensively interlocked through marriage
were also divided into competing factions of merchants, officials, landlords, and
Albany Dutch, and held together more by an increasingly sophisticated pragmatic

politics than by any common set of values and sense of moral purpose. The historical layer of Dutch beginnings, the ethnic and religious diversity, the great variations in landholdings, the presence of manors and tenants as well as freehold farmers, the uneven patterns of city, county, and town governments, and the very landscapes that its diverse peoples had created were all in sharp contrast with New England. Contemporary in development and adjacent on the continent, these two societies further illustrated the remarkable variety of American social regions initiated from the northwest European hearth.

7. Northern Entryways: The Delaware

New Netherland included the lands bordering the South River (the Delaware) as well as the North (the Hudson), but Dutch efforts there were always marginal and less effective. Neither the waterway nor its hinterland seemed as attractive. Delaware Bay was full of shoals, the river ran parallel to the coast for some distance, and just after its course did turn inland navigation was blocked by falls. Thus it did not provide much of a penetration of the continent, and it did not tap a very rich fur country nor major Indian societies ready to become partners in trade. Even as merely an anchorage, the estuary proved to be dangerous country. A Dutch whaling colony set up just inside Cape Henlopen was soon destroyed by Indian attack.

After the Dutch West India Company had shown relatively little interest in the area for many years, several Dutch entrepreneurs went to Sweden and there gained royal support for a diversified colonization program. Thus with the founding of Fort Christina in 1638, a New Sweden began to take shape along the lower Delaware. A number of forts and trading posts and a trickle of Swedish, Finnish, and Dutch farmers were planted along both sides of the river for forty miles below the Schuylkill. The Dutch had not relinquished their claim to the Delaware, and as this sector of the American coast also lay within the limits of English charters granted by the Crown, the area became a complex though very minor international battleground. The most substantial among various English ventures came from New Haven Colony when some local leaders sought to make the Delaware a major frontier for Puritan expansion. In 1641 they set up a fur trading post on the Schuylkill and a small farming colony on Salem Creek. The post was soon seized and dismantled by the Dutch, and the settlers at Salem were pressured into accepting Swedish rule. New Haven made several other unsuccessful attempts to gain a foothold. In 1655 the Dutch company reasserted its claim, expelled the Swedish officials, and began a program of development. However, before much could be accomplished the English captured the whole of New Netherland, only to lose it again to the Dutch briefly in 1673–74. The reestablishment of English control in

1674 marked the sixth change of flag in fifty years among three European states, but such a sequence represented more the reverberations from larger rivalries than an intense interest in the Delaware area itself.

Nevertheless, over those years some of the qualities of the land had been tested and a loosely coherent colonial region had gradually emerged. It was largely an agricultural colony, with forest products and some local fur trade as supplements. Settlement was rather widely dispersed along the river and in a number of localities several miles up small tributaries (as at Swedesboro). Wheat, rye (the bread staple of the Swedes and Finns), maize, tobacco, and livestock thrived, and it became increasingly realized that the Delaware Valley was attractive ground for farmers if not especially so for traders and speculators. Such colonists proved relatively indifferent to which flag was flown before the governor's house as long as they were left undisturbed in their lands and their religion (mostly Lutheran or Reformed), and Finns, Swedes, and Dutch continued to trickle in well after the English took over.

The first headquarters of New Sweden was on the west bank at Fort Christina (now Wilmington). The Dutch eventually shifted the focus a few miles south to New Amstel, which the English later renamed New Castle and confirmed as the capital. In substance it was little more than the largest among a handful of tiny villages.

The creation of New Jersey broke the geopolitical unity of the Delaware Valley as it did of the lower Hudson. On the severed western bank the English formed three counties, but undertook no particular program for development. Some infiltration of English settlers, chiefly from neighboring colonies, now began, and a few of the Swedes moved across the river to get away from the adminstration at New Castle. The first major geopolitical impact of English rule came with the subdivision of New Jersey and the sale of the western half to a group of Quaker proprietors, who immediately set about to create an American commonwealth of tolerance and prosperity. Their first settlement was at Salem in 1675 and within a few years about two thousand Quakers arrived from England and settled in localities all along the east bank of the Delaware from Greenwich north and east through the Swedish districts and beyond as far as the falls. The first capital of West Jersey was established in the new Quaker town of Burlington. Like the Puritans of forty years before, these were an uncommon type of emigrant: mostly middle-class, literate, prosperous, strongly conscious of their religious identity (though as Quakers inherently less cohesive as social groups than the congregational Puritans), and determined to create a better society in America.

Thus, when William Penn arrived in the fall of 1682 to inspect the land of his vast new proprietary grant lying to the west of the Delaware, a Delaware settlement region, created by the efforts of Swedes, Finns, Dutch, and English during the half century preceding, was clearly evident. But it was a fragile creation. It contained only a few thousand inhabitants, it had been cleaved into separate jurisdictions by the arbitrary divisions of the Duke of York, and its eastern side was taking on a strong Quaker coloration quite divergent from the west bank. Thus what might have seemed to be the natural integrity of such a riparian region had already been disrupted, and the sudden creation of Penn's greater inland Quaker commonwealth would soon make this Delaware estuary little more than the threshold of a major new American region.

8. Pennsylvania

William Penn had become involved with American colonization several years before he founded Pennsylvania in 1681. He was a trustee for the estate of one of the original Quaker proprietors of West Jersey in the 1670s, and soon thereafter participated as one of several smaller proprietors in East Jersey. Thus he became well acquainted with the practicalities of land allocations and town planning, emigration and colonization in both the Delaware and Hudson regions. Furthermore, during these years he was traveling and preaching in Britain and on the continent and learning of the plight of Quakers and other pietist sects. Thus when he obtained his enormous proprietary grant (in payment of a large debt owed his father by the king) he was ready to move quickly to create the great commonwealth of tolerance he had envisioned.

He sent agents on ahead of the first colonists to begin the survey of land patents and to locate and lay out the design of a capital city that would be the focus and the symbol of his "Holy Experiment." Twenty-three vessels, loaded with settlers and materials, arrived in the first year and many more were sent in years immediately after. Thus Pennsylvania, founded relatively late (fifty-three years after the Puritan hegira to Massachusetts Bay), and carved out of the hinterland of the meager estuarine settlements on the Delaware, became almost instantly a region of major substance and significance in the North Atlantic world. Dutch, Swedish, and English forerunners had demonstrated the productivity of the lands; a large area was cleared for colonization through peaceful negotiation with the Indians; and the Quaker leadership had the vision, dedication, and resources to design and initiate a society attractive to thousands of family migrants. Within a few years, Philadelphia, the model city of the model colony, was competing strongly with older centers for the premier position on the British American seaboard.

Three distinct groups of people who sought this "virgin elysian shore" in the first three years represented the fruits of Penn's wide European contacts and the kind of society he had initiated. The first and largest group was the English Quakers,

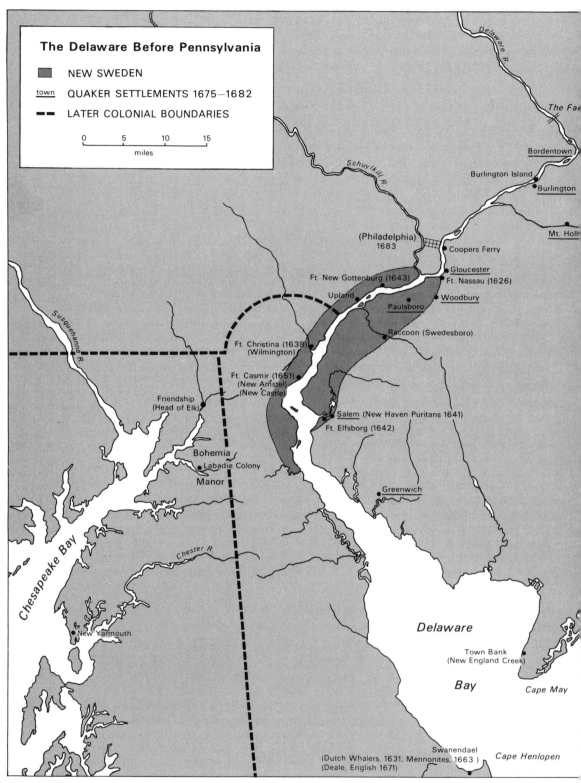

27. The Delaware before Pennsylvania.

chiefly from London and Bristol and various western and northern counties. A small minority were families of some wealth who had purchased extensive lands and were thereby entitled to the most desirable lots in the city. The majority were manual workers, tradesmen, shopkeepers, or farmers of modest means. However, the prominence and promise of this new commonwealth also attracted the attention of other Quaker entrepreneurs who had left England some years before to escape religious harassment and had sought opportunities in the more relaxed atmosphere of overseas colonies. Thus the early nucleus of wealthy merchants in Pennsylvania became dominated by English Quakers who had flocked in from such places as Barbados, Jamaica, New York, and West Jersey.

A second group was the Welsh Quakers, who purchased lands west of Philadelphia. They had sought 40,000 acres for one "undivided barony" wherein they might transplant their Welsh culture intact. They received several smaller blocks instead, but close enough together to create a "Welsh Tract" in which some ethnic identity was preserved for several generations despite the fact that many of these people became active and prosperous participants in the life of the capital and province.

The third people was a group of Quakers from the lower Rhineland, who purchased a tract a few miles north of Philadelphia in order, as their leader put it, that "we High-Germans may maintain a separate little province, and thus feel more secure from all oppression." Therein he laid out Germantown, or "Germanopolis," which became the nucleus of a thriving community of linen makers, artisans, merchants, and farmers with its own burgomaster, court, and local law within the bounds of Penn's tolerant commonwealth.

These Quakers, like the Puritans with whom they shared a number of traits and many social antecedents, were a selective and highly self-conscious group whose combination of religious intensity and determination to exert their talents and energies to the utmost in this world gave them an extraordinary potency for creative colonial development. The "spiritual dynamic" of Quakerism also combined a strong sense of both individualism and community, but with a rather different balance and tension than in Puritan congregationalism. Penn's charter gave him extensive powers to shape the settlement pattern and he believed that "ordered space would mean orderly and happy lives." He wanted to avoid uncontrolled allocations, excessive speculation, and the creation of "Wilderness vacancies" characteristic of so many colonies (most notably New York). Penn sought a degree of authority, proportion, and contiguity that would foster genuine communities: "I had in my view Society, Assistance, Busy Commerce, Instruction of Youth, Government of Peoples manners, Conveniency of Religious Assembling, Encouragement of Mechanicks, distinct and beaten Roads." He further stated, "We do settle in the way of Townships or Villages, each of which contains 5,000 acres . . . and at least ten Families. . . . Our Townships lie square; generally the Village in the Center . . . for near neighborhood."

But this was in his report of 1685 and it was more an expression of his intentions than of what would actually take place. His control over land allocations soon diminished in the face of mounting complexities and pressures from the inflow of so many purchasers and settlers in so short a time. Pennsylvania lands were surveyed in an orderly but piecemeal fashion, not in conformity to any overall grid or standard pattern. Elements of the formal Philadelphia plan were incorporated in the design of many interior towns, but their location, spacing, and relationship to rural allotments followed no uniform system. Most of the area was simply sold in individual lots of a few hundred acres, and except for a number of sectarian communities, farm families were dispersed over the countryside. Many of the churches, meetinghouses, taverns, inns, and mills were also scattered about, and villages and towns only gradually emerged out of local needs and initiatives, rather than from proprietary planning. Penn's heirs did retain control of the creation of counties and the location of county seats, and it was these rather than the township and village that provided the principal administrative, judicial, and, to some extent, social framework and focus.

As Lemon notes, this pattern of rural settlement is not to be explained by ethnic attitudes, deep European antecedents, or the transforming influence of the American environment: "The fundamental force leading to dispersion was the rise of individualism over peasant values in western Europe." By the late seventeenth century the agricultural village was becoming a social anachronism in Europe. Manorial patterns had been greatly weakened, churches were losing community discipline, there was greater political tolerance of social and religious variety, and the agricultural scene was increasingly characterized by owner-operators participating in an expanding market economy. Created half a century or more after most American colonies, Pennsylvania was a display of current European trends on a new expansive and uncluttered stage.

And a very attractive stage it was, physically as well as politically and socially. The rolling Piedmont hills back from the Delaware "shore" proved relatively good country by either European or American standards, and it got better further inland on the numerous limestone valleys and plains. Beyond South Mountain, opened after purchase from the Indians in the 1730s, lay the Great Valley, the first and broadest of the linear lowlands within the distinctive corrugations of the Ridge and Valley Province. Soon famous as "the best poor man's country," Pennsylvania drew a continual stream of immigrants, a large proportion of them families attracted by its agricultural opportunities. It was soon the premier "bread colony"; its output of grains and livestock, orchard and garden produce, flax and hemp made it the most productive mixed farming region in America. Contrary to the harsh experiences of so many pioneers in earlier, experimental colonies in less favored regions, "early Pennsylvania farmers and their families, with few exceptions, ate heartily, were well-clothed, and sold a surplus of goods."

The detailed geography of this colonization was very complex. It was not a contiguous advance inland from the Delaware. The proprietors secured large areas by treaties from the Indians, and individuals and groups ranged well beyond the margins of general settlement in search of the best lands and locations at a good price. Thus the overall pattern of any year showed a wide scattering of new districts, but the influx and local growth were sufficiently large and continuous to cause a rapid filling in. By 1755, when immigration virtually ceased for more than a decade, the whole area of the Great Valley and the Piedmont had been essentially settled. Although the main directions of this flow of settlers were northward and westward within Pennsylvania, it also spread beyond the bounds of the colony: northeastward across the Delaware into West Jersey, and southwestward following the grain of the terrain into western Maryland and northernmost Virginia.

A special feature of this expansion was the absence of any serious clash between the Europeans and the Indians. This unusually benign history was certainly in part the result of the firm policy of conscientious negotiation and purchase by Penn and his successors, but it was also made possible by the weakness of the Indians. The Delaware tribes had been reduced through sixty years of contact before Penn arrived. One band was allocated a small reserve west of Philadelphia; the rest agreed to retire northward. For many years Burlington Island was kept in public ownership (by West Jersey) as a seasonal entrepôt for the upriver Indian trade. To the west the Susquehannocks, who had dominated a broad region during the Dutch and Swedish eras, had suffered heavily in conflicts with the Iroquois to the north and the English settlers of the Chesapeake to the south. When Penn arrived, most of them had shifted to the middle Susquehanna and become clients of their recent enemies, serving to guard the southern margins of the Iroquois Confederation. Thus most of Penn's domain was very thinly occupied if at all. Conestoga, connected by wagon road to Philadelphia, long served as the chief center for the

---

28. Pennsylvania in 1687 (*overleaf*).
This "Mapp of ye Improved Part of Pensilvania in America" was drawn by Thomas Holme, an Irish Quaker who served as the first surveyor general of the province. Holme came to America with William Penn in 1682 to lay out Philadelphia and then proceeded to mark off the larger framework. The map well displays several important features of this colonization: a comprehensive but highly varied internal pattern for orderly contiguous settlement; the variety in sizes of farm lots and manors; the special townships and tracts reserved for Germans, Dutch, and Welsh; the delimitation of counties. (Courtesy of the Library Company of Philadelphia)

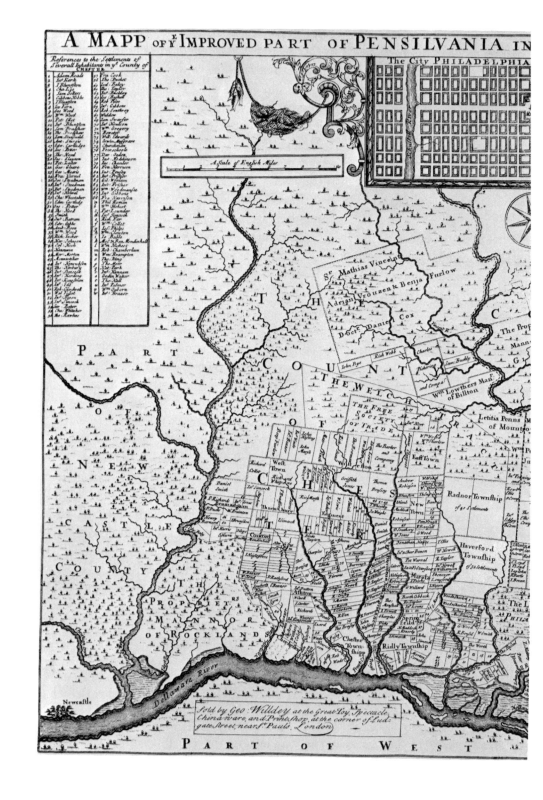

A MAPP OF Yᵉ IMPROVED PART OF PENSILVANIA IN

References to the Settlements of
Severall Inhabitants in yᵉ County of
CHESTER.

A Scale of English Miles

Sᵗ Mathias Vincen

Adrian Vrouzen & Benja Furlow

Docᵗʳ Daniel Cox

John Bye   Rich Webb   Charles

Sam Buckby

Wᵐ Lowthers Manᵗ of Bilton

THE WELCH

THE FREE SOCIETY OF TRADE

Letitia Penns
of Mountio

THE

T COUNT

COUNT

Radnor Township
of 40 Settlements

West Town

Richard Collet

Daniel Smith

East Town

New Town

CHES

CHE

Haverford Township
of 32 Settlements

Concord

Marple

Ridly Township

Chester Town ship

Aston

THE
PROPRIET
MANNOR
OF ROCKLAND

P   A   R   T

O F

N   E   W

C A S T L E

C O U N T Y

Newcastle

Dellaware River

Sold by Geo: Willdey at the Great Toy, Spectacle,
China ware, and Print Shop, at the corner of Lud=
gate Street, near Sᵗ Pauls London

P A R T   O F   W E S T

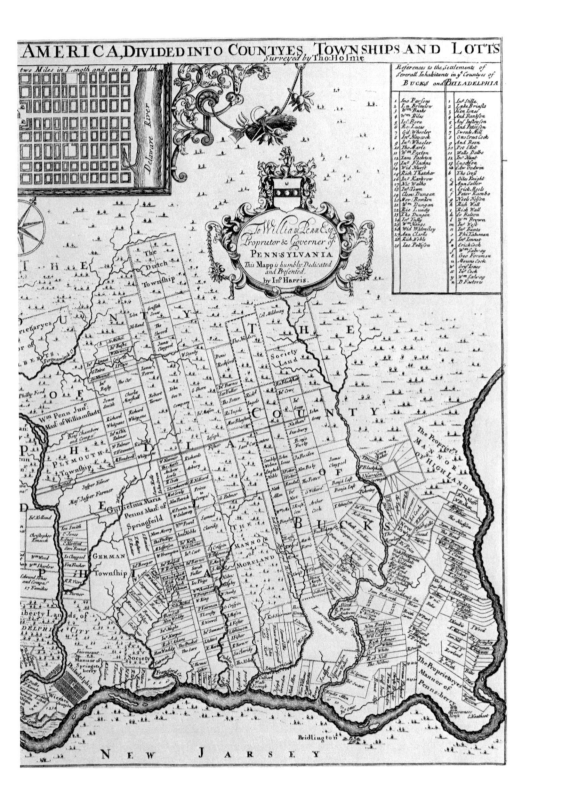

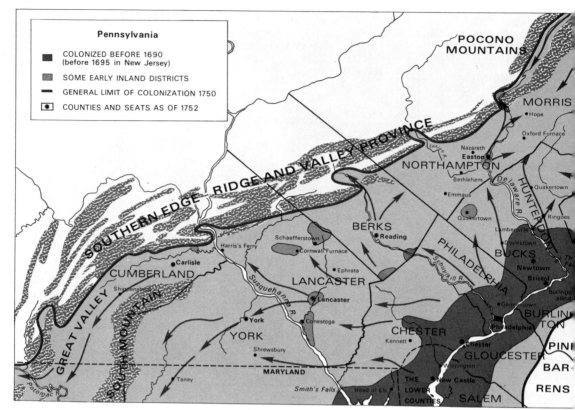

29. Greater Pennsylvania.

Indian trade of the Susquehanna. The Iroquois followed a policy of inviting other Indian groups who had suffered serious depletion and expulsion to join them as political subordinates but social equals (intermarriage was encouraged as a means of expanding populations). Thus, just as Penn's policies of active tolerance brought a diversity of Europeans to the area, so by 1750 there were Susquehannocks and Delawares, Conoys and Nanticokes from the Chesapeake Bay area, Tuscaroras and Tutelos from Virginia and Carolina settled in the Wyoming, Shamokin, and other valleys just north of the European frontier.

South of that frontier the ethnic and religious variety was even more complex. The English (at first mostly, but never exclusively, Quakers) dominated the first tier of counties along the Delaware. There were numerous localities of Welsh also, but Welsh immigration dwindled after 1710 and the forces of assimilation steadily diminished their identity. English immigration continued after the initial surge and spread into all of the later colonization districts, but beginning in the 1720s it became overshadowed by the prominence first of the German and then of the Scotch-Irish migrations. The framework of English-named counties (and seats: Easton, Reading, Lancaster, York, Carlisle) that formed the second tier, from Northampton on the Delaware to York beyond the Susquehanna, was the great receptacle of the German inflow. Experimental religious communities, such as at Ephrata, Bethlehem, and Nazareth, and pietistic sects, such as the Mennonites, were the most visible groups in this ethnic landscape, but the majority of the Germans were Lutherans and Reformed (Calvinists), who were far more individualistic. Although these latter two groups were almost always from different districts in Europe, they became much intermingled in Pennsylvania, often sharing the same church building for awhile. The general regional pattern of German settlement was therefore broadly ethnic rather than one of tight religious clusters. It was the result of large numbers who arrived about the same time in an English colony amidst a variety of peoples and, although they may have come from many different European areas—the Palatine, Alsace, Hesse, Baden, Bavaria, Switzerland—they quickly gained a new awareness of how much they shared in language and general culture and sought to settle amongst their own kind.

The Scotch-Irish began to migrate to America in rapidly increasing numbers after 1718. Although they came to all the British colonies, they did not find the Anglican dominance in New York, the Chesapeake, and coastal Carolinas to their liking, and they were coldly received by their fellow Calvinists in New England. Thus Pennsylvania, where they were welcomed by officials, offered good land at a reasonable price, and extended full religious toleration (there were a dozen Presbyterian churches—English, Welsh, Scots—already in the colony), became much the greatest entryway. They spread into all major districts and came to dominate broad sections of the south and west, partly because many disembarked at New Castle and headed directly toward lower Susquehanna lands (whereas after 1725 all German immigrants had to enter at Philadelphia and take a loyalty oath). Lemon's detailed geographical analysis has demolished the long-standing stereotyped contrast between individualistic, mobile Scotch-Irish frontiersmen scattering through the rougher country and stolid, skillful German farmers rooted deeply on the best limestone plains. In fact representatives of these groups shared many localities, on many kinds of soil, on the frontier as well as in older districts, with generally similar farming results.

These broad patterns mask the complexities within all of the counties and many localities. Lancaster County, for example, created just in time to partake of the greatest German influx and famous ever after as a main seat of the most distinctive German sects, had not only many other German groups but large numbers of English (of various religious affiliations) and Scotch-Irish, as well as small communities of Huguenots and Anglican Welsh, a tiny colony of Jews at Schaefferstown, and the mixed residue of the old Conestoga Indian trading settlement. Even Germantown had a good many English and a sprinkling of others from early on, and active congregations of Quakers, Mennonites, Lutherans, Reformed, and Dunkards. The larger villages and towns of Pennsylvania therefore typically had several churches without any clear dominance in members, wealth, or prestige of any one. And the fact that very often none of the church buildings was located on the main street or central square reflected not only the lack of any clear denominational hierarchy but also the emergence of a distinctly American secular, individualistic, commercial society.

The well-justified reputation of Pennsylvania as a haven for ethnic and religious variety should not be allowed to obscure the suspicions and prejudice that inevitably existed under the official and surficial local tolerance when such disparate groups had to share a region and a government. Resentment against the Quaker oligarchy of Philadelphia and the political power of the old "English" counties was common in the interior. The sheer numbers and "clannishness" of the Germans seemed a threat to many of the British settlers. "Palatine Boor" became a common epithet, and "the German Problem," that is, how to disperse, educate, and anglicize such people, was widely discussed and as widely resented and resisted by the Germans. In fact a rapid adaptation and acculturation was taking place, not in the form of the assimilation of one European group into another but in the emergence of a new encompassing American society in which ethnic and religious identities were retained but diminished in significance by the common desire to make the most of this unprecedented opportunity to achieve a new level of individual social and economic status in the thriving market economy of a productive and tranquil colony.

By the mid eighteenth century Philadelphia was widely regarded as a great exhibit of the vitality of British America as well as of the special character of Pennsylvania. The form and landscape of the city were widely admired. Laid out in a rectangular grid across a two-mile neck of land between the Delaware and the Schuylkill, it had sprung "almost at once into brick and stone" to become the major American display of new departures in city planning and architecture. Just as Boston's "maze of narrow winding streets" bordered by half-timbered buildings "recalled medieval London," so the formal and spacious symmetry of Philadelphia showed it "to be a product of Baroque London," of the London created after the Great Fire of 1666. "Again and again travellers commented" on this fresh design, the delightful novelty of its straight streets, paved and curbed, and lined with brick or flagstone sidewalks and evenly spaced trees: "the first important example in America of the order so desired by the merchant and the trader."

Actually the interests and attitudes of those merchants and traders had kept the city from developing quite in the manner its founder intended. Penn had envisioned a "greene Country Towne" spread out so that every owner would have "room enough for House, Garden and small Orchard" and men of means could have estates in the adjacent countryside. But the city grew up compactly from its Delaware waterfront, tightly bound to its commercial core, for its leaders were an urban mercantile class in close touch with their counterparts throughout the

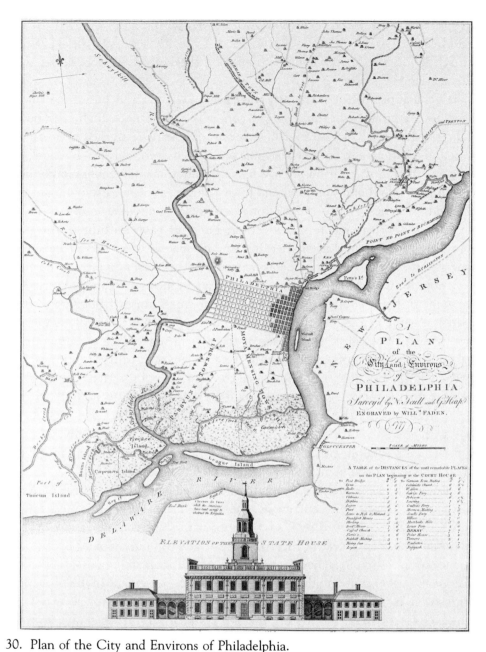

30. Plan of the City and Environs of Philadelphia.

This plan was published in London in 1777 by William Faden, successor to Thomas Jefferys and by then "Geographer to the King." It is essentially the map first prepared by Nicholas Scull and George Heap in 1752, updated in a few particulars. An important addition was the shaded pattern indicating the actual extent of expansion of the city from its Delaware waterfront: to one tier of blocks beyond Northeast (Franklin) Square and Southeast (Washington) Square. Schwartz and Ehrenberg note that Nicholas Scull, born near Philadelphia in 1687, was "the first member of a North American family to engage in cartography as a business"; he served as surveyor general of Pennsylvania 1748–61 and died in 1762. (Courtesy of the Library of Congress)

North Atlantic world, who sought to emulate the best of London rather than become a landed gentry.

The general prosperity of the city was clearly evident in its busy streets lined with close-set brick houses and shops, generally three stories high, the newer buildings reflecting the latest English style but sufficiently restrained in ornamentation and distinctive in detail to become recognized eventually as "Philadelphia Georgian." Rising above were the tower of the handsome new State House (later Independence Hall) and the spires and towers of the Anglican, Presbyterian, and Reformed churches. These promontories on the skyline were marks of Philadelphia as a political and religious center, but they gave no hint of the most important group in the life of the city for such people were served by simple unadorned meetinghouses. The Quakers were now only about a fifth of the city's population, for their main immigration had come in the early years and there had been some drift of more prosperous families to Anglicanism (though the great majority remained steadfast and practiced endogamy within the far-flung Quaker network in the colonies). But although there were now as many Lutherans as Quakers and both German and English were widely used in daily business, the influence of the founding sect still shaped the character of the city. The Quakers no longer dominated the governing councils as they had for several decades, but they continued to set the tone, and their remarkable success in devoting themselves with equal fervor to commerce and culture had given Philadelphia both a prosperity and a set of institutions in the support of education, science, medicine, and charitable works unmatched by any North American city.

Philadelphia was capital of a region that extended beyond the bounds of Pennsylvania, yet did not quite encompass the entire Delaware basin. West Jersey, where settlement developed in a band aligned with the Delaware (much of it by expansions from Pennsylvania), was almost entirely tributary, bound by the convenience of river shipping, the attractiveness of facilities and services, and the lure of the great Quaker center to the many Quakers on the Jersey side of the river. This urban power in Philadelphia dampened the development of towns in all the counties along the river. Burlington, the old capital of West Jersey and now one of the dual capitals of the united Jerseys, remained a relatively small center and minor focus.

Within Pennsylvania nearly the whole of the compact settled area was served by good roads fanning out from the capital. Thus the interior county seats and other market towns, and the farmers themselves, were in rather direct touch with the Atlantic commercial world. The only significant variation in this pattern of flows was in the country west of the Susquehanna. This large river was more a barrier than a boon to traffic. It was too shallow to be suitable for navigation most of the year and too broad to be readily crossed except at a few ferries. As York County became settled and pioneers followed the trend of the terrain southwestward into the Maryland Piedmont, merchants in the town of Baltimore (founded 1729) sought to attract their trade. At mid-century the Chesapeake port was not a major rival to Philadelphia but its rapid rise was based on tapping this westernmost extension of the Pennsylvania settlement area, which was now spreading well beyond the border of Penn's commonwealth.

The one area that Philadelphia failed to dominate as completely as its founder intended was downriver, the west side of the older Delaware estuary region. Penn considered these "Lower Counties" to be included in his grants from the Crown and he regarded control of this shore as being of strategic importance to his colony, but local protests and challenges to the legality of his claim kept their status ambiguous for many years. In 1692 Penn appointed a deputy governor for these three counties and a few years later they obtained a separate assembly. They also became at least a quasi-royal colony but London maintained the tie to Pennsylvania by having the governor of the latter also serve as royal governor of the Lower Counties.

This persistent claim to a political identity was rooted in the distinct history and culture of the area. Although there were fewer than three thousand in the western Delaware estuary in 1692, many of these people had roots in the Swedish and Dutch eras. They had no wish to be absorbed into a Quaker proprietorship and they had good reason to fear their area would become no more than a minor appendage with little political influence in the far greater entity of Pennsylvania.

New Castle continued to be the main focus of that population, but both the town and the county had been caught up in the patterns of Pennsylvanian development. The countryside filled with Scotch-Irish, Lutherans, Welsh Baptists, and Quakers; and New Castle and Wilmington, as ports and milling centers, sought to capture trade from adjacent districts of Pennsylvania. In contrast, the more southerly shore was peopled chiefly by the spread of Anglicans and Roman Catholic planters, some with their African slaves, from Maryland (the boundary between these Delaware and Chesapeake jurisdictions was long in dispute). Thus the three Lower Counties (they had no other official name) were a political framework created around half of an early distinct estuarine settlement region, and they constituted a link between the Pennsylvanian and Chesapeake societies.

There were similarities between the emergence of Delaware and of New Hampshire. New Castle, like Portsmouth, was the seat of an early nucleus of settlement, which was subsequently very nearly swallowed up in the expansive claims and aggressive development of a large adjacent colony, but which successfully maintained sufficient local consciousness to sustain a formal political identity and impose a permanent geopolitical mark upon the American seaboard.

Philadelphia, like Boston, was the focus of a vigorously developing region that overlapped several political jurisdictions and included some distinct subregions. In this geographic sense there was a "Greater Pennsylvania" as there was a "Greater New England," each a very distinctive area created by the initiative of a remarkably energetic sect that had dissented from the established patterns and powers of European society. And there were broad similarities in commercial prosperity, in the importance of Atlantic mercantile networks of kith and kin, and in the concern for education and public morality. But there was also a difference so fundamental as to become the great characterizing contrast in the cultural geography of the two regions: the difference between Puritan corporate self-righteousness and Quaker individual tolerance; between the active discouragement of settlers of different ethnic backgrounds and religious beliefs and the active recruitment of a wide variety of peoples; between a remarkably uniform New England and a strikingly heterogeneous Pennsylvania. Each was a distinctive American creation.

9. Emergence of Greater Virginia

CHESAPEAKE BAY: EARLY VIRGINIA

The first permanent English colony took shape along the lower James River between Point Comfort at the broad entrance and Henrico in the narrows eighty miles upstream. Jamestown was almost exactly midway along this axis, but its selection as the headquarters made more sense within the strategies of seafaring and conquering than from any advantage for planting: it lay somewhat sequestered up a gauntlet from revengeful Spanish vessels and it was a defensible near-island only a few miles across the peninsula from the headquarters of the most powerful Indian leader of the region, but it was a swampy, malarial site that would never become an important agricultural settlement.

Europeans were here intruding upon the lands of agricultural Indians and they were soon embroiled in disputes. Powhatan, the principal chief of a loose confederation, shifted his seat some miles further away up the York River and made no concerted effort to halt this encroachment, but in 1622 his successor attempted to destroy the entire string of European settlements. Despite heavy losses the English invaders withstood this attack and countered with a systematic harassment designed to clear the Indians from the James River area. A second retaliation by the Indians begun in 1644 killed about five hundred colonists but finally failed and resulted in the imposition of a treaty that formalized the decisive shift in the balance of power. All Indians of Virginia were declared to be tributary to the government at Jamestown; the Lower Neck (between the James and York rivers) and Southside (south of the James) were to be cleared of Indian settlement;

blockhouses were to be erected at the falls of the tributary streams and Indians could enter the European area only by special permission. Thus the English created a Virginia "Pale," a clear demarcation, as in Ireland, between (in their terms) "civilization" and "savagery." The success of this conquering effort was quickly followed by an extension of planting. With this initial tidewater foothold secure, settlers soon spread into the succession of long parallel estuaries to the north, up the York, Rappahannock, and Potomac, staking out plantation sites in every little creek and bay along this intricately indented coastline. Others moved to the similar country on the long peninsula of the Eastern Shore above Cape Charles. By the time the Virginians reached the far side of the Northern Neck along the Potomac, settlers of different origins and auspices were creating a Maryland of generally similar character along the opposite shore.

These relentless pressures upon the Indians and the rapidity of settlement expansion were of course directly related to the success of tobacco as a profitable crop and export. That success came only after a decade of desperate search for riches, a decade also of bare survival of the colony. The Virginia Company was never modest about the agricultural potentials of its great province:

> The soile is strong and lustie of its own nature . . . [and] if bare nature be so amiable in its naked kind, what may we hope, when Arte and Nature both shall joyne, and strive together, to give best content to man and beast? . . . We doubt not but to make there in a few yeares store of good wines, as any from the Canaries, by replanting and making tame the Vines that naturally grow there in great abundance. . . . There grows hemp for Cordage, an excellent commoditie, and flaxe for linen cloth. . . . We intend to plant there (God willing) great plentie of Sugar Canes, for which the soyle and clymate is very apt and fit; also linseeed and Rapeseed to make Oiles. . . . Wee must plant also Orenges, Limons, Almonds, Anniseeds, Rice, Cummin, Cottonwool, Carowey seeds, Ginger; Madder, Olives, Oris, Sumacke, and many such like, . . . all very good merchandize.

This is of course a promotional effusion typical of the company's literature, but in fact at least some slight attempt was made with many of these crops (and with a good many others, such as pineapples, peppers, pomegranates, and figs) in the frantic speculations of these first years. The list reflects the common reasoning of the time that climate could be inferred directly and simply from latitude:

> What hope there is els to bee gathered of the nature of the climate, being answerable to the Iland of Japan, the land of China, Persia, . . . the Ilands of Cyprus and Candy [Crete], the South parts of Greece, Italy, and Spaine, and of many other notable and famous Countreys, because I meane not to be tedious, I leave to your owne consideration.

A few full seasons in America quickly undermined confidence in such analogies, although the reasons for such transatlantic differences would remain unclear until some sense of the global system of circulation was grasped.

But once the great success of tobacco was manifest the Virginians showed little interest in anything else. The company and later governmental officials repeatedly attempted to foster diversification. Laws were passed requiring every householder to plant winegrapes, mulberry trees, hemp, and flax; subsidies and prizes were offered for good crops of hops and wheat; skilled persons were sent to assist; but all with little effect. Despite increasing problems of surpluses, competition, quality control, and an erratic market, tobacco remained the one great staple throughout the first century of the Virginia colony.

Although the Virginia Company declared its intention "to Plant an English nation" in America, it was basically a commercial speculation and its overriding concern was with profits rather than the creation of a self-sustaining colony. Its early expeditions were quasi-military operations sent to develop some sort of marketable commodity from the company's lands. Only gradually and reluctantly was land allocated to the control of individual settlers or investors. A critical shift in policy came after a dozen years of major expenditure and meager accomplishments when it was decided to authorize the creation of smaller companies, each to be given a large block of land on which it was "to erect and build a town and settle and plant dyvers inhabitants there for the advancement of the general plantation of that country." Viewed by the larger company primarily as a means of building up the population, these subsidiaries became in fact autonomous little colonies within Virginia, each with its own organizers and backers in England, each responsible for recruiting, transporting, and governing its settlers, and each in control of its land, produce, and commerce. Not all were successful but enough prospered to provide a new impetus and a new pattern for Virginian settlement. Spaced along the James River (by company decree they were to be at least ten miles apart), these little corporate "colonies" or "hundreds" soon evolved toward control by individual families and became the model for the Tidewater "plantation." An adjunct of this program, by which such proprietors were granted a special allotment of fifty acres for every person brought to Virginia, was also to have a profound effect. Begun as an expedient to foster the importation of large numbers under some sort of indenture, this policy rather quickly evolved into the concept of "headright," applicable to any person who paid for his passage, and additional rewards of fifty acres for each family member and servant he might bring with him. Thus landholding in Virginia was from a very early date distributed among a wide range of people in widely varying amounts.

A further feature was the absence of any general system of land survey by which some sort of geographical order might be imposed on these allocations. Plantations were marked out by individual metes and bounds; a headright was not a specific

The Chesapeake

- ■ EARLIEST COLONIZATIONS
- ▢ COLONIZATION TO 1700
- → EXPANSIONS TO 1750

31. The Chesapeake and Greater Virginia.

piece of ground but a right to stake out fifty acres wherever it could be found unclaimed by another. Thus settlement expanded in piecemeal and almost chaotic fashion under minimal oversight, a procedure certain to create a maze of disputes over land boundaries and titles.

In 1619 the Virginia Company divided its James River realm into four "incorporations," and fifteen years later these together with recently settled areas were organized into eight shires or counties. Thus the bare semblance of an English spatial order was traced upon the Tidewater region. It was expected, indeed ordered, that the administration of each of these counties would be seated in a convenient town, but there was yet hardly any place resembling a town in all of Virginia, despite persistent governmental efforts to initiate them, as Reps has noted: "If laws and proclamations could have created towns and cities, early Virginia would have been an urban civilization and Jamestown would have become a frontier metropolis." Jamestown was a persistent, and to some a puzzling, exhibit of the failure of such laws and proclamations. As the Virginia Company headquarters it was the seat of important facilities from the first (governor's house, fort, church, storehouses) and it continued as the capital for nearly a century, yet it never grew beyond a disheveled village, which officials and visitors repeatedly described in disparaging terms. It was not only the political center; it was for years the only legal port of entry, but lack of enforcement brought no great traffic into focus upon it. In 1633 the government ordered the establishment of "stores" at five convenient locations to be legal tobacco market centers, but no commercial towns resulted.

This failure of towns to emerge commensurate with population growth and economic prosperity was regarded as an annoying anomaly by London officials, and they repeatedly sought to remove it, as, for example, in the instructions of 1662 to the governor "that care be taken to dispose the planters to be willing to build towns upon every River which must tend very much to their security and in time to their profit, of which they cannot have a better evidence and example than from their neighbors of New England. . . . We wish that there may be at least one Town upon every River and that you begin at James River." But the only result was the building (and in part rebuilding) of a few houses in dilapidated Jamestown. As Reps observed with reference to these instructions, "it was truly remarkable that a colony with a population of perhaps forty thousand persons still had no town worthy of the name." And so it struck commentators of the time, who then reasoned that it was the result of the configuration of the coastline and the liberty of the land policies, both of which allowed the colonists "to seate in a stragling distracted Condition" with a consequent dispersal of trade. Whatever the reason, it was clear that "neither the Interest nor Inclinations of the Virginians induce them to cohabit in Towns," and we may be quite certain that they would have been contemptuous of any instruction that they might best follow the example of "their neighbors of New England"—both the suggestion and the phrase reveal how little London officials understood the realities of the emerging English America.

During its seventeen years in America the Virginia Company sent over about 6,000 persons, but at the end of its tenure, in 1624, the European population was only about 1,200. The thousands lost (and to the 4,800 difference in these figures we must add those born in America during these years) are stark testimony of the difficulties the English had along the James River: a small proportion had simply given up and returned home, but the great majority had met an early death from the terrible demands of conquering and planting. However, thirty years later there was no doubt but that "an English Nation" had been planted successfully in

Virginia. The population was about 20,000 and growing rapidly, the Tidewater Indians had been conquered and largely expelled, and the tobacco staple was firmly established.

It was, of course, a special kind of "English Nation." It was a hierarchical, Anglican, rural commercial society, but it was far from being a simple transplant. A good many English noblemen and gentry were involved in the Virginia Company; some came to America, but very few created major plantations. The successful planters of the first generation were mostly tough, energetic, rather crudely ambitious entrepreneurs. As the colony emerged as a flourishing economic enterprise toward the middle of the seventeenth century, a new infusion of gentry and younger sons of rising merchants (infusions partly impelled by the political turmoil in England) began to arrive with ample capital to carve out extensive estates and establish themselves as the social and political elite of the colony. But probably three-fourths of the colonists came under some form of indenture, bound to the company or a proprietor for a period of service. "Indentured servants" was a very broad category. It included regular servants, persons in normal apprenticeship, freemen who bound themselves as a means of paying their passage, debtors, orphans, runaway children, vagrants, the poor, convicts, the kidnapped, prisoners of war; it included skilled and unskilled, farmers and laborers, literate and illiterate. It included male and female, young and old, but a large majority were young men. It also included Blacks as well as Whites.

There were only a few hundred Blacks in Virginia in the 1650s and they varied greatly in status: some were free, a few owned property, most were under some sort of indenture, and others were in virtual slavery. All Blacks arrived in Virginia under force, having been seized or purchased in the West Indies and brought on speculation for sale to planters. From the first, all had been routinely categorized separately as "Negroes," but such importations were an episodic and very minor part of the labor supply system and there had as yet been no uniform definition of the status and prospects of such persons nor of their offspring born in Virginia. Breen and Innes have shown that there were at this time free Blacks on the Eastern Shore who were apparently full participants in the civil society and in its economic and social competitions.

It was therefore a very distinct Virginia variant of an "English Nation" that had developed over these first fifty years. English certainly, almost wholly so, drawn from all over the country, though most heavily from London and its environing counties; Anglican, insofar as it gave any attention to ecclesiastical affairs, although with some Puritan influence; and hierarchical, a society led by a small planter class that aspired to the privileges and pleasures of the county elite of Stuart England. But a Virginian county had but a slight and crude resemblance to its English namesake. Surrey, York, and Gloucester in Virginia were thinly populated frontiers with almost no formal institutions and with a loose and unstable social pattern. Land was available, and a wide range of people were getting hold of some of it; yet all the while a large share of the population was bound in legal servitude as the importation of indentured immigrants expanded. Furthermore, this Virginian immigration was only to a small degree a family migration and the marked preponderance of males tended to make marriage more a privilege of the social elite and economically successful. Without a city or towns or family life, clustered on lonely plantations or scattered thinly between them on little patches of clearing in the thick woods of this ramifying, riverine, subtropical coast, most inhabitants of Virginia could have no more than fading memories of English country life or indeed of civilization in general. The ship from London or Bristol calling seasonally at the plantation wharf provided their only recurrent contact. Viewed from those vessels it would have been as yet difficult to imagine such persons as laying the foundations of a major American society. Rather they would have been regarded as Englishmen living in dangerous and squalid exile at the extremity of an oceanic commercial system, producing an annual cargo of an exotic plant that had become of value through a rather bizarre change in public habits.

CHESAPEAKE BAY: EARLY MARYLAND

While the Virginians were still painfully and precariously shaping a colony along the James, a new settlement was implanted with contrasting efficiency and success on land once claimed by the now-dissolved Virginia Company. The contrast arose from differences in leadership and concept and, most of all perhaps, from the lessons provided by that harsh Virginian precedent.

Maryland was the product more of a man than of a company. It was undertaken more as a conscious social design than as a commercial venture, and it was initially formed around a socioreligious group rather than a rabble of speculators. Its creator, George Calvert, had already been deeply involved in colonization activities for more than twenty years, first as a London associate of the Virginia Company; then in Ireland where he became Lord Baltimore, one of the peers created as an enticement to a new plantation scheme west of the Pale; next in Newfoundland where he fostered an English colony for seven years before deciding to leave that niggardly ground for a more hospitable latitude. He visited both Newfoundland and Jamestown in 1629 and returned to request a grant of lands immediately to the south of Virginia. As these had already been claimed and as the Crown was concerned about possible Dutch encroachments from the Delaware, he was encouraged to accept a grant encompassing the upper Chesapeake. He died before the first boats could be sent, but his son took effective hold of the enterprise and the *Ark* and the *Dove* arrived on the lower Potomac in the early spring of 1634.

The founding of Maryland was a convincing exhibit that at least some Englishmen had by now learned some of the basic rules for planting a successful colony. The newcomers were welcomed by the Piscataway (Conoy) Indians, who felt the need of allies against the Susquehannocks and whose assistance was sought in selecting a location and getting established. Well aware of the early miseries of Virginia, Baltimore insisted that all efforts be first directed toward local subsistence. Hogs, cattle, and poultry were picked up en route at Jamestown. By negotiating for the site of an Indian village and its fields they "found ground cleered to their hands" and ready for immediate planting. They readily accepted instructions from the Indians in planting, food preparation, hunting, and fishing. To ward off improvident speculation in tobacco, the proprietor had warned all planters not to grow "any other commodity whatsoever" before a "sufficient quantity of corn and other provision of victuall" was secured. At this site, on a bluff five miles up a fine estuary from the Potomac, they laid out the town of St. Mary's and built a fort, storehouse, church, governor's seat and other houses, and a watermill. An early report stressed that "without boasting it may be said that this colony hath arrived to more in six months then Virginia did in as many yeers," but readily recognized that "if any man say, they are beholding to Virginia for so speedy a supply of many of those things which they of Virginea were forced to fetch from England and other remote places, they will confess it, and acknowledge themselves glad that Virginea is so neere a neighbour." Thus, with subsistence readily secured, tobacco as a proven staple, and the continuing oversight of an intelligent, influential, and nurturing (though absentee) proprietor, there was a rapid expansion from this first nucleus.

But Maryland was also an exhibit of the fact that even such experienced Englishmen as the Calverts had other lessons yet to learn about American colonization. Lord Baltimore had requested and received Maryland as a palatine province, a medieval concept designed to give quasi-royal powers to a noble proprietor in return for settling and stabilizing some dangerous frontier zone. He envisioned baronies, manor courts, and a quasi-feudal society. For him land was more a measure of social status than a means of wealth. That was an ancient and still-common view but it was under extensive challenge in Protestant and mercantilist Britain, and it had already been greatly modified in nearby Virginia. Other colonies had been initiated with similar intent but, as was so often to happen in America, the ready availability of land and the shortages of labor and skills overwhelmed programs of privilege. Land was a necessary inducement to emigration and investment, and it was allocated to almost everyone, in amounts varying from fifty-acre headrights to whatever the wealthy could afford. Thus immigrants sought to become individual entrepreneurs as soon as possible, and they scattered along the "paisley-like pattern of crenated estuaries and necks" in search of whatever land they could warrant or obtain. Although at the very outset the social system reflected something of the proprietor's plans, it came more and more to resemble the patterns of Virginia. Manor courts existed briefly in name but local government soon became a minimal pragmatic negotiation between freemen and a few officials in a population spread thinly within a spare framework of counties. Despite all programs for civic life, even the capital, St. Mary's, like Jamestown, was never more than a rude village.

The concept of Maryland as a strongly hierarchical society was presumably reinforced by the fact that in his young adult years the first Lord Baltimore had embraced Roman Catholicism and had specifically promoted the colony as a refuge for English Catholics. The Calverts themselves were an anomaly: they were personal favorites of King James and then of Charles despite their religion, whereas in general English Catholics lived under chronic suspicion, restrictions, and recurrent persecution. The leading families and most of the first colonists were Catholics (including some Irish servants). Two Jesuits accompanied the first contingent, offered mass at the first Potomac landfall, and set immediately to work among the local Indians. Even though the Roman Catholics were soon outnumbered in the colony by other peoples, there was established here a relatively cohesive network of families who dominated politics and society for decades and remained influential for generations. Socializing and marrying with one another, maintaining connections with Catholic kin surviving in England or in refuge in Flanders or France, supporting local priests and a rudimentary cycle of religious observance, this little society scattered along the southern margins of Maryland had no counterpart in English America, and it became the main seedbed for the slow growth of a firm ecclesiastical presence of the Roman Catholic Church in the emergent nation.

It was not politically possible nor was it the proprietor's personal inclination to make Maryland exclusively a Catholic colony. There were Anglicans in the first contingent and in others that followed. The first important alteration in the social geography of the young colony came from a direct invitation to a group of Puritans as part of a strategy to secure the upper Chesapeake. The proprietor's position had been challenged by the existence of a large trading settlement on Kent Island, established in 1631—with the support of Virginians opposed to the intrusion of the Maryland grant—as a forward position for trade with the Susquehannocks. The leader of that outpost defied Maryland officials until the place was forcibly seized in 1637. A few years later the governor of Maryland (a Protestant) learned that a group of English Puritans, who had settled in the Nansemond district just in from Hampton Roads, was restive under Virginian governors and ready to move, so he invited them to form a colony in the Severn River district opposite Kent Island. Several hundred did so, laying out a town and forming Providence County; they were joined by others from England. Almost immediately, however, they caused the proprietor great difficulty, for when the Puritans came to power in

England these Maryland Puritans rebelled against Baltimore's control, came to dominate the province for several years, and only yielded after explicit assurances of tolerance and equality. Although this group never had the social vigor and cohesion of some New England Puritan settlements (some became Quakers in the 1670s and most eventually merged into dominant regional patterns), the very existence of this nucleus initiated a geographic tension in Maryland and made the Roman Catholics in the southern counties a more obviously discrete society, a small distinctive piece in a broadening, rapidly emergent Chesapeake region.

GREATER VIRGINIA

A century of vigorous expansion extended the social and economic systems from these early nuclei of the James, Potomac, and Severn to create one of the most populous, prosperous, and distinctive areas of colonial North America. Whereas in 1650 there had been no more than 20,000 Europeans and a few hundred Africans clinging closely to a few main estuaries, by 1750 there were perhaps twenty times that number in all, of whom thirty-five to forty percent were Blacks, and they were spread thinly but, in general, contiguously over all the necks and sandy plains of the Tidewater zone from the head of the bay to Albemarle Sound and westward up a dozen streams into the rolling hill country halfway or more to the great ridge. The Indians had very nearly disappeared. Caught between punishing raids of the Iroquois from the north and the chaotic, bloody harassment of frontier settlers from the east, they had retreated farther and farther into the swamps or toward the mountains, until most of the remnants made peace with the Iroquois and sought refuge under their protection in northern Pennsylvania.

Although politically partitioned among the jurisdictions of Maryland, Virginia, and North Carolina, this area had been created by similar peoples working in similar ways with similar results. It was in fact a remarkably uniform region and widely recognized as such at the time. It was still tobacco country. Through a century of erratic market conditions the great staple had persisted as the central commodity of the commercial system, but the whole area was becoming more diversified, not in the direction of those exotic products so prominent in the visions of early speculators, but in the mundane items of corn and wheat, hogs and cattle. A rising export trade in flour and meat was now a significant supplement to the tobacco trade. Harvesting the forests for timbers, planks, shingles, staves, pitch, and tar also provided important shipments, in part as an adjunct of the tobacco culture with its insatiable demands for fresh soils. Hunting and fishing continued to be major sources of subsistence, and the export of furs and skins a minor source of income.

Yet for all this growth in population and commerce the Chesapeake region remained a peculiarly rural country. There was no city, no regional focus, and, despite a century of repeated governmental decrees to induce them, no substantial set of market towns. Instead there were a few small ports of recent growth and uncertain prospects, two small provincial capitals enlivened only in the political seasons, and a scattering of ramshackle river hamlets. The Chesapeake was an important part of the Atlantic commercial world, but its oceanic trunk line had no American focus; instead, west of Cape Charles it frayed into a vast dendritic pattern of fine threads, as the several hundred ships that annually carried this most valued trade of North America ascended the rivers and creeks to hundreds of collection points dotted through this water-laced countryside. The great majority of the settlers lived within a few miles of ocean shipping. Some of these landings were private plantation wharfs; others were at storehouses, "factories," or "rolling houses" (referring to hogsheads of tobacco) serving a local district, the larger of which may have had several British (mainly Scottish) agents in residence competing for the trade. Thus Chesapeake commerce was unusually simple and direct between American producers and European shippers, without the mediation of American services in American towns, a feature strongly rooted in the historic patterns of the tobacco trade.

Only where other commodities requiring more local handling and destined for other markets were most prominent—for example, Norfolk, with its forest products and livestock trade to the West Indies, or Chestertown, in a part of upper Maryland that was diversifying into wheat and becoming an outlier of an enlarging Philadelphia grain trade—was there significant variation in this geographic pattern, a consequent growth in urban functions, and regular links with other North American regions.

To the traveler from another country Virginia and the Chesapeake margins may have seemed no more than semisettled or even half-abandoned after more than a century of colonization. It was an unkempt landscape, a disorderly pattern of natural woods and swamps, half-cleared land studded with stumps and skeletons of giant trees, old fields disappearing under a ragged regrowth, with farming confined to a patch of tobacco and few small fields of corn and wheat. Long narrow tobacco barns, rough outbuildings, and rude dwellings, some of these standing unused, characterized a common scene. Yet the land was all owned, mostly by local persons, and much of it was being used, despite the appearance of so much waste. Tobacco was an intensive crop, harsh in its demands upon labor and soil. Thus it was grown in small acreages and shifted onto plots of fresh ground every few years, while the old fields were given over to natural recuperation. Although no more than a tenth or so of the land was in cultivation at any time, over the course of a few generations much of it was cropped and most was used casually for lumbering, grazing, and hunting all the while. It was a form of shifting cultivation, and the simple buildings, including at times the house, might be shifted to or replaced at new sites periodically. "Tidewater landscapes, atrophied and in disarray, sacrificed esthetics for economics and ecology," as Earle has observed; "the deterioration of buildings and land was integral to the functioning of the system." Such a system could only operate where land was cheap and held in large amounts. Most farms were a few hundred acres but a good many were several thousand acres in size.

All farms were "plantations" within common usage of the term, but it was the largest of these, under the hand of well-established families, that punctuated the landscape with an exceptional scene and would give the word a special Virginian connotation. By the 1750s manor houses of some pretension could be sighted along many of the Tidewater bays and rivers. Most were not very large; some were of wood and some of brick, but they displayed in general design and interior furnishing the direct influence of Georgian London, and the best of them, embowered on a rise well back from the water's edge with their hipped roofs, high corner chimneys, symmetrical facades, and a touch of Palladian detail, had a rural dignity quite sufficient to serve as an enduring model of country life. Such houses were an exhibit of wealth but not of leisure. They were centerpieces of an ensemble of lesser dwellings, kitchens, storehouses, workshops, sheds, stables, and slave quarters, which contained a population whose size and diversity of age, status, skills, and duties equaled that of a thriving village. Successful management of such an estate required uncommon skill and energy.

Such planters together with a few merchants and lawyers were the local rulers of a strongly hierarchical society. Local and provincial governments, the established church, and much of the wealth of the Chesapeake were controlled by no more than a couple of hundred families, a provincial gentry bound together by intermarriage and common interest. The great majority of the people lived beyond the bounds of large plantations, and the basic social geographic unit was the county. The persistence of that early colonial pattern well into the twentieth century has been succinctly described by Arensberg:

> The distinctive community form of the South was and is the county. Dispersed a day's ride in and around the county seat, that community assembled planter and field- or house-land from the fat plantations, free poor White or Negro from the lean hills and swamps for the pagentry and drama of Saturdays around the courthouse, when the courthouse, the jail, the registry of deeds, and the courthouse square of shops and lawyer's row made a physical center of the far-flung community.

This geographic order was established by the government. When a county was created, its officials were typically instructed to select a central site, lay out the most convenient ways to it, and "take care that a court house, prison, pillory and stocks according to law be erected at that place with all convenient speed."

Although the facilities listed in these two descriptions were common to any formal English community, their prominence here as the civic focus reflected a society that was not only completely rural but was at bottom peculiarly coercive and chaotic: a small elite poised upon a large body of persons in some form of legal servitude—slaves, bondsmen, short-term tenants; and a landed society formed without an orderly land survey system, leading to "cadastral chaos" (in Earle's words) and chronic litigation. Lacking any regular marketing functions, these county seats remained tiny country hamlets enlivened only by the socializing, horse racing, cock fighting, and ephemeral fairs that accompanied periodic court sessions. It was a rural society with few formal institutions. The most prominent one, the Anglican parish, enfeebled by the absence of an American-resident bishop, became a creature of local privilege and a relatively ineffective means of religious ministration.

Arensberg's point that the physical and social patterns of the southern county were the rural American counterpart of the European baroque capital, the city of the palace and the parade, was most directly expressed in the unmistakably baroque forms of the new capitals of Maryland and Virginia, which had been laid out within a few years of one another by the same man, Francis Nicholson, who served as royal governor of these colonies in rapid succession. Maryland had made the more drastic move, abandoning St. Mary's in the old Catholic area in favor of a new Annapolis (surveyed on or near the town lands of the old rival but long-dispersed Puritan colony), which was more central within the Chesapeake shores of Maryland. The shift to Williamsburg was a local move expressing the chronic dissatisfaction with swampy Jamestown as well as the power of the older Tidewater gentry to resist demands for a capital more convenient to the whole province. But although impressively elaborate in plan, with wide avenues and squares, imposing capitols, governor's houses, and colleges, Annapolis and Williamsburg were not essentially different in type from the country county seats: seasonal centers of public activities with little commercial function; neither had more than a few hundred families in permanent residence.

The people of this rural society were almost entirely of English or African origin. African laborers were not part of the original scheme in either Virginia or Maryland, and few were imported until late in the seventeenth century. As the slave system gradually became well established in practice and formalized in law, shipments from the West Indies and Africa increased. By the mid eighteenth century Blacks constituted at least a third and sometimes more than half of the population in the older Tidewater counties. Despite continual importations the majority were now "country-born" (American) rather than "outlandish" (African), a shift which gradually altered the sex ratio from its early male preponderance and established the basis for a rapid natural increase. The ever-apparent mulatto population disclosed the role that local White males played in such growth. Slaves were unevenly distributed within any county: absent from the majority of landholdings, present in small numbers on many, and clustered by the score on the largest plantations. Wherever they were they likely worked in some association with indentured White laborers. Cargoes of bondsmen, many of them criminals, male and female, continued to be sent to these colonies and to be peddled by shipmasters and agents in a manner not unlike the sale of slaves. Thus both groups of immigrants were distributed broadly within areas already settled. On the other hand, free Whites of small means headed for the frontier to seek some patch of land. Free headrights were no longer generally available, but land was cheap and such persons were also often taken on as short-term tenants by proprietors opening up frontier estates.

This English population was thus extensively (but not rigidly) differentiated by status, but was relatively homogeneous in terms of other social fundamentals. Most persons were nominally Anglican but largely inactive (or, more accurately, unserved). There was a scattering of Quaker meetinghouses, but no major clusters of Nonconformists. However, Maryland Roman Catholics persisted as a recognizable group. Now numbering no more than a tenth of that colony's population, they were still mainly concentrated in the oldest southern districts, but they had also participated in the expansion of settlement and now had half a dozen churches in the upper Chesapeake. In 1741 a Jesuit Academy was opened near the head of the bay. But such formal facilities were not an adequate measure of extent and vitality. Roman Catholics still lived under severe legal restrictions and services were more commonly held in homes than in churches. The rich planters sent their children to schools in Europe, and through ties of kinship and neighborhood the group as a whole maintained a strong if quiet social identity.

In the early 1700s an important geopolitical change in Great Britain quickly brought a new people to these colonies. The Act of Union in 1707 removed prohibitions against Scottish firms in English colonial commerce and prompted so quick and thorough a penetration of the lucrative tobacco trade that a later Virginian historian, echoing the distress voiced by English interests of the time, referred to the "invasion and commercial domination of the colony by the Scots." Glasgow merchants initiated systems of stores at collection points run by resident agents (the English had worked mainly from ships on annual runs), and by the 1750s Lowland Scots were prominent in Norfolk and many smaller ports and had taken the lead in establishing stores to tap the inland country, as at Falmouth, Dumfries, and Alexandria. Thus there developed a strong link between the Chesapeake and the Clyde, giving a sudden spurt of prosperity and growth to Glasgow. However, it was very largely a commercial rather than a cultural tie across the seas. Most of the Scots who came to the Tidewater region were young males, salaried sojourners rather than family settlers. For the moment such persons made an ethnic distinction between these tiny prospective towns and the countryside they served, but they were not sufficiently numerous nor rooted to constitute a major cultural presence. Little clumps of Ulster Scots farm families in various districts and especially on the Eastern Shore of southern Maryland were more firmly implanted and had organized the first Scottish Presbyterian churches in North America. With the influx of large members of their countrymen to Pennsylvania, these Tidewater churches became affiliated with the synod of Philadelphia, another small addition to the ties developing between the major American metropolis and the Chesapeake.

In view of these general historical geographic features it is not inappropriate to think of this entire colonial region as "Greater Virginia." Certainly the dominating culture patterns derived from those that gradually and painfully took shape along the lower James River in the first decades of the seventeenth century. Maryland had been conceived as a distinctive scheme and of course remained as a separate jurisdiction, but its small Roman Catholic subsociety was the only enduring feature discordant with the Virginian mode. As a much smaller territory lying well behind the Atlantic threshold of Virginia, Maryland was widely regarded as essentially a commercial, cultural, and even political adjunct of the older, larger, and more famous colony. The Albemarle district was even more clearly so. The area lay within the limits of the early Virginia charter and its inclusion in a subsequent Carolina was long disputed and resented. It had been settled almost entirely from Virginia, by land seekers skirting the Great Dismal Swamp, moving down the Blackwater, or crossing the Nottoway into the lower Roanoke River country. Its commerce, originally dominated by traders from Bermuda or New England, had become largely tributary to Norfolk and the Nansemond, either along an expanding network of roads or by coastal vessels threading the dangerous passageways through the Outer Banks that oceanic captains were happy to avoid. Edenton was the local focus of this backwater area. It had served as the de facto capital for some years, but it was culturally and commercially more closely a part of Virginia than of the North Carolina now seated at New Bern.

Furthermore, by the 1750s the concept of a Greater Virginia can be given additional meaning, for the area under settlement was being rapidly extended along the many rivers reaching westward into the "uplands" or "middle country" (Piedmont). Thus *Tidewater* and *Chesapeake* were becoming less appropriate terms for this enlarging contiguous region.

Through destruction, pressure, or negotiation the entire area east of the Blue Ridge had years before been cleared of Indians, excepting only a few tiny pockets of families allowed to remain along the rivers and swamps of the Tidewater. In the 1740s the governments of Maryland and Virginia had gotten the formidable Iroquois Confederation to agree to avoid use of the Great Valley west of the Blue Ridge for hunting or traveling. With this accord, the colonies had secured a large elongated district that had been well explored and that governors, proprietors, and land speculators were eager to have settled. The northern half of the Shenandoah Valley lay within the western reaches of the huge Northern Neck Proprietary of Lord Fairfax. In 1753 "he took the extraordinary step of leaving England . . . and settled in the lower valley at Greenway Court near Winchester, thus becoming the only resident peer in the American colonies." Fairfax supervised the disposal of lands to Tidewater planters and thus the development of a strongly Virginian nucleus beyond the great ridge. Tidewater entrepreneurs also obtained a few large grants in the upper valley, farther south, and by 1755 several wagon roads connected these remote districts with the towns that were now developing along the fall line to serve this whole broadening western region. In all that frontier country, farming was rather more dependent upon grain and livestock, but wherever Virginians settled tobacco was the preferred money crop, slaves were used if they could be afforded, and the great plantation exemplified the rural ideal.

Although the Tidewater pattern was thereby being extended a hundred miles or more beyond the reach of ocean shipping, it was in this most remote inland district fully within their own political bounds that Virginians for the first time encountered streams of land seekers from another region. For while Virginians were moving westward through the gaps, considerably greater numbers of Pennsylvanians were moving southwesterly along the inland side of the Blue Ridge. This convergence was in no way a political or overt cultural challenge between these two major colonies. Indeed, in the interests of revenue and security against the Indians, Maryland and Virginian leaders had taken the initiative to attract settlers from Pennsylvania and other northern colonies into their western lands.

Thus in 1732 Calvert offered 200-acre farms to Pennsylvania German families who would settle in the area between the Susquehanna and the Patapsco. That started a trickle of immigration that soon swelled and spread into other areas. The Monocacy became a major entryway and by 1750 Frederick had emerged as the inland focus of a new western district, and Baltimore, founded in 1729, was its thriving port. Maryland's western realm was truncated by the northerly trend of its Potomac border, but it was sufficiently large and fertile that its colonization mainly by migrants from the north created a major cleavage in the province. In terms of cultural geography, Maryland was, broadly speaking, being transformed into half Pennsylvanian and half Virginian.

While this southward movement from Pennsylvania into Maryland can be seen as a not-uncommon kind of local discordance between political and cultural boundaries, a strong thrust out of Pennsylvania deep into the western reaches of Virginia was a more startling development. This, too, was by invitation, from a

Virginia governor who granted large blocks of land in the Shenandoah Valley to entrepreneurs from Pennsylvania and New Jersey, who then energetically peddled smaller parcels to settlers and lesser speculators from their own region. These promotions, plus the fact that northern Virginia east of the Blue Ridge was being settled from the Tidewater, served to channel this southward movement into the Great Valley and beyond Fairfax's Virginian outlier to the upper Shenandoah. In the early 1750s this migration was just beginning to gather force, but it was already the leading source of settlers in this long corridor. A straggle of more or less discrete German and Scotch-Irish districts had been implanted almost to Roanoke Gap, and some land seekers were moving through the gap and on south to inspect widely advertised lands in North Carolina.

Thus at mid-century two vigorous American colonies were beginning to expand much more deeply into the continent, so much so that they could no longer be accurately described simply as seaboard societies. Typical of British America, such geographic extensions were shaped more by the lineaments of nature than by the geometry of political territories, and thus Virginians following their rivers westward across the Piedmont and funneling through the few natural gaps in the Blue Ridge encountered Pennsylvanians moving in the trough of those great corrugations that curve on southwesterly from the very heart of their home region. Even without the specific lures offered by local governors, people from Pennsylvania would have followed these corridors of good lands. This southwesterly movement introduced new peoples into western Virginia, but it was as yet too slight to have created major cultural districts or internal sociopolitical tensions. Yet even though it was not a self-conscious cultural invasion, it was more than simply an inflow of settlers, for not only did these Germans, Scotch-Irish, English, and others from heterogeneous Pennsylvania—as a general group and as distinct peoples and sects—have many social and cultural differences from the people of Tidewater Virginia, but they were also, for the moment at least, firmly tied in all but political identity to Philadelphia. With this migration a road had been extended along the route of the great Indian path as far as the upper Shenandoah Valley. This Great Philadelphia Wagon Road became the main avenue of commerce as well as migration, and it bound these remote new districts of Pennsylvania settlement to the familiar facilities on the Delaware that offered a range of services far beyond the capacity of meager Tidewater ports. Thus in the larger patterns of culture and circulation Greater Pennsylvania had cast a long thin line across the whole breadth of the western frontier of Greater Virginia.

10. Tropical Islands

In the larger strategies of the time we can regard the English programs for planting in Virginia and Guiana as attempts to gain footholds on the continental flanks of

Spanish Tropical America. Their subsequent occupation of three small islands, Bermuda, St. Christopher, and Barbados, provided bases for a more direct penetration of the long archipelagic screen into the Spanish American seas. Before the end of the seventeenth century these three islands had become important to both seafaring and planting in several ways: as bases for plundering and illegal bartering forays into Spanish waters, as important nodes in the circumatlantic traffic system, as successful tropical plantations, and as source areas from which several other colonies were established. They became, in short, the primary nuclei of an English Tropical America. Furthermore, these English patterns were almost from the start complexly involved with analogous and at times fiercely competitive strategies of the French, for whom St. Christopher and Martinique served as St. Christopher and Barbados did for the English. And all these English and French planting enterprises became closely involved for several decades with the seafaring services of the Dutch, an involvement which would have major impact upon the islands and ramify widely upon European colonial positions in North America.

Bermuda is an anomaly in the Atlantic World: a solitary bit of land (actually a compact set of tiny coral limestone islands) in the midst of the Western Ocean, almost equidistant from the Grand Banks, Virginia, and Hispaniola. It was at first developed as an adjunct of Virginia. Colonization was initiated by a subsidiary of the Virginia Company, and tobacco became the agricultural staple, although many other crops were tried. Land was divided among a few major planters and worked by servants and tenants. The initial labor force was mainly English and Irish. A privateer peddled the first Africans, seized in the West Indies, in 1616, and later Indian and Scottish prisoners of war were also brought in. The legality of Black and Indian enslavement developed gradually, concurrent with Virginia. Freed Blacks and mulattos were supposed to leave the island, but the law was rarely rigidly enforced. In general there was a good deal of coming and going, and the population fluctuated often directly with developments elsewhere in the western Atlantic rim. Several thousand Europeans arrived during the first two decades, but in 1700 there were only about six thousand inhabitants in all, of whom about twenty-four hundred were Africans.

With severe limitations in local resources Bermudians turned increasingly to seafaring and to the development of other islands and coasts. Excellent small sloops, constructed from local cedar, became an important product, and Bermudians were widely involved as carriers of cargo in the developing Atlantic system. The island itself was a port of call on the most direct, although not most heavily trafficked, route between the Carolinas and Madeira, and its strategic importance was repeatedly enhanced by the recurrent naval wars with the Dutch and the French.

Early Bermudian leaders had close Puritan connections and the first colonization parties sent out from Bermuda were part of the wide-ranging ventures impelled by the politico-religious pressures in England. The first of these, initiated by a Bermuda Puritan proprietor, was an audacious and short-lived thrust deep into the Spanish seas in 1631 to implant a colony on Providence Island, within three hundred miles of the critical Panamanian nexus. The new colony was used mainly as a base for preying upon the Spanish, who seized the island in 1643 and expelled the survivors, most of whom went to Barbados.

A more fully Bermudian enterprise was that of the "Company of Eleutherian Adventurers," which established the Puritan colony of New Providence in the Bahamas in 1648. It was a small affair, the early settlers eking out a living from beachcombing, turtles, and timber. Gradually small plantations growing cotton, tobacco, and sugar were developed. But here, too, freebooting was a major attraction and brought retaliation from the Spanish. The settlements on New Providence were destroyed in 1684. The governor of Bermuda initiated a resettlement in 1691, laying out the town of Nassau as a fortified focus. But the Spanish sacked this also and for twenty years this broad Bahaman archipelago became the lair of pirates who raided the shipping of any nation. In 1718 the English government, working out of Bermuda, reestablished control at Nassau and organized the Bahamas as a separate crown colony. Gradually piracy was suppressed and plantations developed. By the 1740s the population was about thirteen hundred Whites and one thousand Blacks, the small total reflecting how little fertile land there was on these many islands. Most of these people lived in or near Nassau, whose position near the Florida Strait, the great sea-lane between Spain and her American colonies, was the primary reason for this repeated reassertion of an English presence.

Bermuda was taken out of company control and made a royal colony in 1684. Its Puritanism waned and St. George, the capital, began to take on much more substantial shape around the Anglican church and waterfront warehouses as the earlier wood, plaster, and palmetto-thatched makeshift houses were replaced by small-windowed, thick-walled, English-looking limestone structures. Tobacco faded in significance; the land was given over mainly to gardening to serve the local population; and the large estates were in the hands of families whose wealth was based upon commerce. Bermudians had wide-ranging connections, not only through commerce, but through the links with those who left, year after year, to seek opportunity beyond this crowded little isle. Bermudians had joined in the settling of Virginia, Jamaica, many of the Lesser Antilles, and Georgia, as well as the Bahamas. The population in 1749 was recorded as 5,290 Whites and 3,980 Blacks. The majority of the slaves were household servants or crew members of ships. It was also a place of seasonal resort for those seeking to escape the winters of New England or the miasmas of the tropics. Bermuda was, therefore, a significant point in the spatial systems of the Atlantic world. Had Bishop Berkeley been successful in his famous plan to establish on this benign isle an Anglican college to serve the sons of English planters and Indian converts, it might have become a strategic cultural center as well.

At the other end of the long, arcuate, insular screen of the tropical American seas northwest Europeans faced two formidable enemies, the Spanish and the Carib Indians. The former were based upon the big islands of Puerto Rico, Hispaniola, Jamaica, and Cuba; the latter were lodged in the jungly mountains of the Lesser Antilles. The English and the French made their first effective penetration by gaining control of St. Christopher and a cluster of small islands nearby, precisely intermediate of these strongholds. However, the choice of St. Christopher as the base for this development was local and opportunistic rather than the product of larger strategies. The English colony was initiated in 1624 by an entrepreneur who had spent some years trying to get some sort of project started in this general area. A small group of Frenchmen came the next year, attracted by the presence and prospects of the English. The leaders of the two groups agreed to apportion the island between them out of the need for mutual defense in so hazardous an area "at the entrance to Peru" (as the French charter described it). The dangers were real. The English and French banded together to exterminate or expel the Indians on the island and then had to fend against Carib retaliations for years thereafter. The Spanish destroyed the first settlements, and although they tried to maintain an uneasy local truce, the English and French on St. Christopher inevitably got caught up in the sequence of wide-ranging wars between their two countries and recurrently ravaged one another. As Dunn observed, "long years of warfare . . . taught the island planters to flee rather than fight, to accept frequent demolition of their property as a fact of life, and to lobby for compensation from the home authorities."

In fact, neither colony had extensive backing in funds or at court and so development was "a slow and turbulent process" as planters hacked out small tobacco-growing estates on the steep fringes of this little volcanic island. In both cases, labor was at first from indentured servants, in the one English and Irish, in the other, Norman and Breton. Black slaves taken from the Spanish were made available but were not in great demand during the early stages. The arable area was very small; consequently, even though development was slow, entrepreneurs were soon looking to nearby islands. Thus within a few years, the English had planted on Nevis, Montserrat, Antigua, and Barbuda, while the French had settled on St. Bartholomew, St. Martin (shared with the Dutch), and St. Croix. All of these were essentially extensions from the initial nuclei on St. Christopher, and each national set was placed under the authority of a governor seated, initially, on that island. However, such expansion had not been undertaken as part of a general program and the result for each country was not so much an enlarged colonial system as an array of quarrelsome, jealous little insular parts. Eventually these islands would become more clearly a part of a broader West Indian society and economy, even while retaining a degree of fierce individuality, but the model of that society and the basis of that economy were first developed on larger islands to the south.

Barbados was anomalous in important ways. It is not a volcanic mountain rising almost sheerly out of the sea but a limestone block mostly terraced into a succession of gentle slopes; it is not part of the closely spaced Windward chain but stands alone in the Atlantic a hundred miles to the east; and, when the English arrived, it was uninhabited. Colonization was undertaken simultaneously and competitively in 1627 by two speculative companies, one of which, after bitter disputes, gained control. Liberal land allocations and the prospect of rivaling Virginia in the lucrative tobacco trade attracted considerable investment and immigration to this benign island. However, tobacco proved disappointing in quality and planters experimented with many other crops, including sugar cane. They had learned something about cotton culture from Surinam Indians (and also perhaps from the well-developed Brazilian industry via Dutch traders) and cotton became the most important export. At first Barbadian society was not significantly different from that of St. Christopher—better financed and of more substantial growth but similarly reflective of a struggling planter economy based upon indentured labor from Ireland and England. Some Blacks captured from the Portuguese were part of the first settlement; life slavery was formalized in 1636, but despite a growth in numbers Black slaves were secondary to White servants for the first twenty years.

In the middle of the seventeenth century, however, Barbadian development took a rather sudden and decisive turn. Three quite independent events were important. First, a plague hit the island and killed several thousand Whites, planters and servants alike, causing the sale of many properties and an intense labor shortage, leading to the formation of larger estates and a sharpened demand for Black slaves. Second, a number of royalist families fled to Barbados to escape the severe political turbulence in England. Relatively wealthy and well connected, able to buy estates outright, such persons were immediately influential locally, and they enlarged commercial connections between the island and other parts of the Atlantic world. Third, at this same time the Portuguese succeeded in prying loose the Dutch from their brief but richly productive hold upon northeastern Brazil, and many of those ousted from their "New Holland" came to Barbados. Each of these events altered the structure and composition of Barbadian society; what bound them together with major effect was a single element: sugar.

When the Dutch captured Pernambuco in 1630 sugar had been the chief basis of Brazilian wealth for nearly a century and Brazilians had dominated the European market for decades. But the Dutch gave a new spurt to the industry, not so much in cultivation (relatively few became planters) as in financing and marketing. They brought in fresh capital to expand and improve production, moved in upon the transatlantic slave trade, enlarged and improved refineries in Amsterdam, and vigorously promoted the demand for high-grade sugar. All of this was part of the rapid rise of the Dutch in the European commercial world. Dutch agents resided in every port of consequence open to them, and Amsterdam was the main metropolis of the Atlantic trading system. In the West Indies, St. Eustatius, a tiny island adjacent to St. Christopher, became the chief focus of Dutch seafaring, and the English and French islands lay along the main routes between that busy entrepôt and major Dutch holdings in Guiana and Brazil. Having moved strongly in upon the Portuguese-African trade also, the Dutch became the chief marketers of slaves to all these American plantation areas.

Thus, the links between Barbados and Brazil suddenly became direct and close in the 1640s and the English, with Dutch help, quickly improved upon their struggling efforts to establish a sugar industry. The boom was in fact already under way before the Dutch were finally expelled from Brazil, and thus Barbados was much the most attractive refuge for those who sought to continue in the industry. With the addition of Dutch knowledge and skills, capital (especially in the form of credit) and equipment, and unparalleled commercial connections, Barbados underwent an explosive development to become the very archetype of the West Indian planter society and economy.

Dunn has given us a striking glimpse of the structure of that society as it was in 1680:

> Like the terraced cane fields of the island, Barbados society rose level by level, from the roughly 40,000 slaves occupying the lowest tier to the 2,300 servants at the next tier, ascending past the 1,300 freemen, the 1,000 small planters, the 400 Bridgetown householders, and the 190 middling planters, to the 175 big planters at the summit who held the best land, sold the most sugar, and monopolized the best offices. In only one generation these planters had turned their small island into an amazingly effective sugar-producing machine and had built a social structure to rival the tradition-encrusted hierarchy of old England.

This sudden growth had made this little island the richest (with exports more valuable than the total from North America), most populous, and most congested (c. 50,000 on 166 square miles) colony in English America. It was also the most fully domesticated landscape, completely apportioned into farms, all but the cliffs and ravines under cultivation. The average estate was rather small (rich planters usually owned several) and the rural population was thickly distributed. The wealthier planters now lived in substantial houses, adjacent to makeshift clusters of storehouses, sheds, and shelters for servants and slaves, but the most striking landscape feature was the great windmills, used to grind much of the cane, sym-

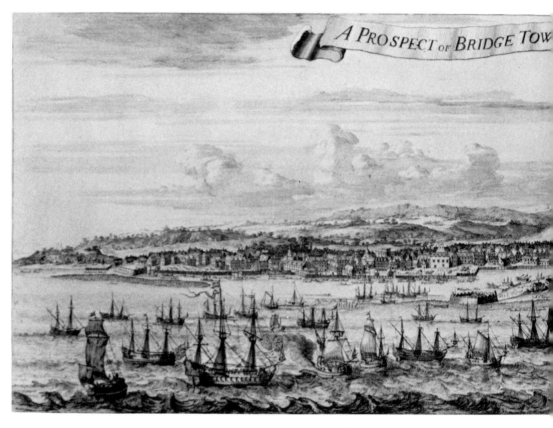

32. Prospect of Bridge Town in Barbados, 1695.
Carl Bridenbaugh has called this sketch, prepared from the deck of a ship by Samuel Copen
and engraved in London by Johannes Kip, "the finest and most accurate seventeenth-
century view of an English seaport in the New World." He also emphasizes the strong
Dutch influence on this flourishing English port, noting the architecture of the great

bolic of the creative Dutch impact. By 1680 the Anglo-Dutch wars had crippled
the Dutch mastery of Atlantic commerce but their mark was imprinted upon the
landscape and society of Bridgetown, the capital and chief port, in the stepped and
ogive gables and red-tile roofs, and in the tight little cluster of Sephardic Jews
(Marranos expelled from Brazil) around Synagogue Street. However, the Dutch
themselves who had remained rather quickly merged into the upper reaches of
Anglican society.

Yet, as Dunn has further observed, Barbados was a paradox, the richest but "in
human terms the least successful colony in English America":

> By crowding so many black and white laborers onto a few square miles they [the
> planters] had aggravated health hazards and overtaxed the food supply, condemning
> most inhabitants of the island to a semi-starvation diet. Those who had money
> squandered it by overdressing, overeating, and overdrinking and by living in ornate

warehouses lining the waterfront as well as the twenty or more windmills. Having suffered heavily from fires (1668, 1673) and a hurricane (1675), the town had been largely rebuilt, and the Dutch had provided much of the capital and leadership in these reconstructions. (Courtesy of the John Carter Brown Library at Brown University)

English-style houses unsuited to the climate. Even the rich were unhappy in Barbados, for they suffered from claustrophobia, heat, and tropical fevers and longed for the dank, chill weather they were used to at home. Most of all they hated and feared the hordes of restive black captives they had surrounded themselves with. The mark of a successful Barbados planter was his ability to escape from the island and retire grandly to England.

Only a few could escape in such fashion but a great many escaped in other fashions and other directions. Some fled the tropics to northern American colonies, following commercial and social links to Newport, Providence, Boston, or New York, or purchasing estates on Narragansett Bay, in the Hudson Valley, or Tidewater Virginia. But a far greater number and variety—aspiring planters of some means, young males of little property, White servants who had completed their term of indenture—looked to other tropical islands where it was hoped that the sensational economic success of Barbados might be repeated. Thus this little

island became a major source of colonists for plantation undertakings (not all of
which were sustained) on many other islands and coasts: Guiana, Trinidad, Tobago, St. Lucia, Jamaica, Carolina. Those who had the means usually took some
slaves with them, but this exodus was mainly of Whites and it was sufficiently large
to be a cause in the decline in the White population. By the 1750s there were about
75,000 people on Barbados but only about twenty percent of these were Whites,
and their number had declined by nearly a third since the 1670s.

The success of the Barbadian sugar industry quickly reverberated to St.
Christopher and its insular environs and transformed these colonies in similar
ways. By the 1750s these small islands were as densely settled as their mountainous
character allowed and parceled into sugar estates worked chiefly by slaves. St.
Christopher, Antigua, Nevis, and Montserrat had a total population about equal
to that of Barbados, and nearly nine out of ten were of African rather than
European origin.

Furthermore, just as the French had closely followed the English in the initiation of West Indian planting on St. Christopher, so also their developments on the
larger Windward Islands were basically similar to and influenced by that of the
English on Barbados. French efforts here were focused upon the two largest of the
chain, Guadeloupe and Martinique. Although undertaken in the same year, 1635,
these were separate and rather different operations, the colonization of the first
being directly from France and that of the second from St. Christopher. Both
colonies faced severe resistance from the Caribs, but Martinique, led and peopled
by experienced personnel, got a more substantial start and was soon modestly
prosperous from tobacco. Sugar growing was tried but the industry developed
slowly until the 1650s when a considerable number of wealthy Dutch planters and
merchants came in from Brazil with their slaves and milling equipment. From this
impetus the two islands developed into a West Indian planter society and economy
broadly similar to that on Barbados, although far less populous and intensive. By
the 1680s the two islands had about 30,000 people, of whom about seventy percent
were Blacks. Martinique emerged as the principal focus of the French West Indies:
it was the seat of the government (shifted from St. Christopher), the religious
orders, and the wealthiest and most influential families, and it was the principal
base from which footholds were attempted on a number of other shores.

This broad analogy and sequence in development between the English and the
French continued in their westward outreach from the Lesser into the Greater
Antilles. Again the English took the lead, this time in 1655 with Cromwell's grand
strategy to oust the Spanish from major islands. They struck first at Hispaniola but,
failing to capture Santo Domingo, sailed on to Jamaica where the thin and feeble
Spanish presence was soon effaced by the large English force of soldiers and
colonists. Despite immense difficulties and high mortality, Jamaican prospects
attracted large numbers of people, chiefly from Barbados, but also from Nevis,

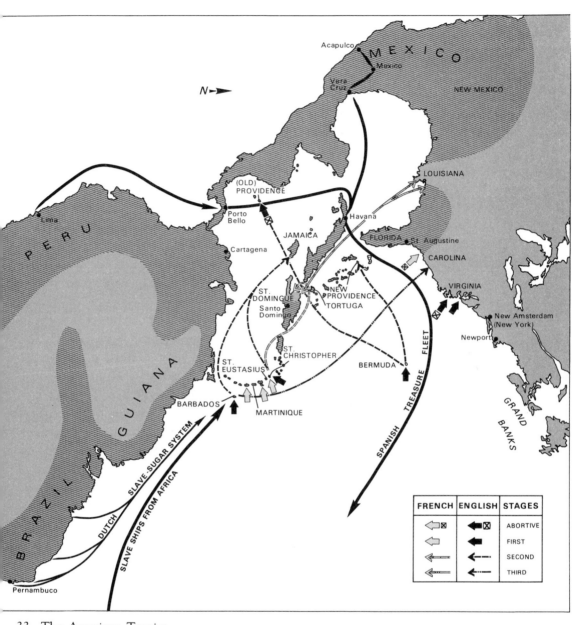

FRENCH	ENGLISH	STAGES
◁☒	◀☒	ABORTIVE
◁	◀	FIRST
⇐	◀──	SECOND
⇐	◀─·─	THIRD

33. The American Tropics.

The parallelism in the French and English penetration of these Spanish seas can be traced from their abortive colonizations in Florida and Roanoke, their successful footholds in the Lesser Antilles, conquest of important islands in the Greater Antilles, and eventually firm footholds in Louisiana and South Carolina.

Surinam, and Bermuda, as well as from England and Ireland, and within a generation it was emerging as a major sugar producer. The economy was in fact based jointly upon planting and plundering.

English buccaneers had been invited to join in this national thrust against the

Spanish, and thus Port Royal, perched at the end of a long spit sheltering the best harbor, was not only the commercial focus of the planter economy, but also the great seat of privateers who, with at least tacit official approval, continued to ravage the Spanish seas and coasts. This place and practice were abruptly altered, however, in 1692 when a great earthquake plunged the town into the sea with large loss of life. Kingston was laid out as a replacement, but changing international political conditions encouraged a suppression of piracy and the new town was never quite as lively a center. Jamaica was a large but difficult area. The mountainous interior harbored several thousand Maroons ("Cimarrones"), a population derived chiefly from escaped slaves and African-Indian mixtures, who resisted English authority and posed a chronic threat to lowland settlers. Thus the plantation population of this large island did not equal that of Barbados until well into the eighteenth century, but Jamaica clearly displayed a Barbadian form of economy and society from the outset.

The English success in Jamaica had a direct influence upon the French. In the 1660s Colbert, like Cromwell, wanted to seize a major Spanish island as part of his program for rationalizing the French imperial economy. The first step was to establish French authority over the tumultuous pirates' lair on Tortuga, a small island just off the northwest coast of St. Domingue (the French name for Hispaniola). This task was made somewhat easier by the fact that many of these buccaneers were French, as most of their English associates had been lured to Jamaica. The local French governor then laid out a new capital, Port au Paix, just across the narrow channel on St. Domingue and began the systematic colonization of coastal lowlands. An attractive area east of Cap Français (Cap Haitian) was the first to be settled, and footholds were soon established at several localities along the west coast. Colonists were lured from St. Christopher, Martinique, and France by the excellent prospects for tobacco, cocao, cotton, and sugar. All of the buccaneers were eventually removed from Tortuga, but, as in Jamaica, they remained "privileged gangsters" and launched audacious attacks against the Spanish from St. Domingue ports. In 1697 a gravely weakened Spain formally ceded the western portion of Hispaniola to its de facto rulers. With this France began to suppress the buccaneers, and the development of St. Domingue as a great tropical plantation was given new impetus. In 1714 it was made a separate colony (it had been under the governor at Martinique), and a new capital was established at Leogane. A boom in coffee and sugar was attracting much investment and immigration from France, including a good many wealthy and influential families, and St. Domingue was well on the way to becoming the key holding of the French in America, the base for even grander strategies of political and economic development. By the 1750s the population was nearly 200,000, a new capital had been laid out at Port-au-Prince, and St. Domingue, like Barbados, had become one of the greatest exhibits of a West Indian planter society.

St. Domingue and Barbados were distinctive national versions of a single social type. They were similar in general structure and proportions: a tiny White oligarchy and small White layers of petty bourgeois, impoverished freedmen, and bondsmen all resting upon a huge Black base. And there was much similarity in the style of life of their ruling elites: a peculiar compound of imitation and adaptation, civilized tastes and colonial crudities, elegance and extravagance, formality and licentiousness. But they were not quite the same in critical aspects of race relations. Such differences are reflected in the contrasts between the Barbados slave code of 1660 and the Code Noir of 1685, which, given the lag in French West Indian developments, are directly contemporary in stage. The contrasts were deeply national: the former a local, empirical compilation arising from the practical problems of English masters learning how to control a captive alien labor force—a common law creation; the latter a magisterial decree from the king arising from the need to define the basic human rights of slaves in order to curb abusive practices of their French masters. Of course one must not assume that stark differences in treatment actually flowed from these pronouncements. In both cases slaves were the property of their owners; their debasement was fundamental and cruelty was endemic. But there were important cumulative differences. For the English (and Dutch), slavery was an economic system, a means of wresting profits from the earth; the Barbados code defined the slave as a chattel, a species of property and a defective creature never to be prepared for full Christian citizenship. For the French (as for the Portuguese and Spanish), slavery was a social as well as an economic system, a means for the slave-owner to achieve high status within a regional community. The Code Noir insisted on the basic humanity of the slave: each was to be instructed, baptized, and ministered unto as a Christian, families were to be recognized, and freed slaves were to receive the rights of common citizens—in theory an African could aspire to become a Frenchman. French racial attitudes were softer and were subtle, and the results showed in acculturation, miscegenation, and manumission: in a burgeoning Afro-Catholicism with its syncretic rituals and festivals, in the large numbers of mulattos and the common social recognition of many degrees of color, in the free Black planters served by their own Black servants and slaves, in the more open and intimate daily life of a vigorous creole society. Barbados was also a creole society, but less complex and flexible, more rigidly cast into a stark biracial structure whose rulers longed to leave rather than to settle in as the patriarchs of a colonial community.

In either case, of fundamental importance was the fact that because of Black slavery these American colonies had become in many ways more African than European, not just in numbers of people (eight or nine times the number of Whites) but in basic elements of culture. For even though Black slaves had been wrenched from African societies, subjected to the trauma of transatlantic shipment, and scattered to labor under European masters on a dozen West Indian

Islands, they were not shorn of African culture nor entirely severed from African contact. There were, despite severe losses and impoverishments, strong continuities in foods and shelter, tools and techniques, language, music, dance and artistic motifs, religious practices, family patterns, and community activities. Every shipload of new slaves from Africa reinforced those continuities. Thus the wooden and thatched huts and garden plots of the slave quarters and the vibrant bartering, socializing, and celebrating by the Blacks among themselves on Sundays, holidays, and evenings were, in the long run, more powerful and pervasive evidences of the cultural transformation of the West Indies than were the manor houses and windmills, wharves and warehouses of their European masters. Furthermore, despite the basic dehumanization from the institution of slavery and despite often-crippling local distortions, the Africans were on the whole a more vigorous population than the Europeans. They had a better demographic structure in terms of sex ratio and age groups; without the freedom to search for opportunity elsewhere, they were more stable and rooted in place; they were more resistant to numerous tropical diseases and afflictions; and it can be inferred, if never proved, that the peculiar workings of the slave procurement and marketing system that, following long-standing African practice, tried to seize the elites of enemy tribes and obtained the best prices for the most physically fit, brought to the Americas a rather better-selected stock. Bridenbaugh asserts that African slaves "represented a choice of human beings that was superior to the selection of white Europeans who were sent to the West Indies. From a social point of view, it may be said that in the English West Indian colonies, a body of inferior whites was supplanted by a much more numerous and superior body of blacks from West Africa." If true, it was one of the deeper ironies of the slave system.

Thus the English and the French broke in upon the Spanish seas, created sets of rich colonies, added important nodes and links to the Atlantic system, and became heavily involved in the implantation of Africans in America. They began by occupying or seizing some of the smallest and most accessible islands, then thrust westward in upon some of the largest. Having secured holds upon Jamaica and St. Domingue they began to look to the mainland. While seafarers, lured by the centers of Spanish commerce, sacked Havana, Cartagena, Porto Bello, and Vera Cruz, other strategists looked to the margins of Spanish settlement to see what coastlands might be appropriated and planted. Thus, these island societies became springboards and cultural sources for colonization of the North American subtropics.

11. Carolina and the Carolinas

The long coastline curving southwesterly from Virginia to Florida was the scene of the earliest attempts by the Spanish, French, and English to plant colonies on the

Atlantic mainland of America. In each case the failure of these sixteenth-century undertakings could be attributed to inexperienced man rather than to inhospitable nature. Thus in the next century, as the success of the English plantings along the James and of their intrusions in the West Indies became manifest, this long unoccupied subtropical strand again became a focus of attention.

The entire area was imprinted with a name when Charles I granted all the land between 31° and 36° latitude to Sir Robert Heath in 1629. Heath's plan for his new "Carolana" had an old, and melancholy, ring to it: it was to be a colony for French Protestants who had flooded into England in the wake of their most recent disaster, the fall of La Rochelle—a distant echo of America as a Huguenot refuge first tried on this very coast seventy years before. Advance agents conducted a reconnaissance and came to Virginia to obtain supplies and workers but the enterprise disintegrated at the English end, and no colony was implanted by Heath or his successors. All was dormant until the Restoration, when a second Charles granted a "Carolina" of the same dimensions to a group of eight proprietors in 1663, a charter which was soon redefined to include an even broader swath (29° to 36°30′). These Carolina promoters included men of wealth, influence, and experience, with an avid interest in colonial speculations. Within a few years several of them would become variously involved in the Royal African Company, the Hudson's Bay Company, New Jersey, and the Bahamas. Their plan for Carolina was first of all to lure experienced settlers from other colonies; they sent invitations to Barbados, Bermuda, Virginia, and New England and soon had responses.

Interest in this long segment of coast focused more upon the attractive series of tidal-scoured estuaries to the south rather than upon the large bays of the north that were shielded by long and dangerous outer banks. The first party to arrive was a group of Massachusetts Bay Puritans who came to the Cape Fear River, the northernmost of these estuaries, but they were soon disheartened with the area and returned home. However, the leader of their exploring party went on to Barbados and helped convince a group of planters there of the excellent opportunities in Carolina. Thus in 1664 a party of about eight hundred colonists from Barbados arrived in the lower Cape Fear valley and began to lay out plantations in the hope, based on the latitudinal climatic reasoning of the day, of producing such Mediterranean commodities as wine, olive oil, and citrus. But the enterprise was quickly debilitated by internal factions and difficulties with the Indians on top of the usual hazards of planting, and after three years the colony was abandoned, many of the settlers moving on to Virginia. However, there were some Carolina proprietors and Barbadians who were ready to learn from such experience, and within two years a much more elaborate program for colonization was initiated, drawing upon leaders, settlers, and resources from both England and Barbados. The intended site was Port Royal, a well-known capacious anchorage, but after landing there they were persuaded by local Cusabo Indians to shift to another estuary sixty miles up the coast. Here, in 1670, they laid out Charles Town and began the search for attractive lands and immediate resources.

This colonization was ostensibly undertaken within the framework of the Fundamental Constitutions of Carolina, a detailed program for the creation of a manorial system and landed aristocracy on American ground. Two-fifths of the land was to be laid out in 12,000-acre baronies and allocated to two levels of local nobility, the rest to be in colonies of similar size but subdivided into small units for freemen and tenants. A hierarchical social structure, including a category for serfs and an oligarchical political system, was also defined. But here as elsewhere there was a marked difference between the plan and the performance. That difference arose not only from the usual exigencies of actual colonization but from the contrasting ideas and motivations of the proprietors resident in England and the Barbadian entrepreneurs who shaped the actual substance.

Carolina was essentially "the colony of a colony," primarily an offspring of Barbados, a reaching out from the constrictions of that congested little island to the expansive possibilities of the continent. Although settlers came in from a number of sources, the largest and much the most influential body came directly from that richest of English colonies, and they drew upon that successful experience in the hope of generating the same kind of sudden wealth on an even larger scale. They went about the business of colonization in their own way, disdainful of inexperienced agents, paper programs, and directives sent out from England, and they repeatedly forced the proprietors to modify their plans in the interests of profits and peace. Thus only a few baronies were even surveyed, few of these were ever occupied, and no real manorial system was established because there was not the capital, the economy, nor the right kinds of colonists to create such things. Instead, aspiring planters made use of an expedient system of headright grants to carve out estates of a manageable size with the expectation of working them with slaves. The proprietors had ordered settlement to be in the form of towns to avoid the "Inconvenience and Barbarisme of scattered Dwellings" (the "Chiefe thing that hath given New England soe much advantage over Virginia"), but settlers, seeing no such advantage, sought out the best lands wherever they might be found along the inlets and creeks between the Edisto and the Santee, and Charles Town emerged as the only town. All the affairs of the colony were permeated by this kind of discordance. The proprietors formally affirmed religious toleration; the Barbadian leaders sought local domination through an established Anglican church. The proprietors frowned on the use of or trade in Indian slaves; colonial entrepreneurs found this to be an immediate source of profit. Yet, in a broad sense, they agreed on the fundamental idea of a strongly hierarchical social and political system featuring a small landed gentry and a large subordinate body of laborers. Carolina had that from the very beginning, but it was derived far more from the living example of Barbados than from the theoretical model of the Fundamental Constitutions.

The Barbadian leadership in Carolina became known as the Goose Creek men, from the main district of their concentration just inland from Charles Town. Energetic efforts by the English proprietors to populate and secure their new colony soon resulted in other districts dominated more or less by a religious or ethnic group, such as that of English Dissenters west of the Edisto, French Huguenots on the Santee, and Presbyterian Scots at Port Royal. This active recruitment of Nonconformists heightened religious contention in the colony, which, ironically, led to the establishment of the Church of England and the division of the countryside into parishes ruled by local vestries.

Despite the commitment both of proprietors and Barbadians in the initial undertaking, Carolina developed very slowly. It was an area of certain dangers (the Spanish destroyed the Port Royal Scottish colony two years after its founding) and uncertain riches. Sugar, citrus, cotton, tobacco, and numerous other crops were tried but with indifferent results. There were great hopes that French colonists would show the way with their special skills ("he perfectly understands Silke, wine and [olive] oyle," wrote the proprietors of one man they had eagerly recruited), but little came from these either. For thirty years there was no agricultural staple. Planters survived chiefly on the production of lumber and naval stores, cattle and hogs, mostly to serve the needs of bare and crowded Barbados. The most valuable commodities came from the Indian trade, especially deerskins and Indian slaves. The establishment of South Carolina created an alternative market for the Indian trade, intruding upon that of the Virginia traders handled through the Occaneechee entrepôt on the Roanoke and that oriented to various posts in Spanish Florida. As such trade drew upon a huge hinterland by means of Indian intermediaries, this new outlet disrupted established patterns and intensified often-bitter rivalries among Indian groups. After an initial battle with them, the Carolina traders began to work through the Westos, an aggressive, well-armed Iroquoian enclave who readily preyed upon their neighbors. The Barbadians routinely accepted slavery as a normal and profitable business, and thus, as Nash states, "by the early 1670s slave coffles were marching through the Carolina backcountry to the coast as much as they were filing through the African interior to the trading posts on the African coast. Once in Charleston, they were transferred to ship for the 'middle passage' to other colonies." Most were shipped to the West Indies, but some were sent north, and many remained in Carolina.

In the first decade of the seventeenth century, however, a new crop wonderfully well suited to those swampy river-laced Carolina lowlands was being rapidly developed as a staple export. The beginnings of rice culture in Carolina are obscure and controversial. It is certain that rice was tried very early and that seed from several sources was brought in at various times. But the growing of rice in flooded fields is a complicated process that would have been unfamiliar to British immigrants either from Europe or the West Indies. Wood has put forth the most plausible argument: the critical element was the knowledge of Black slaves from the lowlands of westernmost Africa where rice was a basic crop. The early methods and tools used in Carolina are congruent with those in Africa, and the development period coincides with the time when the number of Blacks became equal to the number of Whites.

In fact, in no other American colony were Europeans, Africans, and Indians so equally and intricately involved during the critical experimental period of working out ways of living in a new plantation region. Nor was this vital process simply an encounter among three peoples. There were Europeans from several sources, especially England, Ireland, and France, as well as Whites with years of experience in the West Indies, local Indians, Indian slaves from various inland tribes, and Blacks from many parts of Africa, some of whom had spent some seasons or years in the American tropics. In the structure of colonial society and polity these peoples were differentiated into categories of occupation, status, privilege, and wealth; in the daily realities of colonial living and the development of a regional economy they perforce worked intimately together. Thus in major commercial activities, such as forestry, livestock raising, and rice production, as well as in the folkways associated with the production and use of foods, medicinals, basketry, shelter, tools, boats, and myriad other things, colonial Carolina drew quite directly upon the cultural traditions of several peoples from three continents. In many cases the European influence may have been the least important. Thus, this small foothold in the southerly subtropics of North America was a distinctive and significant culture hearth.

Rice is an intensive crop that requires special facilities for water control. Once these were established production could continue in the same fields for many years. Thus, unlike the tobacco colonies on the Chesapeake, expansion was neither rapid nor seemingly limitless in extent, nor was there the need for a recurrent shifting from old fields to fresh ground within each plantation. Lands along the Ashley, Cooper, and Wando river systems immediately back of Charles Town and those along the lower Santee and Edisto provided ample ground for the development of a very productive district within a relatively compact area, with possibilities for extension along the coast in either direction. Lacking the long deep estuaries of Virginia, planters and traders made use of boats and pirogues on the intricate pattern of shallow creeks, swamps, and inlets to bring all into focus upon Charles Town. Relocated a short distance from its original site to a commanding position at the point of the peninsula between the Ashley and Cooper, Charles Town was the only urban and commercial center. Despite the organization of the countryside into parishes, it was essentially the only political and social center also. There were few churches and hardly the semblance of a village elsewhere despite various plans and attempts. A census of 1708 counted 4,080 Whites, 4,100 Blacks, and 1,400 Indian slaves in the entire colony, and evidence indicates that the number of Black slaves was rapidly increasing as the success of rice became apparent.

The development and expansion of this promising nucleus was abruptly halted in 1715 when the Yamasee Indians, living immediately adjacent to the west, reacted to chronic grievances against Carolina traders and attacked plantations in the Port Royal area. Other Indian tribes joined in and, combined with the ever-present threat from the Spanish, threw the entire colony into desperate measures of counterattack. The Indians were finally expelled beyond the Savannah and an uneasy peace established.

This apparently inevitable interdependence of planting and conquering was made clear in the other parts of Carolina during this same time. The proprietors of Carolina showed little interest in the northern half of their long segment of coast. The Albemarle district developed slowly by infiltration from Virginia. In 1691 the governor at Charles Town appointed a deputy for that remote corner, but it remained virtually without public authority. The first settlement south of Albemarle Sound was made by a few French Huguenots from Virginia (remnants of an ill-conceived English scheme originally intending to plant them on the Florida gulf coast) who came to the lower Pamlico River, where the town of Bath was laid out as their seat in 1704. In 1710 a much more formal and ambitious program was initiated along the lower Neuse by a Swiss Protestant entrepreneur who founded New Bern as the nucleus for a large refugee colony. Both of these plantings were encroachments upon the lands of the Tuscarora Indians, and they added to such a long accumulation of Indian grievances held against White traders that the New Bern colony had hardly begun when it was very nearly destroyed by Indian attack. With the help of expeditions from Virginia and southern Carolina the Tuscaroras were finally defeated with heavy losses; they withdrew from the region completely, migrating north to join their Iroquois brethren. But even though this altered the context for planting, the ravages of the war had been so severe and the prospects for development remained so problematical that these lands behind the great Carolina Banks remained a backwater for many years.

There were important political legacies of these events. In 1712 the Carolina proprietors formally divided their holdings, creating a North Carolina under a separate governor. The boundary was set approximately midway in their coastal segment between Virginia and the Savannah River (the de facto frontier with Spanish Florida), and well away from any European settled districts. A few years later, in the aftermath of the Yamasee War, the South Carolinians became so exasperated with the disinterest and ineffectiveness of their distant proprietors that they rebelled and succeeded in persuading the Crown to assume control. Thus the two parts of Carolina, unlike and unrelated as colonial developments, were given distinct formal identities.

Within a few years, however, colonizations along the empty coastal border zone imposed a cultural blurring of this clear geopolitical separation. Planters searching for new opportunities began to range beyond the Santee to Winyah Bay and its attractive tributaries and soon on to the next large estuary of the Cape Fear River. These were folk migrations rather than formal settlement schemes, a movement of individuals and families together with their servants and slaves, a mixture of Anglicans, Huguenots, various Dissenters, and Africans directly out of older districts. Georgetown was established as the port for Winyah Bay, Brunswick and New Liverpool (Wilmington) for the Cape Fear. Although one attraction of the latter district was its location beyond the political jurisdiction of South Carolina, which meant that its shipments did not have to pay duties at Charles Town, it was entirely a creation from South Carolina and in every other way bound to Charles Town. At this same time, Beaufort arose as a similar outport west of Charles Town, serving the steadily developing hinterland of Port Royal.

The 1730s mark a new era. By then the Crown had bought out the proprietors and made both South and North Carolina royal colonies. In South Carolina, especially, a major new geographic strategy was undertaken by royal governors. The population of South Carolina was estimated at this time to be about 30,000, of whom 20,000 were Blacks. That was a total, a ratio, and an indication of a trend that caused a good deal of concern. Colonial leaders began to be haunted by the specter of Barbados. With the rapid increase in slave imports to serve the now-flourishing rice economy, the child was beginning to resemble the parent all too closely. In the rice districts Blacks far outnumbered Whites and the insecurity of the planters, scattered thinly through an area bordered by a vast wilderness into which slaves could escape and from which Indian and Spanish connivance and raids were ever feared, was greater than on the tight little West Indian island. Since slaves were considered essential to the economy there was little support for curbing imports. The alternative was to foster a much larger immigration of Whites and settle them in such a pattern as to augment the security as well as the economy of the colony. Attempts to diversify the labor force by requiring planters to employ White indentured servants in some specific ratio with Blacks or with acreages had little effect, but the old colonial expedient of luring settlers with liberal land allotments did.

The first large program, a 1730 "Scheem . . . for Settling Townships," aimed at establishing blocks of farmer-colonists at strategic locations in the "backcountry" across the entire width of South Carolina. The purpose was to secure the colony

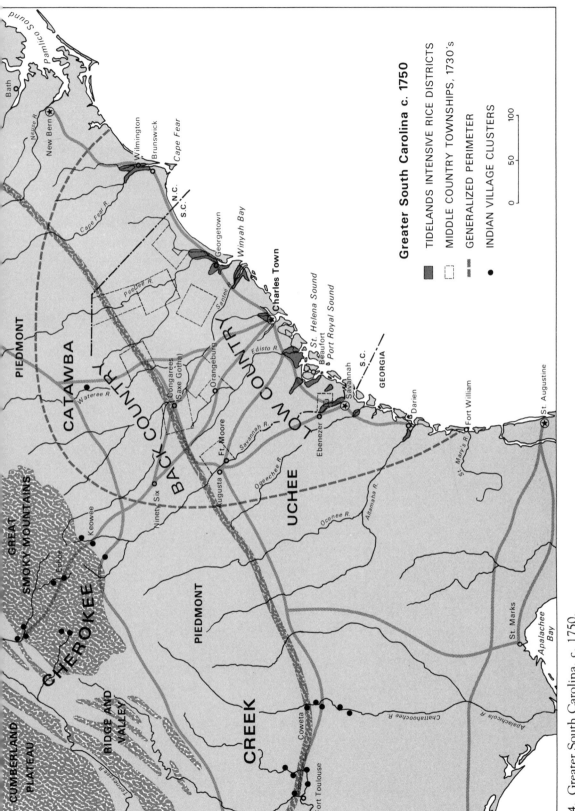

34. Greater South Carolina, c. 1750.

Greater South Carolina c. 1750

- ▨ TIDELANDS INTENSIVE RICE DISTRICTS
- ⬜ MIDDLE COUNTRY TOWNSHIPS, 1730's
- ╍ GENERALIZED PERIMETER
- • INDIAN VILLAGE CLUSTERS

0   50   100

PIEDMONT

CATAWBA

INDIAN COUNTRY

BACK COUNTRY

LOW COUNTRY

UCHEE

GREAT SMOKY MOUNTAINS

CHEROKEE

RIDGE AND VALLEY

CUMBERLAND PLATEAU

PIEDMONT

CREEK

GEORGIA

S.C.

S.C.
N.C.

Pamlico Sound

Bath

New Bern
Neuse R.

Wilmington
Brunswick
Cape Fear
Cape Fear R.

Georgetown
Winyah Bay
PeeDee R.

Santee R.

Charles Town

St. Helena Sound
Beaufort
Port Royal Sound

Edisto R.

Orangeburg
Congarees (Saxe Gotha)

Savannah

Ebenezer

Wateree R.

Keowee
Keowee

Estoe

Ninety Six

Ft. Moore
Augusta

Savannah R.

Ogeechee R.

Oconee R.

Altamaha R.

Darien

Fort William

St. Mary's R.

St. Augustine

St. Marks

Apalachee Bay

Apalachicola R.

Chattahoochee R.

Coweta

Fort Toulouse

Tennessee R.

against Indian raids, implant nuclei from which the interior could be settled, and create a band of dominantly White settlement around the heavily Black "low-country." Over the next decade or so ten such settlement clusters were created, and if the results fell short of the plan, they nevertheless significantly altered the geography of the colony and achieved some measure of the intent.

European Protestants were sought as the most available and reliable colonists. Settlers were offered free passage, supplies and tools, a town lot and a farm lot within a surveyed township. Through various agents, several thousand were attracted. The western townships, along the Savannah River and the Cherokee Trails northwest of Charles Town, were initiated mainly with French Swiss and German Swiss; the eastern ones, north of Charles Town and Georgetown, mainly with British Dissenters: Ulster Scots, Welsh (some from Pennsylvania), and Irish Quakers. In all, and especially in the eastern blocks, there was soon an infiltration of Anglicans, Dissenters, and Huguenots from the Low Country. But there was no great surge into the Carolina interior because it had two serious drawbacks: most of it lay beyond the easy reach of vessels from the coast, and much of it offered poor land for farming. These were patches and strips of rich soil but much larger tracts of "pine barrens," a scrubby growth on a sandy soil. There was little hope, therefore, of extending rice culture into most of it. The Europeans were encouraged to attempt many other intensive crops but few succeeded, and thus most of the colonists had to make a living from corn, cattle, hogs, and various forest products. What was in effect if not in plan a continuation of this township scheme was the colony of Scottish Highlanders on a cluster of grants along the upper Cape Fear River in North Carolina. Initiated by a few hundred about 1739, this Gaelic Presbyterian nucleus would attract several thousand more over the next two or three decades.

A more significant and distinctive extension of this general frontier strategy was applied to the long and dangerous border country beyond the Savannah River. In 1732 the king granted to James Oglethorpe and associates that portion of old Carolina lying between the Savannah and Altamaha rivers. Several distinct interests converged in support of their scheme for the colony of Georgia. Although several investors and officials were probably more attracted by the economic possibilities of lands adjacent to now-prospering South Carolina, Oglethorpe and some of his fellow trustees were strongly motivated by a humanitarian desire to create a place of refuge for various unfortunates who had been caught in an archaic penal system or who suffered religious persecution. With such persons as the main body of settlers, they hoped to foster by careful design a more ideal society devoid of gross differences in wealth and privilege. The Crown was especially interested in creating a much more substantial presence on the borders of Spanish Florida and powerful Indian nations. Furthermore, the prospect of such a buffer was so wel-

come to South Carolinians that they raised no immediate protest at the detachment of this considerable segment of the original Carolina. Actually the Carolina
proprietors had created a precedent in their grant of this same parcel to Sir Robert
Mountgomery in 1717, who, failing to implement his elaborate plan for the
Margravate of Azilia, soon forfeited his rights. Carolina settlers had never established a firm foothold in the area.

Georgia was begun with strong public and official support under conscientious
and resourceful leadership. Oglethorpe, an experienced military commander,
brought over the first contingent of colonists. In consultation with the Indians (a
renegade Creek band), he selected the site for his elaborately designed capital
town on a bluff ten miles up the Savannah, agreed to reserve some coastal tracts for
seasonal use by the Indians, and supervised the initiation of settlement. Later he
set up a series of forts to guard the main estuaries along the southern approaches
and, after negotiating treaties with the Lower Creeks, established the garrisoned
outpost of Augusta far up the Savannah as an advance base to tap the Indian trade.
A group of Scottish Highlander soldier-colonists was sent to Darien (New Inver-
ness) on the Altamaha frontier, but virtually all the other settlers were directed to
lands in the narrow district between the lower Savannah and Ogeechee rivers
within easy reach of Savannah city. The trustees subsidized the emigration of
about twenty-five hundred people within the first ten years and others came at
their own expense. Of the former about a third were non-British, including a group
of Moravians, a cohesive body of Salzburgers (Austrian Lutherans) who developed
the colony of Ebenezer, and about forty Sephardic Jews who needed special dispen-
sation to be allowed in the colony.

Georgia was designed to be primarily a colony of small landholders supporting
themselves by intensive agriculture and associated industries. Settlement was to be
compact, on carefully surveyed village and farm tracts. Land accumulation was to
be limited, its inheritance carefully controlled; ultimate title remained with the
trustees in order to insure compliance. Slavery was prohibited; it was morally
abhorrent to some of the leaders, and considered dangerous and deleterious to
industrious habits by others. The Indian trade was to be closely regulated by
license, and the importation, manufacture, or use of rum and strong spirits was
prohibited. The Trustees Garden was set up in Savannah as an experimental
nursery to test the suitability of a wide range of tropical and subtropical plants.
Great hopes were placed on wine and silk production as intensive industries
yielding valuable produce that England must import; European specialists were
sent as instructors.

Despite much support from the trustees, Oglethorpe's vigorous supervision (he
made several voyages and spent many seasons in his colony), and effective pioneering on the part of some settlers, the results were disappointing and there was much

local dissatisfaction. Georgia was a calculated anomaly, carefully designed to be fundamentally different in society and economy from its neighbor. South Carolina exhibited all that the Georgia trustees wished to avoid, but its example and propinquity proved too powerful. While Georgians struggled to give substance to an untried paper scheme, South Carolinians displayed obvious ways to wealth based upon more than sixty years of hard experience with exactly the same kind of ground. While Georgian colonists laboriously hacked away at the forest, South Carolinian landholders had such work done by slaves; while Georgians experimented with an array of exotic crops and unfamiliar techniques, South Carolinians grew rich on rice, livestock, land speculation, and the Indian trade. Dissident Georgians claimed they could not even take advantage of the obvious market for their forest products because they were prohibited from dealing in rum, a principal form of payment in the West Indies trade.

Two responses to this situation were soon apparent: widespread defiance of Georgian regulations and mounting pressures to change them. Slaves and rum were smuggled in and lands obtained by irregular means. Within five years the land laws were modified slightly, then again, and again, until land could be obtained and held in large amounts in fee simple. In 1742 the prohibition against rum was removed, it being utterly ineffective; in 1747 the law against slavery was tacitly relaxed and three years later, despite the pained resistance of some trustees and Georgia residents, it was formally repealed. Some pressure for these changes came directly from South Carolinian planters and traders who petitioned, connived, and in many cases simply moved, unauthorized, across the border onto attractive Georgian lands. As the model program began to collapse in the late 1740s settlers and speculators surged across the Savannah River.

In 1751 the trustees terminated their proprietorship; admitting the defeat of their program, they were reduced to expressing their concern only that their colony not be simply annexed to South Carolina. The Crown agreed to maintain a separate Georgia. Such geopolitical identity and the remarkable plan of its capital town were about all that remained as bold evidence of the special visions of its founders. What had begun less than twenty years before as one of the most distinctive colonies in America was being rapidly transformed into a replica of its neighbor. In terms of cultural geography, Georgia had become simply the westernmost district of Greater Carolina.

By 1750 this southern half of the original Carolina was one of the wealthiest and most famous American colonies. It was distinct in substance and position, a clearly discernible region: areally discrete, structured, and focused. It fronted the entire coastline between the Altamaha and Cape Fear rivers, and it was set apart from other colonies by a considerable zone of unoccupied ground beyond each of those estuaries: on the south the recent battleground and still-debatable borderland with

Spanish Florida, where Fort William, poised at the entranceway to the St. Mary's, currently asserted the English claims; on the north the broad belt of pinewoods between the Cape Fear River and the Neuse, and the dangerous coast, broad sound, and long estuary of the sea route to the tiny secluded nucleus at New Bern. Within the region the land lay in belts of markedly different ground parallel to the coast. There were perhaps 75,000 settlers in the region as a whole, the great majority of them in the Low Country, the half-drowned tidewater zone of bays, estuaries, inlets, rivers, and swamps. This was the definitive Carolina plantation country, the source of the rice, most of the indigo (a new and booming export crop at mid-century), and much of the naval stores production (especially in newer districts such as Winyah Bay and Cape Fear). Settlement was neither dense nor clustered, but all the land had been claimed and most was divided into plantations of anywhere from a few hundred to a few thousand acres, only small portions of which were cultivated, but larger parts used for forestry, pasture, and hunting.

This Low Country was defined by nature. Inland the general character of the land changed sharply to some of the poorest ground in the colony: long stretches of level, hard, compacted sandy soil covered with pine. Settlers had learned to seek out the breaks in these monotonous "barrens": the grassy savannas, patches of oak-covered loam, cypress swamps, cane breaks, and bottomlands along the larger streams. Such variations were more common farther inland as the land became more undulating. About a hundred miles from the coast was a line of scrub-covered sand hills, but beyond this, above the shoals of the rivers, lay a broad belt of much richer rolling hill country extending clear to the foothills of the high mountains.

All of this was "Back Country," beyond easy reach of the coast, thinly, patchily settled, and, though much of it was now cleared by treaties, still visited and occasionally raided by Indians. The Uchees along the Savannah River and the Catawbas along the Wateree served as buffers along portions of the western and northern frontiers. Augusta (replacing Fort Monroe set up earlier by South Carolina a few miles downstream) and Congarees Fort were garrisoned outposts on the main trails to the formidable Creek and Cherokee nations. There was as yet little colonization beyond these points; they marked the inland limits of a broad area undergoing varied and in places rapid development. Extensions of Low Country plantation culture reached inland intermittently along some of the larger streams, where rich Anglican planters (or their foremen and agents) produced rice and indigo (which grew best on better-drained soil) with gangs of slaves. In marked contrast were some of the township colonies, such as Ebenezer, Orangeburg, and Saxe Gotha, where European Protestants struggled to survive on small tracts, raising grain, hemp, and livestock, as well as experimenting with more intensive crops (some silk was regularly produced). More common were small pioneer planters, mostly British in origin, who sought to imitate wealthy Low Countrymen by buying whatever slaves they could afford and putting them to scrounging some sort of commercial product out of marginal land. Livestock provided the quickest and least intensive means of income, and this Carolina backcountry was dotted with "cowpens," a form of livestock management that seems to have developed early in the lands between the Edisto and Savannah and readily spread. The cowpen itself was a makeshift enclosure of a few hundred acres of open land, serving as the main holding ground amidst a much larger extent of unfenced (and mostly unowned) "range" in the woods and swamps. The operations were overseen by a cowpen "keeper" or "manager" with the help of several "cattle hunters" (usually Black slaves), who worked with dogs and horses. Their huts, the gardens "to raise provisions for the negroes and horses," and a "Hog-Craul" (kraal, corral?), in the words of a 1733 description, constituted the settlement form. The cattle were British, brought in originally from other American colonies. Cowpens were a form of pioneering, but they were mainly a device of Low Country planters and merchants to glean a profit from their inland speculations rather than a stage in the life of local settlers.

The Indian trade was still a major source of wealth. It reached far beyond the border zone, whose Indians as well as resources had been heavily exploited and depleted, to the Creeks, three hundred miles to the west, and, more recently, to the Cherokees lodged in and along the mountains to the northwest. Augusta and Congarees were operational bases for the traders and packers, but the trade itself was very largely controlled by Charles Town merchants. It is estimated that about 100,000 deerskins were exported in 1750, plus small numbers of various furs. The trade in Indian slaves had virtually disappeared.

Within the whole expanse of this Greater Carolina there was therefore a good deal of cultural variety: different peoples, economies, and settlement forms. The backcountry was to a considerable extent a loose pattern of ethnic districts: from the conglomerate along the upper Savannah, where within a few miles there was the tumultuous motley of Augusta's English and Scottish traders, mixed-blood packers and hunters, remnants and renegades of half a dozen Indian tribes, a Chickasaw encampment downriver, and the dwindling remainder of a German Swiss colony across on the Carolina side; through various German Reformed, Lutheran, Quaker, and Anglican locales, the Presbyterian Ulster Scots and Welsh Baptists on the Peedee; to the Gaelic-speaking Highlanders on the Cape Fear. On the tidewater margins were the Salzburgers of Ebenezer and the Swiss across the river in Purrysburg. In the outports Lowland Scots and a few New Englanders controlled much of the trade (when the new port of Georgetown was surveyed lots were reserved for Anglican, Presbyterian, and Baptist churches).

But such a list can be misleading. Such variety was characteristic of a large portion of the overall area but of a very small portion of the total population. Over ninety percent of the people lived in the narrow tidewater zone; more than two-thirds of these were Blacks, and the great majority of the remainder were Anglican English and Anglicized Huguenots. Carolina culture was essentially Low Country culture: the most heavily slave-based, class-structured, gentry-dominated society in North America. Furthermore, unlike Virginia, it was an urban-focused plantation society: Charles Town was the center of regional life to a degree surpassing that in any other American colony. Although distinctive in many features, the general pattern of this Carolina culture strongly reflected its West Indian antecedents. In its slave plantation system and sudden development of wealth, its "aristocratic elite in which wealth, privilege and power were closely correlated," its "proud and mettlesome school of politics," in Charles Town's "brittle, gay and showy style of life"—in such patterns South Carolina "echoed the Barbados milieu of a century before."

Charles Town itself was a larger and more elegant center than any of its counterparts in the English West Indies. In part that was because it was a somewhat healthier place: its riverine peninsular location jutting into a saltwater estuary removed it from the worst of the swamps; and its cool subtropical winter provided an invigorating seasonal break in the array of tropical afflictions. Thus many planters as well as merchants and officials maintained residences here, and the neat tree-shaded streets of large, closely set Georgian houses with their West Indian piazzas overlooking the Cooper became one of the remarkable urban landscapes in America. These same structures housed the political as well as the social life of the colony: there were no official buildings for the governor, council, and assembly; meetings were simply held in the spacious private homes of the ruling oligarchy of planters, merchants, and lawyers. Such people had extensive connections around the Atlantic world, especially with Britain and the West Indies, and increasingly with New York and Philadelphia in colonial commerce and with Rhode Island and Bermuda for shipping services and as seasonal resorts.

There was a Huguenot church in Charles Town but there were also many French names on the membership rolls of the two Church of England parishes. South Carolina was the locale of what was probably the most fruitful encounter and acculturation between French and English colonists in the New World. They were fellow pioneers from the start. The Huguenots were of a more modest middle-class background, inexperienced in colonization, and they encountered some prejudice in those first aggressive Barbadian planters and speculators, but they quickly responded to pressures and opportunities for assimilation, and after the issue of Anglican establishment was resolved the two peoples grew closely together. Within two generations most of the Huguenot churches had been transformed into Anglican parishes; their ministers had obtained Anglican orders in

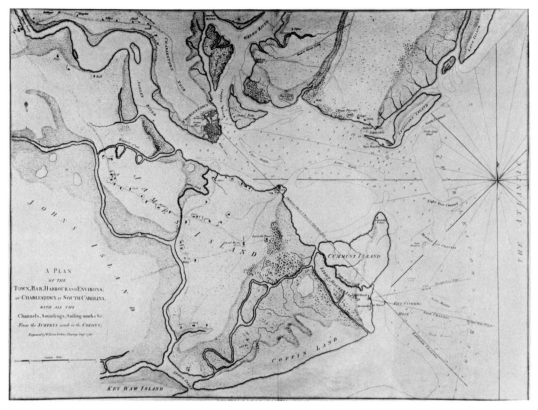

35. Charles Town Harbor.

Thomas James's map well displays Charles Town poised at the end of the Neck within this complicated estuary. The sprinkling of country seats on patches of ground slightly higher than the marshlands and the many waterways providing easy links with the capital are also apparent. The first successful cultivation of indigo was made in 1742 along Wappoe Creek, just across the Ashley west of the city, by a young woman experimenting with seeds sent from Antigua by her father. Imported slaves were usually quarantined on Sullivan's Island just off the North Channel. The two forts (Moultrie and Johnson) commanding the harbor entrance were crude but effective parapets of sand and spongy palmetto logs that could absorb cannonballs with little harm. (Fort Sumter of Civil War fame was only begun in 1829—and unfinished in 1861—on Cummins Point, directly south of Fort Moultrie.) James, a British army officer, prepared this plan in conjunction with the British siege that led to the surrender of American rebel forces in May 1780. (Courtesy of the Map Collection, Yale University Library)

England, services were in English or from an authorized French translation of the Book of Common Prayer, names were being anglicized and intermarriage becoming common. Although they had originally settled in generally separate districts, the two peoples participated fully in the rice boom, the slave trade, the development of Charles Town, and expansion into new areas (a historian of the Georgetown district classified the early families as being twenty-seven English, mostly planters; fourteen Scottish, mostly merchants; and sixteen Huguenot, planters and merchants). By mid-century the Manigaults and the Middletons were equally good measures of success in Carolina society. Although impossible to define in detail, it seems highly probable that the intensity and elegance of the social whirl, the urbane quality of this little colonial capital, owed a good deal to the French as well as to the English background of its leading citizenry; and that in such qualities it might well be considered, as Wilbur Cash suggested, "a miniature London, with overtones of La Rochelle." Similar acculturation trends were discernible in the backcountry. The German Calvinist pastor at Orangeburg, for example, went to England and returned to conduct services in English and German as an Anglican minister. But the process in these outlying areas was uneven and less intense, and by 1750 there were proposals to limit the recruitment of German immigrants and to seek more British.

Charles Town not only set the style but literally controlled the life of the countryside to an unusual degree. For it not only drew all produce to it, but also drained the Low Country of critical talent and leadership and held on tightly to political power. South Carolina was divided into counties and subdivided into parishes and special townships, but these were little more than conveniences for records and elections. There were no county courts, few local officials, no real local government. The fact that the richest of the planters lived in the capital for all or part of the year enfeebled local society. The wealthiest owned thousands of acres and hundreds of slaves and a few of them had built elegant country manors, but their properties were scattered, divided among many operating plantations, cowpens, and speculations of various kinds, run by overseers and agents who had no vested interest in their neighborhoods. There were of course many less-well-to-do planters who could not afford to live in town, but that is what they aspired to do, that was the model of success. Furthermore, that impulse came not just from the lure of a convivial urban society, but from a Barbados-like distaste and deepening fear of the fundamentals of Carolina country life.

For the Low Country, like its West Indian source, was becoming culturally and demographically a true Afro-American region. The Blacks were everywhere a majority, although not commonly by such margins as in Barbados. More than 20,000 slaves had been imported during the expansive times of the 1730s, while the elaborate township scheme was attracting only a few thousand Europeans to the backcountry, and White fears of insurrection had grown commensurately. The Stono Rebellion of 1739, a slave revolt resulting in murder and pillage on several plantations in a country district west of Charles Town, confirmed their fears; its quick and severe suppression, the enactment of a new detailed slave code (replacing the earlier one copied from Barbados), and a heavy tax upon further slave imports were a measure of their continuing anxieties.

The growth of the Black population was therefore markedly slower in the 1740s,

36. View of Charles Town.
This detailed sketch of the solid wall of commercial and civic buildings lining the Cooper
was prepared by W. H. Toms and B. Roberts and published in 1739. They also issued an
"Ichnography" accompaniment showing the location of all buildings on the peninsula at
that time. There are small "bastions" at either end of the waterside, and St. Philip's
Church towers impressively over the scene (the "meeting houses" of five other Christian
groups are noted on the plan). This sketch, with little more than imaginative additions and
rearrangements of ships in the harbor, would serve as the basis for engravings of Charles

although pressures for more laborers were soon reasserted. For the first several
decades nearly all slaves had been imported from the West Indies; in the 1730s
they were virtually all direct from Africa, mostly from Angola. Thus just as in
Barbados, the African influence upon colonial culture was direct and pervasive,
even if blunted and deformed by the harsh rigidities of the slave system. Not just
simple laborers in the rice fields, slaves provided most of the craftsmen as well as
helpers and servants in every kind of activity, and their African knowledge,
techniques, and skills must have been as important in many of these as it is
conjectured they were in rice production. For most slaves, acculturation into the
English pattern must have been slow and selective: "They are as 'twere a Nation

Town for many years, while in fact most of these buildings were destroyed by fire in 1740 and then much of the rebuilt city was demolished in the great hurricane of 1752. Only after the latter date was there a rapid evolution in the style and elegance of its buildings, such that a purist of the time could write that many of its townhouses "have a genteel appearance, though generally incumbered with Balconies or Piazzas." (Courtesy of the I. N. Phelps Stokes Collection, The New York Public Library; Astor, Lenox and Tilden Foundations)

within a Nation, in all Country Settlements," an official reported at mid-century; "they live in Contiguous houses, and often 2, 3, and 4 families of them in one house Slightly partitioned into so many Apartments, they labour together and converse almost wholly among themselves." However, no large group of slaves could converse among themselves without first acquiring a common tongue, for they were drawn from many parts of Africa. Out of the natural tendency to hang onto all they could of their native language and the practical need to grasp a rudimentary English vocabulary there emerged during this era in Carolina a distinct pidgin language, a creolization later known as Gullah. This process and the ingredients were more complex than can be suggested briefly, nor was it entirely an indigenous development. African immigrants first encountered Creole tongues in Africa, not in America; Angolans, for example, almost certainly had contact with a Portuguese pidgin in the slave stations on and near the coast, and then with a partly related maritime English pidgin during ocean shipment and in the receiving station. Furthermore, in Huguenot districts many slaves were exposed more to French than to English. It was this diversity of Black speech added to the more common range of European tongues that made Charles Town at this time "more linguistically diversified than any other spot in the mainland colonies," for its sources of population "stretched from Scotland to Mozambique."

Charles Town, that supreme regional center of 1750, was in fact a good exhibit of such demographic and cultural realities, for a large portion of the inhabitants of its elegant mansions were Black servants, and a larger part of the people on its fringes, on the Neck and along its several waterfronts, were Black laborers, fishermen, watermen, crewmen, artisans, idlers, renegades, hangers-on of many sorts living in defiance of a slave code whose minute regulations were inconvenient or impossible to enforce. In human terms Charles Town might best be described as the capital of an African foothold with a diverse minority of Europeans all under the shaping influence of English West Indian experience, forcibly wedged into American Indian realms.

Savannah was also a capital, but in a very local and as yet limited political sense. The confirmation of Georgia as a royal colony fixed a political boundary but could not interrupt the increasing cultural and commercial influence of Charles Town. Colonization was still so closely confined to a narrow strip of coastal lands that Savannah, the next largest town to Charles Town, was still much more noteworthy for its spacious and elaborate plan than for its actual growth and substance.

On the other side the situation was rather more complex and uncertain. The lower Cape Fear district was clearly an extension from South Carolina and tributary to Charles Town, but the remainder of North Carolina was a huge segment of country with little coherence and no strong focus. Out of competitive pressures from the several small settlement districts on the sounds, New Bern had become the de facto capital in the 1740s, a compromise choice between the Albemarle and the Cape Fear districts. However, by 1750 the most promising areas of growth were not to be found in any of these sheltered tidewater areas, but westward along the Virginia border, and especially far to the west in the rolling hill country where land seekers from Pennsylvania and Virginia were beginning to come in along trails extending south from the Great Philadelphia Wagon Road. In 1750 both North and South Carolina were seaboard colonies, but the tracings of an entirely new entryway and the trickle of what could become a counterbalancing inflow were already visible to anyone who turned away from the coast and ventured deep into the backcountry.

12. Florida

In the late seventeenth century the chronic and rather chaotic imperial contest for control of the tropical seas spread with similar savage intensity onto the subtropical mainland. The creation of English Carolina was soon followed by the initiation of French Louisiana, and both events spurred the Spanish to reinforce their old but meager hold upon intervening Florida. These realms appear as broad colorations on the map of empires, but at first they were perforce no more than grandiose claims anchored upon a few tiny precarious footholds. By 1750, however, a marked differentiation was obvious, reflecting as yet not so much the differences in the colonial possibilities of the areas involved as the differences in motivations, strategies, and agencies of the three European peoples and their governments.

Within a few years of their seizure of the Greater Antilles the Spanish had ranged out to reconnoiter the long broad land lying just to the north of Cuba. They found it to be a projection of the continent, a swampy, sandy, scrubby flatland with little worth plundering. There was a considerable Indian population, but, in the wake of de Soto's ravages, missionaries encountered murderous resistance. Thus the one great importance of Florida was its position alongside the seaway streaming powerfully through the narrow oceanic channel west of the Bahama banks. The moment French buccaneers began to endanger the treasure fleets on this vital passageway the Spanish formally proclaimed Florida part of New Spain and prepared to fasten their hold upon it.

Their initial plan encompassed the entire region: a main naval base well to the north on capacious Santa Elena (St. Helena) Sound, lesser bases along the east coast of the peninsula, and a main supply station on the gulf in ready and secure connection with Vera Cruz and Havana and linked by an overland route to Santa Elena. In 1559 a large party settled on Pensacola Bay to initiate this program, but a hurricane soon destroyed all their ships and supplies. Before a fresh start was made the French were setting up their Huguenot colonies in the key area of the east coast. Sailing north Menendez established St. Augustine as a forward operational base and proceeded to oust the French. He placed garrisons on the French sites and also at Indian River (Santa Lucia), Biscayne Bay (Miami), and Tampa Bay and laid plans for a comprehensive colonial development that would transform Florida into a functional extension of Mexico. But Menendez was soon transferred to other more pressing tasks and the Spanish presence in Florida dwindled rather than expanded. Within a few years they had abandoned or lost to Indian attacks all except Santa Elena and St. Augustine. After the English sacked the latter in 1586, the Spanish withdrew from the north and rebuilt St. Augustine as a more substantial base. Thus Florida was in effect a single, fortified outpost of Havana.

In the seventeenth century, following an extensive official assessment, a modest program to secure the hinterland of St. Augustine was undertaken. Franciscan missionaries began work with the Timucua Indians and eventually developed a network of stations westward across the well-drained limestone country to the Apalachee country (Tallahassee). These missions were small agricultural centers, and although no land was officially granted to any Spaniards a sprinkling of colonists developed, mainly as cattlemen using the attractive small savannas. In 1679 a fort was established at St. Marks, a port off Apalachee Bay, to serve as a western anchor of this line. In 1698, in anticipation of French and English designs upon this coast, the Spanish again sent a fleet from Vera Cruz to secure Pensacola Bay. Thus by 1700 the Spanish had again laid out the framework for a substantial colonial region, but a few years later it was wrecked by raids of the powerful Creek Indians working in conjunction with the Carolina English. All the missions were destroyed or abandoned, and the local Indian groups crippled by slave raids. Gradually the Spanish were able to stem these incursions, establish alliances with some Creek bands, and lure them southward to settle in Florida as a buffer against the English. However, by 1750 they had effective control only at Pensacola, St. Marks, and St. Augustine, and the trail between the latter two was considered too hazardous for travel as it was open to raids by the Seminoles, a new Indian grouping formed from deeply acculturated and embittered remnants who had taken refuge in central Florida.

These three places were northern outposts, garrisons on the fringe staking out the Spanish claim to this bloodied edge of empire. St. Augustine was much the oldest and most substantial, a long, narrow, walled fortress town facing the harbor, focused on the plaza in and around which were the governor's house, main church, guardhouse, and wharf. Despite the fact that it was still a relatively small frontier settlement, nearly two centuries of existence had made it a mature and civilized place of attractive thick-walled houses amidst a profusion of arbors, gardens, and groves, with piazzas and fenestration carefully designed to fend off the tropical sun. Other Catholic churches and a convent displayed the continuing even if geographically confined missionary program. Beyond the walls were a number of straggling settlements, including those of Christian Indian refugees from the inland missions and a colony of free Blacks. The latter were mostly the result of the Spanish policy of encouraging slaves in Georgia and Carolina to escape, offering them small plots of land north of St. Augustine; they became one of the more rooted groups of Spanish Florida. Missionaries worked to Christianize them and they were organized into four companies under their own officers for the military defense of the colony. In addition, there was, of course, the varied array of European, mestizo, and mulatto people in and around St. Augustine common to most Spanish ports.

In 1750, in the wake of the latest battles with the English over the St. Johns–Altamaha border zone, Spain at last decided to augment these garrisons and their

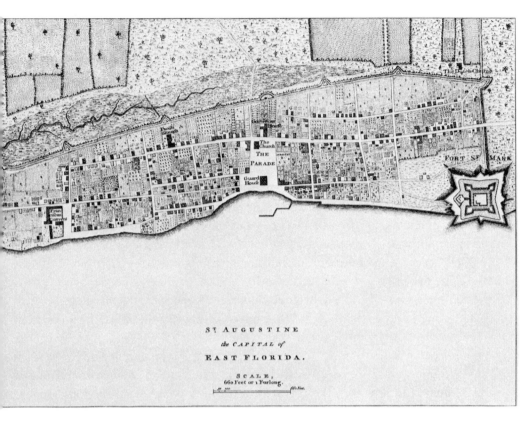

37. St. Augustine, East Florida.
This plan of St. Augustine was rushed into print in William Stork's *Description of East Florida* in 1766 to give English readers a look at the nearly two-hundred-year-old city they had just acquired. It was apparently engraved from "the Survey of Don Luis de Solis, Surveyor who Resided there near Twenty Years," with English labels inserted. It was in fact misleading in one major respect, for by leaving the lower half of the plate blank, omitting Anastasia Island, it failed to show the sheltered position on Matanzas Bay with the narrow entrance guarded by Fort San Marcos, the elaborate Vauban-type bastion just completed a few years earlier. (Courtesy of the Rare Book Room, Olin Library, Cornell University)

motley accumulated populations with a formal colonization program to people all the main localities of their old Florida framework. The first contingents, brought in from the Canary Islands, were to be settled along the St. Johns and in the Apalachee country, but there was so little security that they mostly hung close to St. Augustine. Thus the effectiveness of the program remained in doubt. The Spanish had maintained a firm nucleus in Florida for nearly two hundred years, but they had yet to create a solid self-sustaining, growing colony.

13. Louisiana

Louisiana was an anomaly: it emerged first of all as an extension from Canada rather than an implantation on the seaboard; as a new oceanic terminus for an existing continental system rather than as a coastal foothold for inward expansion. In concept and implementation it stemmed directly from La Salle's descent of the Mississippi in 1682, a southward probing from well-established French outposts on the Great Lakes and in the Illinois country. With this testing of the trunk stream the basic lineaments of a truly continental empire—extending from the Gulf of St. Lawrence to the Gulf of Mexico, commanding the fur trade of a vast interior, containing the English within their seaboard colonies to the east, pushing in upon the border of New Spain to the south and west—seemed readily apparent. It was a vision that excited officials, scientists, and religious leaders in France, and La Salle received quick support for the next obvious move: to secure a hold on the Mississippi mouth.

But Louisiana proved much more difficult to approach by sea than it had by land. The two great natural axes of this imperial design were of utterly contrasting natural character: the St. Lawrence flowing directly and deeply along a great glacial trough that gradually broadened into a sheltered gulf, providing an obvious singular entranceway into the continent; the Mississippi winding, looping its way for hundreds of miles through a broad swampy floodplain, paralleled on the western side of its lower course by an intricate fretwork of sluices and swamps from tributary waters unable to flow into the elevated, alluviated channel of the great stream, until all of these mud-laden waters are fanned out through a vast spongy, vegetation-choked, labyrinthine expanse of half-made coastland to feed a bewildering maze of banks and bars and shoals continuously reworked by the tides and currents of the sea. "Our coast changes shape at every moment," wrote an early Louisiana missionary, and finding any one of the several mouths of the Mississippi was a difficult and dangerous task.

Sailing from La Rochelle via St. Domingue in late 1684, La Salle's colonizing expedition first sighted land more than a hundred miles beyond the Mississippi, kept probing onward, and finally settled far to the west at Matagorda Bay. That was staking out a broad claim, but in that desolate isolation the whole enterprise disintegrated and disappeared while La Salle vainly searched overland for the great river until his death in 1687. European wars delayed further French efforts. In 1698 they were again spurred to action when an English promoter advertised his intention of planting a colony of Huguenots and other "dispersed Protestant refugees" at Apalachicola Bay as the nucleus for a greater Florida. Sensing these moves, the Spanish sent a force from Vera Cruz to occupy Pensacola Bay. The French coming from Europe via St. Domingue found them there, explored further, and set up a base at Biloxi. The advance agents of the English, having wintered in Charles Town, were the third to arrive; they missed their intended landfall but found the Mississippi and sailed up it a hundred miles, where they encountered d'Iberville, the leader of the French Biloxi colony, on reconnaissance. He asserted the French claim, warned them away from the Gulf Coast, and the English scheme, the brainchild of a quixotic proprietor, was soon altered in direction (resulting, before it failed altogether, in the transport of several hundred Huguenots to Virginia, some of whom soon became the pioneer colonists of the Pamlico district in North Carolina).

Thereafter the French met no serious opposition in the immediate area of the lower Mississippi, but it took them twenty years to get anything very substantial started, despite experienced and capable leadership. With the help of local Indians (Houma, Tunica, and Choctaw) the intricacies of the waterways were methodically sorted out. A route inside the shelter of the coastal bars to Lake Pontchartrain and Bayou Manchac became the direct link, suitable for small boats, between the ocean ports and the Mississippi. A port at Mobile, with an outport on Dauphin Island, was established as headquarters in 1701, being judged to have a better hinterland and strategic position than Biloxi. But as a colony Louisiana was at first crippled by a near absence of genuine colonists. It was an imperial design rather than an entrepreneurial venture, administered by the navy, peopled by assignment, sustained by subsidies rather than local produce. Founded during a brief interlude of peace, it was neglected to near destitution during the decade of war that followed. At times critical supplies were obtained from Pensacola, Havana, or Vera Cruz, but the Spanish did not encourage such connections, considering the French to be intruders. Boatloads of flour and furs were shipped downriver from Illinois but these aroused the opposition of officials and merchants in Canada who feared such diversions. Efforts to lure the fur trade of the coastal hinterland ran into the powerful and dangerous competition of Carolina traders and their Creek allies. In 1712 a new approach was tried. A commercial monopoly was granted to a private company in return for certain requirements of colonization and development. Little resulted from this, but a similar concession five years later to another French company under the leadership of the Scottish financier John Law gave a sharp impetus, even though the frenzy of speculation promoted by Law soon collapsed.

In 1718 this company laid out New Orleans at a narrow portage where the Mississippi loops nearest to Lake Pontchartrain. Many tracts of land were granted, and over the next few years several thousand colonists were brought to Louisiana and settled along the river and at various points along the coast. They were of varied origin: French directly from France, from Canada, from the West Indies; Swiss mercenaries who had completed their terms; several hundred Alsatian and Rhenish Germans; and several thousand Black slaves, chiefly directly from Africa. Within a few years indigo, tobacco, rice, cotton, and forest products were being exported, as well as furs and skins from several inland trading posts. These posts marked the effective boundaries of French Louisiana. Natchitoches was estab-

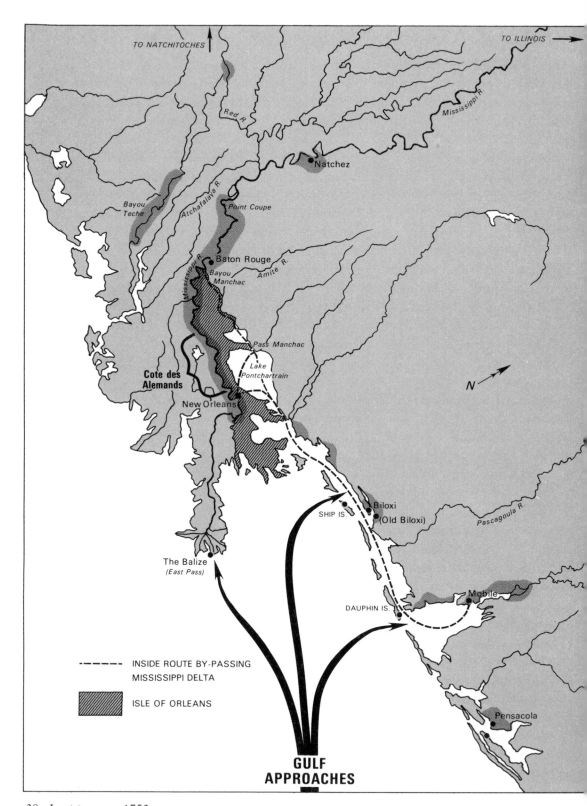

TO NATCHITOCHES

TO ILLINOIS

Mississippi R.

Red R.

Natchez

Bayou Teche

Atchafalaya R.

Point Coupe

Mississippi R.

Baton Rouge

Bayou Manchac

Amite R.

Pass Manchac

Lake Pontchartrain

Cote des Alemands

N

New Orleans

Biloxi
(Old Biloxi)

SHIP IS.

Pascagoula R.

The Balize
(East Pass)

Mobile

DAUPHIN IS.

-------- INSIDE ROUTE BY-PASSING
MISSISSIPPI DELTA

ISLE OF ORLEANS

Pensacola

**GULF
APPROACHES**

38. Louisiana, c. 1750.

lished at the base of the Great Raft, an immense tangle of floating debris that blocked navigation up the Red River. The French hoped Natchitoches might serve as a portal for overland trade with Mexico as well as drawing from its more immediate area, but the Spanish, fearful of encroachment, countered by setting up a garrison at Los Adaes, a few miles to the west, thus fixing a boundary between Louisiana and Texas. On the northeast, the French moved up the Alabama River from Mobile and established Fort Toulouse at the main fork in the midst of the Creek Indians, to try to neutralize the influence of Carolina traders. A third important post was established on the bluffs of the Mississippi in the Natchez country to provide security for travelers and shipments on the river. It was an attractive location on fine soil, and a thriving colony grew up alongside the fort, but it was an intrusion upon the strong Natchez tribe who in 1729 attacked and destroyed the entire settlement. Retaliatory campaigns shattered the Natchez tribe and hundreds of them were exported as slaves to St. Domingue, but the French never achieved a comfortable security along the Mississippi route.

When Louisiana once more came under direct royal control in 1731 it had been significantly altered in shape and substance. New Orleans was now the obvious center, in the midst of the most populous and productive local district, the commercial focus of a huge hinterland, the seat of government (since 1724) for half of a continental empire (the Illinois district having been formally attached to its administration). Nevertheless, Louisiana was still a minor, remote, and costly part of France's global interests, and despite the immense potential for development French officials at home and in America were so immersed in immediate strategic and factional problems, and French entrepreneurs still so restricted by regulations and uncertain of returns, that the colony developed slowly over the next twenty years. The population was augmented by many small immigrations rather than any major program: occasional shipments of families of those already there, selected girls of marriageable age, a few skilled workmen, criminals, orphans, all from France; trickles of Canadian traders drifting down the river and of planters and merchants across from St. Domingue; small shipments of slaves from Africa. Remnants and refugees of Indian tribes clustered closely around the settlements. It was not uncommon for Frenchmen to take Indian wives in Christian marriage (although a change in policy tried to discourage this), and a mixed-race population was everywhere evident. By 1750 there were still probably fewer than 10,000 settlers of mainly French or African origin in all of Louisiana, and they occupied only a minute part of a huge realm. Nevertheless they had hold of and had impressed a distinct mark upon an intrinsically important part of the North American continent. Louisiana had been made into the southern counterpart of Canada: a coastal and riverine settlement area important in itself as well as serving as the base for the control and exploitation of a huge hinterland. Although it was a century younger and far less substantial than New France on the St. Lawrence, Louisiana was considered by many to be at least equal in potential.

The main colonized area was a narrow strip rather like Canada, as long but less continuous and compact, extending from the head of Mobile Bay along the coast and connecting through Lake Pontchartrain with the river district extending for about eighty miles along the Mississippi. It was a pattern primarily shaped by the concern of French officials to secure a grip on this gulf frontage and the Mississippi. By mid-century the sea approaches to Louisiana were of course much better known but they were still indirect and difficult, leading in every case through narrow, changeable passageways. Dauphin and Ship islands were outposts serving and guarding the entrances to Mobile and Biloxi, respectively, and the coastal route to Pontchartrain. The Balize or East Pass marked the main mouth of the Mississippi and was the residence of a small garrison and of the official pilot for the often-tedious sail up the long gauntlet to New Orleans. These three towns were the commercial and strategic anchors of New France on the gulf, though quite unequal in significance. Biloxi and Mobile had been relocated from their initial sites to more advantageous positions, but both former capitals had become quite over-shadowed by the rapid rise of the newest one. Biloxi was a minor settlement but a convenient port midway along the coast. Mobile, now seated on a rise at the northwest corner of its broad but shallow bay, was more substantial, its half a hundred or so houses aligned in formal blocks near the brick walls and parapets of Fort Conde in the midst of the esplanade. Although there were planters, cattle herders, and lumbermen in the area, this elaborate Vauban fortress was clear evidence that Mobile was primarily a garrison town, a major base for French relations with powerful Indians in the interior and a firm emplacement near the frontier of Spanish Florida.

New Orleans was less of a fortress but more of a town: a symmetrical grid of forty-four blocks, partially walled and containing the facilities for a large garrison but protected more by its location than by its fortifications. It stood on the natural levee facing to the southeast aligned with the river, with a road leading from its backside a short distance to Bayou St. John and connecting to Lake Pontchartrain, making it a junction of coastal, river, and ocean routes. At the front and center of its formal layout was the Place d'Armes, an open square faced by government and religious buildings; along the riverfront on either side were commercial areas; behind lay the residential blocks in their tropical exuberance of trees, flowers, and gardens. As yet this original frame was far from filled: a quarter of the squares were still unoccupied. But there had been a steady upgrading in substance as red-tiled brick houses replaced or spread among and beyond the older shingled or bark-roofed wooden structures. In adaptation to this soggy, sweltering site, houses were raised on pillars and most had verandas, often all the way around. There were some

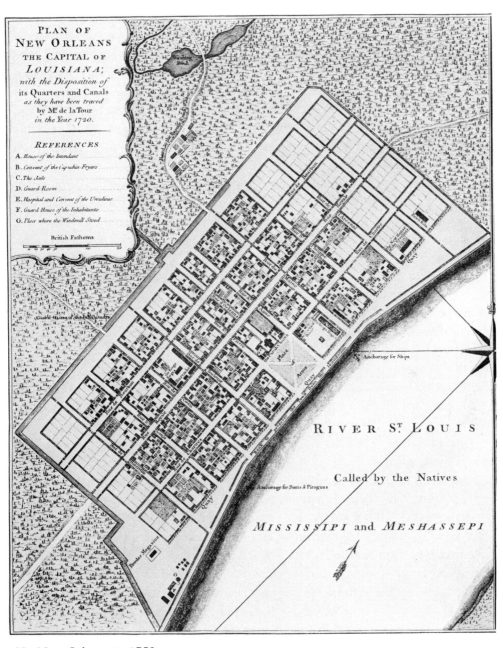

39. New Orleans in 1759.

This plan published by Thomas Jefferys in London clearly displays the symmetry and focus of this fine example of French town-planning. It was designed by or under the direction of the governor, Sieur de Bienville, a Montreal native who had previously prepared the plan for relocated Mobile. The "Mr. de la Tour" in the legend refers to one of the earliest detailed manuscript plans of the city. (Courtesy of the Library of Congress) fine buildings here, as befitting a capital city even if barely thirty years old, and the town throbbed with a vivid social life under the leadership of a governor who delighted in all the pomp and play of French courtly culture. There were cafés, ballrooms, and gambling places catering to the various social levels. There was also an array of religious facilities—churches, offices, hospitals, convent, school, and orphanage—under the direction of the Jesuits, Capuchins, or Ursulines, attesting to the fundamental and exclusive role of the Roman Catholic Church in this entire colonial undertaking.

Commerce was dominated by a small merchant group, mostly family members or agents of La Rochelle or Bordeaux establishments. It was a small group chiefly because the commerce itself was still limited in character, volume, and value. The immediate hinterland produced indigo, tobacco, lumber, and naval stores for export, and rice, vegetables, meat, and fish for local consumption. Much of the produce came from the Côte des Allemands just upriver, where Alsatian and Rhenish immigrants had settled down to become efficient small farmers on their long river-fronting lots. Rice was a staple food but the French would not readily give up bread. They had tried vainly for years to raise wheat locally, and now imported all they could from the Illinois settlements. The Indian trade could yield profitable cargoes of furs and skins from the several interior posts, but it was a highly unstable and hazardous business, suffering spasmodically from intrusions and disruptions by the English and their allies. Louisiana, therefore, was still a minor and marginal province, living more by government subsidy than by its own regional economy. It had little direct commercial traffic with France, being served mostly by shipping from St. Domingue.

Louisiana could be viewed as an outlier of St. Domingue in social and cultural as well as commercial terms. It had been founded just two years after the French had gotten formal control of western Hispaniola, and thus its development as a creole, slave-owning, tropical plantation society was to a considerable degree parallel in time and type. Yet Louisiana was not a direct offshoot of French West Indian society, as South Carolina was of Barbadian, and it did not develop simply as a mainland miniature of the more prosperous and prominent St. Domingue economy and society. Not only was it much less rich, but it was different in important respects. To be sure, some of those differences were related to its relative poverty: Louisianans simply could not afford to buy anything like the number of slaves island planters used. But that in turn was a reflection of the lack of a staple export at all comparable to sugar and the fact that Louisiana had not been initiated primarily as a planter colony but as an imperial foothold. Except for the brief but important interlude of the Law company, Louisiana was a royal project and the government refused to do much of anything to foster the importation of large numbers of slaves. A considerable proportion of those present were servants of officials rather than fieldhands, and plantation production of indigo and rice was seriously limited by lack of manpower. Thus the European-African ratio was very different, the latter making up probably no more than a third of the total. On the other hand, the European-Indian ratio and extent of mixture was different in the opposite way from that of St. Domingue, where most of the native population had been destroyed long before the French arrived. Half a century of missionary work, trade, and increasingly close residential contact had created a considerable number of Christian Indians and an extensive Euro-Indian population. This latter feature had of course been developing for much longer in Canada, and this precedence and the direct participation of some of these tough, energetic, experienced Canadian explorers, traders, and laborers in the founding and expansion of Louisiana was a further distinguishing feature. This new addition to French America had been created and peopled in part by native Franco-Americans.

The pivotal link between Canada and Louisiana was the Illinois Country, a vaguely defined area lying to the west and south of Lake Michigan. It was developed by new religious and commercial enterprise at the same time and in part in direct conjunction with Louisiana. While d'Iberville was probing the Gulf Coast to locate a base for Louisiana, missionaries of the Seminary of Foreign Missions in Quebec were reconnoitering the middle Mississippi Valley and choosing a site at Cahokia, a few miles below the junction with the Missouri, as a base for their new work. The Jesuits soon moved to counter what they considered an intrusion of territory already assigned to them. An adjudication by the Church gave them freedom to work elsewhere in the Illinois Country, and in 1703 they established a mission at Kaskaskia, seventy miles below Cahokia. These initiatives coincided with new official policies designed to reduce the chaotic impact of the fur trade upon the Indians. The idea of a series of permanent French settlements near which Indians could be induced to take root as a Christian civilized community, all under close supervision, was now promoted. The first fruit of this concept was Detroit, founded in 1701, and the Illinois missions were also affected. Colonists settled along the narrow strips of rich alluvial bottomlands paralleling the Mississippi upriver from Kaskaskia. Fort de Chartres, established in 1720 and rebuilt and enlarged several times, became the principal garrison. Across the river Ste. Genevieve emerged as the center for farmers on the west bank and as a base and riverport for the lead mines in the St. François Mountains thirty miles to the southwest. The working of these deposits began in earnest during the Louisiana company era in the 1720s, when skilled men and machinery from France and slaves from St. Domingue were brought upriver.

By mid-century there were probably fifteen hundred French with three hundred or so Black slaves and about sixty Indian slaves living at least semipermanently in this Illinois settlement district. Kaskaskia, sheltered on a small stream just back from the great river, with its substantial church and houses of local stone but with little of the formal symmetry of its Louisiana counterparts, was the principal nucleus, although the commandant at Fort de Chartres served as the chief administrative officer for the region. But the majority of people were habitants living on their long narrow lots extending back from the river. Despite primitive equipment and a shortage of laborers, their farms produced wheat, oats, hemp, hops, and tobacco; they raised corn for their slaves but ate little of it themselves, and their livestock were grazed on the natural prairies of common lands. Within and around these settlement strips were the houses and camps of trappers and traders and of several hundred Indians of various tribes. Much of the population was in some degree involved in the Indian trade, and these Illinois settlements became a great regional focus of trails.

Throughout this time the Illinois Country lay intermediate and ambivalent within the French American system. Its habitants and coureurs de bois were almost entirely from Canada, its officials and entrepreneurs mostly from France or Louisiana; it was administered under the governor of Louisiana, but its powerful religious orders were under the authority of the bishop of Quebec (as was the church in Louisiana); it sent its farming and mining produce down the Mississippi, but its furs east to the St. Lawrence (mainly to avoid damage from the tropical heat and damp); the fur trade was under the control of Montreal firms, but most of the trading goods and other supplies came by way of New Orleans. Located well over a thousand miles west of the one and nearly a thousand north of the other, the Illinois district was a small but significant island of European settlement in the very heart of North America.

14. Texas and the Lower Rio Grande

Texas, like Florida, took form as a Spanish response to French intrusions. Spanish imperial claims in North America had always spanned the full breadth of the continent, and the creation of French Louisiana along the Mississippi axis sundered that pattern, splitting Florida off from the main body of New Spain. However, that was an alteration of the map but not of the substance of empire, for Spain had in fact never secured hold of a single site along the entire coastline from Pensacola to the Panucho. Spanish military or missionary strategists had occasionally envisioned a line of posts along the arc of the coastal plain to bind these parts together, but early reconnaissance had revealed few local attractions and many difficulties, and for nearly two centuries there had been no compelling reason to occupy any of those shielding bars or spacious lagoons, nor any of the monotonous stretches of sand and brush or swamp and forest that lay just behind. Thus despite broad delineations on the map, Florida was an outpost a thousand miles removed from the real empire, which was centered on the rich and populous Valley of Mexico and spread far over the mountains and bolsons of the American cordillera.

Thus counteraction had to reach out across great distances. Warships put out from Vera Cruz to search for La Salle's rumored colony, and a land party was sent out from Monclova, capital of the province of Coahuila in the Sierra Madre Oriental. Coahuila was itself a new piece of the empire. For many years the northeastern Spanish frontier had been stabilized around Saltillo and Monterrey, spring-watered oases on the shoulders of the Cross Ranges, linked by long trails and cartroads across the deserts to the big mining camps to the south and west. In the 1670s a vigorous Franciscan missionary program was initiated amongst many of the small bands of Coahuiltecan Indians spread loosely over the arid country farther north. Civil authority soon followed, and these local developments plus a sudden concern over French intentions led to the formation of a new province and the role of the new villa and presidio of Monclova as an advance base for imperial actions far to the east.

None of these first Spanish searches found any French colonists, but the energetic Franciscans persuaded the commander of the land party to support the initiation of missionary work among the large Indian populations in the forest lands to the northeast. Thus in the 1690s several missions were established in the rolling red hills of the piney woods on the upper waters of the Neches and Sabine, amongst several of the Caddo tribes, who were the westernmost of the great agricultural Indians of the Southeast, cultural kin of the Natchez, Creeks, and others. The region was formalized as the province of Tejas, or Texas (the name a mistaken assumption as to the general term of identity used by the Indians themselves). However, disease and dissension soon brought a collapse of the missionary program and the Spanish withdrew back west across the Rio Grande.

Twenty years later new French actions produced another Spanish reaction. The founding of the French trading post at Natchitoches and a brazen foray by a French entrepreneur to open overland contact with Mexico caused the Spanish to reestablish missions amongst the Caddos and, shortly thereafter, to set up a small presidio at Los Adaes, just to the west of the French post. Thus they hastened to define the border and plug an opening that seemed to endanger, for the first time, the insulation of continental New Spain.

Each of these frontier stations was a feeble terminus of a fragile line, but the French, moving up the great rivers from their bases on the gulf, had a clear logistical advantage over the Spanish operating overland from Coahuila. Nor were distance and mode of movement the only factors. Whereas French voyageurs, as they traced the waterways of the continent over the past century, had created a mode of frontier life intimately adapted to the humid woodlands of eastern America, the Spanish empire, wherever it was something more than Spanish rule over Indian towns or mining camps, was basically a civic-centered ranching society, a cultural form readily transplanted from the semi-arid sierras and meseta of Iberia to the highlands of western America. Coahuila, where towns and ranches had soon been formed around or near the mission nuclei, was merely the newest exhibit of an old process of settlement expansion. Although manipulated by governmental allocation of lands and privileges, the basic lure, there as in scores of earlier districts, was a combination of broad pastures, perennial water, seasonal shelter, and a bit of open irrigable ground. But Texas was a long thrust into a different kind of country. These wet subtropical forestlands, which were often veritable jungles along the streams, could have no attraction to the ordinary settler from New Spain. Despite chronic concern and repeated efforts, Spanish authorities were never able to shore up this critical edge of empire with a reliable, well-rooted population.

Instead, the main nucleus of the new province quickly developed in an area of obvious attractions far to the west of Louisiana. In 1718, while a French company was laying out New Orleans on a bend of the Mississippi, an expedition from Saltillo laid out San Antonio where the long trail from the Rio Grande skirted the curving base of the hill country. Here in the shelter of the Balcones escarpment, amidst the springs and streams, fine pastures and arable bottomlands, between the open plains broadening to the south and the tongues of oak forest thickening toward the east, the full complex of Spanish frontier institutions—mission, pre-sidio, and pueblo—was readily implanted. It was a meager beginning, with cadres scraped together from Coahuila and the newer missions (c. 1700) near the Rio Grande crossing, but it was augmented in 1731 by an importation of families from the Canary Islands and by the shift of some of the missions from eastern Texas to this new area. Memory of La Salle caused the authorities to set up a small presidio and mission near Matagorda Bay as well. However, the Spanish quickly found that the greatest danger to Texas was not the French from the east but the Apaches from the north and west, who raided and threatened all these settlements and trafficways almost at will. By 1750 an uneasy truce had been arranged, but the effects of a generation of conflict showed in the still very limited development at this San Antonio de los Llanos (as the whole complex was termed). The main focus was the Villa San Fernando, laid out formally adjacent to the earlier San Antonio de Bexar presidio to accomodate the Canary Islander colonization. Hardy, frugal, and energetic, these Isleños families were a self-conscious and contentious group that dominated the local society. Their stone church stood on the plaza; their stone, adobe, or wattle houses lined the streets; and their narrow strips of grain, garden, orchard, and vineyard filled the gentle interfluve between the San Pedro and San Antonio rivers. As colonists they had been supplied with horses, oxen, goats, sheep, and cattle, which were grazed on nearby common pastures, but Indian attacks had so far inhibited any rapid extension of ranching. The substantial stone churches, irrigation canals, fields and gardens, flocks and herds of the five missions spaced along a few miles of the San Antonio river displayed the vigorous Franciscan efforts to teach the Coahuiltecan Indians the rudiments of Christianity and civilization, but here too the results seemed meager and uncertain in comparison with perceived potentials and plans.

Small as it was, with no more than a few hundred Spanish and mestizo settlers, soldiers, and officials and a few hundred mission Indians more or less in residence, San Antonio was the only real settlement district on the 600-mile trail undulating across the gentle grain of the country from the Rio Grande to the missions and small presidio on the Louisiana border. The large province of Texas was little more than a few knots on a long thread stretched along the arc of the coastal plain. And the thread was now anchored to Saltillo by way of Laredo and Monterrey rather than Monclova, a southward shift made with the hope of lessening Apache dangers.

At mid-century the southern boundary of Texas was given somewhat clearer definition by the creation of Nuevo Santander as a coastal province between the Tamesí-Panucho and the Nueces. This served as the provincial framework for a considerably larger colonization program along the lower Rio Grande. A capable *empresario* from Queretaro was put in charge and he arrived in the area in 1749 with 750 soldiers, 2,500 colonists, and large herds of livestock. Within six years he had founded twenty towns and settled 6,000 people, mostly along the south side of the river. He established Villa Laredo at the upriver crossing and shifted the presidio originally designed to guard Matagorda Bay to the lower San Antonio (Goliad) in the hope that these outposts and the arid wasteland between them might shield this new region from the kinds of Apache depredation that had kept Texas such a feeble imperial frontier. By this colonization of the Rio Grande Valley the Spanish expanded their control along the Gulf Coast, but in accordance with long-standing policies they did not open a port, even for their own use. Nuevo Santander and Texas were extensions of a vast continental empire officially accessible only by way of Vera Cruz.

15. Encounter and Change: Europeans and Indians

Atlantic America was the scene of a vast unplanned, uncontrolled, unstable, and unending encounter between European and Indian societies. The dual meaning of the word *encounter* had been vividly, sequentially displayed: the benign sense "to meet unexpectedly" was quickly transformed into the root sense "to meet in conflict." It could hardly have been otherwise. Europeans were intruders—in the broad view all were agents of imperialism. Their leaders arrived as military adventurers with charters from home governments granting them authority over foreign lands and peoples. That such charters may have decreed that indigenous people should be dealt with peacefully does not negate the fact that such people were implicitly assigned subordinate status. That these European vanguards, arriving as small forces far from their home base, were highly vulnerable and did perforce negotiate with local Indians in order to gain a foothold does not negate their predatory intentions and imperialist assumptions. That the Indians often welcomed and assisted in the establishment of such European footholds does not mean that Indian motives were any less selfish. Many Indian groups responded avidly to prospects for commerce and the possibilities of allies against troublesome neighbors and rivals. Each party sought to serve its own interests and each necessarily brought to bear its own understanding of the terms of such negotiations. And thus inevitably the disparate nature of the two cultures with reference to such fundamental concepts as authority, property, territoriality, contract, morality, justice, and social prestige meant that what might have begun as a more or less balanced political negotiation soon foundered on the myriad problems of coexistence. Grievances and misunderstandings begat quarrels, quarrels begat violence, local violence begat more systematic coercion, and successful coercion in one locality was aggressively extended to other localities. Much of the violence was gratuitous, powered by a brutal opportunism that in turn engendered hatreds and retaliations.

Overall this encounter can be seen as a vast collision of cultures that produced chaos: a long period of harassment, expulsions, wanton killings, warfare, destruction, punishments, executions, enslavements, and subjugations that sooner or later engulfed every seaboard region and radiated ever more deeply into the continent. It was chaotic because no power could control it, because there was no authority on either side capable of halting it even though many individuals, officials, and leaders tried to do so. Despite all larger assertions, power was in fact local and unstable, often applied opportunistically quite outside of traditional or formal systems. Indians lived within clan-structured local polities in which authority was diffuse, and each unit existed amidst a complex pattern of traditional relations with other Indian groups, with gradations of prestige and power, amity and enmity. The few large confederations were fragile associations dependent upon recurrent internal negotiation and adjustment. Thus in the unprecedented crisis of encounter with aggressive Europeans there was little possibility of concerted resistance at any scale and almost unlimited possibilities for internal division and ready disruption of traditional relations. The European side might appear to be very different but actually there was much similarity. European leaders came as representatives of organized states with elaborate institutions of authority. But

America was a distant and dangerous frontier, far beyond the routine reach of the full apparatus of the state. Furthermore, much of that apparatus was inappropriate to the immediate needs of such transoceanic implantations. Add to this the fact that opportunities for self-aggrandizement in the manipulation or defiance of instruments of authority were so manifold and attractive as to be irresistible, and we begin to understand the ineffectiveness of European restraints. Add further the ruthless competition among the many European colonies and among the European imperial powers, and the fact that treaty relations were too disparate in concept and demeaning in status to be acceptable for long by most Indians, and we can see how there ensued a protracted "kalaeidoscopic combat as each tribe or subtribe and each European province or town or individual strove to expand its power and territory and to increase its wealth." European officials and Indian leaders often sought to stabilize the relations of the two peoples—to adjudicate quarrels, punish wanton crimes, protect allies, license traders, limit contact, and halt warfare—but none had the actual coercive power to do so.

Such abrupt, aggressive, and ultimately massive encounters between disparate societies were of course taking place in Africa, South Asia, the East Indies, and Oceania as well, as Europeans moved in upon all the coastlands of the world. Nor were such encounters unprecedented in world history. The great migrations out of central Eurasia, impacting upon the seats of densely developed civilizations in the Mediterranean, Mesopotamia, India, and North China, offer instructive parallels. Francis Jennings has been a major interpreter of this "invasion of America" and we can adapt his framework for viewing such macroencounter as a general process:

1. contact between previously separate and disparate societies established by massive migrations;
2. catastrophic depopulation through disease and war; deep disturbance of basic social and ecological patterns;
3. reordering of dominance-dependence relationships among competing groups;
4. gradual revival of population growth, with consequent reordering of ecological patterns;
5. establishment of large-scale institutions through acculturation processes; and
6. stabilization of a large society in which all participant groups have undergone cultural change, and in which subcultures continue to display vestigial features of the originating ethnic groups.

By 1750 something like this entire sequence of stages was on display in North America, with many variations among the regions of sustained encounter. The shallow, narrowly focused contacts along the subarctic coasts of Hudson Bay still exhibited features of early contact prior to massive migrations, whereas two centuries of Spanish imperialism in Mexico had produced a relatively stable and markedly synthetic Euro-American society. Most of the areas ranged somewhere in between, with the pressures of contact creating unstable and uncertain relationships.

Viewed broadly, the most obvious variations were more longitudinal than latitudinal: gradations inland reflecting the relative impact of this great encounter. Thus we can readily recognize a coastal zone of conquest and encapsulation, a second zone (partly coastal, mostly inland) of articulation and interdependence, and a third zone deeper in the interior beyond sustained massive conduct but markedly affected by it. Each of these zones had its special kind of geography, history, and portent in European-Indian relations.

In the major areas of European colonization in eastern North America, the catastrophic depopulation, deep social disturbance, and new ordering of dominance-dependence relationships had certainly taken place, indeed so completely in some districts as to make the Indians a memory rather than a presence, although they were actually still to be found in every major region. Some of these remnants lived on designated reserves, tiny enclaves demonstrating the coercive power of the Europeans, their policies of cultural separation, and their legal concepts of exact territorial demarcation and jurisdiction; a good many Indians simply found informal refuge in tracts of forest, swamp, or shore, while others lived adjacent to towns in close dependence upon Europeans. The intensity of relationships differed. In many localities European traders, missionaries, and others exerted pressures for change. Even where there was little regular interaction, adaptations had to be made. Confinement altered economies and ecologies: European tools became necessities, European clothing and housing gradually more acceptable, European languages indispensable to tribal leaders coping with the encompassing imperial society. Such adaptations must not be confused with inexorable processes of assimilation. Even under the heaviest pressures and widest opportunities Indians showed little interest in becoming Europeans. Such changes were a means of survival; the adoption of selected European traits and elements need not compromise the basic integrity of Indian life. Such tenaciousness was generally puzzling and annoying to Europeans who looked upon these miserable remnants with disdain. No longer a threat, with too little land to covet, such people were outcasts, generally treated with contempt and for the most part ignored, especially in the English colonies. Only in French and Spanish areas where European-Indian racial mixtures were more openly accepted and Catholic missionaries had had some success did such people have a recognized place in European-dominated American societies.

Beyond the margins of major colonizations lay a second zone of very different relationships: one of articulation and interdependence. Two rather different geographic patterns are recognizable. In some colonies such relationships were very

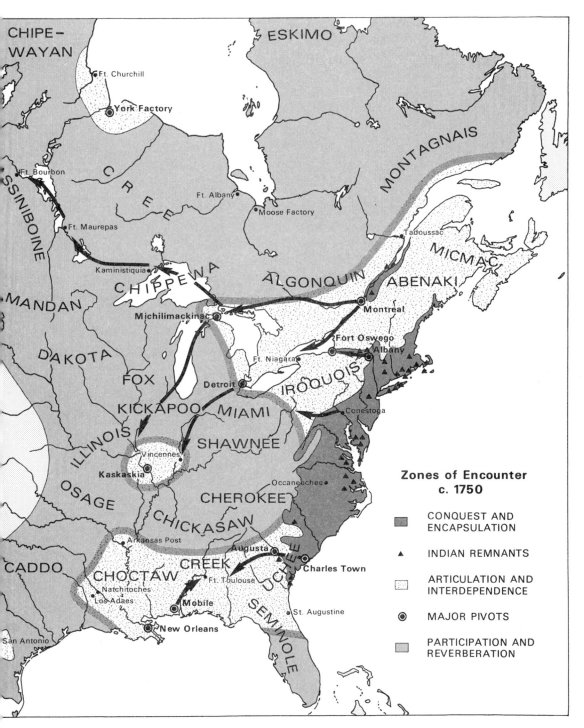

CHIPE-
WAYAN

ESKIMO

●Ft. Churchill

●York Factory

CREE

Ft. Bourbon

ASSINIBOINE

Ft. Albany●

Moose Factory●

MONTAGNAIS

Tadoussac●

●Ft. Maurepas

MICMAC

Kaministiquia●

CHIPPEWA

ALGONQUIN

ABENAKI

MANDAN

Michilimackinac●

Montreal●

DAKOTA

Fort Oswego●

●Albany

FOX

Detroit●

Ft. Niagara●

IROQUOIS

KICKAPOO

MIAMI

Conestoga●

ILLINOIS

Vincennes●

SHAWNEE

Kaskaskia●

Occaneechee●

OSAGE

CHEROKEE

CHICKASAW

Arkansas Post●

Augusta●

CADDO

CREEK

Charles Town

CHOCTAW

Ft. Toulouse●

Natchitoches●
Los Adases●

●Mobile

St. Augustine●

San Antonio

●New Orleans

SEMINOLE

**Zones of Encounter
c. 1750**

CONQUEST AND
ENCAPSULATION

▲ INDIAN REMNANTS

ARTICULATION AND
INTERDEPENDENCE

◉ MAJOR PIVOTS

PARTICIPATION AND
REVERBERATION

). Zones of Encounter, c. 1750.

local and diffuse, a scattering of many points of contact with little systematic development and focus. In these areas much of the trade was carried on as a sideline by both parties, its volume and value relatively minor. This was the case, for example, in Nova Scotia in the contacts between the Acadians and the Micmacs, and along the lower Mississippi between Louisiana farmer-traders and tribes from a wide hinterland. Much more prominent and important in geopolitical and intercultural relations were those extensive, specialized, complex systems anchored on Montreal, Albany, Charles Town, and Mobile.

The critical feature was the obvious interdependence and greater equality of the peoples in contact. European intentions and assertions might be no less imperial than in areas they fully dominated, but here they dealt with as yet unconquered peoples who were still in a position to demand recognition as equals. Formal relations were established and maintained through laboriously negotiated treaties, European agents could safely venture farther inland only on the sufferance of local tribes, trading protocol was very largely by Indian custom, and the terms of exchange were defined by astute bargaining on both sides. The economic basis of the relationship depended on the labor, skills, and cooperation of Europeans and Indians alike, and the two peoples lived in sustained contact in the major frontier entrepôts and outposts. Here were concentrated those facilities and specialists geared to this intercultural system: houses of the chief traders, officers, garrisons, depots, perhaps a chapel and a school; blacksmiths, gunsmiths, boat builders, harness markers, provisioners, translators, and from both sides a wide array of hangers-on. Such intense and sustained interaction inevitably produced changes in the peoples participating. Some alterations were simply utilitarian, such as Indian adoption of iron utensils, weapons, and blankets or European adoption of moccasins, snowshoes, and canoes; some were more complex and mutual, such as the development of pidgin as a language for negotiation and of modes of warfare used by both sides (and usually by forces made up of both Indians and Europeans) that combined in various ways Indian stealth and woodlore and European coordinated movement and attack. Miscegenation was inevitably widespread, and intermarriage of Europeans and Indians had been advocated by a few spokesmen as an obvious means of ameliorating the collision of cultures. That was not widely acceptable to Europeans, although most traders resident in Indian lands took Indian wives, in part for political as well as personal advantage. In all the regions from Virginia to Louisiana a complex mixing of Indians, Africans, and Europeans was widely evident. Indian slaves, African slaves, and European bondsmen might work side by side for the same White master; some Indians held African slaves, and many Africans found refuge and uncoerced incorporation with Indian communities. Thus by 1750 a considerable if never definable proportion of the population of subtropical America was racially mixed, but common terms such as mestizo (or "mustee"), mulatto, zambo, and so forth had meaning only in specific social contexts. It was an important characteristic of this zone that such persons enjoyed greater freedom of action and often played prominent roles as leaders and intermediaries, whereas they would generally be pressured toward the lower levels of the social hierarchy in the more fully Europeanized districts.

There were also special complexities of social identity among the Indians of this zone wherein so many people were refugees displaced by the European impact upon the coastal regions. Some had been absorbed into other tribes, in some cases as subordinates; some kept their own tribal identity within a larger association of Indian groups, such as the Iroquois League, expanding in various ways to incorporate so wide an array of tribal remnants in the north, or the Creek Confederacy, sheltering in makeshift fashion many in the south and itself perhaps as much a product of European as of Indian initiatives.

Of course, many of these features testify that although Europeans and Indians were here locked together for mutual advantage, they were not really on equal terms in a larger sense. They were interdependent within the commercial system they had together created, but they were not equally dependent on that system. Europeans could shift to trading opportunities elsewhere or settle down within a diversifying European colony, whereas Indians could not go back to old ways, for they had lost lands and skills and could never again insulate themselves from European pressures and dangers. The whole relationship was unstable, as history and geography attested. Even the major pivots in these intercultural systems were not necessarily durable points of encounter wherein new complex societies might eventually take root and flower into distinct regional forms. Montreal might appear to be such a place, but Albany had faded over the last twenty years, as had such lesser stations as Conestoga and Occaneechee; Augusta, the main entrepôt of Charles Town traders, was relatively new and there was little reason to believe that it would be any more permanent than its predecessors on the volatile Carolina frontier.

Westward, farther inland, lay a third zone, as yet beyond extensive, sustained encounter yet very much a part of this larger Atlantic World. Here Europeans were very few and sporadic; the commercial system was operated mainly by Indians, as trappers, hunters, carriers, traders, and various production specialists across a broad span of tribal territories. Such activities demonstrated that here as in earlier areas of contact the expansion of the system was the result of powerful forces of attraction as well as of destruction and domination. These forces of change continued to penetrate ever more deeply into North America in part because Indians as well as Europeans were ready participants. Some tribes became less fixed in place as males spent more time away from the villages hunting, while women spent more time in the dressing of furs and skins; as animals became commodities Indian economies and ecologies were altered, with unforeseen social effects. Although this zone was as yet beyond the effective reach of imperial power, it resounded with political reverberations rolling inward from the great collision of cultures. Relative power among tribes had been altered, alliances rearranged, factionalism magnified, warfare intensified. It was therefore in some ways the most volatile zone of all. There was competition and intrigue from a multitude of European agents, whether as representatives of rival empires, companies, or simply themselves. Year by year the points of contact, the pathways of commerce, the patterns of allegiance might change. Under such conditions each European interest felt the pressure to obtain further control of strategic sites and was usually supported by some Indian tribe or faction to do so. Each new outpost altered the geography of the networks and the context of the encounter. The trading posts and missions on the Great Lakes and in the Illinois Country were outliers of zone two, points of articulation and interdependence in the midst of the much broader realm of participation and reverberation.

Anyone who pondered the geographical dynamics of this encounter on this continental scale in 1750 was confronted with an obvious question of great importance: were these three zones an inevitable sequence, historical phases of the encounter, rather than a set of areas that might endure however much altered in form? Would Europeans and Indians share North America in some broad geocultural sense, with stable points of articulation and continuing interdependence, or was drastic reduction and encapsulation to be the eventual fate of all Indian groups—those that survived at all? The prospect might look different when viewed from Canada or Massachusetts, Virginia or Louisiana. The most obvious, and to Indians the most ominous, feature was the fact that the English had demonstrated over the course of their century and a half of American activities that they had neither the will nor the way to accommodate Native Americans as an integral part of an Anglo-American society. They refused to recognize Indian rights of sovereignty, property, or corporate entity except in temporary, manipulative fashion, and could not envision a genuinely plural society that would encompass tribal, non-Christian peoples. English missionary efforts were belated, sporadic, fragmented, and largely ineffectual, for they demanded fundamental alterations in Indian life. To the English "Christianization" involved a process of "civilizing savages," that is, the Indians must settle permanently in towns, live by European modes of agriculture and industry, and adopt European styles of shelter, dress, and decorum. In 1750 the results of such efforts might be seen at a thin scattering of localities, such as Stockbridge, Groton, Martha's Vineyard, or on the Pamunkey River, but might better be read simply in the absence of Indians over so much of the colonized seaboard.

The broad map of Indian-European relationships must be understood basically as a set of patterns produced by force: by pressure, coercion, physical destruction, social disruption—ultimately, terror. In 1750 the eastern half of North America was a ragged, bloody edge of empire, and the disastrous impact upon the Indians of that encounter, the continuing immigration, the now-rapid natural increase in the colonial population, and its organization into large coherent societies ensured European dominance over the arable seaboard. Because such dominance was relentlessly extended, interpretive studies long concentrated on this European success, on the "march of civilization" across the continent, relegating the Indians to a colorful but ephemeral role at "the outer edge of the wave—the meeting point between civilization and savagery." In such a view the "frontier" was essentially a European phenomenon, the Indians primarily an obstacle to be removed, and European-Indian relations a passing phase in the central themes of American history. Obviously no interpretation of that history can ignore the drastic results of this encounter and the ultimate and complete supremacy of Europeans on the continent, but we must fix in our minds the simple but long-neglected truth that Indians were critically involved in the creation of every European mainland colony. As Jennings has stated, Europeans did more than fight their way into America:

> [they entered into] symbiotic relations of interdependence with Indians (and Africans), involving both conflict and cooperation. . . . Every European "discoverer" had Indian guides. Every European colonizer had Indian instruction and assistance. . . . Indians brought to their symbiotic partnership with Europeans the experience and knowledge of millennia of genuine pioneering.

And if we add the critical Indian participation in the vast harvest of resources and the mercantile system that were the great instruments of this European penetration, we may well conclude with Jennings that "what America owes to Indian society as much as to any other source, is the mere fact of its existence." Furthermore, the evidence of 1750 indicates that even where Indians became encapsulated remnants under the heaviest pressures of acculturation, they were not simply absorbed—they did not become European facsimiles, nor were their societies little more than variously proportioned composites of Indian and European elements. Wherever they survived at all such societies were contemporary versions of their particular Indian culture, displaying through their variegated adaptations the continuous vitality of Indian life. That is how they had survived decades and even centuries of encounter to 1750, and that is how they would survive as Indian societies for centuries thereafter. For such peoples coping with imperialism is an ongoing reality.

16. Migration and Change: Europeans Overseas

By 1750 the Europeanized North American sector of the Atlantic World was a complicated mosaic of places and peoples. Migration to America had drawn upon all the regional and religious diversity of Europe from Göteborg to Gibraltar, the Europe directly involved in this Atlantic system. Few people had come from lands bordering the more inland seas, the Baltic or the Mediterranean, and in general the catchment area within the Atlantic states was relatively shallow, migrants being drawn most heavily from districts in routine traffic connection with ocean ports. The principal exception was that long Romano-Germanic borderland that had been so ravaged by the wars of the Reformation. Here the Rhine served as a great conduit, connecting dissidents and refugees from as far inland as Switzerland and Salzburg with Dutch and English ports of embarkation.

Large numbers of people had also been taken from a long stretch of the African coast, from Senegambia to Angola and even from parts of East Africa. But that diversity of peoples was deliberately scrambled on the beaches, in the shiploads, and in the slave markets of America. Thus group identity was generalized from the intricate living ethnicity of African tribalism into the crude racial and national categories of European imperialism. In the most general sense, Africans in America became a single body of people subdivided on the basis of the European language they had been forced to learn to serve their masters.

These transatlantic movements created an American mosaic, but any attempt to specify its pieces is fraught with difficulty. Table 1 represents such an ordering, and requires several cautionary remarks. The areas listed are those on the mainland that have quite clear identity in 1750, plus certain tropical islands that were closely connected to colonies on the continent (here a case could be made for others, such as Cuba and Jamaica).

The selections and labeling of ethnic and religious groups have been governed more by their identities in America than in Europe or Africa (Indian remnants are not included). All Englishmen not otherwise classified have been grouped under "Anglican," a term with both national and religious connotations. The West Country is the only English region recognized; such persons were mostly Anglican in religion but are not here categorized as such. Because French regional identities do not seem to have been clearly sustained overseas, only religious categories are given, except for French-speaking Swiss and Walloons who migrated and settled amongst those of another tongue. The many German groups pose a problem. Palatines, Alsatians, and various Calvinists have been labeled as "Rhenish-Reformed"; Mennonites, Schwenkfelders, Dunkards, and others, as "Pietist" sects; the Moravians are listed separately because of their clear identity in Georgia.

The marks indicating the presence of a group within a particular area are even more arbitrary. Local identity and significance rather than mere presence or numbers are important. Major ports, such as New York, Philadelphia, and Boston, had a greater variety of individuals than shown or even listed in the table (Portuguese, Italians, Norwegians, etc.), but our concern is to note those clusters of people who helped to shape the cultural character of communities, districts, and whole regions. Similarly, this table does not conform exactly to lists and maps of churches as of this date because many of these were very small or new and were not clear signs of a shaping presence. On the other hand, while each mark for Sephardic Jews indicates a single congregation, such people had a high ethnoreligious and socioeconomic significance within this Atlantic World.

There is, of course, an enormous variation in the numbers and importance of these peoples, and in their ethnic visibility. Several of these groups, such as the Welsh and many of the Dutch, were rapidly assimilating to a larger society, while others, such as some of the Germans, were shedding many of their local European particularities and blending into a more generalized ethnic identity. And of course other social processes had already created rather distinct new American identities that are not listed on the table, such as the Spanish Catholic mestizo population of Texas and the French Canadians who could be readily recognized as a distinct group amongst the other French peoples of Louisiana.

A simple tabulation of the marks on table 1 gives 130 regional-ethnoreligious pieces to this American mosaic of 1750. That in itself is not a particularly useful figure. It tends to exaggerate the actual diversity because the areal units are not in every case societies well differentiated from their neighbors. Nevertheless, it provides an emphasis appropriate to our theme.

However, we must also be concerned with more than mere identification of American peoples in terms of their regional and religious antecedents in Europe. We must pay some attention to the processes of transatlantic movement, to the impact of migration and colonization upon such identities. For Europeans could cross the Atlantic but Europe could not. The migrants inevitably carried something of the culture of one of these many ethnoreligious groups, shaped in detail by personal experience, but they could not carry and recreate on American shores a fully European society, no matter how intent some of them were on doing so.

Emigration is selective. Except in the most unusual episodic cases whole populations do not uproot and move to another land, especially not across an ocean under harsh and hazardous conditions. Such selection is not simply of number but of type. The degree to which it is selective of psychological types remains uncertain and controversial, and the topic is complicated by the fact that an unknown but larger than commonly acknowledged proportion of these Europeans did not come of their own free choice. If America was seen as opportunity by some, it was an uncertain refuge or unwelcome exile for others. What is certain is that there were classes and kinds of Europeans who never came to America: "The nobles, the wealthy, the established and the contented, stayed at home; it was the aggrieved middle classes and the impoverished who found themselves, voluntarily and involuntarily, becoming American." Thus they were not a full cross section, but a skewed sample in which certain classes and occupations, roles and relationships that were an integral part of every European society were missing or barely represented. A simplification took place at the source in the selection of emigrants from the whole.

Table 1
European and African Peoples in Selected American Areas, c. 1750

	Hudson Bay	Newfoundland	Nova Scotia	New Hampshire	Massachusetts	Connecticut	Rhode Island	Canada	New York & E. Jersey	Delaware Estuary	Pennsylvania	Maryland	Virginia	North Carolina	South Carolina	Georgia	Florida	Louisiana	Bermuda & Bahamas	Barbados	St. Domingue	Texas & Lower Rio Grande
ENGLISH																						
Anglican	X		X	X	X	X	X		X	X	X	X	X	X	X				X	X		
Puritan & Sep.			X	X	X	X	X		X		X			X	X				X	X		
Baptist					X	X	X				X		X	X	X							
Quaker					X	X	X		X	X	X	X	X	X								
Catholic											X	X										
West Country		X																				
SCOTS																						
Lowland									X			X	X	X	X							
Highland									X					X	X							
Orkney	X																					
IRISH																						
Ulster (Scotch-Irish)			X	X					X	X	X	X	X	X	X							
Quaker											X											
Catholic		X							X		X			X								
WELSH																						
Baptist										X	X			X	X							
Quaker										X	X			X								
FRENCH																						
Catholic		X						X										X			X	
Huguenot									X				X	X	X		X	X				
Swiss		X									X			X	X			X				
Walloon								X	X													

	Hudson Bay	Newfoundland	Nova Scotia	New Hampshire	Massachusetts	Connecticut	Rhode Island	Canada	New York & E. Jersey	Delaware Estuary	Pennsylvania	Maryland	Virginia	North Carolina	South Carolina	Georgia	Florida	Louisiana	Bermuda & Bahamas	Barbados	St. Domingue	Texas & Lower Rio Grande
GERMANS																						
Rhenish-Ref.									X		X											
Swiss									X		X				X	X						
Moravian											X			X	X	X						
Lutheran			X						X		X	X	X	X	X	X						
Catholic											X	X										
Quaker											X											
Pietist											X											
Salzburger																X						
FLEMISH									X													
DUTCH									X	X										X		
SWEDISH										X												
FINNISH										X												
SPANISH																						
Peninsulares																	X	X				X
Isleños																		X				X
JEWS																						
Sephardic							X		X		X				X	X				X		
AFRICANS																						
English					X	X	X		X	X	X	X	X	X	X	X			X	X		
French																		X			X	
Spanish																	X				X	X

Furthermore, a large proportion of those who moved to America had already moved from their native localities. They had left the farms and villages of their youth and were living in or near one of the larger towns, seaports, or capital. Many had lived for a time in various counties or provinces, or even in different countries; some had traveled extensively in Europe or in the larger Atlantic world before settling in North America. Such people knew what it was to pack up and leave home, to settle amidst people unlike themselves in surroundings unlike that of their childhood, and to make adaptations to ease the way. These generalizations are pertinent to many kinds of emigrants, not only to those who came as officials and agents, merchants and speculators, artisans and missionaries, but to those who came as soldiers and seamen or who came out of the almshouses, orphanages, prisons, brothels, dockside slums, and refugee camps. In our search for definition of the peoples who came to America, therefore, it would be useful to know more than birthplaces and ports of departure; one would like to know something of the sociogeographic experience of every shipload. The Midlands laborer who had spent a decade in London before emigration was already an Englishman in a larger sense; the Glaswegian agent bound for the Potomac who had done a tour of duty in the West Indies was already in some degree a British American; the man who in his youth had left a Tipperary cottage for the docks of Kinsale or Youghal was no longer an Irish peasant. Tracking such movements is particularly pertinent to the many European refugees, for whom departure for America was merely another stage in a sequence of residential shifts: Huguenots who may have spent years in the Channel ports of England; Flemish and Walloon artisans from the depressed textile towns of Kent and Norfolk; Palatine Germans marooned for months in London before being shipped to the Hudson Valley. For these and for many others the sharpness of ethnicity had been eroded; the English tongue and English ways were not unfamiliar. Thus the geographical and social mobility that was especially characteristic of English society and the dynamic, often turbulent conditions of the entire northwest European culture hearth were fundamental preparations in the formation of American societies.

It took many weeks to cross the Atlantic. From the time of assembly in the port of embarkation to the landing on American shores, people were forcibly associated, and the shared experience in cramped quarters for the tedious and often painful passage was a socialization that must also have had some effect. Most emigrants came as individuals, some as families, only a few as cohesive congregations. Most shiploads were diverse, although at times mainly gathered from the same general district through the efforts of some emigrant agent; very few were made up entirely of a group already closely associated in Europe. This shared experience of emigration may have further modified differences stemming from the variety of European backgrounds.

The acculturation resulting from such resorting of people within Europe and en route to America represents another kind of simplification of society. However, there is another side to these processes that had quite the opposite effect. For these American societies were being formed at a time when the boundaries between certain social groups were being more firmly defined. The reverberations of the Reformation echoing down through the generations in warfare, persecutions, legal discrimination, and social pressures together with the enlarging possibilities of personal choice in religious affiliation and a broadened sense of nationality heightened ethnoreligious consciousness. It was not that a high proportion of emigrants were especially pious, or even regular churchgoers, but that such identities, whether consciously selected or merely assigned, were a major feature in the reordering of European societies. And it was the kind of social mobilization that might be intensified through the trauma of emigration and the challenge of pioneering. Thus some groups undertook colonization in America with a sense of identity and purpose surpassing anything they could have developed in Europe.

These same kinds of contradictory trends were apparent on the North American side of this transatlantic movement. There were further simplifications as well as diversifications. The American setting precluded any real duplication of European landscape, economy, or society, whatever the plans of proprietors. It was not so much the different character of American natural conditions; in some areas the differences were marked and more or less expected, but the terrain and climate were not wholly alien in type over much of the northern seaboard. Rather it was the utterly undomesticated condition of American lands for European-style living: the need to fell trees, break ground, build houses, set up mills, establish ports, and seek markets. Land was cheap, labor dear—the exact reversal of European conditions. Thus every colonizing group was faced with heavy common tasks, every able-bodied person was a valued resource, every commercial venture was fraught with uncertainty. While this did not bring about an equality of status and opportunity, it brought a degree of leveling, a marked erosion of economic and social differentiations, of occupational distinctions and patterns of deference. This reduction in the range and rigidities of the old European social hierarchies was apparent in both rural and urban settings. Although in every region cumulative developments through several generations would tend to strengthen and elaborate economic and social differentials, the ever-present possibilities for migration to fresh ground, for land or mercantile speculation, and the far fewer institutional and legal restraints kept colonial social structures more open and moderate than any of their European antecedents. Thus from the very first implantations there was built into the American system a further simplification.

Europeans came to America from an immense number of localities, a diversity of places that, despite whatever acculturation had taken place in the years prior to emigration, remained fundamental to the diversity of peoples. But there were strong erosive forces at work in America. As Cole Harris noted:

> European regional customs were thrown together in [colonial] societies, often within individual households. Emigrants brought a wealth of different local superstitions, accents, dialects, languages, social customs, and material cultures, but most of this would not survive where, suddenly, there was no longer a sustaining society of people steeped in the same traditions. The first colonial marriages were powerful cultural mixers; the marriage of their offspring stirred the brew further. Microregional differences in the settlers' collective heritage were quickly lost in a process of simplification and generalization. The many different house types that immigrants had known gave way to a few, accents converged, dress became more nearly common, and many local European demons and sprites must have disappeared from view.

Such acculturation would work most readily where the imported differences were minor regional variations within a national pattern, as those among Anglicans from the south and east of England, or among Catholics from the north and west of France. In this way the intermingling of diverse people in the new communities of America produced a further simplification of European patterns.

This general process of culture change arising from close association was selective and uneven in result. Some differences faded rapidly, some gradually, and others not at all, as was commonly the case, for example, with dress, language, and religion, respectively. So much depended on the proportions, propinquities, and character of the diversities involved. The American mosaic was everywhere different from that of Europe, different in sizes, shapes, colorations, and arrangement of the pieces. A Pennsylvania county with half a dozen German religious groups, Quakers, Anglicans, Welsh, Huguenots, and Ulster Irish; a Louisiana parish with Parisian French, Creoles, Canadians, Alsatians and Swiss, Africans and Indians; a Massachusetts frontier town with Puritans and a few Ulster Irish, but no Anglicans: these were distinctly American patterns in the social geography of local life. Such groups affected one another. If in many cases there was a reduction of differences, in others there was an intensification, an ethnoreligious militancy to protect the integrity of the group against the power of erosive forces. Furthermore, such patterns were complicated and recurrently altered by American religious developments, by the splintering of sects and the sweep of evangelistic movements. The Great Awakening not only gathered many unchurched people at least momentarily into the fold of a revitalized Christianity, but also put pressure on every existing church, and helped make both instability and denominationalism powerful features of American religion.

Even where acculturation is strong the mingling of peoples of different heritage does not result in a culture that is simply "intermediate" or "average." The variety among the elements affected—accents and folklore, mannerisms and dress, foods, houses, tools, etc.—is shaped toward some dominant pattern, the features of which may be the result of selection of a particular form from the initial variety or something new that emerges from cultural interaction and the colonial experience. Such selection and emergence may reflect the utility of the form, as in the case of many material elements, or may reflect the precedence, prestige, or power of one particular group, as in the case of many other elements, especially the less tangible, such as accent and social behavior. Colonizations were planned, undertaken by a sponsoring group with a program designed to achieve certain ends (the long-unauthorized, unorganized, cumulative development in Newfoundland is the only obvious exception). Whatever the specific character of such programs, whether an elaborate design for an improved society, a crass economic speculation, or something in between, all provided a legal framework for governance, public order, allocation of lands, and regulation of commerce. No matter how extensively actual developments diverged from original intentions, some sort of leadership working within some such framework gave a degree of stability and structure to the emerging colonial society.

Thus initial status and sequence may be more important than the size of immigrant groups in shaping the character of a regional society, as the Quaker imprint on Pennsylvania attests, and thus we must pay close attention to Zelinsky's "Doctrine of First Effective Settlement":

> Whenever an empty territory undergoes settlement, or an earlier population is dislodged by invaders, the specific characteristics of the first group able to affect a viable, self-perpetuating society are of crucial significance for the latter social and cultural geography of the area, no matter how tiny the initial band of settlers may have been. . . . Thus, in terms of lasting impact, the activities of a few hundred, or even a few score, initial colonizers can mean much more for the cultural geography of a place than the contributions of tens of thousands of new immigrants a few generations later.

John Porter had earlier enunciated the same concept with reference to Canada:

> The first ethnic group to come into a previously unpopulated territory, as the effective possessor, has the most to say. This group becomes the charter group of the society, and among the many privileges and prerogatives which it retains are decisions about what other groups are to be let in and what they will be permitted to do.

Porter's version may exaggerate the conscious decision-making power of such local colonial groups, who could not always control the kinds of people shipped in by homeland authorities, but the general idea is important and the term *charter group* is a useful addition to the vocabulary of colonization.

We must not allow these emphases upon the diversity of peoples, on the one hand, and the general process and directions of culture change, on the other, to obscure the geographical variations in such matters in Atlantic America. We must look beyond the tabulation of ethnoreligious groups colony by colony and identify types of societies with reference to the degree and structure of such variety. The many specific regions in fact vary from a remarkable homogeneity to several kinds of heterogeneity.

The two most *homogeneous* societies of European North America in 1750 were Canada and Yankee New England. Compared with most others they were astonishing in their uniformity, compared with one another they were interestingly unlike in origin and structure. They illustrate well the selective impact of European religious mobilization in the prelude to colonization.

Canada developed under strong central authority. Immigration was controlled, non-Catholics were not officially allowed, non-French were not really welcome. The French who came, however, did not immigrate as a cohesive body of colonists, and certainly not, in general, as a militant religious group. They came chiefly as individuals, diverse in background from many different districts of France. Most came over during a few decades of the seventeenth century. Thus the homogeneity of the habitants of the côte in 1750 was primarily the result of acculturation within a national group resulting from vicinal association and common pioneering experience in North America. However, Canada as a whole was an explicitly structured society. The officials of church and state and the commercial leaders were urban dwellers who sustained French institutions and customs in the colonial environment. This social hierarchy and a rather marked separation between the urban and rural sectors in New France was a pattern somewhat simplified but not basically unlike that of France itself.

New England, quite the contrary, began as a coherent society rather than a mere collection of individuals thrown together in a colonial project. Its nuclear area was established by the immigration of a group strongly conscious of a common identity, a group which set about to create in New England the Christian commonwealth they had failed to establish in old England. The continued influx over several years of many young families gave this initial nucleus the demographic power to expand rapidly over an extensive region. Later immigration was a mere trickle and had to conform to the general social pattern already established. Despite intense endemic factionalism a general Puritan ethos remained the shaping influence; other faiths were unwelcome, and attempts were made to banish internal dissenters and to select the population for frontier colonization. Life in rural towns had evolved under the same type of leadership and culture as that in the capital and seaports, and the entire region was laced together by familial and other social networks. Despite a lessening of such controls and increasing differentiation in socioeconomic status there had been an unusual continuity: "In no place in colonial

America did the earliest forms of social development—land use, social differentiation, labor force, mode of production, religious ideology, political institutions,
legal codes, and moral discipline—remain so close to the founding patterns as in
the relatively homogeneous communities of New England." Such communities
displayed little of the range or rigidities in social structure apparent in England or
even in Canada. In New England a European fragment had become the whole, a
selective simplification from English society of immense importance to America.

At the other extreme, the most heterogeneous societies were Pennsylvania and
New York–East Jersey. Similar in the sheer range of their diversity, they were
rather different in elements, structure, and social geography. The Quakers, like
the Puritans, were a self-selected group, a prominent example of religious identity
by adult choice, a minority withdrawing from the encompassing society of England. But although they too were the sponsors and shapers of their American
commonwealth, their ethos was one of general tolerance, sympathy, and even
direct recruitment of numerous other peoples. Some of these came in the first years
and helped lay the foundations of Pennsylvanian society. New people continued to
arrive, but these later arrivals also had relatively ready access to land and commerce, and the social structure remained relatively loose and open, despite the
maintenance of many ethnic identities and the persistence of petty prejudices.
Because so much of the colonization was undertaken by ethnic groups, not necessarily as people acting in close concert but simply as miscellaneous families arriving
on the same ship bound for lands in the same district, the countryside tended to
develop as a rather fine mosaic of these different peoples. The scale of this patterning was such that almost every county was a patchwork, every county seat a point
of contact. There was thus an implicit alternative for any group: to band more
closely together and reinforce the social boundaries between themselves and others, as did some of the German Pietist sects, or to associate freely with others in the
routines of daily life and let acculturation erode the sharpness of ethnoreligious
distinctions, as happened with many other Germans, the Huguenots, Welsh, and
Ulster Irish. The first alternative led toward a segmentation of society, the second
toward the kind of fluid diversity that made Pennsylvania the most extensive
example of a *pluralistic* society, in which a variety of ethnoreligious groups participated in some degree of equality (though never of course perfectly so) in the
ongoing life and development of the region.

The Hudson Valley was a more complicated case. North of Westchester the
social geography was a mosaic of larger pieces forming a simpler pattern than that
of Pennsylvania. The Dutch dominated many districts, the English others, and
some of the later groups, such as the Germans and Scots, were shunted to the
northern frontier, quite removed from easy social contact and the main avenues of
commerce. So, too, the social structure was much more obvious and rigid, chiefly

as a result of land policies that favored the creation of large estates with tenants more than the freehold family farm so dominant in Pennsylvania. In the lower Hudson the diversity in peoples and in social structure was intensified. The Anglo-Dutch landed and mercantile gentry, the gradations of imperial officials, and the many ranks in status down to the relatively large number of Africans, some free but mostly slaves, reveal a hierarchy that was American in its components, factions, and seething instability, but almost European in its visibility and complexity. In its variety of peoples it was pluralistic, but it was so much more stratified in structure that one feels uneasy about putting it in the same category as Pennsylvania.

Several types intermediate in this range from near uniformity to high diversity may be recognized. There were clear examples of *segmented* societies, made up of two or three clusters of significant groups that were quite visibly distinct, geograph-ically and socially, and to a considerable degree functionally independent, except for the encompassing framework of colonial administration. The separate West Country–Anglican and Irish Catholic fishing hamlets of Newfoundland provide an example, and the alteration of Nova Scotia by the creation of an Anglican Halifax and an enclave of German Protestants within the old colony of rural Acadian Catholics was an even clearer one.

A further variation in type was the *racially stratified* society. Northern Mexico, of which Texas was a tiny outlier, composed in simplest terms of Spanish (*penin-sulares* and *isleños*), mestizos, and Indians, was an example. In many areas (but not all) such groups were not sharply segregated. The very concept of mestizo defines an intimate relationship, and the gradations of racial mixture through several generations gave rise to subtle but socially recognized strata maintained by an elaborate code of behavior. The Creole society of French Louisiana was more complex because the mixtures involved three races instead of two.

The simplest of the English slave societies, such as Barbados, Bermuda, and Virginia, are examples of still another variation that deserves recognition as a basic type: the *biracial* society of Europeans and Africans. There is a simplicity to these because of the special severity of the English code that relegated all "colored" persons to a single category, and by law forbade racial mixture. Of course such mixture took place, but the various gradations of mulatto were not given formal recognition in the social hierarchy (although individual observance of such varia-tions occurred, as in the selection of lighter-skinned mulattos for house and body servants). Such a society was stratified, but in much cruder terms than the mestizo and Creole societies, and it was distinct from segmented societies in that here the two peoples were in direct interdependent association, sharing farms and shops and even houses in an intricate pattern of segregation, under a rigid code of social deference of Black African to White European, whatever the relative status of the latter in other contexts.

Such categories provide a useful basis of generalization, and most American societies of 1750 can be classified without undue strain. But the typology must serve the reality, and some cases exhibit a combination of features to such an important extent that they may best be thought of as *complex* societies. In South Carolina and Georgia, for example, the coastal plantation zone, an offspring of Barbados, was a relatively simple biracial society with Huguenot and Scottish Lowlanders as well-integrated participants alongside the dominant English. However, the backcountry township belt was clearly a pluralistic society, with some degree of segmentation, while further inland were Indian and mixed-race groups and the new southward influx of intermingled English, Scotch-Irish, and German pioneers from Virginia and Pennsylvania. Thus there was a rather marked geographical differentiation of social patterns within Greater South Carolina.

As already hinted, it would probably be advantageous to recognize the Lower Hudson, perhaps the most heterogeneous of all colonial areas, as a *complex* society as well, setting it apart from the rest of the province of New York. Simply to refer to its "stunning diversity" glosses over its partial segmentation into ethnoreligious villages that were "homogeneous and hostile to strangers and change," the vivid biracial structure of much of the Dutch countryside and many villages as well as New York City itself, and the overall stratification of these complexities.

Table 2
A Classification of Colonial Societies

Type	Colonial Society
Homogeneous	Canada
	Massachusetts–Connecticut
	New Hampshire
Pluralistic	Rhode Island
	Pennsylvania–West Jersey–Delaware Estuary
Segmented	Newfoundland
	Nova Scotia
	Upper Hudson
Racially Stratified	Texas
	Florida
	St. Domingue
	Louisiana
Biracial	Bermuda
	Barbados
	Virginia
	Maryland
	North Carolina
Complex	South Carolina–Georgia
	Lower Hudson (including East Jersey and west Long Island)

A tabulation of these categorizations provides a useful perspective on colonial America (see table 2). In each type the specific societies are ranked from the clearest example to the more complex. The very attempt to make such assignments requires a certain arbitrariness. Several of these societies exhibit features of more than one type, though not so extensively or proportionately as to warrant grouping with South Carolina and the Lower Hudson. It is obvious, then, that this list of categories is not a spectrum, not a continuous gradation from uniformity to high heterogeneity. Rather, five *kinds* of heterogeneous patterning are included; the most important departures from a simple scale of diversity are those types structured according to race. Indeed, the incorporation of Africans into Euro-American societies is so fundamental and so diverse as to deserve its own explication.

17. Enslavement and Change: Africans in America

The ancient institution of slavery took on new forms in America and became so immensely magnified in scale and specialized in people as to leave an indelible African imprint on many of the new Europeanized areas. As we have already seen, the basic pattern was worked out in the first localities of the emergent Atlantic World. In Madeira and the Canaries, the Cape Verde Islands, Senegambia, and São Tomé, systems of labor supply and plantation production were developed in forms readily extended across the broader seas to Iberian footholds on Hispaniola and Brazil. Thus an inflow of Africans became a routine part of European conquering and planting in America, slowly swelling in size so that by the mid-1700s it was running at 50,000–60,000 a year, far exceeding that of any other group in the catalogue of peoples in these transatlantic migrations.

And indeed the volume of this traffic in human beings still staggers the imagination, even though we are becoming more commonly informed about how many centuries and what a broad stage the whole process involved. Philip Curtin's landmark reassessment of numbers set total slave imports from Africa at nearly ten million. According to his estimates about 3,800,000 had been shipped across the Atlantic by 1750. Just over half of these people had been taken to Brazil and Spanish America, the remainder (approximately 1,700,000) to the British, French, Dutch, and Danish colonies. Only a small proportion (totaling about 120,000) of this latter group had been shipped directly to the North American mainland (north of Florida and Texas). For several decades these continental colonies were supplied almost entirely from the West Indies, but as the market expanded toward mid-century direct imports from Africa became much more important. Buyers preferred new slaves from Africa, considering them more industrious and tractable than those experienced in the planter colonies of the Caribbean.

The broad circuits of this traffic were recurrently altered in detail, reflecting major geopolitical shifts, economic developments, and many local factors in every sector. Lisbon's long domination gave way to that of Amsterdam, London and Bristol, La Rochelle and Le Havre, which were in turn challenged by Liverpool and Nantes. And there were of course fluctuations in the availability of slaves from the scores of African stations over these two and a half centuries, but from the early Portuguese period on, the entire coastline from Gambia to Angola was involved, and there were occasionally cargoes from East Africa and Madagascar. Santo Domingo was the first receiving station in the American tropics; later Spain allowed direct shipments to Cartagena, Vera Cruz, and Havana. With the intrusion of the Dutch, English, and French, Curaçao, Barbados, and Martinique became the major West Indian depots, and these small islands (especially the latter two) continued to be important way stations even as Surinam, St. Domingue, and Jamaica became the greatest consumers and important sources for export to lesser American markets.

By 1750 this Atlantic traffic was dominated by big European companies specializing in the trade, using large, specially designed vessels and networks of agents. But all the while dozens of smaller firms and individual shipowners and traders, European and American, were involved as well. Some of these, including several from Bermuda and Rhode Island, competed in the transatlantic trade, but many more dabbled in the dispersal of slaves within the American sector, peddling Blacks along with other cargo up and down the North American coast. By 1750 Charles Town had become much the most important entryway and would thereby, as Peter Wood has emphasized, take on major significance in North American development:

> Here was a thin neck in the hourglass of the Afro-American past, a place where individual grains from all along the West African coast had been funneled together, only to be fanned out across the American landscape with the passage of time. Sullivan's Island, the sandy spit on the northeast edge of Charlestown harbor where incoming slaves were briefly quarantined, might well be viewed as the Ellis Island of black Americans. In fact, the colonial ancestors of present-day Afro-Americans are more likely to have first confronted North America at Charlestown than at any other port of entry. It has been estimated that well over 40 per cent of the slaves reaching the British mainland colonies between 1700 and 1775 arrived in South Carolina.

Because our concern is more with significant presence than with dominant numbers we need to pay more attention to the wide dispersal than to the narrow funnel. The dispersal Wood refers to is primarily that within a later Greater South; the one we are concerned with is the presence in 1750 of Africans in every seaboard society from New Hampshire to Louisiana. As we have seen, that North American seaboard contained half a dozen types of society, with the presence and

position of Africans a definitive factor in some cases. And now we must confront a
further, special complexity: that Blacks were, in almost every case, at once within
and apart. That is to say, they were a significant component, an important people
among the various peoples in these colonial societies, but because of European
(and especially English) racial prejudices they were all—free Blacks as well as
slaves—defined legally and socially as a category of people to be denied any
prospect of assimilation or even full incorporation into the larger regional society.
Thus in all of these regions there was to be found an Afro-American society within
the encompassing Euro-American society. As the circumstances of this relationship differed among the several regions, we must bring this special complexity
of American human geography into clear perspective.

Ira Berlin has given definition and emphasis to this "striking diversity in Afro-
American life" in British North America. Drawing upon his regional characterizations and adding other sectors in our particular perspective on Atlantic America,
we can recognize four basic types of Afro-American society.

Obviously, the most strongly African of these new American societies were the
tropical planter colonies of the West Indies, where Blacks outnumbered Whites
several times over and their Africanness was annually reinforced by new importations of slaves. Here Africans worked and lived in large groups, generally apart
from any close contact with Europeans. The slave plantation system itself was
European in design and control, but many of the patterns of work, local trade,
social life, and cultural forms were African. Europeans wanted as little contact as
possible with their brutalized labor force; thus the slaves were left a good deal to
themselves, and even under the harsh limitations of their circumstance their
African culture provided them with more effective ways of adapting to the American tropics than anything the Europeans could provide. Therefore, distinctly
Afro-American communities emerged on these islands, characterized by a peculiar
degree of cultural autonomy within the bounds of political and economic
captivity.

The South Carolina Low Country became a North American version of this
kind of Afro-American society. Although initiated primarily out of Barbados, it
could not be a simple transplant because it took two generations of hard pioneering
to create a prospering planter society on the mainland. During that formative
period Blacks and Whites worked closely together, but as the rice economy expanded and slave imports increased, South Carolina evolved toward the English
West Indian type. Some differences persisted, such as the greater role of Indians as
participants and Indian tribal societies as refugees, and the greater importance of
Charles Town as an urban focus with its mulatto, creole subculture, but by 1750
the human geography of the Low Country of Greater Carolina was, as in the
islands, more African than European.

Louisiana also had close affiliations with the West Indies and came under increasing influence from St. Domingue, the French archetype of planter society, but it remained distinct. There was an important difference in the proportions, complexities, and relationships of its peoples. Unlike the islands, in Louisiana Africans were no more than a third of the population, and the more thorough mixing of Africans, Indians, and Europeans had created even more complex gradations of color and physique. Most Africans were slaves but a good many were not, and although European prejudice pressured toward an Afro-American segregated subsociety, the legal and social distinctions were less sharp, the possibilities for acculturation much greater. Baptism, marriage. manumission, and civil rights were demonstrably even if not readily nor reliably available. Thus Blacks and mulattos were laced all through Louisiana society: they were to be found in all settings—urban, plantation, small farm, backwoods; at many levels—from gang slave to plantation owner, from household servant to prosperous tradesman; and often in intimate, regular association with Europeans, Indians, and mestizos—as husbands, wives, mistresses, children, and partners of various sorts. We may assume that slavery was no less harsh on individuals here than elsewhere (and no less harsh under a Black than a White master), and it is clear that most Blacks here as elsewhere in America lived on the lowest levels of society, but it is also important to recognize that the overall context of Afro-American life in this multiracial, stratified society was critically different from that in other North American colonies.

A third Afro-American society gradually emerged in Greater Virginia. Here Blacks were present almost from the beginning but relatively unimportant for half a century, during which time they were part of a variously indentured labor force composed more of Europeans than Africans. The regional economy shifted toward ever-heavier dependence on slave labor, but the social context and consequences differed from those of the West Indies. Tobacco was a more exacting and a less dominant crop; slaves worked less in gangs, at more varied tasks, and under greater supervision than in the sugar islands. There were more Whites about and at various levels, as fellow laborers, as foremen, as artisans and tradesmen, and as landowners large and small. As there were no real urban centers, Africans and Europeans, Blacks and mulattos, field hands and domestic servants lived together in a patriarchal, rural society. White owners and overseers intervened in the daily and even the family affairs of their slaves, yet treated them as a separate caste. Thus Blacks were an integral part of every Tidewater rural community and thereby under heavy White influence, yet they had been given a single social identity and were numerous enough and in close enough contact among neighboring farms to sustain a subsociety of their own. Therefore, as Berlin concludes, "Afro-American culture in the Chesapeake evolved parallel with Anglo-American culture and with a considerable congruence."

A final regional type of Afro-American society was that found in the northern colonies, and this category can without strain be extended to Bermuda. The basic characterizing feature was the fact that Blacks were a minority who lived and worked in close proximity with Whites, who indulged in slavery more as a matter of social prestige than from a need for labor. Blacks served as domestics, stable hands, and gardeners for most of the wealthy and many of the middling classes in all the northern cities; they were to be found as laborers, artisans, and sailors around the docks in every seaport; they groomed the estates and helped man the vessels of Narragansett and Bermudian planters and traders; they were common on the farms of the Dutch and English of the lower Hudson, and employed in the ironworks and tanneries of New Jersey and Pennsylvania. Living amongst Whites, in back rooms, lofts, alley shacks, stables, and farm sheds, "they also rubbed elbows with lower-class Whites in taverns, cock fights, and fairs where poor people of varying status mingled." Because they were costly to maintain and a nuisance to supervise, they tended to be given a good deal of freedom, often being allowed to hire themselves out for wages. Northern and Bermudian Blacks, therefore, learned the ways of the dominant society quickly but were not severely suppressed in their Africanness, and thus still another form of Afro-American society emerged.

In all these areas there were some important features internal to Afro-American life: the presence of free Blacks as well as slaves, of dark-skinned and light-skinned, of African-born and American-born, of locally born and those shipped in from other American regions; but the incidence and significance of these features, too, will be affected by the larger regional context.

These several regions, therefore, are basic to any understanding of the transformation of Africans into Afro-Americans. We would expect those in the northern colonies to conform most rapidly and fully to Euro-American patterns, those in the West Indies and South Carolina to retain more of their Africanness, and those in Louisiana to have the greatest African influence upon the encompassing society. But such generalizations need a great deal of refinement. They gloss over complexities at every stage of the process of culture change inferred.

"African" itself, of course, is a European-imposed category and much too general for many purposes. African-born Blacks were in fact usually identified with a tribal or geographic origin (although the latter was often the place of export rather than the actual homeland), and dealers and buyers in the main marts developed strong preferences for certain peoples over others. In the 1750s, for example, Charles Town buyers stated preferences for Gambians and natives of the Gold Coast and strong prejudices against "Calabars" (Ibos) as being less durable and tractable, although they were actually supplied with more Angolans than any other. Nevertheless, the systems of marketing and plantation management worked effectively against the creation of African ethnic clusters in North America, although individuals might retain and indeed pass on to descendants a specific ethnic identity. Yet even if they came from dozens of different tribes, such groups were not sharply differentiated in many basic features. The peoples of Guinea, Western Sudan, and the Congo had a common heritage in the same sense that "Europeans" did. Being uprooted, exported, and thrown together under slavery forced them to search for that which they had in common and define it in terms viable under radically different conditions. Thus the "African" component in emergent Afro-American societies was itself an American creation.

There was much that they could not bring with them or recreate on American shores. They could not transfer any large part of their social and political structures with all their richly developed practices and paraphernalia, nor any of those ways dependent upon particular African ecologies and territorial organization. But there was a good deal that they brought that could survive or be adapted to needs and possibilities in America even under the constrictions of enslavement: a cosmology and a wide range of religious practices, especially those related to rites of passage and to personal problems; folk medicine and pharmacopoeia; food preparation; aesthetic expression in music, song, dance, and work rhythms, and in the plastic arts of woodworking, basketry, and weaving; architecture in self-built slave huts; the intricacies and nuances of family life; language.

All of these things were altered in transfer. There were reductions, selections, blendings, and adaptations; some features, such as family life, were subjected to severe limitations, distortions, and capricious disruptions. What must be stressed is the fact that their persistence in any degree in any form represented the vitality of African culture under unusually severe pressures of acculturation. Despite all that was forced upon them, Africans themselves were, basically and ultimately, the creators of Afro-American life. The point needs emphasizing because time-worn simplicities about "slaves" and "Blacks"—as uniform categories of hapless people severed from their past, with no control over their future—still have an insidious power even though thoroughly refuted. Just what Africans did bring across the Atlantic, what they retained, adapted, adopted, created, contributed remains uncertain in many respects, but the importance of the topic to any interpretation of the shaping of America can no longer be denied. We have, at last, begun to recognize that Africans, too, were immigrants, pioneers, participants in the creation of most American societies and regions.

18. Defining Areas

PARTITIONING THE CONTINENT

In 1750 eastern North America and the West Indies were a patchwork of European claims and jurisdiction. The partitioning of America was part of a vast Euro-

peanizing process and experiment, an ongoing development of a worldwide imperialism that did much to shape modern concepts about relationships between
polity and territory, leading toward a comprehensive division of the globe into
exactly delimited sovereign compartments. The very lines on the map exhibited
this imperial power and process because they had been imposed upon the continent with little reference to indigenous peoples, and indeed in many places with
little reference to the land itself. The invaders had parceled the continent among
themselves in designs reflective of their own complex rivalries and relative power,
and the particular geopolitical impress of the Spanish, French, and English empires upon North America represented the distinct ways each had created, partitioned, and governed its overseas territories.

Florida, Coahuila, Texas, and Nuevo Santander had been created by governmental orders, developed directly as extensions from adjacent parts of the Spanish
empire, elevated into provinces and routinely administered through the centralized imperial hierarchy. Florida was a province of the *audienca* of Santo Domingo, the other three were provinces of the *audienca* of Guadalajara, and all were
within the viceroyalty of New Spain seated in Mexico City. Any vagueness of
provincial boundaries would be resolved by decree whenever required by the needs
of effective administration.

The French empire had also developed under close governmental authority, at
times with the assistance of private companies. Technically all New France was
under the jurisdiction of the governor-general at Quebec, but Acadia, Canada,
and Louisiana had emerged from three distinct initiations in very different areas,
and Louisbourg, Quebec, and New Orleans each had direct connections with
Paris. The three territories were based chiefly upon the broad pattern of nature, on
hydrographic basins and the insular remnants of Acadia.

The English pattern reveals a striking contrast to these relative simplicities. In
1750 the seaboard south from the Gulf of St. Lawrence was segmented into fifteen
political jurisdictions greatly varied in size, shape, and types of boundaries. It was
the result of such a complex accumulation of decisions by a succession of monarchs
over a span of 126 years (from the Virginia Company of 1606 to Georgia of 1732),
responding to such a variety of agents and motives, and employing such different
and often conflicting criteria for the definition of areas that it seems hardly representative of a system at all. The map was in fact a reflection of an empire distinct in
history, structure, and meaning from its continental competitors.

A good deal of the complexity of this English pattern resulted from the use at
different times of different criteria for the allocation of territory to particular
colonial undertakings. There is a basic problem, quite apart from whatever the
contending factions of the moment might be, in the task of partitioning such a
lengthy coastline from across the seas without reference to local peoples. Nature
offers immense variety but few compelling boundaries. Man must select some basis

for demarcation. He may choose to anchor his territorial pattern upon what he discerns to be prominent points and lineaments of nature, or he may draw upon an arbitrary system of his own design anchored, as it were, upon the stars, the geodetic system of latitudes rather than a terrestrial set of landmarks. Seafarers were routinely familiar with both: they navigated the oceans by the one and coasted the continents by the other. And cartographers made use of both as they slowly improved the accuracy of position, shape, and scale of the America looming ever larger along the western edge of Atlantic charts.

The first charter of the Virginia Company (1606) made use of a purely astral definition: that portion of America lying between 34° and 45° north latitude. The second (1609) defined a latitudinal belt in terms of a landmark: the boundaries to be drawn from coastal points two hundred miles to the north and two hundred to the south of Point Comfort, the latter being the northern promontory as one entered the estuary of the James River. Typically neither charter endured, and the northern and southern boundaries of Virginia became fixed by later charters defining Maryland and Carolina, the former following the south bank of the Potomac, the latter a westward latitudinal projection from the northern end of Currituck Inlet. Such combinations of criteria so clearly reflective of seafaring perspectives were not uncommon.

Great rivers offering passage into the continent were major features of obvious interest to seafarers, but they provided alternative possibilities for the demarcation of territories. They could of course be used directly as boundaries, but that would disrupt the natural integrity of the river basin, a unity of basic importance to any people depending upon waterways for transportation. Thus, for example, Canada and New Netherland were at least implicitly defined in terms of hydrographic basins, along watersheds rather than waterways.

Over many decades, involving a long sequence of patents and grants and the annexation of territories from the Netherlands and France, the English made use of all these methods, and, with the added complication of incomplete and often inaccurate maps, they thereby created a great deal of complexity, confusion, and conflict within their own imperial structure. Thus the St. Croix, Kennebec, Piscataqua, Merrimack, Connecticut, Delaware, Potomac, Savannah, and Altamaha rivers were used in some way as intercolonial boundaries. New York and the Lower Counties along the Delaware still reflected in part the hydrographic definition of New Netherland, the boundary between the Lower Counties and Maryland having been translated into an approximate geometric equivalent to the actual watershed between the Delaware estuary and Chesapeake Bay. At the same time, portions of the boundaries of Massachusetts, Connecticut, New York, Pennsylvania, Maryland, Virginia, and the Carolinas were set along specific latitudes, while those between the Carolinas, between New Jersey and New York, and much of Rhode Island's bounds were drawn at angles projected from some base point.

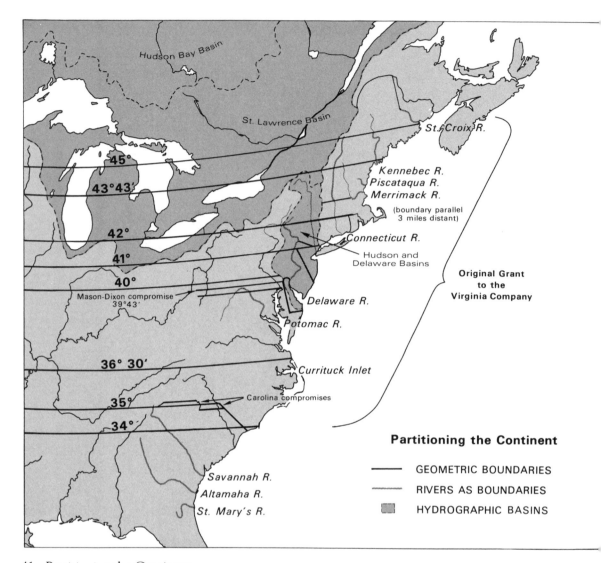

41. Partitioning the Continent.

The northern boundary of the Lower Counties was unique in being a portion of a circle drawn from a twelve-mile radius centered on the capital town of New Castle.

There were enormous geopolitical consequences and implications in this patchwork of empire. Leaving aside the many contentions over the exact designation or positioning of particular boundaries, several colonies were brought into broader disputes arising from the application of different boundary criteria in the charters to adjacent lands. Thus the latitudinal claims of Massachusetts and Connecticut extended directly across large portions of New York, New Jersey, and Pennsylvania, which had been defined in part by hydrography. Virginia and North Carolina had apparently unimpeded latitudinal swaths westward, but analogous claims of South Carolina and Georgia were as yet complicated by the uncertain extent and legal definitions of their other boundaries along rivers. With the Savannah River marking its western bounds, South Carolina was an angled coastal segment truncated by the latitudinal extension of North Carolina, making it a very small piece of the grand belts of the earliest Carolinas. Maryland was similarly pinched between the northwest trend of its Potomac boundary and its geodetic border with Pennsylvania. Three political units, the Lower Counties, New Jersey, and Rhode Island, were already fixed as seaboard colonies without prospect of inland extension.

Great differences in size were apparent. These must obviously have some bearing upon potentials for development, but were not a direct cause of political strain within the empire because it was not run as a coherent system of reasonably balanced parts. Little Rhode Island was not really anomalous; it happened to be a survivor among several colonies of similar size in the area: Plymouth, New Haven, and early Connecticut. Both Rhode Island and the Lower Counties were larger in area than Bermuda, Barbados, and several island colonies. In daily economic and cultural life, ready access to the sea was more important than potentials for westward expansion beyond the mountains, and Rhode Island, especially, was a thriving exhibit of that fact. All the mainland colonies had direct access to the sea, all had begun at tidewater, but they differed greatly in sea frontage and quality of such entryways. Pennsylvania was the most constricted, served only by the relatively shallow Delaware. Penn and his successors long sought to enlarge their frontage, by trying to annex the Lower Counties (an area which the Baltimores claimed as rightfully part of Maryland), and by insisting upon an interpretation of their charter that would place the head of Chesapeake Bay within their southern boundary (a claim steadfastly resisted by Maryland). Chesapeake Bay and New York Harbor were also major seaways shared among political jurisdictions. In the north Piscataqua Harbor was divided between New Hampshire and the Maine district of Massachusetts.

This geopolitical impress of empires is fundamental. It will be further altered, grossly or in detail, but never fully effaced as regards any one of these many units. These basic territorial compartments of political life are of course the most common framework for the description and analysis of this "colonial era." However, they coexist without exact concordance with the actual societies that developed from the many nuclei implanted on these shores. An important link between these two sets of patterns is another: the spatial frameworks of local administration, which reflect some special characteristics of each society within its larger political bounds.

FRAMEWORKS FOR LOCAL GOVERNMENT

Segmentation of the continent into large political territories provided a gross framework for potential development, but life is localized and daily routines were more intimately shaped by areal patterns of a different scale. Some program for local government, for the administration of law and order, was an essential part of all organized colonizations and an important framework for community life. Such designs reflect basic philosophies held by colonizing authorities, and in these as in so many features of colonial life, developments would reflect conditions and experiences in America as well as traditions and designs transplanted from Europe.

The emergence of the local geopolitical framework was usually slow and intermittent. Initially the nucleus was the whole, so that the central authority of the colonizing agency was the local government; only as settlement expanded was subdivision into additional territorial units necessary.

The contrasting character of the three empires was reflected in their local political geographies. Florida was an early and Texas a late example of the routine imposition of order upon a new area according to the minutely detailed regulations of the Laws of the Indies. The Spanish empire was a civic-centered system. The colonizier or *adelantado* was required first of all to select a site and lay out the plan of his capital town, designating the position of the plaza, church, and municipal building. He was empowered to distribute lots and to appoint a council (*cabildo*), and his authority extended over the surrounding countryside to whatever extent required by the developing colony. In both Florida and Texas military and ecclesiastical orders were concomitant with this civic order: presidios and missions were established alongside the pueblos. Thus in terms of local political structure and geography, Spanish imperial provinces were essentially collections of municipalities.

In contrast, New France was a pattern of districts and regions, each with its local governor, *intendant* (civil administrator), *conseil supérieur*, courts, and vicar general. A town was simply part of the district, rather than the countryside an extension from the town as in the Spanish system. Thus the settled area of Canada was divided into three regions, administered from Quebec, Trois-Rivières, and Montreal. The outlying districts of Labrador, the St. Lawrence below Eboulements-Rimouski, and the interior above Veudreuil-Chateauguay were each a *domaine du roi* reserved for fishing or the fur trade under the eye of a local commandant. Similarly, Upper Louisiana (Illinois) was a district with a commandant under the authority of officials seated in New Orleans. French Acadia was a loosely organized unit governed from Louisbourg. Some parts, but far from all, of these districts were also organized into parishes, wherein a very minimal civil administration was provided by the local captain of the militia. This last feature was a telling exhibit of the strongly military character of government in New France.

English America was a radically different creation. There was no consistent territorial hierarchy in England to draw upon, and no standardized policy of colonization ever formulated to give common shape to the local geopolitical patterns of the many implantations. The terms that appear in the colonies—*shire, county, hundred, township, parish, manor, town, precinct, borough, city*—all derived from English usage, but variations in their incidence and meaning were bewilderingly complex at home and some of their applications in America were without obvious precedent. Each colony created its own system; although there were numerous similarities and convergent development, the full structure was never exactly duplicated between one colony and another. Nevertheless, several types of local patterns can be recognized.

The most common administrative subdivision was the *county*. These existed in all of the colonies that had established internal units by 1750 (Nova Scotia and Georgia had none) but they varied greatly in significance. Counties were the principal local political entities in Virginia, Maryland, North Carolina, and Delaware; they were very important in Pennsylvania, somewhat less important in New Jersey and New York, still less in Massachusetts and New Hampshire, no more than judicial districts in Rhode Island, and little more than that in Connecticut. Counties had been proclaimed quite early in South Carolina, and county courts were later created, but none of these had any effect, for the province was in fact run by the oligarchy and central court in Charles Town, and divided into parishes for ecclesiastical and minor administrative purposes.

The weakness of the county in New England was a reflection of the strength of the *town* as the primary local unit. The New England town is an American creation, combining features from various English precedents of parishes, towns, and hundreds. It refers to what elsewhere is more commonly called a township, an area of several square miles, usually containing one or more villages or larger settlements. It became the central unit in these colonies because of their foundation by relatively homogeneous and initially cohesive groups: it was the convenient territorial dimension of the implanted community that was zealous in establishing its local political authority. The powers and importance of these towns were at their maximum in Connecticut and Rhode Island, where the central government was considered more as a federation of towns than as a superior sovereign authority. Towns were basic in Massachusetts and its New Hampshire satellite, but here counties were also given certain judicial, fiscal, and administrative powers.

When the English took over New Netherland they established the town as the basis of local government, in part to accommodate the Dutch patchwork of self-governing villages, municipalities, manors, and thinly settled rural districts. In both New York and New Jersey rudimentary counties were also created, and later these were reorganized and so empowered as to create a division and in considerable degree a territorial hierarchy of local authority. Counties were governed by boards of supervisors elected from each town in a structured relationship unique to these two colonies. Towns continued to have important powers; a few of the old manors functioned in effect as towns (and three of the largest were, like counties, electoral districts for representation in the colonial assembly); and areas too sparsely populated to support town government were formed into precincts.

Pennsylvania was a further and important variation. Here counties formed the chief basis of local government, with towns assigned little significance, but a number of *boroughs* were established independent of towns, giving the larger settlements chartered authority distinct from that of the county. As such centers developed so did their local powers, giving an ever-clearer political distinction between rural and urban life.

South of Pennsylvania, where counties were fully dominant, some kind of subdivision for minor electoral and administrative convenience was common. In Delaware the old English term *hundred* remained in use for such districts; in Maryland and Virginia the original hundreds had been replaced by *parishes*, which in keeping with Anglican practice were both ecclesiastical and civil in function; in North Carolina resistance to Anglican domination resulted in the creation of *precincts* rather than parishes for local administration.

A further colonial complexity was the wide disparity in the political status of municipalities. In England boroughs or cities had gradually attained more and more self-government by contracting out from the jurisdiction of and the obligations of service to encompassing local authority, whether manor, hundred, or perhaps even the county. Such places were recognized more as corporations, a bundle of privileges, than as territories or units in a national hierarchy. Most colonial charters gave the proprietor or governor power to incorporate boroughs or cities, but the interpretation, motivation, use, and results of such privileges over the years varied greatly. Incorporation seems to have been used less in response to the actual political needs of a growing settlement than as a device to foster the emergence of cities out of the wilderness. The earliest municipal incorporations were those of Bermuda City, James City, Henrico, and a few other "plantations" along the James River, a program probably modeled after that of Ulster and envisioned as a means of implanting civilization around urban nuclei of officials, artisans, and shopkeepers. These Virginian paper cities were only the first of many such fruitless attempts in the Chesapeake region. They also established a precedent for the inclusion of an extensive countryside within the bounds of the municipality, as was done in a number of later charters elsewhere. Capitals were sometimes given the dignity of formal incorporation even if they were no more than small settlements (as in the case of Burlington and Perth Amboy, Williamsburg and Annapolis) compared with the genuine city capitals of Pennsylvania and New York. In Pennsylvania and West Jersey the *shire town* was formally recognized as a distinct type of municipality, with special market privileges as well as judicial and administrative functions. But the elusive and uneven incidence and imprint of the city as a geopolitical entity in English America is attested by the continuing uncertainty as to just how many charters were issued and to what effect, by the incongruities between incorporation and population, and by the fact that several of the largest communities were not municipal incorporations at all: Boston, Newport, and New Haven were governed as New England towns, Charles Town by a parish vestry and various boards. The most comprehensive and democratically elected city government was that of New York City, the chief center with Dutch as well as English antecedents.

This brief review can no more than hint at the actual internal variety in the forms and workings of English local government in America. Our chief concern is with the territorial patterning, the areal framework of community life. In these we find no common hierarchy, scale, or political meaning. In New England initially the territory was formed around the community, and that concept of the town became the model framework for the formation of new communities as settlement expanded. In Virginia the community gradually formed within the arbitrary bounds of the county, and was most visible in seasonal gatherings to the county seat. The New England town and the Virginia county were well suited to the rural society each encompassed, but only the former was of a scale readily adapted to serve the internal burgeoning of a city as well. Hence New England municipalities were simply densely settled towns, whereas a genuine Virginian city, such as Norfolk, had to seek separate incorporation. Pennsylvania's concept of boroughs and shire towns was a more consistent structuring of rural and urban relationships, while New York (and to a large extent New Jersey) created a truly interlocking hierarchy of counties, towns, and precincts, with ready accommodation of chartered municipalities as separate features. Thus the English colonies in America displayed something of the diversities of their antecedents, the marked variety of their initiators, and the continued vitality of the English genius for adaptation, for endless tinkering with both forms and substance. Even if an occasional parallel to these adaptations might be discerned in some detail of Spanish and French colonial administration, overall the English empire was a starkly different creation in local government as in so many other features.

PATTERNING THE COUNTRYSIDE

Within these jurisdictional territories of civil authority lay the more intimate and pervasively influential patterns of land parcels, those units marked off for specific tenure, the frameworks of actual settlement. Colonization requires some method of land allocation, and as Jordan has stated,

> few, if any, choices and decision are more permanent and prominent in the cultural

landscape. In some parts of the Old World, divisional patterns created by surveyors now thousands of years in their graves remain visible and functional today, while in North America the handiwork of early colonial surveyors is still vividly marked on the land.

And few, if any, decisions of this kind were so free of local precedents and constraints as those in Atlantic America. By refusing to recognize any indigenous order upon the land, the invaders and colonizers created a tabula rasa upon which they could impose any kind of design their minds could conceive for such purposes.

As Reps demonstrates in his series of great books on town planning in America, an assiduous reconnaissance can turn up some very imaginative designs indeed— arcs and circles and diagonals and elaborate sets of nested squares and much more in many variations. But, ultimately, colonization was not an abstract process, and both Old World precedents and New World practicalities favored simpler, more efficient methods of fixing a pattern upon the ground. Northwest Europeans were not unfamiliar with the process; Ireland, Aquitaine, and new polderlands provided examples and experience. The sheer scale and the rawness of American landscapes and the high costs and weakness of control overseas tended to defeat elaborate paper designs. We are concerned here with general results rather than the full process in each case. In that broad view we can readily recognize three quite distinct types of patterns impressed upon the American landscape, and we can define a fourth rather less obvious in character but widespread in occurrence.

One basic type, *metes and bounds*, arises from the particular process of land allocation in which recipients are given claims not to a designated parcel but to a specific quantity of land wherever it can be found unclaimed by another. Claimants therefore were free to draw the boundaries of their holding in any way so as to include the most valuable resources—the best soil, woodlands, access to water; such boundaries need not be in any prescribed shape nor such claims contiguous with any others. Later claimants might take up some but not necessarily all of the land remaining. In this method the cadastre is created by the process: the design takes shape in piecemeal fashion with each successive individual decision rather than the whole being predetermined by a single authority. A map of the overall result will likely seem a crazy quilt with little discernible order, but if taken into the field it may be seen to reflect the varying qualities of nature as perceived by pioneers. In that simple geographic sense metes and bounds is a very rational system. It is also a strongly individualistic, competitive system in which those who get there first can claim the best as defined by their own judgment. Thus in a sociopolitical sense it reflects the lack of any central authority concerned with regularizing or equalizing access to resources or with shaping the pattern of settlement. The process of allocation becomes a scramble of random withdrawals from an initially enormous fund; boundary conflicts become endemic; and the complex

42. Some Survey Patterns.

Upper: metes and bounds patterns. *Left:* a portion of All Hallow's Parish, tidewater Maryland; courtesy Carville V. Earle (1975). *Right:* metes and bounds patterns applied to an area of rugged terrain near the Delaware Water Gap; adapted from Peter O. Wacker (1975). **Lower:** riverine long lots. *Left:* area of Palatine German settlement along the Mohawk River; a portion of *DeWitt's State Map of New York, 1793*. *Right:* portions of Ile d'Orleans and north bank and south bank of the St. Lawrence River, Quebec; adapted from Gédéon de Catalogne map, 1709.

pattern finally produced might pose serious problems for social interaction and provision of services. Such a system found great favor in British North America. It was used in the opening of various tracts in New York and New Jersey, and it prevailed in all the colonies south of Pennsylvania.

At the opposite extreme were those highly *regularized surveys* wherein land was marked off in uniform blocks, usually *rectangular*, prior to allocation to claimants and purchasers. Such a superimposition of a rigid geometry upon the varying qualities of nature suggests a greater concern for orderly procedures and standardization of parcels than for individual freedom to search out the richest resources. Such simple rectilinear systems were also easier to survey and denominate and therefore greatly reduced boundary controversies, but they also tended to spread the population thinly over an area without close reference to natural features, and this might pose awkward problems in actual land utilization and communications. The most common application of such gridiron patterns was at the local scale of town plans, as exemplified early in the case of New Haven, later in the famous design of Philadelphia, in elaborate form in Savannah, and in various forms in many others. The township settlements in interior South Carolina were laid out as nested rectangles of village, township, and parish. A good many larger tracts in Pennsylvania and frontier New England were subdivided into more or less rectangular parcels, but with various base lines and orientations. Such uniform geometric survey systems were not rare but they were not applied to the whole of any of the colonies.

A third type applied something of both of these concepts to a particular kind of physical environment. It was logical for seafarers moving up the estuaries and rivers to lay claims to blocks of land lying back from river frontages. The seigneuries along the St. Lawrence, the patroons along the Hudson, and the plantations along the James displayed this simple riverine type. The much more distinctive variation of *riverine long lots* developed along the first of these rivers but not the latter two. The difference arose from variations in control, economy, and the settlement process. As there was little basis for profitable speculation in land, Canadian seigneuries were subdivided into family subsistence farms, with each habitant having a frontage on the great river highway. Further subdivision through the generations imprinted the entire valley with an almost uniform pattern of narrow lots with straightline boundaries running back from the river. There was an unusual equality built into such a land system. Each settler had access to the main trafficway and the same sequence of lands from riverbank through a succession of higher terraces and of locations from the water's edge to a deep hinterland. The narrowness of the lots made possible the development of close social proximity in the line of farmsteads parallel with the river, and the eventual emergence of a distinctive *strassendorf* pattern as churches, mills, and other services were added.

There were local areas of riverine long lots in many colonies, such as along portions of the Connecticut, Mohawk, Delaware, and Savannah rivers, and this form predominated along the Mississippi in Louisiana and in the bottomlands of Illinois. Long lots also show up in Texas as irrigation strips along the San Antonio River. Occasionally long lots were laid out fronting on a road rather than a river, as in parts of Bergen County, New Jersey.

These three land survey types—metes and bounds, uniform (rectangular), and long lots—left their distinctive marks upon various colonies and land tracts, but a general view of the northern English colonies suggests recognition of a fourth type as the most common pattern. It may well be called survey by *adaptive order*. Lots were laid out prior to sale in orderly fashion in contiguous plats, or nearly so, often rectilinear, or nearly so, but varied in sizes, shapes, and orientations, fitted in some cases to major natural features, or to main roads, or to the geometric boundaries of large land grants, or to some other base line. The well-known map of Pennsylvania in 1687 by Thomas Holme (see figure 28 above) with its composite of rectangles, riverine strips and other long lots, and even lots radial from a town square, all laid out in various sizes within many separate but contiguous tracts, is a fine display of this kind of land survey. The pattern of New England towns and lots is another version of the same type. General policies in that region favored contiguous expansion by town units of a size and compact form appropriate to community needs, marked out in at least vaguely rectangular fashion with town and lot boundaries adapted to local landmarks and terrain features.

Thus there was as much variation in land survey patterns as there was in local government and the size and shape of the colonial territories themselves, and for the same reasons. All of these things reflect the absence in the English empire of a centralized imperial program with prescribed ways of planting and governing in the wake of conquering. They spring from a great variety of European motivations and American circumstances, from opportunism and empirical adaptation rather than a single system of colonization.

These survey patterns are important because they set the spatial matrix for local life. They define the basic settlement form, with direct influence upon the arrangement of population upon the land, the shapes of fields and the lines of roads, upon proximities and possibilities for contact and services. And despite the regional and local diversities of such patterns, in the broader view one important general feature was apparent: the dominance of dispersed over clustered settlement. There were many examples of the latter in Atlantic America, many attempts to transplant or to foster close-knit communities gathered around a church or meetinghouse of some kind, but in most regions these stand out as curious exceptions to the common pattern. The one region where clustered settlement was unexceptional was New England, where the Puritan attempt to build a Christian commonwealth laid great stress upon social cohesion. The very distinctive patterns of Wethersfield and other early Connecticut Valley towns, with their central set of home lots, commons, and outlying arable strips, have been reprinted time and again as representative of the geographical form of this New England ideal (see figure 18 above). But these American versions of the communal farm-village were never the dominant form. Although the concept of community remained unusually strong, and the lack of a speculative commercial crop and the relatively small farms held New Englanders rather more thickly on the ground than in other regions, the tendencies there as elsewhere were toward dispersion. And that was a simple reflection of the great fact that Atlantic America was being parceled out in farms; leaving aside many technicalities of tenure, most of these were essentially owner-operated farms, and people sought to live on the land they owned and worked.

Survey systems, settlement forms, and society are intimately related. Maps of America at this very local scale display distinctive regional landscapes, but they can also help us to discern some basic common emphases in colonial life: apartness, individualism, privatism. And indeed, in defining areas at this scale the kind of map we rarely see may be the most important of all for the intensive study of society, then or now: the cadastral map of properties. However, we cannot bring such matters into effective focus from our chosen perspective, and we must now shift our view from this nested set of jurisdictional areas to the broader impress of peoples, societies, and cultures.

19. The Europeanized Area: Populations and Regional Societies, circa 1750

By 1750 Europeans had fixed their hold upon and put to regular use harbors, bays, and river entranceways from the Arctic to the tropical seas. But the attractions varied greatly from place to place, and over long stretches of the North American coast their hold was marginal and sporadic. In the north were the scattering of seafarers along the rocky promontories and islands from Cape Ann to Labrador, the naval bastions of Halifax and Louisbourg, the Acadian farmers edged around the tidal marshlands, and, lightest of all, the half-dozen fur trading posts on Hudson Bay, the most minimal fixations on American shores. On the southeastern margins of the continent European rivalries and imperial policies had created a few outposts as at Fort William, St. Augustine, Mobile, and Biloxi, but had rendered many other good harbors too dangerous for planting and had inhibited any broad colonial development. Where settlement had taken more extensive hold in these northern and southern sectors, along the lower St. Lawrence and the lower Mississippi, it was still so narrowly riparian that virtually every habitation was within sight of the waterway.

NEWFOUNDLAND

ACADIA

CANADA

NEW ENGLAND

HUDSON VALLEY—EAST JERSEY

GREATER PENNSYLVANIA

GREATER VIRGINIA

BERMUDA

ILLINOIS
COUNTRY

GREATER SOUTH CAROLINA

FLORIDA

BAHAMAS

LOUISIANA

3. Europeanized Area, c. 1750.

But in between, while much of the actual strand was nearly blank on the map of settlement, harboring at most an occasional seafaring cluster of fishermen, whalers, smugglers, or pilots, a series of bays and passageways through the sandy coastal shield now led to the thresholds of productive regions where conquering and planting had established Europeans as the dominant population over a highly uneven but essentially contiguous zone of settlement from New Hampshire to Georgia. From the anchorages along the Piscataqua one might trace the marchlands of these colonizations westward and southward, reaching inland along the Merrimack, Connecticut, Hudson, and Mohawk, blunted along the higher, rougher ground toward Monadnock, the Berkshires, and the Taconic Range. West of the Hudson the line curved southward and west along the base of the Helderbergs, Catskills, Poconos, and the long wall of ridges just beyond the Great Valley, trending ever deeper into the continent, culminating in a narrow salient of settlements tucked in the mountains of western Virginia two hundred miles from the nearest tidewater.

South from the Potomac the edge of the main settlement regions followed along the eastern base of the Blue Ridge, trending southwesterly to the upper reaches of the Roanoke and Dan rivers, defining the broadest body of Europeanized lands in North America. Farther south the pattern was much more frayed and rapidly chang-ing as pioneers converged on the rolling red hills of the Carolina Piedmont. Native Virginians and new immigrants were moving southward into a succession of dis-tricts along the Yadkin, Pedee, Catawba, Saluda, and Congree, and in any of these valleys they might meet other land seekers coming up from the tidewater country.

The shape of this European margin was closely related to terrain along some bold natural features but in other places it reflected colonial land policies, the presence of still-strong Indian nations, and imperial rivalries. The Iroquois, Cherokees, and Creeks were bulwarks stabilizing long sections. The experience of recurrent bitter warfare in the wilderness border zone between New England and New France was a deterrent to any rapid northward thrust of the generally expansive Yankees, and a similar situation toward the frontier with Spanish Florida confined Georgian set-tlers near their early footholds. Much the most vigorous expansion was into the western districts of Virginia and the Carolinas. It was a response to the ready availability of good lands widely advertised, a broad belt of country opened to speculators and settlers after a century of wanton destruction, expulsion, and withdrawal of the Indians from all the country east of the mountains between the Potomac and the reserve of the enfeebled Catawbas in South Carolina. That this surge was more a southerly extension from Pennsylvania and Virginia than a direct inward reach from the Carolina seaboard was an expression of the greater popula-tion base and demographic vigor of Virginia and Pennsylvania as well as the strong channeling of European immigration through the ports on the Delaware.

In the tropical seas the demographic imprint of the European intrusion took on further complexities. Some islands were completely and densely occupied, such as Bermuda and, to an almost incredible degree, Barbados. On many others nearly all the coastal lowlands and readily accessible slopes suitable to commercial agriculture had been developed, as was the case on St. Christopher, Martinique, Guadalupe, and to a larger extent French St. Domingue and English Jamaica. But on Spanish Hispaniola, Puerto Rico, and Cuba there were large areas once well settled but now empty of Indians and Spanish alike, the legacy of a sudden and vicious exploitation, the gradual enfeeblement of colonial enterprise, and long neglect in the face of greater attractions in Mexico and other mainland provinces. In this old Spanish threshold the European presence was focused on a few major harbors and old administrative centers, such as Santo Domingo, San Juan, and Havana.

In 1750 there were perhaps 1,300,000 living within the European-dominated areas north of the Rio Grande, and another 300,000 in those French and English tropical islands most closely linked to the mainland. Such figures are necessarily general and inferential, for few regular or careful enumerations had been made in many districts.

Estimates for the various political units reveal very great differences in size of populations (see table 3), and these also reflect, of course, great differences in density of settlement, from the more than 450 per square mile on the slave-intensive island of Barbados to the thin scatterings on many mainland frontiers, but such calculations can be seriously misleading unless one knows what area and type of settlement are being measured. For example, about twenty percent of the

Table 3
Estimated Populations of Colonies, c. 1750
(In Thousands)

Hudson Bay (Europeans only)	.1	The Lower Counties	15
Newfoundland	7	Maryland	130
Acadia–Nova Scotia	15	Virginia	260
New Hampshire	35	North Carolina	65
Massachusetts & Maine	230	South Carolina	70
Connecticut	100	Georgia	4
Rhode Island	35	Florida	3
Canada	55	Louisiana & Illinois	10
New York	75	Bermuda & Bahamas	12
East Jersey	34	Barbados	75
West Jersey	36	St. Domingue	200
Pennsylvania	150	Texas & Lower Rio Grande	5

Note: Calculated from Wells, Green and Harrington, and various local studies.

population of Canada, Rhode Island, and New York lived in Quebec and
Montreal, Newport, and New York City, respectively, an urban population that
reflects the major role of seafaring, administrative functions, and in some cases
military activities in these areas, whereas Philadelphia and Boston, the two largest
cities of North America, accounted for ten percent or less of the populations of
their colonies. If we exclude these cities, rough estimates for the densities of the
essentially rural populations within the settled areas of the mainland vary from
about thirty per square mile in Massachusetts to sixteen in Pennsylvania, eight in
Virginia, and six in New York.

Such populations were very largely sustained by a distinctly new North American ecology that was a complex of European and Indian (and in places other)
elements. The formation of this new subsistence complex had begun almost immediately from necessity rather than choice. Europeans generally attempted to transfer familiar homeland systems to American soil but that was never an easy task, and
often a hazardous and sometimes impossible one. Jamestown is only the most
famous among many early colonizations saved from complete starvation by the
purchase or plunder of Indian food stocks. Incorporation of Indian crops and
techniques followed, reluctantly, experimentally, but ultimately routinely. The
great American contribution was, of course, maize or Indian corn, in many varieties suited to local conditions. Beans, squash, pumpkin, and sweet potato were
also in time adopted by European colonists, together with a wide array of Indian
food preparation techniques. The great European contributions were cereal grains
and livestock, together with a wide variety of vegetables, fruit, and, more gradually, pasture grasses. In general the balance between the native American and
imported European elements in this new North American agriculture tended to
vary with latitude, the American being predominant in the subtropics where the
wider array and more elaborate developments of native crops were a reflection of a
location closer to the tropical origins of that agriculture, whereas northward this
indigenous agriculture became more limited and the European component much
greater in lands more nearly like those of colonial homelands. But there was much
variation in detail. The patterns among imported elements were often quite dissimilar to those in Europe. For example, despite repeated and extensive efforts,
especially by British colonists, sheep never became important in any of these
colonial regions, whereas in some hogs thrived beyond all expectation. Sheep
suffered from harsh winters, dense forest, poor fodder, natural predators, and a
shortage of shepherds, while swine, omnivorous, prolific, and fiercely protective of
themselves, ran wild to become a staple and a nuisance, especially in the woods
and swamps of the more southerly regions. Hogs "swarm like Vermine upon the
earth," a colonial visitor wrote, "and are often accounted as such." That twen-

tieth-century Americans consume nearly twenty times as much pork as lamb and mutton is a direct legacy of this seventeenth-century pattern.

Thus in most of the well-domesticated regions of these seaboard colonies a large proportion of the population was relatively well fed from the produce of a new agriculture compounded from American and European sources, varied by region and everywhere supplemented by the yields from hunting, trapping, fowling, fishing, and gathering, activities which also made use of various combinations of Indian and European techniques and tools. Such a diet was basic to the vigorous population growth of so many areas by the mid eighteenth century.

The most important geographic framework, however, is neither these two dozen geopolitical units nor the broad ecological zones of the American seaboard, but the half-dozen major regional societies on the North American mainland from the St. Lawrence to the Altamaha (see table 4). Together these comprise ninety-seven percent of the population within the Europeanized sector of the mainland outside of New Spain. These regional societies were the main geographic creations of a century and a half of conquering and planting out of northwest Europe. These were profound and permanent alterations of the human geography of North America. They were not readily denoted and defined; they were not geopolitical units nor sets of units. Indeed, their borders rarely coincide with political boundaries, and such discordance was telling evidence that these imperial creations had not taken place under tight imperial control. Once firmly implanted overseas, colonies tend to take on a life of their own, growing from natural increase, pressing against limits, expanding wherever opportunity beckons, shaped more by the decisions of countless individuals and local groups than by policies proclaimed from the imperial center. Which is not to suggest that such larger political decisions were unim-

Table 4

Estimated Populations of Major Mainland Regional Societies, c. 1750
(In Thousands)

Canada	55
Greater New England (including eastern Long Island)	400
Hudson Valley (including East Jersey)	100
Greater Pennsylvania (including West Jersey and parts of Maryland and Virginia)	230
Greater Virginia (including Tidewater Maryland and parts of North Carolina)	390
Greater South Carolina (including Georgia and parts of North Carolina)	90

portant, but only to emphasize that whatever geopolitical changes might be imposed upon them from afar as pawns in the vast worldwide game of European politics, these major American regions were by now so firmly rooted in place that they could absorb such shocks and would endure as geographic areas distinct in peoples, economies, and cultural landscapes.

These six regions had all begun as European footholds on American shores, but they now differed considerably in sea frontage, focus, general shape, and inland extent. Canada and the Hudson Valley remained utterly simple in structure with everything bound into their great riverine axes connecting estuary and entrepôt at the head of navigation. Greater Pennsylvania was strongly focused on Philadelphia and the Delaware, but expansion westward beyond the Susquehanna had given rise to Baltimore and the Chesapeake as a competitive orientation for an increasingly important sector. New England and Greater South Carolina each had a dominant focus, but also much longer stretches of coastline and numerous ports, some of which had direct connections overseas. In marked contrast to all the others was Greater Virginia, with the most extensive coastland and no major center at all, a large, prosperous, and populous region without a focus, boasting the most valuable export economy of the mainland but no oceanic entrepôt, no urban intermediary between its rural districts and European ports.

The five British American regions were contiguous along the seaboard (except for the minor wedge of Pamlico North Carolina) but were far from being fixed in shape. They were expansive not only into their own Euro-Indian hinterlands but along their interregional borderlands. Such competition was especially apparent where the western margins of New England settlement pressed upon the Hudson Valley. It was also discernible in New Jersey, western Maryland, and the Great Valley of Virginia; it was incipient in the scramble for lands in the Carolina Piedmont where regional character and orientations to the seaboard were as yet uncertain.

Thus the regional geography of North America was now being shaped by internal dynamics, developing and diverging from the European charter societies initially implanted on the American seaboard. We may well conclude our reconnaissance of these many footholds with a brief summation of how such variety can be connected to the same culture hearth.

Northwest Europe's great instrument of expansion was commercial capitalism. The elemental geographic form of that instrument was still apparent in the fur trade, in York Factory, Montreal, and Albany, overseas entrepôts at the western end of the trunk line linking the resource area with the European metropolis. Ideally, for the operation of that system the resident population of such places should be no greater than that needed to carry out effectively the critical business of exchange. But Montreal and Albany were now more than mere commerical outposts: they were diversified centers at the inland end of extensive settlement regions, and those riverine societies of Canada and New York illustrate some of the modifications and complexities that had developed out of the early speculative probes of commercial entrepreneurs. They displayed the demographic, social, and political results of early decisions to provide local subsistence and security by the planting of small colonies, of attempts to attract capital investment and to promote diversified development by the lure of landed estates and privileges, and of the superimposition of imperial programs and the regional pressures of worldwide European rivalries.

Canada and its other neighbor, New England, represent starkly divergent developments of another central feature of this transatlantic outreach. The relationship between capitalism and Protestantism is one of the most controversial of historical topics precisely because it is at once so critical and complex, because it seems certain in importance even if elusive to specify. Northern America was an emanation from the area most intensely associated with the upheavals of the Reformation. The Separatists of Plymouth and the Puritans of Massachusetts Bay are the most famous overseas inseminations of one of the most powerful strains of this European movement, and by 1750 Greater New England provided the world's best exhibit of a regional society in which the compelling commercial drives of capitalism had become fused with a prevailing sense of moral purpose.

Canada represents the other side of the Reformation, which had its own characteristic vigor and moral purpose. The emergence of New France mirrored important phases in the course of events in the mother country. Initiated by entrepreneurs of Atlantic France, American operations had a "fleeting, commercial, bourgeois—even semiliberal—phase" but the shift from company to royal control in 1663 transformed it into "a deliberate and official projection into the New World of a dynamic, authoritarian society at the zenith of its power." Thus Quebec was a North American display of the Counter-Reformation as Boston was of its adversarial Calvinism. By 1750 each society had taken distinct American directions, the mutation of imperial conscripts into habitants matching that of Puritans into Yankees. Both were by now demographically vigorous populations but they differed markedly in total size (Greater New England was more than sevenfold greater than Canada), a feature also related to national religious policies. During the violent course of the Reformation France drove some 200,000 Huguenots into exile, but excluded them from New France:

> The effects on France itself were severe enough, but for Canada the consequences were even more profound. Had the colony offered a place of refuge, an escape for dissenters along New England lines, for even a modest fraction of these exiles, the subsequent history might have been vastly different.

Greater Pennsylvania represented still another manifestation of this Protestant commercial thrust. If its initiation more than half a century after its neighbors was a measure of how long it took for capitalist entrepreneurs to focus on the most suitable seaboard environment for the easy planting of northwest Europeans in American soil, its growth over so short a time was in part a measure of how rapidly and how well those attractions had been appreciated. Its leadership and the prominence and variety of its sects were also a display of the religious dimension of that thrust, but one quite different from that of New England. It was in fact a peculiarly American echo of a later stage of Reformation reverberations, for the Quaker Commonwealth of Pennsylvania was a regional society of unprecedented tolerance, a society exhibiting the deep erosion of the very ideas of centralized authority and conformity in either church or state.

Farther south the religious dimension of the European outreach was submerged under a simpler, cruder commercial thrust, as evident in the feeble Anglicanism of Virginia, the mild and diffuse influence of Puritans and Quakers, the minor localized importance of the string of ethnoreligious settlements in the South Carolina backcountry, and, most obviously, the rapid subversion of Oglethorpe's Georgia. As planter societies with a strong African complexion, Virginia and South Carolina, and Louisiana as well, seem a special type amongst the many regional creations of European capitalism: mainland footholds of a slave plantation system intensively developed in tropical America and inherently driven toward geographic expansion. But such broad characterizations mask some important differences in lineage and character.

Virginia began as a direct English thrust into the subtropics, a commercial speculation that eventually found a staple export and thereby fostered the emergence of an indigenous planter society. Africans were certainly not basic to the success of the colony, for they were relatively unimportant for half a century. Slavery was only gradually grafted onto the economic and social system, and Virginia grew all the while from White immigration as well as Black importation and expanded as a rural society of small farms as well as large estates. Thus Virginia was neither a forerunner nor an offshoot of the characteristic societies of tropical America, but a distinctive subtropical creation.

On the other hand, a central strand of the lineage of South Carolina leads back through Barbados to Brazil and São Tomé, making it an extension, through English and Dutch intermediaries, of a commercial thrust and social type initiated by the Portuguese two hundred years before. So, too, Louisiana was in important ways an outlier of the much larger planter society of the French Antilles of similar general antecedents, although here, as in Canada, the commercial dimension remained subordinate to the strategic designs of a centralized imperialism. Thus, these more southerly societies were indeed the mainland margins of a Greater

Tropical America formed initially out of those Atlantic circuits that bound Europe, Africa, and America into a single system.

As the Dutch and eventually the French and the English took greater control of the Atlantic slave trade, they more effectively empowered the expansion of these staple export economies and made all the coastal districts from Maryland to Loui-

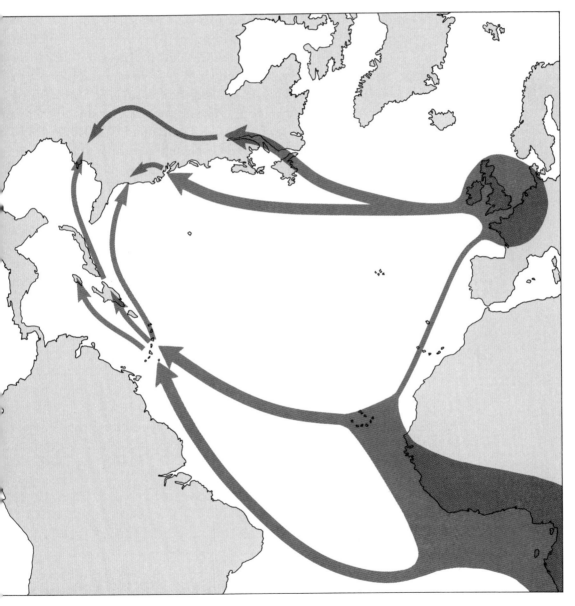

. Thrusts and Convergence.

siana more closely akin to the American tropical type and ever more deeply a part of an enlarging Afro-American world. Yet in every case there was a counterforce, arising from a critical difference between continent and archipelago. For each of these mainland societies had a backcountry, an immense frontier beyond ready exploitation by the plantation system but reasonably accessible and increasingly attractive to individual land seekers. In the broader view we can see the spread of settlers into these interior districts as competitive with the inland reach of these plantation footholds along the coast. And because so much of this European pioneering was in fact a southward drift within the continent—up the Great Valley, across the Virginia Piedmont, into the Carolina backcountry, downriver to Baton Rouge—movements traceable mainly back to Delaware and Laurentian entryways, the general pattern appears as a convergence of two great thrusts along this North American rim of the Atlantic World, the one reaching directly across to Northern America, the other following the natural circuit into the tropical seas, two expansions from the same northwest European culture hearth, but now preponderantly of very different peoples, the one a miscellany of European land seekers, the other a captive variety of African slaves. As of 1750 it was still a convergence without a collision, a fluid, tentative contact in nearly empty country, but the lands were so good and the momentum so great that it would have been hard to imagine in the longer run such an encounter without contest.

This broader view leads us back to seeing all these local and regional areas as parts of a whole. The Europeanized margins of North America were but one side of a transoceanic system, one vigorously expanding periphery beyond the northwest European core of the modern world-system. We must now take a closer look at this larger structure and search for some other geographic patterns and processes that can help us find a way through the labyrinth of this history.

PART THREE
REORGANIZATIONS: THE CREATION OF AN AMERICAN MATRIX

Imperialism is fixed into the historical record of every nation that has an ascertainable past at all.

A. D. Thornton

Prologue

We now need to bind these localities, societies, and regions back into the larger Atlantic World. We begin with a generalized description of the several networks that actually, functionally, bound Northwest Europe and North America together as of about 1750. That will bring into focus a set of points and areas and peoples to form a panorama of empire within which we can identify some systems of interaction, gradations of political power, and directions of cultural change.

We must then deal with the series of great upheavals that radically altered those patterns of empire during the next few decades. First there was the great simplification of the map of European control following the British triumph over the French, and then, astonishingly, the disintegration of that enlarged and prosperous empire and the emergence of an unprecedented federal republic, transforming the whole geopolitical configuration and character of North America. Here again we deal with famous, complex events in a limited and specialized way. But empires and federations and nations are kinds of structures and systems that require and reward geographical interpretation and we may hope to gain a fresh perspective on some familiar features.

We end our reconnaissance in the year 1800 as a convenient moment to assess a North America that was still in many ways an important part of an Atlantic World but was also a direct participant in a larger world of commerce and, at the same time, a kind of new world in itself wherein the dominant actor was an American nation anchored firmly on the Atlantic but moving relentlessly into the heart of the continent.

1. A Geographical Transect of the Atlantic World

By 1750 half of North America had become bound into the Atlantic World. That is to say that it was bound into intercontinental systems of operations anchored in Europe. That these American regions were part of a neo-European world, that they were colonies within imperial structures and production zones in a European-dominated economy, is obvious but insufficient. We need a much more refined geographic understanding of such relationships. In the immense literature bearing upon European penetration and colonization of North America there is surprisingly little explicit geographical formulation of these connections.

Of course, the simple geographic structure of a Europe and an America, separated by the Atlantic, is recognized and signified in various ways. Pairs of terms— homeland and colonies, metropolis and frontier, center and periphery, and variations thereof—are loaded with meaning, carrying as they do implications of old and new, dominance and subordination, innovation and diffusion; but even where some such meaning is specified such crude bipartite structures provide no real basis

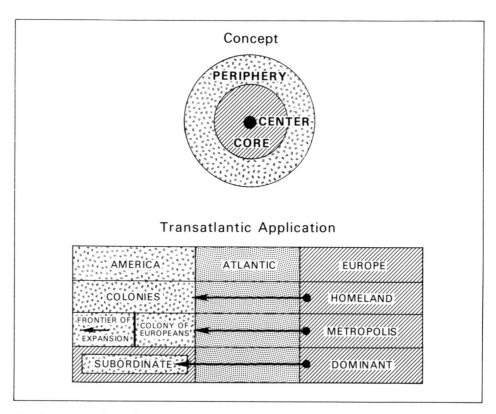

45. Center-periphery Concepts.

for geographical analysis. We may wish to generalize in such broad terms, but we should do so with a clear understanding of what we are generalizing from. We need to penetrate this simple dualism and identify a more intricate set of geographic parts if we are to bring such a vast transoceanic creation into clearer view. Let us therefore review these overarching European-initiated systems that by 1750 had created a single great geographical field extending from the seats of imperial and commercial power in London and Paris to the deep interior of North America (the system extending from Madrid to New Mexico was generally analogous, but is not central to our main concerns in this era).

Our inventory of geographical parts begins (reading figure 46 east to west, as it were) with the European *centers,* the capital cities that served as headquarters for the control of financial resources, commercial intelligence, and marketing systems. The regions lying beyond these metropolitan centers developed industries specifically in response to American needs, for example, blankets from the factories at Stroud and iron tools and utensils from forges in the Forest of Dean; these *hinterlands* supplied the major *Atlantic ports* that served as primary bases for the procurement of ships, trading goods, and tools. On the westernmost fringes of Europe, as in Brittany, Devon, and southern Ireland, Atlantic *outports* provided last-stage provisions and manpower for the oceanic voyage.

On the American side, assuming for simplicity the most direct route to the mainland colonies (Newfoundland or the West Indies were outports on some important circuitry), there was the *colonial port,* complementary in functions to that in Europe, receiving, disassembling, storing, and arranging for distribution, and drawing upon the European *colony* for food and other materials and perhaps for additional trading goods, especially alcohol from local distilleries. Near the inland edge of this colonized area was the *frontier entrepôt,* seat of the principal traders and various specialists serving the interior economy, and the main point of periodic contact with Indian leaders. Further inland were *outposts* staffed by local traders and the *Indian core area* of the powerful intermediary tribes who fostered procurement from a wide hunting *hinterland* and tried to control distribution of trade goods to the most remote participants.

Because our main purpose is geographical rather than economic, the diagram draws attention to the furthest reaches rather than to the greatest volumes of transatlantic traffic. It illustrates the fur trade rather than the far larger volume of commerce between Europe and the colonized areas on the American seaboard, which was largely an exchange of a wide variety of manufactures for a few primary products of the sea, farms, and forest. On the other hand, in the case of Hudson Bay there was no colonized area and York Factory served as both port and frontier entrepôt. Such variations can be readily fitted into the scheme; it should be noted, however, that such a simple transect cannot purport to display the complexities of

AMERICA

PRODUCTION HINTERLAND	INDIAN CORE AREA	OUTPOSTS	FRONTIER ENTREPÔT	COLONY	COLONIAL PORT

COMMERCIAL SYSTEM

PRODUCTION HINTERLAND	INDIAN CORE AREA	OUTPOSTS	FRONTIER ENTREPÔT	COLONY	COLONIAL PORT
OHIO MISSISSIPPI VALLEY Village Clusters	ONONDAGA COWETA	OSWEGO	ALBANY AUGUSTA	NEW YORK SOUTH CAROLINA	NEW YORK CHARLESTOWN
GREAT LAKES	Indian middlemen	DETROIT local traders gunsmiths and blacksmiths	MONTREAL chief traders Indian provisionmen	CANADA Euro-American agriculture local industry distilling	QUEBEC mercantile leaders marketing warehousing local capital
trappers and hunters preparation of furs and skins					
canoes and porters	canoes and pack trains		riverboats, wagons, pack trains		

POLITICAL SYSTEM

PRODUCTION HINTERLAND	INDIAN CORE AREA	OUTPOSTS	FRONTIER ENTREPÔT	COLONY	COLONIAL PORT
OHIO MISSISSIPPI VALLEY	ONONDAGA COWETA	OSWEGO	ALBANY AUGUSTA	NEW YORK SOUTH CAROLINA	NEW YORK CHARLESTOWN
GREAT LAKES		DETROIT	MONTREAL	CANADA	QUEBEC
client and allied tribes	capital town chiefs of confederation	lieutenant garrison	commandant garrison licensed traders	counties parishes towns	capital governor local Assembly
Indian-Indian treaties and warfare		Indian-European treaties and warfare		colonial charters	

SOCIAL SYSTEM

PRODUCTION HINTERLAND	INDIAN CORE AREA	OUTPOSTS	FRONTIER ENTREPÔT	COLONY	COLONIAL PORT
MIAMIS, etc. CHICKASAWS, etc.	IROQUOIS CREEK	ENGLISH, SCOTS, DUTCH, MIXED BLOODS INDIAN		ENGLISH, SCOTS, DUTCH, ULSTERMEN, GERMANS, HUGUENOTS, AFRICANS	
CREE, etc.	ALGONKIANS	FRENCH, METIS CHRISTIAN INDIANS INDIANS		FRENCH	FRENCH
Indian social hierarchy dominant tribe incorporated clients allies slaves		ethnic stratification		colonial hierarchy officials merchants tradesmen and artisans laborers and servants African slaves Indian remnants	
dislocated tribes	dominant Indians	sojourners and settlers Indian collaborators and refugees		settlers	sojourners and settlers
standard Indian tongues incorporating European terms		Trade Pidgin bilingualism		regional versions of American English & French (Koine)	

46. A Geographical Transect of the Atlantic World, c. 1750.

EUROPE

ATLANTIC	OUTPORT	ATLANTIC PORT	HINTERLAND	CENTER
	IRELAND DEVON	BRISTOL	FOREST OF DEAN STROUD	LONDON
company and contract shipping	BRITTANY oceanic provisioning recruitment of seamen and laborers	LE HAVRE LA ROCHELLE shipping services boat-building marketing	NORMANDY ATLANTIC FRANCE iron utensils, weapons, blankets, cloth, foodstuffs	PARIS headquarters entrepreneurs state & corporate systems commercial intelligence
ocean vessels		riverboats, wagons coastal and river vessels		
	IRELAND BRITTANY subordinate provinces	BRISTOL LE HAVRE LA ROCHELLE outlying counties political interests in overseas affairs		LONDON PARIS capital and core area crown, courts Parliament colonial bureaus church
maritime law	imperial rule regional institutions		national law and institutions	
DEVONSHIREMEN DUTCH	SCOTS IRISH ANGLO-IRISH	WEST COUNTRYMEN		ENGLISH
NORMANS ROCHELLAIS mercantile networks of kith and kin	BRETONS FRENCH ethnic stratification; source regions	NORMANS major source regions of overseas settlers and sojourners full social hierarchy		FRENCH
maritime lingo	Celtic or Anglo-Celtic } dialect Franco-Celtic }	regional dialects		standard tongue

transatlantic and intercolonial traffic, though it can help organize our thinking about these economic relationships.

The Atlantic was of course a distinct area requiring special shipping services, and a supplemental way of defining such a set of areas would be to identify the transport facilities—the vessels and vehicles, pack trains and lines of human porters—carrying out the transatlantic contracts involved in this intercontinental exchange. The deep penetrations of North America afforded by the St. Lawrence, Hudson, and Great Lakes are so well known that it may be useful to call attention to the largely overland network of commerce reaching inland from Charleston as well.

When we shift our focus to the political system we can recognize many of the same centers and areas though they are somewhat differently connected and less far-reaching. The trunk line of empire connects the imperial capital to the colonial capital, overarching the local center-periphery patterns within the European states. Britain, especially, was an internally complex geopolitical structure, but our concern here is with those features directly bound up with the larger imperial system, such as those special political interests in American affairs generated in the Atlantic ports and outports. The imperial trunk line was actually several strands of administrative, military, and ecclesiastical links. The French system was a geopolitical hierarchy of military officials, from the Crown and heads of departments in Paris to the governor-general in Quebec, to regional commandants, as at Montreal, and lieutenants in outlying districts. The British empire seems in comparison hardly a system at all. Each colony was unique in the details of local government and there were differences in the connections each had with various departments in London. The most important feature was the fact that each colony was so connected to the imperial capital; there was no governor-general for the American colonies (although there had been an attempt to establish one for the northern colonies in the abortive Dominion of New England 1685–88). Such complexities preclude simple diagrammatic representation. What should be emphasized in this transect is the connection and overlap of the European political system with that of the Indians. In their rivalries the European powers laid sovereign claim to all the lands of their Indian allies, but the Iroquois chiefs who periodically assembled at the central council fire at Onondaga or the Creeks who gathered at Coweta would have been contemptuous of such assertions. They had not been conquered; they held sway over their own geopolitical systems involving an array of confederated, allied, subordinated, and client tribes.

At this point it is also pertinent to note that our transect along the most direct axis binding Europe and America together includes evidence of a far older imperialism within Europe. Insofar as those Atlantic ports and outports are in Scotland, Ireland, Wales, or Brittany, they are not only a part of these transatlantic connections but are locked into the relentless pressures of the English and the French upon these ancient Atlantic societies. We have noted that Ireland and America are analogous and concurrent in certain ways, and if this geographic formulation were applied in detail to all this Atlantic fringe of northwest Europe, it would reveal a more local imperialism little less complicated for being at a different scale.

These several areas were bound together through colonial charters, administrative decrees, and treaties, which were put into practice by the various officials and intermediary agents noted in the diagram, but of course the actual operation of the system may not accord precisely with formal definitions of relationships. Nevertheless, such a scheme can serve as an initial geographical guide to the several kinds of areas within such an imperial structure, each with its own interests and potentials for generating particular kinds of pressures upon the system; it is also a guide to those localized points of authority where decisions may be made and from where coercive action might be taken in event of trouble. Furthermore, the simple relation of these political areas with those of the economic system is enough to suggest the likelihood of marked differentials within this set of geographic parts in response to the various issues of imperial concern.

Implicit in these sets of commercial and political parts are concordant patterns of society. Here we face some special complexities, however, because "society" and things "social" are not so readily comprehensible as a system of points and parts. The terms may encompass the several deep-rooted societies of particular areas, migrations of people from one region to another, and the variety of sojourners stationed for a period of assigned duty at various points in the political and commercial networks. Here we will emphasize some of the important connective features in this panorama. Although emigrants were drawn from much of western Europe, the main Atlantic ports and their hinterlands were commonly the most productive catchment areas and thus became the principal homeland anchors of those transatlantic networks of kith and kin that were most likely to generate and channel further emigration. Outports on the Atlantic edge, as in southern Ireland and the Orkneys, might have similar intensified links with particular areas overseas, and the oceanic shipping services were also operated by closely linked networks of persons along the trunk lines of empire.

On the American side an important feature inherent in the very concept of these kinds of imperial colonies is the coexistence but different roles and divergent interests of sojourners and settlers. The latter, derived increasingly not just from emigrants but from American-born citizens, made up the bulk of the population, and by definition were spread over the whole colonized area. The sojourners were to be found at operational points in the imperial networks, most prominently in the colonial port and capital and in the frontier entrepôt and outposts. Of course, this distinction could be blurred. As a colony developed an increasing share of the offices and agencies on the American end of these networks would likely be held by American-born persons rather than Europeans on colonial assignment, and many an agent sent over for a tour of duty elected to stay on as a permanent settler. Nevertheless, a differentiation between these two groups of colonial residents remained, and that could become critically important when an empire was brought under internal stress.

Figure 46 enables us to shift our focus to yet another level of the transatlantic system, the social complexity arising from the sustained encounter between the invaders and the invaded. In major frontier centers, such as Montreal, Albany, Augusta, and nearby districts, one might find a varied assortment of Europeans, Indians of the powerful tribes who were partners in this intercontinental system, refugee Indian groups, new associations formed of remnants of shattered tribes, Christian Indians, detribalized mixed bloods, all in complex stratifications and segregations. Some such variety might be found in many localities scattered over the entire Europeanized areas, and in many colonies the importation of Africans and subsequent consequences of miscegenation, emancipation, and escape created further social complexities.

As an example of another way of looking at society in such a geographic scheme we might look at language, analogous in a way to transport, each a medium of communication linking these sets of peoples and areas. Such a view would not only take note of the range of languages and dialects in these several parts but bring into focus those areas and points of contact characterized by bilingualism, translators, and trade pidgin in this overall network, spanning the great geographical and cultural separation between the dominant tongue of the imperial capital and the unaltered tongue of the most remote American Indian participants. Such a simplified momentary transect can of course no more than hint at the dynamics of linguistic change induced by these encounters and associations, migrations and separations.

Thus by looking more closely we can penetrate any simple core-periphery or metropolis-frontier concept of intercontinental empire or system and identify almost a dozen geographic parts, each with its own characteristic peoples, activities, and qualities. By displaying these several topical patterns on the same chart, so that we can easily relate the economic, political, and social characteristics of any one geographic part or set of parts, we provide *context* for the consideration of particular elements or processes, anchoring them within particular types of geographic areas. We may also attempt to envision this whole span of areas as a *system*, with arteries pulsating with the circulation of persons, goods, money, and messages, a network connecting a series of stations where decisions are made, policies applied, transactions negotiated, goods exchanged. Of course it was not a simple system of centralized authority and subordinate parts, but was in fact several systems, interlocked in various ways and degrees and complicated by numerous subsystems. In the British case, especially, the political and commercial systems were relatively autonomous and often discordant with one another, and some of the concomitant social changes were quite unmanaged, unforeseen, and unwelcome to London authorities.

We can also try to envision this transect as a *spectrum* showing gradations in power, intensity of interaction, and social character. We might generalize that imperial power declined with distance from the European capital until it became feeble and indirect in the interior of North America where it was represented by European seasonal agents and Indian allies. And we might generalize an analogous cultural gradient from, say, a basic "Englishness" as defined by a social elite in London, through many shadings and transitions until it fades to the faintest evidence of things "English" and disappears in the still strong "Indianness" of the

DISTANCE DECAY

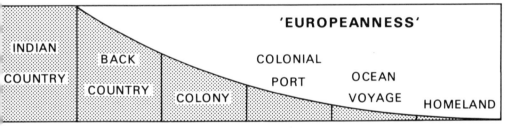

INCREMENTAL PROCESSES

7. Cultural Divergence.

American interior. To put it in such terms may suggest a European view of Americans as fading versions of European archetypes. That the sense of such things on the American colonial side would be rather different needs no emphasis. We may need reminding, however, that the most directly opposite view would be to stand with those as yet barely affected Indians of the interior and look with fear and wonder at the apparent precipitous gradations of "Indianness" as one went eastward.

The cultural divergence developing between mother country and overseas colonies lies at the very heart of American history. At the simplest geographic level we might think of such divergence as a function of distance, or perhaps of "effective distance," taking into account the decreasing efficiencies of transport as Europeans moved farther and farther away, ever less closely in touch with the full force of their homeland culture. Of course it was much more complex than that. To see such a spectrum of change as a "distance decay" effect does not explain anything. One has to examine the actual processes of change in the constituent elements of the system. We have already noted some of these, beginning with the selectivity of migration, simplifications associated with oceanic emigration, and adaptations arising from local circumstances of colonization. Migration into backcountry districts further strained the connections with the homeland culture. Here we refer not just to a transitory pioneer phase of differentiation between colonial metropolis and frontier, but to a divergence arising from new environments and experiences, new problems and a new sense of future possibilities. Such a perspective suggests not so much a spectrum as an incremental divergence, area by area, from center to periphery. We must, of course, remember that processes are bound up with events, and that at any stage and in any of these zones the results of such changes take on special meaning when they are self-consciously asserted by the peoples themselves, when emigrant and stay-at-home, colony and mother country, backcountry and seaboard, begin to declare their differences and even cultivate a sense of separateness, transforming colonists into nationalists, frontiersmen into regionalists who seek to give geopolitical expression to distance and divergence.

But it should also be emphasized that even a long period of differentiation arising from transoceanic movement and colonization may not be so divergent as to be disruptive in either a cultural or political sense. Such overseas colonies begin as European enclaves and they may long develop simply as additional regional versions of the mother culture, distant provinces not essentially different in kind from counties on the homeland fringes of such composite kingdoms as England and France. Any analysis of these processes of differentiation must also take into account those systems of spatial interaction binding center and periphery together and thus serving to counter pressures toward separation. By 1750 there were evidences of all these kinds of cultural changes, clues to all these types and scales of divergence at work within this overarching Atlantic imperial system. There was not as yet, however, obvious evidence that such forces were so powerful, advanced, or inexorable as to bring about the disintegration of the system as a whole. Rather, what was obvious was the chronic rivalry between the European powers that had built this system, and the assumption that the specific political divisions and networks held and operated by the English and the French remained subject to recurrent warfare and redefinition.

2. The Great War and Its Alterations of Empires

In American history books the most common titles for the wide-ranging struggle between the great European powers that erupted just after the middle of the eighteenth century are the "Seven Years' War" and the "French and Indian War." The first, common to European histories, defines the span of time between the formal declaration of war in 1756 and its termination in the Peace of Paris; the second refers to the North American sector of the contest, which began in 1754 and was essentially over by 1760; neither one nor both together are adequate terms for such extensive and transforming events.

In the longer view this war was but one in a sequence involving many of the same states, a series of great outbreaks separated by festering intervals of diplomatic maneuver, aggressive commercial rivalry, and local fighting. Yet by several measures it had unprecedented significance. It has been called "the first of the 'People's Wars'" in that it was "conducted by great 'popular' war-leaders strong in the hearts and imaginations" of their countrymen, who aimed at "the attainment of vast objectives in which the commercial life of the whole nation was deeply concerned." Those objectives involved the commerce of colonies and trading stations, which were now considered fundamental to the expanding prosperity of the mercantilist state, and thereby the Atlantic European powers were engulfed in a contest that transcended economics and became "cultural, ideological, religious, nationalistic." This intense rivalry among these great maritime powers was inevitably contested upon the high seas and carried to many sectors of imperial concern, so that battles in such distant places as Bengal, Canada, and Cuba proved far more decisive than those fought over German and Italian states, the chronic focus of European dynastic concerns. Thus it was the first of the truly "world wars" and whereas in Europe peace brought essentially a restoration of the *status quo antebellum,* in America and India and elsewhere it brought changes of such enormous consequences that some historians have come to refer to the whole affair more descriptively as "the Great War for Empire."

On the eve of war there were conflicting claims along almost every border in North America. In the far north the French had formally renounced their claims to Hudson Bay in 1713, but nevertheless were extending their fur trade system beyond Lake Winnipeg in a direct encroachment upon Rupert's Land, defined by the English to include the entire hydrographic basin of the bay. So, too, the eastern limits of Canada were in dispute: the English claimed that the transfer in that same treaty of "Nova Scotia or Acadie, with its ancient boundaries" meant the entire mainland east of the St. Croix and north to the St. Lawrence, whereas the French insisted it meant only the great peninsula, and in 1750 set up forts on the Chignetco Isthmus to sustain that definition. French assertion of sovereignty over the drainage basin of the St. Lawrence and Great Lakes, though clearly based on early exploration and active exploitation, was disputed by the English, who insisted on rights to much of it through treaty cessions from the Iroquois. French claims to a Louisiana defined to encompass the entire Mississippi Basin cut across the inland latitudinal extension of a whole series of English coastal grants and seaboard colonies. On the Gulf Coast the de facto French-Spanish boundaries appeared to be stabilized between pairs of border outposts (Mobile and Pensacola on the east, Natchitoches and Los Adaes on the west), but between English Georgia and Spanish Florida lay an uncertain zone ravaged by recent raids. The actual chartered limit of Georgia was the Altamaha but an earlier English definition of Carolina had included northern Florida.

These three imperial competitors were the greatest powers of their time and their conflicting claims would be resolved or further altered as they had been in the past: by the results of warfare ranging over half the world and complex negotiations in the courts of Europe in which specific issues and areas in North America might be regarded as no more than minor matters. Our concern is not with the patterns of war but with territorial alteration resulting from that war, and although our study is centered in the North Atlantic arena, especially the North American sectors of this momentous contest and settlement, it is important to set these within the larger global context. In India the rivalry between the trading companies of England and France for domination of the Carnatic coast and Bengal was transformed into a more directly imperial war, and the English military victories were confirmed by the treaty that left the French confined within their coastal trading stations and opened the whole subcontinent to opportunistic English expansion.

Within the Atlantic World, the most difficult negotiations arose over the Lesser Antilles and the Great Fishery, two resource-rich areas long in contention between the English and the French. The sugar islands were considered the most valuable of all colonies. By crippling the French fleet, Britain was able to seize Martinique and Guadeloupe, as well as occupy the string of islands to the south—Dominica, St. Lucia, St. Vincent, the Grenadines, Grenada, and Tobago—that had been declared neutral ground after the indecisive contest of the 1740s. Of these latter, Britain retained all except St. Lucia, which was allotted to France in conjunction with the return of Martinique and Guadeloupe. Although there was a strong temptation to hang on to such rich islands, or at least Guadeloupe, leaving the French only their old central colony of Martinique, powerful English sugar interests, fearing severe competition and oversupply, pressured against retention. Partly to support this expansion in the American tropics, the English also held on to St. Louis and command of the Senegal River, giving them a larger base for the slave trade. However, here too the complex negotiations of the two war-weary states ended in the return of Goreé to French control. This horse-trading of strategic islands typified the treaty settlement: Mauritius (Ile de France), a useful way station to India, was given back to France, while Minorca, an English base in the Balearics lying off from Toulon that the French had seized early in the war, was given back to Britain.

It was a measure of not only the ready riches of the seas but of the peculiar importance of the activity to these maritime mercantilist powers that "the most important bone of contention was the future of the French fishing rights off the coasts of North America." Early in the several stages of negotiations France had indicated her willingness to surrender Canada but tried to insist on retention of Cape Breton Island and extensive fishing privileges in the region. Ultimately the French hold was reduced to two tiny islands, St. Pierre and Miquelon, and rights to fish off the northern coast of Newfoundland.

The contrast between these niggling negotiations over little islands and harbors and the casualness with which huge continental expanses were transferred from one flag to another is difficult for the modern mind to comprehend and a hard lesson in the need to reimagine the imperial perspectives of the time. The French gave up the remainder of Acadia, all of Canada, and any claims to the Ohio Valley with little objection raised in France itself. The chambers of commerce of La Rochelle and Bordeaux protested the harm to their local interests, but could not rally any wide backing. And in a separate treaty France quit the continent entirely by transferring all of Louisiana to her ally Spain to compensate for the loss of Florida, which Spain had been forced to cede to England (along with logwood rights on the Honduras coast) in return for their evacuation of Havana (the English so dominated the seas that they had taken Manila as well).

Thus the French American empire dwindled to St. Domingue, three islands in the Lesser Antilles, a foothold in Guyana, and two tiny bases for a limited fishing ground. The mainland of North America was partitioned between Spain and England along the line of the Mississippi River (excepting the Isle of Orleans below Bayou Manchac, containing the main settlements of Louisiana, which was in-cluded in the transfer to Spain). In the fullest continental perspective another division seemed pending along the Pacific slope. For several decades Russian explorers and fur companies had been working along the Alaskan coast, and although still confined to high latitudes, the movement would soon prompt the Spanish to extend their imperial system upon Alta California, a coast they had lightly reconnoitered long ago but had left unsecured. Spain and Portugal had been drawn into this great war as opponents in its late stages, and the general triumph of England allowed her Portuguese ally to force Spain formally to discard claims derived from the famous fifteenth-century papal division of the world and to recognize boundaries more in keeping with the realities of the Portuguese position in Brazil, although contentions over the southern borderlands in the Plata sector remained unresolved.

The treaties ending this great war formalized a vast reordering of the overseas empires of the European states, and "more American territory changed hands at the Peace of Paris than by any other international settlement before or since." In general, North America had been divided in half between Britain and Spain along the Mississippi and the Missouri-Saskatchewan watershed. But our major concern is with that which was of minor concern at best to the political leaders and negotiators: the impact upon the human geography of the many North American societies involved. We shall focus on this impact and subsequent changes in several broad sectors until the eve of another great imperial convulsion a dozen years later, a mighty event which would produce even more drastic geopolitical and social transformations.

3. Reorganization: Northern America

The capture and annexation of French Acadia and Canada ramified through all Northern America with powerful but markedly different effects upon the several regional societies.

The most drastic change involved the remaking of the cultural geography of Nova Scotia. The earlier British annexation of mainland Acadia in 1713 had produced some common kinds of imperial problems. The Micmacs feared encroachment on their lands; the Acadians resisted giving an unqualified oath of allegiance and lay under suspicion of conniving with the Indians, their land titles were beclouded, and their commerce subject to closer scrutiny. Some of the French moved across the narrow seas to Ile St. Jean or Cape Breton Island, but neither was very attractive, the former because lands had to be won by felling the forest rather than by dyking the marshes, the latter because there was little land worth winning by any means. Insecure English officials in this demonstrably dangerous region had for some years considered expelling such a people, who were not

"Natural British Subjects," and replacing them with reliable Protestants. Yet it would be a formidable task to uproot and transport so many thousands—and to where? During the most volatile years of the 1740s the chief British official at Annapolis, Mascarene, sought a more conciliatory policy. As a "bilingual old Huguenot" he was sympathetic to the plight of a people who through no choice of their own had been "grafted" onto the "Body of the British Nation" and thus needed to be nurtured into "good Subjects." Even Governor Shirley of Massachusetts, who for a time played a powerful role in Nova Scotian affairs and who had been a strong advocate of expulsion, came to modify his views and suggest no more than a local resettlement of the French amongst new colonists so as to "reclaim" them "by a constant inspection of their behaviour, promoting Traffik and all manner of Intercourse between them and the English, [and] gradually introduce the English manners, customs, and language among them." The importation of the Lunenburgers with the idea of distributing them amongst the French was part of the same concept of a routine acculturation through the agency of good Protestants, even if not in their case of "natural English." But a new governor was sent over in 1754 and in the heat of the war, following the capture of the French forts on the Chignetco, this "inflexible and insecure military man" suddenly decreed a complete removal of all the French from the region.

Thus began "le grand dérangement," a complicated extirpation, detention, dispersal, reshipment, wandering, and resettlement of some ten thousand Americans over a span of thirty years, which touched in some degree nearly every part of the English and French Atlantic worlds. There were several stages in this diaspora of one of the oldest European peoples of North America. Within the first three years, between six and seven thousand Acadians were rounded up by British soldiers and shipped out for distribution among the other mainland English colonies. Nearly all of the remainder had fled to Ile St. Jean, into wilderness districts to the north of the Fundy settlements, or on to Quebec. However, after the fall of Louisbourg and Quebec several thousand of these and other Acadians were now deported to France. In the meantime, no British American colony had been pleased with this sudden gift of hundreds of persons who had been branded as unreliable citizens. New Englanders could hardly welcome French Catholics whom they had so long hated and feared; Virginia soon reshipped her large allotment (about eleven hundred) off to England; and little effort was made in any of the colonies to find a place for the exiles, nor did they do much to impede any Acadian attempts to move elsewhere. The treaty settlement of 1763 initiated further movements, especially to the few remaining French American colonies, Louisiana, and again to France itself, where the Acadians were never happy nor well received. But the treaty also marked the beginnings of a strong drift back to Nova Scotia, a move officially allowed under certain circumstances after 1764, but

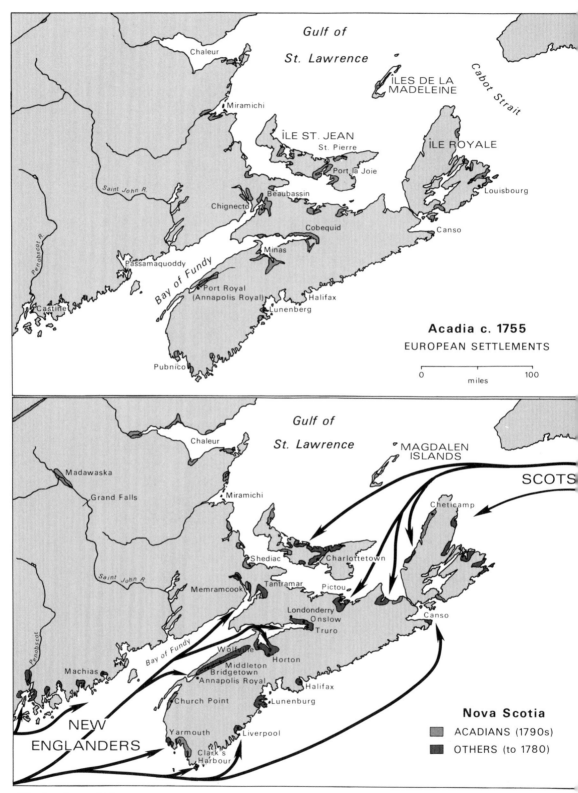

Gulf of
St. Lawrence

Chaleur

ÎLES DE LA
MADELEINE

Cabot Strait

Miramichi

ÎLE ST. JEAN
St. Pierre

ÎLE ROYALE

Port la Joie

Louisbourg

Saint John R.

Beaubassin

Chignecto

Cobequid

Canso

Penobscot R.

Minas

Passamaquoddy

Bay of Fundy

Port Royal
(Annapolis Royal)

Halifax

Castine

Lunenberg

Acadia c. 1755
EUROPEAN SETTLEMENTS

Pubnico

0   miles   100

Gulf of
St. Lawrence

Chaleur

MAGDALEN
ISLANDS

SCOTS

Madawaska

Grand Falls

Miramichi

Cheticamp

Shediac

Charlottetown

Saint John R.

Memramcook

Tantramar

Pictou

Canso

Londonderry
Onslow
Truro

Penobscot

Bay of Fundy

Wolfville

Horton

Machias

Middleton
Bridgetown
Annapolis Royal

Halifax

Church Point

Lunenburg

Nova Scotia

ACADIANS (1790s)

OTHERS (to 1780)

NEW
ENGLANDERS

Yarmouth

Liverpool

Clark's
Harbour

48. Acadia and Nova Scotia.

still much discouraged by most local British officials. As their farms were now occupied by new colonists, these returnees had to find some niche in a wide scattering of localities around the margins of the older region, such as along St. Mary's Bay (where they were first authorized to build a church, at Church Point, in 1770), deep inland at Madawaska on the upper waters of the St. John, and on the north coast, as at Cheticamp, and especially in the many harbors between Shediac and the Gaspé; only at Memramcook, off the head of Chignetco Bay, were they within sight of their old farms on the Fundy marshes. In a number of cases the chief assistance was provided by commercial companies eager to extend lumbering, fishing, and fur trading into new districts; company agents were often bilingual Huguenots or Jerseymen, so that these refugees found support within an American extension of the old Anglo-French Channel community.

Some further shiftings took place during and after the American Revolution, which reopened French-English hostilities. When these were completed, thirty years of such reshufflings after 1755 had left few Acadians in France or England or any of the English colonies, had pretty well integrated several thousands into the rural life of French Quebec, and had created a sizeable colony in a distinct Acadian district in Louisiana. But most important, perhaps as many as five to six thousand—almost as many as initially expelled—were becoming well rooted in half a dozen scattered nuclei of a new Acadia on the margins of the old, offering quiet evidence that the very attempt to efface such a French presence had insured its survival, through the intensification of regional ethnic identity by so harsh an experience.

In 1758 the British began their program for the recolonization and expanded development of an enlarged Nova Scotia. Much of the best land was soon in the hands of various officials and favorites, but there was a need for actual settlers and an obvious source lay nearby: New England, whose seamen had long been familiar with every little harbor, whose merchants had long dominated the trade, whose soldiers had marched here against the French, and whose families had had more than a century of colonizing experience. Counties and townships were laid out, liberal land allotments offered, tolerance of Dissenters declared, and assurance given that local government and courts were "constituted in like manner with those of Massachusetts, Connecticut and other Northern colonies." And so within a few years several thousand Yankees, drawn from coastal Connecticut, Rhode Island, and eastern Massachusetts, had taken over nearly all the former Acadian farms, filled in the Annapolis valley and Minas townships far more thickly than the French had done, occupied every good harbor along the southerly coast, and were sprinkled here and there in the old contested borderlands of the northern Fundy shore, as at Passamaquoddy and the lower St. John. And thus much of the domesticated landscape and social geography of Nova Scotia—its busy seaports, its close-set villages with their greens and Congregational or Baptist churches, its farmer-forester-fishermen, its many cultural and commercial connections with Boston and other ports—displayed the unmistakable mark of Greater New England.

This northeasterly thrust across the local seas weakened rather quickly, however. It was but one edge of a broader northward surge that had followed on the elimination of the French threat from North America, and New Hampshire and especially the upper Connecticut Valley offered a greater array of attractive lands on generally better terms. And despite enticing representations there were basic differences in the political system, for Nova Scotia could not be simply an extension of New England. It was a New England thrust into an old military colony, and the ruling oligarchy at Halifax was unsympathetic with Yankee proclivities toward local autonomy and democracy. And although New England contributed much the largest body of colonists, the numerous land promotions lured a considerable variety: a few from other American colonies; groups of Ulster Irish to Truro, Onslow, and Londonderry; about a thousand Yorkshire Methodists, chiefly to the margins of the Tantramar; and the first contingents of Highlanders to give firm evidence of a New Scotland, most notably to the fine harbor at Pictou on the north coast. And all the while the Acadians kept turning up, catching on as laborers, drifting about, searching for a bit of ground in which to reroot themselves in their native land; so, too, their old friends and allies the Micmacs, though pushed aside from some of their best fishing and fowling grounds, were still present in many a forest village, and the Malecites seemed a dangerous obstacle to any expansions up the St. John.

Thus Nova Scotia had been reorganized and essentially remade in twenty years. It was doubled in size by the amalgamation of French Acadia (though Ile St. Jean was set apart as a separate jurisdiction—with few inhabitants—in 1769), had nearly doubled in population, and, more important, had been drastically altered in character and cultural geography. In 1755, Halifax was a new English capital imposed on the captive portion of an old French colony. By 1775 it was still very much an imperial outpost, the obvious English and Anglican center, but was now the capital of a peculiarly American colony, composed very largely of new communities of Yankees and Acadian returnees, two of the oldest European peoples in North America.

Meanwhile Ile St. Jean was altered in more than name. All but a few hundred of the French had been expelled, and the entirety of St. John's Island was surveyed into 20,000-acre blocks, a capital, and two other county towns, and all these allocated by lottery in London among several dozen petitioners. As usual, most of these recipients were merely speculators, but a few, chiefly Scots, undertook the actual planting on their lands required by their charters. By 1775 there were perhaps thirteen hundred people on the island, mostly Scottish Highland Catho-

49. Halifax in 1759.
This view, taken from George Island, of Halifax and its fine harbor full of British warships displays the liveliness and importance of the place on the eve of the assault upon French Canada. It is by Richard Short, a naval purser who had arrived a few weeks earlier. Short completed six sketches of the town, and after the taking of Quebec he made twelve of that city. The two sets were engraved in London shortly thereafter and became popular items; they are now valuable documents on the character of the two cities at this important time. The dedication is "To the Right Honourable George Dunk, Earl of Halifax," head of the Board of Trade and Plantations, for whom the city was named. (Courtesy of the Picture Collection, Public Archives of Nova Scotia)

lics, under the English governor at the new capital of Charlottetown. Acadian returnees continued to trickle in to the more remote western districts, but the dominantly British imprint was unmistakable.

In contrast to this drastic remaking of the Atlantic margins of former French America, the British annexation of Canada was a simple imperial process: the substitution of one government for another, without major social upheaval. While the English military governor and his lieutenants took charge at Quebec, Trois-Rivières, Montreal, and the various inland outposts, senior French officials and eventually a few leading families departed, but the majority of even the upper levels of society—seigneurs, clergy, lawyers, merchants—remained. Such con-

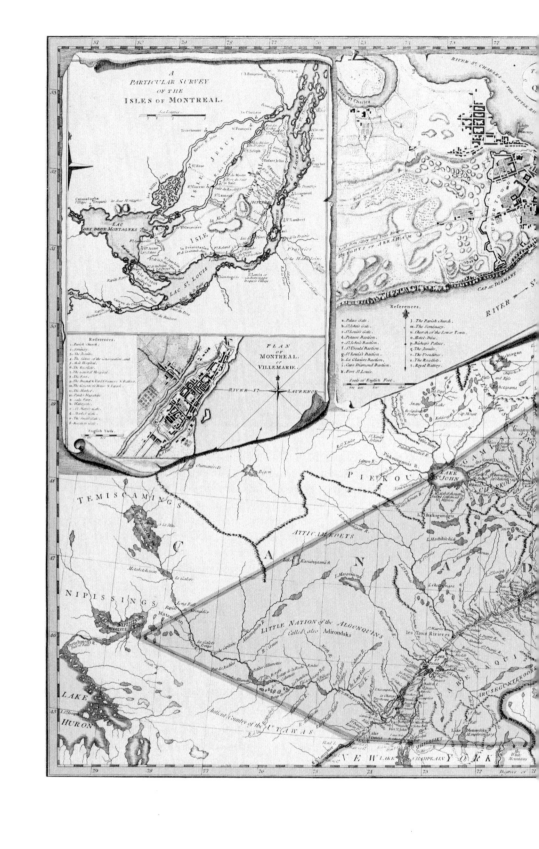

A
PARTICULAR SURVEY
OF THE
ISLES of MONTREAL.

ISLE JESUS

ISLE DE MONTREAL

ISLE

LAC DES DEUX MONTAGNES

LAC ST. LOUIS

PLAN
OF
MONTREAL,
OR
VILLEMARIE.

RIVER ST. LAURENCE

References.

TEMISCAMINGS

C   A   N   A   D

ATTICAMEGUES

PIEKOU

LAKE ST. JOHN

NIPISSINGS

LITTLE NATION of the ALGONQUINS
called also Adirondaks

les Trois Rivieres

LAKE
HURON

Antient Country of the OUTAWAS

NEW
LAKE CHAMPLAIN
YORK

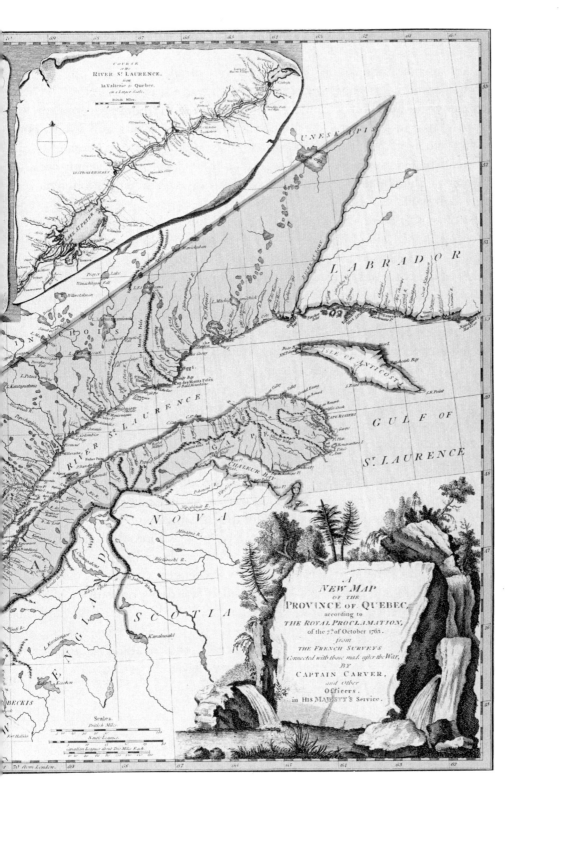

tinuity was not surprising in this case. A shift of allegiance from one king to another was of course not an uncommon European experience. As in all older colonies there had been chronic grievances against the home government, to which were now added the shock of abandonment, for it was well known how readily French officials had traded "snow for sugar"—Canada for Guadeloupe—in the treaty negotiations. Mainly, of course, all these people stayed simply because Canada was their home; they were North Americans, several generations removed from their French roots.

At the outset there was in fact a good deal of talk in London about promoting extensive immigration from nearby British American colonies and fostering acculturation through contact with such Protestants. But no such colonization took place because there was no ready source of colonists. A broad tract of wilderness lay between Canada and colonies to the south, Yankees had their own northern lands to fill, and there was no influx of Europeans, for as the English governor observed in 1767, such persons "never will prefer the long, inhospitable Winters of Canada, to the more cheerful Climates, and more fruitful Soil of His Majesty's Southern Provinces." And it was a matter of more than proximity, climate, and soil, for few prospective emigrants would willingly be joined to the solidly French society of the St. Lawrence. And so the population of Canada grew vigorously, but by its own demographic power rather than by immigration. And despite any programs for Anglicization, local British officials, seeking tranquility in their jurisdictions and predisposed by their own military-aristocratic backgrounds to the virtues of an orderly hierarchical structure, in practice supported the ongoing life of French institutions and customs, even working out an accommodation of the Roman Catholic Church within the framework of the British empire.

In the geopolitical integration of this captive province into their empire, however, the British imposed new and much narrower boundaries upon Canada, limiting it to the general St. Lawrence Valley. In deference to West Country and American fishing interests, the eastern boundary was drawn so as to exclude the Gulf of St. Lawrence coasts and islands, lumping Labrador, Anticosti, and the Magdalens with Newfoundland; and in order to give the well-entrenched English-Dutch merchants of Albany advantageous access to the Great Lakes, an arbitrary western boundary was set just west of the Ottawa River. Thus Canada was politically severed from its major fishing and fur trade frontiers.

---

50. Province of Quebec, 1763 (*overleaf*).
The map clearly shows the constricted boundaries imposed by the British immediately upon annexation. This plate of maps and plans was published in William Faden's *North American Atlas*, 1776, but, as the inscription indicates, was based on detailed French maps; few of the names have been anglicized. (Courtesy of John W. Reps)

The French economy had operated as a relatively stable system under rather close governmental supervision. The British quickly opened up the whole structure to new markets, new sources of capital, new contracts for governmental supplies, new licensees to foster competition and expansion. An influx of merchants and opportunists—mostly Scots, English, and Irish—avidly moved in upon the fur trade and the timber industry, encouraged the commercialization of agriculture, and searched for other profitable activities. Congregating primarily in Montreal, the pivotal entrepôt between ocean and interior, now with attractive alternative connections to New York, these persons soon dominated an expanding commercial life of Canada. Backed by greater capital and political favor, enterprising Scots working in close association with the experienced French took over leadership of the Canadian fur trade. Although set back awhile by the Pontiac-led rebellion of the Indians against the British and their new tactics, these invigorated Canadian operations, spurred by a strong sense of competition with those of Albany and Hudson's Bay, were soon building larger vessels and dominating the Great Lakes as well as reaching deeply into the Saskatchewan country, two thousand miles to the west.

Thus the main alteration in Canada during these years was an abrupt change in political and economic leadership, a decline in the relative influence of the old hierarchical society and the rise of a strongly entrepreneurial bourgeoisie; it was a shift in the balance of power between Quebec and Montreal, between the old citadel of political, ecclesiastical, and military authority and the upriver seat of the vigorous new British commercial community. In all of this there was no strongly overt ethnic conflict. Canada remained basically and almost fully a French society. And this social continuity was given formal recognition and support in the Quebec Act of 1774 by which the British Parliament guaranteed the "ancient laws, privileges, and customs" of the French with respect to the church, civil law, and seigneurial system, and reestablished an appointive legislative council (to include both French and British members). The act also abolished the restrictive 1763 boundaries, reincorporating Labrador, Anticosti, and the Magdalens on the east, restoring most of the Great Lakes and the lands north of the Ohio and east of the Mississippi to Quebec jurisdiction.

The Quebec Act was a conciliatory move during a tempestuous time. If in the main it did little more than give legal recognition to existing practice, it did so because British rulers acknowledged their basic dependence upon the support of the French, and it was prompted by the mounting rebelliousness of the British colonies to the south. It reinforced a classic imperial relationship, an alliance of convenience between the imperial power and the local elites (the French clergy, lawyers, and seigneurs) to sustain the privileged positions of each. Although the British "Montrealers" objected to such strong support for the French system, they were richly served by the restoration of the west to Quebec jurisdiction, which enhanced their competitive position in the fur trade.

Thus by 1775 the British had consolidated their imperial hold upon the 75,000 French of the St. Lawrence, and their characteristic politico-economic policies had lured 2,000–3,000 British into Montreal, creating a bicultural city and locking the two peoples together in a dual society.

4. Reorganization: Tropical America

The annexation of Florida was more an accident of war than a premeditated imperial objective. Florida was the ransom for Havana, a province reluctantly given up by a Spain humiliated by the loss of its key American bastion. As a country Florida appeared to have little intrinsic value and many considered it unequal to so great a prize, but the chance to expel an old enemy from this corner of the continent and put an end to the raids and conspiracies endangering the British position in Georgia seemed sufficiently attractive within the overall treaty settlement. So, too, the French transfer to Spain of her remainder of Louisiana was an unexpected outcome that greatly altered the political geography of North America. Thus even as the old troublesome borderland south of the Altamaha was removed, a far longer boundary was created along the Mississippi in a manner certain to generate new trouble, for the English were given a frontage on all except the most essential sector: the lands commanding the mouth of that greatest of waterways.

The British applied the name Florida across the entire span of their new southern frontier and organized it into two provinces, East Florida and West Florida, divided at the Appalachicola River and significantly different one from the other in character and circumstance.

Although the treaty guaranteed that all the residents of Spanish Florida could remain and be undisturbed in their basic properties and privileges, very few chose to do so. The province had only rarely, and not recently, been much more than an outpost of Havana and a frontier refuge area; there was no large body of deeply rooted colonists as in Canada. Spanish officials urged all to leave and offered lands and assistance to resettle on the real "mainland," Cuba. And thus within a year there was an even more complete replacement of peoples than in Acadia, as about three thousand peninsulares, isleños, Creoles, mulattos, Negroes, and Christian Indians left and an influx of officials and opportunists transfused British life into the two-hundred-year-old Spanish shell of St. Augustine.

This old outpost now became the capital of a province that encompassed the peninsula from St. Mary's River (a compromise between competing claimants of the land between the Altamaha and the St. Johns) to the Florida Keys (valuable turtling grounds, which remained in dispute between England and Spain). Nego- tiations with the Lower Creeks soon cleared a northeastern section for White settlement and here, especially along the St. Johns River, a number of extensive plantation projects were attempted. East Florida was the most popular of England's newly acquired territories among the great throng of petitioners for crown lands (among whom were many Scots who had risen to prominence in imperial service during the long war). More than two hundred grants were issued, but actual colonization was undertaken in fewer than twenty, and most of these were rather meager affairs. It was an era of intense speculation, and there were the usual shortages of capital, capable managers, and colonists. There was now official discouragement of emigration from England itself, and any who did wish to go to America had a wide choice among colonies of proven attractions. Thus promoters turned to Scotland and Ulster, to areas of distressed Protestants on the continent, or to overcrowded tropical islands (such as Bermuda, from which forty families came in 1766). Much the most notable colony in size and character was New Smyrna, established by a wealthy Scottish physician, Dr. Andrew Turnbull, at the site of an old Spanish mission sixty miles south of St. Augustine. Turnbull was married to the daughter of a Greek merchant of Smyrna and had extensive ac- quaintance with Mediterranean lands. He recruited his colonists from southern Europe, chiefly from British-held Minorca in the Balaeric Islands; together with many Greeks, including some from Corsica, and some Italians, they formed a tenantry well-suited to the development of a subtropical economy. Over fourteen hundred were brought over in 1768 and began clearing and ditching for rice, citrus, indigo, and other export crops.

By 1775 British East Florida had a population of about three thousand, exclud- ing Indians, about the number that had left for Cuba twelve years before. St. Augustine was still the main center, but the general pattern of settlement and the composition of peoples were rather different. It was very much more a planter economy, spread out intermittently along the rivers and coast; African slaves were common and the Minorcans, a new isleño group, more numerous than their Canarian predecessors. The Indian trade was more extensive and, along with the rest of the commerce of this small, raw tropical colony, was handled by a network of mostly Scottish agents working out of Charleston.

British West Florida was a new and much less coherent creation. Its capital was set up at Pensacola, replatted in the wake of the complete withdrawal of the Spanish to Vera Cruz. But it also included the French settlements westward along the coast, and the northern boundary was soon shifted to the mouth of the Yazoo River, thereby including the attractive Natchez district as well as the Alabama lands behind Mobile.

Pensacola was a fine harbor backed by poor ground; it remained little more than a government center. French officials departed but most of the settlers around Mobile, Pascagoula, and Biloxi remained. The British moved in mainly as Indian traders and soon diverted to Mobile a good deal of the traffic that had formerly taken the long trails to Augusta and Charleston. Lands along the Mississippi were of greatest interest, especially two localities: at Manchac where the lateral (and now border) waterway from the Gulf Coast via Lake Pontchartrain connected with the river, a strategic point for intercepting the river trade; and the rich, better-drained blufflands at Natchez. Although much of the country remained tied up in fruitless speculations, by the early 1770s a considerable immigration was underway, drawing primarily from the older American colonies. The Company of Military Adventurers, for example, made up largely of officers who had served in New England, had brought in more than a hundred families to their Natchez townships by early 1774. The population of the province in that year was estimated at about 5,000, exclusive of Indians, and including about 1,200 slaves; there were also a good many free Blacks and mulattos, especially among the French creole settlers. The pattern was thin and intermittent along the southern and western waterway edge, with Pensacola increasingly eccentric from the districts of greatest interest.

The great complication and focus of attention in this sector was the Isle of Orleans and the juxtaposition of British and Spanish territories. Spain viewed Louisiana as a costly burden, accepted only to keep it from the British in the hope that it might serve as a rampart for all New Spain. The transfer itself was badly handled. A long delay in the arrival of the Spanish governor and ensuing ambiguity about his purpose and powers, the resentments of the inhabitants in general at being so arbitrarily abandoned by their mother country, and the great fear of the merchants in particular of crippling restrictions on their commerce all combined to produce a revolt in 1768, forcing the Spanish governor and his small retinue of soldiers to withdraw to Havana. For ten months Louisiana was essentially independent, without, however, pushing toward formalization and defense of such independence. Most of the leaders hoped at best for a retrocession to French rule, at least for special status as a Spanish protectorate. But such ideas found little favor in either Versailles or Madrid and in 1769 Spain sent a new governor with a powerful force that reoccupied New Orleans without opposition, executed the principal leaders of the revolt, and proceeded to incorporate Louisiana formally into the rigid structure of the Spanish empire.

However, although there was an official change in language and laws, the society continued much as before, and although external commerce was legally confined to Cuba and six ports in Spain, clandestine traffic with British traders flourished. Such diversion continued because it was advantageous to so many local interests and because Spanish governors were helpless to halt it. The British held treaty rights to navigation on the entire length of the Mississippi, although they were not supposed to conduct trade with settlers on the Spanish bank nor within the Isle of Orleans. They also had access to the river by way of Manchac, bypassing New Orleans, and it was impossible to police any considerable stretch of these long boundaries. Thus much of the produce and profits of Spanish Louisiana flowed through British Florida.

Furthermore, the "Frenchness" of Louisiana actually increased following its accession to Spain. For some years after this long awkward transition Spain had no program for the development of Louisiana. It was administered as an outlying province of Cuba and there were no ready sources of Spanish settlers. But in the late 1750s the first trickle of Acadians drifted in, at first from various British colonies; after 1763 they came in larger numbers direct from Halifax or from the French West Indies. By 1775 about three thousand had arrived, been given some sort of public assistance, and offered land in various outlying areas: upriver above the Germans (to form in time the "Acadian Coast") and at Attakapas and Opeloussas to the west along the natural levees of Bayou Teche. Such people were much the most important addition to the colony during these years, creating distinct Acadian settlement districts, enlarging the small farm and livestock economy, grafting an Acadian ethnicity onto the larger Creole culture of what was still, despite the change in flag, a French Louisiana.

Thus the human geography of Florida, like Nova Scotia, was largely remade, with a complete replacement of one population for another in an old district and the extension of settlement into several new districts. And Louisiana, like Quebec, underwent a change of imperial authority with little disturbance of local cultural patterns but a strong British intrusion into commercial affairs, although the British had not as yet moved directly into New Orleans as they had into Montreal. The flow of colonists into these northern and southern British lands was not heavy, but it was part of a larger plan designed to deal with their new dominion over the whole of eastern North America. As a preliminary proposal put it:

> It might also be necessary to fix some line for a western boundary to our ancient provinces beyond which our people should not at present be permitted to settle hence as their numbers increased they would emigrate to Nova Scotia or to the provinces on the southern frontier where they would be useful to their mother country instead of planting themselves in the heart of America out of the reach of governments.

And, indeed, British policymakers had good reason to be more concerned about the vast interior between Canada and Florida than about their newly acquired Atlantic corners of America.

5. Reorganization: Interior America

The Great War had begun in battles with the French over control of the Ohio Country, and it reverberated on and on after the signing of the European treaties in a series of bloody terrorizing campaigns between British forces and the Pontiac-led alliance of Indians for control of that same area. Having expelled the French from the continent the British were faced with a formidable set of challenges on a grand scale in that "heart of America": the need to reassure the Indians of British protection and fair treatment, a difficult task in the aftermath of a long history of vicious competition with the French for the allegiance of these many peoples; the need to protect and support British traders in Indian country so as to revive and expand a commerce that had been profitable to important mercantile interests; the need to respond to powerful pressures from land companies and from colonial citizens who were determined to enter and settle in these newly secured regions; and the need to face the strong political pressures from the several colonial governments that sought confirmation of their claims to jurisdiction over these western lands as defined by their charters. There was of course no way of really satisfying such a set of different and in part contradictory interests. At best there could be an attempt to formulate a general policy within which conflicts and change might be reasonably managed.

The great step toward meeting that need was the royal proclamation of October 7, 1763. The opening paragraphs defined the bounds of and intentions for civil government in Quebec, the Floridas, and Grenada (to include all the newly acquired islands in the Lesser Antilles). But the main purpose was to deal with the problems of the interior, and the main device was geographic: the establishment of a boundary to separate the European settlers from the Indians. It was an old imperial concept and it had been used recently by the Pennsylvania government to preserve as Indian land all "West of the Allegany Mountains." Now it was applied on a continental scale, using a more precise natural demarcation to forbid European intrusion into "any lands beyond the heads or sources of any of the rivers which fall into the Atlantic Ocean from the west or northwest."

This simple definition of an Indian interior and a European Atlantic America was in fact a crude expediency. The Great Proclamation was an emergency measure designed to quiet the fears of Indians and to block the advance of land seekers until more detailed empirical policies could be put in force. Such a simple watershed boundary did not fit the actual human geography of 1763: settlers were already established west of the line in some areas and Indians still dominated important areas to the east of it in others. To require that all "who have either willfully or inadvertently seated themselves upon any lands" beyond that boundary "forthwith . . . remove themselves from such settlements" was an imperial edict impractical to enforce. Implementation of the Proclamation Line was necessarily

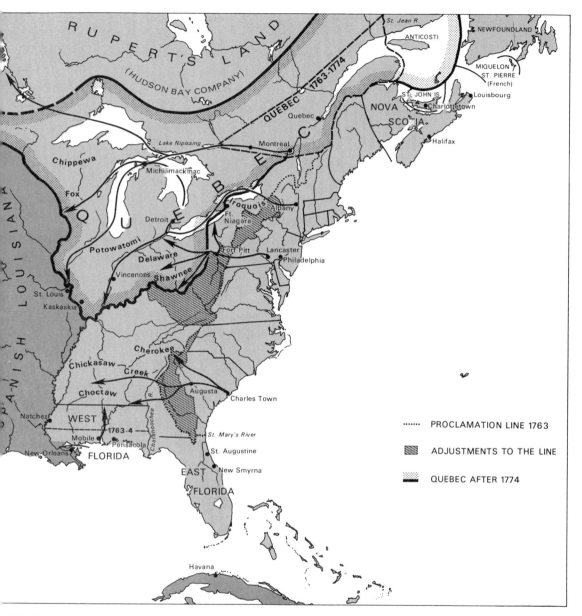

51. British North America, 1763–74.

accompanied by a series of negotiations with Indian nations and various colonial interests so as to define a boundary more in keeping with the existing settlement frontier.

These adjustments and the survey of the separation line were carried out under the authority of the two superintendents of Indian affairs, William Johnson in the Northern Department and John Stuart in the Southern, the two jurisdictions being divided along the Ohio River. Broadly, there were three long sections of the line and two kinds of adjustment made. In the south, from Florida to the southern boundary of Virginia, settlers had not reached the headwaters of Atlantic-flowing streams, nor had land cessions up to that divide been extracted from the still quite powerful Creeks and Cherokees. The Creeks had long been allies of the British and principal intermediaries in an extensive commerce, and the boundary in Georgia was set only a short distance west of the settlement frontier anchored on portions of the Altamaha and Ogeechee rivers. The Cherokees, occupying the southernmost Appalachians, had long tried to stay free of extensive relations with the Europeans. However, mounting pressures from South Carolinians had forced them to yield to the establishment of military trading posts within their mountain homeland, and a brief bitter war in 1760–61 had wrested some of their Piedmont hunting grounds from them. After much haggling the Proclamation Line was drawn near the northwestern edge of the European frontier but still well short of the Atlantic watershed.

Similarly, in the north the Iroquois, who had served as major allies and intermediaries of the Dutch and English for well over a century, still ruled most of the country beyond the Catskills and Poconos and thus new treaties fixed the Proclamation Line along various portions of the upper Susquehanna well east of the natural divide and as yet removed from major pressures. But in a long central section between the Iroquois and the Cherokee, the situation was quite the opposite. And it was so precisely because such lands had for many decades been disputed ground between these two Indian nations, and had lain unoccupied by any other. Such an expanse where Indians appeared only as occasional hunting or raiding parties was a power temptation to European speculators and settlers, and it lay directly in the two intermingled westward thrusts of two of the most vigorous seaboard societies, Greater Virginia and Greater Pennsylvania. These pressures were focused along two quite divergent paths. The northern one led from the western waters of the Potomac and Juniata across to the Youghiogheny and Monongahela and converged on the Great Forks of the Ohio. As early as 1748 the Ohio Company of Virginia had obtained a large grant of land between the Monongahela and the Kanawha rivers. They failed in their plans for development and eventually lost their charter, but their activities initiated much interest in the region and were a factor in the outbreak of war with the French, and as soon as the French were expelled from the area speculators and squatters swarmed in. The other advance was a continuation of the spread southwestward in the Great Valley behind the Blue Ridge that led up the Shenandoah and across a slight divide to the New River, a tributary of the Kanawha, and thence on across another low interfluve to a set of valleys and coves along the upper waters of the Tennessee. There were several hundred settlers in this complicated intermontane alcove by the mid-1750s, and although many were forced out by Indian attacks during the Great War, these and many more returned and pushed on further in the years just after, while a vanguard of land company agents and hunters were following the old Indian trail through Cumberland Gap (first reported in 1750) in avid reconnaissance of Kentucky.

Thus vociferous colonial interests and several thousand settlers were lodged west of the great watershed by the mid-1760s, and, as there were no Indians actually resident in any part of this broad sector and the two major Indian nations that claimed or made some use of it had been much weakened by war, a series of large cessions were obtained so that by 1771 the Proclamation Line lay along the Ohio all the way from the Great Forks at Fort Pitt to the Kentucky River, demarcating a huge wedge of country largely mountainous but with many attractive valleys and streams and opening out to the rolling richness of the Kentucky basins and the grand waterways of the West. Here speculation in land and dreams of great inland provinces took on a feverish intensity. The most substantial project envisioned the creation of a large separate colony called Vandalia in the Kanawha-Kentucky area. Endorsed by London authorities through several stages and redefinitions, it failed to receive final approval and collapsed with the onset of the Revolution.

With these major adjustments the Proclamation Line did serve, momentarily, as a separation line between European settlers and the main territories of Indian nations. Yet conditions west of the line in the great interior explicitly reserved "under our sovereignty, protection, and dominion, for the use of said Indians" became increasingly chaotic. They did so because the British were unable to control participation in and conditions of the Indian trade. A closely regulated system of licenses and designated centers favored by London officials and some of their deputies was never effectively confirmed, lost amidst the welter of competing colonial interests, Indian factions, and aggressive individual ventures. The several regional systems and the character of the trade were rapidly altered after 1760. Whereas the French merchants of Montreal and the Dutch of Albany had worked very largely through Indian intermediaries, Scottish traders now moved in on both systems, especially by ranging westward from Pennsylvania, and carried the trade directly deep into Indian lands with an increasingly lavish use of rum (which the French, especially, had long tried to keep under close control) as the main basis of exchange. These two networks intersected at Niagara and Detroit, and by the 1770s unregulated competition had virtually destroyed the fur trade of the Lower Lakes. The Montreal network continued to prosper on the better furs of more northerly lands and vigorous westward extension, but the New York system dwindled to minor importance, and Albany merchants turned to the developing trade and government contracts in their immediate hinterland.

In the south the old Carolina network reaching inland from Charleston and Augusta developed a profitable northward extension into Cherokee country, but suffered serious diversions to the new British footholds on West Florida. And although the British flag now flew over the Illinois nucleus at Kaskaskia, a rival center had sprung up just across and up the river in Spanish Louisiana where two French agents of a New Orleans firm had laid out the new town of St. Louis as a base for the trade of the Missouri and other western branches of the upper Mississippi. Established in 1763, St. Louis was designated as the new capital of Upper Louisiana (all north of the Arkansas); it lured from various Illinois posts many of the French, who preferred to shift their allegiance to the Spanish rather than to the English empire, and it became a thriving center in a Mississippi network, anchored in New Orleans, which competed with the British over the whole of their western interior.

By the mid-1770s the Indian trade over most of the lands south of Detroit had nearly collapsed from a decade of chaotic activity and from severe restrictions on trading goods, especially rum and blankets, resulting from mounting disruptions of commerce between Britain and its seaboard colonies. This welter of troubles was expressed in and exacerbated by the drastic geopolitical change included in the Quebec Act of 1774, by which this entire interior bounded by the Ohio and the Mississippi was placed under the jurisdiction of Quebec. Ostensibly designed to restore a familiar kind of civil government to the French settlers in Detroit and Illinois, it was an admission that earlier London-designed policies and any hope of cooperation from the British colonies had failed. In effect it restored the St. Lawrence–Mississippi axis, confirmed the dominance of Montreal enterprise over all the Great Lakes, and implicitly testified to the fact that only the Canadians had demonstrated an ability and a willingness to deal at all satisfactorily with the Indians. It was also a calculated act of conciliation to a captive Canada and a restrictive move against rebellious colonies and their aggressive settlers to the south.

6. Expansions, 1750–1775

Benjamin Franklin, viewing the basic conditions of American life from prospering Pennsylvania in 1751, concluded that for British North America as a whole "our people must at least be doubled ever 20 years." Later in the same essay he suggested, only a bit more conservatively, that our "supposed . . . upwards of One Million" may be expected to double in twenty-five years. The lack of reliable data precludes accurate measure, but apparently he was not far off the mark.

The best assessments of the colonial population, excluding Indians, suggest a growth from about 1,300,000 (including the then-French areas) in 1750 to somewhere between 2,325,000 and 2,600,000 in 1775. Much the greatest proportion of this increase was, as Franklin reasoned it would be, an internal growth, although his specific assumptions about earlier marriages and many more children per family in the colonies compared with the mother country may have been a bit exaggerated. There was, in addition, always some immigration and it rather sharply increased during the last few years of that third quarter of the century. Here, too, the data are incomplete, but it is almost certain that the largest body of newcomers, perhaps 125,000, was Black slaves, mostly direct from Africa; and it is quite certain that the greatest European addition came from Ulster, which supplied as many as 100,000 or more. A newly prominent influx was that from Scotland, numbering more than 20,000 in 1768–75 alone, two-thirds of whom were Gaelic-speaking Highlanders. In contrast, there was considerable official discouragement to English emigration at this time (a feature incidentally deplored by Franklin in the conclusion of his essay: "why should Pennsylvania, founded by the English, become a colony of *Aliens,* who will shortly be so numerous as to Germanize us instead our Anglifying them . . .").

The real basis of this demographic power, Franklin observed, was cheap land readily available, and "so vast is the Territory of North-America" that "notwithstanding this Increase . . . it will require many Ages to settle it fully." The British triumph over the French and the subsequent clearance of large areas through treaties forced upon the Indians opened up large new portions of that potential territory, and, powered by intense speculations and an apparently insatiable appetite for fresh land, the frontier of colonization was pushed forward in several major sectors. Thus the years after 1760 were a generally expansive and prosperous time, and despite considerable growth in urban areas and intensification of developments in some older regions, the most obvious geographic feature was a series of thrusts into new ground.

New England was much the most densely occupied large region in British North America, and the removal of the chronic French threat was followed by a strong surge northward. Some of this "swarming," as it was often later termed, was by organized groups from particular towns; some of these had arisen from dissension within local churches, but on the whole it was a colonization process that only faintly resembled the early Puritan mode. Land was being offered by many speculators and jobbers, and most settlers scattered out over the hastily surveyed townships to pick out the best land and set up their homesteads, leaving church and village to develop in due course as a maturing response to settlement rather than forming these as an essential initial focus.

The Yankee influx into Nova Scotia in the wake of the Acadian deportations was of course an easterly branch of this northern movement, which also included the spread of footholds farther along the granitic coast of Maine and up the Kennebec. But much the strongest advance was more directly north from the main body of the region: up the Merrimack and especially up the relatively broad and rich Connecticut Valley and its numerous tributaries, extending a salient of settlement more than a hundred miles beyond the 1750 frontier. Furthermore, Yankee home seekers, encouraged by aggressive New Hampshire governors, moved across the Green Mountains into attractive valleys leading to the upper Hudson and Lake Champlain. But here they entered disputed ground. As a successor to New Netherland, New York claimed all this northerly land lying west of the Connecticut River, whereas New Hampshire governors interpreted their vague charter as license to extend their jurisdiction (and their personal speculations) as far west as had Massachusetts. A ruling from London in favor of New York did little to deter Yankee promoters and settlers, and attempts by New York officials to form jurisdictions and extract fees or to grant lands to their own citizens ignited open frontier conflict. Such pressures and antagonisms remained unresolved by the Crown's suspension of further granting by either authority, and talk of forming a new separate colony (perhaps called "Verd-Mont") began to enliven local discussions.

New York had long felt this kind of encroachment from New England: on Long Island, in Westchester, and all along the Connecticut and Massachusetts border. This northwesterly thrust simply extended the de facto Yorker-Yankee divide that for some years had lain only a few miles back from the Hudson and well west of the political boundary. Furthermore, other New England migrants now passed right across the main body of New York and took root in lands far to the west, beyond the Hudson Valley and the Catskills, including several small colonizations on the uppermost waters of the Susquehanna just beyond the pioneering Scotch-Irish settlement at Cherry Valley. The boldest of these thrusts was farther south in the Wyoming Valley, where a Connecticut land company established a colony centered on Wilkes-Barre. This was an audacious assertion of Connecticut's claim to its original "sea-to-sea" charter rights, and it led to outright battles and harassments and the failure of Pennsylvania to dislodge or effectively incorporate these people. In 1774 the Connecticut Assembly formally annexed this Westmoreland District with its two thousand settlers, an action which only served to intensify the resistance of Pennsylvania officials and rival claimants.

These Yankees were able to preempt the Wyoming Valley because Pennsylvanians had so much good land lying nearer at hand. By 1775 they had spread broadly northward along the Susquehanna and generally up its western tributaries to the abrupt Allegheny Front, but with many farm sites still available in all these new districts. After 1768 the principal focus of speculation was the Great Forks of the Ohio. Several million acres were marketed by a welter of companies and agents to several thousand settlers, who scattered into the valleys and coves of the Youghiogheny and Monongahela, and to the south on the upper Potomac. Here, too, serious conflicts arose between rival claimants to land and jurisdiction in this broad and ragged advance of the frontier well into the Appalachians. Virginia contested Pennsylvania over the southwest corner of the latter's claim, hoping to gain a foothold at the Great Forks itself, while Virginia and Maryland disputed the land between the north and south branches of the Potomac. For all these parties the real prize was access to the waters of the mighty Ohio, the obvious axis of the Transappalachian West.

One of the greatest areas of growth came from the enlargement of a movement already underway just before mid-century. That trickle of land seekers along the Great Philadelphia Wagon Road, passing through Roanoke Gap and on southward into the rolling red hills of the Carolina Piedmont, soon swelled into a flood. Such a large empty country of cheap lands well advertised caught the attention of many people in the older regions, especially in Virginia, Maryland, and Pennsylvania.

The rather diffuse patterns of pioneering began to take on some focus in the 1750s with the emergence of several trade centers and some rather distinctive settlement districts. Hillsborough, at the junction of two emigrant roads, was founded as the seat of the first county in the area by associates of the North Carolina governor, but in general developments in this western country were not part of an inland reach from coastal Carolina. Thus Salisbury, seat of the second county and principal center of the Yadkin district, which seemed to display the marks of the colonial establishment with its Anglican Church and courthouse sharing the central square, had in fact been founded in the midst of his sizeable purchase by a Virginian developer from the Shenandoah Valley. Much the most famous colonization was Wachovia, a tract of 100,000 acres purchased in 1753 by Moravians from Bethlehem, Pennsylvania. After a dozen years of pioneering, they laid out the town of Salem to serve as their principal social and industrial focus, and it drew traffic from well beyond their own lands. There were a good many other Germans as well, Reformed or Lutheran, in this general overland influx, and just to the east of Wachovia was a strong cluster of Quaker settlements in Guilford County. Treaties restricting the Catawbas and Cherokees quickened the flow of land seekers on southward. York, Chester, and Lancaster (towns and later seats of counties of the same names) were evidence of this Pennsylvania imprint across the recently adjusted boundary in new Scotch-Irish districts of South Carolina. Along the southeasterly margins of the Piedmont these migrations from the north did meet and mingle with those moving inland from the seaboard, but the latter drew more largely from immigrants than from the Carolina Low Country. Some immigrants came by sea from the northern colonies, but a good many arrived directly from Europe, such as the several thousand Scottish Highlanders in the Cape Fear district, a considerable group of Palatine Germans and a sprinkling of Irish Quakers along the Broad River, and the Huguenot colony of New Bordeaux on the Savannah.

A View of S.A.L.E.M. in N. Carolina 1787

52. Salem, North Carolina in 1787.
This well-known watercolor by Ludwig Gottfried von Redeken shows one of the least typical landscapes of the Upland South. Twenty years after its initiation, this largest of the Carolina Moravian settlements reflects its close congregational emphasis in the large dormitories (for single members), store, school, and meeting hall clustered at the square on the hill and the close-set but individual family houses, each with an ample garden, just downslope to the left. The density of other structures for crafts and industries, the flourishing orchards, the well-cultivated hillsides (all neatly fenced, and more with the labor-intensive post-and-rail than with the simpler cross-and-rail worm fences of the foreground) all attest to the kind of communal industriousness for which this central European sect had already become famous in America. The artist was a new member of the congregation at Salem who had emigrated from Germany to Bethlehem, Pennsylvania, the year before. (Courtesy of the Wachovia Historical Society, Winston-Salem, North Carolina)

Such ethnic and religious groups gave the Piedmont a diversity not unlike that of the loose belt of townships fostered in the 1730s along the inland margins of the South Carolina Low Country, but, with the important exception of Wachovia, settlement was much less programmed and clustered, much more opportunistic, dispersed, and intermingled. Furthermore, whereas in 1750 this backcountry was only a minor fringe of the colonized area, by 1775 it was the home of well over a hundred thousand people, and thereby this great immigration had transformed the geographic character of both colonies. Now containing more than half the population of North Carolina and perhaps half that of South Carolina, these interior districts, settled by peoples whose origins, social character, economic interests, and political concerns differed sharply from those of the older coastal societies, created a profound geopolitical tension within each of these colonies. Indeed, by 1775, such sectionalism was already a harsh reality, smoldering in the aftermath of several years of chaotic violence that was generated by the failure of either colony to provide effective or equitable government for these remote areas as settlement developed. In general, such administrative and judicial inadequacies were a commonplace of new frontiers, but they took on a special significance in the Carolinas from the peculiar geography of these colonization movements, in which the backcountry was so largely settled by a southward influx from northern colonies, and so little by an extension inland from the maturing Anglo-African planter societies of the coast wherein the power of government resided.

A minor branch of this long southward movement, augmented by refugees from the North Carolina turmoil, created a quite separate pocket of settlements along the several headwaters of the Tennessee River in the farthest reaches of the Great Valley, between the Appalachian Mountains on the east and the Cumberland Plateau on the west. Generally known as the Watauga Settlements, from a local protective association formed in 1772, it was an unauthorized thrust into uncertain and disputed ground. The early settlers assumed they were within Virginia; British and Indian officials declared it an illegal invasion of Cherokee lands; and in fact most of it lay within the western claims of North Carolina. In 1775 the local dangers of this encroachment were eased by purchase from the Cherokees, but such negotiations were technically illegal, and the political status of the area remained uncertain.

Fifty miles to the west of Watauga, beyond Clinch Mountain, was Cumberland Gap, gateway to Kentucky. In March of 1775 the same bold North Carolina speculator who had purchased large tracts (including Watauga) from the Cherokees sent a vanguard of axemen under Daniel Boone to transform the ancient Indian pathway into a wagon road across the rugged Cumberland Plateau to the edge of the Bluegrass Country. It was to be the avenue to "Transylvania," his grandiose scheme for a large proprietary colony in this New West. By summer land seekers were making their way to Boonesborough, the rude hamlet that had sprung up at the end of this new Wilderness Road, or were branching off to stake out claims in various other attractive localities. Transylvania was an audacious ploy; before any degree of legal recognition could be obtained from the Crown or colonial authorities, all were engulfed in the turmoil of the Revolution. Thus, although actually occupied by no more than a few hundred claimants, Kentucky by 1775 was already famous ground certain to attract a flood of immigration, and it stood as a major unresolved geopolitical issue that would have to be faced by whatever government or governments might survive or emerge from the convulsion.

This incipient problem of the formation of new inland colonies was but one of the major geographic features of these years. Another was the irruption of long-latent intercolonial conflicts arising from vague or overlapping charters. There had also been a reconfirmation of the old imperial truth that conquering must precede planting, most especially exhibited in the treaties forced upon the Cherokees and in the punishing defeat by a Virginian militia of the Shawnees who had dared to threaten the Ohio route to the West. But the most important feature of these years was the fact that North American growth was not only vigorous, as Franklin had noted, but was to a large degree translated into a "geographic growth," into a strong outward expansion of the inland margins of the European colonized area. And the power behind that expansion was not simply demographic, vigorous as that certainly was, for there remained a great deal of land as yet undomesticated within all the older regions and a chronic shortage of labor in nearly all cities, towns, and countrysides. The real driving power was an avid and widespread interest in *new lands* as the quickest way to wealth and status in America. Every new region was thick with speculators and land jobbers, but it must be emphasized that pioneering, the creation of actual farms out of the wilderness, could also be a form of speculation. Many of those flocking to these frontiers to begin new farms had not been landless in their former homes—they were farmers who had sold out and moved on in the hope of bettering themselves. Such an attitude and process, apparent from the early stages of European colonization, had become a powerful dynamic in North American life.

There had also been a strong if somewhat less obvious expansion in another important direction: toward greater American command of North American sea-lanes. American commerce was growing rapidly and colonial merchants, investors, shippers, and seamen had an increasing share in it. By 1775 about a third of the British ocean fleet was American-built, and American-owned vessels carried a high proportion of the traffic on most of the major routes. British ships were dominant only in the direct transatlantic staple export trades of the Chesapeake, Carolina, and Canada. The North American colonies traded as heavily (measured in vessel tonnage) with the West Indies as with Great Britain, and mostly in American bottoms. Somewhat less in total tonnage, but greater in the number of vessels and more important in its implications, was the marked increase in coast-wise traffic. Yankee traders called at every mainland port; Philadelphia merchants cultivated connections with Chesapeake and Charleston firms; the mercantile, insurance, and shipping interests of Boston, Newport, New York, and Phila-delphia developed ever-closer working relationships. Thus within general Atlan-tic circulations and the British imperial system, distinctly American networks were emerging more strongly, binding backcountry to seaport, seaports together, and all of these to a nexus of northern commercial centers. This shuttling of more and more vessels—offering more frequent contact among all the regions, helping a broadening selection of Americans to deal with one another, depend on one another, know one another—was a dynamic of more than economic significance in the life of Atlantic America.

7. Divergence

It is one of the ironies of history—though not an uncommon type—that from the moment the British peoples on either side of the Atlantic shared in the great triumph of 1763, with those on the American side taking great pride in being part of an empire so externally powerful and internally beneficent, the relationship between them deteriorated so rapidly that a dozen years later they were openly warring with one another. Although in the nature of history such an outcome was not inevitable, a basic divergence in interest and outlook had been developing for a long while only to be revealed and intensified by a series of policies designed specifically for this enlarged empire. For whereas the American colonists saw the expulsion of their French and Spanish rivals from the eastern half of the continent as a sudden opening of vast new opportunities, British officials in London charged with the care and costs of this huge structure were keenly aware of new burdens and moved toward a rationalization of the whole imperial system. Thus the one side foresaw a loosening of constraints and a time for expansion, while the other saw it as a time to tighten controls and bring order and efficiency to a complex and cumbersome historical creation.

To put the issue in such terms is of course to abstract from an intensely complicated history and to ignore the role and motives of specific actors and a labyrinth of group interests. At best we can only sketch a broad framework within which to identify the general issues of this dispute as they were publicly presented and perceived, and suggest how these were related to the resulting geopolitical divergence.

British intentions during this time may be summarized in terms of four basic problems:

1. *how to control the internal dynamics* of this imperialism—that is, how to keep colonists and Indians from preying upon one another and turning the outer margins of the empire into a zone of chronic violence and instability;
2. *how to manage the empire* more efficiently—that is, how to bring the great diversity of executive relationships between London and the several colonial capitals into some semblance of uniformity, and how to impose some greater coordination in support of general British aims among the notoriously parochial, selfish, and competing interests of these many colonies;

3. *how to defend the empire*—that is, how to maintain a military establishment commensurate with the enlarged scale of responsibility within a highly dangerous international world in which France, especially, was still seen as a formidable adversary; and

4. *how to make the empire pay*—that is, how to apportion costs and regulate commerce so as to support the most basic reason for having an empire.

In very general geographic terms these four may be translated into problems in which the focus was primarily on control over the interior, the seaboard, international frontiers, and oceanic commerce, respectively.

Unfortunately for the British government, attempts to solve these problems by what it considered to be perfectly ordinary and sensible political measures came to be seen by many people in America as calculated assaults upon some of the very principles and privileges basic to their pride in being part of this grand and peculiarly British creation. Each London action produced an American reaction, with a heightening of awareness and a sharpening of the definitions of differences. Thus step by step the very attempts to solve perceived problems generated an unforeseen problem that grew so rapidly and powerfully as to engulf the whole process and cause a ragged sundering of the British Atlantic world.

As we have noted, for London policymakers the Proclamation Line of 1763 was an emergency measure to halt chaos and bring law and order to Indians and colonists alike, both of whom were constituents of this empire. The West was a protectorate, an outer zone annexed by treaties with native peoples, which offered guarantees of protection and a concern for mutual interests. But for many Americans this West was seen as their future, a vast frontier for expansion and wealth in which the Indians were at best an obstacle and at worst an enemy. Now that the chronic French threat was gone, it was widely assumed that the Crown should give high priority to removal of the Indians and to provision of basic jurisdictional support for colonial developers and settlers.

More general managerial reforms foundered on similar divergences and oppositions. Enforcement of customs laws to halt widespread and notorious smuggling in American ports threatened a freedom colonists had come to take for granted and produced violent resistance. New vice-admiralty courts to try such offenders (first at Halifax, later at Boston, Philadelphia, and Charleston) brought accusations of discrimination against Americans in that such courts were given greater arbitrary powers than their counterparts in Britain. Attempts to regularize appointments and payments of various imperial officials under a new Colonial Office in London were protested as a usurpation of the power of colonial assemblies and a direct infringement of basic principles of government long endorsed in practice. And, most critically, proposals to alter various colonial charters, especially with reference to the appointment and power of the governor, so as to bring them all into a common royal pattern, were viewed as an act of tyranny, a calculated blow at the very basis of representative government.

And so, too, with the military. Imperial officials saw the need for an unprecedented peacetime military force to oversee newly captured territories, police the Indian country, and guard the frontiers, and they considered it only reasonable that the colonies should share in the costs of their own defense; the colonists saw no need for such a large establishment and stoutly objected to paying for it. In general they felt no great insecurity and they preferred to depend on local militias called up only when needed, whereas the British commanders considered such irregular units demonstrably unreliable and ineffective. The colonists regarded the common European practice of quartering regular troops in private homes and halls as an odious burden, which indeed it could readily become in burgeoning colonial cities where housing and labor were always in short supply. In fact the disposition of troops in the aftermath of the war was heavily concentrated in Canada, Nova Scotia, and the Floridas, with small garrisons in various interior outposts. But as tensions mounted New York City, with its corridors to Canada and the West and its location central along the seaboard between the Great Fishery and Florida, backed by the principal naval base at Halifax, became the main pivot of North American operations. With this, objections in principle to a standing army in peacetime as being destructive of local morals and a threat to civil liberties became more shrill. Americans increasingly perceived imperial strategy as designed more to suppress the colonies than to defend them.

The most pervasive problem arose over the very rationale of empire. The idea that "empires should pay" was a commonplace of the times and it had particular force in a British system whose overseas colonies were so largely the result of commercial entrepreneurial initiatives. That until 1768 imperial affairs were primarily the responsibility of a "Board of Trade and Plantations" suggests how this American empire was more the product of a series of uncoordinated speculative ventures than of a comprehensive strategic design. The general mercantilist concept of the mother country as the entrepôt and manufacturer with colonies as suppliers and a captive market had been widely understood as a reasonable principle, and navigation acts to regulate commerce toward such objectives date from the early Anglo-Dutch wars of the seventeenth century. In practice it was never a tightly controlled, self-contained system. Colonies were allowed to trade directly with foreign markets in certain commodities, and to manufacture goods that were not seriously competitive with those made in Britian; if the mother country gained the largest share of the profits, it also subsidized various productions in the colonies. Until the 1760s the system had worked without serious strain; indeed the British American colonies were one of the most thriving economic regions of the world, so it was hardly surprising that the British government thought it entirely appropriate for this developing part of the realm to carry a larger burden of revenue production, in part by the imposition of new taxes and in part by more effective collection of those long and widely evaded.

But leaders in the American colonies not only opposed the imposition and collection of such taxes, as most people might be expected to do, but also soon challenged the right of Parliament even to propose and undertake such actions. It was this drastic unprecedented position and its rapidly evolving rationale that created a crisis, for it struck at the whole concept and structure of the empire. There is no need to detail the intensifying sequence of events in the ten years between the passage of the Stamp Act and the commissioning of George Washington as commander in chief of the Continental army. Once begun, given the fundamental nature of the central issue, the process seems simple and ordinary enough. The colonists denied the right of Parliament to legislate for the colonies on such matters, Parliament and the Crown insisted that such a right was essential to the very nature of imperial government, attempts to enforce such laws met defiance, defiance begat coercion, coercion resulted in bloodshed, bloodshed led to open rebellion, and attempts to put down rebellion soon engulfed British North America in civil war. This progressive hardening of positions and the emergence of extremists as leaders on either side is hardly an uncommon sequence in human affairs. What may be less obvious is the remarkable transformation in the internal character of the British empire that took place during this process. To see that more clearly, we must sort out some complexities and ambiguities in the very terms *empire* and *imperialism*.

As we have emphasized, the European invasion of America was a stark form of imperialism, a trespass upon and seizure of the territory of another people, subjecting those people to alien rule. In the 1760s the British were still heavily involved in this kind of imperialism in North America, as their attempts to control and stabilize relationships with the many Indian tribes and confederacies through coercion, treaties, and the Proclamation Line attest. So, too, their conquest of Canada and acquisition of Florida represent a variety of the same kind of imperialism, in this case the imposition of British rule upon non-British peoples as the result of the defeat of rival empires. But the other seaboard colonies were now imperial in a different sense. It is true that in every case conquering had preceded planting, but the Indians had been eliminated or reduced to insignificance, and these units of empire were literally *colonies* in the sense of having been created by the emigration of Europeans (primarily British) across the ocean to take root in American soil. For such people, *empire* referred to a structure embracing a mother country and her offspring. Some sense of a dominant-subordinate relationship in such an obvious old-new sequence and center-provincial form was matter-of-factly accepted, but it was not *imperialism* in the classic sense of one people subjugating another: they were, proudly, the *same* people, Britishers all; the colonies could regard themselves as simply transatlantic extensions of the homeland.

This sense of unity with the mother country was basic to the colonial sense of grievance at what they considered to be discriminatory treatment. Benjamin Franklin, in the very last stages of dispute, put the question succinctly: "why English subjects who live three thousand miles from the royal palace should enjoy less liberty than those who are three hundred miles from it?" But that issue had come to the fore so rapidly because prior to the 1760s he and his fellow Pennsylvanians and other colonists had in fact enjoyed so much liberty, in some ways even more than their compatriots only three hundred miles from London in Northumberland or Scotland. "Government by consent of the governed" and the protection of "the people" from arbitrary political authority had emerged as basic principles of British government out of a long, arduous, and famous struggle. But the existence and recognition of these had never been clearly formulated or rationalized within the structure of empire. The colonies did not elect members of Parliament nor had they seriously sought such privilege, and they were technically subordinate to Parliament in numerous and obvious ways. In practice each colony was represented in London only by an agent, a lobbyist who sought to influence legislation and rulings so as to protect and promote the interests of that colony. On the other hand, each colony had its own parliament, an assembly of elected representatives which, under the provisions of the colonial charter, had power over a wide range of affairs. By the 1760s most of these colonial electorates were more broadly based than that in Britain, and these colonial legislatures were certainly more responsive to local constituencies than to London-appointed officials. Indeed a large part of colonial political experience had to do with the opposition of these local assemblies to the executive actions of the king's men.

Thus the British empire was a peculiarly loose and complex structure. While it was certainly an imperial structure operating under the general supervision of the Crown and Parliament, with governors sent out from London, and a bureaucracy laced through with networks of influential military officials, the American colonies had increasingly developed as a set of more or less self-regulating parts with reference to much of their domestic affairs. Initiative and resolution were more often local than imposed from afar. Pride in basic British freedoms was as important on one side of the Atlantic as the other, and the American side was rapidly emerging as a major portion of the British Atlantic world. As Franklin had pointed out, given current trends it did not take much calculation to figure the time when "the greatest number of Englishmen will be on this Side of the Water." However, there had been no general formulation of an explicit concept of empire to accommodate such an implicit geopolitical evolution. The crisis of the 1760s arose from the fact that London's perception of empire was too discordant with the realities of empire already apparent in America. Parliament's attempts to rationalize the imperial system were grounded on principles no longer applicable or acceptable on the other side of the Atlantic.

Under the pressure of those measures and the crises produced by colonial resistance to them, proposals for a radical reconstitution of empire on quite different principles quickly emerged, especially from Americans, but from a few concerned persons in the mother country as well. There is no need to detail these new geopolitical designs, for none came even close to adoption. Suffice it to note that they tended toward some kind of federal or bipartite concept of empire in which the American side would be placed on some more or less equal footing with Great Britain. Some would have recognized each colonial assembly as a counterpart of Parliament, while others proposed an all-American council of delegates elected on some proportionate basis from each colony; all envisioned home rule under a common British sovereign. Such designs were by no means wholly new. As early as 1697 the Board of Trade had entertained proposals from William Penn tending in this direction, as did those in 1739 of Martin Bladen, a member of the board, and the well-known Albany Plan of Union, drawn up largely by Benjamin Franklin for presentation to a congress of colonial delegates assembled at the invitation of the Board of Trade in 1754. But the main impetus for all these early plans was a desire for closer coordination among the colonies in support of common interests; they may be seen as attempts to formalize some intercolonial networks along the seaboard in support of the London-America trunk line. What was new in the 1760s was the emergence of a rationale, a radical ideology in support of a bipartite transatlantic structure of empire.

That new rationale rested on the proposition that Americans were a separate political people. It argued that the very act of transoceanic emigration and successful colonization in a new land had set such people free. They had created their own states and it was simply by their choice that they had sought charters from and given their allegiance to the British sovereign. As Richard Bland put the case in 1766, the colonies were distinct states, "independent, as to their *internal* government, of the original Kingdom, but united with her, as to their *external polity, in the closest and most intricate* LEAGUE AND AMITY, under the same allegiance." Variations of this concept were quickly elaborated, culminating in the forceful and widely read statement in 1774 by another Virginian, wherein Thomas Jefferson compared the early American colonizers to the Saxons who had crossed the sea to settle in Great Britain, carrying with them their familiar system of laws and continuing to acknowledge the same king. By that geographical shift they had become fundamentally independent, the territory they settled was theirs, not the king's, and therefore the king had no right to send a force across the sea to coerce his subjects, for that would be applying the power of one of his states against another. His sole right and duty was to execute the laws of *each* of his kingdoms.

Such tendentious arguments found little support in England, although there were a few, such as Thomas Pownall, who saw in "the progressive encrease of the territories, trade and power of the American colonies" the necessity of a drastic revision in formal imperial relationships. Pownall, who had served as governor of Massachusetts Bay, pointed to the fact of a great British Atlantic commercial and cultural system, and argued that it only needed to be infused with the great spirit of the British constitution by the direct and substantial representation of the colonies in Parliament (on the model of Scotland) "so as to form . . . A GRAND MARINE DOMINION . . . UNITED IN ONE EMPIRE, IN . . . ONE CENTER, WHERE THE SEAT OF GOVERNMENT IS." But neither the Pownall plan nor the alternative bipartite concept of John Galloway—a conservative Pennsylvanian whose Plan of Union, based upon the formation of an American Grand Council of Colonies to share with the English Parliament jurisdiction over imperial affairs, was presented to the First Continental Congress in a desperate attempt to hold things together—was given serious consideration by those of commanding influence on either side.

Whereas such proposals assumed that only reform could prevent rebellion, the king and Parliament, ever concerned as any imperial government must be to protect its ultimate powers, insisted that rebellion must first be stamped out, that the foundations must be made secure before the superstructure could be altered. Thus in 1768 British troops were hastily assembled from Halifax and Ireland and dispatched to Boston. It was an unprecedented move and it had a catalytic effect. For the first time, a British military force had been sent against a British American colony. Although it landed without incident, resentment was intense and provocations soon followed, culminating in a clash between the troops and local mobs made instantly infamous in the colonies as the Boston Massacre. Although London undertook no immediate retaliation, its forces were now widely viewed as an army of occupation. Attempts to enforce the navigation acts were violently repulsed in ports throughout the northern colonies, including a direct assault upon and destruction of a naval patrol vessel in Rhode Island waters. In the aftermath of the Boston Tea Party Parliament, determined to assert its control over what it considered to be a brazenly rebellious, mob-ruled colony, passed a set of "regulating" bills that included revision of the Massachusetts charter so as to curb local rule, closure of the port of Boston until restitution for damages was received, and strengthening the power of quartering a larger imperial military force. Important leaders in nearly every American colony read these as confirmation of their suspicions of a calculated design by tyrannous interests to take away long-enjoyed civil liberties. Thus these "coercive acts" led directly to Lexington and Concord and a rapidly spreading civil war.

The dispatch of British troops to Boston marked a shift in the internal balance and thereby in the apparent character of the British geopolitical system. That peculiar empirical balance "between metropolis and provinces, coercion and consultation, military-imperial executive and civilian-localist legislature" had endured so well for so long as to have masked the most fundamental feature of such a system. Although much more loosely structured than others of its time, it was after all an *imperial* system and, as Stephen Webb has emphatically reminded us, "there are no empires without armies." The American colonies had long existed routinely within such a military context but they had never for any extended period of time nor in any comprehensive way chafed under the direct rule of "garrison government." Such military authority had been applied only to newly acquired territories or frontier provinces. The crisis in Boston brought this inherent military dimension of empire to the fore, and thereby transformed the American perception of the geopolitical structure of which they had always been a part. Instead of an empire in the sense of a mother country and its distant offspring, they now saw an imperialism in which one people asserted its coercive power over the territory and life of another people. And thereby the pressures that had been forcing the rapid emergence of an American ideology in support of new civil relationships also brought to the fore a sharpened sense of American identity. The British people of the Atlantic World had become two peoples, separated by much more than an ocean.

A large part of that sense of identity was of course grounded in the geographical separateness and scale of America. A hundred and fifty years after its initiation British America was now by many measures a very substantial *new world*. It was a spacious world, more than half as big as the whole of Europe, many times the size of the mother country. And it was a prospering and growing world. Behind its urbane seaport capitals more than two million people were spread out in farms, villages, and towns amidst a comfortably but far from intensively domesticated landscape. Its several regional societies were growing, and some of them seemed certain soon to surpass Scotland in population and productions; indeed they were luring thousands of Scots across the ocean every year. And there had been a rapid expansion of institutions as well as industries, a growing sophistication, cultural sustenance, and confidence that could not but strengthen a self-image of British America as destined to be an important part of the world.

Less obvious and more ambiguous but of increasing interest was the emergence of a *new society*. British America was undoubtedly British, even narrowly English, in many ways. Through direct transfer, careful nurture, conscious imitation, and the routines of daily life, there existed a British Atlantic World that was matter-of-factly apparent and accepted through all these tumultuous years. To quote one historian among many on this reality:

> There was . . . a standard culture throughout the colonies, not strictly American, but one heavily indebted to England. For the most part the institutions of politics and government on all levels followed English models; the "official" language, that is, the language used by governing bodies and colonial leadership, was English; prevailing social values were also English.

And another has emphasized that "the American mind . . . was thoroughly, compulsively English in almost all its articulated manifestations": "a web of nostalgia, shared tastes, psychic needs, and habit, as well as geopolitical realism and political connection bound the colonies to the mother country."

And yet all these students of colonial history have noted that there were at the same time many distinct American departures from English norms, differences in content, emphasis, interpretation, direction. Some of these were common American features, others more characteristic of particular regional societies; some became the focus of attention, others were hardly articulated or even apparent at the time. The very nature of the quarrel between the imperial government and its transatlantic subjects quickly exposed and magnified differences in political character. Excepting only the most recent royal foundations (Nova Scotia and to some extent Georgia) and annexations (Canada and the Floridas), all the continental colonies had over many decades hammered out a basis, style, and philosophy of local and colonial government that varied from Britain's in being more democratic and distrustful of arbitrary power and privilege. Such a pattern in large measure reflected critical differences in social structure, particularly the broader base of property owners and voters and the absence of an aristocracy. Thus the intricate, pragmatic set of checks and balances involving the king, the House of Lords, and the Commons that had evolved over centuries in England simply could not be reproduced across the seas. As the soldier-aristocrat Sir Guy Carleton, governor of Quebec, tried to explain to his London superiors in 1768 (he was arguing against the creation of a popular assembly in Canada): "The British form of government, transplanted into this continent, never will produce the same Fruits as at Home, because it is impossible for the Dignity of the Throne, or Peerage to be represented in the American Forests." Politics in the colonies was therefore a much more direct and simple contest between executive and legislative authority, between the king's appointees and colonial assemblies, between what came to be perceived as *external* power and local rule. Thus under the pressure of political crisis the concept of "the people" as the basic authority quickly emerged as central to the colonial argument. Such a single focus on but one facet of the complex English polity marked a critical divergence in political perspectives.

The peculiar intensity of this American fear of hierarchical authority came out in the widespread opposition to the appointment of an American bishop to serve the established church in the colonies. Nor was this simply the result of the far more influential role of Dissenters overseas than in the mother country, for even though such an episcopal presence was fundamental to the Church of England and essential to its full operation in America, and would be an obvious mark of the emerging maturity and equality of the colonies, such an appointment was also opposed by many Anglicans in America as being politically undesirable and ecclesiastically archaic. Such an unorthodox reaction was one indication among many of how far the religious character of America had diverged from that of Britain itself.

The most obvious difference, as we have seen, stemmed from the very foundations of these British colonies: the great variety of religious groups arranged in patterns and proportions to form a mosaic unknown in the Old World. There was no majority religion in the colonies as a whole; among them there were two deeply antithetical established religions (Puritanism and Anglicanism), but in several of these colonies establishment had little practical effect (New Jersey, Maryland, North Carolina, Georgia), in others it did not exist (Pennsylvania, Delaware), and in one establishment was formally prohibited (Rhode Island). One of the most important features was the power of militantly Nonconformist groups, such as the Quakers from early on, but most notably by mid-century the Baptists, an expanding egalitarian movement.

Over the years such variety had produced immense sociopolitical stress and strife—long reverberations of the Reformation reinforced and modulated by links with ethnicity—but out of the experience had come an unprecedented degree of religious toleration, not so much grounded in argument from principles as simply, grudgingly acknowledged as the only practical basis for civil life in such a pluralistic society. It was a toleration sorely tested but probably strengthened in the fires of the Great Awakening, which swept over the full length of the seaboard at midcentury. In its fervent attacks upon insitutionalized religion and its insistence on a more direct personal access to and outward expression of God's grace, this powerful evangelical movement undermined all structures of authority, splintering congregations and denominations, and did much to make the seething instability of "popular" religion a dominant American feature.

Richard Hofstadter concluded that the Great Awakening intensified what America was already: "in religion the most Protestant of Protestant cultures and in morals the most middle-class country of the emergent bourgeois world." His reference to British America as a middle-class country is not to suggest the absence of the rich and the poor—indeed these were expanding in numbers and significance during this very era—but only to emphasize "the overwhelming weight and presence" of the middle class compared with any other complex society of the time; Hofstadter offered a telling summation of just what this meant:

What distinguished the colonial world of the mainland was that here, much more than elsewhere, the thoughts of both rich and poor were so much directed toward the middle. Here, more than elsewhere, the poor man, if white, could really hope to edge his way into the middle class. And here, more than elsewhere, the rich man had to exercise his power in the knowledge that his way of doing so must not irritate a numerous, relatively aggressive, and largely enfranchised middle-class public. Here there were harassed governors, but no Court; there were rich men and influential councillors, but no nobility; there were churches, two of them with thin legal claims of establishments, but no Church with a full hierarchical panoply and a deeply rooted place in the texture of society; here there were struggling colleges, competently educating the future rulers and ministers of the provinces, but no ancient universities fit to serve as the hiving places of boisterous young aristocrats; here there were stunningly large tracts of land put at the disposal of favorites and speculators, but on them no magnificent estates manned by scores of servants and capable of feeding scores of brilliant and fashionable guests. This was a scene in which the basic institutions of Old World society were represented by shadowy substitutes, but in which the simpler agencies of the middle class were in strong evidence: the little churches of the dissenting sects, the taverns (then known as "ordinaries"), the societies for self-improvement and "philosophical" inquiry, the increasingly eclectic little colleges; the contumacious newspapers, the county courthouses and town halls, the how-to-do books, and *Poor Richard's Almanack*.

Again, there were marked regional variations in this pattern, but even in South Carolina where the middle class was least powerful it was there, it was growing, and, as the Up Country filled, the middle class gave notice that it would challenge the tight hold of Low Country planters.

Reference to South Carolina, where in fact the majority of the people were black slaves, leads to the very existence of slavery as one of the most obvious differences between the social character of the colonies and that of the mother country. But it was a difference rarely mentioned in the discussions of the day. Black slavery was so deeply and broadly a feature of the Atlantic World that it was taken for granted as part of colonial society. Only as British Americans began to talk more shrilly about "freedom" and "equality" and "natural rights of man" did an occasional response point to Afro-Americans as a stark contradiction of such concepts in America. (Most aptly summarized in the now-famous remark of Dr. Johnson: "How is it that we hear the loudest yelps for liberty among the drivers of negroes?") But since most British on either side of the Atlantic routinely placed Blacks in a separate category, apart from common connotations of "society" or "the people," the presence of slaves had little bearing on discernments of divergence and separation within the British Atlantic world.

Thus, as with all peoples, Americans' own perception of their differences from others was selective in content and tended toward idealization. Americans had always been conscious of being "colonials" and "provincials" within the larger British world, but as the imperial center came increasingly to be seen as an adversarial society the colonists increasingly turned common pejoratives of provincial life into virtues. Thus their relatively undeveloped and unsophisticated social institutions were proclaimed as a becoming simplicity, a recovery of natural innocence, their rustic manners a democratic dignity, their contentious politics an expression of vitality and freedom, their uncontrollable religious diversity an exhibit of tolerance, their middle-class materialism an industrious practicality. In all of this, American spokesmen drew ideas and support from the Enlightenment, that powerful intellectual movement of the eighteenth century that focused a penetrating rational, secular critique upon European society, which it considered to be pretentious, extravagant, priest-ridden, and corrupt. Such intellectual leaders were quite ready to seize upon America as a symbol and a hope, and thus the term *American* became heavily invested with meaning.

When Christopher Gadsden of South Carolina fervently urged his fellow delegates, gathered from nine colonies in emergency congress in 1765 to deal with the Stamp Act, that "there ought to be no New England man; no New Yorker, known on the Continent; but all of us Americans," he was asserting a goal, for he was using a term that as yet had rarely carried the weight he wanted it to have. When Patrick Henry, nine years later, declared to the Continental Congress that "the distinctions between Virginians, New Yorkers, and New Englanders are no more, I am not a Virginian, but an American," he was, as usual, exaggerating for rhetorical effect. Nevertheless, if such a goal had not yet been reached, by 1774 *American* had indeed become a widespread term of special meaning. Whereas prior to 1764 "His Majesty's subjects," "British colonists," and "Americans" were essentially synonymous in newspapers on both sides of the Atlantic, ten years later *American* referred not simply to a body of people resident in the colonies, but to a vigorous movement, an elaborating set of arguments about the nature and existence of a particular polity and society, and a growing sense of identity among a people ready to claim a place among the other major peoples of the world.

As those ringing statements of Gadsden and Henry imply, there were in fact two major alterations in perceptions and identities taking place simultaneously. There was the concept of "American" as distinct in content and direction from the mother country, and there was the concept of "American" as a drawing together on the continent, superseding primary identifications with the different provincial ("Virginian") or regional ("New Englander") parts of the continent. Both changes were empowered by the growing sense of common grievances within the structure of empire, and that sense emerged from intensifying intercolonial discussions and recognition of shared values; these in turn were grounded upon long-evolving patterns of political, social, and commercial life and of facilities for interaction.

In a mere twelve years, the attempt to rationalize the empire led to the disintegration of that empire; imperialism begat nationalism; nationalism required that a periphery of many parts become joined together into some sort of confederation of parts; and a truly national confederation had to be something more than a mere association—it had to find a new structure and assert a new kind of meaning as a cultural and political creation. In a single generation, in the view of its ardent spokesmen, *American* shifted in connotation and claim from "colonial" to "equal" to "separate" to "superior." But we must be careful about such summations. It was not a simple translation of British American into American, for not all the parts of British America and not all the British Americans in any one part chose to identify with this new geopolitical creation. Transatlantic divergence within the British empire led to a disruption that, far from being a clean break of the New World from the Old, plunged all British America into the complex geography of civil war.

8. Disruption

The overt disintegration of the British American empire passed through three general geographic phases, each an increase in scale: regional, continental, and an Atlantic interimperial phase. Our concern here is not with the specific battles and policies and personalities but only with the general context of the conflict in each stage and the responsive strategies designed to hold the imperiled structure together.

Although some concern over the treatment of the colonies was voiced in all parts of the empire, the intensifying events leading toward armed challenge to imperial authority were primarily associated with a single province. It was Massachusetts that proposed a congress of delegates from all the colonies to oppose the Stamp Act, Boston that took the lead in boycotting British goods, and Boston harbor into which the fateful cargo of tea was dumped; and thus it was to Boston that the British first dispatched troops, Massachusetts that was singled out for radical "regulating" under the coercive power of Parliament, and the hinterland of that colony's port and capital that became the scene of the first conflict between armed forces of the contending parties. Opposition to arbitrary British rule welled up in other colonies too—there were brief clashes between rebels and loyalists in the Norfolk area—but New England was clearly the seedbed of the revolt. When, gathered in Philadelphia, the Second Continental Congress reluctantly authorized the creation of a Continental army in the aftermath of Lexington and Concord, it in effect adopted the spontaneous New England army that already held

Boston under siege. And before the new commander in chief, George Washington, could actually take charge of that irregular regional force, it inflicted heavy damage upon British troops when they attempted to break open that siege in the Battle of Bunker (actually Breed's) Hill. Such actions by the Congress and American militias, together with a rising flood of other evidence, forced upon British leaders a clearer sense of the scope and depth of this imperial crisis and they began to adjust their responses to deal with something more than a regional revolt.

In August 1775 the king declared the American colonies to be in open rebellion and the government determined to suppress the insurrection by means of a full continental strategy. The general plan was relatively simple, as good strategies ought to be. It envisioned firm control of the northern approaches (Newfoundland, Nova Scotia, and Canada) and the southern approaches (East Florida, the Bahamas, and coastal Georgia and South Carolina) and concentration of a powerful force at New York City, a position pivotal to movement up the Hudson-Champlain corridor (thereby severing New England from the colonies to the west) and to movements by land or sea along the central seaboard from Newport to the Delaware and the head of the Chesapeake (which would give control over major commercial centers and productive districts). Accordingly, the British evacuated Boston, pulling all of those troops back to Halifax, and began to build up a large army to be installed in New York City. If they could control these points and corridors, blockade all American ports, and hunt down any rebel army the British had every reason to be confident of success.

This strategy was such an obvious reflection of some broad physical and cultural patterns of British North America that it had been anticipated by American rebels, and they had already taken steps to thwart it. Shortly after the battles at Lexington and Concord other New England irregulars had boldly seized the virtually undefended forts of Ticonderoga and Crown Point. The Continental Congress was momentarily startled and disturbed by such action but soon authorized a military expedition to Montreal with the intent of establishing firm control over this northern entryway and inducing the French Canadians to join in the rebellion. However, although the Americans took Montreal without a shot and moved on to lay siege to Quebec City, they failed to find any significant support among the Canadians; their overt assault upon the British garrison at Quebec was a bloody failure, and eventually the meager remnant of this expedition made a disorderly retreat before a reinforced imperial army.

But the British also found their grand plan beyond their means. The northern approaches were secured, but the southern were not; for if there were too few rebel sympathizers in Nova Scotia to threaten the key base at Halifax, there were too many for the British in the Carolinas. An attempt to reestablish control over Charleston in 1776 failed, and they were left with only marginal footholds in

ARMY GARRISONS (+25 MEN) IN NEWLY-ACQUIRED
COLONIES AND THE INTERIOR, NOVEMBER 1766 (Cappon)

FORMAL PORTS OF ENTRY, AMERICAN BOARD OF
CUSTOMS 1768 (Cappon)

X   ANTI-CUSTOMS RIOTS 1764-74 (Brown)

V-A   VICE-ADMIRALTY COURT FOR AMERICA 1764-68

V-a   ADDITIONAL VICE-ADMIRALTY COURTS 1768

Savannah   COLONIAL CAPITALS

St. John's

Charlottetown

Halifax V-A
(NAVAL HEADQUARTERS)

Quebec

Portsmouth
Boston V-a

Newport
New Haven

New York City (ARMY HEADQUARTERS)
1764ff

Perth Amboy
Burlington
Philadelphia V-a

Newcastle
Annapolis

Williamsburg

BERMUDA

New Bern

Charles Town V-a

Savannah

St. Augustine

Pensacola

New Providence

. British Imperial Positions.

Florida and the Bahamas. That failure in itself was not decisive, but the inability to carry out their strategy pivoting on New York was. In the summer of 1776 they landed a large army and seized control of New York City, driving Washington out, but despite various campaigns in this central sector, including the capture of Philadelphia, they were unable to corner and destroy Washington's army; the collapse of their three-pronged movement to take command of the Hudson, Mohawk, and Champlain corridors, culminating in October 1777 in the surrender of Burgoyne and his entire army after defeat at Saratoga, changed the whole complexion of the contest. Now, for the first time, in the eyes of the world an overall American victory and the actual dismemberment of the British empire appeared to be a credible possibility. And thus France, which had been covertly supportive of the rebellion, now joined openly in the war, seeking to insure the defeat of her great imperial rival.

The entry of France following upon the failure of their continental campaigns caused the British once again to make a radical change in general strategy. Now the North Atlantic was the main theater; the entire empire was at stake and Britain was determined to protect the most valued parts of it. The rebellion on the continent became secondary to dominance in the West Indies and destruction of the French fleet wherever it might be found. Therefore the British moved quickly, seized St. Lucia, an island adjacent to Martinique, the key French possession in the Lesser Antilles, and deployed naval forces, hoping to lure the French into battle as well as to protect Jamaica, their own most valued island. Meanwhile on the continent they withdrew from Philadelphia, retaining a narrowed enclave firmly anchored on New York City, and shifted their attention to Georgia and Carolina, assuming that capture of Savannah and Charleston would greatly amplify loyalist support in the southern colonies and that a base could be created from which they could eventually move relentlessly northward. All the while they would harass continental ports and cripple American commerce.

But this plan also proved to be more than the British could manage. They took Savannah, much of Georgia, and eventually Charleston but they failed to generate anything like the local support anticipated, and their army became mired in a chaos of bitter partisan warfare in the Carolina backcountry. Meanwhile Spain joined in alongside her ally, France, and soon captured all of West Florida. And although the British ranged boldly through the tropical seas, landed forces in Central America, and grabbed all the Dutch islands (having declared war on the Netherlands), it was all to little effect and the prospect of a combined French and Spanish fleet kept Jamaica and all other British islands in jeopardy. In 1781 the British program was disintegrating. Powerful French forces recaptured the Dutch islands, moved in upon the British Leeward islands, threatened Barbados, and deployed for an assault upon Jamaica. On the continent a decision was made to abandon Carolina and shift the main army to Virginia where it might operate in conjunction with other army and naval support based in New York. But this was a salvage operation designed more to hang on and harass than a means toward ultimate victory, and it foundered on a momentary loss of naval supremacy to the French, whereby American and French armies could be rapidly shifted to the Chesapeake to bring the stranded British army at Yorktown under relentless siege. The surrender of Cornwallis on October 19, 1781, forced the British government to realize that it had lost the major portion of the American empire and that the time had come to seek a peace.

Negotiations over the terms of the dismemberment took a long while. The Americans signed a separate treaty with Britain, but their geopolitical situation was also affected by the settlement obtained by France and Spain with Britain. Thus on September 3, 1783, thirteen colonies were formally severed from the empire and recognized as the United States of America, with the Mississippi and the Great Lakes as the western and northern boundaries of the new state; two colonies, East and West Florida, were returned to Spain after twenty years under British rule. Spain also recovered Minorca; France gained Tobago, Fort St. Louis on the Senegal, and several slave trading stations on the Guinea Coast in this conclusion of what had become a global interimperial war.

Dismemberment was not simply a matter of the separation of political territories; it involved a resorting of people as well, for the American revolt was all the while and everywhere a civil strife, a fierce internal struggle that shattered communities and colonies and uprooted tens of thousands of people. The great exodus of nearly 30,000 civilians accompanying the official British withdrawal from New York City after the treaty of 1783 was merely a late phase of a process that had begun with the emergence of revolutionary agitation years before.

The topic is fraught with difficulties of interpretation. A basic problem is the lack of a generally satisfactory term for those people who chose alignment with Britain. *Tories* and *loyalists* are the most common labels, as they were in the later stages of the war, but the former implies a rather specific ideological stance and it beclouds political interpretation in that it had little relevance to most of the people so labeled; the latter term embraces many gradations of behavior and has been used in widely different ways. The most obvious, but narrow, use has been to equate *loyalists* with *exiles*, applying it to those who declared themselves unmistakably by their departure from the new American state in order to continue as British citizens on British soil. These loyalists are an important body of people because they represent an actual spatial resorting with decisive effects on the human geography of several colonies. But it must be emphasized that such a definition obscures the important fact, recognized by all students of the Revolution, that a far larger number of people with similar general sympathies chose in the end to stick it out in their American homeland and make the best of it in the new republic. It is quite obvious that at the outset of hostilities most Americans were matter-of-factly loyal to the Crown, wanted to be left alone, and certainly did not want to get chewed up in a rough-and-tumble fight. It is the special agony of civil wars that such indifference or neutrality cannot be allowed by the contending forces. Sooner or later people are forced to declare their allegiance. It is also clear that the basis of such decisions in this case were unusually complex and varied. All British Americans found themselves caught in a struggle that began as a political protest, turned into a regional rebellion, spread as a civil war, and quickly took on the intensity of a national war of liberation. If choosing sides was a matter of explicit ideology for some, for many more it must have been a matter of personal interests, community ties, an assessment of current and future opportunites and risks (especially whose troops offered local protection), and a gamble on the fortunes of war. Thus the loyalist exiles do not in themselves provide an adequate measure of the extent and patterns of the contending parties within British America.

A further problem with the term *loyalist,* less commonly recognized, is that to restrict the term either to the exiles or even to all those of British sympathy within the Thirteen Colonies loses sight of the fact that the great majority of the residents of adjacent colonies—Canada and Nova Scotia, the Floridas and Bermuda and the Bahamas—did not rebel and therefore might be thought of as loyalists also. Such allegiance cannot be dismissed as simply an untested routine commitment, for these colonies were not beyond the bounds of this great imperial crisis, but were in fact very directly involved in and affected by it. The peculiar neglect of such a perspective testifies that the topic of the "loyalists" has been shaped almost entirely by narrow nationalism, either Canadian or American, rather than by the larger inclusive context of the British Atlantic empire.

If we wish to get some sense of the cultural geography of the American Revolution we may well begin with just this kind of simple geopolitical classification of *loyal* colonies and *rebel* colonies. And we may limit the former to those colonies on or near North America that were in some way directly involved in the civil strife. A brief survey of their behavior under such stress will give a clearer sense of what *loyalist* might mean in such regions.

In the Northern Approaches Newfoundland was still much more a fishery than a colony; it had no local council or assembly, it was exempt from the navigation acts, and it shared none of the grievances of the continental colonies. It felt the conflict in the interruption of trade and in numerous raids by American privateers plundering ships and stores. Local authorities considered the Irish population unreliable under such circumstances, but the West Countrymen and Jerseymen remained firmly loyal. After France came into the war its tiny footholds of St. Pierre and Miquelon were quickly seized and Newfoundland braced for a major naval assault

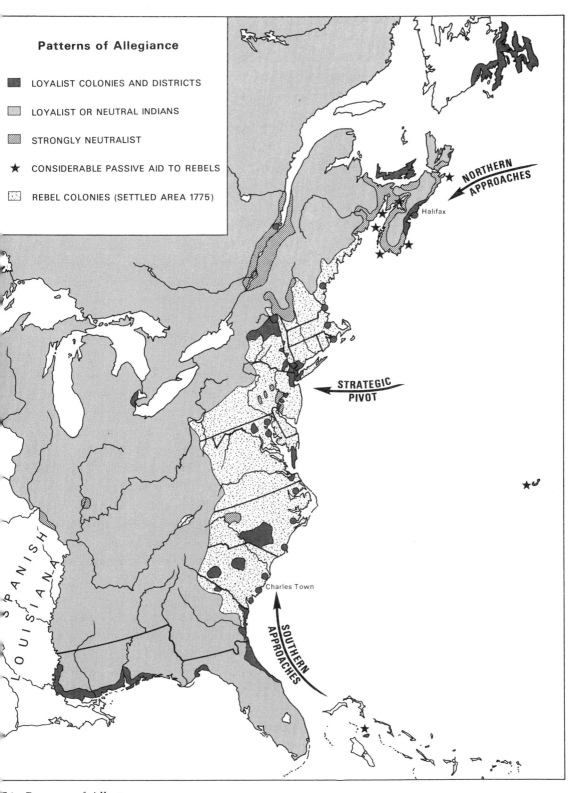

from France, but it never came. Cut off from regular contact with New England, Newfoundland became completely bound to Britain economically as well as politically. St. John's Island, a fresh creation of empire marginal to its main trafficways, was hardly touched by the American Revolution, suffering only a few privateer raids, one of which had been encouraged by rebel sympathizers from Pennsylvania across the strait at Pictou.

Nova Scotia was a far more complex colony and therefore more divided in attitudes and allegiance. Testing came early. When the government sought to draft men to serve in the army at Boston many of the towns petitioned to be exempt because as one (Yarmouth) put it: "We were almost all of us born in New England, we have Fathers, Brothers & Sisters in that country," and thus were "divided betwixt natural affection to our nearest relations, and good Faith and Friendship to our King and Country." As these Yankees made up more than half the population of the colony, Halifax officials—faced with another potentially traitorous people (lured in to replace the Acadians expelled just thirty years before!)—reluctantly allowed them a kind of de facto neutrality. But there was much sympathy with and some minor overt actions in support of the rebellion, especially amongst the Bay of Fundy settlements that lay beyond easy surveillance. Small groups based on the St. John River and west along the coast at Passamaquoddy and Machaias petitioned for union with Massachusetts and pleaded with the Continental Congress to send troops and supplies. Response was slight, however, because those beleaguered officials viewed any venture in this region as marginal, costly, and risky. They had no help to spare and without strong naval support there was little hope of sustained success so far from Boston and so near to Halifax. Thus only a few of these Nova Scotia Yankees took up arms in support of the rebellion, and with little effect; a good many abetted American privateers that raided or traded in nearly every harbor except Halifax itself through most of the war; but most remained inactive if not altogether indifferent to the larger issues. Although they had many ties to New England and knew about the protests, they had been detached from the intensifying buildup to the Revolution. A scattered population of farmers and fishermen still creating homes in new ground, they had no urban focus of their own, and the powerful military base at Halifax was a strong deterrent. By the war's end detachments from that base had quelled all uprisings and fastened a British hold on the coast as far west as the Penobscot. Thus Nova Scotia remained in the empire through a markedly localized pattern of British (and Lunenburger) loyalty and Yankee neutrality.

Canada displayed a similar combination of loyalty and neutrality for quite different reasons. Although American leaders very early sought to lure the French Canadians to their side and were confident that an American invasion and defeat of the British garrisons there would bring Canadian support, they were largely deluded. The Quebec Act of 1774 had given Canada formal cultural autonomy within the empire; the American grievances had little relevance, and an American presence was more to be feared than favored for still-fresh historical and cultural reasons. Thus the principal rebel sympathizers were found among the English-speaking merchants at Montreal (most of whom were American-born) who had lobbied hard but failed to obtain a local assembly dominated by themselves. There was some support from a few French who sensed an opportunity for profit and revenge and who resented the seigneurial and clerical clique cooperating so avidly with British imperial rule. The Continental Congress authorized formation of a Canadian regiment under an American officer. A few hundred French joined, many of them remained in service throughout the war, and some became *rebel exiles* from Canada after 1783, eventually obtaining land grants in the northeast corner of New York State. The prospect of France joining against Britain could not but raise the hopes of many Canadians for a retrocession in the eventual dismemberment of the British empire. But American leaders greatly feared such a restoration and obtained formal assurance in the treaty of alliance that the king of France renounced forever his right of possession over Labrador, Acadia, or Canada. Furthermore, an American right to retain Canada after successful conquest was also recognized. Such clauses were kept secret at the time, but the failure of the French fleet to reappear in the St. Lawrence or the American army to reappear before Montreal dampened any French Canadian hopes. Thus Canada, too, was in undisturbed British control at the end of the war, although its final disposition awaited treaty negotiation.

The situation in Tropical America and the Southern Approaches was rather simpler. Officials and merchants in the various islands shared some concerns with those on the mainland over the impact of new taxation and commercial regulations, and any prospect of interruption of trade with North America was alarming. The assemblies of Jamaica, Grenada, and Barbados formally declared their sympathies for the American cause in its early stages, but the possibilities for overt action were sharply limited by the power of the British navy as well as other political and economic interests; a bit of opportunistic trading with American privateers and nearby Dutch and French islands was about all that could be done.

Bermuda and the Bahamas were more closely involved. The British blockade of the continent caused a crisis over food supply in Bermuda that deeply factionalized colonial leaders, some loyally insisting that relief must come from London, others (many of whom had close family ties with the mainland) ready to risk connivance with the rebels. Several parishes sent a delegation to the Continental Congress to plead for food, with a tacit assumption of arms and powder in return. Similarly Bahamians offered no resistance to an American squadron that appeared in 1776 to seize all their military stores. Formally Bermuda and the Bahamas remained loyal colonies, and probably the majority of their leaders opposed the rebellion in principle, but economic needs and opportunities and the obvious sympathy of many others led to widespread smuggling and aid, and these colonies served in effect as passive allies of theAmericans throughout the war (the Bahamas were not captured by the Spanish until months after Yorktown).

The pattern was rather different on the continent in this southern sector. Still heavily subsidized by the British government, the Floridas were relatively new royal colonies, whose populations were strongly in favor of a military presence to secure the area with respect to the Indians and the Spanish. Many of the planters had been in imperial service, many were Scots, and all were still struggling to create viable estates. Local government was minimal and quarrels over alleged imperial usurpation of colonial autonomy had little meaning. Rebel attempts to rally the New England colonists and French residents of West Florida were briefly troublesome, and the Minorcan tenants of New Smyrna were suspected of having Spanish sympathies (their Catalan-speaking homeland was a restive part of the British empire), but there was no serious threat of rebellion in either colony. Indeed, East Florida became a major bastion of the British and as the war spread its population was swollen and its economy stimulated by the influx of loyalist refugees from other colonies. Having staved off an early attempt by southern rebels to conquer and make it the fourteenth member of their coalition, East Florida became the base from which British forces reconquered Georgia and parts of the Carolinas.

We should also note that nearly all the Indians of the British American interior were loyalists in some degree. Most would have preferred to remain neutral in this White man's quarrel, but under the pressure of events they gave their allegiance to the king who had given them formal assurances of his protection and whose agents had long provided essential supplies. American diplomats worked hard to keep the Indians neutral, but had little to offer and a bitter history of aggression to overcome. The Delaware Indians in the Ohio Country actually made two attempts to form an alliance with the American rebels but could gain no effective commitment. That initiative was taken in self-interest, of course; it was an attempt by a client tribe to free itself from Iroquois dominance. The complicated legacies of disruption from more than a century of European intrusion had generated such factionalism within and among the various Indian groups that no confederacy or nation could muster really concerted and sustained action in support of any part of this intraimperial struggle.

Thus a mere list of *loyal colonies* obscures the range of behavior on the part of major constituent peoples, varying from staunch support of British imperial prerogatives, through various gradations of neutrality, to expressions of sympathy for and very practical aid to the rebel colonies. If we now look within the Thirteen Colonies we may expect to find some analogous variations and complexities, and we should note the obverse bias in the evidence for here it reflects very largely those whose loyalism resulted ultimately in exile rather than those who stayed in place. Wallace Brown has carefully assessed a wide range of evidence and ranked the rebel colonies according to the numbers of loyalists (see table 5). On the face of it such lists seem rather a geographic muddle. The sequences and groupings do not appear to fit very consistently with the broader patterns of regional cultures. But as with the loyal colonies, we must look more closely within these political units to see what correlations may be found. Moreover, in assessing such evidence relating to rebel colonies, we need to take into account the geographic structure of empire as well as the regional patterns of colonial peoples.

The most obvious persons who might be expected to oppose the dismember-ment of the empire are those whose lives were directly dependent on that empire: government officials at all levels (and this included a large number of appointees to petty offices), clergymen of the Church of England, agents of firms providing goods and services in support of imperial operations, and various professional people, especially lawyers and others closely affiliated with British institutions. Add to these agents of empire those persons who sought to identify themselves closely with the upper classes of the imperial power, who saw themselves as overseas

Table 5
The Thirteen Colonies Ranked by the Number of Loyalists

Proportionate Numbers		Absolute Numbers	
Georgia New York South Carolina	strongholds	New York	3 or 4 times greater than any other
New Jersey Massachusetts	relatively strong	South Carolina Massachusetts New Jersey Pennsylvania	relatively strong
Rhode Island North Carolina Connecticut Pennsylvania New Hampshire	middling	North Carolina Connecticut Virginia Georgia	middling
Virginia Maryland Delaware	weak	Maryland Rhode Island New Hampshire Delaware	weak

Note: Adapted from Wallace Brown, *The Good Americans: The Loyalists in the American Revolution* (New York: William Morrow, 1969), 228–29.

members of a British elite, and we have a cluster of people who may be called the imperial establishment in the colonies. It was made up of both sojourners (those on assignment in the colonies) and settlers. Most of the latter may have been native-born Americans. It is important to see that prior to the rebellion the upper levels of this imperial establishment were merely part of a broader colonial elite that included an American gentry, prosperous merchants, and professional people whose ties with Britain were by now much less direct and important. It was only under the stress of civil strife that distinct American and imperial components of this body took on clear identity, and it was an agonizing process for many of the people caught up in it.

The geographic distribution of this imperial establishment was closely related to centers in the network of empire: capital cities and towns, major entrepôts, garrisons, and outposts. The premier exhibit of this kind of imperial political and social center was New York City. By the 1760s it had become the principal American terminus of the transatlantic trunk line of imperial operations and its large and varied array of officials and agents was closely intertwined with the more deeply rooted merchant, professional, and gentry class of this most aristocratic and Anglican colony. Identification of this type of imperial cluster helps explain what seems at first glance the surprisingly high ranking of Massachusetts in Brown's lists. Why so many loyalists in the primary seat of rebellion and one of the most homogeneous colonial cultures in America? But Boston, the third largest city in the colonies, was also an important imperial center. Moreover, this old capital of Dissenters had in some ways become more closely aligned with the mainstream of English society, as evidenced, for example, in the fact that some of the leading merchant and professional families had become Anglican. Similarly, Newport was the seat of a prosperous social elite of conservative merchants with strong ties to the West Indian planter class as well as to London, and its loyalism was reinforced by a deep-rooted Baptist concern over the aggressive inclinations of their old Puritan neighbors. And so, too, in Portsmouth and Falmouth and in every capital and port along the seaboard of America there was a strongly loyalist nucleus made up of those in the pay and those in the sway of the power and prestige of the imperial state. Viewed in these terms, it is Philadelphia that seems somewhat anomalous, for the number of loyalists does not appear to be commensurate with the population of this the largest city in British America. It did have, of course, a considerable body of people aligned with imperial interests, but the empire claimed much less support from the larger colonial elite. The Quakers, oligarchy and common people alike, were pacifists by creed and tended to stay neutral as long as possible, and both the Quaker and the large German element were less attracted by English models of society and culture than were most colonial elites. This prosperous industrial, commercial, and cultural center, backed by a rich and expanding hinterland, was more of an American-based city and less dependent upon imperial support than others. No doubt the difference in loyalist numbers between New York City and Philadelphia was accentuated by the long and strong presence of the British army in the former and its late and brief tenure in the latter, but we must not let that obscure the more basic imperial and cultural contrasts.

This religious and ethnic component in Philadelphia calls attention again to regional cultural patterns in relation to loyalist strength and behavior. Much the clearest equation of loyalism with ethnicity is that of the Scots. The great majority of Scottish Highlanders appear to have been strong supporters of the Crown despite the long and still-fresh legacy of punishments inflicted upon their homeland in the struggles within the older English empire. They were very largely recent emigrants, grateful for generous land grants, still responsive to a clan leadership that was closely entwined in military and administrative lines of imperial service. On the other hand, Scottish Lowlanders were conspicuous as loyalists because so many were agents of mercantile houses prominent in the tobacco and other staple trades, especially in the southern colonies. A good many were sojourners and all such agents found themselves resented as middlemen and money changers, symbols of indebtedness and commercial exploitation, and thus vivid targets of rebel pressures and abuse; most were driven out early in the war. The prominence of this mercantile role amidst the predominantly English rural societies of the south probably exaggerates the loyalist proclivities of this ethnic group, for there were a good many other Lowlanders, farmers and tradesmen, as well as teachers, clergymen, and doctors (for Scottish influence was especially strong in these professions) scattered through the colonies who ended up on the opposite side.

In striking contrast was the fact that the Scotch-Irish were almost entirely aligned with the Americans. These Ulstermen, whose very ethnicity was a byproduct of a drastic English imperial program, had little reason for allegiance and ample grounds for antipathy to English lords and rulers. Indeed, to a large degree they had come to America as exiles from another part of this complex empire. They were very largely a rural population with little direct tie to the imperial system, and it is rare to find any of their number active in its support.

Beyond these British folk, however, relationships between ethnicity and loyalism blur. In general new immigrants settling more or less as groups in the backcountry tended to be loyal because they were primarily concerned about their titles to land and felt dependent upon the services and protection of civil and military authorities. Too new to be caught up in American political issues, most would have preferred to stay neutral but few could escape the relentless pressures of a civil war that was not at all of their own making. Among the older non-British groups the pattern was much less clear. The Dutch of New York and New Jersey were deeply factionalized by religion, culture change, and locality. The more conservative groups had retained institutional ties to Holland and resisted Anglicization but tended to be strongly supportive of authority and therefore loyalist. Yet there were conservatives in the Albany area who resented the imperial role of Sir William Johnson and his Indian allies in the Mohawk Valley and western territories and therefore leaned toward favoring the rebellion. And in most Dutch areas resentment of economic and political pressures from neighboring Yankees added a further complication.

As these several references to religion suggest, the alignment of the many church groups was complex. If we lift religion out of its ethnic contexts we can generalize that the Quakers, the various pietist sects, and other pacifist groups tried to remain neutral as long as possible and when they had to make a hard choice they tended out of their own doctrines to respond more to claims based on individual liberties than to the claims of institutional authorities. Calvinists also generally supported the rebellion, drawing upon a rich tradition of dissidence from what they regarded as corrupt state and ecclesiastical power and their quest for acceptable concepts and structures of authority for the local congregation. Such general tendencies of these churches make the Anglican response all the more anomalous. The Church of England was an integral part and symbol of the very core of English culture and society and therefore of the imperial establishment. Its structure was hierarchical and ultimately authoritarian, modified but without drastic departure from its Catholic antecedents. That the established Church of England should serve as a focus and emblem of loyalism in America was to be expected, and was widely manifest, as in New York City, Boston, and other colonial capitals. What was anomalous was the drastic deviation by the Anglican gentry of Greater Virginia and many of the Carolina planters, who were among the strongest supporters of the rebellion. In such areas the Anglican Church had become captive of an American rural society: it had in effect if not in formal rule become detached from its larger ecclesiastical and cultural context and been made into a local, almost congregational, institution strongly under the influence of those rural elites. This pattern of Anglicanism suggests that under the stress of the rebellion, regional culture was stronger than doctrinal religious systems, that religion, too, had been profoundly but selectively affected by cultural divergence.

If we now review these American colonies we can see that once we extract the loyal establishment from the centers of the imperial network we can readily recognize some general correlations between the allegiance of various peoples and the patterns of regional culture and types of societies. The most homogeneous societies were not deeply torn apart by the crisis. Thus, aside from its imperial centers, New England displayed little evidence of loyalism, except to a modest degree in pluralist Rhode Island. The rapidity and comprehensiveness of its mobilization in support of the rebellion, the work of its dense network of committees, the response of town militias, and the spontaneous emergence of a broad leadership were without parallel. French Canada was similarly united, but in a quiet neutralism or loyalism. The only serious restiveness came from the Anglophone merchant group whose influx in the 1760s had transformed Canada into a segmented society. The stress on that kind of society varied with proportions and specific content. The Newfoundland Irish were too few and scattered to cause any disruption, but Nova Scotia was quite clearly divided between the loyalist areas of English, Scots, and Lunenburgers and the areas of Yankees, Pennsylvanians, and Acadians that graded (largely by location with reference to American incursions) from neutrality to connivance to overt support of the rebellion. In the segmented society of the Upper Hudson the Scottish Highlanders were loyal, but the Albany Dutch and evolving Yorker societies were much more divided, reflecting in part stages of acculturation, and this kind of blurring becomes even more marked in the Lower Hudson and the pluralistic society of Greater Pennsylvania. There was a recognizable ethnoreligious pattern in the response of these many peoples to the crisis, but the scale of this social mosaic, the close intermingling in many districts and counties, and the absence of British protection put loyalists and neutralists under severe pressure and undoubtedly magnified apparent rebel support. One group of German Mennonites, for example, became loyalist exiles out of what they considered to be intolerable pressures on their pacifistic neutrality. The sufferings of complex societies under this kind of stress were more vividly apparent in backcountry Carolina, a region of new colonization into which no stable government had been fully extended. Its diverse ethnoreligious groups, each with marked tendencies toward loyalism or rebellion or neutrality, were ravaged by a chaotic struggle among bandit gangs, local militias, continental armies, and several British expeditions. Here, especially, the grand issues of empire and nationalism became beclouded by local social and economic animosities.

The biracial societies of Greater Virginia and Tidewater Carolina also came under special stress. Virginian support of the rebellion was grounded in a society shaped in America over a century and a half, long essentially autonomous, self-confident, and jealous of its local authority, but the concerted vigor of its response was a reflection not only of the relative homogeneity of its White population but of the fears engendered by the presence of its Black population. When Lord Dunmore, the highly unpopular royal governor, issued a proclamation in late 1775 promising slaves their freedom if they would desert their rebel masters, come to him, and join an "Ethiopian Regiment" to serve the king in suppressing the rebellion, he galvanized White Virginians in response and made neutrality or loyalism intolerable among them.

In time similar inducements were advertised from East Florida, but with considerably less effect, at least for a time, in Georgia and South Carolina. There was a big difference between Dunmore's precarious enclave at Norfolk and vicinity and the very substantial British army and loyalist presence in East Florida. There was also a great difference in the history and character of Virginia and Georgia. The latter was a royal colony barely forty years old, still dependent on British subsidies, with a far higher proportion of its population in some way involved with or dependent upon the imperial system. The specter of slave insurrection and armed Blacks was as terrifying here as in Virginia, but for many Georgians, and some South Carolinians, the coercive forces, civil and military, of the empire seemed to provide the best insurance. Thus at the outset Georgia had a higher proportion of loyalists than any of the thirteen colonies, and Savannah and Charleston ranked along with New York as strongly loyalist centers. Yet the failure of the British to capture and hold coastal Georgia and Carolina undermined such confidence, and the escape of many Blacks to asylum in Florida drove planters toward united action in guarding against slave uprisings and in support of the American cause.

Biracial societies were, by their nature, peculiarly vulnerable in such a civil war. Despite general official policies intended to avoid the dangers and complications associated with the arming or freeing of slaves, both sides tried to manipulate Black allegiance to their advantage at every opportunity. Blacks served in some local militias, in the Continental army, and in the British army; some remained slaves, some were freed on condition of such service, some free Blacks enlisted for duty. The interest of Blacks themselves was obviously in their own freedom and improvement of status; the interest of Whites, British or American, was in winning the war. At its end the tens of thousands of dislocated Blacks were a vexing problem for both sides, and complications arising from this disruption would ramify widely through the British and American Atlantic worlds.

"Loyalists were everywhere, delineated more mentally than geographically." Such a statement from a specialist merits respect and has a ring of truth, for many a British American was forced to make a conscious decision about ultimate allegiance. Yet it seems to do less than justice to the geography of the topic. If it is obvious that this civil war in America was not so clear a territorial conflict as was the one between the North and the South, perhaps those differences are too easily exaggerated. The 1860s struggle also tore apart families and communities and states and regions and produced a body of exiles, and we would likely be more conscious of some basic parallels between the dismemberment of an empire and the dissolution of a federation if the latter had succeeded.

Certainly there were important geographic delineations to the patterns of loyalism in this great convulsion. Viewed in the appropriate Atlantic context there was the differentiation of the geopolitical units between the loyal colonies of the northern and tropical sectors of America and the contiguous bloc of thirteen rebel colonies. Within the latter bloc there was a pattern of loyalism closely correlated with the functional geography of imperial networks, and within all twenty of these American colonies there were discernible relationships, however complex and blurred in some areas, between the patterns of allegiance and the internal geography of their various culture groups.

Furthermore, loyalism had a profound effect on the subsequent geography of North America. It is generally agreed that somewhere between 80,000 and 100,000 civilians left the rebel colonies during and immediately following the war. Just what part of the larger body of loyalist sympathizers these people represented and why they chose to leave rather than stay can never be fully known. It is well documented that they came from all walks of life, from town and country, from seaboard and frontier. Although they represented some occupations and levels and localities disproportionate to the whole they cannot be explained by simple categories of class or wealth or domicile. But we must leave further interpretation to others and keep our focus on geographic matters. Having gained some sense of where such people were when the crisis came upon them, we must now pay some attention to where they went as exiles in search of a home. The topic is important because such people were and for the most part remained Americans. This imperial dismemberment was not simply a contest between imperial armies from overseas and colonial forces defending their homeland but was also a civil war between North Americans, and nothing so demonstrates this fact as the plight of the tens of thousands of defeated Americans who looked to the remnant pieces of the British American empire for a place to start life anew. Few had either the choice or the desire to return to Britain itself; some who did found that they were indeed North Americans in spirit and longed to make their way back across the Atlantic. Thus these loyalist exiles (and another eight to ten thousand uprooted from the Floridas) altered the character of several of the remaining colonies and provided the basis for some new ones. Therefore, before turning our attention to the remarkable new federation wrenched out of the body of British America we shall consider some of the geographical alterations the Revolution caused in the surviving imperial territories. That will help provide an appropriate geographic context for the assessment of this new state, for it will define the nature of its borderlands. The Revolution might dismember the British empire and profoundly alter many relationships; it could not affect the most basic geographic realities of North America and the Atlantic: whatever the change in flag or name or settlement, the great patterns of land and sea continue to provide an essential framework.

9. Reorganization: British North America

The loss of the main body of its continental empire left Britain not simply with a remnant of the old structure and system but with a still-productive realm deeply altered and affected by that upheaval. Her control over the two richest resource realms of northern America, the Great Fishery and the fur trade, was not seriously impaired. But the need to find places for thousands of exiles and discharged soldiers had an impact upon some older settlement areas and created important new ones, and the presence, activities, and demands of these new colonists prompted some major geopolitical changes. The general result therefore was a British North America much narrowed in its Atlantic front but reaching deeply into the continent, organized into a new set of colonies now juxtaposed for twenty-five hundred miles with a new and expansive American state.

As in previous treaty settlements, the fishery was the focus of some of the most intense negotiations. St. Pierre and Miquelon were returned to France (only to be seized and evacuated again in 1793) and the French shore rights on Newfoundland were shifted toward the western coast away from the main British sector. But American fishermen were excluded from the great island entirely and only granted seasonal access to "any of the unsettled Bays, Harbours and Creeks of Nova Scotia, Magdalen Islands, and Labrador, so long as the same shall remain unsettled." English West Country interests sought to specify in law their wartime dominance over the provisioning and carrying trade, but it was soon apparent that cheap American foodstuffs were basic to the Newfoundland economy and Yankee traders were tacitly accepted. The most important change, developing gradually over many years but accelerated by the long interruptions of the American, and soon thereafter the French, revolution was the rise of locally based fishing. By the 1790s half the annual catch was taken by Newfoundland boats, to which may be added the tonnage from Cape Breton Island, which had become a similar local base for resettled loyalist fishermen.

The treaty definition of a continental boundary reaching from the mouth of the St. Croix on the Atlantic to the uppermost waters of the Mississippi underscores one historian's conclusion that the negotiations were conducted "in conditions of precipitancy, lack of confidence, lack of knowledge." Lack of accurate maps and of familiarity with the lands they were dividing resulted in lingering disputes over both of these terminals (which stream was the St. Croix? where precisely was the source of the Mississippi?) and over various details in between. The precipitancy and lack of confidence on the part of the British negotiators was apparent in their readiness to give up their initial claim of the Ohio River as an appropriate division of the interior (it was part of the southern boundary of Quebec, with no substantial American presence to the north of it) and agree to the American compromise of a line drawn through the four Great Lakes and the Rainy River waterway (a backing-down by the Americans from extension of a line from the St. Lawrence at 45°N to Lake Nipissing—the Quebec boundary of 1763–74—and thence to the source of the Mississippi). This unprecedented political boundary through the Great Lakes cut across the southwestern sector of the Montreal fur trade, severing the still-productive districts west of Lake Michigan and leaving the pivotal posts at Niagara, Detroit, and Michilimackinac, as well as the critical Grand Portage to the Rainy River, on the American side.

Yet it was not a crippling blow to the trade. Although the Montrealers petitioned London repeatedly to renegotiate such a gross and careless giveaway, they continued to operate unhindered in the American sector until well after Jay's Treaty of 1795 and by then they had stripped much of that area, had entered richer realms far to the northwest in the Athapascan country, and were preparing alternative posts and routes within British territory. These years were in fact a period of vigorous growth marked by the rapid emergence of the Northwest Company, the great Montreal partnership that kept broadening its participation and expanding its operations into ever-greater dominance of the trade. In the 1790s this distinctive Canadian association of Scottish partners and traders, French Canadian canoemen and woodsmen, and Algonkian and Athapascan hunters and trappers was working toward a transcontinental system. It had its own London agency, specialized canoe-building centers at Trois-Rivières and Michilimackinac, a major forward entrepôt at Grand Portage, and a new "emporium of the north" at Fort Chipewyan from which its explorer-traders were reconnoitering far to the north and west. By so doing, the Montreal firm had cut across and outreached the London-based Hudson's Bay Company and stimulated competition on a vast scale.

It was the resettlement of the loyalist refugees that really transformed the remaining American empire. That such a program should have full and liberal support from the imperial government was assumed from the first. As early as July 1775 the governor at Halifax was directed to be prepared to "make gratuitous grants to all persons who may be driven to seek shelter in Nova Scotia, from the tyranny and oppression that prevails in those colonies, where rebellion has set up its standard." Actually little was needed to accommodate these people until the war was lost, the dismemberment defined, and the person and property of the loyalists stood unsecured amidst the triumphant rebels; then the trickle turned into a deluge: in 1783 alone some 32,000 refugees arrived in Nova Scotia, and thousands more made their way across the new international boundary into Quebec. Halifax, Sorel, Montreal, and other large towns were swollen with refugee camps, while thousands of people were landed at spacious but essentially empty anchorages, such as Annapolis Gut, Spanish Harbour, and Port Roseway, creating instant new towns (named after prominent British officials of the day): Digby (after the admiral in charge of the evacuation), Sydney (after the secretary of state for colonies), and Shelburne (after the prime minister who negotiated the treaty); the last of these, with 10,000 people, was suddenly, momentarily, the largest settlement in British America.

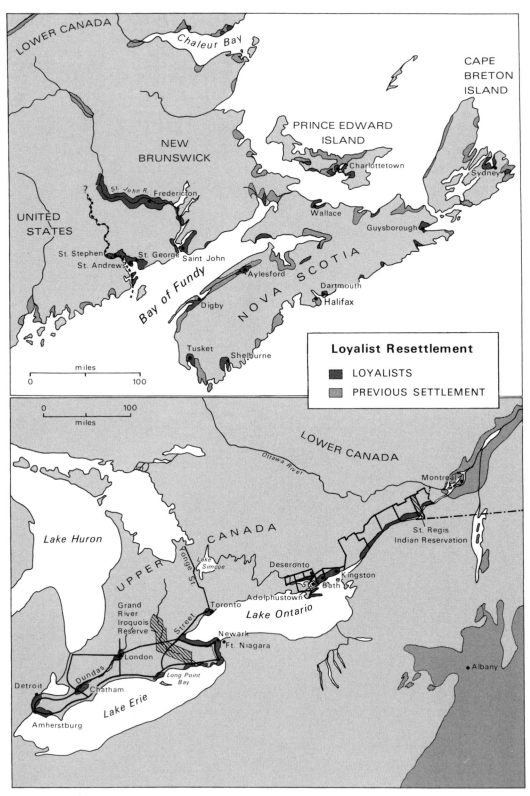

Loyalist Resettlement

- ■ LOYALISTS
- ▨ PREVIOUS SETTLEMENT

55. Loyalist Resettlement.

This great influx was a varied lot. It included thousands of discharged soldiers (perhaps twenty percent of the total) as well as American civilians, several thousand Indian allies, about four thousand Blacks (of whom more than a thousand were still slaves), a good many religious congregations (especially Quakers and German Pietists), and others, primarily from military units, who came as organized ethnic groups. While surveyors hastily measured out new townships, land parcels, and towns, imperial commissioners assessed petitions for recompense. In general land was allocated according to type and length of loyalist support or military rank and service, all in liberal amounts (one hundred acres minimum, generally about five hundred acres to an ordinary family, up to several thousand acres to those of higher rank), together with provisions and tools to sustain life and to get new homes and farms and industries under way. Even those of some means who set up businesses in Halifax and other towns laid claim to sizeable grants.

There was ample acreage to allocate in Nova Scotia (most of it resumed from earlier grantees who had failed to fulfill the terms of their grants), though much of it was of uncertain quality. A good many new settlers were dispersed among dozens of harbors around the mainland peninsula, several thousand to Cape Breton, several hundred to St. John Island, and a sprinkling far to the north on the Bay of Chaleur. In most of these places there was little land worth cultivating, and the colonists struggled to find support from forestry, fishing, and shipping. There was space to fit in only a few in the proven farmlands of the narrow Annapolis Valley (such as at Aylesford), and therefore much the largest blocks for newcomers were laid out on the other side of the Bay of Fundy along the St. John River and around Passamaquoddy Bay, areas inhabited at the time by only a few Yankee entrepreneurs, Acadian returnees, and remnants of the Malecite Indians. Within a few years about 15,000 settlers had been implanted in this new sector, creating an area so homogeneous in origin and so consciously distinct from peninsular Nova Scotia that it sought and received status as a separate colony in 1784. Thus New Brunswick appeared, giving reality to a goodly portion of the "New Ireland" that had been energetically promoted during the late stages of the war after Britain had seized firm control of this coastline as far west as the Penobscot. Fredericton, on the St. John midway between the coast and the Madawaska Acadians above the Grand Falls, was designated the capital.

As refugees began to accumulate in Quebec late in the war the governor-general of Canada, Frederick Haldimand (a Swiss Huguenot soldier of long experience in British imperial service in North America), laid plans to disperse them to Gaspé, Bay of Chaleur, or Cape Breton, well away from the French population. He was strongly against settling them in the empty country south and east of the seigneurial strips along the St. Lawrence and the Richelieu, considering these areas too close to the French on the one side and to the Americans on the other, and he wanted to reserve the West for Indian allies and refugees. But in 1783 the magnitude of the influx forced him to relent and make extensive use of this immense interior region. The arrival of two hundred families at Cataraqui led to the restoration of that old strategic point (Fort Frontenac) as a main base centered on the new town of Kingston, complete with barracks and hospital, wharf and mills. Meanwhile, two series of townships were surveyed. One set of five along the St. Lawrence west from the uppermost French seigneury was allocated to specific army units and religious groups to form, initially, an ethnoreligious sequence of Catholic Highlanders, Scottish Presbyterians, German Calvinists, German Lutherans, and

56. A New Loyalist Town: Kingston, 1784.

This "View of Cataraqui . . . taken from Capt. Brant's house, July 16th, 1784," is a good example of an instant loyalist town and of the role of the military in creating it. It is one of several sketches of the place drawn by James Peachey, a surveyor and topographic artist attached to the Office of the Surveyor-General in Quebec. He had first sketched it the year before while a member of a party sent to assess the area for loyalist colonization. The town site was surveyed in the fall of 1783, and most of the buildings shown here had been built since that time. The large military barracks and storehouses in the center stand on the ruins of French Fort Frontenac; nearby are the gristmill and waterfront warehouses; large timbers are being dressed on the shore at the extreme right; the two ships belong to the Provincial Marine. The Indians are camped in front of the house that the government built for Joseph Brant, the famous Mohawk leader and ally, who was by now looking to the Grand River as a more suitable location for the Iroquois loyalists. (Courtesy of the Public Archives of Canada)

Anglicans. The other set was laid out in the Bay of Quinté country to the west of Kingston. Here, too, there were clusters of particular groups, such as Quakers (mostly from the Hudson Valley) at Adolphustown, German Lutherans at Bath, and Mohawks at Deseronto. This last group reflected factionalism generated by the pressures of the war, for the largest body of the Iroquois settled along the Grand River Valley, nearly two hundred miles to the west, a reserve selected by Joseph Brant as being excellent land at some distance from White colonists and strategic for contact with western Indians. A smaller but intense focus of loyalist resettlement was the Niagara peninsula, across the river from the fort that had served as a major wartime refuge. The pattern at Detroit was similar though on a lesser scale. By 1790 this extensive region of new colonizations contained perhaps 20,000 Whites and, as in the case of Nova Scotia, there was strong agitation to set it apart as a new province, a movement in this case intensified by the clear geographic demarcation and obvious cultural distinction from the old French area downriver. Thus in 1791 the huge territory of Quebec was divided along the Ottawa River and the western boundary of Longueuil seigneury to form a Lower Canada and an Upper Canada. The first governor of the latter, John Simcoe (another American-experienced military leader), arrived that fall, set up his temporary capitol at the new town of Newark (across the river from Fort Niagara), and began an energetic program to develop and secure this first wholly inland colony of British America.

Both the human geography and the geopolitical structure of the empire had therefore been greatly modified. The old historic colonies of Atlantic Nova Scotia and Laurentian Quebec had been subdivided and deeply altered in context and potential. It has been said that "the Maritime world of islands, peninsulas, and river valleys, lacking a single entrance or unifying principle, has always been unusually divided against itself and from the earliest times to the twentieth century it has bred small-scale competition and cross purposes." Any such natural tendency was greatly magnified by the events and policies of this short period of intense reorganization. The British government, following the ancient imperial maxim of "divide and rule," further partitioned Nova Scotia in 1784 (St. John Island having been set apart in 1769) by separating Cape Breton Island, making it another Newfoundland wherein householders were allocated licensed fishing lots rather than freeholds, and creating New Brunswick, thereby interposing a fully loyalist colony between a Yankee-permeated Nova Scotia and the Maine district of rebellious Massachusetts. Halifax remained the principal imperial center for the whole region, the seat of the first American bishop of the Church of England (a loyalist, former rector of Trinity parish, New York City), but it was now one among five colonial capitals, each with at least some direct ties to London and its own contentious little establishment (creating places for loyalist leaders was an added incentive for setting up these new geopolitical units).

In Canada all was on a grander scale. The division of Quebec left two still very large territories. Although the boundary between the two was a clear severance of the new loyalist colonizations from the old seigneurial lands along the lower St. Lawrence, it could not become a simple division between French and "English" Canada for it left the British merchants of Montreal and other cities as islands in a French sea. However, the power of that already influential minority was magnified and formalized in the new governmental structure. The British were given a majority of the appointments in the upper house and executive council, and under the new county and municipal apportionment they won nearly a third of the seats in the lower assembly. Although English was the only language formally recognized by London, a de facto equality of French and English was quickly negotiated locally for the official business of Lower Canada. Meanwhile, Simcoe was working energetically to place a firm English stamp on the official character, in language and religion, law and polity, of Upper Canada. Thus an indelible dualism, that central geopolitical feature of Canadian history, was formalized along this great Laurentian axis. Although separate provinces they were not merely juxtaposed, but were locked together by geography, for Montreal, the historic frontier entrepôt at the head of navigation, was now the port of entry for Upper Canada, crucial, pivotal to the economy and security yet beyond the jurisdiction of this huge new interior province.

A more radical restructuring of empire was strongly advocated by some knowledgeable leaders during the consideration of this partition of Quebec. The governor of Canada and his chief justice, both widely experienced in America, formally proposed "that all the provinces of British North America be brought together into one general government, under a Governor General, with a bicameral legislature to be drawn from the several provinces." Such a federal union, they argued, "would prevent the northern colonies from developing those dangerous tendencies which had produced rebellion in the old colonies to the south." London made no response, but the concept of a Canadian confederation had been launched, and London's insistence on a direct Montreal-Halifax postal route rather than the Canadian preference for reestablishing the Montreal–Albany–New York City service spun a thin thread linking these parts together.

Thus a very extensive reorganization of northern America was in place by the early 1790s. The gross geopolitical framework designed to accommodate these reverberations from the Revolution would prove largely immutable, but the human geography created by the loyalist resettlements proved far from stable. In the Atlantic region there was a good deal of shifting about and a considerable exodus. Nova Scotia fell far short of expectations for so large an influx of farmers and merchants. New Brunswick replaced Portsmouth and Maine in supplying masts for British shipping, but pioneering was too harsh a life for many of the loyalist gentry and there was soon a drifting away. Within fifteen years nearly half of the colonists around Passamaquoddy Bay had emigrated, chiefly back to the United States. And there were others who went much further afield. About ten percent of the Nova Scotia loyalists who filed claims for compensation were Blacks. Some were given minimal land grants, but few could pursue all the legal steps to obtain actual title. With few resources or skills these people were an indigent and unwanted population, and officials seized upon the chance to ship them off to a floundering, newly established colony for "repatriated" Africans sponsored by British abolitionists. It is uncertain how many Blacks really wanted to go, but in 1792 nearly twelve hundred of them sailed from Halifax for Free Town to start life anew under the auspices of the Sierra Leone Company. They were soon joined by another shipment of about five hundred Jamaican Maroons who had surrendered to British authorities and been exiled to Nova Scotia. These Afro-Americans, very largely American-born and including many mulattos, became the nucleus of a Europeanized Christian community, dominating a colony that was soon enlarged and diversified by thousands of Africans freed by British antislave trade patrols. Thus the American Revolution reverberated around the Atlantic world to create a new cosmopolitan Creole center on the coast of West Africa; in a sense it was a minor reversal of the vast Luso-Afro-American system initiated in Cape Verde-Senegambia three hundred years before.

The situation and prospects of Upper Canada were quite different. There was much good land available and Governor Simcoe was convinced that it could be used to lure thousands of people from the new republic who would really prefer to live on British soil. A new act of 1789 had made land available in generous amounts to almost anyone willing to swear an oath of allegiance. Those who responded over the next few years became known as "late loyalists," and in some degree they really were, for many of them were relatives and friends of those farmers of New York and Pennsylvania who had come in as refugees after the war. Simcoe had served in the British forces in Philadelphia and now made a special effort to advertise in that region; he presumably attracted some people of like sympathies who only now saw migration and resettlement as a feasible alternative to sticking it out in the United States. But of course there were others for whom political allegiance was unimportant compared with the offer of land in larger amounts on easier terms than it could be had from any of the various companies peddling that of western New York and Pennsylvania and large parts of Ohio. In this sense one may agree with Burt that Upper Canada's policies and geographical position simply "pulled the American frontier north into British territory."

The governor was of course very concerned that his province not become enveloped by the westward thrusts of Americans. He laid out a strategic design to make Upper Canada a defensible part of the empire. When the Americans finally occupied Fort Niagara he shifted his seat of government across the lake from Newark to Toronto, where he laid out the new town of York. From here military roads led north (Yonge Street) to Lake Simcoe (which he had renamed after his father) opening a way to the upper Great Lakes, and west (Dundas Street) to the Thames River (where he founded London, designating it as his eventual capital) and on to Detroit; Chatham and Long Point Bay were nominated to become navy yards. Two-sevenths of the land in every township was set aside in crown and clergy reserves. The governor pushed hard, though unsuccessfully, for a university, and did all he could to foster the growth of a local gentry. He was quite explicit that the object was to counter influences from south of the border by "forming the Character, Temper, and Manners of the People of this infant Colony to British Habits and to British Principles."

And it is clear that this and similar policies did stamp a British imprint on Upper Canada and New Brunswick, and strengthen it in Nova Scotia. The true loyalist exiles had of course explicitly rejected American citizenship, and there were plenty among them willing to respond to a paternal imperial government that sought to aid them in their struggle to preserve or attain a proper station in life. Yet the imprint could never be simply British. If, as Lower so aptly put it, "Canadians are children of divorced parents and they know the bitterness that comes from a broken home," they were not simply shaped thereafter by the parent they had chosen to live with. Canadians were "children of both parents, British and American," as MacKinnon observes:

> Their role in the war and their consequent sacrifices had them lay stress upon British ties and institutions. But the majority were American bred and shaped by the land, and no amount of rhetoric could quite disguise the desire of the great mass of Loyalists for a more participatory, democratic form of government, a more egalitarian society. . . . Moreover, within a decade of their exile the ties with America were revived and extended so that much of what was American in thought and practice made its way easily into [these British colonies], making [them] . . . British in rhetoric, quite American in reflex.

Thus, "the American Revolution produced not one country but two: a nation and a non-nation"; the non-nation was still part of the British empire but it too had taken on a new identity within a profoundly altered North American world.

10. Destabilization: Tropical America

The impact of the 1783 treaty on the tropical margins of the continent was more drastic yet less decisive than in the north. Here it involved not simply the contraction of the British empire and the definition of loyalist colonies alongside the new nation, but the giving away of a firmly loyalist colony to a long-hated rival empire as well. By all logic of the American situation, Florida, especially East Florida, already swollen at war's end with thousands of loyalist refugees from Georgia and the Carolinas, should have become a southern counterpart of Nova Scotia and New Brunswick. But European logic ruled that Florida be sacrificed for Gibraltar, even though many high government officials (including the king himself) were distressed with that decision. Such a retrocession after twenty years of British rule and stoutly loyal performance caused a profound shock among British citizens and their Indian allies in that part of the world. Giving up a colony of such obvious strategic and speculative interest could only be understood by such persons as a momentary maneuver amidst the ever-shifting rivalries and alignments among the great European powers. And so they, and some of like mind in London, acted as if this particular treaty had settled nothing in this sector, and by so acting they helped to insure that it had not.

The accumulation of loyalist refugees in East Florida began with those fleeing the chaos in the Carolina backcountry in 1778, and after the evacuations of Savannah and Charleston the population of 16,000 (more than half of which was Black) was several times the prewar total. Such an influx together with infusions from British military operations had created boom times in St. Augustine. A good many of the earlier exiles had obtained land and were busily carving out new plantations, confident that Florida would remain a British stronghold. Once they recovered from their dismay and anger at having the whole province given over to the detested Spanish, they looked southward to search for some niche in which to carry on their speculations and commerce. Thus British refugees fanned out over the tropical seas from Belize on the western mainland to Grenada in the Windward Islands. By far the greatest number went to Jamaica or the Bahamas, where the total influx (8,000–10,000 and 6,000–7,000 respectively) included a considerable number of evacuees from New York City and a trickling from Nova Scotia as well.

In Jamaica such people added to an already populous and thriving island. In the Bahamas the impact was much more dramatic, for population was tripled, Nassau became a lively center of commerce and politics, and planters took root over a wide scattering of islands from Grand Bahama and Abaco nearest to Florida clear to Caicos and Grand Turk six hundred miles to the southeast. By 1789 the total population was about 11,800, including some 8,000 slaves, and this infusion of people, capital, and energy had transformed the Bahamas into an important addition to the planter colonies and a principal source of cotton for the new textile factories of Britain. Furthermore, Bahamans did not feel entirely severed from the adjacent mainland. There was still trade, legal and otherwise, with Florida and there were visions and projects aplenty that looked beyond current geopolitical arrangements to some reassertion of British power in these continental margins.

Not all British subjects fled on the return of the Spanish to the Floridas. Blacks who had in one way or another gained freedom during the Revolution had little interest in risking their status by further emigration. Most of the survivors of New Smyrna stayed on. The colony had disintegrated from internal abuses during the war and the people had been given small plots of land on the northern edge of St. Augustine. Within a few years these Minorcans, Greeks, and Italians were merging into a single people and as farmers, artisans, fishermen, and mariners were the most vigorous nucleus in all the province. Even a few British planters stayed on, mostly along the St. Mary's somewhat removed from Spanish surveillance and often with landholdings across the river in Georgia as well. The Spanish governor arrived in 1784 with a large retinue of officials and soldiers but as before it was hard to find genuine Spanish colonists for this remote corner of their American empire. Spanish Louisiana was somewhat more attractive and considered more important. There in the years 1779–83 a sizeable body of settlers had been brought from or by way of Havana into the bayous, including nearly two thousand Canarios (some of whom may have left Florida in 1763), the last of the Acadians (after an unhappy sojourn in France), and about five hundred Spaniards (founders of New Iberia on Bayou Teche), but the prospect of obtaining many more seemed so dim that the governor of Louisiana set forth a bold plan to admit Protestant Americans who might be converted and their progeny assimilated through the use of English-speaking Irish Catholic missionaries. His concern was actually not so much with luring such colonists as with how to deal with those already there, as in the Mobile and Natchez districts (which latter Spain claimed as part of the Florida cession), and with those poised to come in whether authorized or not, as had happened at New Madrid, a colony founded far upriver by an aggressive American promoter. For a few years his plan was in effect (he even obtained several Irish priests), but without major results, and his successor turned to other tactics to secure Spanish control of this strategic province.

The support of the much-harried but unsubdued Indians was critical to any imperial position in this gulf region, and here the British continued to play a major role. For many years these tribes had been dependent upon the services and supplies of Scottish traders, a relationship so pervasive and intimate that mixed-blood offspring had become very influential, most notably in the case of Alexander McGillivray, hereditary chief of the Lower Creeks. These people had long regarded British support essential to any hope of stemming the aggressive Americans. The Spanish, realizing that they were quite unable simply to take over these roles, decided to work through such British agents, and they granted a monopoly over the Indian trade to a Scottish firm. Working out of Pensacola, backed by a secure warehouse in the Bahamas, this company soon had outposts at St. Marks, Mobile, New Orleans, and Baton Rouge and a network of pack trains ranging widely through the interior. Thus the old but always meager town of Pensacola took on a vitality it had never enjoyed, even during its term as capital of West Florida. Lying at some distance from the main Spanish centers at St. Augustine and New Orleans and from the administrative and ecclesiastical supervision of Havana and Santiago, it was an entrepôt on Spanish ground of a British-dominated Indian trade, with legal links to Nassau; furthermore, its harbor was soon enlivened much more by illegal American vessels than by those of Spain or Britain.

Although the Treaty of 1783 had apparently placed the entire mainland coast from Texas to Georgia under Spanish rule, a decade later it was clear that such a simplification was superficial, for there were at least four, perhaps five, powers contending for position, all operating on the assumption that current boundaries and treaty arrangements in that part of America were subject to change. To the Spanish the whole area was an imperial fringe valued as a buffer against encroachment upon Mexico and its vital sea-lanes. The great Bourbon reorganization of the empire toward greater administrative efficiency in the 1780s could have little impact here, for the Spanish simply lacked the resources to populate, develop, and defend these largely empty areas. In 1783 they had been suddenly faced with a long border with the aggressive new republic and were immediately embroiled in bitter disputes over the boundaries of West Florida. It was soon blatantly apparent that American traders, speculators, slave hunters, rivermen, and mariners showed little respect for such international borders anywhere. When Spain attempted to pressure the Americans by closing the lower Mississippi to their traffic, it induced such ominous counterpressures throughout the Mississippi Valley that the Spanish soon backed down. It became obvious that American expansionism carried out by well-armed settlers was the most powerful force in this region.

The Indians who suddenly found themselves on lands claimed by the United States were a major and volatile participant in these rivalries. They disputed the right of diplomats in Paris to barter away their lands, they still looked to George III as their protector, and they were willing to listen to anyone who offered help against the Americans. The region was sprinkled and edged with British schemers who were only too willing to pledge such help. Loyalist opportunists were poised in the Bahamas to reenter once a shift in the fortunes of war or diplomacy opened the way. Many persons anticipated the secession of the western transmontane territories from an impotent and antagonistic government anchored on the seaboard; indeed a more general disintegration of the United States was not an uncommon assumption at this time in Europe or America. Thus intrigue with and among Indian tribes and factions was endemic. The boldest scheme was the "Muskogee" of William Bowles, envisioned as a large territory of Creek and Seminole lands to be brought under formal British protection.

In the 1790s the French suddenly reappeared as a major factor in the region as the result of two tremendous upheavals. The first and nearest and most fearful in America was the revolt of the mulattos and slaves on St. Domingue in 1791. Momentarily suppressed after great loss of life, rebellion flared up again even more widely the next year and planters began to flee the island. The crisis for this local ruling elite was compounded by the fact that just at this time the great revolution in France itself was moving into its massive terrorist phase of radical change. In 1794 the revolutionary government heeded the logic of the initial catalytic call for liberty and equality and declared slavery abolished in all French territories. Faced with the beheading of their king and destruction of the aristocratic order in France and with death or chaos in St. Domingue the French planters turned in desperation to the British, asking them to place the island under their protection and restore order. The British, once again officially at war with France and alarmed at the implications of the revolt for their own slave colonies, landed at the main ports and undertook a reconquest. But it proved a costly and impossible task. The Black revolutionary forces, dominant in numbers and operating from the rugged backcountry under skilled leaders, proved a formidable foe while on the coastal plains yellow fever took an appalling toll of the European troops. In 1798, after five years and the loss of 20,000 men, the British gave up the task and pulled out. That left the entire island, the Spanish half as well as the French, under the rule of the Black dictator Toussaint l'Ouverture. It was an event of enormous implications. For the first time in the American Indies, the Afro-Americans had successfully revolted against their masters, defeated imperial armies, and now commanded not just one island among the many but the oldest and one of the greatest seats of Europe in America, a highly valued colony, long a major source of sugar and coffee, and the very archetype of planter society.

The great convulsion in France soon engulfed all of Europe in war and spread rapidly outward to the American tropics. In the latter 1790s the West Indies was once again the arena of savage, chaotic conflict involving fleets and armies, privateers and local renegades; islands were taken and retaken, plantations plundered, slaves dispersed. On the mainland, Spain, faring badly in Europe, sought to placate the Americans and lessen its burdens. By formal treaty in 1795 Spain accepted 31°N as the northern boundary of West Florida, yielding to the American claim of the broad Yazoo Strip and its productive Natchez district, and also recognized American navigation rights on the entire Mississippi and privileges of deposit (without customs fees) in New Orleans. The result was a riotous surge of Americans into these borderlands and an ominous whetting of their appetites for more. A beleagured Spain now set up a small garrison on the overland trail to Mexico at Nacogdoches, deep in the piney woods of east Texas, and made overtures about returning Louisiana to France. The new French government had already indicated its interest in the Mississippi Valley in 1793 by dispatching to the United States a minister (Citizen Genet) who so brazenly plotted with American filibusters for an attack on Louisiana that an embarrassed American government had him recalled. By 1796 Britain was at war with Spain as well as France, reviving hopes for a whole array of geopolitical speculations. Loyalist planters suffering from a sharp decline in cotton yields from shallow soils and insect damage in the Bahamas now agitated openly for a reconquest of Florida. William Bowles suddenly reappeared after some years in Spanish prisons to invade West Florida at the head of a motley band of Indians and Whites; he seized St. Marks and invited British loyalists and French royalists to join him in making Muskogee a reality.

Meanwhile, New Orleans, the obvious strategic center of these continental margins, was booming along unscathed by direct warfare. It had been almost completely consumed by fire in 1788 and again six years later, but each time it was rapidly rebuilt and enlarged. Although the new *cabildo* and cathedral were architectural emblems of the Spanish presence, the governing power was so weak that the whole province had been pretty much left on its own resources, and these were being altered and enlarged in important ways. The French influence had remained strong all the while—by the 1780s Louisiana's main link with the world was more by way of St. Domingue and Bordeaux merchants than with Havana and Cádiz, and after 1793 French refugees began to come in. Planters from St. Domingue brought new varieties of sugar cane and applied their expertise to the marginal conditions in frost-endangered Louisiana; within a few years sugar had replaced indigo as the principal export from bayou plantations. Meanwhile cotton was rapidly expanding upriver, especially in the Natchez area, and American merchants were setting up in the city to handle the burgeoning Mississippi trade. Near the end of the century New Orleans was a cosmopolitan center of nearly ten thousand people, and the remarkable variety of its citizenry, including French creoles in all gradations of color, refugees from St. Domingue and France itself, Acadians, Spaniards, Canarios, Canadians, Americans, and British traders, plus a wide variety of visiting Indians, was an excellent display of the geopolitical complexities characteristic of these tropical margins during the century since d'Iberville first reconnoitered this deltaic labyrinth.

In 1799 events in Europe took another decisive turn and quickly reverberated across the Atlantic. The master strategist Napoleon was now dictator of an awesomely powerful France. The defeat of Britain, the reconquest of St. Domingue, the return of Louisiana, and the recreation of a great French American empire suddenly became specific and seemingly realistic goals. In fact, in October of 1800, Spain formally (and secretly) transferred the whole of Louisiana back to France in return for some petty dynastic gains in Italy, although this retrocession was not publicly confirmed in America until the following March. Once again the fate of

American regions seemed likely to be altered by a turn of the European ka-
leidoscope and huge areas bartered away with little thought of their inhabitants.
Yet such decisions could not have quite the impact as before, because America was
not quite the same kind of place. Current events in St. Domingue and the Mississippi Valley, like those enacted twenty years earlier all along the North American seaboard, had demonstrated that Africans and Americans would have something important to say about decisions made in Madrid, Paris, and London. If in
1800 it seemed obvious that all was in flux as to the future of these lands, it was also
apparent that there were now forces in those lands that might impose an American
rather than a European definition of the future.

11. Unification: Forming the United States

The United States was born in travail over a span of years. In a simple and narrow
sense that period may be defined by the Declaration of Independence in July 1776
and the signing of the Treaty of Paris in September 1783, that is, from the formal
transformation of civil strife within the empire into a war of liberation from that
empire on to the formal completion of that struggle. But of course declarations and
treaties do not create enduring federations and nations. The shaping of a nation is
always a much longer process involving conception and internal growth and the
provision of a substantial shelter within which to nurture the newborn state and
political society. It is therefore more appropriate to consider the twenty-five years
between the Stamp Act Congress of October 1765, the first intercolonial political
assembly called on American initiative, and the full ratification of the new federal
constitution in May 1790 as a convenient political definition of this formative
period.

As has been noted, the British American empire of the eighteenth century was a
loose and complex structure of many semiautonomous parts, each part connected
directly across the Atlantic to London with no formal political bonds between
adjacent colonies on the seaboard. Long ago, in 1643, the Calvinist colonies of
Plymouth, Massachusetts, New Haven, and Connecticut had formed the "United
Colonies of New England" as a "firme and perpetual league" to confront common
enemies and resolve intercolonial problems, but it faded away after a couple of
decades. The Albany Congress a century later was the first substantial indication of
some sentiment for a wider union. Although called by London officials, partly in
response to the urgings of colonial governors, to consider greater coordination of
policies relating to defense and Indian affairs, delegates of the seven colonies
represented endorsed a committee report on "A General Union of the British
Colonies on the Continent" to include all those from New Hampshire to South

Carolina (excepting Delaware, which was still considered a subordinate of Pennsylvania). The proposal (mostly by Benjamin Franklin) envisioned a limited federation within the imperial structure by which a Grand Council elected by the colonial assemblies would be empowered to deal with Indian affairs, frontier expansion, and military matters essential to these tasks. However, the plan was never submitted to Parliament or to any of the colonial assemblies for ratification.

Failure to act upon this or any of the other paper plans for some sort of union that had appeared from time to time simply underscored the basic reality that competition was far more compelling than cooperation among these many units. These colonies, after all, had been created very largely as opportunities for private gain and it was therefore not surprising that they were blatant displays of self-interest, fiercely jealous of one another, enmeshed in chronic and often bitter rivalries over territories, trade, and various prerogatives. Colonial assemblies were responsive to local constituencies, which were deeply committed to factional interests, and even where it was obvious that broader policies were needed, as in some aspects of Indian and military affairs, it was expected that the Crown would provide such leadership. Cooperation between the colonies was episodic, sporadic, and grudgingly given. Only when important economic interests of constituencies in all the colonies seemed threatened by Britain itself did an upwelling of common action become manifest in America.

In 1765 Massachusetts called for a congress of delegates to gather in New York City to formulate a concerted response to the Stamp Act. By the time the representatives from nine colonies assembled (New Hampshire had declined, and the governors of Virginia, North Carolina, and Georgia prevented the election of delegates) a good deal of informal intercolonial consultation had taken place. Formal action at the congress resulted in no more than a number of petitions and memorials to Parliament and the king, and even these were not signed by all delegates owing to differing instructions and uncertainties as to their powers. But during the course of this crisis an organized intercolonial resistance movement had emerged all along the seaboard. It sprang up independently in a number of seaports, but the most intensive efforts began and remained centered in New York City, from where traveling agents and couriers reached out as far as Portsmouth and Albany on the north and Savannah on the south to form a loose association of local groups known as the Sons of Liberty. The degree to which the widespread and often violent resistance to the Stamp Act may be credited to this movement is uncertain, but even though the Sons of Liberty organization faded away after the repeal of the act, the intercolonial correspondence networks it had so vigorously fostered were firmly established and informally continued and expanded.

Thus when in a resurgence of crisis in 1773 the Virginia House of Burgess called upon all the other colonial assemblies to join in establishing a Committee of

Correspondence "whose business it shall be to obtain the most early and authentic intelligence of all such acts and resolutions of the British Parliament or proceedings of Administration, as may relate to or effect [sic] the British colonies in *America*" and to disseminate such intelligence quickly to all, it got a quick response, and with the creation of such a formal network designed to promote intercolonial solidarity "a revolutionary political union was in the making." It was this organization that paved the way for the call, again from Virginia, to convene a Continental Congress in Philadelphia in September 1774.

Fifty-five delegates from twelve colonies attended the first Continental Congress, but they differed considerably in just what bodies they represented. Three delegations had been sent directly by their colonial legislatures (Massachusetts, Rhode Island, Pennsylvania), six others had been elected by some sort of provincial congress or convention of county or town officials, but three (Connecticut, New York, South Carolina) carried no formal authorization, and Georgia was not represented at all. This gathering tabled the Galloway Plan, the only major geopolitical proposal put before it, and created no intercolonial structure, but it was in itself a new level of association and out of such experience the convening of a Second Continental Congress in the aftermath of Lexington and Concord was almost routine. To this second Philadelphia meeting in May 1775 came sixty-nine delegates from thirteen colonies (Georgia now included); those from Rhode Island, Connecticut, New Jersey, Pennsylvania, Delaware, and South Carolina had been sent by their colonial assemblies, and all the others had been authorized by some kind of representative gathering. This body quickly created a Continental army, appointed George Washington as commander in chief, and began to define the terms of their association.

Franklin's Albany Plan was taken as a basis for discussion and given to a committee for reworking. It did not reappear for a year, being presented to the delegates in July 1776 shortly after they had declared that "these United Colonies are, and of Right ought to be FREE AND INDEPENDENT STATES," and it was little more than a formalization of the de facto operations of the Continental Congress. It took the Congress, absorbed in the imperatives of the war, more than a year to endorse a final document, which strongly emphasized state sovereignty and the limitations of congressional power. Each state was accorded one vote and all important measures required nine votes to pass. As Gordon Wood has noted, "The 'United States of America' thus possessed a literal meaning it is hard to appreciate today"; it was "a firm league of friendship" among the thirteen for "common defence, the security of their liberties, and their mutual and general welfare," with no central executive power. The terms of this limited association were then submitted to the states and were soon mired in disagreements over very basic issues. Major contentions involved proposals to substitute some sort of proportionate representation related to the great variations in population and wealth among the states (as Franklin had originally proposed at Albany in 1765), and the disposition of western lands to which the several states had very unequal claims and access. Final ratification came only after the first steps were taken to resolve the latter issue by the cession of such lands to Congress for the good of the whole. Thus, not until March 1, 1781, nearly four years after they had been first presented, were the "Articles of Confederation" officially signed, defining the mode by which the thirteen members of the United States of America were formed into and agreed to conduct themselves as a "perpetual union."

However, the Articles of Confederation only defined half of the new geopolitical creature, and the members of the union were confronted with the grave difficulty of defining the other half. By the terms of the 1783 treaty the territory of the United States was more than doubled from that under effective occupation or jurisdiction of the seaboard colonies. A vast new West between the mountains and the Mississippi had been appended to Atlantic America, and, although the states had agreed to cede to Congress their claims to that West, the exact terms and timings of those cessions and just how Congress would organize and manage this immense realm remained uncertain. A crucial basic principle had been established in 1780 when Congress stated that this national territory would be "settled and formed into distinct republican states, which shall become members of the federal union, and have the same rights of sovereignty, freedom and independence, as the other states." This principle had emerged from intensifying discussions since 1776 on the vexing problems of western lands, and was explicitly endorsed as an inducement to bring about such cessions.

Thus at issue thereafter was the size, number, and boundaries of such states and the procedure by which they could become members of the union. A committee assigned to prepare a plan for "the temporary government of the Western Territory" presented a report in March 1784. It recommended subdivision into fourteen new states, as illustrated in a rough sketch drawn by its chairman, Thomas Jefferson, whose influence and predilections were plainly apparent in the geometric pattern aligned on a central meridian and parallels, together with a suggested list of contrived polysyllabic names (such as Assenisipia, Cherronesus, Metropotamia, and Michigania—but also Washington). Congress amended the report, eliminating the names but modifying only slightly the basic geometry, and spelled out provisions for the formation of temporary governments that would control each district until it had a free population equal to that of the least populous of the thirteen original states, whereupon it could petition for admission to the confederation as an equal member. This Ordinance of 1784 did not become the actual tool by which the West was shaped because Congress ruled that it should apply only after all states had actually ceded their western claims. Nevertheless, it stood as a statement of principles, the basis for further debate in the formulation of more specific legislation.

Pressures for actual implementation of a plan for the West rapidly intensified. The Land Ordinance of 1785, defining a system of surveys and sales of congressional lands, was a first attempt to bring some order to the frenzied scramble among a welter of avaricious interests, large and small, local, national, and international, to reap some profit out of this vast national domain. In strategic locales all over the West earlier traders and squatters were becoming outnumbered by speculators of one kind or another. National leaders saw an imperative need to impose some kind of legal government upon such populations in remote districts. Congressional attempts to prohibit intrusions and expel squatters from the homelands of the Miami and Shawnee Indians failed. As new legislation to deal with chaotic and dangerous conditions in the area between the Ohio and the Great Lakes was being debated, Congress was further impelled by the highly effective lobbying of the Ohio Company, which connived with officials to obtain a huge block of land in that area and sought government protection of its interests. A definitive response came in 1787 when Congress created "the territory northwest of the River Ohio" as a temporary jurisdiction. That act specified that not less than three nor more than five states should be formed within this area (a reduction from the eight and a half proposed in Jefferson's sketch), and defined the boundaries for three eventual states lying between the Ohio and the lower Great Lakes. This "Northwest Ordinance" also laid down a three-stage process for the transition into statehood. Initially the territory was to be served by a governor, a secretary, and judges appointed by Congress; as soon as a district had five thousand free adult male inhabitants it could choose an assembly, which body could nominate a list of candidates from which Congress would select a council, with the congressionally appointed governor retaining full veto power over all legislation; when this district had 60,000 free inhabitants it could petition for admission as a state on an equal footing with the original states. This 1787 ordinance was clearly an adaptation of that of 1784, but the differences were important. It dealt with only the northern half of the West, the only lands that had as yet been fully ceded (except for a Western Reserve of Connecticut) to Congress, it defined fewer and larger states, it significantly strengthened the hold of Congress over the territorial phase of government, and it altered the minimum population essential for statehood. If, as many historians maintain, the major change was the fact that it lodged political control of the West "in the hands of Eastern promoters instead of Western squatters," it retained the really fundamental guarantee of eventual statehood as a full partner in the union.

In fact it turned out to be a guarantee of partnership in a very different association than the one in being during the debate. For the Northwest Ordinance was a last act of Congress under the Articles of Confederation, completed while the Constitutional Convention was under way in Philadelphia with a radical revision in the very basis of the union. That convention came about because many influential persons and interests became convinced that the United States could not survive unless the power of the central government was greatly strengthened and the course of direction sharply altered.

Out of bitter experience with an arbitrary imperial government Americans had at first devised a union that kept power in the constituent state governments, which were considered to be closer to the people and more responsive to local interests. But once the emergency of war had passed, state governments proved to be extremely self-centered, contemptuous even of the very limited authority they had granted the Congress:

> They violated the Articles of Confederation by ignoring the nation's treaties with foreign countries, by waging war with the Indians, by building navies of their own. They sent men with less vision and less ability to represent them and at times failed to send any, so that Congress could scarcely muster a quorum to do business.

Most serious of all, the states rendered Congress impotent by failing to answer requisitions for money while at the same time taxing the commerce of one another, issuing paper money, and undermining the credit of and confidence in the parts as well as the whole. Attempts to amend the Articles to give Congress power to levy a modest tax on foreign imports were twice defeated by the negative vote of a single state. Such pervasive and progressive internal weakness left the United States helpless in a perilous world. Its credit was no good, its ships were seized, it had no leverage to pry the British out of their old posts on American soil or to pressure the Spanish from interfering with Mississippi traffic. Out of such experience came a broadening consensus that the initial terms of the union must be revised.

The direct lineage of the Philadelphia Convention of 1787 is traceable to Mt. Vernon, where in 1785 George Washington, as president of a company formed to promote the building of a canal connecting the Potomac with the Ohio, hosted a meeting of commissioners from Maryland and Virginia to work out a basis for cooperation on this interstate project. This led to a proposal to invite representatives from Pennsylvania and Delaware to join in creating a commercial policy for the whole Chesapeake-Delaware region, and this idea soon expanded to an invitation to all the states to gather in Annapolis in September 1786 to deal with general commercial problems and possible amendments to the Articles of Confederation. The response to that call was disappointing; only five states sent representatives, but one of these was Alexander Hamilton of New York, who took the lead in getting the Annapolis group to urge Congress to call a special convention of delegates from all the states to consider all changes necessary to create a "federal government adequate to the exigencies of the Union." Eventually, reluctantly, Congress did so, spurred on by local rebellions and rumblings throughout the country so ominous as to cause George Washington, along with many others, to express fear that "we are fast verging to anarchy and confusion."

Twelve states responded, Rhode Island alone refusing to participate, and as most of the men they sent were influential leaders convinced of the need for a much stronger central government, work on a comprehensive revision got under way rapidly. The fame of the debates and decisions of the 1787 Philadelphia Convention has been justified by the results: a constitution that has stood the test of two centuries of experience in an often-tumultuous and ever-expanding nation. We must limit our focus here to the central geopolitical issues, one of which was crucial to everything else. Put in terms of high principle, the question was how to create a strong national government that would be responsive to the people yet operate within a genuine federal system of states. Put more baldly, it was the problem of how to allocate power amongst the varied constituent parts of the union. The issue, inherent in the nature of federations, had been long recognized but never fully confronted and resolved. After festering for a dozen years it was laid bare in the opening discussions and its ominous character revealed. The Virginia delegation proposed that state representation in Congress be proportionately based on population or wealth, whereupon the delegation from Delaware threatened to withdraw from the convention and, by implication, from any union so designed. The issue thereby became immediately defined as one of the small states versus the large states, with spokesmen for each group arguing from reason and equity, the former unwilling to be at the mercy of Virginia, Massachusetts, and Pennsylvania (understood by all to be the largest in population by a considerable margin), the latter unwilling to be at the mercy of a coalition of tiny states and finding it unconscionable that the fewer than 50,000 inhabitants of Delaware should balance the more than 600,000 of Virginia. Such arguments quickly exposed the most basic question: was this political creation a *nation* or a *confederacy of sovereign states?* Were the states mere districts of people composing one political society or were they thirteen distinct political societies? Was it "We the People" or "We the States" that sought to establish a more perfect union? A deadlocked convention referred the matter to a committee for resolution.

The famous compromise finally hammered out declared that the United States of America was at once a nation and a federation, a union of people and a union of states. The creation of a bicameral national legislature in which states were given an equal voice in the upper house and representation proportionate to population in the lower, together with the specification of certain powers, terms of office, and modes of election for each house, ultimately gained the support of the convention. Such a solution required definition of how representation on the basis of population would be calculated and that exposed another division of interests, but this one, as Madison observed, "did not lie between the large and small States: it lay between the Northern & Southern" and this "principally from their having or not having slaves." The existence of slavery itself generated angry debate but no decisive action; the problem of whether slaves, being denied most of the rights of citizenship, should be counted in the population base for political representation was resolved by extension of an existing compromise formula, used in taxation, of calculating a slave as three-fifths of a person. Each state was to have at least one representative and not to exceed one for every 30,000 inhabitants (excluding Indians not taxed), based on an official census to be taken every ten years. As no reliable enumeration existed at the time, the need to reach an agreement led to an initial lower house of sixty-five representatives, allocated among the thirteen states in proportions determined in committee by drawing upon various estimates of populations and wealth. The results of the first national census, taken in 1790, necessitated major adjustments in the 1787 proportions and total (see table 6).

The divergent interests of north and south shaped other important compromises built into this national framework. Northern shipping interests, shorn of British markets and maritime protections, wanted Congress to have the power to regulate commerce and create a strong national policy in their support, whereas southern-

Table 6
Proportional Representation

	1787 (initial allocation in the Constitution)	1793 (on the basis of the 1790 census)
Vermont	—a	2
New Hampshire	3	4
Massachusetts	8	14
Rhode Island	1	2
Connecticut	5	7
New York	6	10
New Jersey	4	5
Pennsylvania	8	13
Delaware	1	1
Maryland	6	8
Virginia	10	19
North Carolina	5	10
South Carolina	5	6
Georgia	3	2
Kentucky	—a	2
Total	65	105

aNot yet a state.

ers, heavily dependent upon staple trades, sought the least possible regulation in order to foster the cheapest possible rates. Furthermore, a glaring feature of American commerce was the slave trade. After it was made clear very early that any attempt to abolish slavery in all the states would immediately dissolve the convention and doom the union, the antislavery forces narrowed their focus to prohibiting further imports. There was powerful support for this not only among northerners but from influential delegates from Virginia and Maryland as well (which states had already passed such laws, in part, it was alleged, to protect the value of their own rapidly increasing slave populations). However, spokesmen from the Carolinas and Georgia flatly declared that they would never be at the dictate of Congress on the matter and that to prohibit such trade was in effect to exclude these states from the union. Out of these controversies came the compromise wherein Congress was given the power "to regulate Commerce with foreign Nations, and among the several States, and with the Indian Tribes" in return for a specific assurance that "the Migration or Importation of such Persons as any of the States now existing shall think proper to admit, shall not be prohibited by Congress prior to the Year one thousand eight hundred and eight."

Such patterns of divergent regional interests underlay many of the most intensive discussions of the constitutional convention, as they had throughout the life of the confederation to that point. And much of this was explicitly expressed as regional simply because it was routine to think in geographical terms, and an aid to that was subtly built into the formal procedures of this political union. From the very first meeting of the Continental Congress in 1774 the roll call of colonies/states was geographical, from north to south ("New Hampshire, Massachusetts . . ."), rather than alphabetical ("Connecticut, Delaware . . .") or historical ("Virginia, Massachusetts . . ."), or some other sequence. Such a pattern, derived from well-established British usage in late colonial times, was commonplace (as displayed in the list of states in the Articles of Confederation and in the Constitution) and convenient because it translated so readily into those regional groupings, eastern (or New England), middle, and southern states, or, more simply, northern and southern states, which everyone understood as referring to important differences in "staple productions," "religion," "manners," and "other circumstances" (to use some of Madison's terms); indeed, regional stereotypes abounded. On the other hand, knowledgeable people were also well aware that such state groupings did not represent clear or rigid divisions of interests and attitudes, and despite strong regional prejudices and jealousies political alignments were only occasionally concordant with such simple patterns, as perhaps most notably and bitterly in the north-south cleavage (along the Mason-Dixon Line) on the proposal to relinquish navigation rights on the lower Mississippi (1786).

Something more expressive of the underlying complexities of regionalism in

America was revealed in the ratification of the Constitution. The Federalists dominating the Philadelphia Convention took the bold step of ignoring the amending procedures of the Articles of Confederation, bypassing the state legislatures, and going directly to the people by requiring ratification from a popularly elected special convention in each state. They further decreed that ratification by nine states would be sufficient to proceed with the formation of this new union. This radical process immediately generated intense political activity in every state, and subsequently a great deal of intricate political analysis of personalities and processes by students of American history. Here again we need consider only the more obvious geopolitical features. Suffice it to note that the forces in support of ratification held a great many advantages, inherent and in particular: they presented a positive plan already shaped by intensive debate among some of the best minds of the country, they were men of wide personal influence, they controlled in some degree much of the press, and they had defined the rules by which the whole process was to be carried out. Furthermore, the very nature of their concerns and experience had made them men of nationwide vision and contacts, whereas those opposed to the Constitution ("antifederalists") were for the most part more locally oriented, strongly protective of their own state's interests, with less knowledge and less care about what went on in other areas, and they had no common alternative plan to cure the manifold dissatisfactions with the Articles of Confederation.

The pattern of results offers no obvious reflections of size or broad regional groupings. The Delaware, New Jersey, and Connecticut conventions quickly ratified; the first two were unanimous in support, but so was that of Georgia, a potentially large state, spurred to such action by the help that a strong central government might give on a dangerous frontier. Two other indisputably small states, New Hampshire and Rhode Island, did not at first support ratification, and although the former eventually became the decisive ninth state, Rhode Island remained steadfastly antifederalist, and only joined the new union in May of 1790, long after the rest and even then by a very narrow vote. North Carolina at first rejected the Constitution by a large majority, and New York accepted it by a margin of three votes (with seven abstentions) only after the most intense lobbying and a clear threat from the Federalists that New York City would ratify and secede if necessary. These last two cases provide clues to the most obvious geographic pattern, for North Carolina was virtually all backcountry and New York City a major seaport. With few exceptions (for example, Rhode Island, Baltimore, Cape Fear), the seaboard strongly supported the new federal structure, while in general the interior regions strongly opposed it. Thus there were fierce political struggles over ratification within all those states large enough and old enough to contain well-settled inland districts as well as seaports and tidewater regions: Massachusetts, New York, Pennsylvania, Virginia, and South Carolina. In these particular cases as well as in the overall view (wherein New Hampshire and North Carolina were largely hinterland areas) we can see in the most general sense a set of center-periphery patterns. That geographic concept in itself explains nothing, but may be translated into a whole series of contrasts—metropolis-frontier, mercantile-agrarian, urban-rural, cosmopolitan-provincial, wealthier-poorer, dominant-subordinate—that are directly pertinent in varying degrees to the analysis of this topic.

Certainly the issues relating to the Constitution were extremely complex, and there is ample indication that they generated discussion and disagreement within every substantial community in America. Neither the creation of the document itself nor the reactions to it yield to any simple set of geographical explanations, but no assessment can get very far without taking into account the complex regional patterns imprinted upon Atlantic America over the course of nearly two centuries. The United States of America over which George Washington assumed the presidency in April 1789 was in formal terms a much more united body than its predecessor, an unprecedented federation of states based on the consent of the people. It was an immense and remarkable political experiment and its success as a federation and a nation would be determined in no small part by how well it might cope with problems deeply embedded in its historical human geography.

12. Emergence of a Federal Nation

The first years of the United States, say the two decades including the confederation and the testing of the new Constitution under the first two presidents, were a creative geographic as well as political period in American history. It was a time of expansion into new ground under new auspices in the midst of a new North American imperial situation. How to extend, colonize, develop, integrate, and secure a democratic federal republic spanning half a continent was a new experiment on a grand scale. Whether it could be done or not was a matter of debate. There were pessimistic predictions to match all the exhilarating visions; the only safe assumption was that there would likely be as much trial, adaptation, and amendment involved in the shaping of its new geographic as of its new political system.

Despite all the disruptions of the Revolution and its aftermath it was a period of continuing vigorous growth. The census of 1800 reported 5,305,937 persons, an increase of thirty-five percent in the ten years since the first national enumeration (3,929,827 in 1790) and more than double the more generous estimates for this United States area in 1775. There was growth everywhere except in the most confined of the older areas (e.g., Rhode Island). Hundreds of thousands pushed the frontier of settlement northward in New England, westward in New York and across Pennsylvania, southwestward filling in the Piedmont from Virginia into Georgia; and by 1800 there were 325,000 people in the new interior states of

Kentucky and Tennessee. There was nothing really new in the general directions of these outward surges, for they were well under way or incipient by the eve of the Revolution, nor in the general problems they presented to a central government in the conflicting jurisdictional claims, the continuing presence of the Indians, the intense competitions for lands, and the tenuous connections of such outlying parts with the older regions. What was new was a sociopolitical context that was now American, national, federal, and state rather than British, imperial, and colonial, and a geographic context that in some large areas favored the convergence of migrations from distinct seaboard societies rather than simply regional expansion.

Resolution of the overlapping territorial claims of the states to these interior lands, a complicated task essential to the continuation of the union, was accomplished in principle and very largely in fact by 1790. One of the most complex and aggravating was the chronic dispute in the northern interior over the area between the upper Connecticut River and Lake Champlain. In 1777 delegates from most of the towns in this area proclaimed the independent State of New Connecticut (named for the source of most of the settlers). A convention later that year changed the name to Vermont (because of the prior claim of another New Connecticut in the Wyoming Valley) and drew up a constitution. In 1779 this government annexed thirty-two towns on the east side of the Connecticut Valley that had voted to secede from the remote and oligarchical rule of Portsmouth, and two years later a bordering tier of New York towns east of the Hudson voted to join Vermont also. However, New Hampshire and New York refused to give up any of their overlapping claims to the area or recognize the legality of any of these moves, and they kept the Continental Congress from doing so. The area seethed with factions whose only common aim was to secure title to their lands but who differed deeply on how to do so. With initial expectations of joining the new union thwarted, an independent Vermont began to look to other possibilities. It was increasingly neutral as the war dragged on, and, although the whole wedge of territory was given to the United States in the Treaty of 1783, Vermont remained in fact a sovereign state outside the confederation. Influential Vermonters began to discuss special relationships with Britain, some envisioning an imperial protectorate, others a Switzerland-like neutrality. But such interest was largely confined to the Champlain Valley where commercial access to the St. Lawrence was considered essential. Statehood remained the obvious goal for most of the people, and once the contending border states relinquished their claims that became possible. New Hampshire, fearing its own dismemberment, withdrew in 1782 after the union of its Connecticut Valley towns with Vermont was dissolved; New York only gave up in 1790, accepting payment to compensate its grantees (its seceding towns had been returned some years before). Thus in 1791 the independent republic of Vermont became the first addition to the United States of America.

In 1781 New York took the lead in ceding to Congress its very uncertain rights (based on treaties with the Iroquois) to lands west of a boundary line drawn south from the westernmost point of Lake Ontario. Massachusetts subsequently ceded its "sea-to-sea" charter claims to lands beyond that same line, and the two states then resolved their dispute over territory east of that boundary by recognizing New York sovereignty over it all but granting Massachusetts property rights over a large part of western New York and a small detached block (the "Boston Ten Towns") just to the east. By prearrangement those cessions left a small triangle of land fronting on Lake Erie, which Pennsylvania then purchased from the federal government in 1792 to obtain direct access to the Great Lakes. Meanwhile the bitter dispute between Connecticut and Pennsylvania was adjudicated by a special congressional

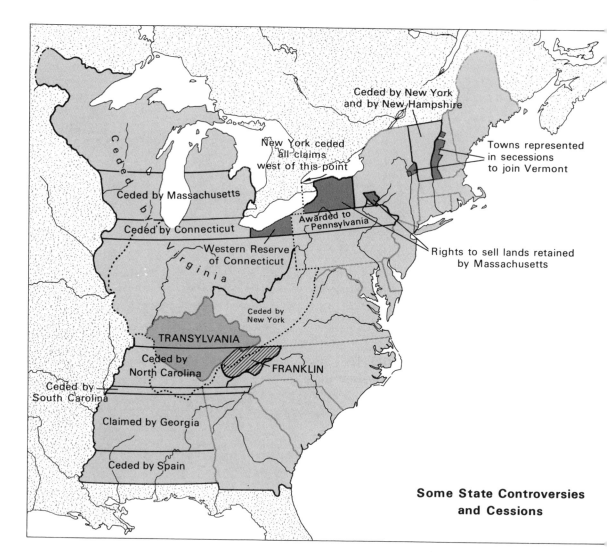

57. Some State Controversies and Cessions.

court in favor of the latter, and Connecticut subsequently gave up the remainder of its "sea-to-sea" claims in 1786, except for a 120-mile strip (the "Western Reserve") that it held until 1800. As Virginia had ceded its claims to territory beyond the Ohio (except for an area contingent on the need for military bounty lands) in 1784, Connecticut's action opened the way for Congress to establish the Northwest Territory, the first such jurisdiction created by the new Union.

There also were great contentions and complexities south of the Ohio. In 1775 the audacious Transylvania Company organized at Boonesborough a proprietary government and proceeded to petition the Continental Congress for admission of their huge Kentucky-Cumberland land claim as a fourteenth state. That was firmly blocked by Virginia and North Carolina; the company soon collapsed, and in 1776 Virginia organized the whole of its territory south of the Ohio and west of the Big Sandy River and Cumberland Mountain as Kentucky County. From 1784 on, the future of Kentucky was debated in a long series of local conventions, some factions toying with the idea of an independent Mississippi Valley republic. Separatist sentiment was fanned by the apparent ineptness of the confederation and by uncertainty about its future, and especially by the anger at the demonstrated indifference of the northern states to the basic western interest in Mississippi navigation. But an outright revolt against American authority was never very likely, and the statehood movement gathered strength until it was arranged in 1792 for Kentucky to be simultaneously granted independence from Virginia and admission to the United States.

A slightly different sequence took place in the band of territory just to the south. In 1784 settlers in the mountain valleys along the uppermost waters of the Tennessee, a district by then considerably expanded from the original Watauga nucleus, assembled at Jonesboro and proclaimed the independent State of Franklin with the expectation of joining the confederation on the terms laid out in the ordinance of that year. But opposition from both North Carolina (which had rescinded its initial cession and regarded Franklin as a land grab and rebellion) and the United States (angered at violations of Indian treaties in the area) and internal strife brought a collapse of this movement in 1788. Two years later North Carolina again ceded its western lands, which Congress organized into the Southwest Territory. A new treaty with the Cherokees opened more land, settlers poured in, and Tennessee soon had more than the 60,000 to qualify for statehood, which was granted in 1796, making it the first to be admitted under the Ordinance of 1787. Farther south, South Carolina's narrow western band proved illusory, based on inaccurate maps, while Georgia's claim to a broad swath of territory became so mired in the most flagrant attempts by speculators, many of them members of the legislature, to reap benefits prior to or under some condition of cession that a transfer acceptable to Georgia and Congress alike was not worked out until 1802. Meanwhile, following the treaty settlement of the boundary with West Florida and

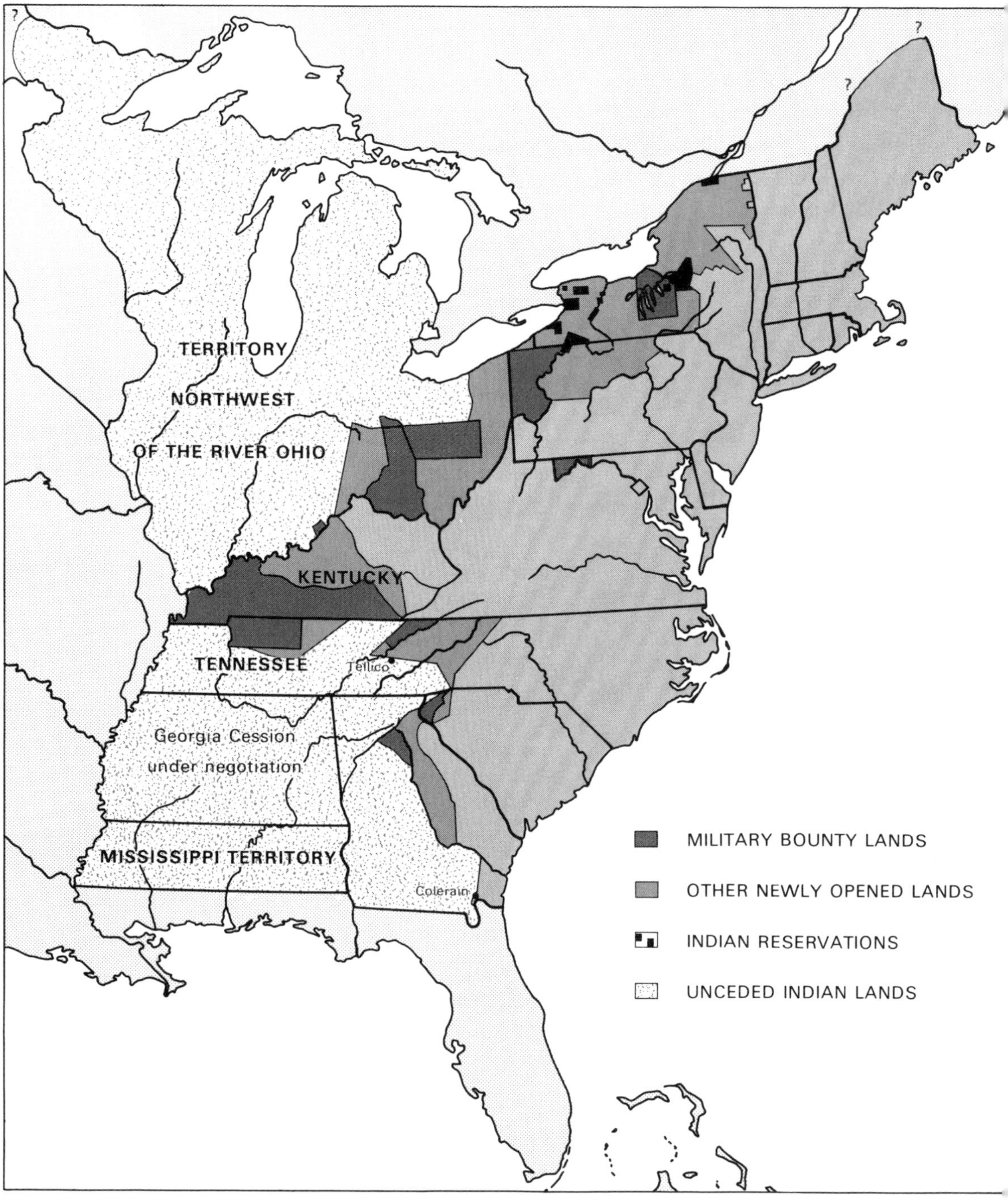
TERRITORY
NORTHWEST
OF THE RIVER OHIO
KENTUCKY
TENNESSEE
Tellico
Georgia Cession
under negotiation
MISSISSIPPI TERRITORY
Colerain
MILITARY BOUNTY LANDS
OTHER NEWLY OPENED LANDS
INDIAN RESERVATIONS
UNCEDED INDIAN LANDS

58. Categories of Western Lands.

Spanish evacuation of Natchez, the southernmost strip of long-disputed ground lying west of the Chattahoochee was organized as Mississippi Territory in 1798.

Any hope for an orderly advance of settlement into this huge western region required that these decisions about state and national political jurisdiction be accompanied by treaties with the Indians to arrange for cessions of lands and definitions of reserves. There were four main sectors involved, each with a different set of actors and issues. In the north the long-formidable Iroquois Confederation was a shambles, its immemorial council fire at Onondaga extinguished, its dominance over the broad region from the Mohawk to the Maumee at an end. The war had dissolved the league into tribes and factions. Most had been active allies of the British, bringing terror and destruction to the New York and Pennsylvania frontiers. But in retaliation a large American force had left a swath of devastation through the richest of their lands, destroying crops, orchards, and villages as far west as the Genesee, forcing most of the nation into refuge and dependence upon the British. As defeated enemies the Iroquois were vulnerable to the intense pressures of speculators and officials to eliminate them from the region. Many fled to Canada; those that remained ceded their western lands to the United States, and in the confused times that followed New York State officials and land companies negotiated treaties with the separate tribes that reduced and fragmented the Iroquois homeland into ten small reserves. Meanwhile Pennsylvania gained title to all remaining Iroquois and other Indian lands for a small payment.

The Ohio Country was a much more troublesome area. In 1783 the Ohio River was the de facto boundary between a loosely associated group of Algonkian tribes to the north (principally the Shawnee, Delaware, Wyandot, Chippewa, Ottawa, Potawatomie) and Americans in the western lands of Virginia to the south. All United States policies were geared toward clearing the entire Ohio Valley for land sales and settlement, and there was neither the will nor the way for the government to keep Americans from moving up the Muskingum, Scioto, Miami, and other attractive tributary valleys. Some of the Indians, however, sought to create a concerted militant resistance against any such encroachment. Initial Congressional actions sought to establish a clear separation line between Whites and Indians, opening up huge new areas. But no such line (there were several different ones suggested through a sequence of proposals) could gain general Indian endorsement. Therefore Congress, in its eagerness to create a Northwest Territory, negotiated treaties with whatever tribes or factions it could and ostensibly cleared the way as far west as the Wabash. But opposition from other Indians soon led to clashes and then open warfare. In 1790 and again in 1791 a large American militia ranging north from the Miami Valley was defeated with heavy losses. Such events not only heartened the Indians but emboldened British officials, working out of their old forward post at Detroit, to come to their support. The British hoped to create some sort of Indian buffer state in the region. But such a proposal was utterly rejected by the United States, which proceeded to create a national army, and in 1794, under the leadership of General Anthony Wayne, this force defeated a large Indian contingent at Fallen Timbers on the lower Maumee. These Indians had taken their stand near a newly constructed British outpost on American soil (Fort

Miami), and the pointed refusal of the British to risk coming to their aid against an American army, together with their defeat and devastation of their fields and villages, ended Indian hope of holding the Americans to the Ohio River. By the Treaty of Greenville in 1795 a large area was ceded by the Indians and the Territory Northwest of the River Ohio was decisively opened for development.

Another chronically troublesome area was the Cherokee country amidst the southern Appalachians. Here the confrontation was intense because White settlers were advancing along two distinct fronts, southwestward in the Great Valley and northwestward on the Carolina-Georgia Piedmont, directly in upon the Cherokee homelands. The onset of the Revolution had generated chaotic conflict that left a great many Indian villages and frontier farms destroyed and had driven many of the Cherokees into refuge with other Indians or the British. After the war congressional officials tried to hold speculators and frontiersmen at bay and restore much of the area to Cherokee control. They disallowed treaties made by Franklin officials and other opportunists, but could not control depredations by the many factions on both sides. They set up a government supply station at Tellico, but the Cherokees resented it as an intrusion and claimed the goods provided were inferior to the British standard they had become used to. In the 1790s the Cherokees formally gave up the northern half of their old homeland and shifted south and west along the upperwaters of the Coosa and toward the middle Tennessee. Here they were increasingly turning to the raising of cattle and hogs and were seeking plows and other tools and teachers to develop a more secure agricultural base and a firmer hold on ancestral lands, but there was little to suggest that pressures from local Whites would not be reasserted or that the protections guaranteed by a distant American government would have any real effect.

To the south on the broad coastal plain the situation was also volatile but less confrontational because the main base of the Creeks lay 150 miles west of the Georgia frontier and that of the Choctaws lay well back from Natchez and the Mississippi. After the Revolution the remarkable Creek leader, Alexander McGillivray, ranged widely over the continent, visiting Ohio Indians, New York City, New Orleans, and Pensacola in complex intrigues to preserve the integrity of tribal lands. In 1790 he ceded a long strip of country west of the Ogeechee that Georgians had long coveted and penetrated, relieving the most immediate pressures. In 1796 the American government set up a store at Colerain, thirty miles up the St. Mary's River, in an attempt to lure the Creeks into greater allegiance and dependence. But McGillivray's death (1793), the Spanish cession of the Yazoo Strip, the reappearance of William Bowles and his Muskogee scheme, and a host of local factors kept these southern borderlands in turmoil. By the end of the century the Creeks and Choctaws, and the Chickasaws to the north and west, still held official title to a huge realm between the Oconee and the Mississippi, but it was a region so large, so attractive, and so thinly held that it obviously could not continue long as it was. Drastic alteration of its tenure only awaited resolution of the intense rivalries among American governments, companies, and individuals for the first chance at marketing these lands to others.

Thus a greatly broadened and rather jagged wedge of country angling from northern New York and southern Georgia westward to the point where the Tennessee joined the Ohio was cleared for White settlement in the first years of the new republic. However, even though the central government had devised a system for orderly survey and sale of federal lands, it had little direct control over the disposal of these particular western districts, because the various states had very largely reserved that right to themselves. There were two major forms of transfer of public lands into private holdings during this period: by allocation to those who had qualified through military service and by sale to land companies. These two forms were used in separate areas, each was applied in total to nearly half of the land available, and both involved a great deal of land jobbing and speculation.

The practice of paying soldiers in scrip redeemable at a future date in land warrants was initiated during the Revolution by an impecunious Continental Congress and soon followed by most of those states that had western lands available: New York, Pennsylvania, Maryland, Virginia, North Carolina, South Carolina, and Georgia. Eligibility varied from state to state but all apportioned acreage by rank (to be selected within designated military land districts) and all allowed veterans to sell their scrip to nonmilitary persons. Virginia, lavish in payment to large forces, had early reserved the whole of southern and western Kentucky for such purposes, and in 1790 it exercised the right it had specified in its cession to Congress to create an additional Virginia Military District north of the Ohio between the Scioto and Little Miami. Also set aside was a small area on former Virginia lands, downriver just north of the Falls of the Ohio, for George Rogers Clark and members of his western army. In 1787 the federal government created a military district on the upper Muskingum, and this United States reserve was later enlarged westward to allow for additional claims from more recent service. Little of the land in most of these designated areas was actually settled by military veterans, for many of them turned their scrip into some more readily negotiable form of payment. And there were often long delays before such lands were actually made available to claimants. Indian opposition quickly forced New York to suspend allocations in its very attractive original reserve for seven years, until it had arranged purchase from the Onondagas and Cayugas.

Most of the rest of the western land made available during this time was first sold in large blocks directly to land companies, which might in turn sell to other companies; a series of such speculative wholesale transactions might precede sale to an actual settler. Such was often the case in Kentucky, where an array of Virginia companies had been vying for twenty years for the chance to deal in these fabled lands. Heritage, geography, and current circumstances made New York the scene of some of the most intense and complex activity. Long confined to little more than the Hudson and Mohawk valleys by the presence of the Iroquois, the remainder of this large state was now suddenly available. State land commissioners made some gestures toward arranging for sale to settlers, but there were other pressures and precedents and for the most part they simply marketed huge acreages to the highest bidder. There was no shortage of buyers. New York had a long history of speculation and also of a landed gentry, and the syndicates of investors that quickly formed were propelled not only by the prospect of profits but by the vision of handsome country estates on English—and Hudson Valley—models. The convergence of a variety of monied interests upon upstate New York is readily illustrated by reference to a few of the largest transactions. Alexander Macomb, a New York City merchant-adventurer who had made a fortune in furs, bought most of northern New York lying between the Adirondacks and the St. Lawrence (including ten still-empty townships that had been earlier laid out as a strategic plan to induce settlement opposite the new loyalist towns across the river) and quickly resold large parcels to other wholesalers. An association of Yankee investors headed by Oliver Phelps and Nathaniel Gorham contracted for the entire block of Massachusetts land, the western third of New York. Unable to make their payments, they soon had to give up a large portion of it and sold the rest to Robert Morris of Philadelphia, who in turn repurchased that which they had forfeited and then sold most of his holdings, one large block to Sir William Pulteney and a group of British capitalists, and an even larger one encompassing the western end of the state to the Holland Land Company, a syndicate of Dutch bankers that had already invested in smaller tracts in New York and Pennsylvania. Several of these land companies spent a good deal of money on roads, mills, stores, and the systematic survey of land into farm-size parcels for sale to actual settlers, envisioning a long-term income from their investment. Much of the rest of the land in New York was peddled by similar if smaller syndicates, entrepreneurs, and aspiring country gentlemen.

New Englanders were heavily involved in land sales and development schemes all across the northern states and territory. The Connecticut Land Company was formed to purchase the entire Western Reserve of that state on the south shore of Lake Erie, and in 1796 it began surveys and sales in the area east of the Cuyahoga, the only part as yet ceded by the Indians. And the main forerunner of these organizations was the Ohio Company, by which Yankee speculators had wangled a million and a half acres in the Muskingum area and then put pressure on Congress to follow through with the Act of 1787, which opened the region to settlers. In fact, this new Northwest Territory was the best exhibit of all the main varieties of land disposal schemes of the day. Just downriver from the Ohio Company lay the large tract claimed by the Scioto Company, a disjointed and dishonest speculation whose extravagant promotions had sold thousands of acres to credulous Frenchmen, resulting in the hasty creation (actually on Ohio Company lands) of the rude village of Gallipolis ("City of the Gauls") to receive an unexpected vanguard of settlers; later a small French grant was provided by Congress to succor these defrauded immigrants. West of the Scioto was the large Virginia Military District, and beyond that, between the Miami rivers, was the Symmes Purchase of a wealthy New Jersey developer. Inland from these river frontages a block of congressional lands and the United States Military District had been designated. However, up to 1799 the only federal land actually surveyed and offered for sale directly to intending settlers was in what was known as the Seven Ranges, a strip of land adjacent to the Pennsylvania border wherein the new "township and range" system defined in the Ordinance of 1787 was first applied. In accordance with that initial federal land act, alternate townships were "sold entire" (thirty-six square miles) and "by lots" (of one square mile each), a compromise designed to accommodate the interests of New Englanders who wanted the opportunity to settle by groups and create their traditional township communities and of Virginians and others who were militantly in favor of individual purchase of family-size lots.

The expansion of settlement into these post-Revolution frontiers was therefore shaped by the availability of land in these various forms and in these many separate tracts, as well as by the sources and pathways of settlers. We can generalize these movements into a few broad regions, each area characterized by some dominant features. Thus we may for convenience group the many districts lying between Lake Champlain and the Cuyahoga River—including much of New York, northern Pennsylvania, and the Western Reserve—as a northern landscape of glaciated terrain being given a strong imprint of New England colonization. Old political claims and avid commercial promotions combined with relative accessibility, strong cultural aspirations, and demographic pressures to create a powerful westward surge of Yankees into these newly opened lands. The town of Utica, laid out just beyond the limits of colonial settlements in the famed Mohawk corridor, became the principal gateway to the new "Western District" of New York. From here the Genesee Road, skirting the edge of the plateau and touching the remarkable sequence of narrow lakes, led to coveted lands made famous by the Iroquois and by the expeditions against them. Geneva and Canandaigua were focal points for major tracts, and just to the west Joseph Ellicott set up a supply center for the surveys preparing the Holland Company lands for sale; the road led on to Black Rock and access by lake or by land to the Connecticut Land Company's new headquarters village of Cleveland in the Western Reserve. There were numerous branches from this trunk line—southwesterly to the Chenango and the Boston Towns, northwestward to the Black River Valley—and there were parallel pathways: out of Vermont along the northern base of the Adirondacks to the St. Lawrence, out of Connecticut across the Hudson and the Delaware into northernmost Pennsylvania.

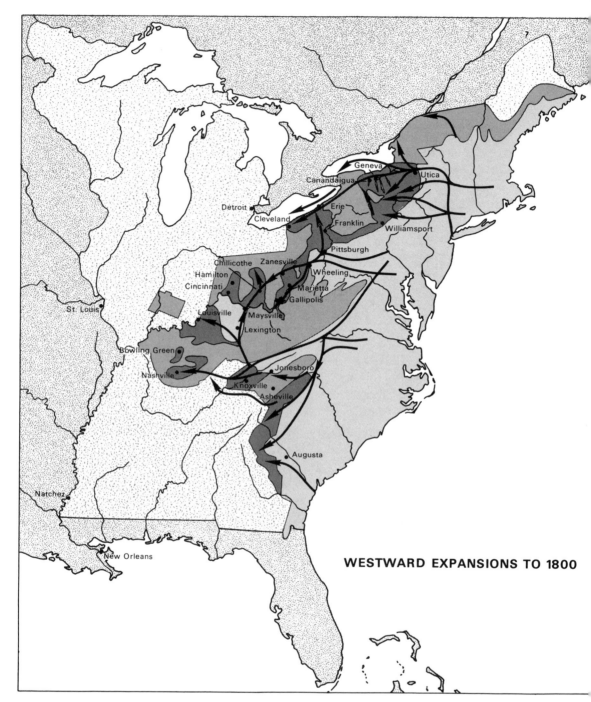

59. Westward Expansions to 1800.

However, although New England was the principal source of settlers and developers in this broad region, it was not the only one. Yorkers of various kinds from the Hudson Valley and New York City were to be found in many districts; Pennsylvanians edged northward or westward into nearby valleys, and some of the most important land promotions were based in Philadelphia. Williamsport on the West Branch of the Susquehanna became an important southern portal. Charles Williamson built a road from there to his "capital" at Bath by way of the Lycoming and Tioga valleys to help lure colonists from Pennsylvania and New Jersey to the "Geneseo" lands of his proprietors. Similarly, the various Holland Land Company operations in western New York and northwestern Pennsylvania were being managed and supplied out of Philadelphia. And still farther west the towns of Franklin, Meadville, and Erie were laid out in 1795 along an improved road following the old trail that connected the Forks of the Ohio to the Great Lakes.

60. The Genesee Country in Western New York.
This 1800 map of the "Middle States of North America" is one of successive versions in various promotional publications by Charles Williamson showing where "Geneseo" was and how to get there. Several other large tracts of speculators, such as that of Alexander Macomb, are also shown. Robert Morris had not yet sold the western end of the state to the Holland Land Company. The "Lands granted to the American Army" refers to the new military tract of the State of New York. (From the collection of the Geography and Map Division, Library of Congress)

Thus, although these tens of thousands of Yankees must inevitably have had a great influence upon the character of many, perhaps most, towns and countrysides of this northern frontier, they could not make it simply a grand extension of New England, however much some of their leaders and spokesmen may have wished. The Hudson Valley, dominated by a different set of people (although heavily infiltrated by Yankees at numerous points), intervened between the old homelands and these new settlements, and the influx of settlers from other sources introduced into most districts a social variety unprecedented in colonial New England. It was too early to tell just what the social geography of the region would be, but even amidst this first swirl of promotion, immigration, and pioneering the convergence of settlers from several colonial source regions signaled that an important national, Americanizing, process was taking place.

The pattern for another convergence of major potential was taking shape in the Ohio Valley. The mighty Ohio provided a great natural waterway to the West. Cutting across the margins of the Appalachian Highlands, the broad river wandered southwesterly through a country of dense forests and steep hills, and the succession of tributary valleys provided the obvious entryways to the more attractive lands. Marietta, the New England town of the Ohio Company platted amidst the curious Indian mounds at the mouth of the Muskingum, and Cincinnati, facing the Ohio with ready access to the Miami rivers on either side, were the first and most famous portals. There was no similar town serving the Scioto Valley because most land seekers in the Virginia Military District came by way of the Kentucky settlements, crossing the Ohio at Limestone (later Maysville) and moving inland from Manchester (platted in 1791). Promoters were soon laying out towns in the midst of these tracts, such as Hamilton (1794) and Chillicothe (1796), but much of the country was too rugged to lure large numbers. The Ohio Company had trouble peddling its lands, and sales in the Seven Ranges brought only a disappointing trickle of funds into famished federal coffers.

In 1799 the first of the congressional tracts lying well in from the river was opened for sale, and the enterprising Ebenezer Zane undertook the building of an access road along the old trail west from the family base at Zanesburg (later Wheeling) to Chillicothe and on to Maysville, founding towns at the crossings of the Muskingum (Zanesville) and the Hocking (Lancaster). The first stretch of Zane's Trace opened a direct route across gentler country toward the broadening plains and provided another important entryway. With three main routes in place, by river and by road out of Pennsylvania and from the south by way of the Kentucky trails, connecting the variety of land promotions in the Northwest Territory with source regions from Virginia to New England, the framework for another broadly national expansion was in place, although here too it was too early to tell just what the regional cultural pattern would be.

There was little doubt about the incipient character of regions father south. Virginians, Marylanders, and North Carolinians were spreading broadly beyond their rapidly filling forward base in the Bluegrass into the knobs and barrens of western Kentucky, as well as grabbing the former Cherokee lands and reaching across the Cumberland Plateau to the rich limestone country of northern Tennessee. Knoxville and Nashville, connected in 1795 by a new wagon road, were soon thriving centers in these new districts. Still farther south pioneers were pushing westward into the long strip of newly released Indian lands. The old Indian country entrepôt of Augusta had been formalized, incorporated, and was not only the civic and commercial focus of this colonization frontier but the temporary state capital of Georgia as well. There were no federal lands in any of these sectors, nor were there as yet any extensive systematic surveys, state or private. There were in fact almost no institutional impediments to the taking up of land. The old southern practice of allowing individuals to claim land in any shape, defining its metes and bounds by reference to particular rocks and trees and creeks and other landmarks, prevailed, as did the ensuing chaos of conflicting claims, a problem only modestly mitigated by a requirement in North Carolina and Tennessee that the claimant's filing at the land office be confirmed by an official surveyor before title be conferred.

This continuity in the mode of land disposal was merely one exhibit of the important fact that, unlike the development of the Ohio Valley and northern frontier, this southern expansion was really nothing new. There were no federal, state, or elaborate private programs for development; there was no convergence of settlers from markedly different source regions. All these movements were simply westward extensions out of the Piedmont and Great Valley, in large part a reassertion of thrusts that had been interrupted, blunted, or temporarily repelled by the exigencies of the Revolution. There was a complete continuity in peoples and practices, in culture: Scotch-Irish, English, German, and a few other pioneer families searching out the valleys and coves and meadows and grassy uplands, forming closely clustered "stations" where Indian dangers still existed and dispersed kin-structured "settlements" in safer country, carrying on their hunting, stockraising, farming way of life with intermittent connection by way of primitive trails and trackways and stretches of open river with a thin sprinkling of trade centers and county seats. What was new was the extent and strength of this American type. What was important was the expansion and clearer expression of a major regional culture, for we are dealing here not simply with a phase of backcountry pioneering, but with the emergence of the Upland South as a growing force in the new nation.

These new frontiers, especially the transmontane country, constituted a vast national hinterland only tenuously connected to the main body of the nation. A slow throbbing of the national pulse might be discerned in the thin arteries of the postal service reaching west to Canandaigua, to Pittsburgh, and via the Great Valley to Lexington and Knoxville, but other movements were imbalanced and divergent. Migrant families with all their livestock and paraphernalia, and a great assortment of agents, merchants, and promoters trekked westward along these roads and trails, but there could be little return movement of western produce, for overland freighting costs were prohibitive on anything from west of Pittsburgh or the Valley of Virginia. Only goods that could be driven on foot or that were of sufficient value to be carried in pack trains could cross the mountains; the rest of the traffic was drawn inexorably to the waterways and on downstream to the Mississippi or the St. Lawrence, diverging into foreign territories and foreign ports. There were persistent efforts to open up these exits and insure American privileges. Pinckney's Treaty of 1795 secured navigation and deposit rights on the Mississippi, but soon the rumored possibility of the transfer of Louisiana from feeble Spain to powerful France revived American anxieties. In the north this same French power actually helped the new republic, for once again the English were willing to placate the Americans in order to concentrate attention on their great imperial rival. Thus Jay's Treaty brought about evacuation of the Champlain forts, Oswegatchie, Oswego, Niagara, Detroit, and Michilimackinac (which the British had held ostensibly as hostages for debts relating to loyalist indemnities), finally clearing this annoying foreign presence on American soil. There was at the moment some local trade and immigration across this border, but here, too, a larger and longer-term dependency upon the St. Lawrence seemed an unsatisfactory prospect, and talk of purchase, secession, or seizure of these two strategic borderlands was commonplace amidst the volatile politics of the day.

These divergences and dependencies might be undercut by drawing traffic directly eastward to American ports, but the practicality of doing so was yet to be demonstrated. George Washington's early and serious scheme for a Potomac-Monongahela canal was generally regarded as impracticable after engineering reconnaissance revealed a much longer and more difficult connection than originally thought, and in the north the shallow ditch across the old fur trade portage between the Mohawk River and the creek flowing toward Lake Ontario was barely serviceable. Whether the West could be effectively bound to Atlantic America, therefore, loomed as a geographical problem of imperative political and commercial concern for the new nation in the new century.

Meanwhile the main body of the nation in the seaboard states was becoming more densely populated, domesticated, and integrated, at least in part. The reach of various seaports into more immediate hinterlands was being improved. There were now canal bypasses around the falls of the Potomac above Alexandria and Georgetown, around Conewago Falls on the lower Susquehanna, Little Falls on

61. Turnpike Bridge.
This handsome nine-arch stone bridge was completed in 1800 as part of the Philadelphia-Lancaster Turnpike, America's first superhighway. Sketched by Benjamin Latrobe in 1801, the bridge crossed over the Conestoga River just east of Lancaster. The center building at the west end was a roadside tavern, which still stands; the bridge was in use until 1932. (Courtesy of the Maryland Historical Society, Baltimore)

the Mohawk, and South Hadley Falls on the Connecticut. More ambitious canals were under construction to give Boston direct access to the Merrimack, and in South Carolina to give Charleston a direct waterway to the Santee. There were major improvements in land travel as well. The completion of the Philadelphia to Lancaster turnpike in 1795 after five years of work was a major event. This first superhighway bridged the rivers and, by the careful construction of a stone and gravel base, lifted the road out of its seasonal mire; its success soon touched off a flurry of turnpike chartering, especially in New York and New England.

Pressure for the improvement of roads mounted with the expansion of stage-coach service. By 1800 scheduled stages radiated from Boston and Philadelphia and connected New York northward to Albany with branches on to Rutland and Utica. Even more important to the emerging nation were the lines connecting these major ports along the seaboard. There were regular stages between Portland (formerly Falmouth) and Richmond, with daily departures provided between New York and Baltimore, and one-day service between New York and Philadelphia. The portion of this lateral link between the Piscataqua and the Potomac was emerging as a basic axis of the nation. Philadelphia (69,403 in the census of 1800) and New York (60,489) were now much the largest cities, with Boston (24,937) and Baltimore (26,114) next in size, and these four served as regional centers for the most concentrated body of people (circa 2,800,000 between the two rivers and excluding the more remote populations of New Hampshire, Vermont, and western New York and Pennsylvania) and industry (ironworks, glassworks, potteries, paper mills, textile mills, distilleries, sugar refineries, shipbuilding), as well as several productive agricultural districts.

Such a concentration contrasted sharply with the pattern south of the Potomac (and including southern Maryland) where all was more purely rural and agrarian, with a population of about 2,000,000 (of whom almost forty percent were slaves) spread over a considerably broader area. Charleston (20,473; its name changed from Charles Town in 1783) was the only real urban center in the south, several times larger than the places next in size (Richmond, 5,737 and Savannah, 5,166), and it was enjoying a surge of activity from the emergence of cotton as a promising staple. Planters were finding it a profitable replacement for indigo, and new varieties were proving successful farther inland. The new canal was designed to improve access to that hinterland, but such a facility could be no more than a localized answer to a broad regional need. A great variety of boats and barges, arks and rafts and pirogues served for seasonal shipments downriver, but there was hardly a decent stretch of road or substantial bridge to be found anywhere in the south. The question of how and where to bind the rapidly developing Upcountry (of South Carolina), Backcountry (of North Carolina), and Middle Country (of Virginia) more effectively to the Low Country or Tidewater remained a matter of intense concern in all these states.

That concern was first of all commercial, for all those hinterlands, no matter how remote, in the south as well as the north, aspired to be part of the Atlantic capitalist world. The actual American links with that world had been seriously disrupted by the Revolution and still seemed far from restored or stabilized in new patterns. A few places, most notably Newport, had been so heavily ravaged by raids and lost so much entrepreneurial talent that they simply never recovered their former prosperity. Although nearby ports such as Bristol and Providence were soon expanding their general commerce and slave trading, Newport seemed destined to become "a small summer residence for idle people of easy fortune only." But much the most serious handicap of the new nation was to have Britain close its home market and West Indies to American vessels. Shipbuilding and the New England economy were heavily affected. The opening of the French West Indies, a few Spanish ports (Havana, Trinidad), and use of Dutch and Danish entrepôts in the area could not make up so great a loss, and there began an unprecedented probing of far more distant seas. In 1784 a partnership of Philadelphia and New York merchants outfitted a large vessel, renamed it *Empress of China,* and sent it off

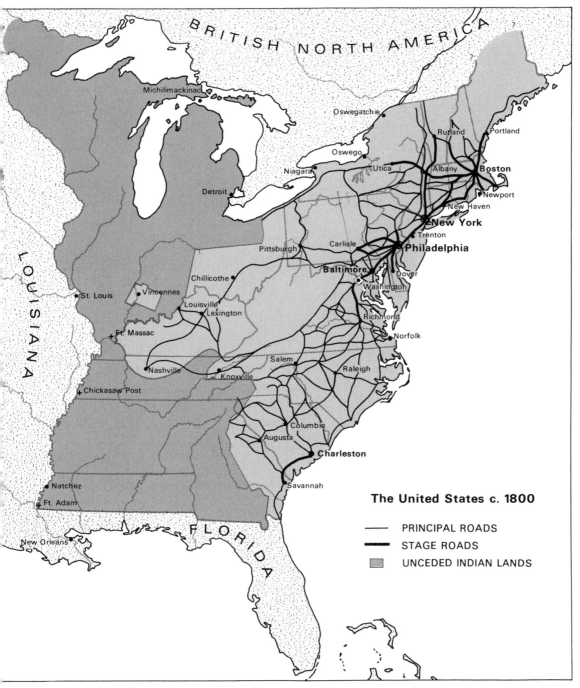

2. The United States, c. 1800.

The United States c. 1800

—— PRINCIPAL ROADS

—— STAGE ROADS

▨ UNCEDED INDIAN LANDS

from New York City to Canton, from whence it returned the next year at a handsome profit. In 1786 an American commercial house opened in Canton and the first vessel from New England arrived; in 1790 the *Columbia* returned to Boston having traded for a cargo of furs off Vancouver Island, exchanged these in Canton for tea and silks, and sailed on around Africa to complete the first American circumnavigation of the globe. By 1800 the China trade had become routine, spurring the building of bigger ships, the taking of greater risks, and the spread of chinoiserie in the furnishings of the wealthy in the seaport cities. Meanwhile, Salem merchants had established trade with India and the East Indies, and whalers from New Bedford, Nantucket, and a number of small ports were roaming the South Atlantic and South Pacific. In the 1790s the turmoil in Europe caused further shifts in and stimulus of American commerce. Increasingly France became the enemy and Britain much more of a friend. The British West Indies were at least partially reopened, and to serve that market New England reasserted its role in the Great Fishery and extended its operations to Labrador and the Bay of Chaleur. In Europe American vessels skirted the war zones and reached into the Baltic and the eastern Mediterranean. The European conflict made everything uncertain, but by 1800 American foreign commerce was far more vigorous and its major ports were clearly prospering as points on an expanding global rather than merely Atlantic system.

That concern of southern seaports over how to make more effective connection with developing hinterlands was political as well as economic, and one direct geopolitical impact of inland expansion had already been felt in every southern state: the transfer of the capital to a more central position. Virginia had taken the lead, in 1779, although in this instance the impetus had come more from wartime fear over the exposed position of Williamsburg than from the power exerted by the interior districts. At the border of the Tidewater and Piedmont, Richmond was considered "more safe and central than any other town situated on navigable water," and was an excellent intermediate position (although not exactly safe, being sacked by the British in 1781). The moves from New Bern to Raleigh (authorized in 1788), Charleston to Columbia (1786), and Savannah to Louisville (1789), in each case to new towns laid out for the purpose, were directly responsive to the rapidly changing geography of settlement. Shifts of such economic and symbolic importance could only come out of intense political struggles, and none more so than that in South Carolina in which the Low Country oligarchy success-fully retained dominance in representation and enough special offices to make Charleston in some degree a dual capital.

There were a few such shifts in northern states as well: from Philadelphia to Lancaster (1799), New York City to Albany (1797), the lesser move from New Castle to Dover in Delaware (1777), and the selection of Trenton as a single and central capital for New Jersey (1790). There were no such changes in New England, although in 1780–81 the western towns in Massachusetts attempted to pry the government out of Boston. All these cases reflect the more or less free play of local geopolitical forces within each state made possible by their independence, which released them from the external power that had kept capitals on the seacoast as beachheads of imperial authority.

None of these geopolitical struggles, however difficult, could match the long acrimonious debate, political maneuvering, and trading of favors among regional interests relating to the momentous decision on where to locate the capital of the federation. For years after the war Congress was migratory, meeting in Annapolis, Trenton, New York, and Philadelphia, but all the while there were great pressures to establish a permanent home. It was generally agreed that the capital should be reasonably central along the seaboard and placed in its own territory apart from the states; location on a navigable stream providing some access toward the interior was also considered desirable. That left open a wide range of possibilities, and offers came in from many places, from as far afield as Kingston on the Hudson to Williamsburg near the James, but the debate soon narrowed the focus to locations on the Delaware, the Susquehanna, and the Potomac. In 1789 the House voted in favor of the Susquehanna; the Senate amended this to designate Germantown, Pennsylvania, near the Delaware, and no further action was taken. However, in the following year they agreed upon the Potomac, with a provision that Congress meet in Philadelphia until 1800. A committee soon selected the actual site, in 1791 the "District of Columbia" was proclaimed, and the French engineer Pierre Charles L'Enfant was set to work to lay out the "City of Washington" on the Maryland side of the river just below the old port of Georgetown.

Thus the permanent capital of the federation was to be almost exactly central along the seaboard between Maine and Georgia, on the most westerly indentation for ocean vessels, with the Potomac pointing toward the Ohio River, the obvious axis of the Transappalachian West. But it was a location less central in other ways, south of the median of population and barely in contact with the busiest commercial networks of the nation, and approval came only after northern delegates agreed to support the southern preference for the Potomac in return for southern support of Hamilton's bill on the federal assumpton of state debts incurred during the Revolution. That a decision on the matter had to come out of a compromise between north and south reflected a major geopolitical reality of this federal nation; that it resulted in a site almost exactly at the fulcrum of these two emerging sections was an appropriate solution of an inherently difficult problem.

The new city arising on the Potomac, like the famous one created on the swamps of the Neva ninety years before, was conceived on a grand scale to serve as the seat of a great "Empire." With a contiguous area of more than 900,000 square miles, the United States was one of the world's largest political units, surpassed only by Russia, China, and Turkey. But those were Old World empires; as a republic the United States was utterly unprecedented in scale, a prodigious experiment in democracy. If there was reason to doubt whether an Atlantic America

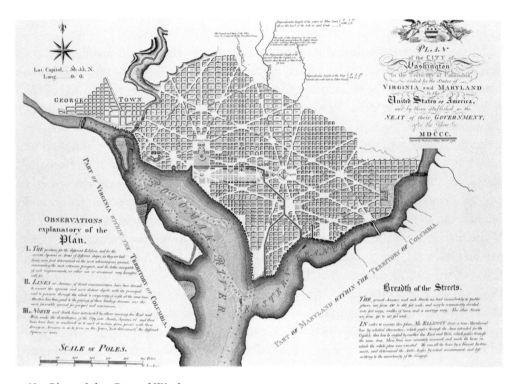

63. Plan of the City of Washington.

This grand baroque design fitted upon the modest heights of an undulating segment of
ground between the old river port of Georgetown and the small Eastern Branch (Ana-
costia) of the Potomac remains one of the really remarkable feats of individual urban
planning. This is the 1792 version, prepared by Andrew Ellicott and differing slightly from
that of Pierre Charles L'Enfant, who was at the time embroiled in the dispute with the
commissioners of the new District that would soon result in his dismissal. But the whole
concept—all the essentials and most of the details—was Major L'Enfant's, a French
military engineer who had served as a volunteer in the American forces under Washington
and whom the President personally selected for this great task. The only important feature
never built was the canal angled across the city below the capitol. The diagonal avenues
were named after the fifteen states of the time; it was expected that each state would
contribute to adorn with suitable monuments the squares its street intersected. (Courtesy
of the Rare Book Room, Olin Library, Cornell University)

could extend and sustain itself as a viable geopolitical system across half a continent, there was no doubt at all about Americans themselves spreading across such
an expanse, for they were busily doing so. The only uncertainty about that advance
was how far they might go, for there was little reason to think that they might halt
at the Mississippi or be deterred by the bounds of other political claims. Fervent
spokesmen were already declaring a transcontinental destiny for the American
people and asserting that "westward the course of empire" must indeed soon take

its way. Bishop Berkeley's famous phrase was of course a vision of "empire" as the seat of civilization, the vehicle of progress, "Time's noblest offspring." Whether America was to be such a vanguard of culture was surely uncertain, but we do well to remind ourselves that it was, in 1800, certainly an empire in a more basic, bloody sense. Conquering must precede planting; it had done so for two centuries in North America and there could be no reason to believe that it would not continue to do so in the century ahead.

Nearly half (about forty-five percent) of the national area of the United States was unceded Indian lands. On the maps of the time, and on the historical reference maps of today, that area is encompassed in two formal territories, parts of four states, and a broad swath of unresolved jurisdiction (Georgia's western claims), but the actual American hold on that very large expanse was minimal at best and nonexistent over much of it. In the Northwest Territory the little enclaves of French traders and settlers at Detroit, Vincennes, and the Illinois Bottom now sent elected delegates to Chillicothe (before 1796 they had sent them to the assembly of Upper Canada) but had only the most tenuous ties to the main body of the nation. In the southwest the Americans were moving into Natchez (Spanish officials had only just left, in 1798) and the government had hastily constructed three forts overlooking the great waterway: at the southwest corner of the nation (Fort Adam), at the old Chickasaw post (Memphis), and near the strategic junction of the Tennessee with the Ohio (Fort Massac); but except for these localities the whole area was legally closed to American settlers. By treaty or by assertion all this Indian country was a protectorate, a large realm of dependent peoples, recognized as distinct tribes and territories—"resident foreign nations"—under the sovereignty and care of the United States. In reality most of it was unsecured, even in part unknown, territory that the United States could neither protect nor serve in any effective way. What it could do, as demonstrated by very recent events, was to punish, devastate, conquer, expel any people that stood in its way and challenged its authority. That was understood even by those Indians so far away as never to have seen an American, for they could not be unaware of the larger, terrible history of North America.

The birth of the United States—republic, federation, empire—was indeed a momentous event, but we should keep in mind that it had a very different portent to the different peoples within its bounds. If those who now proudly called themselves American saw it as a transforming moment of independence and freedom, those who were far more deeply American in another sense could only regard it as an ominous transformation of one empire into another, from one whose distant king had actually made some real effort to befriend and protect them to an empire run by the very people who had proved relentless in their destructive advance. For indigenous peoples in the outlying territories who had no wish to be part of the United States, the American president was a man to be feared, the direct analogue of czar, emperor, and sultan; for Creeks and Cherokees, Chickasaws, Shawnees, Winnebagos, and many others, the new city of Washington was what St. Petersburg was for the Finns, Peking for the Miao, or Constantinople for the Serbs: the seat of a capricious, tyrannical power.

13. Generalizations: The Disintegration of Empires

A MODEL OF EMPIRE

The essence of empire lies in the coercive dominance of one people by another in a territorially structured relationship. The conquest of a contiguous nation and its incorporation as a distinct outlying province, subordinate to the central government of the conquering power, express the process and pattern in elemental form. Even so simple a model of empire contains a geographic complexity that needs to be made explicit, however, for in addition to the bipartite division of conquering state and conquered province, each of these has its basic areal parts.

It is useful to recognize within the aggressive imperial state itself a *capital*, a *core*, and a *domain*. The *capital* is the seat of authority, principal locus of the elite, and focus of communications. The *core* is the secure and productive area sustaining that headquarters, the most densely populated, intensively developed, thoroughly integrated portion of the state; its common patterns of culture are considered representative of the society's norms, its routine allegiance essential to the survival of the government. The *domain* refers to the remaining area dominated by the same general people as that of the core, but this area is less densely settled, less intensively developed, less closely bound to the power and influence of the center; domains lie farther afield and may have once been quite distinct and separate— they are outlying provinces now integral parts of the central state but displaying important variations from normative patterns, areas of different geographic character, and strong localisms, with perhaps ethnic minorities resisting acculturation.

Similarly, in the conquered territory we must recognize the *provincial capital*, the local headquarters or "beachhead" of imperial authority, and a hinterland or umland, which may also contain important geopolitical differentiations. Three kinds of imperial territories are most common: 1) *areas of conquered people under direct rule* of alien imperial officials (the simplest form of imperialism); 2) *areas colonized* by migrants from the conquering state (those literal "colonies" created by "planting"); 3) *marginal areas under indirect rule*, that is, areas allowed to remain under native authorities who have acknowledged their ultimate subordinance to the imperial power (areas often called *protectorates*, from the reciprocal support

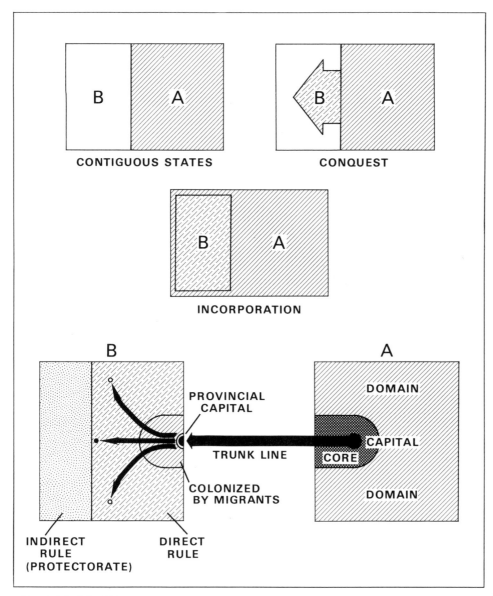

64. A Model of Empire.

promised by the imperial ruler). The trunk line of empire is the link between the capitals of the two parts; the essential bond is the ability of the imperial government to deploy its power over the imperial province; and the subordinate position of that province exposes it to penetration by agents, institutions, colonists, and influences from the dominant society. The capital and other points and areas affected by such penetrations become in some degree bicultural localities in which the political inequalities of the two peoples are reflected in social stratification and segregation.

We may add to these simple geographic patterns some common concerns and tendencies within imperial structures, those pertaining to conquerors and those pertaining to the conquered. The most basic concern of an imperial administration is the integrity of the overall structure, which ultimately rests upon military supremacy, upon the ability to apply force when and where necessary to maintain order and to hold the parts together. A general tendency of imperial government is to seek uniformity of administration, a bureaucratic pressure toward a single standard pattern in all those relationships basic to imperial objectives. There will be a strong tendency to impose the conqueror's laws, courts, revenue systems, concepts of property, and most basic of all, language, the insistence on use of the conqueror's tongue as the standard medium and symbol of empire. Thus there will be pressures toward conformity and acculturation to achieve what the ruling power regards as an appropriate level of integration of the imperial province with the imperial center.

We may assume that the most basic concerns of the conquered people are to survive and to preserve their cultural integrity and as large a degree of political autonomy as possible (perhaps, but not necessarily, looking toward eventual independence). A general tendency in the imperial province, therefore, is to resist change, to alter local ways of life as little as possible. Such resistance will tend to be uneven in kind, because some pressures for change are easier to resist than others; and it will tend to be uneven among people, because some members of the conquered population will see personal advantage in responding to change. Such persons may cooperate with and adapt to the imperial authority and culture so as to obtain for themselves greater security, wealth, skills, or status. It is in the interest of the imperial power to seek the support and the active participation of such persons as agents of imperial administration. Thus there will develop a bilingual, increasingly acculturated cadre of persons, concentrated mainly in the provincial capital, who serve as basic links between conqueror and conquered.

Of course in some cases successful conquest may be a testimony not only of superior force but of a more complex and sophisticated culture. Affiliation with such an imperial core culture may be perceived by some members of the conquered population as advantageous not just for themselves but for their native society, as a means toward an enlarged, richer, more satisfying future. If such attitudes are widespread, acculturation will tend to lead to assimilation. Even in such circumstances, however, there will be resistance to overcome; the more common pattern within imperial structures is one of chronic tension between the forces of change and the forces of resistance to change. "The difficulty of striking a satisfactory and enduring balance between central authority and peripheral autonomy is such as to verge on an impossibility." Nevertheless, after the early stages of conquest and incorporation such forces tend to come into fragile balance, allowing the empire to function without serious internal disruption, whatever the long-term direction of change may be.

As multicultural, bipartite territorial structures, empires, by their very nature, are potentially vulnerable to disintegration. Given the basic antithetical interests and tendencies of the two parts, any marked alteration in the balance of forces may bring the system under stress. An unusual pressure upon the subordinate people will tend to produce more intense resistance; a strong challenge to the prerogatives of the ruling power will likely evoke a coercive response. Such stress may be resolved by crushing the resistance, or by yielding to it on such terms as to establish a new working relationship between the peoples and parts of the empire. But imperial authorities will generally resist such a redefinition of relationships because it may appear as an admission of weakness. Because empires rest ultimately upon force, there is a natural fear that compromise in the face of one challenge will encourage further challenges, leading to progressive loosening and eventual disintegration. This tendency to resist compromise and to react with force poses a vital threat to the challengers, who will therefore attempt to pressure the provincial population into a unified opposition. Thus an imperial system under stress tends to generate extremism on either side.

The outcome of any such threat to the integrity of an empire is obviously affected by many factors. Much depends upon scale and context, upon the relative sizes of populations and resources of the adversaries and upon the larger geopolitical circumstances of the empire. Because we are primarily concerned with a particular case we shall give attention to a particular kind of imperial disintegration, that is, successful revolt initiated in some part of the periphery. We may note in passing two other kinds of disintegration: collapse from within because the center has become so enfeebled as to be unable to serve or to deploy force upon outlying provinces; and dismemberment upon defeat by a rival external power. In any case, because empires are a patchwork they tend to come apart along the seams; that is, because they are geopolitical structures in which the captive, subordinate peoples have territorial identity as outlying provinces each with its own capital city, such units provide the framework of successor states.

The victorious revolt of an imperial periphery brings into focus two interdependent topics: the effective mobilization of forces within the periphery and the ineffective application of imperial coercion against that rebellion. The first calls attention to the common fact that in any mature empire revolt is most likely to be initiated and led by those in the periphery who are most familiar with the imperial system. Those who know the language and understand the social and political institutions, those who have had their horizons broadened by participation in the larger imperial society, those, in other words, who have become acculturated to a considerable extent are the ones most likely to dream larger dreams, recognize opportunities, and rally a provincial population toward secession. In such ways does imperialism beget nationalism; cadres trained in the tools of empire turn them to the dismemberment of empire. Geographically this means that revolt is likely to begin and to be based in the provincial capital area more than in the margins of empire; therefore, the most critical point in an imperial system is the provincial terminus of the trunk line.

In any revolt of a periphery against the center, distance becomes a major factor. Distance is not to be measured simply in miles, but in time and costs, in reaction time to directives from the center, in the need to delegate authority to imperial officials operating in the provinces, in the inevitable disparity in perceptions between center and periphery as to problems and needs, issues and opportunities. The pertinence of this principle was put to Parliament by Edmund Burke in a famous speech on the American problem:

> Three thousand miles of ocean lie between you and them. No contrivance can prevent the effect of this distance in weakening government. Seas roll, and months pass, between the order and the execution; and the want of a speedy explanation of a single point is enought to defeat a whole system. . . . In large bodies, the circulation of power must be less vigorous at the extremeties. Nature has said it. The Turk cannot govern Egypt, and Arabia, and Curdistan, as he governs Thrace; nor has he the same dominion in Crimea and Algiers, which he has at Brusa and Smyrna. . . . The Sultan gets such obedience as he can. He governs with a looser rein, that he may govern at all. . . . This is the immutable condition, the eternal law, of extensive and detached empire.

In this the specific geography of empire becomes critical: the patterns of populations and resources, the trunk lines and networks of circulation, the points of strategic control. An imperial government must seek to develop a logistical system for the efficient application of force to any point of possible stress; a successful revolt must interrupt that system or make its use so costly as to be unworthy of support. Military forces and the logistical system place a costly burden on empire and thus tend to be held to a minimum. Heavy stress at a major point may cause withdrawal of forces from and loss of control over less valued parts of the periphery. Open warfare impels decisions as to allegiance and prompts a sorting and redistribution of populations seeking the protection of the side with which they have aligned. Rebel control of centers and countrysides not only interrupts connections with the imperial state but tends to undo acculturation, for the provincial culture is now seen as the model and imperial influences a taint; if the imperial power is one of great cultural prestige the rebellious leadership at least seeks control over contacts and over the processes and degree of culture change. Such movements intensify the formation of the core of the emergent successor state.

THE PATTERN OF THE BRITISH EMPIRE

Such a basic model helps make clear what a complex and unusual structure the British empire was in the late eighteenth century, even if we focus on only the North Atlantic portion of that far-flung system. A basic feature, so often overlooked, is that the British empire was a centuries-old growth whose earliest patterns were forged by the aggressive expansion of the English against the other peoples of the British Isles. Wreford Watson has summarized this expansion:

> Stage by stage, the seizure of the continental coign of Britain, the mastery of its interlocking plains, the encirclement of the uplands, the use of the Atlantic approaches, and the integration of all these around the great node of London, saw the rise of a centralising power in the British Isles that came to link and cement together most of its parts, making something distinctive out of Britain as a whole.

This aggressive, integrative movement proceeded apace with the creation of a vast new American extension of empire. By the 1760s the British Atlantic World might best be seen as consisting of two major sectors separated by an ocean but bound to a common center and imperial core. Although greatly different in geographic scale, these sectors were not so different in population and developed resources and in the complexity of their imperial character.

Thus the British Isles themselves were a complicated imperial realm, with half a dozen major parts bound to the densely developed English core. Wales was a fully incorporated province under heavy pressures of acculturation. Lacking a single center and core of its own, Wales had yielded grudgingly to English power. Its laws and administration had been brought into conformity, and its borderlands had been heavily penetrated by the English and English influences, but the main body of Wales and its people tenaciously resisted full anglicization and their ethnic identity was still apparent. In contrast, Scotland was a major province with a highly developed capital and core. The Scots had been repeatedly defeated in battles but never directly conquered, and by several stages they had become junior partners in empire. In the Union of 1707 they had given up much of their political autonomy, partly in return for full access to personal and commercial opportunities in the imperial system (and it was their vigorous pursuit of those opportunities that

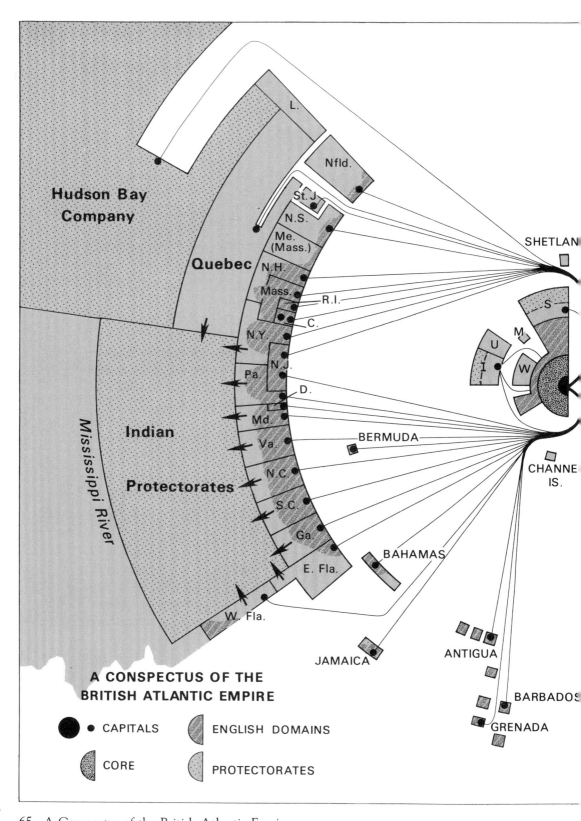

65. A Conspectus of the British Atlantic Empire.
The initials in the British Isles denote London, Scotland, Wales, Isle of Man, Ulster, and Ireland.

made it increasingly common and appropriate to speak of a "British" rather than "English" empire). The ambiguity of Scotland within that system was apparent in the fact that the Scots retained a deep sense of ethnic identity, their own religion, and a large measure of their own institutions, and yet had made Edinburgh a rival of London as an intellectual center of the English-speaking world. Furthermore, Scotland itself was a province still strongly divided in language and society between the Anglo-Scottish Lowlands and the Gaelic Highlands. The latter, long a violent frontier of empire, only recently quelled by force of arms and exile of captives, was still considered a turbulent periphery.

In Ireland the complexities of empire were even greater, with all three types of areas of our imperial model apparent in various gradations. Technically Ireland was a separate kingdom with its own Parliament at Dublin, but despite retention of some Irish institutions, it was under English and Anglo-Irish rule backed by imperial force. Dublin, the southern ports, and a hinterland rather larger than the old Pale formed the core of a dominant Anglo-Irish society that exerted powerful pressures of acculturation. Ulster was the very archetype of an imperial "plantation" from which many of the conquered people had been expelled; most of the land had been confiscated and given to English proprietors, who had colonized it with new tenants, mostly from nearby Scotland. The west of Ireland, more remote and less attractive in resources, was still densely Irish and Catholic, a people resistant to anglicization or any thought of being British. Some portions were essentially protectorates under native rulers, but all of it was demonstrably under the ultimate control of coercive imperial force. Ireland, in fact, exhibited all the patterns, concerns, and tendencies of our model of empire. Even without adding the Isle of Man and the Channel Islands, both ancient suzerainties of the king with separate legislatures and many distinctions in institutions and language (French in the Channel Islands), the complexity of this archipelagic base of the empire is manifest, and it helps put the American sector in clearer perspective.

We can readily recognize some of the same categories of imperial provinces on the other side of the Atlantic. The simplest kind, conquered peoples in a separate province under direct imperial rule, can be found in Quebec. Here English was imposed as the official tongue, but after initial intentions of fostering closer conformity to English ways, the Quebec Act explicitly recognized local language, religion, laws, and customs; moreover, the influx of British merchants and colonists was so small and geographically confined as to have relatively little cultural influence upon this French Canadian province. Very different was the fate of other colonies seized from European rivals. The Acadian returnees of Nova Scotia and the French creoles of West Florida were soon minorities within their old provinces as British colonization followed hard upon conquest. The fading strength and visibility of the Hudson Valley Dutch as an ethnic group bespoke a century of benign acculturation following imperial transfer.

The transappalachian interior was essentially a vast protectorate established by assertions of imperial force followed by treaties recognizing the cultural integrity and political autonomy of the various Indian nations, with the imperial power represented by a few officials, garrisons, and commercial agents. A variation of this sequence and pattern was to be found in the Hudson's Bay Company territories where the Indians had never been sufficient in numbers or organization to resist encroachment and had generally regarded British commercial expansion as to their advantage.

Most prominent, of course, was a third type of imperial province, that in which conquest was followed by colonization to such an extent that the native population was reduced to impotence. The colonists had originally been drawn, and were still arriving, from the eastern sector of the empire, and at times and in some cases more heavily from the imperial provinces of Scotland and Ireland (especially Ulster) than from the English core culture. There had been many additions from the European continent, but such migrations were not a peculiarity of the American sector. Many of these people had come by way of London and the core, where some of their compatriots had stayed behind, and others had settled in imperial provinces nearby: there were Huguenots and Palatines in Ireland as well as America, offshoots of the same exodus. It was such migrations as well as those of countless predecessors that prompted Watson to speak of Britain as "Europe's first America": "[Britain] was the beckoning frontier, it was the second chance, it was the last refuge to hundreds and thousands of adventurers, homesteaders, and refugees from Europe over hundreds and indeed thousands of years." It probably takes a Scot with a long experience in both sides of this Atlantic World so readily to liken Britain with America in such terms. If we add to his characterization just a bit more stress on the coercive force involved in some of these migrations and pioneerings, from Romans, Saxons, Danes, and Normans in Britain itself and from their descendants in America, we might gain a better sense of parallels and continuities in this British Atlantic empire. Certainly during the crisis of empire those arguing a case for a particular policy often drew upon their versions of such parallels between provinces in these two sectors.

We may therefore envision this British empire as two great sectors of concentric patterns, a radiating set of provinces—anchored on a single point—ringing much of the North Atlantic. Such a conspectus also illuminates some major differences between the western and eastern sectors that were significant to the disintegration of this imperial complex.

A critical difference was the fact that except for recent acquisitions most of the American colonies were actually cultural *domains* of England. For all their diversity of peoples, they were in origin (except for New York and parts of New Jersey) specifically *English* in sponsorship and institutions, and they had evolved under the dominant influence of English culture. Their diverse charters and local governments were simply regional variations characteristic of domains, not essentially different from those found in Durham or Lancashire or Devon or other outlying areas of England itself. Yet they were governed as imperial provinces; unlike Durham, Lancashire, or Devon they had no representation in Parliament nor direct access to all the agencies of the English government. Like Ireland each had a local parliament, and these American parliaments were similar to that of Ireland in that the unassimilated conquered people, the Indians like the Roman Catholic Irish, had no representation. But because the Indians in the seaboard colonies had been broken and reduced to such impotence, these provinces were no longer considered imperial in that basic sense. They were now English colonies, extensions of the homeland rather than areas of conquest, and thereby had been allowed a larger measure of local freedom than had Ireland, where the local government was itself a device to foster acculturation and expand English control over the Irish. Benjamin Franklin and other English Pennsylvanians may have thought that similar pressures for acculturation should be exerted on their German neighbors but those Germans were fellow colonists and citizens, not a conquered and captive population.

A second difference was the fact that many of the American mainland colonies bordered on a vast imperial protectorate that they considered an obvious frontier for expansion. Ten of the seventeen continental colonies had direct access to that western interior and two others (Massachusetts and Connecticut) had charter claims to swaths across it. There was some parallel here with the outer provinces of the British Isles wherein the Scottish Highlands and the west of Ireland were possible areas for colonization and development, but the enormous differences in scale and potential were critical. In America these borders lay in backcountry, distant from provincial capitals and difficult to control. Furthermore, such borders could not be regarded in the colonies as anything but temporary. Their current position was in most cases the result of conquest, expulsion, and colonization, and the attitudes and actions of American officials and common citizens alike gave every indication that such local imperialism continued to have great power. The tropical island colonies had no such frontiers for expansion. The mountainous Cockpit section of Jamaica was in effect a protectorate following the treaty ending bush warfare with the Maroons in 1738, but it contained no land fit for colonization. British West Indian planters seeking new areas could only look to the subtropical mainland of North America or hope for the conquest or treaty cession of the larger Spanish islands as a result of further European warfare.

Perhaps the most obvious difference between the two sectors was the sheer distance from the imperial center: the three thousand miles of rolling seas separating London from its American provinces, which Burke so eloquently emphasized. Communications across the Atlantic took at least four weeks and not uncommonly twice that long or more, and thus exchange between London officials and provincial governors rarely took less than four months, often half a year or more. But we must remember that time is relative, to be measured by possibilities and expectations appropriate to the routines of the day. Such response times were very good in comparison with common imperial operations of the eighteenth century, for North America was the closest of the transoceanic imperial realms. Much more significant was the separation in experience and outlook. Ireland was an overseas colony, too, but by sheer proximity it was much better known by London officials. Several important ministers of Parliament in the 1760s had served in Ireland, some as lord-lieutenant or viceroy, but none had ever lived in America (although some had investments there). Most high imperial officials were sojourners who spent only part of the year in Dublin, whereas an increasing number of American officers, including a few governors, were American-born. Such was the case in part because the American colonies were extensions of the English domain rather than conquered provinces; their citizens were unquestionably British in every political sense, whereas in Ireland questions of allegiance were ever present. And so distance was a factor in the great degree of local self-government in America as well as in the very limited acquaintance of imperial leaders with the local issues and perspectives of such governments. Of course distance was a factor in the cultural divergence between America and the mother country, but the implications of that for the operation of the imperial system must not be exaggerated. Ireland and Scotland were in many ways more deeply different from England than were most of the British American colonies. Americans entered into rebellion insisting that they were good British citizens defending fundamental principles of English polity against the tyranny of the imperial government. Their interpretations of those principles did in fact reflect a divergence, but one in which distance was only an elementary part of a complex process.

Another obvious feature of the American imperial sector was its great size, its division into so many separate provinces, and the many trunk lines between the imperial capital and the provincial capitals. Such geopolitical realities became important when the system was brought under stress. Here, too, we must not overemphasize distance as a problem. The British military system could send a formidable force across the sea to Boston as it had to Belfast many years before; if it had been required to deal only with Massachusetts there is little reason to think that it might not have eventually gotten the capital and core of that province under pretty firm imperial control. The critical feature of the North American sector was that for all their regional differences, the British colonies from Maine to

Georgia had enough in common to make possible a concerted revolt and thereby not only greatly magnify the scale of opposition but multiply the points that would have to be captured and occupied to suppress it. Not every colony had an obvious core (take, for example, North Carolina), and presumably not every capital would have had to have been seized to reestablish British dominance over the American sector, but population and resources were so widely distributed over so lengthy a seaboard that there was no obvious strategic focus for the suppression of rebellion. To move against the capital and core of key provinces in each region would necessarily be very costly. The particular geopolitical structure of the American sector made it intrinsically a difficult kind of empire to control.

THE PROCESS OF DISINTEGRATION

Viewed against the basic model of empire, the famous convulsion and disintegration of 1775–81 appears to be a fairly typical sequence. Of course, such historical processes are not inexorable; we may assume that bold shifts in policy might have interrupted the sequence and altered the result, but these would have been more anomalous than the actual course of events. Similarly, in this broader view, attempts to assess the relative blame of London and the colonies for such a bloody resolution of their disagreements do not seem to be particularly pertinent, for once set in motion the process has a certain symmetry in which center and periphery are locked together in an incremental action-reaction dynamic.

It is clear that the process of disintegration was impelled by the attempt of the center to rationalize the imperial system, and those policies reflected the pressures common to this kind of geopolitical structure (though long subdued in this particular empire) toward closer integration in the interests of efficiency and conformity. Such an abrupt alteration in the relationships between center and periphery inevitably created stress since the imperial provinces followed their inherent self-interest to resist change and to preserve as much political autonomy as possible. Resistance in the periphery was met with coercive force because imperial leaders were deeply convinced that "the constitutional authority of this Kingdom over its colonies must be vindicated and its laws obeyed throughout the whole empire." To do otherwise, the colonial secretary went on to say in 1774, would threaten "not only its dignity and reputation, but its power nay its very existence . . . ; for should those ideals of independence . . . once take root, that relation between this Kingdom and its colonies, which is the bond of peace and power, will soon cease to exist and destruction must follow disunion." In this, too, there was nothing exceptional. As the center marshaled its forces to crush the rebellion, leaders in the periphery worked frantically to broaden and strengthen resistance; that is to say, they pressured the provincial populations toward conformity with

the rebel cause and the many colonies toward a common and coordinated response. Under such stress, "the sense of superiority and the snobbery that underlay
all the theory" of imperial relationships gave a rasping edge to the rhetoric on both
sides. Thus as one side talked endlessly about "our possessions," "our subjects,"
and "the children of the Mother Country," the other talked ever more shrilly
about the arrogance and corruption of a tyrannous government bent on reducing
them to vassals or slaves. And so the process impelled the contestants into extreme
positions.

Overt rebellion was initiated primarily by a cadre of people in the provincial
capital of Boston, the terminus of one of the several important trunk lines of
empire. As in the model case, such persons were thoroughly familiar with the
imperial system and culture. There were no keener students of English political
history and philosophy than these New England rebels. They were rooted in a
colonial society that from its beginnings had focused much of its intellectual and
emotional energies precisely on issues concerning the legitimation of authority and
proper relationships among individuals, congregations, and the larger polity.
Their knowledge of English ways allowed them to argue cogently how these new
imperial policies and attitudes contradicted basic principles of the ruling society
itself. Thus did they draw upon the ideas and examples of the imperial core culture
to formulate a rationale for the disintegration of that empire and the creation of
something better in its place.

The direct application of imperial military power against a provincial center, at
Boston, dramatically exposed and accelerated the cultural differentiation between
center and periphery. Once a substantial number of Americans began to see
themselves as a people subordinated by force within an imperial structure, their
determination to resist that force gave them a common sense of identity as well as
purpose. Cadres in other colonies were rapidly augmented, splitting the colonial
establishment between a rebel elite and loyalist elite. Forced demonstrations of
allegiance and the uprooting and resorting of peoples began to spread throughout
the continental empire.

The initial seat of rebellion was readily accessible to imperial power projected
along the London-Halifax axis, with the garrisons and depots of Ireland, the
principal problem area in the European sector of the empire, poised along the way.
But once it became clear that the rebellious colony could not be subdued merely by
control of its capital city and ports, and, further, that rebellion was far from being
confined to one colony or one region, the particular geographical complexity and
character of the North American sector put the imperial military system under
enormous strain. The shift to New York City was an obvious move, for that point
was the nearest thing to a strategic center for control of the continent. But the
nature of the rebellion combined with the geography of empire to limit the signifi-

cance of that center or even of a set of such provincial centers. General deploy-
ment of British forces over much of the seaboard axis of population and commerce
between Newport and Philadelphia failed to curb the revolt. British control of the
urban centers could not cripple the Americans because the basic subsistence of the
colonial population was not absolutely dependent upon the services of those
capitals and entrepôts. On the other hand, the revolt had wide enough support to
make American areas unreliable sources of supplies for the imperial forces. Even in
the New York area repeated forays in search of such basic needs as hay and
livestock and firewood both revealed the problem and exacerbated it, for such
"foraging operations were never gentle affairs" and they deeply antagonized local
populations. The British armies were therefore critically dependent upon transatlantic shipments for almost every need and thus the logistic lines of empire were
put under unprecedented strain. Furthermore, the sheer size and depth and undomesticated character of America, the crude state of roads and waterways, the
absence of bridges and ferries, all made the movement of large forces difficult and
expensive. Under such circumstances responsible officials tend to become cautious
and conservative, and campaigns become ponderous, intermittent, and irresolute.

In contrast, these conditions greatly favored guerrilla activity, at which the
Americans became increasingly adept. At home in the environment, sustained by
the countryside, skilled with axe and rifle, they could harass outposts, routeways,
and the flanks of imperial forces almost at will. They could also terrorize the people
of any locality not directly protected by the British army. Thus the British were
faced with the problem of conquering and holding and policing large territories.
But this was an extremely costly and uncertain task to which they never committed
themselves. As one of the king's German generals complained, the land was "too
large, and there are too many people. The more land we win, the weaker our army
gets in the field." Rather than expand, they tended to withdraw from some areas in
order to concentrate their power on localities considered more important to a
particular strategy. But such a policy, routine in the standard European wars of
maneuver between opposing armies, was disastrous in a civil conflict, for it meant
the abandonment of loyalists and neutralists in those areas, leaving them open to
the intimidation and revenge of the rebel populace. Once it became clear that the
center could not be relied upon to protect those substantial populations in the
periphery that supported its basic objective of holding the empire together, it
became quite certain that the empire would come apart.

As it became increasingly apparent to the center that it could not hold the
entire periphery at a reasonable cost, there followed a succession of strategies
designed to hold on to the most valuable parts. The abandonment of most of New
England was followed by the withdrawal from Pennsylvania and the Delaware
Valley, the reluctant loss of Georgia and Carolina, and finally the surrender of

Virginia and New York City, saving the West Indies and the Great Fishery. Canada remained in the system more by the will of its people, by their preference for autonomy within the empire over association in a republic, than by its high importance to the British empire. Such a pattern accorded with the theory of empire then dominant as well as the realities of the war, wherein those colonies producing obviously profitable export staples not in competition with the imperial core were valued far above settler colonies in the middle latitudes. Thus as some losses became certain there were proposals to hold on to (or recapture where necessary) Nova Scotia, Canada, Staten Island, Manhattan, Long Island, Norfolk, and coastal South Carolina and Georgia as a means of securing to Britain "all the trade of America which was worth having" and at much less burden than before. Securing these commercial areas was not an unreasonable military proposition at the time, but it did not draw sufficient political support in the midst of the disintegration. In the end this empire came apart along the seams, along the boundaries of preexisting territorial units, wherever such geopolitical fracture lines were firmly incised on the ground (as they were along the seaboard but not in the Indian protectorates), rather than being carved into new parts through the retention of imperial military footholds as some proposed.

Despite strong moral as well as strategic arguments in favor of retaining Florida, which had remained loyal and was already the refuge of thousands of loyalist exiles, it was sacrificed in order to retain Gibraltar, which was deemed to be of far greater importance to the security of Britain itself. And essentially the same was true of the whole of America. Ultimately the greatest importance of the distance between America and Britain was that it made the American sector less critical to the security of the British capital and core than the provinces in the British Isles and the bases and allies on the European continent. All through the deepening crisis British leaders repeatedly expressed their fear that loss of the American colonies would weaken and expose England itself to grave danger from her imperial rivals, but they came reluctantly to believe, or simply felt forced to take the risk, that such transatlantic areas could be given up without disastrous geopolitical consequences. It would be more than a century and a half before English leaders could, reluctantly and in the midst of another ugly war involving rebels and loyalists, admit the same about adjacent Ireland (and had the ocean been far narrower it is reasonable to assume that the rebellion of the 1770s would not have been confined to the American sector alone but would have enflamed the British archipelago; the Continental Congress sent an appeal to the Irish people for help and got a sympathetic if not directly effective response).

We may summarize by saying that the disintegration of this particular empire began with the government's failure to appreciate the divergence that had long been developing between the center and the periphery; that it could not be halted because the center never understood what it was up against in that periphery; and that it was accepted when and on the terms it was because the government decided that the loss of even so large a portion of that distant periphery would not be crippling to the center and core of a continuing imperial system. If the general process itself was far from new in history, there were basic features of the particular case that had at the time no obvious precedent, as Mackesy has noted: "In the American War there first appeared the fearful spectacle of a nation in arms. . . . A revolutionary struggle which involved an armed insurgent population was unique in the memory of the age." And here the stress must be on the emergence of a "nation" out of this "revolutionary struggle," for it was the first such case to arise in the Neo-European world. For well over two hundred years European seafaring, conquering, and planting had been creating a new macrocultural realm in the Americas and a few other parts of the globe. In British North America, in contrast to Latin America, there had been no significant fusion of conquerors and con-quered, and no significant residue of native populations on the seaboard colonies; therefore, these parts of the empire were essentially extensions of the homeland, overseas *domains,* in the culturo-geographic sense of that term. Hence the re-bellion of the 1770s did not arise as an ethnic protest against a foreign ruler, as in the most common imperial disintegrations, but as a civil war over the treatment of overseas "Englishmen." The mutation of this civil strife into a national war of liberation—transforming those Englishmen into Americans—was something that the rebels had not planned and that the imperial government did not understand until this "long, dirty war" drew to a close and both were confronted with the reality of and the problems of coping with a brand new nation.

14. Generalizations: The Problems of Federations

Federalism is a means of coping with geopolitical diversity. The essence of federalism is the binding together of several distinct geopolitical entities whilst preserving the basic integrity of those entities. It is a device for being united without becoming unitary. In a federal state two sovereignties coexist over the same territory, each with respect to specified realms of authority, and this allows the coexistence of dual allegiances in the citizens of that territory.

Logically a federal structure might be created by a process of "devolution", by a reduction of the authority of the central government and an empowerment of constituent regional governments—a degree of disintegration. But the great his-torical examples of successful federation were created by acts of controlled integra-tion, by agreement among several geopolitical units to join together to form a new larger complex. Such a sacrifice of some measure of local independence to a central and encompassing authority is most likely to be taken at a time of crisis as being essential for survival in a threatening world.

The United States of America became the greatest, most famous exhibit of federalism and its characteristics and experience have, more than any other case, influenced general discussions of the topic. Our concern here is not with the intricate structure of the American government but only with a few very fundamental geographic issues apparent in the formation and first trials of this particular case of this most fundamentally geographic of political types.

The most basic problem inherent in all federal states is how to allocate power between the central government and the member units. James Bryce put the matter forthrightly in his famous assessment, written as the American commonwealth was completing its first century:

> The problem which all federalized nations have to solve is how to secure an efficient central government and preserve national unity, while allowing free scope for the diversities, and free play to the authorities, of the members of the federation. It is, to adopt that favorite astronomical metaphor which no American panegyrist of the Constitution omits, to keep the centrifugal and centripetal forces in equilibrium, so neither the planet States shall fly off into space, nor the sun of the Central government draw them into its consuming fires.

The American union found itself immediately in difficulty on this basic matter and only resolved it by a complete redefinition of the terms of agreement. The replacement of the Articles of Confederation with the Constitution markedly increased the substance and power of the central government, giving it authority over external and interstate affairs and the power to generate the resources to carry out those duties and in general to support the common welfare. Federal executive and judicial branches were created alongside a restructured legislature.

The enlarged cluster of central institutions magnified the pressures to resolve the question of where to seat the federal government. The selection of a capital city, always a momentous decision, is likely to be especially contentious in an incipient federation wherein there is no obviously dominating member or city. However limited the scale and power of the central government may be, it has inherent symbolic as well as economic and experiential significance and is a geographic prize likely to excite intense regional jealousies. Theoretically, the problem is not necessarily a matter of selecting one place over all others, for it is possible to have capital functions shared among two or more places, either in some rotation (as, in effect, had been the case with the Continental Congress), or by assigning the different branches of government to different places (as was later done in South Africa). Despite a widespread sense of interregional stress within the American federation, apparently neither of these alternatives was considered.

There had been considerable despair in the last years of the confederation over holding the union together, and the alternative most commonly anticipated was three regional confederations (New England, Middle, Southern), but this pattern of thinking apparently did not lead to proposals to disperse the federal government of the thirteen in some such regional manner. In the early stages of constitutional design one of the delegates in Philadelphia argued strenuously for a plural executive, with one member to be drawn from each of these three main groups of states, but his concern was more to guard against a too-powerful executive than to appease regional interests; the idea gathered no support.

The conditions set forth to guide the selection of a location for the federal capital were unexceptional. It was implicit that centrality and accessibility were to be interpreted with reference to the constituent members of the federation, that is to say, in terms of the settled regions of Atlantic America. *Centrality* applied to the whole national territory would have called for a location on the middle Ohio rather than the Potomac. The provision of a separate federal district for the capital city was an obvious means of denying the prize to any one state and it simplified the matter of territorial jurisdiction. It also implicitly sustained another condition generally supported at the time, for in practical terms it meant that such a federal area would not include an existing urban center (for presumably no state would give up a major city). Recent history in America had provided ample reason for political theorists to argue the need to insulate government from the pressures of special interests and, especially, from intimidation by mobs. Hence the separation of the political center from leading commercial centers was accepted as a basic geopolitical principle. All in all, despite the intense political maneuvering over several years, the selection of a capital site did not put alarming strain on the federation. The choice of the Potomac reflected a balance of power between north and south calculated in terms of a whole set of issues, and the site seemed sufficiently central, accessible, and neutral to serve the new federation reasonably well for the time being.

A second basic problem inherent in federations is how to allocate power among unequal member units. In any complex union there are likely to be important differences in numbers of people, wealth, area, and geographic position, the last two having some bearing upon prospects and interests. How to recognize these variations without compromising the intrinsic equality of each unit as a freely associated member is likely to be a formidable challenge. Under the Articles of Confederation the United States was a union of political equals; each member state had one vote. Such an association asserted the sovereignty of each unit and its integrity as a full, functioning political society, whatever its size or history. But the confederation proved to be little more than a league of friendship among broadly similar states in support of uncertain long-term goals. It became clear to those who desired a more effective, integrated union that they must find a way to bring relative political power into closer concordance with the relative contribution of each member state to the population and wealth of the whole.

The inequalities among the thirteen units, the great geopolitical legacy of empire, were well appreciated even if inexactly known. Only crude estimates of populations and partial measures of wealth were available, but these were quite sufficient to support common categorizations. Everyone understood that Virginia was the largest and most populous state and would remain so even after the Kentucky counties were cut loose to form a new state. That in itself was not alarming, for the magnitude of Virginia did not overbalance the rest; unlike Holland in the Dutch confederacy (a common example of the time), it did not violate the principle of federal stability (as enunciated later by John Stuart Mill) that "there should not be one State so much more powerful than the rest as to be capable of vying in strength with many (or all) of them combined. If there be such a one and only one, it will insist on being the master of the joint deliberations." Virginians did take the lead at Philadelphia in insisting on some sort of proportionate representation, but opponents pointed not to Virginia alone but to the great disparity between the three largest states (Virginia, Pennsylvania, Massachusetts) and those that were both small in population and prospects (Delaware, Rhode Island, and, to a lesser extent, New Jersey; Georgia was small in population but understood to be large in potential). Spokesmen for the small states repeatedly insisted that they would "never accede to a plan that would introduce an inequality and lay 10 states at the mercy of Va. Massts. and Penna." Attempts to assuage such fears called attention to the actual human geography of Atlantic America. It was emphasized that these three large states lay separated from one another, each in a different region with its own kind of society and economy, and therefore they could have no common interest upon which to combine against the rest. Quite the contrary, experience demonstrated that "rivalships were much more frequent than coalitions" among preeminent states. There was some general recognition of the fact that a federation of thirteen or more members might be less endangered from internal stress than a union of only a few, for it would provide more flexibility, more room for political bargaining on special issues and less need to adhere to fixed groupings in order to survive. Common interests would produce regional alignments but it might be hoped that these would not be so rigid and confrontational as to put the whole structure under chronic strain.

The problem of inequalities among the states was sufficiently vexing to the delegates at Philadelphia as to produce a suggestion "that a map of the U.S. be spread out, that all existing boundaries be erased, and that a new partition of the whole be made into 13 equal parts." The idea was put forth in a complicated debate but it was not considered preposterous. Benjamin Franklin stated that he found the proposition an "equitable one."

> I should, for my own part, not be against such a measure, if it might be found practicable. . . . Small states are more easily well & happily governed than large ones. If therefore in such an equal division, it should be found necessary to diminish Pennsylvania, I should not be adverse to the giving a part of it to N. Jersey, and another to Delaware.

But he noted that such changes could only be done with "considerable difficulties," and the balance attained would soon be upset by further inequalities in population growth; therefore, he did not regard it as an effective solution.

The very idea of so reconstituting the member units was a radical concept that went to the heart of the question of what kind of political creature the United States was or should be. In this view states were little more than administrative conveniences, a scale of government intermediate between local and national, mere "districts of people" within one great political society. States were to be shaped by the central government to serve the larger interest. Such a view conflicted totally with the idea, and the fact, that these thirteen states were preexisting sovereignties, each a full political society rooted in time and place; as "free and independent states" they had created the federation and they had done so to serve *their* mutual interests, not to dissolve their identities within a powerful new unit. There were obviously deep differences of opinion on these matters in Philadelphia and, as attested by the ratification debates, in the country at large, and this tension between nation and federation was necessarily built into the system. The United States was formed as a federation of dual sovereignties; delegates did find a way to resolve the deadlock over the allocation of power to member states. If there was never much likelihood of any significant reshaping of the founding states (although there was talk of subduing and dividing a recalcitrant Rhode Island between Massachusetts and Connecticut), it was certain that the shaping of new states would be a recurrent general issue as the western half of the country was colonized.

In the debates at Philadelphia common assertions of the magnitude of difference in populations between the largest (Virginia) and smallest (Delaware) states varied from 16 to 1 to 13 to 1. The initial allocation of seats in the House of Representatives reduced this difference to 10 to 1, but the census of 1790 produced a ratio of 19 to 1, which became the basis for representation after the first reapportionment. There were numerous other shifts in relative weight at this time, with a few substantial gains (most notably, besides Virginia, North Carolina), and losses (e.g., Georgia, Delaware, South Carolina), but the full order of adjusted numbers of representatives (1, 2, 2, 4, 5, 6, 7, 8, 10, 10, 13, 14, 19) displayed what a relatively even gradation in size and voting power there was in this federation. More important, perhaps, was the fact that in this first reapportionment the ratios of the commonly accepted regional groupings of the original thirteen remained unchanged, with New England having about twenty-six percent of the seats, the middle states twenty-nine percent, and the southern forty-five percent. The very idea of regular reapportionment was radical democratic sense. Federations of this general kind, being particularly balanced combinations of unequal units laboriously negotiated at a historic moment, are peculiarly vulnerable to the stresses of geographic changes in population and wealth. To have so simple a method of keeping relative political power in half of the federal congress so closely conformed to the relative population of the member states gave the United States a self-adjusting quality of incalculable importance.

By the time of that first reapportionment there were actually fifteen states; the addition of Vermont and Kentucky, and soon thereafter Tennessee, began to modify those basic regional proportions, and indeed the adequacy of this old threefold division. Here as well, the United States had established certain principles and procedures to regularize the handling of an inherently difficult and fundamentally important geopolitical matter. How to enlarge a federation, how to cope with external geographic expansion must be a delicate and possibly perilous problem for this type of structure, for any such alteration must ramify through the whole, affecting existing patterns of relationships and balances of power. Vermont, for example, was but a small wedge in the national territory but it was thoroughly Yankee in people and added two senators and two representatives to the New England alignment.

It was a problem that could be anticipated since the United States began with half its territory as yet politically unorganized. The principle of enlargement of the federation through the accretion of units fully equal and alike in basic political powers was formalized as early as 1780, but, like virtually everything else, it became a topic of debate in the Constitutional Convention. Gouverneur Morris of Pennsylvania pushed hard "to secure to the Atlantic States a prevalence in the National Councils." Morris was one among many who saw the main object of government to be the protection of "property," that is, the provision of order, a basic stability and security to society. Morris worried that the new states would have less concern for the general interest and that their expansionism might get the federation involved in wars, the burden of which would fall on the Atlantic states. Such an argument was yet another expression of the idea that the thirteen original states were sovereign historic societies whose qualities and experience could never be duplicated in the new settlements taking shape in the transmontane West. Morris's argument sprang from the struggle to work out a basis for representation and came before the idea of dual forms in a bicameral legislature was presented, but the still-fresh experience of empire and the very principles of the Revolution could be called up against any such attempt to build a permanent inequality of parts into the federal system. Those settlers in the western lands were Americans, it was pointed out, the vanguard of our own people who deserve the same opportunities for freedom and self-government as those in the founding states. To discriminate against them in such a way would be to reconstitute the empire, subjugating American citizens to distant and unresponsive rule.

The Ordinance of 1787 defined a standard procedure for the formation of republican states under the supervision of the central government. However, Vermont and Kentucky were directly admitted without prior territorial status. Tennessee was the first to go through the process, and that very rapidly, but there had been a number of abortive starts and irregularities in Tennessee's case, so that the territorial system of state-formation can hardly be said to have been tested and regularized as yet. That would have to come in the huge Territory Northwest of the River Ohio and in the broad swath of lands lying west of Georgia. And there was much yet to be tested that was not spelled out in the ordinance. Basic procedures as to the institutions of government were defined, but portentous geopolitical decisions remained to be decided case by case: how to carve these huge areas into appropriate units for federation. What sizes, shapes, types of boundaries, positions with reference to major geographical features should they have? Some general ideas and precedents were at hand, but they were hardly sure guides. Vermont was not a useful reference, for it was a remnant defined by preexisting boundaries. Nor were Kentucky and Tennessee obvious models. These new units were simply the western halves of the old sea-to-sea claims of Virginia and North Carolina, respectively, and such elongated strips stretching over four hundred miles across diverse country were at considerable variance from general ideas then current about the kind of compact, coherent territories best suited for a democratic republic. The discussions relating to Jefferson's committee on the "Western Territory" in 1784 dealt extensively with the topic. Rough sketches displaying Jefferson's plan showed tiers of states two degrees of latitude wide fitted into the general framework of the West in the simplest geometric form. In correspondence on the matter he argued for states of no larger than about 30,000 square miles ("not quite as large as Pennsylvania") as being appropriate to the character of American society. It was generally agreed that new states should be of "moderate" size, but the concept was open to broad interpretation. The admission of more Delawares and Rhode Islands was clearly out of the question, and, at the other extreme, the severance of their western territories had been, in part, a recognition by Virginia and North Carolina that these constituted more area than could feasibly operate under a single democratic government. Kentucky and Tennessee could in fact be taken as "moderate" in size, being somewhat smaller than Pennsylvania and New York and considerably smaller than their parent states. On the other hand, they were 10,000 to 12,000 square miles larger than Jefferson's recommendation (his plan showed two states in the area of Tennessee and one and a half in that of Kentucky), and whereas he had parceled the area north of the Ohio into eight and a half units, the Ordinance of 1787 stipulated that at least three but no more than five states should be formed in that expanse. Jefferson protested such a change as a dangerous one, in that it appeared to serve the interest of the "Maritime" states over that of the "Ultramontane" ones and would cause resentment and possibly revolt and secession on the part of the latter. All that was speculation but the matter of size and therefore numbers was clearly fundamental. The maximum of five new states in the Northwest Territory and another two in the lands west of Georgia added to Kentucky and Tennessee would make a total of nine new western states. Adding Vermont and an eventual Maine (the only eligible "maritime" area left) would make eleven new states alongside the original thirteen. The prospect of such numbers as these could not but cause a good deal of unease about the future character and survival of the federation.

And of course there was more to it than just numbers of new states, for their particular sizes and shapes would affect economic and cultural patterns in the developing nation. Jefferson wanted to serve Western interests equitably so as to insure their allegiance to the union, but he also had Virginia's interests very much in mind, arguing for the voluntary cession of its Western lands so that it might thereby define the separation line to Virginia's advantage by retaining the Great Kanawha river and valley as a critical passageway for commerce. Jefferson's geometry for the West was not accepted, no general pattern for the anticipated formation of states was defined, and the eventual character of the federation could hardly be foreseen. If it might be argued that these new western states would not develop as discrete cultures in the same sense as had those drived from the British colonies of the seventeenth century, that was not to say that they would be no more than arbitrary territorial segments of "American" culture. Each new state would perforce develop its own social character based upon the influx of particular peoples in particular proportions and distributed in some distinctive pattern in relation to its particular economy, with its own set of commercial centers and links with adjacent and distant regions. Each new state would have its special interests, and in support of these would look to some members of the union more than to others. The impact of each addition had to be read in how its human geography related to the complex regional geography of the United States as a whole, and indeed to the larger North American context, for Maine would surely be interested in the Great Fishery, new western states in Mississippi navigation, and new southern states in relations with the Floridas. Such divergences in interests constitute centrifugal forces that must be countered by careful balancing and strength of commitment to the center. One might expect attempts to maintain some symmetry in the admission of new states relating to the different regional groupings. In this sense it might be advantageous for a federation to be able in some degree to program its expansion through the admission of many new members rather than having to adjust to the accretion of only one or a few.

The problem of how to integrate disparate peoples, a problem often handled in federations by recognition of special territorial status, was avoided, ignored, or temporized by the United States. Had French Canada joined the original union, as provided for in Article 11 of the Confederation, that issue would have had to have been faced very directly. And so it would should such areas be purchased or conquered; Gouverneur Morris, reflecting upon the structure designed at Philadelphia, confided in a letter that "I always thought that, when we should acquire Canada and Louisiana, it would be proper to govern them as provinces, and allow them no voice in our councils." But the Revolution had not led to the accretion or conquest of non-English-speaking colonies, nor had it created any obvious territorial bloc of political dissidents, for the most resolute opponents had taken refuge beyond the bounds of the new republic, causing the British to add new geopolitical units to its empire in Upper Canada and New Brunswick.

Indians dominated nearly half the territory of the United States but had no stable position or prospect in the federation. The central government assumed jurisdiction over all that area and over relations with its people. Treaties recognized in effect that

> The Indians were *resident* "foreign" nations. . . . The North American continent was their homeland. It was a problem for which the nationalism of a new country had no solution. With its exclusive claims to sovereignty and territorial control, nationalism did not even provide a vocabulary suitable for discussion of the problem. There was no conceptual category for resident "foreigners" who did not think of themselves as clients of the United States, much less as dependents, and who showed no signs of wanting to become a part of the new American nation.

Through warfare and various negotiations a line of separation between Indians and Whites from Lake Erie to Florida was established in the 1790s, but there was no American expectation that Indian tribal areas should endure as geopolitical entities. Responsibility for Indian affairs was assigned to the War Department, and although it was federal policy to stop encroachment on unceded Indian territories, it was assumed that such land would, under formal treaties, eventually be ceded to the central government for disposal to White settlers. There had been glimmers of the idea of an Indian state, but no more than that. A 1778 treaty with the Delaware Indians negotiated at Fort Pitt stipulated that they and associated friendly tribes might, with congressional approval, enter the confederacy as a state, but that was a military expediency that never came close to a test. Nor did McGillivray's offer of 1787 to form an Indian state or territory based on the Creek Confederacy, an attempt to stem Georgia's expansionism. Such gestures could not be taken seriously because it was clear that in general Americans regarded Indians as enemies and encumbrances. The only long-term geopolitical accommodation Indians were likely to be given was on display in the tiny reserves of tribal remnants scattered about the Atlantic seaboard.

The other obviously disparate people, the Blacks, by the very nature of their distribution and status could not warrant special federal territorial provisions for themselves, but their presence as slaves in some units of the federation put a grave stress on this federal design from its inception. The division was becoming starkly regional, for by 1786 all states from Pennsylvania northward (except New Jersey) had either abolished or made provision for the gradual abolition of slavery over a specified term of years. National abolition was too dangerous a topic to bear decisive discussion at Philadelphia. The slave trade could only be halted twenty years hence, and proportional representation was resolved only through an utterly artificial formula. Such avoidances, postponements, and compromises indicated that despite the intricate structure that emerged out of all that brilliant debate and negotiation, this federation was a precarious patchwork of regions. That was all it could be at the time, for that was all the human geography and the human feelings bound into that geography would allow.

Like most federations, the United States was an expedient developed under duress. Having bound themselves together to fight their way out of an empire, these former colonies felt it imperative to stay together to keep free of other empires and to prevent chaos from erupting among themselves. That some of their leaders envisioned something utterly new and grand, a polity and society more effectively promoting human happiness than any heretofore conceived, was also apparent but not as yet particularly convincing, for it was too soon to know how well the design created at Philadelphia might serve. And in fact it remained unclear just what had been created, for that elaborate set of offices and powers and checks and balances incorporated so many ideas, so many shades of meaning, so many compromises that it lay open to widely varying interpretations. As one modern student of those proceedings concluded, there was true consensus only on one principle, that of "duality articulated in a single constitutional system of two distinct governments, national and state, each acting in its own right, each acting directly on individuals, and each qualified master of a limited domain of action. . . . All else was controversial presumption, inference and supposition." The United States was certainly, fundamentally, a federation, and a very remarkable one of many parts, already expanding its membership and programmed for further expansion. But that only emphasizes what an uncertain creation it was: complex, asymmetrical, incomplete, unstable—and grandiose in scale and pretension. If federalism by its very nature involves duality, compromise, and delicate balances among the territorial parts, the need to cope with so much more internal geopolitical change would surely keep this new structure under heavy stress for some years ahead.

15. Generalizations: Nation-building

The essence of a nation is a state of mind amongst a large number of persons by which they see themselves as a people in the most fundamental sense of being bound together by a common heritage and set apart from all other peoples; to that identity they give their highest emotional loyalty. The Constitution of 1789 defined a nation as well as a federation, a union of people as well as a union of states. The basic concept of dual sovereignty acting directly upon individuals required of every citizen an allegiance to something single, unitary, overarching all the units of the federation. Thereby all the peoples in the several states were also joined together as *a* people, as "Americans."

The actual basis for such bonding together is highly varied among nations. Nationalism can be contrived from whatever characteristics and experience may be available. Every nation claims a heritage but it need not be deep-rooted nor grounded very firmly in the facts of history, and every nation asserts its special character but this may be derived from any number of things. Hans Kohn interpreted the case of the United States:

> The new nation was clearly not based upon common descent or upon a common religion and it was not separated by its own language or its literary or legal traditions from the nation from which it wished to differentiate itself. It was born in a common effort, in a fight for political rights, for individual liberty and tolerance,—English rights and traditions but now raised into inalienable rights of every man, universalized as a hope and message for the whole of mankind. . . . What held the new nation together was an idea, the idea of liberty under law as expressed in the Constitution.

In giving the United States a national government and a national idea the Founding Fathers had not so much invented a nation (as they had a federation) as completed one, or rather completed the foundation of one. For with the ratification of the Constitution the geopolitical movement that had irrupted in Atlantic America such a few years before had been carried into the third stage of a sequence we now regard as typical of nationalism: 1) the initial stirrings of self-awareness and a sense of grievance, 2) the struggle for independence, and 3) the consolidation, purification, and reinforcement of the emergent nation. The emergence of so many nations over the past two hundred years, indeed the redefinition of the entire world order primarily in terms of national units, has stimulated considerable attention to "nation-building" as a general process. Such formulations have necessarily a strong geographic dimension. A nation fully realized becomes a nation-state and a nation-state fully realized encompasses the national homeland, the area actually occupied by that particular body of people or claimed as an essential part of the national heritage. Furthermore, nation-building is an internal process of areal integration. As one major theoretician has put it, the politics of nationalism involves the development of "the economic, intellectual, and military resources of a population, . . . [knitting] them together in an ever tighter network of communications and complementarity based on an ever broader and more thorough participation of the masses of the populace."

Those first stirrings of national feeling typically arise in particular localities and tend to create fields of activity that come into focus and crystallize in some area of special advantage within the larger geopolitical context. That area forms the geographical nucleus of the incipient nation. It is the principal seat of its leadership, the intelligence center and main focus of the communications network, and the main source of manpower and resources marshaled in the nation-building effort. The principle of location theory that "initial location advantages at a critical stage of change become magnified in the course of development" may be applied to such geopolitical situations. Having taken the lead in the popular effort, such areas attract talent and capital from outlying areas, which in turn reinforce that lead: being the seat of the leaders tends to make this nuclear area (as a delegate from outlying Georgia complained in 1787) "a vortex for every thing."

In this nuclear area, or core, the earliest mobilization of the general population in support of the national ideals and objectives takes place, and from this area such activity spreads into other regions. Such expansion and intensification are carried out by small groups of political activists (usually labeled "elites" in the model case) in a pattern of hierarchical diffusion, that is, from the main center in the core to outlying provincial centers, and in any one region from the main center to lesser centers and outward to the countryside. There may of course be impediments to that process: special resistances and selectivities, arising from regional differences and relative locations, may result in lags and lower intensities of participation. Center-periphery, heartland-hinterland, core-domain relationships—and tensions—are part of the generic structure of every nation of considerable size or complexity. Such nations will be subdivided into administrative areas, and these may represent preexisting geopolitical units relating to a particular group of people or tributary to a particular city, or they may be more arbitrary divisions created by the national authority for its own administrative convenience. There will of course be an outer limit to this diffusion of the national ideal and mobilization of people in its support. At some point local populations will be encountered who steadfastly refuse to give willing allegiance to the nationalism being promoted. In the model case the national boundaries should coincide with such barriers to that diffusion; in historical cases it is more common to find nations extending their boundaries as far as they have the coercive power to do so.

In geographic terms we may summarize by saying that every nation seeks to become a sovereign state, to develop and maintain a high degree of areal integration of the national territory, and to protect that territory from all undesirable external influences. In historical terms we may note that the simplest test of such integrity is whether the people of all parts of the nation stick together under stress.

To think of the American Revolution in terms of spatial diffusion and areal integration is to reduce the agonies of civil war to bloodless abstractions. To speak of such times as a phase of "creative turbulence" in which there is a breaking of old patterns and the forming of new is to impose a euphemism on agonizing, deadly disagreements over issues, methods, and objectives. But the very concept "American nationalism" binds the particular to the general and invites a broader view. From such a perspective the United States, despite its size and complexities, shows extensive concordance with this simple model of nation-building. It had, of course, the incalculable advantage of being able to ennoble its side of a bloody civil war with a powerful ideal and translate its own struggle for independence into a symbolic effort for all mankind. Basic to the success of that nationalizing experience was a common culture that was at once obviously English and latently American. As the movement for independence gathered momentum the common Englishness emphasized in the opening phases of the dispute gave way to a newly articulated Americanness, a discovery and emphasis and idealization of cultural differences that had actually been developing ever since Englishmen had begun to create an Atlantic America. Thus, as is usually the case, national independence and national integration were concurrent and interdependent movements, although they were not of equal velocity, for the latter was far from complete at the achievement of the former.

The most remarkable aspect of this particular case is that the creation of an American people and an integrated state was not impeded by the variety of peoples who continued to characterize this population. Of course, some ethnic differences had been eroded and self-identities altered by the experiences of living in America. More important, perhaps, was the fact that the national ideals of individual liberty and tolerance for all transcended such differences; indeed, they could be interpreted as formulas for pluralism. While there may have been in fact an ethnic factor in some local conflicts during the tumultuous course of the Revolution, which may explain the presence of particular bodies of Scots or Germans or others among the loyalists, such people were not excluded by the terms or emphasis of American nationalism. And it was of immense importance that there was no overt religious dimension to this national movement. The Church of England came under attack because of its political status as an official institution of the imperial power and it was badly mauled in the conflict, but American nationalism was in principle inclusive rather than selective of religious groups.

However, despite these transcending ideals and inclusive principles, we may assume that the integration of an American nation would have been more difficult had this ethnoreligious variety been patterned in large territorial blocs rather than scattered over the seaboard in an uneven but detailed mosaic of localities and districts. Having failed to lure or conquer or negotiate French Canada, the fledgling nation had to deal with no non-English state; if some German groups consciously resisted acculturation they did so as small minorities with no prospect of formal geopolitical recognition. Thus for all its remarkable diversity, the human geography of this portion of British America did not hinder the formation of a national state.

But these broad patterns were merely potentials for nation-building. The rapid mobilization of so many people over so broad an area was made possible not just by common characteristics but by extensive networks of contact already in place. Through intercolonial travel, transactions, and correspondence, from summering in Newport or Boston, wintering in Bermuda or Charleston, through sojourns in England or Scotland on business or in school, seminary, or law courts, through membership in fraternal or philosophical societies, by tightly knit associations of blood and belief (Puritan, Quaker, or Jewish), in one way or another or indeed in several ways together, the leading people in every important business and profession—merchants and shippers, industrialists and investors, lawyers and politicians, clergyman, doctors, scientists, teachers, publishers, artists, and musicians—knew others of their kind within the whole British Atlantic world. How readily such relationships could be harnessed to the work of nationalism was demonstrated in the first committees of correspondence of 1765, which bound together leaders of like mind in every mainland colony and several of the islands. Informal networks intensified with the mounting crisis, and the move in 1773 to formalize the links among the colonial legislatures, with the directive that each of these would in turn establish connections with every county or town, was the very model for the mobilization process.

Such rallying was more readily accomplished in some areas than in others. The almost instantaneous appearance of more than 15,000 armed men around Boston in the aftermath of Lexington and Concord was an expression not only of a well-developed militia system but of the density of networks long in place in this homogeneous regional society. Most areas were far less cohesive and responsive.

The ideas of resistance to British authority, independence for the colonies, and the formation of an American nation spread in various forms and mixtures throughout the British Atlantic world. There were sympathizers everywhere, including England, active agents in most of the colonies, but effective positive response only in some. Viewed as a diffusion process American nationalism ran into a virtually impenetrable barrier in French Canada, made only slight headway into the Floridas, and found Nova Scotia, Bermuda, and the Bahamas more permeable but was ultimately resisted by the majority of the people in each case. Within the rebel colonies nationalism also encountered varied resistance but became powerful enough to dislodge and expel the most stalwart opponents, the loyalists, and to surround and swamp, as it were, the rest. Clearly not all of the population of the new United States had been mobilized into effective support of the idea of an American nation, but those who opposed independence yet remained within its bounds were effectively quelled. Just what the balance of their loyalties to the union and to their own state should be might remain uncertain, but commitment to some form and scale of American nationalism was no longer debatable, for, once triumphant, nationalism demands allegiance.

The American case displays a geographical dynamic typical of the formative stages of nationalism. Overt violence against British authority broke out at many points along the seaboard between Falmouth and Norfolk and as far afield as St. Kitts, and the idea of regularizing intercolonial resistance sprang up simultaneously in several colonies. Political action networks were initiated from Boston, Newport, Providence, New York City, and Charleston; under the Sons of Liberty organization these were quickly connected, extended, and bound into primary focus on New York City. An important center in the imperial system, New York City had been a major base for operations and supplies in the war against France in the 1750s and continued thereafter to grow as a focus of shipping and a center of commercial and political intelligence. That role expanded with the developing crisis, but the strength of British officials and loyalists in the city and its hinterland made it an increasingly dangerous place for American revolutionaries. The Continental Congress convened in Philadelphia, on safer and still central ground. The British domination of New York City for most of the war was a major impediment to American operations. A minimal national network was patched together from parts torn from larger British Atlantic circuits, such as the postal system and coastal shipping, supplemented by expedients formed amidst the shifting fortunes and foci of war. Despite the density of specialized contacts among individuals, the direct intercolonial infrastructure was very thin. The imperial system had always operated as a multitudinous set of transatlantic connections, so there was no substantial bureaucracy or facilities for direct interaction among the seaboard colonies that could be subverted or imitated. The desperate efforts to sustain an army shifting about between the Hudson and the Delaware, to supply the essential needs of regional populations, to improve communications within and between the colonies, to bring leaders together for periodic conference—all these contributed to the nation-building process, and all these fields of wartime activity were brought into primary focus on one small area.

The new nation took shape around a nuclear area anchored on Philadelphia and New York City. The former, now just a hundred years old, the largest in size and long the main ornament of urban America, had embellished its preeminence as a commercial and cultural center with its recent political role, giving it a name famous in the world and secure in the heritage of the new nation. But New York City was the most vigorously developing center in America and indeed in the Atlantic World. Its intrinsic qualities were demonstrated in how quickly it recovered from the great loyalist exodus that momentarily halved its population and disrupted so much of its life. Within months its famous Chamber of Commerce and other institutions were reconstituted and invigorated. Exodus was followed by influx, including many persons of wealth and talent, from New England and New Jersey, from Philadelphia itself, from Britain, and especially from Ireland, from Germany, France, and the West Indies. By 1800 its growth rate and total commerce exceeded that of Philadelphia.

New York City was a compelling exhibit of the "urban crucible," of cities as centers of economic, social, and political change. The revolutionary era had brought an unprecedented turbulence to civic life in all the major seaports, which ramified through all levels of society and radiated through the hinterlands. Mass meetings and mob actions were vivid momentary displays of a radical mobilization process; less obvious were the breaking down of traditional ways, the challenge to entrenched interests, the scramble for position in the changing order, the sheer energy released by the glimpse of new opportunities. What was especially important about New York City, and to a great extent Philadelphia as well, was that in these cities such changes clearly constituted a mobilization for *national* life, with relatively little concern for or consciousness of state or regional interests as such. And that was a logical development from earlier patterns. These states and this section had never had the strong identity of some others. "Middle" colonies or states referred to an obvious geographic position rather than to an obvious culture region; the label lumped together states with similar types of societies—pluralistic, complex—but could not refer to a single society. But it was now becoming apparent that *middle* could be translated to mean "central within a system, nodal, nuclear." New York City and Philadelphia thrived on their interaction; each drew daily upon the trade and talent of three states in its immediate hinterland and thereby bound together a belt of country extending from the Susquehanna and Head of Elk (tapping the Chesapeake) to the lower Connecticut Valley. That

66. Financial Focus, New York.
This well-known painting by Francis Guy exhibits the commercial vitality and intensity of New York City at the end of the century. The scene is focused on the corner of Wall and Water streets; the view covers the block from the East River docks to the new Tontine Coffee House on the left. The Tontine, built in 1792, was the most important amongst a cluster of coffeehouses serving the busy area. It housed the Stock Exchange and major insurance offices and was a principal meeting place of merchants and traders. As John Kouwenhoven has noted, Guy's paintings, done in 1798 or 1799, "marked an important change in ways of looking at the city. For the first time the bustle of human activity in the streets was as interesting as the buildings themselves." (Courtesy of the New-York Historical Society)

functional area, taking shape well before but compounded and crystallized out of the fields of activity generated during the birth of the United States, was clearly the incipient core of the nation.

Such delineations are geographical abstractions designed to summarize and illuminate some basic features of national life. It will be noted that the nuclear area thus defined does not include the full length of the Baltimore-Boston axis nor all of the most intensively developed part of the new nation as described before. That is because such extensions reach into areas rather distinct and divergent from the Philadelphia–New York City nucleus. Boston was the hub of a very self-conscious region. New Englanders were heavily involved in nation-building and were knitting themselves ever more closely into New York, city and state. Yet in national

GEOGRAPHICAL MORPHOLOGY OF A NATION

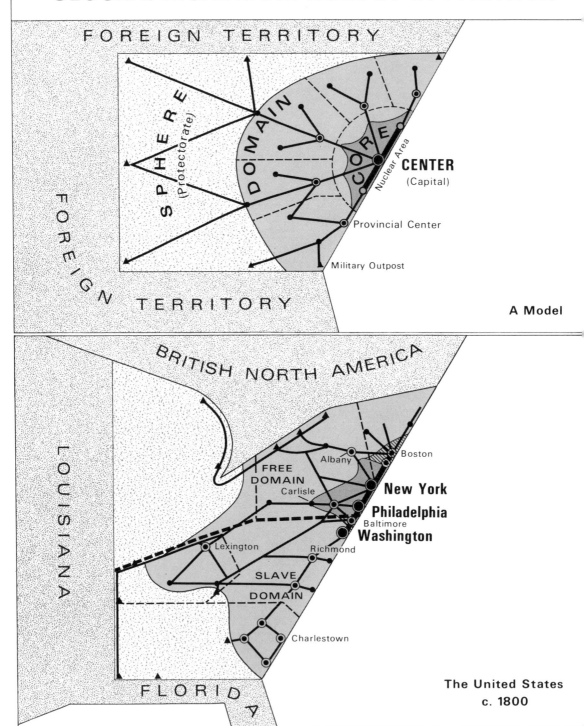

67. Geographical Morphology of a Nation.

deliberations they tended to speak with a clear sense of their own regional interests. The reality of New England as a geopolitical bloc was often asserted; the
possibility of it as a separate confederation remained latent; and its position within
the new nation was eccentric and contingent. Baltimore was itself a more ambiguous case: a burgeoning seaport in many ways similar to and competitive with
Philadelphia. But it lay south of the Mason-Dixon Line and faced the world
through the Chesapeake, and that bound it into a critically different context.
Maryland was historically part of Greater Virginia and a slave state and was
therefore southern in a sense that had taken on an importance greatly magnified in
a union of states in which half were to be "free" and half "slave." It was in this that
the variety of peoples within the American people impinged most directly upon
nation-building: not simply the presence of Blacks, for they were in every state, but
the presence of Black *slaves* and in great numbers. Where Black slaves had been
few their emancipation could be regarded as both desirable and feasible; where
they were many their emancipation might be considered humane and desirable, as
it was by some prominent leaders in Greater Virginia, but such persons could find
no feasible way of instituting emancipation without unacceptable risks of sociopolitical disruption. Thus while Boston and Baltimore were important centers on
the main axis of national development, they were not centers of nation-building in
quite the same way and degree as New York City and Philadelphia. New England
and the southern states were areas of strong regionalism and therefore of strong
dual allegiance committed to the building of a *federal* nation, whereas New York
City and Philadelphia commanded a nuclear area wherein statehood had faded as a
loyalty and their region was itself the center of a truly *national* structure. That
seems to be the fundamental geographical reality of this new United States,
whatever the detailed arguments and conclusions about specific political structures
and issues at various Philadelphia conventions.

This geographical view reveals a more important incongruity in the American
nation-building process: neither the nuclear area nor the longer axis of intensive
socioeconomic development touches Virginia, yet that state was much the largest
in area and population and Virginians had been the most influential leaders of the
union from the time of the first Continental Congress onward. It was of course
connected to those northern ports through Norfolk and lesser shipping points and
overland by stage from Richmond, but the intensity of interaction was low; it had
its sprinkling of forges and ironworks and flour mills but nothing to compare with
the density of industry developing along virtually every stream of any size from the
Brandywine to the Merrimack; it had a college, a few academies, societies, and
newspapers but it remained very largely a townless agrarian region little touched by
the kind of mobilization experienced in northern seaports. Virginia was reaching
westward rather than northward. Geographically its greatest contribution to na-

tion-building was the sending of tens of thousands of its citizens beyond the mountains to add a whole new domain to the American structure. But the distances and difficulties of transport precluded close integration of these western regions with their Virginian source. The Wilderness Road could not serve as a trunk line for commerce eastward to some prospering Virginian port. Prying the national capital out of Philadelphia and drawing it to the Potomac, together with the possibility of a canal from there to the Ohio, might stimulate developments so as to stretch the national axis to Virginia's northern border, but as yet this largest member of the union had little connection with the most intensive integrative processes. This eccentricity, this detachment from formative patterns, this incongruity between Virginia's great political prestige and power and its geographic position within the emerging American nation, was a sign of impending geopolitical stress.

The tentative character of all these areal patterns was evidence that the United States was no more than a nation abuilding and it was being shaped not after the design of a simple model but uniquely, experimentally, within the framework of a federation. The core of a nation was discernibly taking shape around an early nuclear area, but anchored on two cities rather than a single dominant center, and neither of these the highest-order political seat. Geographically, Washington was a conscious act of decentralization, a federal compromise rather than an integrative national focus. Beyond this incipient core lay the national domain, the remainder of the area actually colonized and controlled by American settlers. By definition such a domain was as fully American in the basic national sense as anything at the center, but except for southern New England and the Chesapeake and nearby extensions into Vermont, western New York and Pennsylvania, it was a realm barely bound to the nuclear area. In much of the southern and all of the western portions of this domain migration, colonization, community formation, and governmental organization were all in a state of flux. The shift of state capitals inland to more central locations was one important step in providing more effective focus and a means of mobilization of populations, but the human geography of all these states and the orientation of whole regions was still uncertain, and such areas were so distant and divergent from the incipient core that it was hard to discern national integration in the geographic sense of ever-tighter networks of communication and complementarity.

Beyond the margins of this domain lay the sphere of the American nation, areas claimed in this case as integral parts of the national territory but not actually dominated by an American population. By a series of congressional acts, warfare, and intimidation these huge areas had been formalized as protectorates under the authority of the central government. It was a typical colonial system, designed ostensibly to reduce friction between Americans and the other peoples whom they had caught within the broad westward cast of their political boundary, but in the longer view intended to further American penetration, control, and eventual transfer of land. It was assumed that this outlying sphere was to be reduced by orderly acquisition and colonization until it was transformed into an extension of the national domain in which Indians would be confined as minorities on small reserves. Here nation-building and imperialism merged.

But there was more to this American policy than simple expansionism. The United States was bounded by two empires, and the Indians in these protectorates were, with some reason, regarded as tools of the British or the Spanish. Hence the exertion of firm control over these frontier areas was regarded as part of the elemental need of a nation-state to protect itself. It was the difficulties of doing so that caused the United States to create a national military establishment despite strong republican fears of standing armies. This was formed in the wake of the disasters to the patchwork of militias sent against the Indians in Ohio, and its main directives following victory in that sector were to secure the Ohio-Mississippi waterway and guard the northwestern and southwestern borders against British and Spanish encroachments or machinations. This army system of the late 1790s operated out of Philadelphia as the principal depot (backed by arsenals at Carlisle, Springfield, and Harper's Ferry) along two main routes, one west to Pittsburgh and the downriver posts, the other north via Albany and west to Lake Ontario and the former British forts on the frontier of Upper Canada. Lesser tentacles reached the blockhouses in the Cherokee country and by sea and land to Fort Wilkinson and Fort Stoddert on the Creek frontiers. It was a very sparse logistical network. Congress was so niggardly that the army was always understrength and operated in makeshift fashion by purchase or hire of many of the wagons, carts, boats, and packhorses for particular expeditions. But as an instrument of the central government reaching out from the nuclear area to the farthest outposts, it transformed old trading paths into lines of coercive force and was therefore an active agency of nation-building.

A national navy was also created in haste to meet immediate danger when American shipping became victimized in the wide-ranging war at sea between Great Britain and revolutionary France. When that crisis abated in 1800 all military operations were quickly deflated but six naval dockyards, parceled among five states and the new federal capital, were in operation and army engineers were building naval fortifications to guard Atlantic America from foreign attack.

The creation of an American military establishment, belatedly, reluctantly, was a recognition by national leaders that a large position on the North American continent, an oceanic moat, and a policy of neutrality in European affairs did not in themselves secure American national interests. In the larger geopolitical view the United States was surrounded by empires; there was danger on every side. That it must be able to protect its territory against foreign intrusion was not an issue. American nationalism was a firm enough emotional bond among the people to insure that. But beyond such basic patriotism there was less certainty as to what kind of a nation the United States was or ought to be. The first congressional bill to authorize a national navy barely passed. The vote revealed a fairly clear divergence between maritime and interior constituencies, and the debate featured differences between those who favored and those who feared giving the central government greater coercive power. Here was a basic issue: nation-building involves some degree of centralization. Politicians saw this as the problem of allocation of powers among the various levels and organs of government; the geographical corollary is that nation-building involves an imbalance of power among centers and regions. Effective nationalism requires connections among all parts of the nation, networks and systems of circulation, instruments for mobilization of whole populations in support of general policies. Geographically such national integration tends to form around a nucleus, magnify a center, and bind all outlying areas into that focus; thus nationalism is centripetal and tends to generate center-periphery tensions. How much of this kind of geographical centralization was essential or desirable or indeed controllable was also debatable and of major significance to the developing state.

In 1800 the United States was certainly a nation as well as a federation but there was as much uncertainty about the one as the other as to eventual geographical shape and structure and system. At the most basic level nationalism and federalism were complementary, essential to one another; the one providing the emotional bond, the other a workable political system to hold disparate parts together. But beyond that the two were not necessarily concordant. Geographically a national core was taking shape quite at variance from the delicate balances of federalism, and national integration even at a minimal level of effectiveness must further emphasize that area in important ways. Whether the forces and facilities for such integration could overcome the centrifugal tendencies in so large and diverse a state was of current concern. George Washington mentioned the matter in his Farewell Address and urged an end to such speculation. "Let experience solve it," he said, and then went on to warn against opportunistic exaggerations of differences between "*Northern* and *Southern; Atlantic* and *Western*" as being a matter of grave danger to the "community of Interest as *one Nation.*" Clearly regionalism posed a formidable challenge to nation-building in the American case. And, as with federalism, the difficulties and uncertainties were compounded by the fact that the basic form and content of the nation was so obviously incomplete. As a nation the United States was not only large and barely integrated, but was determined to get larger, to spread an American people over the whole of the American territory, and perhaps even to extend that territory in advantageous ways, for none of its boundaries seemed to its people to be impermeable or immutable. Thus nation-building was not only a matter of joining areas together in an ever-tighter network of communications and complementarity; it was also a question of whether such national consolidation could keep pace with national expansion.

16. Generalizations: Expansionism, American-style

Whether the United States of America could survive as a coherent federal nation may have been uncertain but there could be no doubt that it had within it immense vitality. However loosely structured it may have been, it had an inner dynamic of impressive power: exhilarating, awesome, fearful, depending upon just where and what one was in relation to it. However fitfully it functioned as a whole it had momentum, it was expansive, it exerted pressure outward upon everything around it and showed no sign of being content or contained. Indeed, at times it showed little sign of being controlled from within or without.

The United States was an invention, a new design for doing certain basic tasks of society, polity, and economy. It was an unusually large and complicated creation and like most inventions it was a mixture of old parts and new, incorporating some new ideas with well-tested ways of doing things, and the whole structure was put together and its energies harnessed in such a fashion as to provide a new level of efficiency and power. This is readily apparent in any assessment of its ability and propensity to expand. Its very presence over so large a territory was of course a product of three centuries of European expansion into North America. The new state drew heavily upon those antecedents, but it also developed some new techniques and refinements and all of these things were combined and applied in such a way as to warrant recognition as a distinct American mode of geographic growth.

A basic tenet of the European thrust overseas was the claim of sovereignty over the territories of non-European peoples. Declared the moment Europeans set foot on American shores, such an assertion could have meaning only when enforceable; thus conquest was a corollary of such claim. The actual methods of such expansion varied, involving a wide array of pressures and purchases, treaties and alliances, as well as open warfare and undisciplined violence among many different groups of European and Indian peoples. Furthermore, this long and continuous history of European expansion gave rise to a rationale, a set of moral excuses for the dispossession and subordination of non-European peoples. A welter of speculations and sophistries assured Europeans that Indians, for whatever cause, were deficient compared with themselves; unchristian, uncivilized, unenlightened, they were a primitive, savage mode of mankind that in the nature of things must give way to a higher order.

The United States was a ready and willing successor to this older imperialism and set about to give it even greater force. George Washington, awaiting news of the signing of the peace treaties in 1783, set forth in a letter to a congressional committee concerned with Indian affairs the basis for a national policy. The Indians should be informed, he wrote, "that after a Contest of eight years for the Sovereignty of this Country G:Britain has ceded all of the Lands of the United States within the limits discribed by . . . the Provisional Treaty." Because the Indians had ignored American warnings and joined their fortunes with those of Britain, the United States would have every right to make them share the same fate: to be compelled to retire north of the Great Lakes (the situation in New York and the northwest was of immediate concern at the time). But he said that they should be told that the Americans are a generous people who forgive them their delusions, knowing that the Indians will now understand that "their true Interest and safety must now depend upon *our* friendship." Furthermore, they should be told that

> as the Country, is large enough to contain us all, . . . we will . . . establish a boundary line between them and us beyond which we will *endeavor* to restrain our People from Hunting or Settling, and within which they shall not come, but for the purposes of Trading, Treating, or other business unexceptionable in its nature.

Such a line, he advised, should "neither yield nor grasp at too much," but enclose enough to accommodate reasonable needs for growth. If the Indians object to the choice of boundary, they should be compensated for yielding their claims. He emphasized that "none who are acquainted with the Nature of Indian warfare, and has ever been at the trouble of estimating the expence of one" would hesitate to acknowledge the importance of peaceful negotiations for the transfer of land. Such purchases should only be made by the sovereign power, and ideally the Indian trade ought to be a monopoly of the central government as well, but if that were impractical at least "no person should be suffered to trade with the Indians without first obtaining a license, and giving security to conform to such rules and regulations as shall be prescribed; as was the case before the War."

"As was the case before the War"—the whole approach was a reiteration of the kind of order that the British had aspired to create with their Proclamation Line. And, alas for Washington's hopes, such a policy was no more workable in 1783 than it had been twenty years earlier, and for the same simple reason: neither the Indians nor the American settlers would accept such a continental program for the management of their interests. Neither party accepted that view of central sovereignty. The Indians beyond the Ohio River had never been subdued by European or American forces; some had been allies but none acknowledged having been subjects of Great Britain, and they refused to recognize the power of diplomats in Paris to give away their lands. Similarly, American settlers pressing forward in a dozen districts would not be restrained by a distant government from moving in upon any lands that seemed available for the taking. Indians were enemies to be defeated and extirpated, and if any justification were needed it was to be found in local experience of the horrors perpetrated on frontier settlers; any government that did not understand that forfeited the right to govern in the name of "the people." Thus while leaders of the United States enunciated policies of "expansion with honor" in which the Indians' right of peaceable possession was acknowledged until formally extinguished by treaty with the sovereign protecting power, the dynamics of American life resulted in bloodshed and explusion year after year in area after area. This combination of central order and local disorder, this tension between center and periphery, became a distinctive feature of American expansionism.

The pattern was established early on. In the Northwest Ordinance of 1787 Congress defined a geopolitical framework for lands the Indians would not cede and from which settlers could not be restrained. The resulting series of collisions soon produced a decisive alignment of national forces in support of the settlers and subordination of the Indians. The Treaty of Greenville in 1795 recognized the Indians as having prior rights of possession but it made clear who was the ultimate trustee of their lands. Before the large assembly gathered for the signing ceremony, an Indian leader declared: "We do now, and will henceforth, acknowledge the fifteen United States of America to be our father. . . . [We] must call them brothers no more." To which the victorious General Wayne replied: "I now adopt you all, in the name of the President of the Fifteen great Fires of America, as their children, and you are so accordingly." We are occasionally reminded that parentage is a power relationship. We may assume that children alien in race, recalcitrant in character, openly despised but adopted because they hold title to property coveted by their foster parents are more than occasionally aware of that fact.

This display of the role and power of the federal government in conquering was followed by a display in this same area of its new role in planting:

> The Northwest Ordinance of 1787 discarded many of the complexities of the common English law of property. . . . Essentially, once the national government had made the initial sale of a parcel of land, it stepped out of the picture. . . . Generally, a man could buy the land he wanted, sell what he wanted, and grant it by will, in what parts and pieces he pleased. Land had become a commodity and a productive resource privately owned and controlled, a basic part of the system known to the world as American capitalism.

American laws of property were of course rooted in English common law, but they also reflected changes arising from peculiar American experiences and conditions. The colonies had been founded during a period of rapid shift in England toward a more commercial society—indeed they were major emanations and emblems of that shift—but such changes became exaggerated and accelerated in America. Because the full institutional and cultural context could not be transplanted over-seas, all the colonies were necessarily more simple and commercial than the homeland, and those that were founded with the intention of creating more equitable societies undertook reforms in property relationships as a necessary task. Under the township system in early New England, for example, rights to sell, divide, and devise land were very near to the later American version of fee simple. Furthermore, the lack of firm control, the extraordinary looseness of and variety within the English imperial system, fostered further departures from home prac-tices and intentions: "Running a land distribution agency from 3,000 miles across the sea was at best precarious, generally ineffective, and frequently doomed to failure."

Most important of all was that great, exhilarating American feature: immense tracts of land for the taking. That it had to be taken from the Indians could be regarded as incidental, an initial task of officials and frontier militia. That ultimate right to the land was held by the king was no damper on the hopes of a wide range of persons to obtain property in amounts and at a price far beyond any possibility they could hope for in Europe. The actual problems of dealing with such lands gave rise to further changes in laws and practices, all tending toward simplification of property concepts. The first redistribution of land in Virginia, the allocation of garden plots to each man in a desperate attempt to stave off starvation, conveyed a free and simple tenure equaled by few landholders in England at the time. As the colonies developed, the chronic need for labor, the competition for immigrants, the profits to be made from land jobbing, the impossibility of close supervision and enforcement all tended toward a reduction of encumbrances on property. Despite elaborate charters and occasional energetic landlords and the unusual resistances of certain cases (such as in New York where Dutch manorial concepts had been reaffirmed by English law), many forms of entail, escheat, quitrents, and other fees, duties, restrictions, and privileges eroded under relentless pressures from powerful and widespread interests to obtain clear and simple title for a single money payment.

Most colonial companies were, or soon became, primarily land merchandising companies. Land awarded to proprietors could be subdivided and sold on shares and further divided and resold time and again in England even before the grant had actually been surveyed and located in America. Such transactions were claims to specified amounts of land rather than specific parcels of ground, a market transac-tion of speculators with no direct connection to actual development. In the longer run such land could sustain value only as there was labor to make it productive, and the headright system, granting acreage claims for the transport of persons (free, indentured, or slave) was a means of using the plenitude of land to overcome the scarcity of labor with which to work it. Despite some attempts there were no effective limits on the amount of land that could be legally held. Headrights could be accumulated, requirements for planting and seating could be avoided, "indeed the whole spirit of the colonial land policy, like the federal policy of a later date, was to allow the settler as much land as his financial position or business ability would permit." Or, one might well say, as much land as he could get hold of by whatever means. In so many of the colonies at opportune times the system was so complex and dynamic, with so few controls and so many ways of getting around laws and regulations, that land fraud was endemic. It became a widely accepted practice to search out a tract of land, assert occupancy of it in some way, and later try to work out a means of obtaining proper deeds and formal registration. Squatting and preemption, like other forms of speculation, were deeply rooted American practices.

With the Revolution state governments suddenly became possessors of vast quantities of land confiscated from the king, or loyalists, or Indians. There were great pressures to dispose of these "public lands" in some advantageous way, and new land laws and land offices were set up to do so. The most common official objectives were the quick sale of lands to raise revenues and the use of land to pay state debts, as in the grants for military service, essentially a form of headright that the grantee could sell if he wished. The national land policy was formed under similar circumstances, and engendered extensive consideration of regional practices and the national purpose. Basic differences arose from the New England preference for regularity and group purchase as opposed to the old southern tradition of individual location by metes and bounds. Various influences and compromises were incorporated into the principles of a national policy that included survey before sale, a national grid aligned on the global reticule of latitude and longitude, uniform rectangular townships six miles square, each township subdivided into thirty-six rectangular sections of one square mile, land to be sold in specified units at auction with a fixed minimum price, title to be granted in fee simple upon cash payment. There is a faint imprint of New England in the concept and scale of the township as the basic survey unit and in the reserve of section 16 in each township for the support of schools (a proposal to reserve another section in each for the support of religion was defeated). But it was all frame without substance or center. The government was not creating townships in any functional social or economic sense; it designated no square for a village or market or school (it was the income from the lease or sale of section 16 that was to be used for education, not that particular land as a site); there was no focus, no provision whatever for roads, and indeed there could be no square literally central within this particular geometry. The government was not in the business of community formation; it was in the business of peddling land and keeping a clear record of it. A rectangular system served this purpose superbly. There were ample precedents for such surveys in British America. They had been used here and there in various city designs and rural tracts from early on, and despite obvious objections regarding the indifference of such a rigid system to variations in land quality, they became more common in the eighteenth century. The formality, regularity, symmetry, divisibility of such a system made it especially attractive to the more philosophical minds of the day, and Jefferson devised one based on a new decimal system of linear measurement. But most important was the fact that a comprehensive uniform rectangular system provided a quick way to get land on the market in a mode perfect for speculation. Such absolute standardization of units, each efficiently and exactly defined and registered, made the buying and selling of land simple, safe, and fast; together with the simplified concepts of property it made land "a commodity largely separated from the social organism except by strict monetary measures."

The "social organism" was there, of course, spreading and developing by its own processes. Farms were being created, forests felled, mills erected, roads laid out, communities shaped, all by private initiative within a remarkably open system. And by this time in any of the major frontiers of the new nation such things were beginning to be done on such a scale, over so large an area at such a rapid pace, that all became suffused in speculation. Land buyers were perforce engaged in geographical prediction. No matter how astute they were in judging soils or sites they could not know just what the mature patterns of population, circulation, and economy would be. The American frontier was a vast lottery in which people bought sections and subdivisions of sections down to the size of town lots in the hope that the collection of squares they held would prove to be ones of high value. The government was involved only in the most minimal fashion: in the selection of seats for essential political courts and offices; and in the fact that land ownership was not absolute, for land could be taken by eminent domain, or in judgment against private debt, or for failure to pay taxes. All of these were empowerments of local governments elected by the people; the national government did not presume to intervene in the relationships between its citizens and their lands.

Actually the full force of this national land policy was just becoming discernible by 1800. That the initial surveys and sales in the Seven Ranges had been far slower than expected was partly due to the relative quality of those lands, partly to the competition from large private tracts just downriver, and partly to administrative difficulties in getting the system into operation. But all this was changing. The next federal tracts to be offered were in more attractive country, private competition was diminishing as those early special grants were sold, and the system could be improved. Under heavy pressure from Ohio interests there was a modest but significant shift toward making land more readily available to farmers; as a Western congressman argued, the federal government "ought not only to keep a wholesale but a retail store." In 1800 federal land was being surveyed much more rapidly and put up for sale at several convenient regional land offices in units as small as half a section (320 acres) at two dollars per acre on four years' credit. That quickened the pace of things, and as the federal government held such a huge stock of land it was obvious that its new marketing system would be basic to American expansionism for decades to come.

There was, of course, more than the prospect of profits powering this expansion. There was vigorous population growth. The thirty-five percent increase in the last decade of the century was very largely internal growth, for the turmoil in Europe and interruptions to shipping had hindered overseas immigration. In an agricultural society such growth obviously means putting more people on the land. That there was room for more in the older seaboard settlement areas was demonstrated but it would be very hard to measure just what the economic limits of such intensification might have been. Some districts, such as lowland New England, had been fairly densely settled for many years. Declining yields and increasing prices of land were common American complaints, and improvements in farming practices may not have been as readily attainable as assumed by the editors and travelers who so continually recommended them. What is certain is that the expansive pressures of the demand for new land cannot be explained by economics alone; there were powerful social pressures as well.

In an agricultural society ownership of land confers a basic dignity; the amount owned largely defines social status. The relatively ready access to land in America had long been a powerful lure to people in the land-scarce hierarchical societies of Europe. But there was something more, and peculiarly American, in this outward movement than simply the desire of land for social standing. There was the desire for escape: from political restrictions, from authority of any kind, from social strictures, from discord, debt, disappointment, failure. The restlessness of Americans, the instability of American communities, the propensity of individuals, families, small groups to pack up and head for new ground had long become a cliché of commentators on the American scene, native and foreign alike. It was evident everywhere; the possibility of such movement had become regarded as a basic right, one of the dimensions of freedom for which so many people had willingly fought. There had always been those who warned against the evils of such tendencies and tried to curb them by admonition or regulation: proprietors, governors, congressmen, ministers, leaders of many sorts who had an interest for whatever reason in social and political order, in community stability, compact settlement, controlled expansion. But even the early Puritan settlements, wherein social order and community cohesion were held to be central to the whole purpose of colonization, displayed this American response from the very first. Dissidents were expelled, and factions, schismatics, those chafing under authority and those who sought their own brand of authority moved out to start anew in another place. There was room for them to do so and conquering continued to make more. The whole society loosened as Puritan gradually turned into Yankee, and we cannot sort out in their motivations (any more than they could) the lure of new land as capital speculation from the lure of a new place as social freedom. In most other American societies the same processes of change were operating with less, often far less, resistance. Liberty, property, and mobility lay intertwined at the base of American culture.

This unsettling of society was accelerated by the Great Awakening, and subsequent evangelical movements and the most influential trends in American religion continued the momentum. These all constituted a frontal assault upon more formal institutions and hierarchies, stressing a radical individualism in the fundamentals of religious belief and practice, implanting a principle of choice that had civic as well as churchly implications. The rapid rise of the Baptists and Methodists was testimony of such tendencies. They thrived in the backcountry of every region, their farmer-preachers, circuit riders, and traveling evangelists reaching out to the unchurched, the under-served, and the restless churchman. Under these pressures the Presbyterian church, strongly committed "to a formal structure of congregations, presbyteries, and synods . . . came apart in large chunks," and these schismatic churches took on some of the characteristics of and competed in many districts with the Baptists and Methodists. By their widespread presence and their emphases upon individualism and local autonomy, these denominations were an important "Americanizing" force, and their conflicts and volatility were an integral part of that restlessness so common in the nation. The general weakness of institutions, the minimal civic order, the frailty of community were all concomitants of powerful centrifugal forces in American life. That outward spreading was in some large, if unmeasurable, degree the result of a strident individualism that had come to regard migration as a social solution, giving force to Wiebe's summation: "Differences were spread across space rather than managed within it. . . . What held Americans together was their ability to live apart."

All these centrifugal tendencies obviously generated problems for a central government. It was one of the polarities and paradoxes of the new American system: the very existence of a huge, as yet unsecured and unsettled interior made a central government necessary to the union of states, and this central authority was given exclusive power to manage the initial allocation of lands and geopolitical evolution of that area, yet it could not control the fundamental processes of development, and any effort to do so engendered fear and resentment in the people. George Washington had foreseen the problem clearly enough and had issued a warning in 1783:

> To suffer a wide extended Country to be over run with Land Jobbers, Speculators, and Monopolisers or even with scatter'd settlers, is, in my opinion, inconsistent with that wisdom and policy which our true interest dictates, or that an enlightened People ought to adopt and, besides, is pregnant of disputes both with the Savages, and among ourselves, the evils of which are easier, to be conceived than described; and for what? but to aggrandize a few avaricious Men to the prejudice of many, and the embarrassment of Government, for the People engaged in these pursuits without contributing in the smallest degree to the support of Government, or considering themselves as amenable to its Laws, will involve it by their unrestrained conduct, in inextricable perplexities, and more than probably in a great deal of Bloodshed.

His fears were soon confirmed in the Ohio Country and Cherokee lands where the efforts of the national government to halt unauthorized expansions were fruitless and there was indeed "a great deal of Bloodshed."

From the outset the United States exhibited a democratic dilemma: how to empower the people and keep government local and minimal yet have them sufficiently responsive to more general needs so as not to embarrass and endanger the whole. As a British historian has put it, "Americans needed government, but resented and attempted to thwart its operations; they had called an intensely acquisitive and increasingly capitalistic society into being, while frequently denying and disclaiming its moral consequences." That this *could* be the case was not simply because Americans were acquisitive, restless, and individualistic, but because they did not actually need the assistance and protection of the central government in their expansions into new lands. These aggressions into Indian country were often dangerous, but "the westerner in our history has always been a man with a gun," and he has been ready to use it ruthlessly against any opposition. Throughout the history of Atlantic America, conquering was mainly a folk movement; the fighting that paved the way for and protected White settlers was done by frontiersmen working in local gangs or self-appointed militias (George Washington referred to them as "a parcel of Banditti") rather than by regular military forces. That a national army was formed to conquer the Ohio Country was not a significant exception, for it was created to establish the prestige of the United States as well as to retrieve a situation that local militias would have resolved sooner (had they not deferred in some degree to the new federal government) or later (as their numbers were restored and hatreds deepened following their initial defeats). In comparative terms American expansion had "unusually low protection costs" and thereby could afford to be more egalitarian and libertarian than was the case of most settler invasions elsewhere in the world wherein armies and special frontier forces, garrisons and fortresses, and elaborate bureaucracies were a con-comitant of advance and security. If the existence of a generally armed population made such an extensive centralized superstructure unnecessary for expansion, it also made it impossible for the central government of the United States to direct and shape that expansion except in ways those armed citizens approved. On the bloody margins of this empire local interests were more influential than national interests, and expansionism ran essentially out of control despite the federal offi-cials ostensibly at the helm. Like its predecessor in London the government in Washington was faced with the dilemma that any attempt to bring the Western frontier under closer control would require such a severe braking of those forces actually driving it forward that it might create a friction so intense as to ignite and destroy the whole system.

From another perspective, however, the United States was a geopolitical unit of impressive coherence, a single body of people asserting claim to a continent. Expansion had become one of the great unifying themes and processes of American life. This new nation was suddenly, conspicuously, the great power of North America, and its spokesmen were quick to insist that it should be, was destined to be, had a moral right to be in full command of the continent. Nature had set no bounds to its geographical growth short of the Pacific shores; man had made no boundaries that need stand in the way.

There was nothing new in the assumption that political boundaries were altera-ble. The Americans had been given such a generous treaty settlement at Paris because no one there took such boundaries to be fixed for all time, or even for much time at all. Few European leaders expected the United States to survive for long as a political entity; when it disintegrated there would be reorganizations and real-locations, and the geopolitical map of North America would be redrawn, as it had been time and again with every turn of imperial fortunes. On the other hand, American leaders were determined to see not only that the United States survived but that its security be enhanced and that nothing be allowed to impede its development. From the early stages of the Revolution American security was viewed primarily in geographic terms. The conformation of the continent made Canada, Nova Scotia, Florida, and Louisiana pertinent to American strategic interests, and any reduction of European control over these areas would obviously be welcomed. All had been mentioned in the peace conference bargaining; failing to obtain them there, the new nation evolved a rationale for taking them later. By leaps of logic peculiar to American thinking, nationalism and "natural rights" were extended to include territorial rights to the North American continent: a nation conceived in liberty had a right to a homeland; in order to enjoy that liberty the people must feel secure; in order to feel secure and to enjoy the freedom to develop their territory in accordance with the "immense designs of the Deity" they must have control of all areas strategic to their homeland. Such a rationale for expansion arose from expansion itself and the frustrations of Americans in Ohio and Kentucky over foreign control of the lower Mississippi. Early assertions of a "natural right" to complete freedom of navigation on the entire trunk stream were increasingly extended to include rights of deposit and operations in Spanish territory, and on to the extreme claim, formulated by Jefferson in 1790, of a right to firm American control of the Mississippi mouth (he thought annexation of the "Island of New Orleans"—where "nature has decided" the "geography" of the issue—would suffice). It was clear that most American leaders and spokesmen simply recognized no unalterable barriers to expansion. Thomas Hutchins, official "Geographer to the United States," estimated the habitable area of North America to be three and a half million square miles and stated forthrightly: "If we want it, I warrant it will soon be ours." Canada, New Brunswick, Nova Scotia, Florida, Cuba, and Louisiana were all potential accretions, and all by "natural right." How the inhabitants of those provinces might feel about the matter was not important, and there were ready precedents for dealing with such peoples: they could withdraw to other colonies of their imperial parents, as had already happened twice in twenty years in Florida; or be uprooted and expelled, as in Acadia; or subordinated and encapsulated, as in Quebec; or suppressed and assimilated, as with the loyalists who stayed on in the new republic.

Americans read the geography of the continent in terms of their own interests, as any nation might be expected to do, but they then translated those interests into a moral claim of "natural rights" superior to those of other people and thereby gave to nationalism a new dimension and portent. By using such rhetoric promiscuously to promote their special mission to command the continent, they put the full force of nationalism behind American expansionism.

The United States was a successor to three hundred years of European imperial expansion in North America. The marks of northwest Europe—of its peoples; of commercial capitalism, its chief instrument of expansion; of a diversifying Protestantism, its great energizing sociopolitical movement—were everywhere upon it. But the United States was obviously something more than a federation of newly independent commercial colonies of Protestant Europeans, and it was expanding inward upon the continent with a powerful instrument peculiarly its own: a special fusion of capitalism, individualism, and nationalism brought into focus on a huge territory of magnetic attraction. The basic dynamics of American expansion were unprecedented. Never had so many people acting in their own private interest under conditions of great political freedom had access to such a large area of fertile lands, parceled by a simple efficient system into readily marketable units that could be bought and sold under clean rights of property to be used for family subsistence, commercial production, speculative investment, social status, community development, psychological relief, or whatever else one might desire; and never had such a wide array of private interests been further motivated by a deeply emotional corporate interest to act as a unified body of people with a mission to expand relentlessly, subordinating any other people that stood in its way. Out of an Atlantic America created by seafaring, conquering, and planting from the turbulent world of northwest Europe a new nation had emerged and was probing, conquering, and planting in its own restless, violent, creative way on a continental scale.

PART FOUR
CONTEXT:
THE UNITED STATES,
CIRCA 1800

This was the sentiment that generally struck me most forcibly, as I travelled through the states—the appearance every where of a vast outline, with much to fill up.

Henry Wansey, 1794

Prologue

It is time to pause and again ponder the broader view. The end of the eighteenth century is commonly considered an important moment in American history. Our perspective is rather different; we are not so directly concerned with new political persons, parties, and philosophies, but the same date can serve us well, for we are on the eve of dramatic new geographies following upon the sudden surprising addition of the whole of Louisiana to the American republic.

We have come into focus on the United States because it was the most remarkable European creation on this side of the Atlantic World—and because it is, quite arbitrarily, our main concern. Firmly lodged upon the continent, organized on a large scale, and embarked upon a life of its own, it had become the major force in shaping the human geography of North America. But we must resist the tendency among Americans to let their national borders become blinders, closing out all to the north and to the south, while fixing their gaze firmly toward Pacific shores. We must not lose sight of the broader North American context of national life.

And despite its aggressive, assertive political independence, the United States remained a child of Europe, still nourished from the familial hearth in important ways. We need to bring these links into focus as well and attempt some assessment. Even though we can begin to see patterns of American-ness emerging in many aspects of life, it was far from clear at the time just what the potential for genuine cultural creativity and independence might be. In 1800 America was a vigorous but rude, provincial outlier of Western civilization.

What follows is not a conclusion nor even a summation, for the story continues. We pause only to orient ourselves, to get our bearings as to the general shape of things, and to put a few more annotations on the very specialized map we are constructing of the American past.

1. The United States in North America

Three hundred years of reconnaissance and conquest had brought all of North America within the claims of imperial powers, and by 1800 the actual lineaments of the continent were rapidly being sketched in. By land and by sea, from the east, the south, and the northwest, agents of competing empires and commercial systems converged upon the rich fur resources of the rugged, rain-soaked archipelago and fiordlands of the Northwest Coast. The sudden and tense encounters there of Spanish, Russian, British, and American officials or traders marked the closure of globe-encircling networks. There was nothing new in the great distances involved in these outreaches, for European systems had nearly girdled the earth for 250 years. But the Spanish and Portuguese networks never effectively met, with Manila tied to Spain eastward via Mexico and Mação westward to Lisbon via the Indian Ocean. What was new in the 1790s, therefore, was contact, competition, connection, and, especially, the spanning of the great northern landmasses of Eurasia and America.

On the political maps of the time the United States must have appeared as the least among these participants. Although "Boston Men" were very active in Pacific trading, the nation itself was confined to a portion of eastern North America and was bordered by imperial holdings far greater in extent. However, the actual situation was rather different. British North America included half of the continent but, typical still of the English imperial mode, was a set of barely connected and disparate regional parts, which were of varied significance to the strategic interests of the secessionist republic. Americans had little to fear from the local peoples on the other side of their northern border, for the balance of population was heavily in favor of the Americans and it was they who exerted pressures outward. Geopolitical relationships were not quite so one-sided. The British hold upon Newfoundland and Nova Scotia meant that despite the vigor of New England seafaring the Northern Approaches to North America could not be secured against British naval power. In the northern entryways American independence had recreated an old pattern of imperial rivalry between the St. Lawrence and the Hudson for commercial control of the Great Lakes, and the United States was at a natural disadvantage unless it could make the Mohawk corridor an efficient trafficway. If the outright seizure of Canada seemed a tempting alternative to some American spokesmen, the acquisition of Lower Canada would surely produce acute problems of geopolitical integration. That solid French legacy in the St. Lawrence Valley was the major cultural fact facing any imperial strategy in this sector.

Farther inland the Canadians had far outdistanced the Americans. While the latter were belatedly taking over Detroit and Michilimackinac, Montreal traders

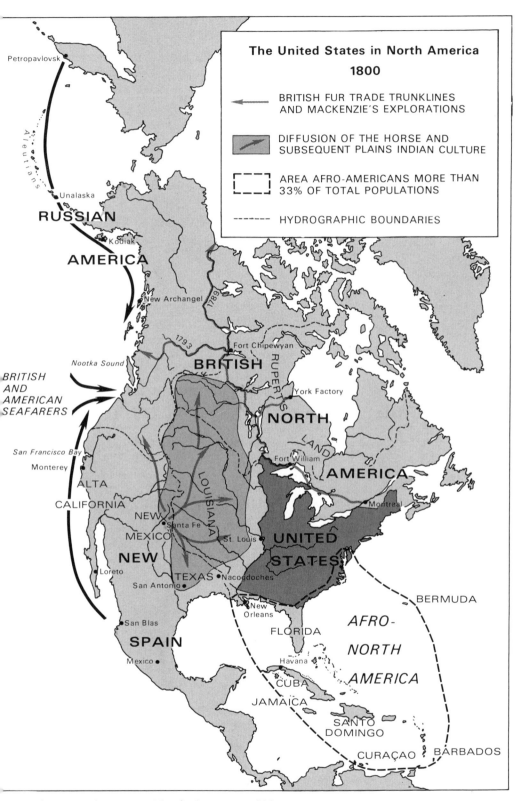

The United States in North America
1800

BRITISH FUR TRADE TRUNKLINES AND MACKENZIE'S EXPLORATIONS

DIFFUSION OF THE HORSE AND SUBSEQUENT PLAINS INDIAN CULTURE

AREA AFRO-AMERICANS MORE THAN 33% OF TOTAL POPULATIONS

HYDROGRAPHIC BOUNDARIES

Petropavlovsk

Aleutians

Unalaska

RUSSIAN

Kodiak

AMERICA

New Archangel

1789

1793

Fort Chipewyan

BRITISH

Nootka Sound

BRITISH AND AMERICAN SEAFARERS

York Factory

RUPERT'S LAND

NORTH

San Francisco Bay

Monterey

ALTA

CALIFORNIA

LOUISIANA

NEW

Santa Fe

MEXICO

St. Louis

NEW

Loreto

TEXAS

Nacogdoches

San Antonio

San Blas

New Orleans

SPAIN

FLORIDA

Mexico

Havana

CUBA

JAMAICA

Fort William

AMERICA

Montreal

UNITED

STATES

BERMUDA

AFRO-

NORTH

AMERICA

SANTO DOMINGO

CURAÇAO

BARBADOS

68. The United States in North America, 1800.

were crossing the continent. In 1789 Alexander Mackenzie of the Northwest Company followed the outflow from Lake Athabasca down to an even greater lake (Great Slave) and greater river all the way to the Arctic. The river would soon bear his name, but he called it Disappointment because it led to the Frozen Sea instead of the Pacific. And so he went off to London for an intensive study of maps extant and mapping techniques and returned to Fort Chipewyan to try again. In 1793 he ascended the Peace River, crossed the mountains, struck a south-flowing stream that proved unnavigable in that section, and, because time and supplies were running short, he turned to the west and struggled across very difficult country to finally reach the Pacific. He had not demonstrated a feasible transcontinental route but he inferred one, for he was convinced that he had been on the upper waters of the Columbia River and from that discovery a grand strategy unfolded in his mind:

> But whatever course may be taken from the Atlantic [Saskatchewan, Athabasca, or Peace], the Columbia is the line of communication from the Pacific Ocean, pointed out by nature, as it is the only navigable river in the whole extent of Vancouver's minute survey of that coast: its banks also form the first level country . . . and, consequently, the most Northern situation fit for colonization, and suitable to the residence of a civilized people. By opening this intercourse between the Atlantic and Pacific Oceans, and forming regular establishments through the interior, and at both extremes, as well as along the coasts and islands, the entire command of the fur trade of North America might be obtained, from latitude 48 North to the pole, except that portion of it which the Russians have in the Pacific. To this may be added the fishing in both seas, and the markets of the four quarters of the globe.

But the Americans were not entirely out of this picture, as the very name *Columbia* attested. In 1792 Captain Robert Gray out of Boston on his second voyage to the Northwest Coast entered and explored the estuary of a great river. As the first to "discover" the fabled "River of the West" he named it after his ship and in good European fashion formally claimed the whole territory for his nation and then returned to tell his Boston merchant backers that it would be a fine place for a major outpost. British seafarers had been the first to open trade with the Northwest a few years before, and later in 1792 Captain Vancouver extended his methodical surveys of these coastal waters to the lower Columbia, and so the British and the Americans became not only rivals for the same resources but claimants of the same ground.

But whereas the British claim to the Northwest Coast was a completion of a transcontinental empire, the American claim to the Columbia was a tenuous legal foothold in a detached enclave of unknown extent a thousand miles or more from the western borders of the United States. The whole of Louisiana intervened, a broad expanse that few Americans had even glimpsed the fringes of and into which even St. Louis traders had not as yet ventured very far. (In response to Mackenzie's feat the Spanish government offered a prize to anyone who would trace a route from the Missouri to the Pacific but no exploring party had gotten beyond the Mandan villages.) Visionary American imperialists scorned the meager Spanish hold upon Upper Louisiana as being of no consequence to the march of their empire, and they paid no attention at all to the Indians, for the rationale and the means of dealing with them had been established.

Yet the presence of the latter was much the most important geopolitical fact of life in 1800 to westward-expanding Americans. Underneath those broad colorations on the map of empires in all the country west of the Wabash and Tennessee was a shifting, complex pattern of Indian tribal territories. Furthermore, within Louisiana but as yet beyond American vision was a new kind of Indian in a very different kind of country: horse-mounted buffalo hunters on the seemingly endless, treeless plains. These were literally a new kind of Indian because they were the result of a great cultural transformation that had been taking place in continental North America simultaneous with the emergence of European Atlantic America. While Europeans were conquering and planting westward from the seacoast, the horse, first obtained by the Indians in raids and trades from the Spanish, was being diffused from tribe to tribe northward in the Great Plains, revolutionizing all economic, social, and political relations, reverberating over a great breadth of country, generating chronic instability and warfare. Initiated in the mid sixteenth century in Mexico, such changes had radiated to the northern plains by the mid eighteenth century. These two great movements had not as yet come into their most critical contact. The westward-expanding British fur trade system had made connections with horse-culture Indians in the Saskatchewan Country and had begun to bind the peoples of the open plains and those of the bordering woodlands together in support of this long tentacle of European commerce, but the inland edge of European conquering and planting still lay in the Ohio Valley several hundred miles to the east of this broad longitudinal belt of buffalo country. Thus American expansionists whose visions were continental in scope and whose far horizon lay on the Pacific could not yet bring this remarkable intervening realm into focus, and thus they could not foresee that the westward march of their empire would inevitably bring about a collision of the two peoples on a very different kind of stage in the heart of the continent.

To the Spanish Louisiana was a huge buffer, which they realized they would have increasing difficulty in sustaining against American and British encroachment; they were therefore willing to transfer it to an ally in the hope that a newly invigorated France could provide a stronger shield. Spain would thereby withdraw to its original frontier province of Texas wherein Nacogdoches stood guard at the overland entryway, although the Tejanos would be preoccupied with guarding themselves against heightened dangers from the Indians of the Great Plains. New Mexico continued in its relative isolation, still anchored on the Pueblo Indian region but now predominantly mestizo Spanish-American in population and also under heavier pressures from radically altered societies on the east (Comanches) and the west (Navahos). And New Spain had been extended in substance in another long northerly salient, partly in response to Russian advances in the North Pacific. While Russian commercial companies, having ravaged the Aleutians, were shifting eastward to Kodiak, the Spanish were creating Alta California with their age-old imperial instruments of presidio, mission, and pueblo, fixing a firm hold as far north as San Francisco Bay.

On the political map the Spanish hold extended across the southeastern corner of the continent. One might read these broad patterns as the continuing confrontation between the two great thrusts across the Atlantic, with the Iberian hold upon Florida and Texas as the essential shield of Havana and Mexico against the predatory pressures from northwest Europe, the Americans on the Georgia coast in 1800 being the latest in a succession commenced by the French Huguenot colonies 238 years before. But it was, always, a volatile and complex encounter. For a period of twenty years the Spanish had been completely ousted from this mainland coast and their present tenure was highly insecure. They had backed down before the aggressive Americans to a narrow strip in West Florida, and they were dependent there on British intermediaries. In any general view of this part of Atlantic America the appropriate stress is on the continuing, seething instability of this tropical planter world.

And here too maps of empires might display the kaleidoscopic geopolitical changes but they consistently ignored the main body of people in the area: the Afro-Americans, who had been the majority population in this tropical realm for more than two hundred years, and who numbered over a million and a quarter in the islands alone in 1800. To bring them into focus inevitably suggests a concomitant broadening of view to include the Afro-American fringes of the mainland as well. That will bring another million Black Americans to our attention and remind us that so far the creation of this Atlantic America had involved a greater transfer of people out of Africa than out of Europe. There were, of course, important differences in the proportions and geographic contexts of Blacks, between the islands and the mainland and in detail amongst the several regional societies. That there were over four times as many Whites as Blacks in North America was a general measure of the circumstances and mortalities of those transfers. By its constitutional commitment to put an end soon to the importation of slaves the United States had made a decision to alter those proportions further. That limited and controversial effort was a first small step toward resolving the blatant contradiction of 900,000 slaves in a nation dedicated to freedom and equality. Today the horrors of slavery and the slave trade are so overpowering that it may be useful to point out a truth inescapable from our historical geographic view of this Atlantic world: by severing this connection with Africa the United States was cutting itself off genetically and culturally from what had been one of the great wellsprings of American vitality.

We may also note that a truly accurate geopolitical map of 1800 would have displayed a sensational change at the very geographic heart of this Afro-American world: a de facto independent Santo Domingo under Black rule. That powerful act of revolt and resistance and revenge in what was the very first seat of Europeans in America reverberated like a drumbeat in the night, stirring up visions of horror or hope in the minds of White and Black over the whole breadth of tropical and subtropical America. To the instabilities endemic in this sector, arising from the complex rivalries of the several European imperial powers, there was now the greatly magnified possibility of contagious unrest and ultimate convulsion within the vast coercive system that Europeans had fixed upon these millions of unwilling Americans.

By 1800 North America had been encompassed and engulfed by the seafaring, conquering, and planting of Europeans. Seafarers had touched all but its most extreme icebound coasts, and the tentacles of transoceanic commercial systems reached deep inland and were on the verge of bridging the continent at its broadest. All of North America was claimed but less than half of it had actually been conquered, and there were great variations in the momentum of this vast invasion on its many different fronts. The zones of most active encounter and pressure were along the wedge of the American westward push into the Mississippi Valley, the highly destructive advance of the Russians along the Northwest Coast, and within the recent superimposition of Spanish rule upon coastal California. Elsewhere there were numerous enclaves and outposts of Europeans amidst Indian country, most of which were initially intrusive but no longer very expansive, as in Florida and Texas. Those variations were of course in part a reflection of variations in the character and success of European planting. The Spanish had long ago taken the lead and created an immense New Spain, but the power of that system to follow its conquests with substantial implantations had long since faded. In great contrast was that remarkable manifestation of two hundred years of planting out of northwest Europe wherein New World Europeans had become Americans in a fuller sense. By freeing itself from European political ties and organizing on such an extensive geopolitical scale, the United States was in a position to project conquering and planting on its own terms well beyond the solid Europeanized seaboard. Such divergence and disruption had broken some and strained other important ties within the grand circuits of the Atlantic world. But many links remained and just how and to what extent the American people, American culture, the

American scene had become something really distinctive within an expanding Western civilization was a difficult and debatable topic in 1800, as it is now.

2. The United States and Europe

The Declaration of Independence was a claim to maturity. It was an assertion that these "United Colonies" were offspring who no longer needed or desired the care and protection of their legal (and to a large degree natural) parent. Their aspiration for a "separate and equal station" among "the Powers of the earth" was not a search for isolation but for acceptance as a full member in the larger family of mature states. The fact that such a move was not accepted without a painful struggle no doubt exaggerated in the offspring a desire to achieve an independence that was more than just political, but something of that larger sense of freedom was also implied in the very idea of equality, for a degree of self-sufficiency or autonomy in certain basic realms of national life would seem to be a prerequisite for recognition as one of the "Powers of the earth." It is appropriate to our task to give some attention to the kinds of connections the United States retained with Britain and Europe and how these bear upon its "separate and equal station" in this larger sense.

A view of these matters is blurred by the turbulent conditions prevailing in the Atlantic World all through the 1790s. The wars on land and sea and the unstable relationships of the United States with Britain and France made it difficult at the time to bring into clear focus just what the "normal" long-term relationships between America and Europe would be like. There was certainly much talk about such matters, and inevitably the greatest attention was given to commercial relations, affecting as these did the daily lives and family fortunes of so many Americans, but in the larger and longer view commerce need not be of greatest concern. America was obviously rich in resources, its seamen ranged the world, and the capitalist system had proved so adventurous and adaptable that one might be confident that commerce would find its way. More important was the degree to which and how fast the United States could become a major producer of more than raw materials and foodstuff. Many saw the question to be more a matter of policy than of inherent potential. Hamilton's attempt to accelerate such developments by tariffs and incentives to nurture American manufacturing foundered in part on the strong regional differentiations already apparent, which such a program would magnify. However, despite a shortage of capital and the high cost of labor there was strong evidence that America could markedly lessen its routine dependence on the great variety, quantity, and quality of European manufactures. One famous development of the time was the covert emigration of the English artisan Samuel Slater, who carried in his head the intricate design of the new power-driven textile machinery and supervised its duplication in a mill at Pawtucket, Rhode Island (notwithstanding English laws prohibiting the emigration of such persons or the export of such technical information). The almost simultaneous invention of an efficient cotton gin by the native New Englander Eli Whitney laid the basis for a modern American textile industry. Whitney's new system for the mass production of army muskets from standardized parts, set up in New Haven in 1799, was an important American contribution to the industrial revolution that had been gathering strength for half a century in England.

The episode of Samuel Slater was indicative that the importance of Europe to America was not so much in commerce as in continuing to be a source of people and ideas. The blockades and dangers on the high seas and disruptions of regular shipping services surely affected the sources and volume of emigration to America. The war itself reemphasized America's role as a refuge from the strife and oppressions of Europe, most obviously in the highly visible influx of several thousand French representing the considerable spectrum of sociopolitical ranks endangered in the successive phases of the Revolution. Most of these cosmopolitan exiles clustered in the coastal cities and formed a restless group longing to return home, but many stayed and some of these, such as the Du Ponts who set up a powder mill at Wilmington and members of the Sulpician Order who opened a seminary in Baltimore, made notable contributions to American development. Near the end of the decade the sharp turn in American attitudes reflecting the undeclared war at sea dampened all relationships with France and emphasized the episodic nature of this particular connection.

Less vivid but more sustained and important were the migrations from Scotland that resumed soon after the American Revolution. Despite recent loyalist alignments, the progression of Highland clearances sent more thousands across the sea, and Glasgow merchants reestablished connections with considerable success, although they no longer dominated the tobacco trade. Most telling were the cultural contacts and infusions. Many of the rising professional class in Scotland were pro-American and, faced with limited opportunities at home, they flocked in as teachers, clergymen, scientists, and physicians. Furthermore, many Americans went to Scotland for training. Edinburgh was considered to be the finest medical school in the Old World, Scottish theologians and philosophers were the most influential on American thinking, and the general character of Scottish society made it more attractive to many Americans than England:

> If . . . Scottish and colonial culture were both "provincial," they could find shared experience and opportunities in this status. Scottish universities were open to all. The social tone of the capital was set by ministers, lawyers, professors and men of letters, not by titled men who lived on rents from inherited estates. In Glasgow the dominant elite was even more decidedly middle class.

Scotland also gave Americans a convenient way of getting around lingering animosities and legal difficulties in their relations with the English and England. The American remnant of the Church of England was reorganized as the Protestant Episcopal Church and got its episcopate legitimized through the Scottish Anglican remnant of early church struggles in Great Britain. In a number of areas the connection with this alternative English-speaking society was foremost at this time.

On the other hand, Americans did not entirely welcome some of these foreign influences. In 1798 the Presbyterian Church voted to require all foreign clergymen to submit their credentials to the Presbytery, undergo an oral examination, and serve on probation for a year. The motives were certainly mixed (including those arising from the strong Ulster element in the American church) but there were clearly assertions here of American separateness, equality, and independence. The general topic of foreigners and citizenship became an impassioned issue in the republic. First efforts to make "naturalization" a long and selective process failed; a congressional act in 1790 required only a two-year residence, but in reaction to the French influx this was changed in 1795 to five years, with the additional specification that all titles to nobility be renounced; four years later Congress decreed a minimum residence of fourteen years to qualify for citizenship. This last measure was one of the Alien and Sedition Acts that many Americans saw at the time as an overreaction to fears generated by the recent mob actions and bloodshed in France and Ireland, and there were counterpressures to block its application, but it represented strong feelings in the United States that the nation ought to be selective as to the kinds of transatlantic influences it should welcome. Those who felt that way might proudly proclaim America as the land of the free but they insisted that it would likely remain so only if its own carefully balanced structure of freedom and authority remained undisturbed. In this view the United States was itself the greatest political creation in the modern world; it did not need to import any new political ideas; on the contrary, it was ready to export those of its own making. In political forms the United States was already proudly "separate and equal" among "the Powers of the earth."

The actual degree of American cultural independence can best be measured by reference to certain types of institutions. Dixon Ryan Fox defined the process by which colonial offspring achieve independence in such professions as medicine and science as a progression through four stages. As applied to the American case this sequence of what he termed "civilization in transit" may be summarized as follows:

1. European specialists emigrate to America and establish their practice;

2. American-born aspirants go to European institutions for training and return to establish their practice;
3. American institutions of training are established, but these remain dependent on Europe for staff, textbooks, and scientific apparatus; and
4. American institutions become sustained in all essentials from the resources of America itself.

The British North American colonies as a whole were just edging into stage 3 by the eve of the Revolution, as evidenced by such things as eight colleges, two medical schools (Philadelphia and New York City), the American Philosophical Society, and general recognition of a number of distinguished American scientists. Following the Revolution there was an acceleration of such developments in the new nation. By 1800 several state universities and seventeen new colleges had been founded; medical societies were organized in most of the states and the first medical journal had begun publishing (1797); various societies to promote science and the application of science to agriculture and industry had been formed; and the American Academy became a New England rival to Philadelphia's American Philosophical Society. These were not simply provincial imitations of European models; they displayed some American innovations (for example, the Chemical Society of Philadelphia was the first of its kind in the world) and they included a few major figures in most fields. Yet by 1800 the United States was really not very far along in stage 3: most of these institutions were callow affairs; America was still heavily dependent on Europe for books and apparatus, still sent many of its sons there for training, and still received important help from skilled emigrants. American scientists and thinkers were active participants in the larger Western world of science and thought, and America itself, land and society, was an area of great interest to Europeans, many of whom visited and reported upon it. And so there was interaction, lots of it and no reason to think it would lessen, but there remained an American dependence, somewhat less than in late colonial times but still large, and little reason to think that it could be overcome very soon. As Henry Adams noted, in 1800 "the task of overcoming popular inertia in a democratic society was new, and seemed to offer peculiar difficulties" for there was no real scientific class to lead the way nor a wealthy class to provide the means of experiment, and Americans would not be "roused to feel the necessity of scientific training" until "they were satisfied that knowledge was money."

We may also note parenthetically that if this same perspective on stages of cultural independence were applied internally in the United States it would reveal important variations among the broad sections of the nation. All the developments cited above were heavily concentrated in the northern cities. The southern states were still largely in stage 2, dependent upon Europe or the northern states for advanced training in most fields. The 1798 formation of Transylvania University in Lexington, Kentucky, offering work in religion, law, and medicine, may be taken as the very first step out of stage 2 in the western states. These kinds of regional differentiation and dependency would continue to be fundamental in the geographical dynamics of American culture.

Architecture offered further evidence of American relations with Europe, showing very active connections and influences, heavy dependence but also experimentation, hints of originality and leadership, and above all a self-conscious national context. Only very late in the eighteenth century did men with professional training in architecture appear in America, and they found at least a few exciting opportunities because the new republic needed public buildings that could symbolize its status and character. Thomas Jefferson took the lead in making this kind of architectural statement. He had been working on the design and building of his remarkable home at Monticello since 1769. While serving in France in the 1780s he made an extensive study of Roman remains and fell "in love" with a building in Nîmes, perhaps "the most beautiful and precious morsel of architecture left us by antiquity." He wrote to Madison that "it is simple, but it is noble beyond expression" and would therefore serve as a perfect example by which to form a proper taste in Americans. Urging that we must "avail ourselves of every occasion when public buildings are erected, of presenting to [our countrymen] models for their study and imitation," he arranged for a halt in the construction of a new capitol at Richmond until he could have a model of this gem built and sent, and thus in the late 1780s "the first example in the modern world of a public building in temple form" came to stand on a height overlooking the James River in Virginia.

Immediately thereafter the embryo City of Washington provided a far grander and more influential setting for the symbolic architecture of the new republic. The whole place was largely the work of emigrés. Within the monumental baroque plan of the French engineer and architect Pierre L'Enfant arose the capitol designed by William Thornton, a gifted Englishman from the West Indies, and the President's House by James Hoban from Dublin. Work on the Capitol was later overseen and redesigned by Benjamin Latrobe (whose mother was American-born), who had arrived from England in 1796. Latrobe's first work was the Bank of Philadelphia in which he displayed his fervent conviction that the new nation should be learning from democratic Greek rather than imperial Roman precedents. That was an argument among specialists that had no critical bearing on the general fact that an American version of neoclassical architecture "was well underway before the first example of it had appeared in Edinburgh, London, or Paris" and, more important, that it was given in America a prominence and meaning that it could not possibly have in the dense historic complexities of European landscapes and polities. These

69. The Capitol at Richmond, 1798.
This striking watercolor view of Jefferson's famous replica was drawn by Benjamin Latrobe, who had come to America from England two years earlier and settled in Richmond hoping to make his fortune as an architect and engineer. In the distance to the left, just above the bridge, are gristmills on the riverbank below the falls on the James. (Courtesy of the Maryland Historical Society, Baltimore)

first symbolic buildings were on a new public scale for America, spacious settings for the political life of a spacious republic, and they would be imitated a thousand times in statehouses, courthouses, and city halls across the land.

Meanwhile in Boston Charles Bulfinch had returned from a leisurely grand tour of Europe and had begun leisurely to design houses adapted from the latest English fashions for a few wealthy clients. However, bankruptcy from a more creative but speculative building project soon spurred him into much more extensive work and by 1800 his mark upon houses, churches, halls, statehouses (for Connecticut and Massachusetts; he later did one for Maine) had brought him fame as the first great American architect. At the same time a number of New England craftsmen-artists, such as Samuel McIntire of Salem and Asher Benjamin, author of the first American architectural treatise and patternbook (1797), were elaborating distinct American versions of the Adamesque and Palladian architecture of Georgian England, chiefly in mansions for prosperous merchants, but in churches and other buildings as well. This first florescence would become known as "federal style" architecture, and it was readily compatible with the neoclassic revival, the one

70. American Classic: Bulfinch in Boston.
This house built in 1800 by Charles Bulfinch for Harrison Gray Otis at 85 Mount Vernon Street became one of the authoritative definitions of what the "federal style" could be. One hundred and fifty years later, Walter Muir Whitehill declared, authoritatively, that it was still "the handsomest house in Boston." (Courtesy of the Library of the Boston Athenaeum)

more often a classical finish given domestic buildings by a carpenter-builder, the other at its best public buildings by professional architects working from classical foundations.

Here then was a telling link between America and Europe. It was a dependence of the newer upon the older, certainly, for the agents were either Europeans who became Americans or Americans who drew heavily upon Europe. But the results were not simply European: it was not an ordinary diffusion from center to periphery, for the products were not provincial imitations of the latest metropolitan fashions but were resurrections and adaptations from a deep layer of European history, selected from a time regarded by the intellectuals of the late eighteenth century as having been a Golden Age, when art and intellect and civic virtue were at their best. The leaders of America saw their country as a new start for mankind, a conscious break from contemporary Europe, and they looked back across the ages for inspiration; thus Greek and Roman temples and colonnades and porticos and domes and balustrades and the restrained detailing appropriate to these forms became the new landscape symbols of American civic life and American private success. It was a highly selective and self-conscious borrowing and not all its implications were obvious. If widely adopted it would impose some peculiar constraints on American architectural development. Could buildings, no matter how "simple and noble," which were originally designed to serve a few specialized functions in Mediterranean societies two thousand years ago really meet the needs of a society now spreading across half the North American continent? The testing of that would in itself be something new and would likely leave its mark on the American scene.

But all of this was in its infancy. These new landmarks had not yet transformed the American landscape. For the moment they were conspicuous, which is to say that they had widened the contrast between the monumental and the vernacular. America was expanding vigorously but that did not mean that it was responding eagerly to these new stylistic influences. Charles Bulfinch's career points to the gap between the new aesthetics and the prosaic demands of everyday life in a developing nation: "He failed twice in business because, reaching desperately for perfection in the art of architecture, he quite forgot that America at the dawn of the nineteenth century was a mechanic's rather than an artist's paradise." Mechanics and carpenters and artisans of many sorts had been at work in America for many generations. They had always tried to build in a European manner, routinely, for they were Europeans, imitatively, for they were provincials, yet they had not actually duplicated in any comprehensive sense the European built environment, because it was quite beyond their power to do so. They had to work with the materials at hand and what people could afford to have shipped across an ocean, and they had to work under very different conditions to serve a much more limited society than those in Europe. They built houses, barns, warehouses, shops, churches, and courthouses according to their deeply European ideas of what such things should look like and how they should function, but the results were never quite the same; often the individual elements themselves, usually the ensembles, and certainly the whole scale and order and finish of the vernacular landscape were distinctly American—as every European who looked upon it confirmed.

This brief glance at architecture suggests three processes at work on the cultural relations between the United States and Europe in these first decades of political independence: *selection, imitation,* and *divergence.* The first was a self-conscious creation of something emblematic of the new republic, a new classicism to house the noble simplicity of the new polity and society. Such actions may be seen as a programmatic attempt to achieve cultural independence through an assertive distinctiveness. A second process was conscious imitation, evident in the better buildings, public and private, everywhere, so as to bring to America a European level of style and comfort. Such actions may be seen as routine attempts to lessen the qualitative differences between the metropolis and the provinces. In the new nation they became a means toward cultural equality, bringing a fuller complement of European civilization to America. The third process arose inevitably from the others, as all sorts of unconscious or at least unplanned divergences resulted

71. American Vernacular: Carolina I-house.
The "Old Red House," built nearly two hundred years ago (1789) on the coastal plain of North Carolina forty miles inland from Albemarle and Pamlico sounds, endures as a simple example of one of the most common regional house types in America. Although modeled in basic form on English originals, such tall, narrow, somewhat ungainly structures took on a thoroughly American appearance during the eighteenth century as they were spread across the whole of Greater Virginia. The combination of one-room deep, two-story, and central entry, in these general proportions, was the distinctive mark; the timber-frame, clapboard siding, and external end-chimneys were one of several variations; the full-length shed-roof front porch and the shed-roof attached kitchen at the rear became standard accretions. (Courtesy of the North Carolina Division of Archives and History)

from the selections, simplifications, and adaptations demanded by the very different conditions obtaining in America, a geographic differentiation arising from cultural diffusion across an ocean and onto a continent that to Europeans was a distant wilderness to be domesticated. Such alterations are usually deplored at first as being makeshift, limited, and unequal, but those that prove to be successful solutions to common problems may come to be regarded as achievements and in time as quite equal to or even superior to their European antecedents. Nationalism may invoke the vernacular in its cause and claim that the common American house, the American farmstead, the ordinary American town have qualities that set them apart from and above equivalent features of European life.

These several and partly contradictory processes may be discerned in various degrees in other realms of American life. For example, Noah Webster set energetically to work to simplify spelling, fix pronunciation, and supply a set of edifying American readings, all with the intent of establishing "a *national* language" superior to that of the motherland, while at the same time most Americans gave routine respect to London's standards in literature and speech. Yet all the while the American spoken tongue was continuing to diverge and differentiate, as it has for generations.

And there was, always, a geography to such things. If we could map architecture classified into these three types, we would find that which was consciously designed to proclaim national distinctiveness on display in the federal and state capitals and in some of the important new buildings in the seaport cities. The imitative mode, which envisioned America as an extension of European civilization, was more evident in the domestic, commercial, and religious architecture in cities and towns and in mansions and larger houses in the countryside, while the divergent architecture of the American vernacular was to be seen everywhere, dominating broad areas. The pattern therefore was not one of three discrete distributions but of three overlapping ones of markedly different extent, showing a layering in those places most closely and complexly related to Europe. Had we maps of these and other diagnostic features we might bring into clearer view the geographical dynamics of American cultural independence.

Certainly that kind of independence was not readily discernible nor generally appreciated at the time. Europe remained the obvious seat of civilization and despite a few shrill spokesmen, America had not declared independence from that. Aspirations for "separate and equal station" as a New World part of Western civilization would imply a more balanced and flourishing interaction across the Atlantic rather than severance and isolation. America was Europe's first independent offspring (Latin America was a child grown huge in stature but still tethered to parental authority) but it remained nourished by and dependent on Europe in innumerable ways, and there was no concerted program to alter that deep-rooted fact. In that sense America was old as well as new, a continuation as well as an invention.

3. *E Pluribus Unum, in Uno Plures?*

"What then is America, this new land?" If we should adapt Crèvecoeur's query of 1782 we will be faced with a question as complex in its own way as was his about "the American, this new man." The queries are of course complementary in some degree and we may well draw upon his response, but we shall have to do much more, not only because of the limitations and biases peculiar to the emigré "American Farmer," but because of the nature and intent of our geographic interpretation.

Broadly we may take the question to be "What was the human geographic result of two centuries of seafaring, conquering, and planting in eastern North America?" To answer that we should like to have a detailed description of the character of land and society place by place. Such a comprehensive review is quite beyond the scope of this study, but we are fortunate to have Ralph H. Brown's carefully contrived *Mirror for Americans* wherein he presents a coherent "Likeness of the Eastern Seaboard," drawing solely upon and written in the style of geographical works extant in 1810. Later Brown offered another treatment of the same topic without that historiographic restriction in his *Historical Geography of the United States*. But valuable and interesting as these gracefully written works are, they cannot adequately serve our purpose. It is not only that they were written forty years ago from a rather restricted concept of historical geography and show how uneven is the coverage in the more obvious documents, but that no single synoptic description could very well encompass or illuminate the several dimensions of the human geography of America we have tried to keep in view. In 1800 the United States was at once a nation, a federation, and a set of sociocultural regions, and we shall conclude this review of the continuous shaping of America with some summary comments on these coexisting dynamic formations.

The United States was an early and prominent exhibit of self-conscious nationhood and of some tendencies associated with the sudden convulsive creation of a nation-state. New national states are inherently fragile and obsessed with survival. A union must imply some degree of unity, and unity may be most readily created where it can be grounded on some degree of uniformity. Henry Adams's remark that the United States in 1800 did not have "enough nationality to be sure that it was a nation" suggests that American political and cultural self-consciousness had not developed commensurately. Yet there was, as he noted, plenty

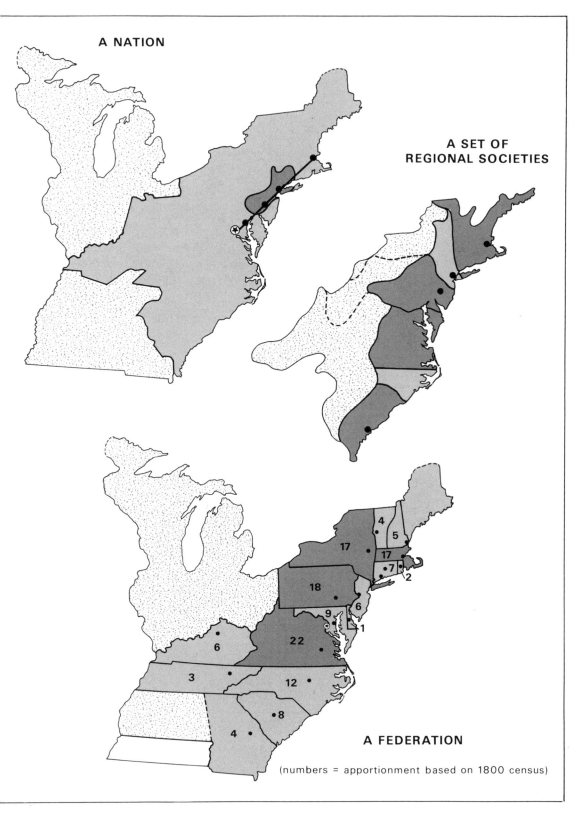

A NATION

A SET OF REGIONAL SOCIETIES

A FEDERATION

(numbers = apportionment based on 1800 census)

. Three Geographic Formations.

of comment, especially from foreigners, about a pervasive "Americanness" of society, culture, and landscape in the new republic. Many features were obvious enough: the general Englishness of language and law and so much else yet all with a difference, for, as Thomas Cooper noted, "although American manners and society approach nearer to English than any other, they are not quite English." There was also the middle-class character of society and economy that had been so apparent for more than half a century. And vivifying all these differences were American traits that visitors found so striking: the informality and egalitarianism in manners, the assertive individualism and independence, the pervasive materialism and commercialism, the restlessness and lack of commitment to place or profession. Such features were clichés laced through the descriptions and assessments of the day, and fervent American spokesmen shaped these into positive images to serve the general concept of an American national character.

"The staple of America at present consists of land, and the immediate products of land," reported Thomas Cooper, and something of these American qualities was directly visible in the landscape. The whole scale of life, the spaciousness, the scatteredness, the relative emptiness never failed to impress European travelers. Even in ostensibly well-settled districts they kept encountering long stretches of forest or more open country uninhabited and apparently unused. Moreover, by any European standard Americans held astonishingly large tracts of land. Ordinary farmers seemed to have a hundred or two or even several hundred acres, and it was obvious everywhere that they held more than they could readily make good use of. Living reasonably well, they farmed only the most productive or convenient portions and let their livestock roam over the rest, while year by year they hacked away at the forest edge. Equipment was scarce, tillage casual, and the entire countryside had a raw, unfinished, and unkempt look. Associated with all of this was a lavish use of wood, for fences, houses, barns, and buildings of every kind. Throughout the newer districts simple log cabins and more elaborate log houses occasioned comment as a distinctive American feature. They were not in fact an American invention but their antecedents were not obvious to travelers from Atlantic Europe and indeed remain controversial today. Terry Jordan has argued persuasively that the Finns and others of New Sweden introduced log construction into North America, with later refinement and amplification by Germanic immigrants. Jordan concludes that "the log house was largely Teutonic in carpentry; the log cabin was Fenno-Scandian." But the important point in 1800 was that these European forms had evolved into what was becoming a major American symbol.

Some common features of the American landscape, like the log cabin, could be understood at the time to reflect a stage of development more than a distinction in culture, with the pioneering phase gradually giving way to a more European-like finish of the domestic scene. Yet even the mature landscape could never become

73. Virginia Log Buildings.

This loose cluster of log buildings in Stafford County, Virginia, about forty miles south-west of Washington, was sketched by Benjamin Latrobe in 1806. Although it was an industrial rather than an agricultural settlement (the quarries preparing stone for the construction of the national capitol), its appearance and Latrobe's commentary on it perfectly exemplify a distinctively American attitude toward wood and design in back-country settlement: "Mr. Robertson . . . fixed upon a beautiful little knoll in the midst of the woods close to his quarry and determined to form a settlement there. In the true Virginia style, he first levelled every tree on the spot in a circle of about 150 yards diameter, in the center of which he built a little log house 24 feet by 18, two stories high, each divided into two small rooms. A loghouse kitchen, a d[itt]o stable, smithshop, hen house, meat house, and tool house, sprinkled irregularly over the knoll, gave to the whole a some what romantic appearance." (Courtesy of the Maryland Historical Society, Baltimore)

truly European. There was not only its spaciousness and loose patterning but also the fact that it was grounded upon a distinct American agriculture and ecology. That in turn sustained an American diet that in its common foods, their combina-tions and proportions, differed from that of any country in Europe. "The prejudice in favor of Indian corn is deeply rooted in this country," noted the Duke de la Rochefoucauld Liancourt, who no doubt found it hard to stomach, and it is unlikely that he or his various hosts in Massachusetts and elsewhere could appreci-ate what a difficult Americanizing process lay behind that mundane fact. Indian corn in many forms, wheaten bread, potatoes, pork, beef, milk, and milk products, supplemented almost everywhere by extensive use of game and washed down with strong drink—rum along the seaboard, whiskey farther inland—was common American fare and together with the manner of its consumption was increasingly viewed as a mark of American character.

All of these general characteristics had emerged from several generations of European planting in North America. They were part of an American folk culture that served more as a common base than as an overt expression of American nationalism. There was also, as we have noted, a highly self-conscious nationalism being applied to political forms, architecture, language, and other selected features, but it was too soon to know just what the imprint of such efforts would be. There were still other processes that may be thought of as intermediate in kind between folk culture and explicit nationalizing instruments, rather more self-conscious than the one but less programmatic than the other. Here we might recall Crèvecoeur's first response to his own rhetorical question, wherein he stated that the American "is either an European, or the descendant of an European, hence that strange mixture of blood, which you will find in no other country. I could point out to you a family whose grandfather was an Englishman, whose wife was Dutch, whose son married a French woman, and whose present four sons have now four wives of different nations." The illustration seems to be drawn from the lower Hudson Valley where he was then residing, but it could be generalized, with variations in elements, throughout the middle states and even in parts of the south. His stress falls on a nationalizing dynamic: out of diversity by way of ethnic promiscuity comes a new creation. The process was widely apparent, but a great deal of diversity remained and no amount of genetic blending could by itself produce an "American." Nevertheless, the presence of such ethnic diversity, a tolerance of it, and, as in Crèvecoeur's illustration, some degree of personal indifference to it figures prominently in an American national character, as did, less uniquely, a deep-seated White prejudice against Blacks.

Something of the same kind of diversity and blending could be seen in American religion. The formal tolerance for a variety of faiths built into the national political system was an American distinction, but there was also an American coloration to many of the specific denominations, for they were suffused with feelings and attitudes that reflected American individualism, informality, voluntaryism and instability, along with the more European rationalism and deism of the day. The family of Mr. Read of Reading, host to Rochefoucauld Liancourt on his travels through Pennsylvania, provides a pertinent illustration: Read had ten children, "two of whom only have been baptized; the rest are left to choose their religion for themselves, if they think proper, when they arrive at years of discretion." Such attitudes accentuated the competitiveness of religious denominations but undermined their historic differences, for as they sought to lure the unchurched adult to their fold the distinctions between them became more and more a matter of style and strategy and less and less a matter of doctrine or ethnic particularity. After the Revolution several major denominations reorganized themselves for comprehensive national efforts to mobilize the large proportion of the population that had no sustaining affiliation with any church. Unhindered by hierarchy the Baptists set avidly to work in all regions. The Presbyterians managed to gather most of their various ethnic, regional, and doctrinal bodies together in one general fellowship and in 1800 were on the verge of working out cooperative relationships with the Congregationalists of New England. But the Methodists were most clearly emblematic of the incipient American nation. Arising as an evangelical discipline within the Church of England, the movement had been carried to America by the Wesleys themselves, among others, in a series of preaching missions in late colonial times. In 1784 the tie to the Anglican Church was formally severed and the Methodist Episcopal Church was founded in Baltimore. Coeval with the republic, it undertook a national mission of Christian conversion and invigoration through a remarkable system of circuit-riding ministers, radiating out of the middle states. By 1800 Methodism was emerging as a major force in shaping American Protestantism.

These church organizations, especially the Methodists and Presbyterians, operating nationwide but dependent for much of their leadership and institutional support upon the resources of the main nuclear area (the College of New Jersey at Princeton was much the most influential theological center) were in fact if not by intent instruments and displays of the geography of nation-building. As in the model case, the power of the center is not only political and economic but also social and cultural. That which is quintessentially American should be most fully expressed in the core of the nation. The leadership of that area molds the patterns of education and thought, defines proper usage and etiquette, initiates styles, arbitrates fashions, and in general sets the standards for the nation. But of course the United States was not a model case. It did not form around a nucleus; rather it was a unique experiment in duality and ambiguity: a federal nation encompassing several regional societies.

In 1800 the United States was still a mere fledgling of a federation. The legal relationships between the parts and the whole were still uncertain and controversial, as exposed by the Virginia and Kentucky resolutions of 1798 that proclaimed the right of states to judge the constitutionality of federal acts and by the tumultuous emergence of political parties and new forms of mass electioneering, which generated strong doubts about the future of republican government. Geopolitical relations were only a little less complex and tentative. Each state was, in certain specified ways, a unit, a single political society, and equal to every other state. Yet each was also unique in its particular composition, and there were great differences in coherence and self-consciousness. There was an obvious contrast between the strong feelings of state pride and allegiance among Virginians and the weak sense of any such identity in a New Jersey with its peculiar heterogeneity and history, and many variants fell between these extremes. Such things are neither fixed nor fully measurable; they may respond to events or be manipulated in causes, and thereby affect the stability and direction of the entire structure. Federalism and nationalism were contingent and contentious.

In simplest political terms the most important difference among the states was in size of populations. In 1800 Congress was poised for its first decennial reapportionment of the House of Representatives according to the self-adjusting device defined by the Constitution. Relative power would be altered, but not dramatically. The margin of the largest (Virginia) over the smallest (Delaware) would be increased by three (22 to 1), while New York would receive the greatest increase (from 10 to 17), making it equal to Massachusetts and one of the "big" states. On the other hand, Rhode Island (2) and Connecticut (7), as well as Delaware, would remain unchanged, and as the total membership in the House would be increased (from 105 to 141) their voices would actually be diminished. Such adjustments must also affect the relative power of common groupings of states, but sectionalism was far from rigid, not only because of the nature and variety of the issues addressed but because of the changing human geography. Reapportionment was a periodic response to differential growth, but there was more to it than numbers. New England might remain the same set of states but New Englanders were spreading by the tens of thousands into other jurisdictions and that must affect the political culture of all such units and thereby the alignments and balances in the whole. Thus the future of the federation was bound up with the underlying patterns and dynamics of its regions.

The regional societies of 1750 were still very much in evidence fifty years later. Whereas nation and federation were new and tentative and to a large degree contrived and intangible, these regions were deep-rooted and distinctive, cumulative creations of several generations, providing physical settings for the routines of American life. Foreign travelers were usually too much impressed with a common Americanness so different from the scenes of home and so concerned with the costs and qualities of lands and goods and services from place to place to give close and systematic attention to regional patterns, but almost any traverse across the grain of these well-settled districts brought some recognition of the emblems and ensembles of this remarkable set of American cultural landscapes: the dense pattern of handsome white houses, red barns, stone fences, and lush meadows of the Massachusetts countryside ("as much cultivated as France"), with every scene punctuated by the fine spire of a white church in the midst of an attractive village; the wider scattering of farms and the few towns along the mighty Hudson, with the

74. New England Farmstead.
The density of settlement and cultivation of taste to be found in some of the older districts of New England, especially where urban commercial wealth could be applied to the countryside, are apparent in this very studied painting displaying the country estate of Ezekiel Hersey Derby, a prosperous Salem, Massachusetts, merchant. Derby purchased this farm, which lay only a mile or so from his town residence and business, in 1800 and promptly set Samuel McIntire to work at embellishing its buildings. The carved adornments (barely discernible) around the barn door and the classical facade of the summer house on the hill are McIntire touches. The capacious three-story house, with gambrel roof and balustrade, was a common type in the prosperous ports of eastern New England. The painting is attributed to Michele Felice Cornè, who arrived in Salem from Italy in 1799 (aboard one of Derby's ships) and was soon making a comfortable living painting the faces, ships, and estates of aspiring Yankee families. (Courtesy of the Peabody Museum of Salem)

occasional appearance of a manor and some telltale imprint of Dutch beginnings in the form and fashion of a house or barn or commercial street; the rich rolling countryside of Pennsylvania where travelers often remarked on the small indifferent houses and great capacious barns of the German farmers and on the many churches and the narrow brick houses hugging the radiating streets of the thriving

75. New England Landscape.
What will become one of the great symbolic landscapes of America, the white church spire pointing heavenward above the embowered New England village, makes perhaps its first artistic appearance in this view "Looking East from Denny Hill" by Ralph Earl in the 1790s. The work was commissioned by Colonel Thomas Denny to record a scene he had loved since childhood. The churches are those of Worcester, Massachusetts, and the naive painting of the hills rolling on to Shrewsbury on the horizon gives an accurate impression of the well-domesticated countryside. (Courtesy of the Worcester Art Museum, Worcester, Massachusetts)

market towns; the water-laced Chesapeake world of plantations and small farms, of Georgian manors, modest cottages, and rude huts, of intensively cultivated plots and extensive tracts of forest and waste, of tobacco landings and courthouse crossroads; the comfortable verandahed townhouses clustered on the narrow peninsula of Charleston in the hope of health-bearing breezes amidst the watery patchwork of the sweltering ricelands.

Such vignettes lend themselves to regional caricature but they accord with general patterns long widely recognized and increasingly tested and refined by detailed studies of enduring evidence in architecture, both folk and formal, in farmsteads and field patterns, village types and town plans. Armed with appropriate guidebooks the traveler of today can make the same traverse and discern upon the earthly palimpsest many of these very marks of 1800. But our principal concern is not with artifacts but with American life, and the importance of such forms lies in the cultures that created them. These several landscapes provide clues to the

76. Hudson Valley Landscape.
We have cropped almost all the drama out of Thomas Davies's sketch of the British attack upon Fort Washington on September 16, 1776 (leaving in a few puffs of cannon smoke), in order to focus upon mundane details of the setting that his keen topographic eye and pen faithfully recorded. Davies was at the time a captain of artillery in charge of a battery covering the flotilla (*left*) moving up the Harlem River for the assault upon the heights. The view is from the Bronx across to the northern end of Manhattan. Although the majestic river is barely visible at the foot of the sheer wall of the Palisades in the right background (with a British frigate anchored at Sputyen Duyvil), this short stretch of well-tended fields, pastures, and woodlots on the hummocky ground, backed by steep forested slopes, with four substantial farmsteads, each with a solid house of brick or stone and at least one with an obvious broad-base Dutch barn, is a fine exhibit of a common Hudson Valley rural scene. (Courtesy of the I. N. Phelps Stokes Collection, The New York Public Library, Astor; Lenox and Tilden Foundations)

basic regions of American society; they indicate the geographic framework of those differences in ethnic content, social character, religious expression, and political culture that are fundamental to the shaping of America. Despite numerous elaborations and modifications in the tumultuous years after mid-century the general

77. Pennsylvania Barn.

George Stoner's farm lay in a steep creek valley just off the Susquehanna downriver from Conestoga rather than in the rich rolling lands common to most of Lancaster County, but his large barn and small house were certainly characteristic of the Pennsylvania countryside. These huge barns of stone or brick base and gable ends, with a wooden forebay projection sheltering the livestock doors below, were a remarkable American creation and found in no other colonial regions. This one was sketched by Benjamin Latrobe in the autumn of 1801. (Courtesy of the Maryland Historical Society, Baltimore)

pattern persisted in 1800, and indeed in these features too, the modern traveler might find today some vestige of the moral fervor of Protestant capitalism in socially conscious New England; of the factious, speculative, secular society of heterogeneous New York; of the pluralism and privatism of the Quaker commonwealth; of the paternal agrarianism of the Anglican gentry in Virginia; of the planter oligarchy and the politics of privilege in the Black lowlands of Carolina.

But if a seaboard traverse would display this clear geography of American society, a short swing inland would encounter some complications. The swirl of movement into New York and northern Pennsylvania had not produced simple westward extensions of seaboard societies. There was a strong Yankee imprint but there were other peoples as well and the great Hudson trafficway worked against sustained connections with New England. The distinction between these northern colonizations and the broad westward extension of Pennsylvania was clear enough, but beyond the Forks of the Ohio interweaving strands of Yankee, Pennsylvanian, Virginian, and other movements were creating new complexities. Thus regional patterns were becoming blurred and difficult to assess. Whether they pointed toward new composite regions or a more comprehensive national integration was uncertain, but clearly an expanding United States was not going to be a simple latitudinal projection of colonial America. That had been clear for several decades farther south where the inland districts had drawn so heavily from the Delaware and Susquehanna valleys and entryways. In 1800 the rapidly extending Upland South appeared to be increasingly detached, divergent, and in some ways alienated from older Virginia and the Carolina Low Country; with no focus as a region and little cohesion as a society, it seemed a "fluid, individualistic, flamboyant, decentralized and conservative culture [that] cried out for containment and direction—for structure."

Thus, even if the pattern of regions brings some basic contexts of American life into clearer focus than do the patterns of the nation and federation, it does not reveal a simple structure or a static scene. Regions and regionalism have their own

78. Pennsylvania Town.
Lancaster was laid out as the county town in 1731. It quickly became a thriving center and well represents such red-brick Pennsylvania boroughs focused on a market square. By 1801, when Latrobe made this drawing, its population of nearly 5,000 made it renowned as the "largest inland town in the United States." In 1799 it had been designated as the capital of Pennsylvania, and the handsome courthouse featured here was serving as the statehouse. (Courtesy of the Maryland Historical Society, Baltimore)

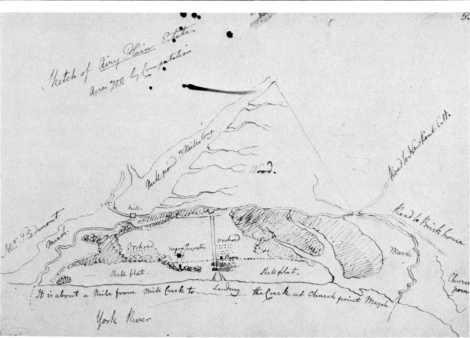

79. Virginia Plantation.

By turn-of-the-century standards this plain Georgian hipped-roof structure perched on the bank of the York River was a not untypical Virginia house on a modest 700-acre Tidewater plantation called Airy Plain Estate. During his sojourn here in 1797 Benjamin Latrobe also sketched a plan of the property, showing the layout of orchards and fields, woodlands (mostly) and marsh, as well as the placement of the barn, mill, and "Negro Quarters." (Courtesy of the Maryland Historical Society, Baltimore)

80. Virginia River Landing.
A view of Rockett's Landing on the James just below Richmond, in the midst of fertile rising country near the head of tidewater. The house and dock directly in the center of the picture was Powhatan estate, on the site of an Indian town at the time the English first ventured up the James River. Sketched by Latrobe, 1796. (Courtesy of the Maryland Historical Society, Baltimore)

peculiar dynamics and, surveying the scene in 1800, we are forced to concur with David Russo's recent observation that "the question of what constitutes a region in the *historical* development of American life is still a vexing one. . . . Regionalism, it would appear, is an important but devilishly uneven force in our historical experience."

European life in America began in localities, was formalized into political colonies, became generalized into regions, and much of it eventually became encompassed by a federal nation. Here we may well caution ourselves about a common assumption of our time: that this successive increase in scale of organization constitutes a set of "natural" stages and a measure of "progress." We are so immersed in a world of national states, so imbued with the dramatic development of the United States from a loose association of colonies to a global superpower, that such endemic expansion, enlargement of scale, and concentration of power have been accepted as part of the natural evolution of successful societies and states. As Jackson Turner Main has noted, there has long been a strong tendency in American historical literature to characterize persons who opposed this trend as

81. Carolina Country Seat.
John Julius Pringle, attorney general of South Carolina, built this house on his plantation a short distance up the Ashley River from Charleston just a year or two before young Charles Fraser made this small watercolor sketch of it in 1800. It is a good exhibit of architectural trends in the Low Country. In this spacious country setting the hipped-roof Georgian house has been raised and wrapped in a verandah, whereas in town it more likely would have had a two-story porch built onto one side. The basic structure appears to be an example of what might later be labeled a Charleston "Huguenot-plan" "double" house. It was destroyed by Union forces in 1865. (Courtesy of the Carolina Art Association/Gibbes Art Gallery)

"men of little faith, petty minded, at best provincial, at worst faintly traitorous." The longer historical and broader anthropological view of mankind might suggest that this kind of geographical growth in the scale of social and political organization is neither inexorable nor essential to human well-being. The more careful historical view will suggest that there may well have been a reasonable doubt about such matters on each occasion and warn against imposing an anachronistic national bias in our judgments.

In the United States of 1800 it seems certain that most of the people and many of the leaders could barely discern a nation and saw the union as a bold experiment rather than an ultimate, as a means (to secure liberty), not an end (an absolute good in itself). The appropriate stress, therefore, is not on a succession of stages but on the continuing coexistence of these several scales of experience; we need to remind ourselves of another commonplace: that life is lived simultaneously within several geographic contexts, that the citizen of 1800, as today, was at once a resident of a locality, a state, a region, a federation, and a nation. Furthermore, while these several contexts are in some degree complementary and may be entirely compatible, they may also be contentious and give rise to serious stress. Each tends to become focused on rather different objectives. Thus nationalism looks for unity and thereby tends to pressure toward conformity and depress diversity. In contrast, regionalism, which tends to be grounded more directly in family and community life, works routinely (and only in part consciously) to sustain local patterns of culture, and thus tends to maintain diversity within the whole. Federalism is a carefully contrived device to balance and harmonize diverse and even conflicting interests, to bring variety into concert for the common good.

The United States was a large and complex creation in which such relationships had not yet been really tested and certainly not stabilized. If there seemed to be serious possibilities of conflict there was also a looseness and openness about the whole structure and system that ought to work to its advantage in coping with internal stress. *E Pluribus Unum,* the inscription on the banner upheld by the national eagle, was a maxim of many possible connotations: out of many states, one state; from many peoples, one people; from a diversity of regions, an American society and culture. But neither law nor logic insists that the one must supersede the many; they might coexist and even be complementary so that the obverse, *In Uno Plures*—within one, many—might be true as well. Could a diversity of peoples and regional societies not only endure but prosper and even flourish into new forms within the body of a single nation and a people united?

Such a question was surely bound up with the geographical shaping of America, with the dynamics of expansion and the attempts to keep an ever-changing set of parts knit together in an ever-changing whole. We have brought a particular kind of geographical perspective to bear upon several centuries of European seafaring, conquering, planting, and development in North America. The year 1800 marks no end to or interruption of these activities and processes but there were indications that this mighty movement had reached the geographic point that a shift in our stance and angle of vision might be advantageous for following its development into the next century.

The French geographer C. F. Volney, one of the more observant of the many foreign travelers who wrote about the new United States, noted that the people on the Atlantic seaboard were accustomed to refer to the country beyond the mountains "by the names of the *back country,* the *back woods,* the *wilderness,* and, more fancifully, the *western waters.* The phrase back country is used by them relatively to their own situation with regard to Europe, the great object and centre of all their thoughts, interests, and speculations." But he noted that in his travels in the spring of 1796 he had scarcely passed the Allegheny when he heard the term *back country*

> applied, by the dwellers on the Great Kenhawah and Ohio, to the maritime country. This is a striking proof that these people have already derived, from their geographical situation, new and peculiar views and interests; that their thoughts tend, like the great thoroughfares, their rivers, to the Gulph of Mexico, and thence to the West Indies, which is the great point of mercantile attraction in America.

At this point the translator of this American edition of Volney's *Travels* inserted an asterisk and appended a cautionary footnote: "M. Volney draws large inferences from a trivial circumstance. The disjunction and opposite direction of the interests of the two great divisions of the empire, together with its causes, are obvious enough, but have little connection with the terms above-mentioned, which are purely geographical." It is of course true that the views and feelings of these new Westerners must not be magnified in meaning. They do not invert center and periphery, undermine the significance of older regions, or nullify America's place in the Atlantic World. But perhaps we have come far enough in this reconnaissance of history to be inclined to rely in such matters rather more on geographers than on translators and to understand that such geographical terms are neither trivial nor inert. (Or should we interpret the translator's intrusion as perhaps an attempt by a patriot to suppress the awful thought of an impending geographical strain on his fragile republic?) In any case, the fact that *back country* had now taken on such utterly contradictory meanings does suggest that, while we must keep Atlantic America always in view, it is now time to begin thinking as well in more continental terms.

Sources of Quotations

PART ONE

p. 8 Sauer, *Early Spanish Main*, 83

p. 9 "trial laboratory": Verlinden, *Beginnings*, 124
Parry, *Spanish Seaborne Empire*, 42
"transplantation": Haring, *Spanish Empire*, 150
"principal architect": Sauer, *Early Spanish Main*, 150

p. 10 "discovery an art and science": Penrose, *Travel and Discovery*, 45
"captaincy system": Burns, *History British West Indies*, 34

p. 12 distinctly "Mexican": MacLachlan and Rodriguez, *Forging of the Cosmic Race*, 198

p. 14 "symbol of Spanish colonization": Lang, *Conquest and Commerce*, 28

p. 16 Paz, *Labyrinth*, 100

p. 17 Boxer, *Portuguese Seaborne Empire*, 27

p. 18 Sauer, *Northern Mists*, 20–21

p. 21 Galloway, "Mediterranean Sugar Industry," 190
"strange company": Duffy, *Portugal in Africa*, 34
"basic machinery": Palmer, *Slaves of the White God*, 10

p. 22 "key region": Curtin, *Economic Change*, 4
on lançados: Duncan, *Atlantic Islands*, 212

p. 23 on São Tomé and Brazil: Rawley, *Transatlantic Slave Trade*, 26, 28

p. 25 Sauer, *Northern Mists*, 54
Quinn, *North America from Earliest Discovery*, 110
on Verrazzano: Morison, *Northern Voyages*, 316

p. 28 "Huguenot circle": Rowse, *Elizabethans and America*, 12–13
Morison, *Northern Voyages*, 486–87
Hakluyt, "Discourse," 271

pp. 28–29 on Eden: Parks, *Richard Hakluyt*, 22

p. 29 Jones, *O Strange New World*, 164
Rowse: *Expansion*, 137
"a country embanked against marauders": Andrews, "Geography and Government," 182

p. 31 "first principle" and "voice of the new nationalism": Parks, *Richard Hakluyt*, 50, 2
Hakluyt, "Discourse," 280, 318, 314, 233, 274, 234, 319, 326, 234

pp. 32–33 "City of Raleigh": Morison, *Northern Voyages*, 659

p. 33 Hakluyt, "Discourse," 318
"foreign and far country": Quinn, "England and the St. Lawrence," 133
Morison, *Northern Voyages*, 434

p. 36 "While the crews were loading the ships": Eccles, *France in America*, 15–16

p. 38 "the . . . most wholesome and fertile place": Hakluyt, *Writings*, 492

p. 39 Quinn, "Munster Plantation," 31
"blueprint for America": Rowse, quoted in Wallerstein, *Modern World-System*, vol. 1, 88
Ulster as regional planning: Orme, *Ireland*, 120, 123

p. 40 Hakluyt: *Writings*, 422

p. 43 Eburne, quoted in Bridenbaugh, *Vexed and Troubled Englishmen*, 401

p. 45 "plundering Muslim villages": Lomax, *Reconquest*, 175

p. 46 "married Atlantic and Mediterranean technology": Hess, *Forgotten Frontier*, 13

p. 48 "Anglo-French Channel community": Rowse, *Elizabethans and America*, 13

p. 49 Amsterdam as "capitalist centre": Ball, *Merchants and Merchandise*, 103
"most dynamic society": Bridenbaugh, *Vexed and Troubled Englishmen*, 475, 28

p. 51 "Ireland and privateering": Rabb, *Enterprise and Empire,* 156

"postponed the application of capital": Quinn, *North America from Earliest Discovery,* 384

p. 53 Dawson, *Dynamics,* 69

p. 55 Spanish America as "normative order" etc.: Lang, *Conquest and Commerce,* 219, 110

p. 56 Cabot quote: Morison, *Northern Voyages,* 203

p. 59 "Mediterraneans exiled in the land of maize": Channu, "The Atlantic Economy," 120

p. 61 "great areas of savage, unorganized conflict": Parry, *Age of Reconnaissance,* 324

"immense increase . . . of robbery and violence" and "an affair of innumerable small ships": Andrews, *Spanish Caribbean,* 253, 252

p. 65 "inland sea of Western Civilization": this phrase was used by Ross Hoffman and quoted in Hayes, "The American Frontier," 207–08

p. 70 on impact of disease: Crosby, *Columbian Exchange,* 31

p. 76 birth of "the modern world-system": Wallerstein, *Modern World-System,* vol. 2, 37

PART TWO

p. 80 Kammen, *People of Paradox,* 16

Davies, *North Atlantic World,* 45

p. 81 "vigorous Anglo-Welsh society": Jenkins, *The British,* 48–49

p. 83 Huggins, *Black Odyssey,* 5

p. 84 "Afro-American community as an alien body": Curtin, *Atlantic Slave Trade,* 700

p. 86 Clark, "Acadia and the Acadians," 90

p. 88 immigrants to Newfoundland: Mannion, *Peopling of Newfoundland,* 7

p. 89 "win farms with spades": Clark, "Acadia and the Acadians," 114

p. 93 on Providence: Davies, *North Atlantic World,* 134

p. 101 "Christian, utopian . . . communities": Murrin, "Review Essay," 234, quoting Lockridge

p. 104 Rhode Island as different from Massachusetts: Perry Miller, quoted in Davies, *North Atlantic World,* 134

p. 105 Morison, *Maritime History,* 21

p. 106 Bridenbaugh, *Pat Mutton,* 69

p. 108 Mather's report: quoted in Charles Clark, *Eastern Frontier,* 13

pp. 111–12 Quebec description: Eccles, *France in America,* 140

p. 113 "polish and social graces": Eccles, *Canadian Frontier,* 102

p. 117 Harris: *Canada before Confederation,* 41

pp. 122–23 on Edmund Andros and New York: Webb, *1676,* 341, 410

p. 126 on Albany: Bonomi, *Factious People,* 40

p. 133 "we High-Germans": Myers, *Narratives,* 381

"ordered space": Lemon, *Best Poor Man's Country,* 98

pp. 133–34 Penn's views: Myers, *Narratives,* 263

p. 134 Lemon, *Best Poor Man's Country,* 108

p. 135 "early Pennsylvania farmers and their families": Lemon, *Best Poor Man's Country,* 216

p. 140 on Philadelphia, Boston, London: Tunnard and Reed, *American Skyline,* 33, 47

"greene Country Towne": Myers, *Narratives,* 243

p. 145 on agricultural potential: "Novo Britannia," 16–17, 22

on climate: Thomas Heriot, "A briefe and true report of the new found land of Virginia," in Hakluyt, *Principal Navigations,* vol. 6, 194

p. 146 companies "to erect and build a town": Andrews, *Colonial Period,* vol. 1, 133

p. 147 Reps, *Tidewater Towns,* 47

p. 148 instructions to governor: Reps, *Tidewater Towns*, 52
"neither the Interest nor Inclinations of the Virginians": Harrison, *Landmarks*, 365

p. 151 on planting and early report: Hall, *Narratives*, 76, 23, 77
"paisley-like pattern": Earle, *Evolution*, 19

p. 155 "Tidewater landscapes": Earle, *Evolution*, 138
Arensberg, "American Communities," 1151
"court house, prison, pillory and stocks": Reps, *Tidewater Towns*, 315

p. 157 "invasion . . . by the Scots": Harrison, *Landmarks*, 371

p. 159 on Lord Fairfax: Mitchell, "Content and Context," 81

p. 163 "long years of warfare": Dunn, *Sugar and Slaves*, 118

pp. 165–67 Dunn, *Sugar and Slaves*, 116; copyright 1972 University of North Carolina Press. Used with permission of the publisher.

p. 170 "privileged gangsters": Roberts, *French in the West Indies*, 70

p. 172 Bridenbaugh, *No Peace beyond the Line*, 265

p. 174 "colony of a colony": Wood, *Black Majority*, 13
"Inconvenience and Barbarism": Lee, *Lower Cape Fear*, 55

p. 175 "he perfectly understands Silke": Hirsch, *Huguenots*, 169
Nash, *Red, White and Black*, 113

p. 184 on cowpens: Dunbar, "Colonial Carolina Cowpens," 126

p. 185 "aristocratic elite," etc.: Dunn, "English Sugar Islands," 58

p. 187 "a miniature London": Cash, *The Mind of the South*, 19

p. 188 "a Nation within a Nation": Bridenbaugh, *Myths and Realities*, 63

p. 190 "more linguistically diversified": Wood, *Black Majority*, 169

p. 194 "Our coast changes shape": Giraud, *French Louisiana*, 65

p. 207 "kalaeidoscopic combat" and "invasion of America" framework: Jennings, *Invasion*, 331, 329

p. 213 "meeting point between civilization and savagery": Turner, "Significance of the Frontier," 200
Jennings, *Invasion*, 173–74

p. 215 on Europeans who never came to America: Hofstadter, *America at 1750*, 32

p. 220 "European regional customs were thrown together": Harris, "Simplification," 472, 474; copyright 1977 Association of American Geographers. Used with permission of the publisher.

p. 221 Zelinsky doctrine: Zelinsky, *Cultural Geography*, 13–14
Porter concept: quoted by Breen in Greene and Pole, *Colonial British America*, 205

pp. 222–23 on homogeneous New England: Nash, in Greene and Pole, *Colonial British America*, 238

p. 225 "hostile to strangers and change": Kammen, *Colonial New York*, 87

p. 227 Wood, *Black Majority*, xiv; copyright 1974 Peter H. Wood. Used with permission of Alfred A. Knopf, Inc.

p. 228 Berlin, "Time, Space, and Evolution," 45

p. 229 Berlin, "Time, Space, and Evolution," 77

p. 230 "rubbed elbows with lower-class Whites": Berlin, "Time, Space, and Evolution," 48

pp. 239–40 Jordan, quoted in Rooney, *This Remarkable Continent*, 54

p. 248 Hogs "swarm like Vermine": Gray, *History of Agriculture*, 206

p. 251 "fleeting, commercial, bourgeois . . . phase" and "effects on France itself": McRae, "Structure of Canadian History," 220–21, 227

PART THREE

p. 267 "first of the 'People's Wars'": White, *Europe in the Eighteenth Century*, 180–81
"cultural, ideological, religious, nationalistic": Savelle, *Empires to Nations*, 137

p. 269 "most important bone of contention": White, *Europe in the Eighteenth Century*, 173

p. 270 "more American territory changed hands": Savelle, *Empires to Nations*, 149

p. 271 on English program to "reclaim" the Acadians: Rawlyk, *Nova Scotia's Massachusetts*, 183–84, 200

p. 273 local government "constituted in like manner": Brebner, *Neutral Yankees*, 22

p. 278 "never will prefer the long, inhospitable Winters": Ouellet, *Economic and Social History*, 95

p. 283 "necessary to fix some line": De Vorsey, *Indian Boundary*, 28

pp. 288–89 Franklin, *Papers*, vol. 4, 228, 233

p. 299 Franklin: as quoted in Christie and Labaree, *Empire or Independence*, 212

p. 300 Bland: as quoted in Christie and Labaree, *Empire or Independence*, 88

p. 301 Pownall, *Administration of Colonies*, 164

p. 302 balance "between metropolis and provinces": Webb, *Governors-General*, 459, xvii

p. 303 "a standard culture": Middlekauff, *Glorious Cause*, 28

"American mind . . . thoroughly, compulsively English": Ketcham, *From Colony to Country*, 12–13, 3

Carleton: quoted in Ouellet, *Economic and Social History*, 100

pp. 304–05 Hofstadter, *America at 1750*, 290, 132–33; copyright 1971 Beatrice K. Hofstadter. Used with permission of Alfred A. Knopf, Inc.

p. 306 Gadsden: quoted in Krause, *Intercolonial Aspects*, 225–26

Henry: quoted in Morris, *Making of a Nation*, 34

p. 314 on divided allegiance: Brebner, *Neutral Yankees*, 271

p. 322 "Loyalists . . . delineated more mentally than geographically": Brown, *Good Americans*, 224

p. 324 on treaty negotiations: Rich, *Montreal and the Fur Trade*, 55

p. 325 "gratuitous grants to all persons": Ells, "Clearing the Decks," 53

p. 329 "Maritime world of islands": Bailey, *Culture and Nationality*, 49

p. 330 "prevent the northern colonies from developing those dangerous tendencies": Craig, *Upper Canada*, 15

p. 331 "pulled the American frontier north": Burt, "If Turner Had Looked at Canada," 69

p. 332 "forming the Character, Temper, and Manners": Craig, *Upper Canada*, 40

Lower: quoted in Brebner, *Canada*, 105

"children of both parents": MacKinnon, "The Loyalists," 89

"American Revolution produced not one country but two": Bell, "Loyalist Tradition," 22

p. 338 "United Colonies of New England": Ward, *United Colonies*, 384

p. 340 on Committee of Correspondence: Gipson, *Coming of the Revolution*, 209–10

Wood: in Bailyn et al., *Great Republic*, 230

p. 341 "distinct republican states": Berkhofer, "Jefferson," 235

p. 342 "Eastern promoters instead of Western squatters": McDonald, *E Pluribus Unum*, 143

p. 343 "They violated the Articles of Confederation": Morgan, *Birth of the Republic*, 124

pp. 343–44 Hamilton and Washington: Morris, *Making of a Nation*, 113

p. 345 Madison: in Ferrand, *Records*, vol. 1, 486

p. 364 Newport as "a small summer residence": Coughtry, *Notorious Triangle*, 237

p. 366 on Richmond: Reps, *Tidewater Towns*, 187

p. 373 "The difficulty of striking a . . . balance": Liska, *Career of Empire*, 88

p. 374 Burke, *Speeches on the American War*, 108–09

p. 375 "stage by stage, the seizure . . . of Britain": Watson, "Individuality," 18

p. 378 Watson, "Individuality," 5–6

p. 381 colonial secretary: quoted in Christie and Labaree, *Empire or Independence*, 192

p. 382 "sense of superiority and snobbery": Middlekauff, *Glorious Cause*, 25

p. 383 "foraging operations": Bowler, *Logistics*, 242
German general's complaint: Higginbotham, *Reconsiderations*, 159

p. 384 "all the trade of America": Knorr, *British Colonial Theories*, 203

p. 385 "revolutionary struggle . . . unique": Mackesy, *War for America*, 4, 31
"long, dirty war": Shy, "American Society," 82

p. 386 Bryce, *American Commonwealth*, 348

p. 388 Mill: quoted in Dikshit, *Political Geography of Federalism*, 239
"never accede to a plan": Mr. Martin of Maryland, in Ferrand, *Records*, vol. 1, 324
"rivalships . . . more frequent than coalitions": Madison, in Ferrand, *Records*, vol. 1, 448
"that a map of the U.S. be spread out": Madison, in Ferrand, *Records*, vol. 1, 177

p. 389 Franklin: Ferrand, *Records*, vol. 1, 180

p. 390 Morris: Ferrand, *Records*, vol. 1, 533–34

p. 393 Morris: as quoted in Pomeroy, *Territories*, 95
"Indians were *resident* 'foreign' nations": Jones, *License for Empire*, 169

p. 394 principle of "duality articulated": Davis, *Federal Principle*, 114

p. 395 Kohn, *Nationalism*, 19–20

p. 396 on politics of nationalism: Deutsch, "Growth of Nations," 184
"a vortex for every thing": Mr. Baldwin (Madison's notes), in Ferrand, *Records*, vol. 1, 372

pp. 406, 408 Washington, *Writings*, vol. 27, 134–36, 138

p. 409 Indian leader's declaration: Smith, "Land Cession Treaty," 96
"The Northwest Ordinance": Hughes, *Social Control*, 25–26

p. 410 "Running a land distribution agency": Harris, *Land Tenure System*, 199

p. 411 "the whole spirit of the colonial land policy": Harris, *Land Tenure System*, 197

p. 412 land "a commodity": Hughes, *Social Control*, 87

p. 413 "ought . . . to keep . . . a retail store": Rohrbough, *Land Office Business*, 18

p. 414 Presbyterian church "came apart in large chunks": Hofstadter, *America at 1750*, 279
Wiebe, *Segmented Society*, 29, 46

p. 415 Washington, *Writings*, vol. 27, 133
"Americans needed government": Pole, *Foundations*, 236
"westerner in our history": Morgan, "Conflict and Consensus," 305
"unusually low protection costs": McNeill, *Great Frontier*, 27

p. 417 Jefferson: *Papers*, vol. 17, 122
Thomas Hutchins: as quoted in Smith, *Virgin Land*, 9

PART FOUR

p. 424 Mackenzie, *Voyages*, 411

p. 429 "Scottish and colonial culture": Brock, *Scotus Americanus*, 170

p. 430 "civilization in transit": Fox, *Ideas in Motion*, 6

p. 431 Adams, *United States in 1800*, 52

p. 432 on Jefferson and the capitol at Richmond: Andrews, *Architecture, Ambition and Americans*, 63–64
neoclassical architecture "well underway before": Mumford, *Sticks and Stones*, 62–63

p. 435 on Bulfinch: Andrews, *Architecture, Ambition and Americans*, 99

p. 437 Webster on "a *national* language": Warfel, *Noah Webster*, 129

p. 438 Adams, *United States in 1800*, 113

p. 440 Cooper, *Some Information Respecting America*, 74, 2
on log cabins: Jordan, "A Reappraisal of Fenno-Scandian Antecedents," 94

p. 441 La Rochefoucauld Liancourt, *Travels*, vol. 1, 398

p. 442 Crèvecoeur, *Letters*, 39
   La Rochefoucauld Liancourt, *Travels*, vol. 1, 26
p. 444 "as much cultivated as France": La Rochefoucauld Liancourt, 396
p. 449 "fluid, individualistic, flamboyant": Calhoon, "A Troubled Culture," 99
   Russo, *Families and Communities*, 104
p. 451 "men of little faith": Main, "American States," 2
p. 453 Volney, *A View of the Soil and Climate*, 17–18

Bibliography

The following list of works used in the preparation of *Atlantic America* is divided according to the four parts of the book. Of course some studies were pertinent to more than one part, but these are listed where first used and are listed again in a subsequent part only if specifically mentioned by author or title in the text of that part.

There are in addition certain materials of general importance that deserve mention at the outset. No one who is not a trained specialist in American colonial history could prepare a book of this sort without incurring a heavy debt to the writers of major university-level textbooks. Fortunately the writing of these remarkable distillations and assessments is a distinguished tradition in American history and new works by leading scholars appear every year. I shared the good fortune of thousands of Americans in having been given my first ordered view of the history of my country with the aid of Morison and Commager, *The Growth of the American Republic*. This famous work has been in print for more than fifty years. Of course it has been revised time and again, but I have kept my well-worn third edition within easy reach as a handy reference on innumerable details. While preparing *Atlantic America* I always had several more current texts at hand as well, and occasionally I paused and looked over a batch of new ones. I probably learned something from every one, but I came to rely most heavily on Bailyn et al., *The Great Republic* as an up-to-date general reference. I

made similar use of an older copy of another hardy perennial of somewhat more specialized focus: Billington's *Westward Expansion*. One becomes also deeply grateful to be able to tune in on historians talking to one another in sophisticated review essays, such as the rich compendiums edited by Greene and Pole and by Michael Kammen.

On the more geographic side I found Theodore Miller's *Graphic History of the Americas* the most useful among several historical atlases and Herman Friis's maps of colonial populations and John Reps's splendidly illustrated book on historical city plans to be major aids. Reproductions of a wide variety of maps of the various American colonies are now available in many forms, including inexpensive individual sheets. I shall cite only one collection and one study of maps and mention the twenty sheets published by the United States Constitution Sesquicentennial Commission as items I referred to most often. Over many years I have found the state guidebooks produced by the Federal Writer's Project of the W.P.A. in the late 1930s and early 1940s to be rich mines of information on localities. They are too numerous and well known to warrant separate listing, but I do wish to testify in general to their value and fascination.

Full citation of the individual items mentioned above together with a few others of general utility are given immediately below.

GENERAL

Bailyn, Bernard, David Brion Davis, David Herbert Donald, John J. Thomas, Robert H. Wiebe, and Gordon S. Wood. *The Great Republic: A History of the American People*. Vol. 1. 2d ed. Lexington, Mass.: D.C. Heath, 1981.

Billington, Ray Allen. *Westward Expansion: A History of the American Frontier*. 2d ed. New York: Macmillan, 1960.

Fite, Emerson D., and Archibald Freeman. *A Book of Old Maps Delineating American History from the Earliest Days down to the Close of the Revolutionary War*. 1926. Reprint. New York: Dover, 1969.

Friis, Herman R. *A Series of Population Maps of the Colonies and the United States, 1625–1790*.

New York: American Geographical Society, 1968.

Greene, Jack P., and J. R. Pole, eds. *Colonial British America: Essays in the New History of the Early Modern Era*. Baltimore: Johns Hopkins Univ. Press, 1984.

Kagan, Hilde Heun, ed. *The American Heritage Pictorial Atlas of United States History*. New York: American Heritage, 1966.

Kammen, Michael, ed. *The Past before Us: Contemporary Historical Writing in the United States*. Ithaca: Cornell Univ. Press, 1980.

Kerr, D. G. G. *A Historical Atlas of Canada*. Toronto: Thomas Nelson & Sons, 1961.

Miller, Theodore R. *Graphic History of the Americas*. New York: John Wiley, 1969.

461

Morison, Samuel Eliot, and Henry Steele Commager. *The Growth of the American Republic*. 3d ed. New York: Oxford Univ. Press, 1942.

Nicholson, Norman L. *The Boundaries of the Canadian Confederation*. Toronto: Macmillan, 1979.

Paullin, Charles O., and John K. Wright. *Atlas of the Historical Geography of the United States*. Washington, D.C.: Carnegie Institution, 1932.

Reps, John W. *The Making of Urban America: A History of City Planning in the United States*. Princeton: Princeton Univ. Press, 1965.

Schwartz, Seymour I., and Ralph E. Ehrenberg. *The Mapping of America*. New York: Harry N. Abrams, 1980.

Van Zandt, Franklin K. *Boundaries of the United States and the Several States*. Geological Survey Bulletin 1212. Washington, D.C.: Government Printing Office, 1966.

Wells, Robert. *The Population of the British Colonies in America before 1776: A Survey of Census Data*. Princeton: Princeton Univ. Press, 1975.

PART ONE

Andrews, J. H. "Geography and Government in Elizabethan Ireland." In *Irish Geographical Studies in Honour of E. Estyn Evans*, ed. Nicholas Stephens and Robin E. Glasscock, 178–91. Belfast: Department of Geography, Queen's University, 1970.

Andrews, Kenneth R. *The Spanish Caribbean: Trade and Plunder, 1530–1630*. New Haven: Yale Univ. Press, 1978.

Baird, Charles W. *History of the Huguenot Emigration to America*. 1885. Reprint. 2 vols. Baltimore: Regional Publishing Co., 1966.

Ball, J. N. *Merchants and Merchandise: The Expansion of Trade in Europe, 1500–1630*. New York: St. Martin's, 1977.

Bishko, Charles Julian. "The Peninsular Background of Latin American Cattle Ranching." *Hispanic American Historical Review* 32 (1952): 491–515.

Boxer, C. R. *The Dutch Seaborne Empire, 1600–1800*. London: Hutchinson, 1965.

———. *The Portuguese Seaborne Empire, 1415–1825*. London: Hutchinson, 1969.

———. *Salvador de Sa and the Struggle for Brazil and Angola, 1602–1686*. London: Athlone, 1952.

Braudel, Fernand. *Capitalism and Material Life, 1400–1800*. New York: Harper & Row, 1973.

———. *The Mediterranean and the Mediterranean World in the Age of Philip II*. 2 vols. London: Collins, 1972–73.

Bridenbaugh, Carl. *Vexed and Troubled Englishmen, 1590–1642: The Beginning of the American People*. Oxford: Oxford Univ. Press, 1968.

Burns, Sir Alan. *History of the British West Indies*. 2d ed. London: Allen and Unwin, 1965.

Burns, E. Bradford, ed. *A Documentary History of Brazil*. New York: Knopf, 1966.

Burwash, Dorothy. *English Merchant Shipping, 1460–1540*. Toronto: Univ. of Toronto Press, 1947.

Butlin, R. A. "Urban Genesis in Ireland, 1556–1641." In *Liverpool Essays in Geography*, ed. Robert W. Steel and Richard Lawton, 211–26. London: Longmans, Green, 1967.

Canny, Nicholas P. *The Elizabethan Conquest of Ireland: A Pattern Established 1565–76*. Hassocks, England: Harvester Press, 1976.

———. "The Ideology of English Colonization: From Ireland to America." *William and Mary Quarterly*, 3d series, 30 (1973): 575–98.

Chadwick, St. John. *Newfoundland: Island into Province*. Cambridge: Cambridge Univ. Press, 1967.

Channu, Pierre. *Seville et l'Atlantique (1504–1650)*, especially vol. 7, *Construction Graphique: Ports–Routes–Trafics* (1957) and vol. 8, *Les Structures: Structures Géographiques* (1959). 11 vols. Paris: S.E.V.P.E.N., 1955–59.

Channu, Pierre, and Hugette Channu. "The Atlantic Economy and the World Economy." In *Essays in European Economic History 1500–1800*, ed. Peter Earle, 113–26. Oxford: Clarendon Press, 1974.

Clark, Andrew Hill. *Acadia: The Geography of*

Early Nova Scotia to 1760. Madison: Univ. of Wisconsin Press, 1968.

Crosby, Alfred W., Jr. *The Columbia Exchange: Biological and Cultural Consequences of 1492.* Westport, Conn.: Greenwood Press, 1972.

Curtin, Philip D. *The Atlantic Slave Trade: A Census.* Madison: Univ. of Wisconsin Press, 1969.

————. *Economic Change in Pre-colonial Africa: Senegambia in the Era of the Slave Trade.* Madison: Univ. of Wisconsin Press, 1975.

Curtin, Philip D., Steven Feierman, Leonard Thompson, and Jan Vansina. *African History.* Boston: Little, Brown, 1978.

Davies, D. W. *A Primer of Dutch Seventeenth Century Overseas Trade.* The Hague: Martinus Nijhoff, 1961.

Davies, K. G. *The North Atlantic World in the Seventeenth Century.* Minneapolis: Univ. of Minnesota Press, 1974.

Davis, Ralph. *The Rise of the Atlantic Economies.* Ithaca: Cornell Univ. Press, 1973.

————. *The Rise of the English Shipping Industry in the Seventeenth and Eighteenth Centuries.* London: Macmillan, 1962.

Dawson, Christopher. *The Dynamics of World History.* New York: Sheed & Ward, 1956.

Duffy, James. *Portugal in Africa.* London: Penguin, 1962.

Duncan, T. Bentley. *Atlantic Islands: Madeira, the Azores and the Cape Verdes in Seventeenth-Century Commerce and Navigation.* Chicago: Univ. of Chicago Press, 1972.

Eccles, W. J. *France in America.* Vancouver: Fitzhenry & Whiteside, 1972.

Elkins, Stanley. *Slavery: A Problem in American Institutional and Intellectual Life.* 3d ed. Chicago: Univ. of Chicago Press, 1976.

Elliott, J. H. *The Old World and the New, 1492–1650.* Cambridge: Cambridge Univ. Press, 1970.

Fage, J. D. *An Atlas of African History.* London: Edward Arnold, 1958.

Foster, George M. *Culture and Conquest: America's Spanish Heritage.* Viking Fund Publications in Anthropology No. 27. New York: Wenner-Gren Foundation for Anthropological Research, 1960.

Galloway, J. H. "The Mediterranean Sugar Industry." *Geographical Review* 67 (1977): 177–94.

Gerhard, Peter. *A Guide to the Historical Geography of New Spain.* Cambridge: Cambridge Univ. Press, 1972.

Goslinga, Cornelis Ch. *The Dutch in the Caribbean and on the Wild Coast, 1580–1680.* Assen, The Netherlands: Van Gorum, 1971.

Hakluyt, Richard. *The Original Writings & Correspondence of the Two Richard Hakluyts,* vol. 2, with an introduction and notes by E. G. R. Taylor; especially "Discourse of Western Planting" [1584], 211–326. London: The Hakluyt Society, 1935.

————. *The Principal Navigations Voyages Traffiques & Discoveries of the English Nation.* Vol. 6. Reprint. London: J. M. Dent and Sons, E. P. Dutton, 1927.

Hamshere, Cyril. *The British in the Caribbean.* Cambridge: Harvard Univ. Press, 1972.

Haring, C. H. *The Spanish Empire in America.* New York: Harcourt, Brace & World, 1947.

Harris, Richard Colebrook, and John Warkentin. *Canada before Confederation: A Study in Historical Geography.* New York: Oxford Univ. Press, 1974.

Hayes, Carlton J. H. "The American Frontier—Frontier of What?" *American Historical Review* 51 (1946): 199–216.

Hess, Andrew C. *The Forgotten Frontier: A History of the Sixteenth-Century Ibero-African Frontier.* Chicago: Univ. of Chicago Press, 1978.

Hillgarth, J. N. *The Spanish Kingdoms, 1250–1516.* Vol. 2, 1410–1516. Oxford: Clarendon Press, 1978.

Jenkins, Daniel. *The British: Their Identity and Their Religion.* London: SCM Press, 1975.

Jones, Howard Mumford. *O Strange New World. American Culture: The Formative Years.* New York: Viking, 1967.

Lang, James. *Conquest and Commerce: Spain and England in the Americas.* New York: Academic Press, 1975.

Lewis, Archibald R. "The Medieval Background of American Atlantic Maritime Development." In *The Atlantic World of Robert G. Albion,* ed. Benjamin W. Labaree, 18–39. Middletown, Conn.: Wesleyan Univ. Press, 1975.

Lockhart, James, and Stuart B. Schwartz. *Early Latin America: A History of Colonial Spanish America and Brazil.* Cambridge: Cambridge Univ. Press, 1983.

Lomax, Derek W. *The Reconquest of Spain.* London and New York: Longman, 1978.

McGrath, Patrick. "Bristol and America, 1480–1631." K. R. Andrews, N. P. Canny, and P. E. H. Hair, eds., *The Westward Enterprise: English Activities in Ireland, the Atlantic, and America, 1480–1650.* Detroit: Wayne State Univ. Press, 1979.

MacLachlan, Colin W., and Jaime E. Rodriguez O. *The Forging of the Cosmic Race: A Reinterpretation of Colonial Mexico.* Berkeley and Los Angeles: Univ. of California Press, 1980.

McManis, Douglas R. *Colonial New England: A Historical Geography.* New York: Oxford Univ. Press, 1975.

———. *European Impressions of the New England Coast, 1497–1620.* Research Paper No. 139. Chicago: Department of Geography, Univ. of Chicago, 1972.

Marshall, C. E. "The Birth of the Mestizo in New Spain." *Hispanic American Historical Review* 19 (1939): 161–84.

Masselman, George. *The Cradle of Colonialism.* New Haven: Yale Univ. Press, 1963.

Meinig, D. W. "A Macrogeography of Western Imperialism: Some Morphologies of Moving Frontiers of Political Control." In *Settlement & Encounter: Geographical Studies Presented to Sir Grenfell Price,* ed. Fay Gale and Graham H. Lawton, 213–40. Melbourne: Oxford Univ. Press, 1969.

Mellafe, Roland. *Negro Slavery in Latin America.* Berkeley and Los Angeles: Univ. of California Press, 1975.

Morison, Samuel Eliot. *The European Discovery of America: The Northern Voyages,* A.D. 500–1600. New York: Oxford Univ. Press, 1971.

Neasham, V. Aubrey. "Spanish Emigrants to the New World, 1492–1592." *Hispanic American Historical Review* 19 (1939): 147–60.

O'Gorman, Edmundo. *The Invention of America.* Bloomington: Indiana Univ. Press, 1961.

Orme, A. R. *Ireland.* Chicago: Aldine, 1970.

Palmer, Colin A. *Slaves of the White God: Blacks in Mexico, 1570–1650.* Cambridge: Harvard Univ. Press, 1976.

Parker, John. *Books to Build an Empire: a Bibliographical History of English Overseas Interests to 1620.* Amsterdam: N. Israel, 1965.

Parks, George Bruner. *Richard Hakluyt and the English Voyages.* New York: American Geographical Society, 1928.

Parry, J. H. *The Age of Reconnaissance, Discovery, Exploration and Settlement, 1450 to 1650.* New York: World, 1963.

———. *The Spanish Seaborne Empire.* London: Hutchinson, 1966.

Paz, Octavio. *The Labyrinth of Solitude: Life and Thought in Mexico.* New York: Grove Press, 1961.

Penrose, Boies. *Travel and Discovery in the Renaissance, 1420–1620.* Cambridge: Harvard Univ. Press, 1952.

Pike, Ruth. *Enterprise and Adventure: The Genoese in Seville and the Opening of the New World.* Ithaca: Cornell Univ. Press, 1966.

Quigley, Carroll. *The Evolution of Civilizations: An Introduction to Historical Analysis.* New York: Macmillan, 1961.

Quinn, David B. "England and the St. Lawrence, 1577 to 1602." In *Merchants & Scholars,* ed. John Parker, 117–43. Minneapolis: Univ. of Minnesota Press, 1965.

———. "The Munster Plantation: Problems and Opportunities." *Journal of the Cork Historical and Archaeological Society* 71 (1966): 19–40.

———. *North America from Earliest Discovery to First Settlements: The Norse Voyages to 1612.* New York: Harper & Row, 1977.

———, ed. *North American Discovery circa 1000–1612.* Columbia: Univ. of South Carolina Press, 1971.

Rabb, Theodore K. *Enterprise and Empire: Merchant and Gentry Investment in the Expansion of England, 1575–1630.* Cambridge: Harvard Univ. Press, 1967.

Ramsay, G. R. *English Overseas Trade during the Centuries of Emergence.* London: Macmillan, 1957.

Rawley, James A. *The Transatlantic Slave Trade, A History.* New York: Norton, 1981.

Reynolds, Robert L. "The Mediterranean Frontiers, 1000–1400." In *The Frontier in Perspective,* ed. Walker D. Wyman and Clifton B. Kroeber, 21–34. Madison: Univ. of Wisconsin Press, 1957.

Rowse, A. L. *The Elizabethans and America.* London: Macmillan, 1959.

———. *The Expansion of Elizabethan England.* London and New York: Macmillan and St. Martin's Press, 1955.

———. *The West in English History.* London: Hodder and Stoughton, 1949.

Ryder, A. F. C. *Benin and the Europeans, 1485–1897.* New York: Humanities Press, 1969.

Sanchez-Alboronoz, Claudio. "The Frontier and Castilian Liberties." In *The New World Looks at Its History,* ed. Archibald R. Lewis and Thomas F. McGann, 27–46. Austin: Univ. of Texas Press, 1963.

Sauer, Carl Ortwin. *The Early Spanish Main.* Berkeley and Los Angeles: Univ. of California Press, 1966.

———. *Northern Mists.* Berkeley and Los Angeles: Univ. of California Press, 1968.

———. *Sixteenth-Century North America: The Land and People As Seen by the Europeans.* Berkeley and Los Angeles: Univ. of California Press, 1971.

Saunders, A. C. deC. M. *A Social History of Black Slaves and Freedmen in Portugal, 1441–1555.* Cambridge: Cambridge Univ. Press, 1982.

Scammell, G. V. *The World Encompassed: The First European Maritime Empires, c. 800–1650.* Berkeley and Los Angeles: Univ. of California Press, 1981.

Schneider, Oscar. "The Brazilian Culture Hearth." University of California Publications in Geography 3:159–99. Berkeley: Univ. of California Press, 1929.

Smith, C. T. *An Historical Geography of Western Europe before 1800.* London: Longmans, Green, 1967.

Stanislawski, Dan. *The Individuality of Portugal: A Study in Historical-Political Geography.* Austin: Univ. of Texas Press, 1959.

Taylor, E. G. R. *Tudor Geography, 1485–1583.* London: Methuen, 1930.

Vance, James E., Jr. *The Merchant's World: The Geography of Wholesaling.* Englewood Cliffs, N.J.: Prentice-Hall, 1970.

———. *This Scene of Man: The Role and Structure of the City in the Geography of Western Civilization.* New York: Harper & Row, 1977.

van Dantzig, Albert. "Effects of the Atlantic Slave Trade on Some West African Societies." *Revue Française d'histoire d'outre-mer* 62 (1975): 252–67.

Verlinden, Charles. *The Beginnings of Modern Colonization.* Ithaca: Cornell Univ. Press, 1970.

Vogt, John. *Portuguese Rule on the Gold Coast, 1469–1682.* Athens: Univ. of Georgia Press, 1979.

Wallerstein, Immanuel. *The Modern World-System.* Vol. 1, *Capitalist Agriculture and the Origins of the European World-Economy in the Sixteenth Century.* New York: Academic Press, 1974.

———. *The Modern World-System.* Vol. 2, *Mercantilism and the Consolidation of the European World-Economy, 1600–1750.* New York: Academic Press, 1980.

Whitehead, A. W. *Gaspard de Coligny, Admiral of France.* London: Methuen, 1904.

Williamson, James A. *The English Channel, A History.* London: Collins, 1959.

———. *The Tudor Age.* London: Longmans, Green, 1953.

Wolfson, Freda. *Pageant of Ghana.* London: Oxford Univ. Press, 1958.

PART TWO

Allen, David Grayson. *In English Ways. The Movement of Societies and the Transferal of English Local Law and Custom to Massachusetts Bay in the Seventeenth Century.* Chapel Hill: Univ. of North Carolina Press, 1981.

Alvord, Clarence Walworth. *The Illinois Country: 1673–1818.* Springfield: Illinois Centennial Commission, 1920.

Andrews, Charles M. *The Colonial Period of American History.* 4 vols. New Haven: Yale Univ. Press, 1934–37.

Anthony, Carl. "The Big House and the Slave Quarters." *Landscape* 21 (1976): 9–15.

Archdeacon, Thomas J. *New York City, 1664–1710: Conquest and Change.* Ithaca: Cornell Univ. Press, 1976.

Arensberg, Conrad M. "American Communities." *American Anthropologist* 57 (1955): 1143–60.

Ashford, Gerald. *Spanish Texas, Yesterday and Today*. Austin: Jenkins Publishing Co., 1971.

Austin, Mattie Alice. "The Municipal Government of San Fernando de Bexar, 1730–1800." *Quarterly of the Texas State Historical Association* 8 (April 1905): 277–352.

Axtell, James. "The White Indians of Colonial America." *William and Mary Quarterly*, 3d series, 32 (1975): 55–88.

Bailey, Alfred Goldsworthy. *The Conflict of European and Eastern Algonkian Cultures, 1504–1700: A Study in Canadian Civilization*. 2d ed. Toronto: Univ. of Toronto Press, 1969.

Bailyn, Bernard. "The Challenge of Modern Historiography." *American Historical Review* 87 (1982): 1–24.

Bell, Winthrop Pickard. *The 'Foreign Protestants' and the Settlement of Nova Scotia*. Toronto: Univ. of Toronto Press, 1961.

Berkhofer, Robert F., Jr. *The White Man's Indian: Images of the American Indian from Columbus to the Present*. New York: Random House, 1978.

Berlin, Ira. "Time, Space, and the Evolution of Afro-American Society on British Mainland North America." *American Historical Review* 80 (1980): 44–78.

Bolton, Herbert Eugene. *Texas in the Middle Eighteenth Century*. Berkeley: Univ. of California Press, 1915.

Bonomi, Patricia. *A Factious People: Politics and Society in Colonial New York*. New York: Columbia Univ. Press, 1971.

Breen, T. H. "Persistent Localism: English Social Change and the Shaping of New England Institutions." *William and Mary Quarterly*, 3d series, 32 (1975): 3–28.

———, ed. *Shaping Southern Society: The Colonial Experience*. New York: Oxford Univ. Press, 1976.

Breen, T. H., and Stephen Foster. "Moving to the New World: The Character of Early Massachusetts Immigration." *William and Mary Quarterly*, 3d series, 30 (1973): 189–222.

Breen, T. H., and Stephen Innes. *'Myne Owne Ground': Race and Freedom on Virginia's Eastern Shore, 1640–1676*. New York: Oxford Univ. Press, 1980.

Bridenbaugh, Carl. *Fat Mutton and Liberty of Conscience: Society of Rhode Island, 1636–1690*. Providence: Brown Univ. Press, 1974.

———. *Myths and Realities: Societies of the Colonial South*. Baton Rouge: Louisiana State Univ. Press, 1952.

Bridenbaugh, Carl, and Roberta Bridenbaugh. *No Peace beyond the Line: The English in the Caribbean, 1624–1690*. New York: Oxford Univ. Press, 1972.

Bruce, Philip Alexander. *Economic History of Virginia in the Seventeenth Century*. 1896. Reprint. New York: Johnson, 1966.

Bushman, Richard L. *From Puritan to Yankee: Character and the Social Order in Connecticut, 1690–1765*. Cambridge: Harvard Univ. Press, 1967.

Cable, George W. *The Creoles of Louisiana*. New York: Charles Scribner's Sons, 1884.

Carter, Hodding W. *Doomed Road to Empire: The Spanish Trail of Conquest*. New York: McGraw-Hill, 1963.

Cash, W. J. *The Mind of the South*. New York: Knopf, 1941.

Cell, Gillian T. *English Enterprise in Newfoundland, 1577–1660*. Toronto: Univ. of Toronto Press, 1969.

Clark, Andrew Hill. *Acadia: The Geography of Early Nova Scotia to 1760*. Madison: Univ. of Wisconsin Press, 1968.

———. "Acadia and the Acadians: The Creation of a Geographical Entity." In *Frontiers and Men*, ed. John Andrews, 90–119. Melbourne: F. W. Cheshire, 1966.

———. *Three Centuries and the Island: A Historical Geography of Settlement and Agriculture in Prince Edward Island, Canada*. Toronto: Univ. of Toronto Press, 1959.

Clark, Charles E. *The Eastern Frontier: The Settlement of Northern New England, 1610–1763*. New York: Knopf, 1970.

Clark, John C. *New Orleans 1718–1812: An Economic History*. Baton Rouge: Louisiana State Univ. Press, 1970.

Clark, John G. *La Rochelle and the Atlantic Economy during the Eighteenth Century*. Baltimore: Johns Hopkins Univ. Press, 1981.

Clark, Robert Carlton. *The Beginnings of Texas, 1684–1718*. Austin: Bulletin of the Univ. of Texas, No. 98, 1907.

Clemens, Paul G. E. *The Atlantic Economy and*

Colonial Maryland's Eastern Shore: From Tobacco to Grain. Ithaca: Cornell Univ. Press, 1980.

Cohen, David Steven. "How Dutch Were the Dutch of New Netherland?" *New York History* 62 (1981): 45–60.

Condon, Thomas J. *New York Beginnings: The Commercial Origins of New Netherland.* New York: New York Univ. Press, 1968.

Corkran, David H. *The Carolina Indian Frontier.* Columbia: Univ. of South Carolina Press, 1970.

Cornell, Paul G., Jean Hamelin, Fernand Ouellet, and Marcel Trudel. *Canada, Unity in Diversity.* Toronto-Montreal: Holt, Rinehart and Winston, 1967.

Coughtry, Jay. *The Notorious Triangle: Rhode Island and the African Slave Trade, 1700–1807.* Philadelphia: Temple Univ. Press, 1981.

Craton, Michael. *A History of the Bahamas.* London: Collins, 1962.

Craven, Wesley Frank. *White, Red, and Black: The Seventeenth-Century Virginian.* Charlottesville: Univ. Press of Virginia, 1971.

Crawford, James M. *The Mobilian Trade Language.* Knoxville: Univ. of Tennessee Press, 1977.

Cronon, William. *Changes in the Land: Indians, Colonists, and the Ecology of New England.* New York: Hill & Wang, 1983.

Crouse, Nellis M. *French Pioneers in the West Indies, 1624–1664.* New York: Columbia Univ. Press, 1940.

Daniels, Bruce C. *The Connecticut Town: Growth and Development, 1635–1790.* Middletown: Wesleyan Univ. Press, 1979.

——, ed. *Town and Country: Essays on the Structure of Local Government in the American Colonies.* Middletown: Wesleyan Univ. Press, 1978.

Davies, K. G. *The North Atlantic World in the Seventeenth Century.* Minneapolis: Univ. of Minnesota Press, 1974.

Davis, H. P. *Black Democracy: The Story of Haiti.* 1928. Reprint. New York: Biblo and Tannen, 1967.

Davis, Harold E. *The Fledgling Province: Social and Cultural Life in Colonial Georgia, 1733–1776.* Chapel Hill: Univ. of North Carolina Press, 1976.

De Vorsey, Louis, Jr. *The Indian Boundary in the Southern Colonies, 1763–1775.* Chapel Hill: Univ. of North Carolina Press, 1966.

Dewhurst, William W. *The History of Saint Augustine, Florida.* New York: Putnam, 1981.

Drums and Shadows: Survival Studies among the Georgia Coastal Negroes. Savannah Unit, Georgia Writer's Project, W. P. A. Athens: Univ. of Georgia Press, 1940.

Dunbar, Gary S. "Colonial Carolina Cowpens." *Agricultural History* 35 (1961): 125–30.

——. "The Popular Regions of Virginia." *University of Virginia News Letter* 38 (1961): 9–12.

Dunn, Richard S. "The English Sugar Islands and the Founding of South Carolina." In *Shaping Southern Society: The Colonial Experience,* ed. T. H. Breen, 48–58. New York: Oxford Univ. Press, 1976.

——. *Sugar and Slaves: The Rise of the English Planter Class in the English West Indies, 1624–1713.* Chapel Hill: Univ. of North Carolina Press, 1972.

Earle, Carville V. *The Evolution of a Tidewater Settlement System: All Hallow's Parish, Maryland, 1650–1783.* Chicago: Univ. of Chicago, Department of Geography Series, No. 170, 1975.

Earle, Carville V., and Ronald Hoffman. "Staple Crops and Urban Development in the Eighteenth-Century South." *Perspectives in American History* 10 (1976): 7–78.

Earle, Swepson. *The Chesapeake Bay Country.* Baltimore: Thompson-Ellis, 1924.

Eccles, W. J. *The Canadian Frontier, 1534–1760.* New York: Holt, Rinehart and Winston, 1969.

Fairlie, John A. *Local Government in Counties, Towns and Villages.* New York: Century Co., 1906.

Faulk, Odie B. *The Last Years of Spanish Texas.* The Hague: Mouton, 1964.

Florin, John. "The Advance of Frontier Settlement in Pennsylvania, 1638–1850: A Geographic Interpretation." Master's thesis, Department of Geography, Pennsylvania State Univ., 1967.

Foner, Philip S. *History of Black Americans.* Westport, Conn.: Greenwood Press, 1975.

Freeman, Douglas Southall. *George Washington, A Biography.* Vol. 1, *Young Washington.* New York: Charles Scribner's Sons, 1948.

Garvin, James L. "The Range Township in Eighteenth-Century New Hampshire." In *New England Prospect: Maps, Place Names, and the Historical Landscape,* ed. Peter Benes, 47–68. Dublin Seminar for New England Folklife: Annual Proceedings. Boston: Boston University, 1980.

Gaustad, Edwin S. *Historical Atlas of Religion in America.* New York: Harper & Row, 1962.

Gerhard, Peter. *The North Frontier of New Spain.* Princeton: Princeton Univ. Press, 1982.

Gerlach, Larry P. *Prologue to Independence: New Jersey in the Coming of the American Revolution.* New Brunswick: Rutgers Univ. Press, 1976.

Gipson, Lawrence Henry. *The British Empire before the American Revolution.* Vol. 2, *The Southern Plantations.* Caldwell, Idaho: Caxton, 1936.

Giraud, Marcel. *A History of French Louisiana.* Vol. 1, *The Reign of Louis XIV, 1698–1715.* Trans. Joseph C. Lambert. Baton Rouge: Louisiana State Univ. Press, 1974.

Glick, Thomas F. *The Old World Background of the Irrigation System of San Antonio, Texas.* El Paso: Univ. of Texas, 1972.

Gottman, Jean. *Virginia at Mid-Century.* New York: Henry Holt, 1955.

Gray, Lewis Cecil. *History of Agriculture in the Southern United States to 1860.* Vol. 1. Washington, D.C.: Carnegie Institution, 1933.

Green, Evarts Boutell, and Virginia D. Harrington. *American Population before the Federal Census of 1790.* 1932. Reprint. Gloucester, Mass.: P. Smith, 1966.

Griffith, Ernest S. *History of American City Government: The Colonial Period.* New York: Oxford Univ. Press, 1938.

Hall, Clayton Colman, ed. *Narratives of Early Maryland, 1633–1684.* New York: Charles Scribner's Sons, 1910.

Haller, William. *The Puritan Frontier: Town-Planting in New England Colonial Development, 1630–1660.* New York: Columbia University Studies in History, Economics, and Public Law, no. 568, 1951.

Hamilton, Peter J. *Colonial Mobile: An Historical Study.* Boston: Houghton Mifflin, 1910.

Hansen, Marcus L. "The Settlement of New England." In *Handbook of the Linguistic Geography of New England,* ed. Hans Kurath, 62–104. Providence: Brown University, 1939.

Harper, J. Russell. *Painting in Canada, A History.* Toronto: Univ. of Toronto Press, 1966.

Harris, Richard Colebrook. *The Seigneurial System in Early Canada: A Geographical Study.* Madison: Univ. of Wisconsin Press, 1966.

———. "The Simplification of Europe Overseas." *Annals of the Association of American Geographers* 67 (1977): 469–83.

Harris, Richard Colebrook, and John Warkentin. *Canada before Confederation: A Study in Historical Geography.* New York: Oxford Univ. Press, 1974.

Harrison, Fairfax. *Landmarks of Old Prince William: A Study of Origins in Northern Virginia.* 1924. Reprint. Berryville, Va.: Chesapeake Book Co., 1964.

Heidenreich, Conrad, and Arthur J. Ray. *The Early Fur Trade: A Study in Cultural Interaction.* Toronto: McClelland & Stewart, 1976.

Higgins, W. Robert. "Charleston: Terminus and Entrepôt of the Colonial Slave Trade." In *The African Diaspora: Interpretive Essays,* ed. Martin L. Kilson and Robert I. Rotberg, 114–31. Cambridge: Harvard Univ. Press, 1976.

Hirsch, Arthur Henry. *The Huguenots of Colonial South Carolina.* 1928. Reprint. Hamden and London: Archon Books, 1962.

Hofstadter, Richard. *America at 1750: A Social Portrait.* New York: Vintage, 1973.

Hubbard, R. H., ed. *Thomas Davies, c. 1737–1812, An Exhibition Organized by The National Gallery of Canada,* Ottawa, 1972.

Huggins, Nathan Irvin. *Black Odyssey: The Afro-American Ordeal in Slavery.* New York: Random House, 1977.

Innis, Harold A. *The Cod Fisheries: The History of an International Economy.* Rev. ed. Toronto: Univ. of Toronto Press, 1954.

Jacobs, Wilbur R. *Dispossessing the American Indian: Indians and Whites on the Colonial Frontier.* New York: Charles Scribner's Sons, 1972.

James, Sydney V. *Colonial Rhode Island, A History.* New York: Charles Scribner's Sons, 1975.

Jennings, Francis. *The Ambiguous Iroquois Empire: The Covenant Chain Confederation of Indian Tribes with English Colonies. New York: Norton, 1984.

———. "The Indian Trade of the Susquehanna Valley." Proceedings of the American Philosophical Society 110 (1966): 406–24.

———. The Invasion of America: Indians, Colonialism, and the Cant of Conquest. Chapel Hill: Univ. of North Carolina Press, 1975.

John, Elizabeth A. H. Storms Brewed in Other Men's Worlds: The Confrontation of Indians, Spanish and French in the Southwest, 1540–1795. College Station: Texas A & M Press, 1975.

Johnson, Sir Harry H. The Negro in the New World. London: Methuen, 1910.

Johnson, Hildegard Binder. "Der deutsche Amerika Auswanderer des 18. Jahrhunderts in zeitgenössiselen Urteil." Deutsches Archiv fur Landes und Volkskunde IV, 2 (September 1940), 211–34.

Kammen, Michael. Colonial New York, A History. New York: Scribner, 1975.

———. People of Paradox: An Inquiry concerning the Origins of American Civilization. New York: Knopf, 1972.

Lauriere, Emile. Histoire de la Louisiane Française, 1673–1939. Baton Rouge: Louisiana State Univ. Press, 1940.

Lee, Laurence. The Lower Cape Fear in Colonial Days. Chapel Hill: Univ. of North Carolina Press, 1965.

Lefler, Hugh Talmadge, and Albert Ray Newsome. North Carolina: The History of a Southern State. Chapel Hill: Univ. of North Carolina Press, 1973.

Lemon, James T. The Best Poor Man's Country: A Geographical Study of Early Southeastern Pennsylvania. Baltimore: Johns Hopkins Univ. Press, 1972.

Leyburn, James G. The Haitian People. 1941. Reprint. New Haven: Yale Univ. Press, 1966.

———. The Scotch-Irish: A Social History. Chapel Hill: Univ. of North Carolina Press, 1962.

Littlefield, Daniel C. Rice and Slaves: Ethnicity and the Slave Trade in Colonial South Carolina. Baton Rouge: Louisiana State Univ. Press, 1981.

Lockridge, Kenneth A. A New England Town,

The First Hundred Years: Dedham, Massachusetts, 1636–1736. New York: Norton, 1970.

McDermott, John Francis, ed. Frenchman and French Ways in the Mississippi Valley. Urbana: Univ. of Illinois Press, 1969.

McDonald, Forrest, and Ellen Shapiro McDonald. "The Ethnic Origins of the American People, 1790." William and Mary Quarterly, 3d series, 37 (1980): 179–99.

Macfarlane, Alan. The Origins of English Individualism: The Family, Property and Social Transition. New York: Cambridge Univ. Press, 1978.

McRae, Kenneth D. "The Structure of Canadian History." In The Founding of New Societies, ed. Louis Hartz, 219–74. New York: Harcourt, Brace & World, 1964.

Mannion, John J., ed. The Peopling of Newfoundland: Essays in Historical Geography. St. Johns: Institute of Social and Economic Research, Memorial University of Newfoundland, 1977.

Marion, John Francis. The Charleston Story: Scenes from a City's History. Harrisburg, Pa.: Stackpole Books, 1978.

Massachusetts Historical Society, Collections. 1st series, vol. 10 (1809): 101–24, 134–37.

Meriwether, Robert L. The Expansion of South Carolina, 1729–1765. 1940. Reprint. Philadelphia: Porcupine Press, 1974.

Merrens, Harry Roy. Colonial North Carolina in the Eighteenth Century: A Study in Historical Geography. Chapel Hill: Univ. of North Carolina Press, 1964.

Merrill, Gordon. "The Role of Sephardic Jews in the British Caribbean Area during the Seventeenth Century." Caribbean Studies 4 (October 1964): 32–49.

Meyer, Duane. The Highland Scots of North Carolina, 1732–1776. Chapel Hill: Univ. of North Carolina Press, 1961.

Mintz, Sidney W., and Richard Price. An Anthropological Approach to the Afro-American Past: A Caribbean Perspective. Philadelphia: Institute for the Study of Human Issues, 1976.

Mitchell, Robert D. "American Origins and Regional Institutions: The Seventeenth-Century Chesapeake." *Annals of the Association of American Geographers* 73 (1983): 404–20.

———. *Commercialism and Frontier: Perspectives on the Early Shenandoah Valley.* Charlottesville: Univ. Press of Virginia, 1977.

———. "Content and Context: Tidewater Characteristics in the Early Shenandoah Valley." *The Maryland Historian* 5 (1974): 79–92.

Mockon, Marion Johnson. "Stockbridge-Munsee Cultural Adaptations: Assimilated Indians." *Proceedings of the American Philosophical Society* 112 (1968): 182–219.

Morison, Samuel Eliot. *The Maritime History of Massachusetts, 1783–1860.* Boston: Houghton Mifflin, 1921.

Mullin, Michael. "British Caribbean and North American Slaves in an Era of War and Revolution, 1775–1807." In *The Southern Experience in the American Revolution*, ed. Jeffrey J. Crow and Larry E. Tise, 235–67. Chapel Hill: Univ. of North Carolina Press, 1978.

Murrin, John M. "Review Essay" [on New England studies]. *History and Theory* 11 (1972): 226–75.

Myers, Albert C., ed. *Narratives of Early Pennsylvania, West New Jersey and Delaware, 1630–1707.* New York: Charles Scribner's Sons, 1912.

Nash, Gary B. *Red, White, and Black: The Peoples of Early America.* Englewood Cliffs, N.J.: Prentice-Hall, 1974.

Newcomb, W. W., Jr. *The Indians of Texas, from Prehistoric to Modern Times.* Austin: Univ. of Texas Press, 1961.

Newton, Milton B., Jr. *Atlas of Louisiana: A Guide for Students.* Baton Rouge: School of Geoscience, Louisiana State Univ., Misc. Pub. 72-1, 1972.

———. "Louisiana Geography, A Syllabus." Baton Rouge: School of Geoscience, Louisiana State Univ., Syllabus Series, 1976.

Norton, Thomas Elliot. *The Fur Trade in Colonial New York, 1686–1776.* Madison: Univ. of Wisconsin Press, 1974.

"Novo Britannia." Peter Force, *Tracts and Other Papers, Relating Principally to the Origin, Settlement, and Progress of the Colonies in North America.* Vol. 1. Washington, D.C.: Peter Force, 1836.

O'Mara, James. *An Historical Geography of Urban System Development: Tidewater Virginia in the 18th Century.* Toronto: Atkinson College, Geographical Monographs no. 13, 1983.

Parsons, James J. "The Migration of Canary Islanders to the Americas: An Unbroken Current since Columbus." *The Americas* 39 (1983): 447–81.

Pomfret, John E. *The Province of East Jersey, 1609–1702.* Princeton: Princeton Univ. Press, 1962.

Prichard, Walter. *Walter Prichard's Outline of Louisiana Studies.* Edited and expanded by Sue Eakin. Gretna, La.: Pelican Publishing Co., 1972.

Prowse, D. W. *A History of Newfoundland from the English, Colonial, and Foreign Records.* 2d ed. London: Eyre and Spottiswoode, 1896.

Quinn, David B., ed. *Early Maryland in a Wider World.* Detroit: Wayne State University, 1982.

Randall, Daniel R. "A Puritan Colony in Maryland." Baltimore: Johns Hopkins Univ. Studies in Historical and Political Science, 4th series, 1886, 211–57.

Ray, Arthur J. *Indians in the Fur Trade.* Toronto: Univ. of Toronto Press, 1974.

Ray, Arthur J., and Donald Freeman. *"Give Us Good Measure": An Economic Analysis of Relations between the Indian and the Hudson's Bay Company before 1763.* Toronto: Univ. of Toronto Press, 1978.

Reid, John G. "'The Beginnings of the Maritimes': A Reappraisal." *American Review of Canadian Studies* 9 (1979): 38–51.

Reps, John W. *Tidewater Towns: City Planning in Colonial Virginia and Maryland.* Charlottesville: Univ. Press of Virginia, 1972.

Reynolds, Helen Wilkinson. *Dutch Houses in the Hudson Valley before 1776.* 1929. Reprint. New York: Dover Publications, 1965.

Rich, E. E. *The History of the Hudson's Bay Company, 1670–1870.* Vol. 1, *1670–1763.* London: Hudson's Bay Record Society, 1958.

Rink, Oliver A. "The People of New Netherland: Notes on Non-English Immigration to New York in the Seventeenth Century." *New York History* 62 (1981): 5–41.

Roberts, W. Adolphe. *The Caribbean: The Story*

of Our Sea Destiny. Indianapolis: Bobbs-Merrill, 1940.

_____. *The French in the West Indies*. Indianapolis: Bobbs-Merrill, 1942.

Robinson, Morgan Poitiaux. "Virginia Counties." *Bulletin of the Virginia State Library* 9 (1916): 1–283.

Rogers, George C., Jr. *The History of Georgetown County, South Carolina*. Columbia: Univ. of South Carolina Press, 1970.

Rooney, John F., Jr., Wilbur Zelinsky, and Dean R. Louder, eds. *This Remarkable Continent: An Atlas of United States and Canadian Society and Cultures*. College Station: Texas A & M University Press, 1982.

Rowntree, Helen C. "Change Came Slowly: The Case of the Powhatan Indians of Virginia." *Journal of Ethnic Studies* 3 (1975): 1–20.

Sauer, Carl O. "The March of Agriculture across the Western World" [1942]. In *Selected Essays 1963–1975, Carl O. Sauer*, 45–56. Berkeley: Turtle Island Foundation, 1981.

_____. "The Settlement of the Humid East." In *Climate and Man: Yearbook of Agriculture, 1941*, 17–30. Washington, D.C.: Department of Agriculture, 1941.

Scharf, J. Thomas. *History of Maryland: From the Earliest Period to the Present Day*. 1879. Reprint. Hatboro, Pa.: Tradition Press, 1967.

Schwartz, Seymour I., and Ralph E. Ehrenberg. *The Mapping of America*. New York: Harry N. Abrams, 1980.

Scofield, Edna. "The Origin of Settlement Patterns in Rural New England." *Geographical Review* 28 (1938): 652–63.

Sirmans, M. Eugene. *Colonial South Carolina: A Political History, 1663–1763*. Chapel Hill: Univ. of North Carolina Press, 1966.

Smith, Hale G. *The European and the Indian: European-Indian Contacts in Georgia and Florida*. Gainesville: Florida Anthropological Society Pub. No. 4, 1956.

Snyder, Martin P. *City of Independence: Views of Philadelphia before 1800*. New York: Praeger, 1975.

Soltow, James H. *The Economic Role of Williamsburg*. Williamsburg: Colonial Williamsburg, 1965.

Sparling, Mary, ed. *Great Expectations: The European Vision in Nova Scotia, 1749–1848*, with catalogue descriptions by Scott Robson. Halifax: Art Gallery, Mount Saint Vincent University, 1980.

Spaulding, H. S. *Catholic Colonial Maryland. A Sketch*. Milwaukee: Bruce, 1931.

Stevenson, W. Iain. "Some Aspects of the Geography of the Clyde Tobacco Trade in the Eighteenth Century." *Scottish Geographical Magazine* 89 (1973): 19–35.

Thwaites, Reuben Gold, ed. *Travels and Explorations of the Jesuit Missionaries in New France, 1610–1791*. Vol. 69, *All Missions 1710–1756*. Cleveland: Burroughs Brothers Co., 1900.

Tolles, Frederick B. *Meeting House and Counting House: The Quaker Merchants of Colonial Philadelphia, 1682–1763*. Chapel Hill: Univ. of North Carolina Press, 1948.

Trelease, Allen W. *Indian Affairs in Colonial New York: The Seventeenth Century*. Ithaca: Cornell Univ. Press, 1960.

Trewartha, Glenn T. "Rural Settlement in Colonial America." *Geographical Review* 36 (1946): 568–96.

Trigger, Bruce G., ed. *Handbook of North American Indians*. Vol. 15, *Northeast*. Washington, D.C.: Smithsonian Institution, 1978.

Trindell, Roger T. "Building in Brick in Early America." *Geographical Review* 58 (1968): 484–87.

Trudel, Marcel. *Introduction to New France*. Toronto: Holt, Rinehart and Winston, 1968.

Tunnard, Christopher, and Henry Hope Reed. *American Skyline: The Growth and Form of Our Cities and Towns*. New York: Mentor, 1956.

Turner, Frederick Jackson. "The Significance of the Frontier in American History." In *Annual Report for 1893*, 199–227. Washington, D.C.: American Historical Association, 1894.

Upchurch, John C. "Middle Florida: An Historical Geography of the Area between the Apalachicola and Sewanee Rivers." Ph.D. dissertation, Department of Geography, Univ. of Tennessee, 1971.

Verrill, Addison E. *The Bermuda Islands*. New Haven: the Author, 1902.

Wacker, Peter O. *Land and People: A Cultural Geography of Preindustrial New Jersey: Origins and Settlement Patterns.* New Brunswick: Rutgers Univ. Press, 1975.

Wallace, Paul A. W. *Indians in Pennsylvania.* Harrisburg: Pennsylvania Historical Museum Commission, 1961.

Wareing, John. "Migration to London and Transatlantic Emigration of Indentured Servants, 1683–1775." *Journal of Historical Geography* 7 (1981): 356–78.

Webb, Stephen Saunders. *1676, The End of American Independence.* New York: Knopf, 1984.

Weddle, Robert S. *San Juan Bautista, Gateway to Spanish Texas.* Austin: Univ. of Texas Press, 1968.

Wertenbaker, Thomas Jefferson. *The Founding of American Civilization: The Middle Colonies.* New York: Charles Scribner's Sons, 1938.
———. *Norfolk, Historic Southern Port.* 2d ed. Durham: Duke Univ. Press, 1962.

Weslager, C. A. *The English on the Delaware: 1610–1682.* New Brunswick: Rutgers Univ. Press, 1967.

Wilkinson, Henry C. *Bermuda in the Old Empire.* New York: Oxford Univ. Press, 1950.

Withey, Lynne. *Urban Growth in Colonial Rhode Island: Newport and Providence in the Eighteenth Century.* Albany: State Univ. of New York Press, 1984.

Wolf, Stephanie Grauman. *Urban Village: Population, Community and Family Structure in Germantown, Pennsylvania, 1683–1800.* Princeton: Princeton Univ. Press, 1976.

Wood, Joseph S. "The Origin of the New England Village." Ph.D. dissertation, Department of Geography, Pennsylvania State Univ., 1978.

Wood, Peter H. *Black Majority: Negroes in Colonial South Carolina from 1670 through the Stono Rebellion.* New York: Knopf, 1974. Reprint. New York: Norton, 1975.

Wright, J. Leitch, Jr. *Anglo-Spanish Rivalry in North America.* Athens: Univ. of Georgia Press, 1971.
———. *The Only Land They Knew: The Tragic Story of the American Indians in the Old South.* New York: Free Press, 1981.

Zelinsky, Wilbur. *The Cultural Geography of the United States.* Englewood Cliffs, N.J.: Prentice-Hall, 1973.

Zuckerman, Michael, ed. *Friends and Neighbors: Group Life in America's First Plural Society.* Philadelphia: Temple Univ. Press, 1982.

PART THREE

Abel, Annie H. "Proposals for an Indian State, 1778–1878." *Annual Report of the American Historical Association* 1 (1907): 89–104.

Acheson, T. W. "A Study in the Historical Demography of a Loyalist County." *Histoire Sociale/Social History* 1 (1968): 53–64.

Adams, Henry. *The United States in 1800.* 1889. Reprint. Ithaca: Cornell Univ. Press, 1955.

Bailey, A. G. *Culture and Nationality.* Toronto: McClelland & Stewart, 1972.

Bailyn, Bernard. "The Central Themes of the American Revolution, An Interpretation." In *Essays on the American Revolution,* ed. Stephen G. Kurtz and James H. Hutson, 3–31. Chapel Hill: Univ. Of North Carolina Press, 1973.

Bell, David V. J. "The Loyalist Tradition in Canada." *Journal of Canadian Studies* 5 (1970): 22–33.

Berkhofer, Robert F., Jr. "Jefferson, the Ordinance of 1784, and the Origins of the American Territorial System." *William and Mary Quarterly,* 3d series, 29 (1972): 231–62.

Billias, George Athan. "The First Un-Americans: The Loyalists in American Historiography." In *Perspectives on Early American History: Essays in Honor of Richard B. Morris,* ed. Alden T. Vaughan and George Athan Billias, 282–324. New York: Harper & Row, 1973.

Bowler, R. Arthur. *Logistics and the Failure of the British Army in America, 1775–1783.* Princeton: Princeton Univ. Press, 1975.

Brebner, John Bartlet. *Canada, A Modern History.* Ann Arbor: Univ. of Michigan Press, 1960.
———. *The Neutral Yankees of Nova Scotia: A Marginal Colony during the Revolutionary*

Years. 1937. Reprint. Toronto: McClelland & Stewart, 1969.

Brock, William R. *Scotus Americanus: A Survey of the Sources for Links between Scotland and America in the Eighteenth Century.* Edinburgh: Edinburgh Univ. Press, 1982.

Brown, Ralph H. *Historical Geography of the United States.* New York: Harcourt, Brace, 1948.

————. *Mirror for Americans: Likeness of the Eastern Seaboard, 1810.* New York: American Geographical Society, 1943.

Brown, Wallace. *The Good Americans: The Loyalists in the American Revolution.* New York: William Morrow, 1969.

————. *The King's Friends: The Composition and Motives of the American Loyalist Claimants.* Providence: Brown Univ. Press, 1966.

Bryan, Wilhelmus Bogart. *A History of the National Capital.* New York: Macmillan, 1914.

Bryce, James. *The American Commonwealth.* 2d ed. London: Macmillan, 1891.

Bumstead, J. M. "Loyalists and Nationalists: An Essay on the Problem of Definition." *Canadian Review of Studies in Nationalism* 6 (1979): 218–32.

Burke, Edmund. *Speeches on the American War, and a Letter to the Sheriffs of Bristol,* with a new introduction and preface by George Athan Billias. Boston: Gregg Press, 1972.

Burt, A. L. "If Turner Had Looked at Canada, Australia, and New Zealand When He Wrote about the West." In *The Frontier in Perspective,* ed. D. Wyman Walker and Clifton B. Kroeber, 59–77. Madison: Univ. of Wisconsin Press, 1957.

Calhoon, Robert McCluer. *The Loyalists in Revolutionary America, 1760–1781.* New York: Harcourt Brace Jovanovich, 1973.

Cappon, Lester J., editor-in-chief. *Atlas of Early American History. The Revolutionary Era, 1760–1790.* Princeton: Princeton Univ. Press, 1976.

Christie, Ian R., and Benjamin W. Labaree. *Empire or Independence, 1760–1776.* New York: Norton, 1977.

Coatsworth, John H. "American Trade with European Colonies in the Caribbean and South America." *William and Mary Quarterly,* 3d series, 24 (1967): 243–61.

Cotterill, R. S. *The Southern Indians: The Story of the Civilized Tribes before Removal.* Norman: Univ. of Oklahoma Press, 1954.

Craig, Gerald M. *Upper Canada: The Formative Years, 1784–1841.* Toronto: McClelland & Stewart, 1963.

Davis, Joseph L. "Political Change in Revolutionary America: A Sectorial Interpretation." In *The Human Dimensions of Nation Making: Essays on Colonial and Revolutionary America,* ed. James Kirby Martin, 184–217. Madison: State Historical Society of Wisconsin, 1976.

Davis, S. Rufus. *The Federal Principle: A Journey through Time in Quest of a Meaning.* Berkeley and Los Angeles: Univ. of California Press, 1978.

Deutsch, Karl W. "The Growth of Nations: Some Recurrent Patterns of Political and Social Integration." *World Politics* 5 (1953): 168–95.

————. *Nationalism and Social Communication: An Inquiry into the Foundations of Nationality.* Cambridge: Massachusetts Institute of Technology Press, 1953.

Dikshit, Ramesh Dutta. *The Political Geography of Federalism: An Inquiry into Origins and Stability.* New York: John Wiley, 1975.

Din, Gilbert C. "The Immigration Policy of Governor Esteban Miro in Spanish Louisiana." *Southwestern Historical Quarterly* 73 (1969): 155–75.

Douglas, Marjory Stoneman. *Florida: The Long Frontier.* New York: Harper & Row, 1967.

Ellis, David Maldwyn. *New York: State and City.* Ithaca: Cornell Univ. Press, 1979.

Ells, Margaret. "Clearing the Decks for the Loyalists." *Canadian Historical Association Report,* 1933, 43–58.

————. "Settling the Loyalists in Nova Scotia." *Canadian Historical Association Report,* 1934, 105–09.

Everest, Allan S. *Moses Hazen and the Canadian Refugees in the American Revolution.* Syracuse: Syracuse Univ. Press, 1976.

Faulk, Odie B. *The Last Years of Spanish Texas, 1778–1821.* The Hague: Mouton, 1964.

Fenton, William N. "The Iroquois in History." In *North American Indians in Historical Perspective,* ed. Eleanor Burke Leacock and Nancy Oestreich Lurie, 129–68. New York: Random House, 1971.

Ferrand, Max, ed. *The Records of the Federal Convention of 1787*. Rev. ed. 4 vols. New Haven: Yale Univ. Press, 1966.

Franklin, Benjamin. "Observations concerning the Increase of Mankind, Peopling of Countries, etc." [1755]. In *The Papers of Benjamin Franklin*, vol. 4, ed. Leonard Labaree, 227–34. New Haven: Yale Univ. Press, 1961.

Galtung, Johan. "A Structural Theory of Imperialism." *Journal of Peace Research* 8 (1971): 81–117.

Gentilcore, R. Louis, and David Wood. "A Military Colony in the Wilderness: The Upper Canada Frontier." In *Perspectives on Landscape and Settlement in Nineteenth-Century Ontario*, ed. J. David Wood, 32–50. Toronto: McClelland & Stewart, 1975.

Gilchrist, David T., ed. *The Growth of the Seaport Cities, 1790–1825*. Charlottesville: Univ. Press of Virginia, 1967.

Gipson, Laurence Henry. *The Coming of the Revolution, 1763–1775*. New York: Harper & Row, 1954.

Goldstein, Jonathan. *Philadelphia and the China Trade, 1682–1846: Commercial, Cultural, and Attitudinal Effects*. University Park: Pennsylvania State Univ. Press, 1978.

Graham, Ian Charles Cargill. *Colonists from Scotland: Emigration to North America, 1707–1783*. Ithaca: Cornell Univ. Press, 1956.

Hansen, Marcus Lee. *The Mingling of the Canadian and American People*. New Haven: Yale Univ. Press, 1940.

Harris, Marshall. *Origin of the Land Tenure System in the United States*. Ames: Iowa State College Press, 1953.

Harvey, Evelyn B. "The Negro Loyalists." *Nova Scotia Historical Quarterly* 1 (1971): 181–200.

Hast, Adele. *Loyalism in Revolutionary Virginia: The Norfolk Area and the Eastern Shore*. Ann Arbor: UMI Research Press, 1982.

Hatcher, Harlan. *The Western Reserve: The Story of New Connecticut in Ohio*. Indianapolis: Bobbs-Merrill, 1949.

Higginbotham, Don, ed. *Reconsiderations on the Revolutionary War: Selected Essays*. Westport, Conn.: Greenwood Press, 1978.

Hofstadter, Richard. *America at 1750: A Social Portrait*. New York: Vintage, 1973.

Hughes, J. R. T. *Social Control in the Colonial Economy*. Chancellorsville: Univ. Press of Virginia, 1976.

Isaac, Rhys. *The Transformation of Virginia, 1740–1790*. Chapel Hill: Univ. of North Carolina Press, 1982.

Jackson, W. A. Douglas. "The Regressive Effects of Late 18th Century British Colonial Policy on Land Development along the Upper St. Lawrence River." *Annals of the Association of American Geographers* 45 (1955): 258–68.

Jaher, Frederic Cople. *The Urban Establishment: Upper Strata in Boston, New York, Charleston, Chicago, and Los Angeles*. Urbana: Univ. of Illinois Press, 1982.

Jakle, John A. "Salt on the Ohio Valley Frontier, 1770–1820." *Annals of the Association of American Geographers* 59 (1969): 687–709.

Jefferson, Thomas. *The Papers of Thomas Jefferson*, vols. 6 and 17, ed. Julian P. Boyd. Princeton: Princeton Univ. Press, 1952, 1965.

Jensen, Merrill. *The New Nation: A History of the United States during the Confederation, 1781–1789*. New York: Knopf, 1950.

Johnson, Cecil. *British West Florida, 1763–1783*. New Haven: Yale Univ. Press, 1943.

Johnson, Hildegard Binder. *Order upon the Land: The U.S. Rectangular Land Survey and the Upper Mississippi Country*. New York: Oxford Univ. Press, 1976.

Jones, Dorothy V. *License for Empire: Colonialism by Treaty in Early America*. Chicago: Univ. of Chicago Press, 1982.

Jones, Francis Godwin. *Ireland in the Empire, 1688–1770*. Cambridge: Harvard Univ. Press, 1973.

July, Robert W. *A History of the African People*. New York: Charles Scribner's Sons, 1970.

Kaminski, John P. "Democracy Run Rampant: Rhode Island in the Confederation." In *The Human Dimensions of Nation Making: Essays on Colonial and Revolutionary America*, ed. James Kirby Martin, 243–69. Madison: State Historical Society of Wisconsin, 1976.

Kerr, Wilfred Brenton. *The Maritime Provinces of British North America and the American Revolution*. 1941. Reprint. New York: Russell & Russell, 1970.

Ketcham, Ralph. *From Colony to Country: The*

Revolution in American Thought, 1750–1820. New York: Macmillan, 1974.

Knorr, Klaus E. *British Colonial Theories, 1570–1850.* Toronto: Univ. of Toronto Press, 1944.

Kohn, Hans. *American Nationalism: An Interpretative Essay.* New York: Collier Books, 1957.

———. *Nationalism: Its Meaning and History.* Princeton: Van Nostrand, 1955.

Kraus, Michael. *Intercolonial Aspects of American Culture on the Eve of the Revolution.* New York: Columbia Univ. Press, 1928.

Lanctot, Gustave. *Canada and the American Revolution, 1774–1783.* Toronto: Clarke, Irwin, 1967.

Leblanc, Robert A. "The Acadian Migrations." *Cahiers de Géographie de Québec* 24 (1967): 523–41.

Liska, George. *Career of Empire: America and Imperial Expansion over Land and Sea.* Baltimore: Johns Hopkins Univ. Press, 1978.

Livingston, William S. "A Note on the Nature of Federalism." *Political Science Quarterly* 67 (1952): 81–95.

McDonald, Forrest. *E Pluribus Unum: The Formation of the American Republic 1776–1790.* Boston: Houghton Mifflin, 1965.

Mackesy, Piers. *The War for America, 1775–1783.* London: Longmans, Green, 1964.

MacKinnon, Neil. "The Loyalists: 'A Different People.'" In *Banked Fires: The Ethnics of Nova Scotia,* ed. Douglas Campbell, 69–92. Port Credit, Ontario: Scribbler's Press, 1978.

McNeill, William H. *The Great Frontier: Freedom and Hierarchy in Modern Times.* Princeton: Princeton Univ. Press, 1983.

MacNutt, W. S. *The Atlantic Provinces: The Emergence of Colonial Society, 1712–1857.* Toronto: McClelland & Stewart, 1965.

Maier, Pauline. *From Resistance to Revolution.* New York: Knopf, 1972.

Main, Jackson Turner. "The American States in the Revolutionary Era." In *Sovereign States in an Age of Uncertainty,* ed. Ronald Hoffman and Peter J. Albert, 1–30. Charlottesville: Univ. Press of Virginia, 1981.

Meekison, J. Peter, ed. *Canadian Federalism: Myth or Reality.* 2d ed. Toronto: Methuen, 1971.

Meinig, D. W. "Geographical Analysis of Impe-

rialism." In *Period and Place: Research Methods in Historical Geography,* ed. Alan R. H. Baker and Mark Billinge, 71–78. Cambridge: Cambridge Univ. Press, 1982.

———. "Geography of Expansion." In *Geography of New York State,* ed. John H. Thompson, 140–71. Syracuse: Syracuse Univ. Press, 1966.

Merritt, Richard L. *Symbols of American Community, 1735–1775.* New Haven: Yale Univ. Press, 1966.

Middlekauff, Robert. *The Glorious Cause: The American Revolution, 1763–1789.* New York: Oxford Univ. Press, 1982.

Minogue, K. R. *Nationalism.* Baltimore: Penguin, 1967.

Mood, Fulmer. "The Origin, Evolution, and Application of the Sectional Concept, 1750–1900." In *Regionalism in America,* ed. Merrill Jensen, 5–98. Madison: Univ. of Wisconsin Press, 1952.

Moore, John Preston. *Revolt in Louisiana: The Spanish Occupation, 1766–1770.* Baton Rouge: Louisiana State Univ. Press, 1976.

Morgan, Edmund. *The Birth of the Republic, 1763–89.* Chicago: Univ. of Chicago Press, 1977.

———. "Conflict and Consensus in the American Revolution." In *Essays on the American Revolution,* ed. Stephen G. Kurtz and James H. Hutson, 289–309. Chapel Hill: Univ. of North Carolina Press, 1973.

Morris, Richard B. *The Making of a Nation, 1775–1789.* New York: Time Inc., 1963.

———. *The Peacemakers: The Great Powers and American Independence.* New York: Harper & Row, 1965.

Mowat, Charles Loch. *East Florida as a British Province, 1763–1784.* Berkeley and Los Angeles: Univ. of California Press, 1943.

Nash, Gary B. *The Urban Crucible: Social Change, Political Consciousness, and the Origins of the American Revolution.* Cambridge: Harvard Univ. Press, 1979.

Newton, Milton, Jr. "Cultural Preadaption and the Upland South." *Geoscience and Man* 5 (1974): 143–54.

Ouellet, Fernand. *Economic and Social History of Quebec, 1760–1850.* Ottawa: Institute of Canadian Studies, Carleton University, 1980.

Padover, Saul K. *To Secure These Blessings: The*

Great Debates of the Constitutional Convention of 1787, Arranged according to Topics. New York: Washington Square Press and the Ridge Press, 1962.

Panagopoulas, E. P. *New Smyrna: An Eighteenth-Century Greek Odyssey.* Gainesville: Univ. of Florida Press, 1966.

Pocock, J. G. A. "British History: A Plea for a New Subject." *Journal of Modern History* 47 (1975): 601–28.

Pole, J. R. *Foundations of American Independence.* London and Glasgow: Fontana/Collins, 1973.

Pomerantz, Sidney I. *New York: An American City, 1783–1803.* New York: Columbia Univ. Press, 1938.

Pomeroy, Earl S. *The Territories and the United States, 1861–1890: Studies in Colonial Administration.* 1947. Reprint. Seattle: Univ. of Washington Press, 1969.

Pownall, Thomas. *The Administration of the Colonies, Wherein Their Rights and Constitution Are Discussed and Stated.* 1768. Reprint. New York: Da Capo Press, 1971.

Prucha, Francis Paul. *The Sword of the Republic: The United States Army on the Frontier, 1783–1846.* Toronto: Macmillan, 1969.

Quarles, Benjamin. *The Negro in the American Revolution.* Chapel Hill: Univ. of North Carolina Press, 1961.

Quinn, David Beers. *The Elizabethans and the Irish.* Ithaca: Cornell Univ. Press, 1966.

Rawlyk, George A. *Nova Scotia's Massachusetts: A Study of Massachusetts–Nova Scotia Relations, 1630 to 1784.* Montreal and London: McGill-Queen's Univ. Press, 1973.

Reamon, G. Elmore. *The Trail of the Black Walnut.* Toronto: McClelland & Stewart, 1957.

Rich, E. E. *Montreal and the Fur Trade.* Montreal: McGill Univ. Press, 1966.

Risch, Erna. *Quartermaster Support of the Army: A History of the Corps, 1776–1939.* Washington, D.C.: Quartermaster Historian's Office, 1962.

Roberts, Leslie. *Montreal, from Mission Colony to World City.* Toronto: Macmillan, 1969.

Robson, Eric. *The American Revolution in Its Political and Military Aspects, 1763–1783.* 1955. Reprint. New York: Da Capo, 1972.

Rohrbough, Malcolm T. *The Land Office Business: The Settlement and Administration of American Public Lands, 1789–1837.* New York: Oxford Univ. Press, 1968.

Sachs, William S. "Interurban Correspondents and the Development of a National Economy before the Revolution: New York as a Case Study." *New York History* 36 (1955): 320–55.

Savelle, Max. *The Diplomatic History of the Canadian Boundary, 1749–1763.* New York: Russell & Russell, 1968.

———. *Empires to Nations: Expansion in North America, 1713–1824.* Minneapolis: Univ. of Minnesota Press, 1974.

Shy, John. "American Society and Its War for Independence." In *Reconsiderations on the Revolutionary War: Selected Essays,* ed. Don Higginbotham, 72–82. Westport, Conn.: Greenwood Press, 1978.

———. *Toward Lexington: The Role of the British Army in the Coming of the American Revolution.* Princeton: Princeton Univ. Press, 1965.

Siebert, Wilburt H. *The Legacy of the American Revolution to the British West Indies and Bahamas: A Chapter out of the History of the American Loyalists.* 1913. Reprint. Boston: Gregg Press, 1972.

Smith, Dwight L. "The Land Cession Treaty: A Valid Instrument of Transfer of Indian Title." In *This Land of Ours: The Acquisition and Disposition of the Public Domain,* 87–102. Indianapolis: Indiana Historical Society, 1978.

Smith, Henry Nash. *Virgin Land: The American West as Symbol and Myth.* Cambridge: Harvard Univ. Press, 1950.

Sosin, Jack M. *The Revolutionary Frontier, 1763–1783.* New York: Holt, Rinehart and Winston, 1967.

———. *Whitehall and the Wilderness: The Middle West in British Colonial Policy, 1760–1775.* Lincoln: Univ. of Nebraska Press, 1961.

Sprout, Harold, and Margaret Sprout. *The Rise of American Naval Power, 1776–1918.* Princeton: Princeton Univ. Press, 1944.

Stanard, Mary Newton. *Richmond, Its People and Its Story.* Philadelphia: J. P. Lippincott, 1923.

Stilgoe, John R. *Common Landscape of America, 1580 to 1845.* New Haven: Yale Univ. Press, 1982.

Stuart, Reginald C. *War and American Thought from the Revolution to the Monroe Doctrine.* Kent: Kent State Univ. Press, 1982.

Tarleton, C. D. "Symmetry and Asymmetry as Elements of Federalism: A Theoretical Speculation." *Journal of Politics* 27 (1965): 861–74.

Tebeau, Charles W. *A History of Florida.* Coral Gables: Univ. of Miami Press, 1971.

Thornton, A. P. *Doctrines of Imperialism.* New York: John Wiley, 1965.

Thrower, Norman J. W. *Original Survey and Land Subdivision.* Chicago: Rand McNally, 1966.

Tucker, Robert W., and David C. Hendrickson. *The Fall of the First British Empire: Origins of the War of American Independence.* Baltimore: Johns Hopkins Univ. Press, 1982.

Ullman, Edward L. "Regional Development and the Geography of Concentration." *Papers and Proceedings of the Regional Science Association* 4 (1959): 179–98.

Upton, L. F. S. *Micmacs and Colonists: Indian-White Relations in the Maritimes, 1713–1867.* Vancouver: Univ. of British Columbia Press, 1979.

Vile, M. J. C. *The Structure of American Federalism.* London: Oxford Univ. Press, 1961.

Wallace, David Duncan. *South Carolina: A Short History, 1520–1948.* Chapel Hill: Univ. of North Carolina Press, 1951.

Walton, Gary M. "New Evidence on Colonial Commerce." *Journal of Economic History* 28 (1968): 363–89.

Ward, Henry M. *The United Colonies of New England—1643–90.* New York: Vantage Press, 1961.

——. *"Unite or Die": Intercolony Relations, 1690–1763.* Port Washington, N.Y.: Kennikat Press, 1971.

Warren, Charles. *The Making of the Constitution.* Cambridge: Harvard Univ. Press, 1928.

Washington, George. *The Writings of George Washington,* vol. 27, ed. John C. Fitzpatrick. Washington, D.C.: Government Printing Office, 1938.

Watson, J. Wreford. "The Individuality of Britain and the British Isles." In *The British Isles: A Systematic Geography,* ed. J. Wreford Watson and J. B. Sissons, 1–19. London: Thomas Nelson, 1964.

Webb, Stephen Saunders. *The Governors-General: The English Army and the Definition of the Empire, 1569–1681.* Chapel Hill: Univ. of North Carolina Press, 1979.

Weinberg, Albert K. *Manifest Destiny: A Study of Nationalist Expansionism in American History.* Baltimore: Johns Hopkins Univ. Press, 1935.

White, R. J. *Europe in the Eighteenth Century.* New York: St. Martin's, 1965.

Whittlesey, Derwent. *The Earth and the State: A Study of Political Geography.* New York: Henry Holt, 1939.

Wiebe, Robert H. *The Segmented Society: An Introduction to the Meaning of America.* New York: Oxford Univ. Press, 1975.

Williamson, Chilton. *Vermont in Quandary: 1763–1825.* Montpelier: Vermont Historical Society, 1949.

Wilson, Bruce. *As She Began: An Illustrated Introduction to Loyalist Ontario.* Toronto: Dunburn Press, 1981.

Wood, Gordon S. "Framing the Republic, 1760–1820." In *The Great Republic: A History of the American People,* ed. Bailyn et al., 171–305. Vol. 2. 2d ed. Lexington, Mass.: D.C. Heath, 1981.

Woodward, Grace Steele. *The Cherokees.* Norman: Univ. of Oklahoma Press, 1963.

Wright, J. Leitch, Jr. *Britain and the American Frontier, 1783–1815.* Athens: Univ. of Georgia Press, 1975.

——. *Florida in the American Revolution.* Gainesville: Univ. Presses of Florida, 1975.

Wynn, Graeme. "Late Eighteenth-Century Agriculture on the Bay of Fundy Marshlands." *Acadiensis* 8 (1979): 78–89.

PART FOUR

Adams, Henry. *The United States in 1800.* 1889. Reprint. Ithaca. Cornell Univ. Press, 1955.

Ahlstrom, Sydney E. *A Religious History of the American People.* New Haven: Yale Univ. Press, 1972.

Andrews, Wayne. *Architecture, Ambition and Americans.* New York: Free Press, 1964.

Archambault, Paul J. "From Grand Alliance to Great Schism: France in America, 1763–1815." *Papers on Language & Literature* 12 (1976): 339–65.

Boorstin, Daniel J. *The Americans: The Colonial Experience.* New York: Random House, 1958.

Brock, William R. *Scotus Americanus: A Survey of the Sources for Links between Scotland and America in the Eighteenth Century.* Edinburgh: Edinburgh Univ. Press, 1982.

Brooks, Van Wyck. *The World of Washington Irving.* New York: E. P. Dutton, 1944.

Brown, Ralph H. *Historical Geography of the United States.* New York: Harcourt, Brace, 1948.

———. *Mirror for Americans: Likeness of the Eastern Seaboard, 1810.* New York: American Geographical Society, 1943.

Calhoon, Robert M. "A Troubled Culture: North Carolina in the New Nation, 1790–1834." In *Writing North Carolina History,* ed. Jeffrey J. Crow and Larry E. Tise, 76–110. Chapel Hill: Univ. of North Carolina Press, 1979.

Carter, Edward C., II, John C. Van Horne, and Charles E. Brownell, eds. *Latrobe's View of America, 1795–1820: Selections from the Watercolors and Sketches.* New Haven: Yale Univ. Press, 1985.

Childs, Frances S. *French Refugee Life in the United States, 1790–1800.* Baltimore: Johns Hopkins Univ. Press, 1940.

Cooper, Thomas. *Some Information Respecting America.* 1794. Reprint. New York: Augustus M. Kelley, 1969.

de Crèvecoeur, J. Hector St. John. *Letters from an American Farmer.* 1782. Reprint. New York: E. P. Dutton, 1957.

Fox, Dixon Ryan. *Ideas in Motion.* New York: D. Appleton-Century, 1935.

Fraser, Charles. *A Charleston Sketchbook 1796–1806,* with an introduction and notes by Alice R. Huger Smith. Charleston: Carolina Art Association, 1940.

Gibson, James R. *Imperial Russia in Frontier America: The Changing Geography of Supply of Russian America, 1784–1867.* New York: Oxford Univ. Press, 1976.

Haines, Francis D. "The Northward Spread of Horses among the Plains Indians." *American Anthropologist* 40 (1938): 429–37.

Hamlin, Talbot F. *The American Spirit in Architecture.* New Haven: Yale Univ. Press, 1926.

Hansen, Marcus Lee. *The Atlantic Migration, 1607–1860: A History of the Continuing Settlement of the United States.* Cambridge: Harvard Univ. Press, 1940.

Jareckie, Stephen B. *The Early Republic: Consolidation of Revolutionary Goals.* Worcester, Mass.: Worcester Art Museum, 1976.

Jordan, Terry G. "A Reappraisal of Fenno-Scandian Antecedents for Midland American Log Construction." *Geographical Review* 73 (1983): 58–94.

Kimball, Fiske. *Domestic Architecture of the American Colonies of the Early Republic.* New York: Charles Scribner's Sons, 1922.

Kraus, Michael. *The Atlantic Civilization: Eighteenth-Century Origins.* Ithaca: Cornell Univ. Press, 1949.

Krout, John A., and Dixon Ryan Fox. *The Completion of Independence, 1790–1830.* New York: Macmillan, 1944.

La Rochefoucauld Liancourt, Duke de. *Travels through the United States, the Country of the Iroquois, and Upper Canada, in the Years 1795, 1796, and 1797.* 2 vols. London: R. Phillips, 1799.

Little, Nina Fletcher. *Paintings by New England Provincial Artists, 1775–1800.* Boston: Museum of Fine Arts, 1976.

Mackenzie, Alexander. *Voyages from Montreal, on the River St. Lawrence, through the Continent of North America, to the Frozen and Pacific Oceans; in the Years 1789 and 1793.* 1801. Reprint. Toronto: Radisson Society, 1927.

Main, Jackson Turner. "The American States in the Revolutionary Era." In *Arms and Independence: The Military Character of the American Revolution,* ed. Ronald Hoffman and Peter J. Albert, 1–30. Charlottesville: Univ. Press of Virginia, 1981.

Miller, John C. *The Federalist Era, 1789–1801.* New York: Harper & Row, 1960.

Morrison, Hugh. *Early American Architecture, from the First Colonial Settlements to the National Period.* New York: Oxford Univ. Press, 1952.

Mumford, Lewis. *Sticks and Stones: A Study of*

American Architecture and Civilization. New York: Horace Liveright, 1924.

Nagel, Paul C. *One Nation Indivisible: The Union in American Thought, 1776–1861.* New York: Oxford Univ. Press, 1964.

Noble, Allen G. *Wood, Brick, and Stone: The North American Settlement Landscape.* Vol. 1, *Houses.* Amherst: Univ. of Massachusetts Press, 1984.

Nye, Russel B. *The Cultural Life in the New Nation, 1776–1830.* New York: Harper & Row, 1960.

Russo, David. *Families and Communities: A New View of American History.* Nashville: American Association for State and Local History, 1974.

Stewart, George. *American Ways of Life.* Garden City: Doubleday, 1954.

Volney, C. F. *A View of the Soil and Climate of the United States of America.* Translated with occasional remarks by C. B. Brown. Philadelphia: J. Conrad, 1804.

Wansey, Henry. *The Journal of an Excursion to the United States of North America in the Summer of 1794.* 1796. Reprint. New York: Johnson, 1969.

Warfel, Harry R. *Noah Webster: Schoolmaster to America.* New York: Macmillan, 1936.

Whitehill, Walter Muir. *Boston, A Topographical History.* Cambridge: Harvard Univ. Press, 1963.

INDEX

Abenaki Indians, 95, 96

Acadia: French beginnings, 33, 36; and fur trade, 64; as a regional society, 89–90; becomes Nova Scotia, 97, 268, 269; in French empire, 232, 236; British annexation, 270–71; French renounce right to, 315

Acadians: 377; and Indians, 210; as segmented society, 224; expulsion and dispersal, 271–73, 283, 334, 337; and American Revolution, 321; returnees, 327, 377

Acculturation: in Spanish America, 14–15; and Afro-Americans, 84, 171, 188–89, 229; and French-Indian relations, 113; in South Carolina, 185, 186–87; as a phase, 207; in American immigrants, 219–21, 265; in Canada, 222; in Pennsylvania, 223; in Wales, 375; and Hudson Valley Dutch, 378; pressures on Germans, 379. *See also* Culture change

Adolphustown, UC, 329

Africa: Portuguese explorations, 9–10, 18, 54; slaves from, 21, 24, 60, 83, 214, 226, 289; crop exchange, 23; Dutch trading to, 41, 62; new human geography, 65; slave system, 72–73, 83

Africa, East, 190, 214, 227

Africa, West: slaves, 20, 21; and Europeans, 22; slave procurement, 64; disease, 72, 73, 172; cultural impacts, 72–75; as source of rice culture, 176

Africans: fusion with Europeans, 22; spread in America, 62, 73, 76, 83, 227; acculturation, 83–84, 172, 214, 230–31; and European-imposed identity, 83–84, 214, 230; in Hudson Valley, 125, 224; in Chesapeake area, 149, 153, 156–57, 252, 321; in West Indies, 161–

72; and rice culture, 176; in Carolina, 176, 178, 187–90, 227, 228, 252; in Florida, 192, 280; complex mixing, 210; in Louisiana, 220, 229; and racial categories, 224; rate of influx to America, 226; types of Afro-American societies, 228–30; in Nova Scotia, 327; sent to Sierra Leone, 331; and status in new USA, 394

Afro-Americans: and American Revolution, 322; and political geography of empires, 426–27

Afro-American society: within Euro-American society, 228; four basic types, 228–30

Afro-American world, 253, 426–27

Agricultural complex: formation of Euro-American, 12–14, 248

Alabama, 281

Alaska, 270, 426

Albany: and fur trade, 126, 128, 210, 211, 250; landscape, 126; diversified center, 251; peoples, 264; British favor to merchants, 278; in American Revolution, 320; Sons of Liberty, 339; stage connection, 363; becomes capital, 366; route to west, 405

Albany Plan of Union, 300, 341

Albemarle district, 158, 190

Albermarle Sound, 153, 177

Alexandria, VA, 157, 362

Algonkian Indians, 35, 112–13, 119, 121, 325, 353

Alsatians, 200, 214, 220

Alta California, 270, 426

Altamaha River, 180, 182, 192, 233, 268, 280, 281, 286

America: as religious refuge, 33–35; and influ-

MAR
DEL
NORT.

FRETUM HUDSON

NOUA
BRITANNIA

AMERICÆ SEPTEN:
NOUA
Canada

Novelle
Biscaie

PRIONALIS

PARS
VIRGINIA

MARE
VIRGIVIVM

COSTA DE LA FLORIDA

La Bermuda

INSVLÆ BAHOVENTO

GOLFO DE NUEVA
ESPAÑA

DEL   L

NVEVA
ESPA

Espanola

INSVLÆ CANIBALES

Vene zuela
Nueva Andalusia

MAR

DEL

ZUR

Milliaria Germanica Communia.